Communications
in Computer and Information Science 1832

Rationale

The CCIS series is devoted to the publication of proceedings of computer science conferences. Its aim is to efficiently disseminate original research results in informatics in printed and electronic form. While the focus is on publication of peer-reviewed full papers presenting mature work, inclusion of reviewed short papers reporting on work in progress is welcome, too. Besides globally relevant meetings with internationally representative program committees guaranteeing a strict peer-reviewing and paper selection process, conferences run by societies or of high regional or national relevance are also considered for publication.

Topics

The topical scope of CCIS spans the entire spectrum of informatics ranging from foundational topics in the theory of computing to information and communications science and technology and a broad variety of interdisciplinary application fields.

Information for Volume Editors and Authors

Publication in CCIS is free of charge. No royalties are paid, however, we offer registered conference participants temporary free access to the online version of the conference proceedings on SpringerLink (http://link.springer.com) by means of an http referrer from the conference website and/or a number of complimentary printed copies, as specified in the official acceptance email of the event.

CCIS proceedings can be published in time for distribution at conferences or as post-proceedings, and delivered in the form of printed books and/or electronically as USBs and/or e-content licenses for accessing proceedings at SpringerLink. Furthermore, CCIS proceedings are included in the CCIS electronic book series hosted in the SpringerLink digital library at http://link.springer.com/bookseries/7899. Conferences publishing in CCIS are allowed to use Online Conference Service (OCS) for managing the whole proceedings lifecycle (from submission and reviewing to preparing for publication) free of charge.

Publication process

The language of publication is exclusively English. Authors publishing in CCIS have to sign the Springer CCIS copyright transfer form, however, they are free to use their material published in CCIS for substantially changed, more elaborate subsequent publications elsewhere. For the preparation of the camera-ready papers/files, authors have to strictly adhere to the Springer CCIS Authors' Instructions and are strongly encouraged to use the CCIS LaTeX style files or templates.

Abstracting/Indexing

CCIS is abstracted/indexed in DBLP, Google Scholar, EI-Compendex, Mathematical Reviews, SCImago, Scopus. CCIS volumes are also submitted for the inclusion in ISI Proceedings.

How to start

To start the evaluation of your proposal for inclusion in the CCIS series, please send an e-mail to ccis@springer.com.

Constantine Stephanidis · Margherita Antona ·
Stavroula Ntoa · Gavriel Salvendy
Editors

HCI International 2023 Posters

25th International Conference
on Human-Computer Interaction, HCII 2023
Copenhagen, Denmark, July 23–28, 2023
Proceedings, Part I

 Springer

Editors
Constantine Stephanidis
University of Crete and Foundation for
Research and Technology - Hellas (FORTH)
Heraklion, Crete, Greece

Margherita Antona
Foundation for Research and Technology -
Hellas (FORTH)
Heraklion, Crete, Greece

Stavroula Ntoa
Foundation for Research and Technology -
Hellas (FORTH)
Heraklion, Crete, Greece

Gavriel Salvendy
University of Central Florida
Orlando, FL, USA

ISSN 1865-0929   ISSN 1865-0937 (electronic)
Communications in Computer and Information Science
ISBN 978-3-031-35988-0   ISBN 978-3-031-35989-7 (eBook)
https://doi.org/10.1007/978-3-031-35989-7

This Springer imprint is published by the registered company Springer Nature Switzerland AG
The registered company address is: Gewerbestrasse 11, 6330 Cham, Switzerland

Foreword

Human-computer interaction (HCI) is acquiring an ever-increasing scientific and industrial importance, as well as having more impact on people's everyday lives, as an ever-growing number of human activities are progressively moving from the physical to the digital world. This process, which has been ongoing for some time now, was further accelerated during the acute period of the COVID-19 pandemic. The HCI International (HCII) conference series, held annually, aims to respond to the compelling need to advance the exchange of knowledge and research and development efforts on the human aspects of design and use of computing systems.

The 25th International Conference on Human-Computer Interaction, HCI International 2023 (HCII 2023), was held in the emerging post-pandemic era as a 'hybrid' event at the AC Bella Sky Hotel and Bella Center, Copenhagen, Denmark, during July 23–28, 2023. It incorporated the 21 thematic areas and affiliated conferences listed below.

A total of 7472 individuals from academia, research institutes, industry, and government agencies from 85 countries submitted contributions, and 1578 papers and 396 posters were included in the volumes of the proceedings that were published just before the start of the conference, these are listed below. The contributions thoroughly cover the entire field of human-computer interaction, addressing major advances in knowledge and effective use of computers in a variety of application areas. These papers provide academics, researchers, engineers, scientists, practitioners and students with state-of-the-art information on the most recent advances in HCI.

The HCI International (HCII) conference also offers the option of presenting 'Late Breaking Work', and this applies both for papers and posters, with corresponding volumes of proceedings that will be published after the conference. Full papers will be included in the 'HCII 2023 - Late Breaking Work - Papers' volumes of the proceedings to be published in the Springer LNCS series, while 'Poster Extended Abstracts' will be included as short research papers in the 'HCII 2023 - Late Breaking Work - Posters' volumes to be published in the Springer CCIS series.

I would like to thank the Program Board Chairs and the members of the Program Boards of all thematic areas and affiliated conferences for their contribution towards the high scientific quality and overall success of the HCI International 2023 conference. Their manifold support in terms of paper reviewing (single-blind review process, with a minimum of two reviews per submission), session organization and their willingness to act as goodwill ambassadors for the conference is most highly appreciated.

This conference would not have been possible without the continuous and unwavering support and advice of Gavriel Salvendy, founder, General Chair Emeritus, and Scientific Advisor. For his outstanding efforts, I would like to express my sincere appreciation to Abbas Moallem, Communications Chair and Editor of HCI International News.

July 2023   Constantine Stephanidis

HCI International 2023 Thematic Areas and Affiliated Conferences

Thematic Areas

- HCI: Human-Computer Interaction
- HIMI: Human Interface and the Management of Information

Affiliated Conferences

- EPCE: 20th International Conference on Engineering Psychology and Cognitive Ergonomics
- AC: 17th International Conference on Augmented Cognition
- UAHCI: 17th International Conference on Universal Access in Human-Computer Interaction
- CCD: 15th International Conference on Cross-Cultural Design
- SCSM: 15th International Conference on Social Computing and Social Media
- VAMR: 15th International Conference on Virtual, Augmented and Mixed Reality
- DHM: 14th International Conference on Digital Human Modeling and Applications in Health, Safety, Ergonomics and Risk Management
- DUXU: 12th International Conference on Design, User Experience and Usability
- C&C: 11th International Conference on Culture and Computing
- DAPI: 11th International Conference on Distributed, Ambient and Pervasive Interactions
- HCIBGO: 10th International Conference on HCI in Business, Government and Organizations
- LCT: 10th International Conference on Learning and Collaboration Technologies
- ITAP: 9th International Conference on Human Aspects of IT for the Aged Population
- AIS: 5th International Conference on Adaptive Instructional Systems
- HCI-CPT: 5th International Conference on HCI for Cybersecurity, Privacy and Trust
- HCI-Games: 5th International Conference on HCI in Games
- MobiTAS: 5th International Conference on HCI in Mobility, Transport and Automotive Systems
- AI-HCI: 4th International Conference on Artificial Intelligence in HCI
- MOBILE: 4th International Conference on Design, Operation and Evaluation of Mobile Communications

List of Conference Proceedings Volumes Appearing Before the Conference

1. LNCS 14011, Human-Computer Interaction: Part I, edited by Masaaki Kurosu and Ayako Hashizume
2. LNCS 14012, Human-Computer Interaction: Part II, edited by Masaaki Kurosu and Ayako Hashizume
3. LNCS 14013, Human-Computer Interaction: Part III, edited by Masaaki Kurosu and Ayako Hashizume
4. LNCS 14014, Human-Computer Interaction: Part IV, edited by Masaaki Kurosu and Ayako Hashizume
5. LNCS 14015, Human Interface and the Management of Information: Part I, edited by Hirohiko Mori and Yumi Asahi
6. LNCS 14016, Human Interface and the Management of Information: Part II, edited by Hirohiko Mori and Yumi Asahi
7. LNAI 14017, Engineering Psychology and Cognitive Ergonomics: Part I, edited by Don Harris and Wen-Chin Li
8. LNAI 14018, Engineering Psychology and Cognitive Ergonomics: Part II, edited by Don Harris and Wen-Chin Li
9. LNAI 14019, Augmented Cognition, edited by Dylan D. Schmorrow and Cali M. Fidopiastis
10. LNCS 14020, Universal Access in Human-Computer Interaction: Part I, edited by Margherita Antona and Constantine Stephanidis
11. LNCS 14021, Universal Access in Human-Computer Interaction: Part II, edited by Margherita Antona and Constantine Stephanidis
12. LNCS 14022, Cross-Cultural Design: Part I, edited by Pei-Luen Patrick Rau
13. LNCS 14023, Cross-Cultural Design: Part II, edited by Pei-Luen Patrick Rau
14. LNCS 14024, Cross-Cultural Design: Part III, edited by Pei-Luen Patrick Rau
15. LNCS 14025, Social Computing and Social Media: Part I, edited by Adela Coman and Simona Vasilache
16. LNCS 14026, Social Computing and Social Media: Part II, edited by Adela Coman and Simona Vasilache
17. LNCS 14027, Virtual, Augmented and Mixed Reality, edited by Jessie Y. C. Chen and Gino Fragomeni
18. LNCS 14028, Digital Human Modeling and Applications in Health, Safety, Ergonomics and Risk Management: Part I, edited by Vincent G. Duffy
19. LNCS 14029, Digital Human Modeling and Applications in Health, Safety, Ergonomics and Risk Management: Part II, edited by Vincent G. Duffy
20. LNCS 14030, Design, User Experience, and Usability: Part I, edited by Aaron Marcus, Elizabeth Rosenzweig and Marcelo Soares
21. LNCS 14031, Design, User Experience, and Usability: Part II, edited by Aaron Marcus, Elizabeth Rosenzweig and Marcelo Soares

47. CCIS 1836, HCI International 2023 Posters - Part V, edited by Constantine Stephanidis, Margherita Antona, Stavroula Ntoa and Gavriel Salvendy

https://2023.hci.international/proceedings

Preface

Preliminary scientific results, professional news, or work in progress, described in the form of short research papers (4–8 pages long), constitute a popular submission type among the International Conference on Human-Computer Interaction (HCII) participants. Extended abstracts are particularly suited for reporting ongoing work, which can benefit from a visual presentation, and are presented during the conference in the form of posters. The latter allow a focus on novel ideas and are appropriate for presenting project results in a simple, concise, and visually appealing manner. At the same time, they are also suitable for attracting feedback from an international community of HCI academics, researchers, and practitioners. Poster submissions span the wide range of topics of all HCII thematic areas and affiliated conferences.

Five volumes of the HCII 2023 proceedings are dedicated to this year's poster extended abstracts, in the form of short research papers, focusing on the following topics:

- Volume I: HCI Design - Theoretical Approaches, Methods and Case Studies; Multimodality and Novel Interaction Techniques and Devices; Perception and Cognition in Interaction; Ethics, Transparency and Trust in HCI; User Experience and Technology Acceptance Studies
- Volume II: Supporting Health, Psychological Wellbeing, and Fitness; Design for All, Accessibility and Rehabilitation Technologies; Interactive Technologies for the Aging Population
- Volume III: Interacting with Data, Information and Knowledge; Learning and Training Technologies; Interacting with Cultural Heritage and Art
- Volume IV: Social Media - Design, User Experiences and Content Analysis; Advances in eGovernment Services; eCommerce, Mobile Commerce and Digital Marketing - Design and Customer Behavior; Designing and Developing Intelligent Green Environments; (Smart) Product Design
- Volume V: Driving Support and Experiences in Automated Vehicles; eXtended Reality - Design, Interaction Techniques, User Experience and Novel Applications; Applications of AI Technologies in HCI

Poster extended abstracts are included for publication in these volumes following a minimum of two single-blind reviews from the members of the HCII 2023 international Program Boards. We would like to thank all of them for their invaluable contribution, support, and efforts.

July 2023

Constantine Stephanidis
Margherita Antona
Stavroula Ntoa
Gavriel Salvendy

25th International Conference on Human-Computer Interaction (HCII 2023)

The full list with the Program Board Chairs and the members of the Program Boards of all thematic areas and affiliated conferences of HCII2023 is available online at:

http://www.hci.international/board-members-2023.php

HCI International 2024 Conference

The 26th International Conference on Human-Computer Interaction, HCI International 2024, will be held jointly with the affiliated conferences at the Washington Hilton Hotel, Washington, DC, USA, June 29 – July 4, 2024. It will cover a broad spectrum of themes related to Human-Computer Interaction, including theoretical issues, methods, tools, processes, and case studies in HCI design, as well as novel interaction techniques, interfaces, and applications. The proceedings will be published by Springer. More information will be made available on the conference website: http://2024.hci.international/.

General Chair
Prof. Constantine Stephanidis
University of Crete and ICS-FORTH
Heraklion, Crete, Greece
Email: general_chair@hcii2024.org

https://2024.hci.international/

Contents

Multimodality and Novel Interaction Techniques and Devices

Perception and Cognition in Interaction

Ethics, Transparency and Trust in HCI

User Experience and Technology Acceptance Studies

HCI Design: Theoretical Approaches, Methods and Case Studies

Human-Centered HCI Practices Leading the Path to Industry 5.0: A Systematic Literature Review

Anja Brückner[1] , Philipp Hein[2]([✉]) , Franziska Hein-Pensel[1] , Jasmin Mayan[1] ,
and Mandy Wölke[1]

[1] Institute for Applied Informatics at the University of Leipzig, 04109 Leipzig, Germany
[2] Ergonomics and Innovation Management, Chemnitz University of Technology, 09111
Chemnitz, Germany
`philipp.hein@mb.tu-chemnitz.de`

Abstract. In the course of digital transformation and advancing automation through artificial intelligence (AI), the manufacturing industry, in particular small- and medium-sized enterprises (SMEs), is under pressure to move forward and face the associated challenge of redesigning both their business processes and their work organization. The importance of this transformation process increases with the introduction of new forms of human-machine collaboration, like Human-AI collaboration. To design digital transformation in a sustainable and value-adding way, well-established human-computer interaction (HCI) practices can be used as a framework. This paper explores the question of how human-centered HCI practices can be adapted to the context of the manufacturing industry, considering their unique characteristics. As a basis for this research, a literature review was conducted, examining English- and German-language articles on common HCI practices with a focus on practical use cases and empirical research in an industrial context. The review's findings show that while traditional human-centered design principles such as user-oriented design and usability engineering are broadly considered in HCI, there are several organizational conditions that need to be considered more strongly, such as the limited resources and expertise concerning digitalization available in SMEs. Therefore, this study examines the extent to which human-centered HCI practices in the manufacturing industry can be tailored to the specific characteristics of SMEs. The findings from this review can be used in future research as a basis for developing guidelines for implementing human-centered HCI practices in SMEs. Building on this, guidelines and frameworks can be developed that consider SME specifics such as flexibility and limited resources and are application-ready for practical use. This will support a human-centric digitalization process that is sustainable and value-adding in the long term.

Keywords: Human-Computer Interaction (HCI) · Industry 5.0 · Systematic literature Review (SLR)

C. Stephanidis et al. (Eds.): HCII 2023, CCIS 1832, pp. 3–15, 2023.
https://doi.org/10.1007/978-3-031-35989-7_1

1 Introduction

While the steam engine or electrification were the first key technologies to decisively change work in the manufacturing sector, the implementation of Artificial Intelligence (AI) technologies is a further evolutionary step towards (smart) industry. Intelligent assistance systems, automation and machine learning systems hold enormous economic value for companies (e.g., acceleration of production, quality improvement or optimization of processes) [1, 2]. However, in addition to the economic benefits, AI applications also offer great potential for the realization of environmental and social goals. From an ecological perspective, better control and use of resources can take place through AI-powered maintenance. From a social point of view, an improvement in working conditions can be ensured by relieving the workload through assistance systems and enabling better ergonomic workplaces with the help of robotics [3]. To be able to profit from these advantages in the long term, measures for a human-centered implementation that focuses on the needs of people are needed. After all, the potential of these technologies can only unfold fully if they are recognized and perceived by the user as an actual improvement and thus accepted as an innovative work tool. The HCI research can be seen here as a key factor for a human-centered implementation of AI.

Since AI and, in particular, the use of deep neural networks acts like a "black box" for the end user, the employee must be given special consideration in the transformation process. Since the user themselves cannot see the basis on which the AI makes decisions, corresponding systems require a high level of trust [4]. To overcome these hurdles and create acceptance, transparency and trust, a human-centered design and implementation are critical. The objectives of the next industrial revolution, Industry 5.0, reinforce the relevance and put human-centered HCI in the focus of future research [5].

For small and medium-sized enterprises in particular, AI offers an important opportunity to survive on the market in the long term and even to expand business areas. At the same time, resources in SMEs are limited compared to large companies in terms of financial, technical and human resources [6]. Therefore, the question arises how to ensure human-centered HCI with low entry barriers and as cost- and personnel-friendly as possible. Current HCI guidelines form an important orientation for agreeing on both maximum automation potential and maximum employee centricity. Currently, existing frameworks relate, for example, to the optimal design of the implementation process or a human-friendly UI design [7, 8]. Our study therefore uses a systematic literature review to examine human-centered HCI practices in the industry with a particular focus on SMEs. The findings of this research can be used as a basis for the development of guidelines for designing and implementing human-centered HCI practices in SMEs.

Our paper is structured as follows: the next section discusses the theoretical background of our research, introducing Industry 5.0, human-centered interaction research and the characteristics of small-and-medium-sized enterprises. Before presenting our findings, we introduce our methodological approach. Finally, we conclude future research areas and discuss research limitations.

2 Theoretical Background

2.1 Industry 5.0

At least since the definition of the term in the European Commission's Policy Brief 2021, the topic of Industry 5.0 has become a major point of discussion in industry and research [5]. While Industry 4.0 focused primarily on furthering the development of technical solutions and their integration (for example, in IoT, digital factory models or cyber-physical systems) [9], the next industrial revolution is shifting the focus to social requirements and needs. These are defined by the three pillars sustainability, resilience, and human-centered work design [10]. The latter is directly linked to existing and future production processes. With a view to Industry 5.0, it will be indispensable to consider cooperation with people and technology when implementing or developing machines.

Aleves et al. conclude in their study, that Industry 5.0 builds on Industry 4.0, with the difference that the human-centric approach forms the basis [11]. This means that, in perspective, the focus will no longer be on the high productivity of technological systems only, but more on the adaptation and orientation for the people in the organization. Derived from this is the objective that human-computer interaction must be improved and become a research focus in the next industrial revolution. Specifically, the European Commission also names the individualization of human-machine interaction as a field of action for Industry 5.0 [5]. For this purpose, the development of new frameworks as well as the further development of existing HCI frameworks is urgently needed.

2.2 Human-Computer Interaction (HCI)

Human-computer interaction studies focus on the intersection between humans and machines to investigate and optimize their interaction. Already in 1993, Fischer emphasized the importance of including more aspects of the interaction rather than just focusing on the interface, as research had done up to that point, to provide a holistic understanding [12]. Since then, the focus of human-computer interaction and human-robot collaboration research has increasingly been on explainability and trust towards those complex systems.

Regardless of the performance of AI systems, their potential can only be exploited in the future if they are accepted by users. This applies to systems that intervene significantly in the autonomy of humans, e.g., by issuing warnings in critical situations or giving instructions to be followed. Particularly in the case of complex systems whose mode of operation is not understood or cannot be comprehended by users, an appropriate level of trust is hard to reach [13].

The perception and assessment of the environment differs in humans and intelligent systems, and learned human behavior patterns or predictions about them are not easily transferable to intelligent systems, as problems are not solved comparably [14]. This discrepancy affects the mental models that users of a system make of it. If the user's mental model differs greatly from how the system actually works, trust and attitude toward the system are impacted [15]. Lack of interaction and poor explanations are cited as the main reasons why AI is often perceived as a so-called black box [16]. Accordingly, explainability and transparency are especially crucial when the system is used by non-experts [17]. Results from the research fields of Explainable AI (XAI) as well as Interactive Machine Learning (IML) show that explanations and the creation of interaction possibilities can increase trust in the AI system [18, 19]. In addition to improving AI-human collaboration through increased trust, transparency of models and decisions is also highly important for democratizing AI. For example, the European General Data Protection Regulation demands a "right to explanation" when humans are affected by automated decision-making [20].

To address the users' needs for trust calibration and transparency, it is necessary to have a comprehensive understanding of the users, their tasks and the task environment. The iterative process for human-centered development of interactive systems (DIN 9241–210) covers these requirements. The design solutions are continuously evaluated by users in an iterative development process and are optimized regarding the users' needs and capabilities. Human-centered design plays an important role in the democratization of AI. Shifting from a "human in-the-loop" mindset to "AI in-the-loop" with humans at the center is an important component of human-centered AI [19]. Collaboration between the research fields of artificial intelligence and Human-Computer Interaction offers potential to address issues such as fairness and transparency of AI systems [21].

2.3 Characteristics of Small and Medium-Sized Enterprises

Small and medium-sized enterprises (SMEs) are often considered the backbone of the European economy, writes the European Commission [22]. In fact, the share of SMEs in the EU-27 non-financial business sector in 2021 was 99,8% and employed about 64% of the total labour force [23]. Moreover, SMEs generated 52% of the total value added in the non-financial business sector [20]. This shows that they are essential for job creation and economic growth. In this context, SMEs are represented in several business sectors. Looking at the manufacturing sector, SMEs are also particularly strongly represented here with 99.3%. The overwhelming majority (83.8%) of these are companies with fewer than 10 employees [20]. For companies of this size, viability and competitiveness are of enormous importance. Digitalization in particular enables SMEs to keep up with larger companies in terms of affordable prices and high-quality products [24]. Finally, the use of digital technologies often creates new opportunities for improved access to knowledge or more efficient communication and collaboration. In addition, more comprehensive product developments, the creation of new business areas and the reduction of bureaucracy can be made possible. Technologies such as AI methods in particular hold enormous potential and, as key technologies, can have a significant influence on the success of a company. The numerous potentials are well known and have already been sufficiently researched, but at the same time, studies repeatedly show that SMEs in particular lag in the realization of their digitalization projects. A closer look at the organizational-structural circumstances of SMEs quickly reveals that due to SMEs often limited financial and human resources, digitization projects often take a back seat to profitable day-to-day business. Digitalization projects, such as the implementation of new software, are often carried out alongside daily tasks [25]. So, SMEs tend to be laggards rather than pioneers when it comes to digitalization projects. Several obstacles need to be overcome for SMEs to move forward with their digitalization plans. A decisive factor here is the lack of a wide digital infrastructure, skills and IT-security [26]. Especially when it comes to the implementation of AI solutions, it is often associated with high effort and investment risks [27]. So, it is often not clear in advance whether the technology will be accepted and used in the long term. Unlike large companies, which can cultivate a culture of trial and error due to increased resources, SMEs are unfortunately less able to do so. Based on the increasing importance of human-centered human-computer interaction and insufficient research results so far, this paper aims at investigating existing HCI frameworks with a special focus on human-centeredness and SME suitability.

3 Method

To address the research objective, our study uses a systematic literature review and investigates HCI use-cases previously presented in research papers, using the citation database Web of Science for English papers and the citation database Springer and Research-Gate for German papers[1]. The contributions were refined by defining the following parameters:

- *Publication language:* German and English,
- *Year of publication*: 2011–2022,
- *Format*: Full Paper (min. Two pages), reviewed journal or conference publications.

Table 1 presents the used keyword-strings and their number of results to generate a list of HCI case study publications.

To investigate human-centered HCI use-cases, we used the approach presented by Große-Schwiep et al. [28] and filtered the search results in an iterative procedure, consisting of four stages of literature screening. An overview of the number of publications for each screening level is listed in Table 2.

---

[1] We had to use different citation databases for English and German because they rely on fundamentally different sources. There are very few German journals in the Web of Science database, which resulted in zero hits in our keyword search.

Table 1. Keyword-strings.

LANGUAGE	KEYWORD-STRING	QUERY	HITS
GERMAN	(KI OR "künstliche intelligenz" OR ML OR "maschinelles lernen" OR "Industrie 4.0" OR "Industrie 5.0") AND (nutzerzentriert OR menschzentriert OR mensch-maschine-interaktion OR mensch-roboter-interaktion OR mensch-computer-interaktion OR MMI OR MCI OR erklärbar*) AND (evaluier* OR interview OR feldstudie OR fallstudie OR nutzerstudie OR nutzertest OR evaluation OR gestaltung OR untersuch*) AND (fertigung OR produktion OR fabrik OR "fabrik planung" OR produktionsplanung OR angebotserstellung OR kalkulation OR produktionssteuerung) NOT (gesundheit* OR mediz*)	ResearchGate	45
		Springer Link	417
ENGLISH	(((AI OR "artificial intelligence" OR ML OR "machine learning" OR "Industry 4.0" OR" Industry 5.0") AND (user-cent* OR "user cent*" OR human-machine OR "human machine" OR HCI OR human-computer OR "human computer" OR explainab*)) OR (HCML OR HC-ML OR XAI)) AND (investigate OR evaluate Or interview OR "case study" OR "user study" OR "field study") AND (manufacturing OR production OR industry OR maintenance OR mechanical OR costing OR "production planning" OR "production sheduling" OR factory OR factories OR fabrication) NOT (healthcare OR medicine OR medical OR "health care")	Web of Science	235

4 Human-Centered HCI Practices in SMEs

Frameworks and guidelines provide orientation for the various stakeholders in AI implementation and create an understanding of the overall process [7, 8, 21, 29, 30]. While they are well founded and provide valuable insight on how to develop and introduce technologies under the human-centered lens of Industry 5.0, there is a gap in making them actionable for practical use cases, especially in the manufacturing industry and SMEs.

Using a systematic literature review, we analyze human-centered HCI practices in the industry and focus on SMEs. Table 3 offers a structured overview of the literature in the following categories: technology, contribution, user group, research design, and practical setting. Regarding the technologies which were used, most use cases in our review involved assistance systems or augmented reality. The technologies were often developed or implemented by using or adapting a user-centered design approach. Emerging technologies like machine learning are only represented in a small number of included papers. This might stem from our focus on practical use cases and the implementation

Table 2. Number of publications per stage.

Stage of literature review	Number of excluded publications	Number of publications for the next stage
0. Total number of publications (result of research string)		697
1. Exclusion of papers by title (relevance)	427	270
2. Exclusion by abstract and keywords (finer relevance analysis)	96	174
3. Exclusion by formal criteria (accessible, peer-reviewed, scientific approach)	32	142
4. Exclusion based on full text analysis (e.g., methodological transparency, dimensions and criteria clearly defined, focus on use-case)	123	18

of HCI research design, where both factors are less often considered with newer technologies. Research designs were primarily focused on qualitive research methods like observation, sometimes in combination with thinking aloud, and interviews. Contributions to the body of literature are mainly in the field of knowledge transfer. Practical use cases were described in a broad range of industries, I.e., automotive, textile, woodworking and aviation. The targeted user groups were predominantly new workers or workers in positions with low skill requirements.

For HCI practices to be applicable to SMEs several factors must be considered. Since SMEs are generally limited in financial and human resources, HCI practices that have a high degree of complexity or require big investments of money or time are not very well suited. SMEs are highly specialized and individually structured. This requires HCI practices to be flexible and adaptable to differently sized and structured SMEs.

Therefore, we characterize HCI practices as usable for SMEs, by the following key factors that need to be considered. Firstly, the practice should already have been implemented in other SMEs, and there should be empirical findings to support its effectiveness. Additionally, it should be adaptable and flexible in use, with low support requirements. This means that the practice can be easily integrated into existing workflows and doesn't require extensive training or support. Another important consideration is the cost-benefit calculation for the SME. The practice should offer a positive return on investment, in terms of both time and money saved. By considering these factors, SMEs can identify and adopt human-computer interaction practices that are well-suited to their needs and resources.

Table 3. Systematic literature review.

Reference	Technology	Contribution	Practical Setting	User research design	User group
Abdul Hadi et al. 2022 [31]	Assistance Systems	Psychological benefits (Visualization)	Use of sensor & guidance devices at assembly stations of a construction machinery manufacturer	Contextualization of sensory data and establishing a dynamic knowledge management system	Assemblers
Aceta et al. 2022 [32]	Language Model	Dialogue Framework	Robot collaboration, Information systems	Prototype testing, questionnaire	Industrial workers
Cabour et al. 2022 [33]	AI-Model	XAI Framework	Aircraft parts inspection	Ethnographic approach, including interviews, observation, field experiment	Inspectors
Foullois et al. 2021 [34]	Assistance Systems	User acceptance model	Two pilot projects: Mixed mock-up in production system planning & Service system for conformity management	Interviews, prototype testing	All process participants
Gloy 2020 [35]	Augmented reality	Knowledge transfer	Weaving machine usage and maintenance (textile industry)	User-centered design-approach, including a requirements survey, expert interviews, workshops, and group discussions	Workers in textile manufacturing
Keller et al. 2021 [36]	Assistance Systems	Knowledge transfer ((Learning) innovation in companies designed context-sensitively)	Scientists collaborate with application partners (EVerAssist project)	Organizational education design-based research approach, integrating processes of reflection, translation, negotiation and visioning as practices of knowledge production in a participatory approach	All process participants
Konstantinidis et al. 2020 [37]	Augmented reality/ Computer vision	Knowledge transfer (reduce the knowledge gap between the manufacturers and maintenance operators)	Automotive industrial asset provided by a collaborative manufacturer (A/C compressor)	Optimization of smartphone and user interaction	Operators with low knowledge and experience/ machine operator

(continued)

Table 3. (*continued*)

Reference	Technology	Contribution	Practical Setting	User research design	User group
Lacueva-Pérez et al. 2018 [38]	Assistance Systems/ Self-learning manufacturing workplaces	Job satisfaction, innovation & problem-solving skills, the productivity of factories	Slovenian supplier of the automotive industry (FACTS4WORKERS project)	Questionnaires, observation, interviews	Shopfloor workers and system creators
Marques et al. 2022 [39]	Augmented reality	Knowledge transfer (Collaboration among remote team members)	Use case in remote maintenance; design and implementation of a participatory design to foster the contributions of domain experts	User centered design-approach, including focus groups	Technicians and experts involved in maintenance tasks
Merhar et al. 2019 [3]	Assistance Systems (smartwatches)	Psychological benefits (Supporting employees in the execution of tasks)	Introduction of a digital assistance system in an SME, supported by Mittelstand 4.0 competence center	User-centered design-approach, including a requirements survey, and workshops	All process participants
Pacaux-Lemoine et al. 2022 [40]	Cognitive Work Analysis & Digital Twin	Knowledge transfer	Decision support system (manufacturing plan, supervisor-worker-interaction)	Cognitive work analysis methodology, including work domain and control task analysis	All process participants
Peruzzini et al. 2020 [41]	monitoring system: eye tracking and wearable biosensor	Physical benefits	Include human data into the creation of the digital twin to optimize the design of the workplace	Theoretical human-centered framework for Operator 4.0 based on the analysis of human behaviors and actions	Assembly operations
Peruzzini et al. 2017 [42]	adaptive manufacturing systems (AMS)	Physical benefits	Large-sized Italian company producing woodworking machine tools	HC redesign of AMS, considering the users, the context, the machine, and the interface; use prototypes	Aging workers
Peruzzini et al. 2019 [43]	Virtual mock-ups, monitoring sensors for tracking	Psychological benefits (Visualization)	Large-sized international company in the field of production of agriculture systems	Analysis of human-machine interaction, based on interaction model by Norman	Workers with machine interaction (health aspects, ergonomics)
Rusch et al. 2021 [44]	Assistance Systems	Knowledge transfer	Production engineering workplaces (e.g., logistics, production)	Integration of the system in practice + usability scale	New employees

(*continued*)

Table 3. (*continued*)

Reference	Technology	Contribution	Practical Setting	User research design	User group
Schönig et al. 2020 [45]	BPM in context IoT, Human-robot interaction	Psychological benefits	Automation and production company	Design science research approach, including prototype testing	Workers with robot cooperation
Stern et al. 2019 [46]	Cyber-physical Production Systems (CPPS)	Psychological benefits	Production lines, Cyber Physical Systems	Observations and user surveys	All process participants
Vanderhaegen 2021 [47]	Unspecified AI-Model	Framework to investigate ethical dissonance	Mobility Safety: Lane Keeping Assist System (LKAS); Automated Speed Control System (ASCS)	Lab experiments, questionnaires	All experts in the field of ethics, developers of mobility assistance systems

In order to assess the applicability of HCI practices we tried to overlay SMEs specific factors onto the use cases we identified through our review. Through this process we were able to diagnose a gap in reporting on factors relevant to assessing the feasibility of HCI practices for SMEs. Authors of included articles often omit key data when describing case studies conducted within actual work environments. Information on company size, expertise in HCI methods or innovation management in general, is usually not included. Also, investment of time and money is not taken into consideration.

5   Conclusion

We examined use cases of human-centered HCI practices in SMEs based on a systematic literature review. The conducted study shows that currently only a few HCI approaches have been evaluated as practical use cases in SMEs. While technical implementation and design principles mostly play an essential role in the described use cases, the flexibility and cost-benefit ratio of HCI practices are usually not evaluated. Likewise, no detailed information on company size and structure is provided by the reporting studies in practical use cases. This gap in data stems from the fact that HCI research usually focuses on the methods themselves, and less on environmental factors influencing their implementation. However, these criteria are crucial for assessing the applicability in SMEs [48]. With the goal of creating resilient, sustainable, and human-centered strategies for the use of AI in the context of Industry 5.0 [10], the applicability of HCI for SMEs must become a strong focus of future research. Therefore, to ensure the transferability of HCI practices, evaluations should also include SME-relevant aspects. One limitation of our systematic literature review is the small number of papers included in the final review. While the literature selection process was rigorous and followed a well-defined set of criteria, the exclusion of papers that did not meet these criteria may have led to a biased sample. Many papers missed an empirical case or did not document the implementation in their work. Additionally, the use of a keyword string to identify relevant papers may have inadvertently excluded practical papers that did not use the same terminology. This limitation may impact the generalizability of the findings and limit the scope of the review. Therefore, future studies may benefit from a more comprehensive search strategy that includes a broader range of keywords and considers a wider range of literature sources, like white or corporate papers. Overall, the small number of results nevertheless provides a statement that there are currently only few practical use cases for HCI methods in context with Industry 5.0 or AI reported in literature, so there is still a considerable need for research in the future. Particular attention should be paid to SMEs and their hurdles, such as limited resources and lack of expertise. Yet, HCI practices are still valuable tools for SMEs. While there are challenges to implementing HCI methods in such settings, the benefits for both employees and the company still make it a worthwhile effort. SMEs can start by adopting application-proven methods or by seeking out external support and expertise where necessary. Hence, our review ought to be a starting point in helping to pave the way to better-suited HCI methods for SMEs by representing the current situation and drawing attention to the special challenges for SMEs.

Author Contribution. All authors have accepted responsibility for the entire content of this manuscript and approved its submission. authors use alphabetical sequence to acknowledge equal contribution (EC).

Funding Information. This research was funded by the Bundesministerium für Bildung und Forschung (BMBF, Federal Ministry of Education and Research) – Project: K-M-I (Grant: 02L19C501).

References

1. Cioffi, R., Travaglioni, M., Piscitelli, G., Petrillo, A., de Felice, F.: Artificial intelligence and machine learning applications in smart production: progress, trends, and directions. Sustainability **12**, 492 (2020)
2. Zinke-Wehlmann, C., Friedrich, J., Kirschenbaum, A., Wölke, M., Brückner, A.: Conceptualizing sustainable artificial intelligence development, pp. 545–554. Springer, Cham (2022). https://doi.org/10.1007/978-3-031-14844-6_43
3. Merhar, L., Höllthaler, G., Berger, C.: Digitale Assistenzsysteme für die Produktion: Von der Zielfindung bis zur Einbindung gemeinsam mit den Mitarbeitern. In: Bosse, C.K., Zink, K.J. (eds.) Arbeit 4.0 im Mittelstand, pp. 279–302. Springer, Heidelberg (2019). https://doi.org/10.1007/978-3-662-59474-2_17
4. Eschenbach, W.J.: Transparency and the black box problem: why we do not trust AI. Philos. Technol. **34**(4), 1607–1622 (2021). https://doi.org/10.1007/s13347-021-00477-0
5. European Commission, Directorate-General for Research, Innovation, Breque, M., de Nul, L., Petridis, A.: Industry 5.0 Towards a Sustainable, Human-Centric and Resilient European Industry. Publications Office (2021)
6. Abdollahzadegan, A., Che Hussin, A.R., Moshfegh Gohary, M., Amini, M.: The Organizational Critical Success Factors for Adopting Cloud Computing in SMEs (2013)
7. Shneiderman, B.: Human-Centered AI. Oxford University Press, Oxford (2022)

8. Amershi, S., et al.: Guidelines for human-AI interaction. In Brewster, S., Fitzpatrick, G., Cox, A., Kostakos, V. (eds.) Proceedings of the 2019 CHI Conference on Human Factors in Computing Systems, pp. 1–13. ACM, New York (2019)
9. Suleiman, Z., Shaikholla, S., Dikhanbayeva, D., Shehab, E., Turkyilmaz, A.: Industry 4.0: clustering of concepts and characteristics. Cogent Eng. **9**, 2034264 (2022)
10. Xu, X., Lu, Y., Vogel-Heuser, B., Wang, L.: Industry 4.0 and Industry 5.0—Inception, conception and perception. J. Manuf. Syst. **61**, 530–535 (2021)
11. Alves, J., Lima, T.M., Gaspar, P.D.: Is Industry 5.0 a human-centred approach a systematic review. Processes **11**, 193 (2023)
12. Fischer, G.: Beyond human-computer interaction. In: Böcker, H.-D., Glatthaar, W., Strothotte, T. (eds.) Mensch-Computer-Kommunikation, pp. 274–287. Springer, Berlin (1993)
13. Rožanec, J.M., et al.: STARdom: an architecture for trusted and secure human-centered manufacturing systems. In: Dolgui, A., Bernard, A., Lemoine, D., von Cieminski, G., Romero, D. (eds.) APMS 2021. IAICT, vol. 633, pp. 199–207. Springer, Cham (2021). https://doi.org/10.1007/978-3-030-85910-7_21
14. Amershi, S., Kamar, E., Kiciman, E.: People and AI see things different implications of mismatched perception on HCI for AI systems. In: Workshop on Human-Centered Machine Learning Perspectives at CHI 2019 (2019)
15. Bansal, G., Nushi, B., Kamar, E., Lasecki, W.S., Weld, D.S., Horvitz, E.: Beyond accuracy: the role of mental models in human-AI team performance. HCOMP **7**, 2–11 (2019)
16. Pena, F.C., Guerra-Gomez, J.: Opening the black-box. In: Proceedings of the Machine Learning from User Interaction for Visualization and Analytics Workshop at IEEE VIS (2018)
17. Molnar, C.: Interpretable Machine Learning. Christoph Molnar, Munich (2022)
18. Gutzwiller, R.S., Reeder, J.: Dancing with algorithms: interaction creates greater preference and trust in machine-learned behavior. Hum. Factors **63**, 854–867 (2021)
19. Shneiderman, B.: Bridging the gap between ethics and practice. ACM Trans. Interact. Intell. Syst. **10**, 1–31 (2020)
20. Goodman, B., Flaxman, S.: European Union regulations on algorithmic decision-making and a "right to explanation." AIMag **38**, 50–57 (2017)
21. Auernhammer, J.: Human-centered AI: the role of human-centered design research in the development of AI. In: DRS2020: Synergy. Design Research Society (2020)
22. eurostat: Kleine und mittlere Unternehmen (KMU). https://ec.europa.eu/eurostat/de/web/structural-business-statistics/information-on-data/small-and-medium-sized-enterprises
23. Gorgels, S., Priem, M., Blagoeva, T., Martinelle, A., Milanesi, G.: Annual Report on European SMEs 2021/2022. Publications Office of the European Union, Luxembourg (2022)
24. Ramdani, B., Raja, S., Kayumova, M.: Digital innovation in SMEs: a systematic review, synthesis and research agenda. Inf. Technol. Dev. **28**, 56–80 (2022)
25. Lindner, D.: Definition und Besonderheiten von KMU. In: Lindner, D. (ed.) KMU im digitalen Wandel, pp. 5–7. Springer Fachmedien Wiesbaden, Wiesbaden (2019). https://doi.org/10.1007/978-3-658-24399-9_2
26. Abel-Koch, J., Obaidi, L.A., Kasmi, S.E., Acevedo, M.F., Morin, L., Topczewska, A.: European SME Survey 2019 (2019)
27. Pokorni, B., Braun, M., Knecht, C.: Menschzentrierte KI-Anwendungen in der Produktion. Fraunhofer-Gesellschaft (2021)
28. Große-Schwiep, B., Bensberg, F., Schinnenburg, H.: Entwicklung eines reifegradmodells zur bewertung des digitalisierungsgrades von geschäftsprozessen. Anwendungen und Konzepte der Wirtschaftsinformatik **11**, 14 (2020)
29. Langer, M., et al.: What do we want from Explainable Artificial Intelligence (XAI)? – a stakeholder perspective on XAI and a conceptual model guiding interdisciplinary XAI research. Artif Intell. **296**, 103473 (2021)

30. Xu, W., Dainoff, M.J., Ge, L., Gao, Z.: Transitioning to human interaction with AI systems: new challenges and opportunities for HCI professionals to enable human-centered AI. Int. J. Hum. Comput. Interact. **39**, 1–25 (2022)
31. Abdul Hadi, M., et al.: Towards flexible and cognitive production—addressing the production challenges. Appl. Sci. Basel **12**, 8696 (2022)
32. Aceta, C., Fernández, I., Soroa, A.: KIDE4I: a generic semantics-based task-oriented dialogue system for human-machine interaction in industry 5.0. Appl. Sci. Basel **12**, 1192 (2022)
33. Cabour, G., Morales-Forero, A., Ledoux, É., Bassetto, S.: An explanation space to align user studies with the technical development of Explainable AI. AI Society (2022)
34. Foullois, M., et al.: Arbeit 4.0 in der Produktentstehung. In: Jeske, T., Lennings, F. (eds.) Produktivitätsmanagement 4.0. ifaa-Edition, pp. 81–113. Springer, Heidelberg (2021). https://doi.org/10.1007/978-3-662-61584-3_4
35. Gloy, Y.-S.: Assistenzsysteme in der Textilproduktion. In: Gloy, Y.-S. (ed.) Industrie 4.0 in der Textilproduktion, pp. 188–256. Springer, Berlin (2020). https://doi.org/10.1007/978-3-662-54502-7_6
36. Keller, A., Weber, S.M., Rentzsch, M., Haase, T.: Lern- und Assistenzsysteme partizipativ integrieren – Entwicklung einer Systematik zur Prozessgestaltung auf Basis eines organisationspädagogischen Ansatzes. Z. Arb. Wiss. **75**, 455–469 (2021)
37. Konstantinidis, F.K., Kansizoglou, I., Santavas, N., Mouroutsos, S.G., Gasteratos, A.: MARMA: a mobile augmented reality maintenance assistant for fast-track repair procedures in the context of Industry 4.0. Machines **8**, 88 (2020)
38. Lacueva-Pérez, F., et al.: Comparing approaches for evaluating digital interventions on the shop floor. Technologies **6**, 116 (2018)
39. Marques, B., Silva, S., Alves, J., Rocha, A., Dias, P., Santos, B.S.: Remote collaboration in maintenance contexts using augmented reality: insights from a participatory process. Int. J. Interact. Des. Manuf. IJIDEM **16**, 419–438 (2022)
40. Pacaux-Lemoine, M.-P., Berdal, Q., Guérin, C., Rauffet, P., Chauvin, C., Trentesaux, D.: Designing human–system cooperation in industry 4.0 with cognitive work analysis: a first evaluation. Cogn. Technol. Work **24**(1), 93–111 (2021). https://doi.org/10.1007/s10111-021-00667-y
41. Peruzzini, M., Grandi, F., Pellicciari, M.: Exploring the potential of Operator 4.0 interface and monitoring. Comput. Ind. Eng. **139**, 105600 (2020)
42. Peruzzini, M., Pellicciari, M.: A framework to design a human-centred adaptive manufacturing system for aging workers. Adv. Eng. Inform. **33**, 330–349 (2017)
43. Peruzzini, M., Pellicciari, M., Grandi, F., Oreste Andrisano, A.: A multimodal virtual reality set-up for human-centered design of industrial workstations. DYNA **94**, 182–188 (2019)
44. Rusch, T., et al.: SynDiQuAss – Synchronisierung von Digitalisierung, Qualitätssicherung und Assistenzsystemen. In: Bauer, W., Mütze-Niewöhner, S., Stowasser, S., Zanker, C., Müller, N. (eds.) Arbeit in der digitalisierten Welt, pp. 289–303. Springer, Heidelberg (2021). https://doi.org/10.1007/978-3-662-62215-5_19
45. Schönig, S., Ackermann, L., Jablonski, S., Ermer, A.: IoT meets BPM: a bidirectional communication architecture for IoT-aware process execution. Softw. Syst. Model. **19**(6), 1443–1459 (2020). https://doi.org/10.1007/s10270-020-00785-7
46. Stern, H., Becker, T.: Concept and evaluation of a method for the integration of human factors into human-oriented work design in cyber-physical production systems. Sustainability **11**, 4508 (2019)
47. Vanderhaegen, F.: Weak signal-oriented investigation of ethical dissonance applied to unsuccessful mobility experiences linked to human-machine interactions. Sci. Eng. Ethics **27**, 2 (2021)
48. Jiwangkura, S., Sophatsathit, P., Chandrachai, A.: Industrial internet of things implementation strategies with HCI for SME adoption. Int. J. Autom. Smart. **10**, 153–168 (2020)

Temperature, Entropy, and Usability: The Theoretical and Practical Resemblances Between Thermodynamics and User Interface Design

Lance Chong[✉]

University of Lethbridge, Lethbridge, Canada
lance.chong@uleth.ca

Abstract. This study explores the possibility of creating a set of new theoretical models and metrics that can potentially serve as portable evaluation tools for user interface-related design and research. With inspirations from thermodynamics and information theory, this study perceives the user interfaces interactivity as binary finite-state machines (BFSM) and as "networked two-way communicational channels" (NTCC), thus bridging the gap between widely applicable fundamental scientific theories and the methodologies that are potentially useful for user interfaces design and research. The new metrics and theoretical models created and examined in this study seem to coincide with empirical experiences and are worthy of further investigation.

Keywords: Usability · User Interface · Interaction Design · Design Evaluation · Information Theory · Entropy · Thermodynamics · Interface Temperature

1 Introduction

Most of our current definitions of "usability" [1] are based on subjective user experiences and expectations instead of based on the objective properties and inner workings of the user interface (UI) itself. Because the user feelings are diverse and the user motivations could be uncertain, it is often complicated to conduct quantitative evaluations for a UI and its related interactions.

At the same time, a user interface is obviously a product that was made to produce or perform functional "work"; it consumes and processes "energy", e.g., information and electricity; and is often subject to performance evaluations such as efficiency, reliability, and "usability". The UI is also a "system", and has inner components not too different from other types of machineries that scientists have been studying for a long time. With such an amount of similarity, it would be logical for us not only to seek possible ways of using well-established scientific theories and methodologies such as those from thermodynamics [2] and from information theory [3] to facilitate our existing approaches in UI research and design but also to examine what these different fields may have in common. Few works have yet been done to analyze such possible inner connections.

C. Stephanidis et al. (Eds.): HCII 2023, CCIS 1832, pp. 16–24, 2023.
https://doi.org/10.1007/978-3-031-35989-7_2

This study aims to examine such potential relationships in hopes of discovering fresh theoretical insights and novel practical solutions.

2 Theoretical Foundation

2.1 Miller's Variance and "Unfamiliar Actionable Interface Options" (UAIO)

In his influential 1956 paper *The Magical Number Seven, Plus or Minus Two* [4], George Miller used several simple and intuitive schematics to introduce the basic concepts and methodologics that are related to Shannon's information theory [3]. His schematics include a localized definition of "variance" and justifications for using "unidimensional stimuli" [4] in user-to-system performance evaluations. By following Miller's paradigm, we can also view the "actionable items" in an interactive UI as "variances" and consider these "variances" as a set of "unidimensional stimuli".

To avoid potential mix-ups, in this study, we can call these "actionable items", e.g., dial knobs on a dashboard or clickable links on a web page, etc., as "actionable interface options" (AIO). We can also categorize these AIO into two types: those that are already known and familiar to the user during the interaction, and those that are still not known or unfamiliar to the user during the interaction. We can call those belonging to the second type as "uncertain actionable interface options" (UAIO). We can consider the tossing of a fair coin as a simple example of interacting with a UI. If we toss this coin for N times, the number of UAIO is N. For the case of tossing a set of N fair coins for one time, the number of UAIO is also N.

We will focus on the UAIO in a UI in this study because they are the determining factor for the level of uncertainty or "unusability" of a UI at a given stage of the interaction concerning a particular user. If we can effectively evaluate the "unusability" of a UI, we are not too far from successfully quantifying its "usability".

2.2 The UI as a Binary Finite-State Machine (BFSM)

The interactions with UI can be easily viewed as finite-state machines (FSM). We can go one step further to consider them as BFSMs by normalizing all the possible UAIO outcomes into two categories: those that are "relevant" (*re*) to the user, i.e., useful, worthy of follow-up actions, and those that are "irrelevant" (*irre*) to the user, i.e., not useful, unworthy of following through. Assuming fair chance, for each UAIO item of x, its equiprobable outcomes will be $X = \{x_{re}, x_{irre}\}$. If the total number of UAIO is N, the number of total outcomes will be $n = 2^N$ (See Table 1).

Table 1. The possible numbers of equiprobable outcomes (*n*) given the number of UAIO (*N*).

Number of UAIO	Number of possible outcomes	Probability for each outcome
0	1	1
1	2	0.5
2	4	0.25
...	...	...
N	$n = 2^N$	$1/n$

When the total number of UAIO is N, the outcomes will be: $X = \{x_1, x_2, \ldots, x_N\}$, their probability distribution of these outcomes will be: $p(X) = \{p(x_1), p(x_2), \ldots, p(x_N)\}$. The Shannon entropy, which in our case represents the amount of "need-to-learn" information, or uncertainty, concerning all the UAIO that are present at a given stage of the UI from a user's perspective will be:

$$H(X) = \sum_{i=1}^{N} p(x_i) log_2 \frac{1}{p(x_i)} \text{ bits.}$$

If all the UAIO have equiprobable outcomes, the entropy (*H*) will be equal to N bits. This synchronizes well with typical user experiences: when the value of N is larger, i.e., the UI is more complicated or more unfamiliar, the Shannon entropy (*H*) is also higher. Such a correlation also resembles *the second law of thermodynamics* [2].

3   The Interface Temperature (IT)

3.1   The Inventions of Temperature in Physics

Scientific terminologies are often selected from plain languages and given new and more precise meanings. The evolutional story behind both the concepts and the measurements of "*temperature*" [2] is a perfect example. We can clearly see that most temperature measuring scales, including Celsius, Fahrenheit, and Kelvin, were designed by first selecting two anchoring numbers (usually 0 and 100) from a decimal scale, associating them with two arbitrarily chosen thermo-equilibrium states that are easily perceptible to human senses, and then dividing the in-between measurements evenly to match per unit. Various types of thermometers were also invented to augment such intellectual innovations. Given such scientific precedence, it is logical for us to also consider the invention of a "temperature-like" new metric to facilitate the measuring and communication of user feelings concerning the UI.

3.2 The Technical Degree ($^{\circ}t$) and the Emotional Degree ($^{\circ}e$)

Let us continue the above thought experiment by calling such a new metric "interface temperature" (IT). Because the number of UAIO is often associated with the feeling of "cleanliness" or "cluttering" of a UI's layout, we can associate the value of N directly to a decimal scale at a 1:1 ratio, and call this measuring scale the "technical temperature scale" (iT) with "technical degree" ($^{\circ}t$) as its unit. For non-technical communications, we can establish another one and call it the "emotional temperature scale" (eT), with "emotional degree" ($^{\circ}e$) as its unit. We can designate 0 $^{\circ}e$ to represent the UI condition of $N = 0$, and designate 100 $^{\circ}e$ to represent the UI condition of $N = 27$, (the 26 alphabets plus *space*). Both IT scales seem to have potential values for applications (See Table 2, and Fig. 1). Given today's technological advancements, we can assume that monitoring the value of N in a UI during the user interaction is firmly within our reach.

Negative temperature measurements are not considered in this study due to the apparent absence of corresponding user experiences. Cases such as faulty or misleading UAIO can be considered as channel noises (η) or UAIO biases in specific situations. The highest possible iT value could be capped by the human retina resolution of 5.76×10^8 or by another limiting value of choice for specific applications.

Table 2. The comparison of the numbers of UAIO (N), the number of possible outcomes (n), interface temperature measurements (IT) in technical degrees ($^{\circ}t$) and in emotional degrees ($^{\circ}e$).

N	n	iT ($^{\circ}t$)	eT ($^{\circ}e$)	Notes
N	2^N	$N/1$	$N/0.27$	
...	...	...	...	...
27	134M	27	100	26 alphabets + 1; water boiling point 100 $^{\circ}$C
12	4,096	12	44.44	Twelve months; twelve hours; a dozen
11	2,048	11	40.07	
10	1,024	10	37.04	Decimal; human body temperature 37 $^{\circ}$C
9	512	9	33.33	
8	256	8	29.63	
7	128	7	25.93	Miller's number of "7 ± 2". [4]
6	64	6	22.22	
5	32	5	18.52	Comfortable indoor temperature 18–24 $^{\circ}$C
4	16	4	14.81	
3	8	3	11.11	
2	4	2	7.41	Binary; duality; on/off
1	2	1	3.70	
0	1	0	0	The lowest possible IT measurement

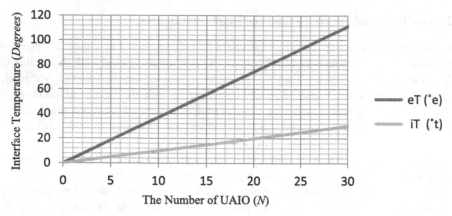

Fig. 1. The correlations between N and the IT measurements ($^\circ t$ and $^\circ e$) are perfect positive.

4 The Networked Two-Way Communication Channel

4.1 The User Interface as a Two-Way Communication Channel (TCC)

When applying Shannon's information theory to our study, if all the available UAIO are the input X; and out of which, those the user will perceive are the output Y. The information-theoretic quantities concerning a UI will be as follows: the input entropy $H(X)$; the output entropy $H(Y)$; joint entropy $H(X, Y)$; mutual information $I(X, Y)$; the equivocation $H(X|Y)$; and the conditional output entropy $H(Y|X)$ [5].

If a UI contains one input message, e.g., a clickable image of a dog, as its input, the information that the user recognizes will be the output. We can view the UI as a one-way communication channel as in Shannon's information theory [3, 5, 6]. Hereby, the input entropy $H(X)$ is the total intended information in the image representing the dog; the output entropy $H(Y)$ is the total output information decodable by the user, which will likely contain the recognizable dog plus *noise information*, such as, a sled in the background of the image; mutual information $I(X, Y)$ is the graphical representation of the dog; output conditional entropy $H(Y|X)$ is the noise information recognizable as the sled; and the equivocation $H(X|Y)$ is the noise information that neither represents the dog nor recognizable by the user. In this example, the number of UAIO is $N = 1$, the number of possible outcomes is $2^N = 2$. The likeliness of the user to click the image should be considered as channel noise, UAIO bias, or user bias depending on the situation. This model also applies to UIs with multiple UAIO.

4.2 Background Information and the Networked Two-Way Communication Channel (NTCC)

During the interactions, the user will gradually learn the UAIO in a UI. Assuming no new UAIO will be added to the UI and the user never forgets, the value of N will either stay the same if the user stops learning, or will decrease over time, causing the input entropy $H(X)$ to decrease with it. This result seems to contradict both the information theory and the second law of thermodynamics, unless we consider the user is building a dynamic mental copy of the UI, and to view the UI and the user as *two information-exchanging objects or sub-systems*, inside a larger "UI-to-user system" (UIUS). In this model, $I(X, Y)$ transfers from the UI to the user and is to be retained by the user. As $H(X)$ decreases during the interaction, $I(X, Y)$ will increases by the same amount if the TCC is noiseless, i.e., no AIO will change and the user never forgets. The $I(X, Y)$ represents user learning; $H(Y|X)$ represents unintended background information the user can decode; $H(Y)$ is the sum of $I(X, Y)$ and $H(Y|X)$.

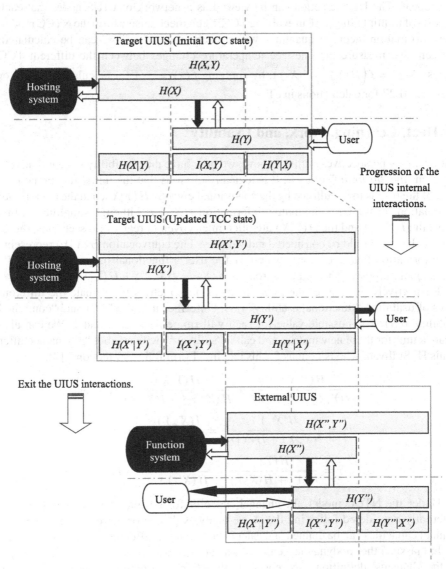

Fig. 2. Networked two-way communication channels (NTCC) and UI-to-user systems (UIUS).

In this model, the mutual information $I(X, Y)$ is only considered as part of the UI's working mechanism that serves the interactive operations. The information that fulfills the user's original functional purposes is $H(Y|X)$. During the interaction, the dynamic flow of information forms a two-way communication channel model, which differs from the one-way communication channel model [3, 5, 6] in Shannon's information theory. The information in $H(Y'|X')$ is subsequently transmitted out of the UIUS at an exit stage and becomes the input information $H(X'')$ of an external UIUS that fulfills the user's original functional purposes (see Fig. 2). Such internal and external processes will repeat. The UI interaction can be viewed as a network of UIUS nodes that each consists of multiple stages of an evolving TCC. Such mechanisms form the NTCC model. The information-theoretic quantities within each stage of a TCC can be calculated. We can also measure the interface temperature changes between the different TCC stages: $\Delta IT = f\left(H(X) - H(X')\right)$, by applying $f(x) = x/1$ for calculations in iT, or $f(x) = x/0.27$ for calculations in eT.

5 Heat, Learning, Work, and Usability

With the new perspectives outlined above, we now have the possibility to quantitatively represent the "*usability*" of a UI. It is logically obvious that the initial functional purpose of the user is to be fulfilled by the conditional entropy $H(Y|X)$, and the operational information for the UI is the mutual information $I(X, Y)$. Although simplified in this study, the $I(X, Y)$ and the $H(Y|X)$ are often interwoven in real-world scenarios, therefore, each case should be considered individually. The equivocation $H(X|Y)$ represents the information that does not serve either the user's functional purposes or the UI's operational purposes. The output entropy is $H(Y) = I(X, Y) + H(Y|X)$.

Respectively, we can create three different new metrics to evaluate the different types of usability: "functional usability" (*fS*); "interface usability"(*iS*); and "combined usability"(*cS*). The possible value for each will range between 0 and 1. We can also create a unit for these new metrics and call it "sullivan" (with symbol "*s*"), named after Louis H. Sullivan, who is famous for his maxim "Form follows function." [7].

$$fS = \frac{H(Y|X)}{H(Y|X) + H(X|Y)} = \frac{H(Y|X)}{H(X, Y) - I(X, Y)} \text{ sullivan.}$$

$$iS = \frac{I(X, Y)}{I(X, Y) + H(X|Y)} = \frac{I(X, Y)}{H(X)} \text{ sullivan.}$$

$$cS = \frac{H(Y)}{H(Y) + H(X|Y)} = \frac{H(Y)}{H(X, Y)} \text{ sullivan.}$$

Under the NTCC model, the channel capacity for UI interactions should also be differently considered following the above analysis. Three or more different types of channel capacities can be defined and calculated, each for different evaluation purposes.

In classical thermodynamics, entropy was defined as $\Delta S = \Delta Q/T$ or $\Delta S = W/T$ by the Clausius' definition. ΔS represents the change in entropy, ΔQ represents the change in heat, W represents work, which is a heat equivalent, and T represents temperature. Since Clausius' entropy (S) and Shannon's entropy (H) both measure the dynamic nature of energy or information in systems, we can hypothetically presume them to be interchangeable ($S \Leftrightarrow H$) in our theoretical experiments. We can also presume that the physical temperatures T and the interface temperature iT are interchangeable ($T \Leftrightarrow iT$). Under these assumptions, we can establish a set of metrics that potentially represent the UI-related *"interface work"* that is done by the user during the interactions, as well as the *"interface heat"* (Q_η) which is associated with $H(X|Y)$, i.e., the UI's input noise (η). We can also follow the convention in physics by creating a new unit of "interface joule" (i-joule, or iJ) for these new metrics:

$$dW_{functional} = dW_{user\_cond.} = (H(Y'|X') - H(Y|X)) \cdot iT(X) \quad \text{i-joule.}$$

$$dW_{learning} = dW_{mutual\_info.} = (I(X,Y) - I(X',Y')) \cdot iT(X) \quad \text{i-joule.}$$

$$dW_{combine} = dW_{user\_output} = (H(Y') - H(Y)) \cdot iT(X) \quad \text{i-joule.}$$

$$\delta Q_\eta = \delta Q_{equivocation} = (H(X|Y) - H(X'|Y')) \cdot iT(X) \quad \text{i-joule.}$$

$$dW_{combine} = dW_{functional} - dW_{learning} \quad \text{i-joule.}$$

The idea leading to the creation of the aforementioned "interface work" and "interface heat" is largely a theoretical experiment and requires further validation and refinement. Random number simulations using these metrics have yielded interesting results, indicating that these new metrics may have potential value and deserve further investigation.

6 Conclusion

In one of the few studies ever done on the relationship between information theory and thermodynamics, E. T. Jaynes commented that the statistical mechanics approach to scientific inference is "a method of reasoning which ensures that no unconscious arbitrary assumptions have been introduced." [8] These scientific methods have contributed enormously to the making of our modern age. They are intellectual instruments that were brilliantly designed by famous scientists and constantly improved by generations of younger scientists thereafter. With this observation, perhaps the most important inspiration we can derive from the present study is that scientific theories and user interfaces are both tools of human creation – they are the results of human design. By learning from the proven-effective scientific methodologies that were developed in the past, maybe we are not too far from inventing equally elegant and powerful scientific theories for our research and design endeavors related to the user interface and interaction.

References

1. ISO: International Standard ISO 9241–11:2018. Ergonomics of human-system interaction – Part 11: Usability: definitions and concepts. International Organization for Standardization, International Electrotechnical Commission, Geneva (2018)

2. Müller, I.: A History of Thermodynamics: The doctrine of Energy and Entropy. Springer, Berlin (2007)
3. Shannon, C.E., Weaver, W.: The Mathematical Theory of Communication, 1st edn. The University of Illinois Press, Urbana (1949)
4. Miller, G.A.: The magical number seven, plus or minus two: some limits on our capacity for processing information. Psychology Rev. 63(2), 81–97 (1956)
5. Stone, J.V.: Information Theory: A Tutorial Introduction, 2nd edn., p. 149. Sebtel Press, Sheffield (2022)
6. Pierce, J.R.: An Introduction to Information Theory: Symbols, Signals and Noise, 2nd edn. Dover Publications, New York (1980)
7. Sullivan, L.H.: The tall office building artistically considered. Lippincott's Mag., p. 408. J.B. Lippincott Co., Philadelphia (1896)
8. Jaynes, E.T.: Information theory and statistical mechanics. Physical Rev. 106(4), 630 (1957)

Wetland Challenge—Using Service Design Research as an Approach to Establish an AR APP for Environmental Education

Wen-Huei Chou[1], Jia-Yin Shih[1(✉)], and Yao-Fei Huang[2]

[1] Department of Digital Media Design, National Yunlin University of Science and Technology, Douliu, Taiwan, R.O.C.
billowinglight082@gmail.com
[2] Department of Graduate School of Design, National Yunlin University of Science and Technology, Douliu, Taiwan, R.O.C.

Abstract. Given the looming threat of catastrophic environmental disasters, there has never been a more urgent need for establishing awareness of the importance of sustainable environments through environmental education. Chenglong Wetland in Kouhu Township, Yunlin County, Taiwan, has been dramatically affected by land subsidence and slow climate change resulting from global warming. This has forced Chenglong Village to abandon its traditional fish farming industry and instead turn to green energy and economic development. However, this shift has led to the loss of wetland ecological resources, highlighting the pressing need for environmental education among the residents. The current study aims to explore how service design, a methodology incorporating input from experts and stakeholders, can facilitate communication with residents regarding the wetland, environmental crises, and associated risks.

This study employed service design methods to explore the experiential and cognitive needs of stakeholders through the Chenglong Wetland narrative project. A digital environmental guide system was created for local elementary school students using a persona and user map developed after interviews. The guide system integrated Augmented Reality (AR) technology and location-based functions to establish a narrative experience flow and provide relevant information for wetland environmental education. The resulting AR environmental guide app is expected to enhance public awareness of climate change issues and increase attention to ecological and environmental conservation.

Keywords: Environmental education · Service design · Augmented reality experience

1 Introduction

Considering the significant impact of climate change on the development of capitalism and the fundamental crisis it presents, humans must take every possible action to combat climate change and minimize its most dramatic impacts to the fullest extent possible.

© The Author(s), under exclusive license to Springer Nature Switzerland AG 2023
C. Stephanidis et al. (Eds.): HCII 2023, CCIS 1832, pp. 25–32, 2023.
https://doi.org/10.1007/978-3-031-35989-7_3

To help students understand climate change and its potential consequences, it is necessary to provide them with a strong foundation in climate science literacy and endow them with the ability to analyze and relate multiple data sources (Lay, 2019). From an international perspective, environmental education is considered a means by which to induce changes in human behavior related to production and consumption, which are necessary when it comes to protecting and restoring the global environment. This change can be reflected in individual choices and broader collective actions mediated by culture (Baker, Crump & Harris, 2019). Children who have received environmental education will develop a sense of autonomy towards the ecological environment and are eager to understand the ecological value of the existing environment (White, Eberstein & Scott, 2018). Therefore, by involving children aged 7 to 9 in environmental education, and prepare themselves for the changing impact of climate warming in the future through reflection (Williams & McEwen, 2021).

2 Service Design in Environmental Education

2.1 Service Design

Service design focuses on conducting preliminary investigations and research, while it also seeks to involve all stakeholders. The service design method emphasizes the use of technology at every touchpoint where users interact with a service; this method also utilizes user experience to enrich the understanding of the value of service components at various levels, thereby finding the optimal path and improving innovation (Sudbury-Riley, Hunter-Jones, Al-Abdin et al., 2020).

2.2 User Experience Design

Public service design has been provided with a novel approach in the digital age, known as "design for experience." It is based on the developments of digitization, user experience, service design, and the integration of service ecosystem concepts. "User experience design" aims to promote the proposition of supporting public service users in co-creating value in their life world. Realizing this requires a multi-level approach, because the user's value creation process is embedded in the configuration of multiple stakeholders and managed by institutions or organizational groups (Trischler & Westman Trischler, 2022). To achieve the goal of service design as a constructive method, this study explores the stakeholders involved in the environmental education experience process and examines the service design process.

Environmental Education and AR.
In recent years, augmented reality (AR) has become a new field in human–computer interaction. It can project interactive graphics into the real-life environment and can be applied to various fields as well as research and business goals. In the field of education, textbooks are still considered the primary tool for students when it comes to learning new subjects. However, since AR requires interaction and exploration, it brings an interesting element that is difficult to replicate with traditional textbooks (El, Mao & Zambrano,

2019). Digital technologies, including mobile applications and AR, can stimulate students' interest, and students can capture experiences of local and remote environments, collect data, and share new knowledge discoveries with a wider audience (Buchanan, Pressick-Kilborn & Maher, 2018). Combining constructionist learning methods with AR technology to present virtual objects can aid in deepening students' understanding of environmental learning (Fuchsova & Korenova, 2019).

3 Service Design Methodology for Environmental Education

3.1 Service Design Methodology

Service design is typically based on qualitative research using focus groups, while information systems and interaction design help service design to achieve service innovation (Joly et al., 2019). The service perspective provides a conceptual framework for value co-creation design within the service system, and design offers methods and tools to support the process of understanding and envisioning new forms of value co-creation through services. Service blueprints include elements of the Contextual Inquiry, while they also clarify the concepts of people, things, time, and place, correspond to the timeline concept, and map out the user's journey.

3.2 Projections and Backcasting in Service Design

Service design has a long history of generating effective solutions to problems that are complex, uncertain, and involve competing interests. Design has been described as "reflection … in action," and the process of "organizing complexity or seeking clarity in chaos." Design research can also support education-related efforts (Kennedy-Clark, 2013). In adaptive scenarios, the path is a combination of projections and backcasting. By establishing expectations for long-term sustainability planning and developing system-based decision-making and research capabilities, the iterative and interactive process also creates opportunities to connect science and policy. Scenario building is a key element in creating future imaginative scenarios, while addressing the future issues of multi-layered sustainable development in organizations relies on climate change scenario building, which can be discussed using multi-dimensional perspectives (Migliorelli & Marini, 2020). Wargo and Alvarado's research on exploring the data generated after making different educational research scenes in the children's environment presented how preschool and elementary school students use the functionality of contemporary immersive simulation technology to create differences (2020).

3.3 Environmental Education and AR

With the help of new technologies and trends, the overall user experience journey of AR has created storyboards and prototypes of user interfaces (Zhang et al., 2020). The overall journey services supported by AR can establish storyboards and prototypes of user interfaces (Heller et al., 2021). The service design of AR also uses anthropological methods to gain a deeper understanding of different cultural groups and subgroups (Zhang et al., 2020).

3.4 Children's Digital Education Materials

Based on the interactive multimedia features of AR, the application of simulated real-world overlays can improve the critical thinking abilities of elementary school students in learning about earth structures and materials science related to fisheries through the guidance and facilitation of those students' teachers (Syawaludin & Rintayati, 2019). In addition to allowing students to personally experience the content, the focus is on the equality of learning. Therefore, considering accessibility in experience design is particularly important for students with different physical conditions. From an educational perspective, it is necessary to increase inclusiveness by considering the learning rights of color-blind or color-deficient students.

4   Service Design Process for Wetland Environmental Education

4.1 Method for Focus Group Interview

The research investigation was conducted in two parts. The first part involved visiting the touch points and recording location and landscape information. The second part focused on understanding the various stakeholders involved in the service design process (Table 1). We interviewed three organizational groups closely related to the Chenglong Wetland environment, namely the Kuan-Shu Educational Foundation, the Community Development Association, and teachers from Chenglong Elementary School who had experience in compiling wetland-themed teaching materials. For each focus group, two semi-structured interviews were conducted, with seven to ten questions listed in the outline for each interview. Following the interviews, the researcher transcribed all of the focus group discussions using the recordings. Grounded theory coding was employed for interview analysis to identify recurring themes.

Table 1. Wetland stakeholders

Stakeholders	
Public policies	Public sectors
Communities	Wetland birdwatching associations; optoelectronics manufacturers; township office
Organizations	Ecological experts; community development associations; elementary school teachers; Kuan-Shu Educational Foundation
Interpersonal relations	Tourists; fishery residents; bird watchers; artists
Individuals	Residents

In the first interview, the main objective was to identify the target users. It was found that students from Chenglong Elementary School exhibited a high level of autonomy in participating in wetland-related learning activities. Students interested in ecology were even more likely to explore wetland-related knowledge outside of class. In addition, it was discovered that the school often collaborates closely with the community association in planning wetland environmental education lessons based on the experience of teachers who have taught wetland-related subjects. In the second interview, there was an exploration of the opinions of community organizations and environmental education groups regarding the camps and environmental education activities held by students. These discussions informed the establishment of the environmental education learning content covered by the AR application. The content includes wetland hydrological information, habitat biology information, local industry information, residential and environmental information, as well as global and Taiwan environmental changes and warming trends information, all of which aim to address climate change.

4.2 User Experience Design

Figure 1 is a user journey map created before the user interface design for children.

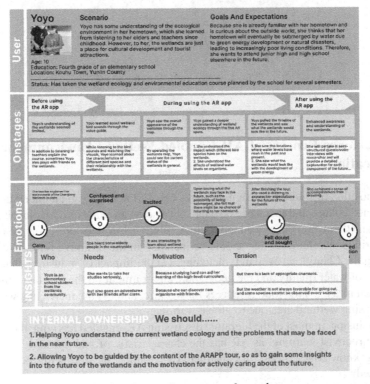

Fig. 1. The user journey map for students

based on interviews with stakeholders and experts; the map includes the planned usage process and insights obtained from the interviews, as well as potential environmental education issues that may arise after the introduction of AR.

4.3 User Interface Design

In the design of the user interface, alongside allowing students to experience the content themselves, emphasis is also placed on the equality of learning, and so accessibility in the user experience design is crucial for students with different physical conditions. In terms of the arrangement of the story plot, not all environmental education narrative content has the same advantage of making people rethink the environment, but all can achieve the goal of imparting scientific knowledge, and visual content is the main factor when it comes to influencing the immersive experience of AR. In terms of presentation, the use of AR in environmental education applications can construct the environment through more imaginative space, rather than being completely confined to the presentation content of scientific textbooks (Fig. 2).

Fig. 2. Voice guide interface

5 Experience Process of AR-Enabled Wetland Environmental Education

The composition of interface design elements is based not only on an understanding of the residents' culture and social background, but also on an analysis of the focal points of daily life and the awareness of wetland ecology (Fig. 3.). Furthermore, ecological experts have identified the elements that should be included in the initiative for environmental changes in the Chenglong Wetland, including: (1) the impact of industrial changes, (2) the impact of water quality and the geographic environment on the habitat of migratory and resident birds, (3) the food resources for wildlife, and (4) the increasing water level and decreasing wetland area due to global warming.

In conclusion, in most of the literature discussing AR-enabled learning, the emphasis is on constructivist learning, as AR has the characteristic of adding more information to existing knowledge. Based on constructivist learning, the following points can be summarized:

AR-enabled education based on constructivism should be able to construct a game narratively, deriving AR learning materials from the primary subject knowledge of students. The narrative description of the specific worldview also helps to increase students' understanding of the chronological order of historical events. Establishing an AR scenario system through location-based navigation can connect more realistically with the physical ecological environment. Exploratory learning makes it possible to

Fig. 3. Interface design overview

achieve immersive learning, while providing maps for users to explore and creating three-dimensional visualizations can provide a more concrete learning experience, making AR for environmental education purposeful and effective.

6 Conclusion and Future Prospects

We propose using the service design process in the context of environmental education. We develop a service design process for environmental education in wetlands, describing the issues that elementary school children may encounter in sustainable environmental learning, and how these issues can be overcome using digital technologies. We also provide environmental elements that should be incorporated into user experience design and AR, serving as a reference for the future development of digital education materials in a sustainable environment. Based on the literature and design guidelines discussed earlier, we propose a user experience flow for wetland AR and design a user interface. Currently, research is ongoing to prepare for the design of the app based on the literature review. In the future, after designing the content of the app, usability testing for elementary school children on wetland-related topics will be conducted. The aim is to evaluate the user experience of using AR as a teaching material in environmental education, as well as to understand the differences in environmental cognition before and after the use of the app. The purpose of this is to verify the effectiveness of the service design process in improving the user experience. Finally, an AR interface design suitable for wetland environmental education will be provided, along with usability guidelines.

References

1. Lay, Y.F.: Integrating environmental education and ICT. Eurasia J. Math. Sci. Technol. Educ. **15**(5), em1707 (2019)
2. Baker, E., Crump, J., Harris, P.: Global Environment Outlook (GEO-6): Healthy Planet, Healthy People (2019)
3. White, R.L., Eberstein, K., Scott, D.M.: Birds in the playground: evaluating the effectiveness of an urban environmental education project in enhancing school children's awareness, knowledge and attitudes towards local wildlife. PLoS ONE **13**(3), e0193993 (2018)
4. Sudbury-Riley, L., Hunter-Jones, P., Al-Abdin, A., Lewin, D., Naraine, M.V.: The trajectory touchpoint technique: a deep dive methodology for service innovation. J. Serv. Res. **23**(2), 229–251 (2020)
5. Trischler, J., Westman Trischler, J.: Design for experience–a public service design approach in the age of digitalization. Public Manag. Rev. **24**(8), 1251–1270 (2022)
6. El Kouzi, M., Mao, A., Zambrano, D.: An educational augmented reality application for elementary school students focusing on the human skeletal system. In: Proceedings of the 2019 IEEE Conference on Virtual Reality and 3D User Interfaces (VR), pp. 1594–1599. IEEE (2019)
7. Buchanan, J., Pressick-Kilborn, K., Maher, D.: Promoting environmental education for primary school-aged students using digital technologies. Eurasia J. Math. Sci. Technol. Educ. **15**(2), em1661 (2018)
8. Fuchsova, M., Korenova, L.: Visualisation in basic science and engineering education of future primary school teachers in human biology education using augmented reality. Eur. J. Contemp. Educ. **8**(1), 92–1021 (2019)
9. Joly, M.P., Teixeira, J.G., Patrício, L., Sangiorgi, D.: Leveraging service design as a multidisciplinary approach to service innovation. J. Serv. Manage. (2019)
10. Kennedy-Clark, S.: Research by design: design-based research and the higher degree research student. J. Learn. Des. **6**(2), 26–32 (2013)
11. Migliorelli, M., Marini, V.: Sustainability-related risks, risk management frameworks and non-financial disclosure. In: Sustainability and Financial Risks, pp. 93–118. Palgrave Macmillan, Cham (2020)
12. Zhang, H., Kim, M., Ye, C., Costa, S.: Service design for mediating technology and experience in augmented reality: a case study of a holistic AR travel service (2020)
13. Heller, J., Chylinski, M., de Ruyter, K., Keeling, D.I., Hilken, T., Mahr, D.: Tangible service automation: decomposing the technology-enabled engagement process (TEEP) for augmented reality. J. Serv. Res. **24**(1), 84–103 (2021)
14. Syawaludin, A., Rintayati, P.: Development of augmented reality-based interactive multimedia to improve critical thinking skills in science learning. Int. J. Instr. **12**(4), 331–344 (2019)

A Case Study: Designing a User Interface for Disconnected Operations of Defense and Security

Sona Dalsania and Devashree Marathe[✉]

SAP Labs, Bangalore, India
devashree.marathe@sap.com

Abstract. SAP provides Enterprise solutions for Defense and Security within the Public Sector area of S/4 HANA Industries. Defense and Security tackles a range of use-cases from organizing personnel and their assignments, management of material, products, and also enabling and keeping track of their maintenance activities. The most recent solution focused on preparing a server from the perspective of the data required for any remote operation. The business user is required to control and utilize the information pertaining to any equipment, personnel or activities that must go on at the remote location.

The early part of this project involved a deep dive into the topic with industry experts to gain clarity on the business processes for disconnected operation scenarios for Defense nations.

These sessions would typically target 2 aspects of the topic:

1. Understanding processes being handled in the situation of a foreseen disconnected operation. This included study and analysis of the existing tools that enable a secure data transfer between communication channels.
2. Understanding various tasks involved in triggering and monitoring data transfers via a user interface in disconnected scenarios for informed decision making.

This allowed for identification of opportunity gaps in the current process and pain points from the business user perspective.

The purpose of this case study is to shed light on:

1. The niche industry requirement and enterprise scenario
2. Collaboration with the end users to align the process
3. Impact of usability on decision making process and efficiency

Keywords: Defense and Security · Design Research · Enterprise Usecase

1 Introduction

1.1 The Challenge

The 'disconnected operation' area focused on a peculiar aspect of defense operations, one which was tricky to grasp considering the lack of military backgrounds of those of us designing it.

C. Stephanidis et al. (Eds.): HCII 2023, CCIS 1832, pp. 33–38, 2023.
https://doi.org/10.1007/978-3-031-35989-7_4

It focused on the disconnected operations that military forces need to perform while heading out for longer duration missions, while conducting relocation projects, and while handling remote location missions.

The challenges were:

1. **To provide a software solution for remote operations, where a military unit would need to self-sustain without accessing the central databases.**

   It required a model that allowed planned availability of data at different stages of the operation. It required a UI capable of conveying the precise location of the dataset, for user to act accordingly.

2. **To handle contingency situations out in the ocean/in the middle of a desert.**

   Remote locations and vessels can be tracked from a central unit, however, this may not cover the aspect of on-site activities. The mission-essential tasks have to be managed and monitored at the locations. In the situation of any step or activity not going as per expectation, the fall-back options are also to be handled on site. The apt availability of data allows the user to take quick and informed decisions.

3. **To ensure operational data is available in order for forces to work optimally even during the 'disconnected' time periods the remote location may experience.**

1.2 First Impressions (Learn Early Requirements, Current Model, Need for Validation from Business Users for Redefined Process)

It quickly became clear that we'd need to generate a model with a UI that would help the user visualize this exchange of data, real-time, between communication systems.

The solution needed to allow:

1. Managing remote servers to allow required data synchronization.
2. Monitoring of data exchanges and data ownership at a given point for reporting purposes.
3. Updates required due to operational changes while disconnected from the communications channel (example – maintenance of machinery onboard, break-fix cases, loss of material, changes in personnel assignments).

The existing method of enabling this data exchange was a subscription model. This subscription model had scope for improvement with UI interventions. The Design direction was based on industry experts validation and end user feedback. The current processes were being handled via multiple UI systems resulting in incomprehensible task flow.

Defence being a sensitive and critical area of work, on-site action is strictly tied to orders, data and authorizations – making the building of this application more of a meticulous process, ensuring we're covering what the user needs to seamlessly perform his tasks.

It was imperative to have end user involvement for design co-innovation and it paved the way for an application that finally seemed 'intuitive' after the final delivery.

2 Use-Case (Impact)

The Business Use Case. Making available all information relevant to all equipment and activities that are to take place in the interval of time that is prescribed to enable operations while disconnected. The purpose of this data ranges from maintenance of equipment onboard, any repair or assembly required, to ensuring the required information is available for any authorized equipment joining the ship after leaving shore – example a helicopter that will land on the ship while it is disconnected from the central servers.

Exception: There is always a possibility to perform data exchange between the central servers and the remote servers as and when network becomes available to the sailing ship. This is referred to as 'delta load'. Accounting the possibility of delta data updates for UI was considered as an improvement.

Sample Scenario. A ship is planned to be on sea for the purpose of a relocation operation, for a given time period. There is a variety of equipment that is being transported on this ship. After a certain time at sea, it will lose its network connectivity to the central servers, however, the ship itself will be hosting a server onboard (also known as the 'remote server').

One ship, and its remote server are tied closely together. Both of these when linked to the central server, form a Subscription. It allows the user to track the various servers to which the central server has to coordinate data with.

User Goals and Pain Points. During design thinking sessions with business end users, we derived user goals aligned to their specific processes. In accordance to the nature of an upcoming remote operation or mission, the end user is required to proactively set up appropriate data pertaining to

1. The material the remote operation would require
2. Personnel it would have assigned to it.
3. Any other remote locations it would need to play host to during its operation period.

The business user is primarily concerned with ensuring the right data is available on the right servers prior to their operation period commencement.

The key pain points noticed during initial discussions were:

1. Multiple transactions on several systems
2. Lack of easy investigation into the root source of any record.
3. Unable to identify the data processing status at a given time.
4. Non-intuitive UI hampering decision making.
5. No ease of triggering data process steps.
6. Lack of mass actions while maintaining multiple scenarios.

Prerequisites/Background. For a given disconnected situation, it is assumed to have a remote location, mobile or immobile, and a server stationed at the site, allowing the user access to all the 'offline' data transferred to it in preparation for the operation.

Significance for the End User. This scenario is significant for the business user for what it allows (all relevant data at the remote location), but also for the consequences of what might happen when this data isn't available at the remote location.

Failing to achieve the required information availability can possibly hinder the operation readiness.

The design for this use-case went through multiple iterations considering the end user pain points, concerns and impact. This posed us with a UI challenge to visualize the exchange of data, the status as well as the progress in a simple design language for easy execution.

3 Design Process: Iterations (How Designs Evolved, Key Stakeholders Involved, Defined Problem Space, Early Ideas of Solution)

Designing for a Defence role, comes with a precedence of a power user. Our target user being an expert, knows required drills and is trained to perform necessary decision making. And hence the UI was required to aid their agility.

The Design process was to work towards the problem space defined by end user concerns and business goal. We iterated design proposals with experts to validate design translation of the business case. This design process impacted scope and feature priority for the release road map.

Continuous feedback cycle with end users allowed incremental improvisations of appropriate scope to be considered for development.

Establishing an engagement model for continuous feedback among primary stakeholders created a self-sustaining iteration model.

The designs were open for constructive feedback from the primary stakeholders, and end users impressions.

4 Design Validations (Validate, Reinforce Correct Understanding, Strengthen Designs)

From the design research methods available at each step of the design process, the formative usability testing was considered at the design stage to validate our initial research and prepare apt designs for implementation.

Formative usability testing was conducted with 9 business end users from various nations. These usability tests were driven by an interactive prototype, which was meticulously constructed on the basis of the testing scenarios prioritized.

Test scripts were prepared well in advance for aligning the prototypes, and to incorporate feedback from the primary stakeholders prior to the testing sessions. The scenarios in the test script were aimed to focus on specific business process steps, to gain clear insights.

Dry run of the usability testing session helped prepare better by testing the prototypes and brought attention to technical glitches that can occur while conducting a remote session.

Key Insights:
Key insights derived through validation sessions with end users were considered for ongoing development for improvisation.

Ongoing Processes Indication. Through the usability tests, it became clear that the users valued seeing an 'ongoing' progress indication on the data processing as a critical decision making factor. Enabling process indication for the first stage of the process was a challenge, considering the 'unpredictable' nature of the quantity it would need to stop the stage at. Knowing definite system status like non-functional / functional came to our notice apart from the process related statues.

Challenge: "How might we enable progress indication on the UI, when there is no defined quantity of a derivation process?".

Proposal: To indicate through growing numbers, allowing the user to know that the system is still working on that step, allowing the user some idea of if the system is hung, or still functional.

Use-Case Reiteration. It also became evident that our understanding of the use-case and the assumptions we had initially started with, were not aligned to their business processes. Given the nature of this project each customer had unique methods to handle the disconnected operations scenarios.

Incomplete Data. One key insight on UI was to be able to indicate when information for a certain data entry is incomplete. Furthermore, preventing the user from taking actions on an incomplete data entry as well from the system side was expected UI behavior.

Business Terminology. Going into the usability tests, certain terminology seemed obvious in its meaning, but from the users' confusions, it was clear that perception plays an important role and naming the different business infotypes needed more careful consideration and expert consultation.

A Lesson in Perceptions for UI Elements
a. "Statuses" on the UI

Status depiction became a rather challenging point to take away from the sessions.

The data transfer stages, each was supposed to indicate 'in process', 'completed' or 'Error'. However, whenever the status showed 'in process', it was tricky to indicate that there were errors within the already processed items, and vice-versa.

b. 'Sections' on a page.

Another lesson in how perceptions affect UI interactions was when the users viewed multiple different sections as something interlinked in terms of interaction. An example was a table row selection in one section before triggering an action on a completely different section.

Validity Periods and Time Depiction. An observation that only would remain relevant to disconnected operations was that validity dates seemed to convey almost little to no meaning to the user. The term 'validity' itself, seemed to not cover the business scenario of how the time is defined for a disconnected operation.

5 Results in Implementation

The final implementation of this application was well received during the customer testing sessions. There was explicit feedback about the UI feeling 'intuitive' to the testers, and the changes that were made to the design proposal as a result of the validation sessions seemed to have an impact at several points in the application.

Design proposals that were finalized from the set of iterations, made intricacies of the use-case clear and comprehensible. User experience matters for industries like defense and security just as much as it does for anyone, as finally, the end user remains a human interacting with a computer.

Acknowledgements. We sincerely thank our fellow colleagues from the Defense & Security product team in SAP, who have involved our UX expertise into this topic. They encouraged and appreciated design research activities with end users along the way. Their openness to adapt to a 'UX' way of approaching the topic, their patience to endure all our questions during project discussions helped us articulate this topic in detail.

References

1. Razzouk, R., Shute, V.: What is design thinking and why is it important?. https://doi.org/10.3102/0034654312457429?journalCode=rera
2. Design thinking an effective tool for innovation. https://d1wqtxts1xzle7.cloudfront.net/27180660/Ispim2012FinalVersion.low-libre.pdf?1390871891=&response-content-disposition=inline%3B+filename%3DDesign_Thinking_as_an_effective_Toolkit.pdf&Expires=1678984888&Signature=HugVrUbUNGpUwFG1lFH4ffIHzKr5d2dwwEkJDQtiHoLl9ww9jt~~arUfHToSDZmr6YhcNIKSfZ9Q7IeV2OeFk6u7GdTKZnBYFvZhjLhmYf-AYhNJBAipX5wFYFQV6Up1EQp0A2JRmSNU7DhrB1TYjqUvYJ9-izCpYuP8zao-0k3huN2QemHnM1pE9YReXJEd0JvcxsmNXXLt2qtlMcL4e2rDrKfJSkC8Fho4JE~ikaVYje9eUCx7R27xeCIy3BsDkRowQtitjHRIRibt9I7g2Loj9cgnoGRanKtJjpZYLBfL0hf4qihb84ilU29DM6vgWqbBcnKJBbeLjzX~DCh22A__&Key-Pair-Id=APKAJLOHF5GGSLRBV4ZA
3. Redish, J., Bias, R.G., Bailey, R., Molich, R., Dumas, J., Spool, J.M.: Usability in practice – formative usability evaluations – evolution and revolution. https://doi.org/10.1145/506443.506647
4. Adinda, P.P., Suzianti, A.: Redesign of user interface for e-government application using usability testing method. https://doi.org/10.1145/3290420.3290433
5. Wynn, D.C., Eckert, C.M.: Perspectives on iteration in design and development. https://doi.org/10.1007/s00163-016-0226-3
6. Nielsen, J.: Iterative user interface design. https://ieeexplore.ieee.org/abstract/document/241424

How to Design Successful Conversations in Conversational Agents in Healthcare?

Kerstin Denecke(✉) [ID]

Institute for Medical Informatics, Bern University of Applied Sciences,
Bern, Switzerland
kerstin.denecke@bfh.ch

Abstract. Conversational agents (CA) applied in a healthcare setting are often designed to mimic healthcare professionals. Inappropriate design of their implemented conversation flow might impact on the achieved outcome, patient adherence and experience, and might even become a risk for patient safety. Objective of this paper is to identify factors to be considered when designing conversations of health CA to ensure that the patient-CA communication is successful. Focus is on rule-based CA-based medical interview assistants, i.e. systems that collect the medical history from a patient implemented using rules. Starting from models, guidelines and best practices for successful healthcare communication (e.g. partnership model, AIDET model and RESPECT model), I derived aspects to be considered in designing successful interactions of health CA with patients. Transferring basic concepts of these models to patient-health CA communication leads to the following conclusions: Health CA should be equipped with certain communication skills, including being empathetic, know how to listen, have respect for the patient, have open-ended skills and be able to adapt to the level of knowledge of the user. Additionally, I derived information on how to structure the conversation flow.

Keywords: Physician-patient communication · Human-computer interaction · Chatbot · Conversational agent · Patient-centered design

1 Introduction

Conversational agents (CA) are dialog-based systems. They are increasingly used in digital health interventions, simulating the conversation between patients and healthcare professionals. While guidelines have been developed to support healthcare professionals in well conducting conversations with patients, this knowledge has not yet been translated into the development of dialogues of CA in healthcare: It is unclear how to best design the conversation in CA-based digital medical interview assistants. To increase the perceived interpersonal communication competence of CA, concepts characterizing human-like behavior like expressing empathy [4] and self-disclosure [7] have been implemented in such systems. But I am not aware of research work that tried to integrate communication skills from patient-doctor communication into health CA. In this paper,

© The Author(s), under exclusive license to Springer Nature Switzerland AG 2023
C. Stephanidis et al. (Eds.): HCII 2023, CCIS 1832, pp. 39–45, 2023.
https://doi.org/10.1007/978-3-031-35989-7_5

I want to identify best practices and guidelines for patient-physician communication and translate these findings to a design of a successful health CA - patient interaction and communication.

I am considering text-based health CA that are implemented as computer-assisted history taking systems, also known as digital medical interview assistant systems [2,5]. These are software programs that enable patients to electronically provide their medical history before the consultation [13]. The CA-based history taking systems are often rule-based, i.e. fix rules determine the conversation flow and pre-defined patterns are used to understand user input.

In the patient-physician relationship in general and in the history taking process in particular, communication is essential. Effective communication improves patient and physician satisfaction, reduces medical errors, decreases patient complaints and improves patient compliance to treatments [6]. It has been demonstrated that effective communication between patients and physicians enhances treatment effectiveness, adherence to treatment, and diagnostic precision [1]. Consequently, the communication between health CA and a patient should be designed effectively. In this paper, I derive recommendations for an efficient health CA-patient interaction from patient-physician communication models.

2   Methods

In this work, I am starting from communication models described below and guidelines as well as best practices from successful patient-physician communication. These models have been identified using a literature search following the snowball strategy. Starting from an overview paper on effective patient-physician communication [11], I collected more details on the mentioned communication models using an inductive thematic analysis. From these models and from guidelines for communication in healthcare, I derived aspects to be considered that are transferable to the interaction between patient and health CA and formulated recommendations for designing successful interactions in CA-based digital medical interview assistants.

3   Models and Guidelines for Patient-Physician Communication

The identified communication guidelines and models focus on different aspects. In this section, I will briefly summarize the models I considered. *The partnership model* is based on a participatory style of conversation, where patient and physician spend an equal amount of time talking [14]. Several basic principles of patient-doctor communication have been described: To optimize the patient-physician relationship it has been suggested to create the conditions for a good environment which supports in establishing trust [15]. Furthermore, it is necessary to know how to listen, be empathetic and convey trust to patients by creating a climate of dialogue. The level of knowledge of the patient regarding the topic under consideration has to be identified. Beyond, the physician has to assess what the patient needs or wants to know. Information should be provided clearly and slowly to allow the patient to understand what is being communicated [15].

The *RESPECT model* presented by Mutha et al. [9,11] addresses race, ethnicity and culture. The seven dimensions include rapport, empathy, support, partnership, explanations, cultural competence, trust. Dimension rapport refers to a connection to the patient on a social level, resisting on judgments and making assumptions. Empathy is demonstrated by acknowledging the patient's feelings and personal situation. Support in the context of communication means to ask about barriers to care and compliance and to create an ambiance that allows the patient to disclose personal health information. The partnership dimensions requires a physician to clarify roles in the patient-doctor relationship and conversation. Explanations include to check for understanding and use verbal clarification techniques. The cultural competence dimension means to respect the patient, their culture and beliefs. It recognizes how race, ethnicity, gender, education, socioeconomic status, sexual and gender orientation, immigrant status, and so forth affect care. Trust must be earned by the physician which can be realized by a relationship that builds upon understanding, power-sharing and empathy [8].

The AIDET model [10] described five fundamentals to be considered in patient communication: Acknowledge, introduce, duration, explanation, and thank you. These fundamentals can help in structuring the patient-doctor encounter and conversation.

Paget et al. described *seven basic principles and expectations* of patient-clinician communication [12]: mutual respect, harmonized goals, a supportive environment, appropriate decision partners, the right information, transparency and full disclosure, continuous learning. Mutual respect concerns that patient and physician engage as full decision-making partners. Harmonized goals comprise a common understanding of and agreement on the care plan. A supportive environment pays attention to the comfort and ability of the patient. Correspondingly, appropriate decision partners possess skills appropriate to patient circumstances and ensure competence and understanding by the patient. The right information concerns best available clinical evidence and choices to be discussed and correct presentation of symptoms, personal practices etc. by the patient. Going along with that is transparency and full disclosure: Patients should be open towards a physician regarding relevant circumstances, preferences, medical history. The physician in turn has to appreciate and understand the patient's circumstances and limits. Continuous learning requires a feedback system between patients and physicians on status, progress and challenges.

Paget et al. described patient characteristics to be considered to tailor the communication for maximizing faithfulness [12]. Among them are the functional capacity of the patient (level of physical or mental impairment), communication capacity (language, literacy, speech disorder), receptivity (motivation, incentives, learning style, trust level), support (skilled family or caregiver, financial capacity), and the living situation (housing, pharmacy, grocery, recreation, safety).

4 Translation of Communication Models to CA Dialogue Design

In the following, I am providing the derived guidelines to design the conversation flow between a health CA and a patient. Communication requires certain skills. In Fig. 1, I therefore list the identified skills together with technologies needed to enable a health CA having these skills.

An essential aspect seems to be empathy - it is part of all communication models - i.e. health CA should be empathetic, at least to a certain extent. This requires sentiment and emotion analysis technologies integrated in the systems. Only when the answers from the patient can be analyzed regarding sentiment and emotions, the health CA can generate an appropriate, empathetic answer.

Another important skill is knowing how to listen. Many rule-based health CA in general and digital medical interview assistants in particular provide pre-defined answers to their questions. In this way, the patients cannot express themselves. Free-text entries should be enabled to be able to listen to the patients. Dealing with free-text entries requires open-ended skills, meaning that the health CA should be able to summarize and paraphrase the user input to demonstrate that it was understood properly. It might be that the user does not understand a question or comment from the health CA - clarification questions should be enabled in such systems to avoid frustration or unsuited answers.

Patients are highly diverse, have a varying knowledge background and an individual health literacy. To address this in a health CA, the system should be able to categorize the knowledge level and health literacy of its user and dynamically adapt the content and language to it. This goes along with the accessibility to such systems. There might be users with cognitive disabilities that are unable to interact with a health CA for more than ten conversation turns. Thus, it is essential to consider this and adapt the conversation length when necessary. Furthermore, a health CA should be able to adapt to cultural, gender and ethnics aspects depending on the user. This can be considered by formulating responses and questions appropriately - which again requires a dynamic adaptation of the health CA outputs.

In Table 1, I summarize the recommendations for designing the conversation flow of health CA, particularly of digital medical interview assistants with conversational user interface. Creating a good environment is essential for a communication and exchange of personal health care. This includes greeting and introduction at the beginning of the conversation and ensuring privacy and data security. The latter are rather technical aspects to be realized on the implementation side of the health CA. However, the health CA should provide information on what will happen to the data and which role the health CA has within the diagnostic or treatment process. The interview itself should include non-focused interviewing aspects and focused interviewing aspects. In this way, the patients can provide the information they want to talk about, but it is also ensured that aspects are asked which are relevant for structuring and preparing the actual encounter.

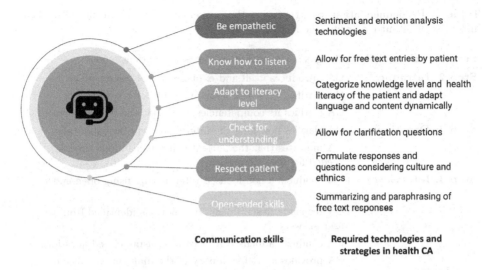

Fig. 1. Required communication skills of conversational agents and how to implement them in a health CA.

5   Discussion and Conclusion

In this work, I identified skills necessary to be implemented in a CA-based medical interview assistant considering guidelines or communication models from patient-doctor communication. In previous work, I developed three digital medical interview assistants [2,3,5]. Experts were involved in the development phase, specifically they generated the questions and answer options for the rule-based systems. I had to recognize that they used a complex language and long sentences. As a result, the interactions with the health CA were rather similar to answering questions of a questionnaire than similar to a conversation with a human. I think, considering the recommendations and guidelines reported in this paper could help a lot in improving the user experience with such CA-based medical interview assistants. It could help in increasing the naturalness of the interaction. In particular adapting language and formulations dynamically to the user could increase the accessibility of health CA for people with varying cognitive skills and different health literacy levels. I focused in this work on health CA-based digital medical interview assistants. The identified skills might of relevance in more complex implementations of health CA going beyond rule-based systems. Future work will have to study this.

Shan et al. [17] studied the language use in health CA. They found out that language cues are important in human-CA interaction: they are essential for promoting user engagement. So far, the impact of linguistics has rarely been studied. Similar to our result that empathy might be a crucial conversation skill, they claimed that "respectful, helpful, supportive and empathetic wording" helps in engaging patients when interacting with a health CA. Interestingly, Seitz et al. concluded "that it is promising to enhance the interaction's perceived naturalness

Table 1. Recommendation for structuring the conversation flow in a digital medical interview assistant (following the AIDET schema).

Step 1: Acknowledge	CA greets the patient and uses the patient name
Step 2: Introduce	CA introduces itself and explains its role or purpose
	CA clarifies what will happen to the collected data
	CA clarifies its competencies and what the user can expect
Step 3: Duration	CA clarifies how long the interaction will probably take
	CA indicates that the patient can take as much time as needed for the interaction.
Step 4: Interview	CA conducts a non-focused interviewing using open-ended questions
	CA responds to sentiments or emotions identified from the user answers
	CA conducts a focused interviewing using closed questions
	CA provides a brief summary of the dialogue or collected information

instead of focusing on human-like cues." [16]. Further, they found evidence that empathy of a health CA may evoke incredibility feelings. More important are a CA's communication competencies [16]. In future work, it should be studied to what extent artificial empathy is accepted by patients and whether it is useful or not. This holds true for all skills that have been identified in this work. It is an open research issue whether these skills implemented in a health CA will really improve the user experience, engagement and outcome of the conversation. Another aspect to be studied is whether these skills can contribute to create an environment that supports in disclosing personal health information with a health CA.

References

1. Davidson, M., Agid, O.: Who has poor insight, my patient suffering from schizophrenia or myself? Eur. Neuropsychopharmacol. J. Eur. College Neuropsychopharmacol. **68**, 27–29 (2023)
2. Denecke, K., Hochreutener, S.L., Pöpel, A., May, R.: Self-anamnesis with a conversational user interface: concept and usability study. Methods Inf. Med. **57**, 243–252 (2018)
3. Denecke, K., Lombardi, P., Nairz, K.: Digital medical interview assistant for radiology: opportunities and challenges. **293**, 39–46 (2022)
4. Fitzpatrick, K.K., Darcy, A., Vierhile, M.: Delivering cognitive behavior therapy to young adults with symptoms of depression and anxiety using a fully automated conversational agent (Woebot): a randomized controlled trial. JMIR Mental Health **4**(2), e7785 (2017)
5. Gashi, F., Regli, S.F., May, R., Tschopp, P., Denecke, K.: Developing intelligent interviewers to collect the medical history: lessons learned and guidelines. In: dHealth, pp. 18–25 (2021)

6. Honavar, S.G.: Patient-physician relationship-communication is the key. Indian J. Ophthalmol. **66**(11), 1527 (2018)
7. Lee, S., Choi, J.: Enhancing user experience with conversational agent for movie recommendation: effects of self-disclosure and reciprocity. Int. J. Hum Comput. Stud. **103**, 95–105 (2017)
8. Mostow, C., et al.: Treating and precepting with respect: a relational model addressing race, ethnicity, and culture in medical training. J. Gen. Intern. Med. **25**, 146–154 (2010)
9. Mutha, S., Allen, C., Welch, M.: Toward culturally competent care: a toolbox for teaching communication strategies. University of California, Center for the Health Professions (2002)
10. Nguyen, T.T.: The Effect of AIDET Communications Delivered by Front Desk Staff on Patient Experience and Satisfaction at a Medical Practice. Ph.D. thesis, Capella University (2019)
11. N.N.: Effective patient-physician communication. Committee opinion. Committee on Patient Safety and Quality Improvement (587), 1–5 (2014)
12. Paget, L., et al.: Patient-clinician communication: Basic principles and expectations. NAM Perspectives (2011)
13. Pappas, Y., Anandan, C., Liu, J., Car, J., Sheikh, A., Majeed, A.: Computer-assisted history-taking systems (cahts) in health care: benefits, risks and potential for further development. BCS (2017)
14. Roter, D.L.: Patient question asking in physician-patient interaction. Health Psychol. **3**(5), 395 (1984)
15. San, L., Arranz, B.: Effective patient-physician communication in the era of neuropsychopharmacology. Eur. Neuropsychopharmacol. **71**, 1–2 (2023)
16. Seitz, L., Bekmeier-Feuerhahn, S., Gohil, K.: Can we trust a chatbot like a physician? A qualitative study on understanding the emergence of trust toward diagnostic chatbots. Int. J. Hum Comput Stud. **165**, 102848 (2022)
17. Yi, S., et al.: Language use in conversational agent-based health communication: systematic review. J. Med. Internet Res. e37403 (2022)

POWER – A User Experience Research Model for Industrial Internet Design Practices

Jiachun Du[✉], Hanyue Duan, Shuoyu Chen, and Wei Zhao

Alibaba Cloud, Hangzhou, China
jiachun.dje@alibaba.inc.com

Abstract. Industrial internet implementations are popular on a global scale. Different types of products, including both hardware and software, are included in industrial internet projects. Due to their complexity and diversity, user experience research for industrial internet products is difficult. To get insights for enhancing the industrial internet product experience, designers need an improved research method. In this paper, the POWER framework for user experience research in industrial internet design practices is promoted. POWER represents 5 factors in industrial internet design, which are people, object, workflow, environment and review. This framework emphasizes interventions of production work flow and user flow. Also, it promotes the importance of industry paradigms reviews to avoid common-sense mistakes. A showcase of how POWER framework helps designers to improve software user experience in car industry is demonstrated.

Keywords: User Research · Industrial Internet · Framework · Human-Computer Interaction

1 Introduction

The importance of manufacturing has grown since the COVID outbreak. Manufacturing's digital transformation is once more a hot topic in the sector. More and more internet companies are shifting their focus to the industrial internet for manufacturing's digital transformation. But manufacturing field entails considerable know-hows, extensive workflow, and numerous stakeholders. When dealing with these complex scenarios and product systems in the manufacturing industry, user experience factors are often ignored. It leads to a system that is difficult to understand and use for end users, consequently making it difficult to meet customer's needs. In order to better improve the user experience of industrial internet products, designers need to implement better design strategies. An improved user research method for industrial internet is essential for these strategies.

This paper will introduce our team's insights and methods for improving user research in the field of industrial Internet. First, this paper will introduce design features in the industrial internet and the challenges they bring. Then this paper will introduce POWER, an improved user research framework focusing on five key elements that affect design decisions in industrial internet scenarios. Finally, this paper will present how these 5 elements can help designers design better experience in a showcase, as well as provide further discussions on this methodology.

C. Stephanidis et al. (Eds.): HCII 2023, CCIS 1832, pp. 46–52, 2023.
https://doi.org/10.1007/978-3-031-35989-7_6

2   Complexities of User Experience Research in Industrial Internet

The manufacturing field is the most traditional field of HCI research, which has developed over the years and formed a certain paradigm [1, 2, 3]. In addition to traditional industrial production control software, industrial internet products have also added some consumer internet features, such as mobilized instant message systems, interactive 3D digital twins, etc. The diversification of products has led to an increase in the complexity of industrial internet platform products. It also brings new complexities in corresponding user researches list as follow:

1. Deep industry know-hows. Manufacturing industries are mostly very mature fields which have a lot of industry knowledge and requirements. This requires designers to quickly understand the basic patterns of the corresponding industry in a short period of time, and avoid common sense mistakes. For example, in production lines most of the workers are wearing gloves when they need to control through the HMI screen. If designers place common interactions behaviours from normal computer such as right-clicking with the mouse, it will disable workers to complete the operation on touchable HMI screen.
2. There are many user roles involved and their relationships are complex. Completing the manufacture of a product may involve hundreds of processes, more than 20 roles, and collaborations of thousands of devices. Software products designed by user experience designers are only one part of these collaborations. It is necessary to clarify which parts are intervenable by designers and which parts are not.
3. Diversity in product design forms. In a certain project of industrial internet, designers need to deal with PC software, mobile application, and digital twin data visualization design. It is not sufficient to apply traditional user research methods directly since they mostly focus on a particular product design form.
4. Data privatization. Due to data security reasons, user behavior data cannot be recorded in private network environments. Internet data-driven design methods is unavailable.

These features make it difficult for designers and developer teams to establish overall cognition and empathy with industry users. This difficulty will further lead to low usability in products and frequent adjustments from the customer, reducing the delivery efficiency. In order to solve these problems, designers need to implement a better user research strategy and pass more insights to the developer team.

3   POWER Framework for Overcoming the Complexities

Based on practices in the industrial internet field, the POWER framework is promoted as an improved user research strategy. 'People' stands for users and stakeholders of industrial internet products. They are usually workers, managers in production line and technology staffs in office. They have direct control in production. 'Object' stands for devices in production line and end-products. 'Workflow' stands for how people and object interact with each other. 'Environment' stands for physical embodiment of a factory. 'Review' stands for know-hows in industry guidelines, standards and paradigms (Fig. 1).

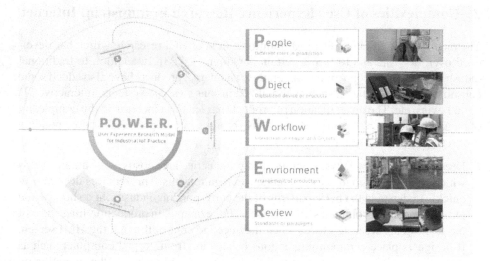

Fig. 1. POWER framework.

Compared with traditional user research method such as user journey map [4], the POWER framework has the following advantages:

1. Highlight the core of the "people-object" relationship in manufacturing, rather than a simple analysis of each user role at each stage of production.
2. Arrange view of the complete production flow, which is convenient for recognizing flow pain points with specific software product features in the subsequent development stage.
3. Increase observation and recording of the environment to facilitate the transfer of knowledge, build empathy, and support possible subsequent digital twin/augmented reality design tasks.
4. Add reviews of industry paradigms to avoid common-sense mistakes.

These 5 factors, which are people, object, workflow, environment, review, can quickly help designers abstract complex working environments in field research and build good perception in different manufacturing environments. Moreover, these factors not only enhance developer team's attention on user experience but also allow developer and business teams to see the intersection of products and business processes. This will greatly benefit cooperation between these teams. In the next chapter, a showcase of automotive factory user research based on the POWER framework and corresponding user experience improvement is demonstrated.

4   POWER Framework in Industrial Internet Design Practices

In the process of digital transformation of an electrical vehicle factory, production data from equipment's needs to be collected and transferred to factory servers for further analysis. However, the client complained that current data collection software was not easy to use and inefficient. To get better understandings designers went to do field research and create a POWER story board shown in the figure below (Fig. 2).

Fig. 2. A storyboard of electrical vehicle production based on POWER framework.

Based on the POWER storyboard, the core problem of the old interface was recognized. It was because of presenting data collection process from a device-centric view and ignoring users' requirements. In fact, there were three different roles of users using this data collection software:

1. Operation technology (OT) engineers for circuit construction. They used the software to complete circuit connections and device data collection. From a web-based list interface, they needed to finish 4 input boxes to record a data point. But it was extremely inefficient to finish thousands of data points.
2. Information technology (IT) engineers for application development. They used the software to get data for further analysis. The current interface was a point list view without any alerts or logs. As a result, if there were any problems occur in the analysis software, they had to go to production line in person to figure out what happened.
3. Project managers. They used the software to monitor the overall construction progress. The current interface had no relevant information. So they tried to get the progress by checking the pagination bar every day and record it on the whiteboard, which is absolutely inconvenient (Fig. 3).

After understanding the situation with POWER framework, the software design was improved to distinguish these three different demands. For OT engineers, an import function of excel lists was added to fit batch data points recording needs. For IT engineers, debug logs and detail records were added to every data points. For project managers, data collection progress bars were added for convenient supervision. As a result, the client provided very positive feedbacks on these improvements (Fig. 4).

With POWER framework, designers can better understand what different users in context really need. Furthermore, they can set DOs and DONTs to avoid common sense

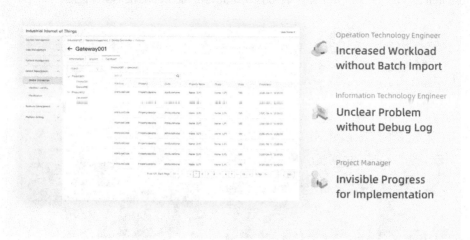

Fig. 3. Withdrawals of old data collection software interface revealed by POWER framework.

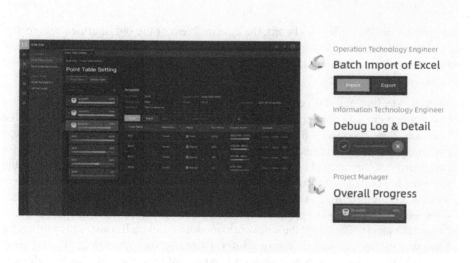

Fig. 4. Improved user experience features for different user cases.

mistakes in certain industry. These will help them design various products in industrial internet with better experience (Fig. 5).

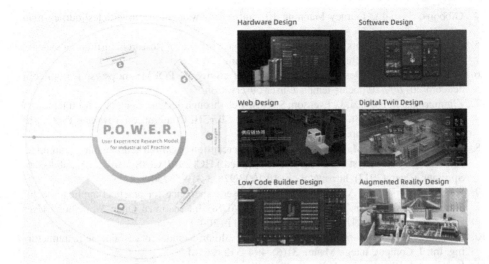

Fig. 5. Different software systems with improved user experience with insights from POWER framework.

5 Discussion and Future Work

Compared with traditional journey map methods, the major contributions of POWER framework are:

1. Emphasize attentions of the intertwined relationship between production flow and user flow.
2. Propose industry paradigms reviews as a key factor in user research.

These two improvements can help designers address DOs and DONTs in industrial internet fields quicker and more precise. Consequently designers can arrange better decisions in product experience design. In addition to the industrial internet, agricultural internet is considered to be potential in applying POWER framework to outline the journey map. Agricultural can be seen as another manufacture behaviour which emphasize the "people-object" relationship with a large amount of industry knowledge. Moreover user experience factors are also often ignored in agricultural digital transformation process. Further practices are expected to introduce the POWER framework in agricultural internet and its relevant software systems.

References

1. Daneels, A., Salter, W.: What is SCADA? (1999)
2. Moencks, M., Roth, E., Bohné, T., Kristensson, P.O.: Human-computer interaction in industry: a systematic review on the applicability and value-added of operator assistance systems. Found. Trends Hum.-Comput. Interact. **16**, 2–3, 65–213 (2022). https://doi.org/10.1561/110 0000088
3. Burkimsher, P.C.: Jcop experience with a commercial scada product, pvss. In: Proceedings of the ICALEPCS (2003)

4. Gibbons, S. (n.d.): Journey Mapping 101. https://www.nngroup.com/articles/journey-mapping-101/

5. Kumar, V.: User Insights Tool. A Sharable Database for Global Research, Institute of Design, Illinois Institute of Technology (2004). www.id.iit.edu

6. Crawford, K. (n.d.): Design Thinking Toolkit, Activity 3 – POEMS. https://spin.atomicobject.com/2017/09/20/poems-template-user-observation/

7. Zimmerman, J., Forlizzi, J., Evenson, S.: Research through design as a method for interaction design research in HCI. In: Proceedings of the SIGCHI Conference on Human Factors in Computing Systems, pp. 493–502 (2007)

8. Du, J., van Rooij, T., Martens, J.-B.: Mirrored perception cognition action model in an interactive surgery assist system. In: Stephanidis, C. (ed.) HCI 2017. CCIS, vol. 713, pp. 300–306. Springer, Cham (2017). https://doi.org/10.1007/978-3-319-58750-9_42

9. Jetter, C., Gerken, J.: A simplified model of user experience for practical application. In: NordiCHI 2006, Oslo: The 2nd COST294-MAUSE International Open Workshop" User Experience-Towards a Unified View, pp. 106–111 (2007)

10. Peruzzini, M., Pellicciari, M.: User experience evaluation model for sustainable manufacturing. Int. J. Comput. Integr. Manuf. **31**(6), 494–512 (2018)

11. Koskinen, I., Zimmerman, J., Binder, T., Redstrom, J., Wensveen, S.: Design research through practice: From the lab, field, and showroom. IEEE Trans. Prof. Commun. **56**(3), 262–263 (2013)

Altruism in Design: Conveying Designers' Thoughtfulness to Users Through Artifacts

Kentaro Go[✉][iD]

University of Yamanashi, Kofu, Takeda 400-8511, Japan
go@yamanashi.ac.jp

Abstract. The COVID-19 pandemic has heightened awareness of the importance of altruistic behavior towards others, making it a timely topic in the field of Human–Computer Interaction (HCI). Altruism, a fundamental trait that distinguishes humans from other animals, can be incorporated into design through two approaches: designing artifacts that encourage users to act altruistically and designing artifacts from an altruistic viewpoint. While the former approach has been the focus of most studies, this paper explores the possibility of "altruistic design" and identifies three factors that hinder it: the distance between the designer and user, contextual dependence of artifact use, and transparency of well-designed artifacts. To address these factors and effectively convey the designer's altruistic wish to the user, three perspectives are proposed. This study provides valuable insights into the altruistic relationship between designers and users and highlights the potential for incorporating altruism in HCI design, which can contribute to a society where people help each other with kindness.

Keywords: Altruism · Altruistic design · Design issue · Thoughtfulness

1 Introduction

In the face of global public health crises such as COVID-19, thoughtfulness for others has become more important among people [5]. Such thoughtful behavior toward others, or altruistic behavior, is an essential characteristic of humans that distinguishes them from other animals [4]. It will contribute to a better future society where people help each other with kindness. In Human–Computer Interaction (HCI), altruistic behavior has been attracting attention in recent years.

The way to treat "altruistic" in design can be broadly divided into two. One is that designed artifacts encourage users to act altruistically. Most of the previous studies have taken this approach. For example, Lee et al. [6] designed the Altruistic Fan to increase social empathy among people. In addition, Mah and Hespanhol [7] proposed an evaluation method for a design solution's "altruistic tendency."

The other is that the act of creating artifacts is done from an altruistic viewpoint. Designers devise artifacts with an altruistic desire to "create something

C. Stephanidis et al. (Eds.): HCII 2023, CCIS 1832, pp. 53–59, 2023.
https://doi.org/10.1007/978-3-031-35989-7_7

useful for someone in the future." Then the designers will convey the wish to the users through the artifact. This study will discuss whether such an "altruistic design" is possible. It further examines three factors that hinder altruistic design: the space-time distance between the designer and the user, the contextual dependence of artifact use, and the transparency of well-designed artifacts. Finally, we discuss perspectives to reduce them and convey to the user the altruistic wish of the designer for the artifact. This study provides a deep insight into the altruistic relationship between designers and users and, in that sense, points to a new direction in how to incorporate altruism in HCI.

2   Related Work: Altruism in Design

There are two main approaches to incorporating "altruism" into design. The first involves designing artifacts that encourage users to behave altruistically. The second approach is to create objects from an altruistic perspective.

2.1   Artifact Design that Encourages Altruism

Lee et al. [6] designed the Altruistic Fan as an example of the concept of "altruistic interaction design," which aims to increase social empathy among people. The paper explains the concept and application process of altruistic interaction design, using the Altruistic Fan as a case study. The study also includes the results of an exploratory user study that utilized this product.

Mah and Hespanhol [7] proposed a theoretical analytical design schema called the Mediated Tendency Towards Altruism (MeTTA), which categorizes various aspects of HCI systems and assesses their "altruistic tendency." The authors suggest that this approach could serve as a model for other moral perspectives and could be used as a basis for further inquiry into understanding and taxonomy of a moral continuum in HCI.

In a broader perspective, this category includes designs that encourage prosocial behavior [2,8,10] . For example, there are designs that encourage environmentally friendly behavior, such as eco-designs, and designs that encourage charitable donations. By promoting the use of these design artifacts, many social goods reflecting altruistic behavior are expected to be realized.

2.2   Artifact Design with Altruism

The alternative approach involves creating artifacts from an altruistic perspective. In this approach, designers aim to create something that will be useful to someone in the future, driven by a desire to do good for others. The act of designing is seen as a means of conveying this altruistic wish to users through the artifact itself.

This approach raises interesting questions about the nature of design and its relationship to ethical concerns. How can designers ensure that their altruistic intentions are effectively communicated to users, and that the artifact is used in a way that aligns with these intentions?

In this study, we will explore these questions in depth, examining the theoretical foundations of altruistic design and the practical implications for designers. By analyzing existing research and case studies, we will seek to identify the key principles and best practices for creating artifacts that promote altruistic behavior. As a preliminary step, this paper examines the complex relationships between designers, users, and artifacts, and considers the challenges that designers face when attempting to create altruistic designs. Finally, we propose perspectives to address these challenges.

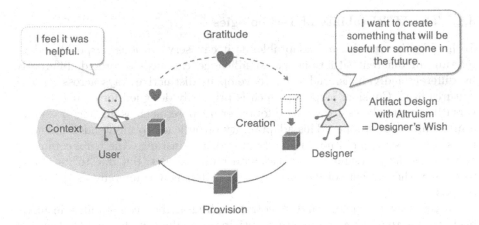

Fig. 1. the "space-time distance between the designer and the user" and the conveyance of altruistic wishes.

3   Conveyance of Altruistic Wishes and Its Difficulty

In modern manufacturing, the "space-time distance between the designer and the user" essentially exists (see Fig. 1). The products developed by designers necessitate the passage of time and spatial distance before they can be delivered to users. Commercial products require manufacturing processes that take a considerable amount of time. Additionally, there exists a time gap between product delivery and its utilization by the user. Moreover, the design field occupied by the designer and the user's usage field are spatially separate. In contemporary society, where the opportunities for creating and utilizing tools autonomously are scarce, synchronizing these two domains has become arduous. Thus, the current design landscape encounters a temporal and spatial discrepancy between designers and users, which necessitates indirect communication through designed artifacts. Although discussions concerning the communication facilitated by these artifacts have emerged, mainly from the perspective of mental models by Norman and following studies, the focus of such discussions has been primarily limited to the usability and user experience of artifacts.

Against this background, there are three factors that make it difficult for the designer's "altruistic wish" to be conveyed to the user through the artifact:

1. the multistability of technologies
2. the contextual dependence of artifact use
3. the transparency of well-designed artifacts

3.1   The Multistability of Technologies

Technology is versatile and adaptable, as it can serve various purposes and be relevant in different situations. Its significance can be interpreted differently by different individuals, and it can develop in distinctive ways across various cultures [3, 9]. Consider a spoon, which is primarily designed for eating, but its versatile nature allows it to be used for other purposes such as digging or even as a makeshift door stopper. This adaptability often leads to unintended usage by users that designers did not originally intend. For instance, the Unix command cat was initially designed to concatenate multiple files, but due to its ability to display the contents of files on the screen, it is now commonly used for this purpose.

In this way, technology and its corresponding artifact can stabilize in unexpected ways that designers may not anticipate, making it difficult for them to predict how they will ultimately converge. Even if a designer creates an artifact with a specific "wish" in mind, it is not guaranteed that the users will utilize it in the intended way, and thus the artifact usage may not reflect the designer's initial wish.

3.2   The Contextual Dependence of Artifact Use

The diversity of contexts in which artifact users are placed also influences the aforementioned multistability of technologies. For example, using a finger to input text on a smartphone while driving a car is a hazardous activity. In this scenario, it is recommended to use voice input instead. However, even with voice input, it is not appropriate to use it in all settings. For instance, using voice input on a smartphone in a quiet meditation room with several people present may not be well-received.

The example highlights that when the same technology and its corresponding artifact is expected to be used differently based on the context, the "wish" of the designer can also be influenced by the user's context. A "wish" that is effectively communicated in one context may not be comprehensible in another, and may even convey the opposite meaning.

3.3   The Transparency of Well-designed Artifacts

For a long time, people have claimed that well-designed tools become "disapear" [11]. Heidegger's famous hammer is a perfect example of this phenomenon. If we consider the hammer as an individual tool, we can identify its various parts and functions. However, when it is utilized effectively, the user's attention shifts to the process of using it, causing the hammer as a tool to become invisible or unnoticeable.

This fact also makes it difficult to convey the designer's "wish" to the user. Effectively designed artifacts "disappear" when they are used, so the "wish" mediated by artifacts will not rise to the user's consciousness.

4   Circulating Altruistic Wishes

The central challenge posed by the "space-time distance between the designer and the user," as explained earlier, involves the designer's altruistic with to create something that will be useful in the future for someone else. It is difficult to determine the effectiveness of the designer's creation for someone else, depending on the extent of the spatial and temporal gap between them, without the opportunity to witness its use. Furthermore, the use of the designed artifact is likely to occur in a future when the designer may no longer exist. To tackle these challenges, we propose three perspectives that can help mitigate them.

4.1   Designer Side: Designer's Immersion

The creative process for designers typically begins with a wish or desire, but as they engage in the act of designing and become fully immersed in it, their original wish may fade away or become unconscious. Csikszentmihalyi refers to this state as "flow" [1]. Achieving this state allows designers to perform at their best and also maintain their own well-being. Our goal is to create a mechanism that can help designers achieve this state of immersion and creativity.

4.2   Provision Process: Artificial Matching the Time and Space

If the space-time distance between the designer and the user, which exists essentially, cannot be changed, it should be matched artificially. There are two possible approaches to this: the designer approaching the user spatio-temporally, and the user approaching the designer spatio-temporally. An example of the former is a user survey in human-centered design. The first step in the altruistic cycle of design is for a designer to visit a user's workplace and life, and build a relationship with the user. Examples of the latter include end-user development and end-user programming, where the user can experience the designer's attitude and mindset by performing the design task themselves. End-user development has a long history in HCI, and we suggest revisiting it from the perspective of the cycle of altruism.

4.3   User Side: Blank Spaces

By incorporating "blank spaces" into their artifacts, designers can enable users to imagine the designer and potentially modify the design. Through intentionally incorporating blank spaces, designers can provide users with room for interpretation and creativity, which can lead to greater user engagement and participation in the design process. This approach fosters a sense of co-creation between designers and users, promoting a more collaborative design process at large. Our goal is to characterize effective blank space for artifacts that facilitates this process of co-creation.

5   Future Directions

As a potential avenue for future research, we propose conducting an analysis of the characteristics of commonly used sticky notes and workarounds in daily life. By investigating these temporary design modifications made to existing artifacts, we can reflect upon the "blank space" in the artifact's design. Sharing the results of this feature analysis between designers and users could help bridge the gap between them and generate new design ideas. Furthermore, participating in designers' ideation activities can provide researchers with insights into the state of immersion in design. Thus, the examination of sticky notes and workarounds is considered a preliminary step in exploring how altruistic wishes can be conveyed between designers and users.

6   Conclusion

In this paper, we have discussed the concept of altruism in design. As an initial step, we examined the complex relationships among designers, users, and artifacts, and considered the challenges designers face when attempting to prioritize the well-being of users. We then proposed three perspectives to address these challenges. Our study provides significant insight into the altruistic relationship between designers and users, and points towards a new direction in incorporating altruism in HCI. As designers increasingly recognize the importance of designing for user well-being and the well-being of designers themselves, we hope that our research will inspire further exploration of altruistic design practices in the field of HCI.

Acknowledgements. Part of this work is supported by JSPS KAKENHI Grant Number JP20K11904 and The University of Yamanashi grand-in-aid, Regional Contribution Promotion Project FY2022. We also thank Dr. Masaya Ando of CIT for his valuable comments and suggestions.

References

1. Csikszentmihalyi, M.: Flow: The Psychology of Optimal Experience. Harper Collins (2008)
2. Damen, I., et al.: MirrorMe: increasing prosocial behaviour in public transport. In: Extended Abstracts of the 2019 CHI Conference on Human Factors in Computing Systems, pp. 1–6. CHI EA 2019, Association for Computing Machinery (2019). https://doi.org/10.1145/3290607.3312961
3. de Boer, B.: Explaining multistability: postphenomenology and affordances of technologies. AI Soc. 1–11 (2021). https://doi.org/10.1007/s00146-021-01272-3
4. Fehr, E., Fischbacher, U.: The nature of human altruism. Nature. **425**(6960), 785–791 (2003). https://doi.org/10.1038/nature02043
5. Grimalda, G., Buchan, N.R., Ozturk, O.D., Pinate, A.C., Urso, G., Brewer, M.B.: Exposure to COVID-19 is associated with increased altruism, particularly at the local level. Sci. Rep. **11**(1), 18950 (2021). https://doi.org/10.1038/s41598-021-97234-2
6. Lee, Y., Lim, Y., Suk, H.J.: Altruistic interaction design: a new interaction design approach for making people care more about others. In: Proceedings of the 2011 Conference on Designing Pleasurable Products and Interfaces, pp. 1–4. DPPI 2011, Association for Computing Machinery (2011). https://doi.org/10.1145/2347504.2347514
7. Mah, K., Hespanhol, L.: Embodying altruism in interaction design: towards moralising HCI. In: Proceedings of the 29th Australian Conference on Computer-Human Interaction, pp. 592–596. OZCHI 2017, Association for Computing Machinery (2017). https://doi.org/10.1145/3152771.3156177
8. Naqshbandi, K., Mah, K., Ahmadpour, N.: Making space for faith, religion, and spirituality in prosocial HCI. Interactions. **29**(4), 62–67 (2022). https://doi.org/10.1145/3544301
9. Rosenberger, R.: Multistability and the agency of mundane artifacts: from speed bumps to subway benches. Hum. Stud. **37**(3), 369–392 (2014). https://doi.org/10.1007/s10746-014-9317-1
10. Steinemann, S., Geelan, B., de Salas, K., Opwis, K.: Simple acts for a better world: a gameful system for prosocial behavior: preliminary design and research plan. In: Extended Abstracts Publication of the Annual Symposium on Computer-Human Interaction in Play, pp. 305–313. CHI PLAY 2017 Extended Abstracts, Association for Computing Machinery (2017). https://doi.org/10.1145/3130859.3131295
11. Wheeler, M.: The reappearing tool: transparency, smart technology, and the extended mind. AI & Soc. **34**(4), 857–866 (2019). https://doi.org/10.1007/s00146-018-0824-x

The Ladder of Participation as a Conceptual Tool for Sustainable Socio-Technical Design of Data-driven Digital Services

Viktoria Horn[(⊠)][iD] and Claude Draude[iD]

Participatory IT Design, Faculty of Electrical Engineering and Computer Science,
University of Kassel, Kassel, Germany
viktoria.horn@uni-kassel.de

Abstract. Participation in the data economy is prone to unjust power imbalances. Individuals function as mere data sources and are left out of decisions on how, when, and where personal data is accumulated and processed. In this paper, we translate Arnsteins' 'Ladder of Citizen Participation' to the field of the data economy to offer a conceptual lens to tackle power imbalances' underlying structures. For this, we derived assumptions from the application's ecosystem. We propose to encase the lowest rungs of the ladder with the term of *involuntary participation* and frame individuals as digital Citizens to avoid a mere focus on the economic dimension of participation. Building on this, we translate the eight rungs of Arnstein's original ladder to the new application field of the data economy through examples and design affordances corresponding with differing degrees of digital citizens' data agency. Eventually, we contemplate implications for socio-technical design resulting from the re-conceptualization of the 'ladder' and formulate future research.

Keywords: Participatory design · Data economy · Socio-technical design

1 Introduction

Society is increasingly data-driven [25]. A huge amount of social processes take place in online settings. Digital services like apps, social networks, and platforms are not just tools but required for social and public participation [29]. These services convert traceable aspects of (online) social life into quantifiable data and embed techniques of digital data processing in economic utilization contexts, framed by the term 'data-economy' [12]. Several researchers state [14,20,29] that there is a problematic power imbalance in the data economy between firms collecting, sharing and accumulating data, while individuals are sources of data extraction but not in control. Thus, individual data agency and fair competition are "at stake" [17]. To provide a conceptual lens on those power imbalances and to uncover possibilities to overcome them, we propose to re-frame Arnstein's

© The Author(s), under exclusive license to Springer Nature Switzerland AG 2023
C. Stephanidis et al. (Eds.): HCII 2023, CCIS 1832, pp. 60–67, 2023.
https://doi.org/10.1007/978-3-031-35989-7_8

'Ladder of Citizen Participation' [2] in the context of the data economy. The original ladder was developed to introduce a typology of citizen participation to encourage more enlightened discourse. Arnstein draws exemplifications from public programs of urban renewal, Model Cities and anti-poverty. The ladder consists of eight rungs, namely *Manipulation, Therapy, Informing, Consultation, Placation, Partnership, Delegated Power and Citizen Control*. To further conceptualize, the first two rungs of the original ladder are encased as Degrees of Non-Participation, followed by the next three rungs encased as Degrees of Tokenism and the last three rungs encased as Degrees of Citizen Power.

We transfer the idea of this typology to participation in the data economy, thereby rethinking the ascending degrees of control for the digital Citizen and elaborating on the different rungs in the context of the novel application area.

2 Theoretical Background

2.1 Participation in Human-Computer Interaction

Mostly, participation in HCI occurs as the question of how to involve users in IT systems design. Relevant literature shows the importance of user involvement reporting challenges but also stressing the benefits [3,15,27]. Notably, involvement does not equal participation. Damodoran [16] states that participation is the most comprehensive stage of user involvement because it means that people hold decision making power for the overall system. This power to make decisions and the understanding of a digital system and, furthermore, its impact on the application domain, defines participation as active, conscious and self-determined. In contrast, users may also hold a merely informative or consultative role [16]. In the data economy we relate citizen involvement or participation to the design and use of IT. Typically though, citizens appear as users of a product or service or, more broadly, as humans affected by the system. The first corresponds with user-centered design [24], the second with human-centered design [10,26]. The question of where in the design process, to what intensity and by which means humans are involved depends on the approach and methods applied. A most comprehensive take towards citizen involvement is participatory design, an approach reaching back to labor unions fights for workplace democracy in the 1970s in Scandanivia [4,11]. Participatory design seeks to increase people's decision making power throughout all stages of development. Through participation "democracy at the workplace and beyond", "empowerment of people through the process of design", "emancipatory practices through mutual learning between designers and people", "seeing people as skillful and resourceful in the development of their future practices" is aimed for [5]. Participatory design entails conceptual considerations, concrete methods and best practices, and its development and adaptability has been widely discussed in the field of HCI [3,21]. While participatory design seeks to increase people's power, the socio-technical approach always considers social and technical aspects as interdependent and equally important in IT design. This means accounting for technical infrastructures, hard- and software, technical requirements along social structures, work tasks and people's affordances, and considering that changes in one component might change the overall system design and use [22]. Socio-technical approaches broaden the view of humans interacting with a service towards a more systemic understanding. For participation in HCI this means that IT design not just affects how a user interacts with a system, but how citizens can participate in society and how their citizenship is affected by digital transformation.

2.2   Socio-technical Challenges in the Data Economy

The ecosystem of the data economy is very complex, not seldom integrating multiple stakeholders in the life cycle of data [14]. Production and contribution of personal data happens intentionally. Individuals use fitness trackers or give status updates on social media. Conversely, data contribution also happens unintentionally through digital services use being tracked by third-party cookies, advertisers, data brokers and credit-scoring companies [14,20]. Here, data is traded between firms as a 'good'. This leads to the assumption that personal data may be considered neutral or value free and leaves out contextual effects [14]. Not just in Nissenbaum's [23] concept of contextual integrity, a framework for understanding privacy as a social construct shaped by context-specific norms, values, and expectations, this becomes highly problematic when taking ethical aspects of personal data into account. For instance, the accumulation of personal data is processed by sophisticated algorithms to measure and infer "increasingly sensitive features of our lives (e.g., purchasing behaviour revealing our political or sexual preferences, our state of mind, or our likely future behaviour)" [20].

The data economy has given rise to several socio-technical problems, notably the asymmetric distribution among firms and individuals of the means of data-based knowledge production, leading to the emergence of surveillance capitalism as conceptualized by Zuboff [29]. As the researcher states, this form of information capitalism seeks to predict and modify human behavior as a means to generate revenue and control markets, which has resulted in the commercialization of everyday life and the blurring of societal boundaries. In response, Zuboff has introduced the concept of an 'information civilization' to address questions of authority and power, particularly with regard to who learns from global data flows and who ultimately has decision power. Additionally, the data economy expands the data lens beyond past virtual behavior to current and future actual behavior, enabling the manipulation of behavior through reward and punishment mechanisms, with individuals being left without a fair share of the resulting benefits. Therefore, big tech firms, such as Apple and Google, now hold significant power through pervasive and continuous recording of transaction details to impact the economy in the foreseeable future [29].

3   Reframing the Ladder of Citizen Participation as a Conceptual Tool for Data-Driven Digital Services

Since Arnstein's ladder was developed as a frame to show power imbalances in decision processes between powerholders and those effected by the decision, 'climbing up the ladder' means reaching for equal participation to overcome those imbalances and to aid citizens to be deliberately included. Thus, the concept of the ladder should help to address the named power imbalance between firms and individuals by conceptualizing different levels of participation of individuals in the data economy and through the corresponding socio-technical design of the anchored data-driven digital services. The ladder of citizen participation has already been transferred to several fields, for instance Political Science [19], Public Health [9, 28] and Media Studies [8]. To introduce the ladder of participation to the data economy, we reframe the rungs as different levels of data agency, thereby making the conceptualization accessible to the field of Human-Computer Interaction. Mortier et al. [20] define agency as follows: "Agency, concerned with giving people the capacity to act within these data systems, to opt-in or to opt-out, to control, inform and correct data and inferences, and so on. Additionally, the authors state that even if people do not make use of their agency often the capacity to do so has to be guaranteed. Lehtiniemi & Haapoja [17] identify data activists' stating that individuals' lack of agency over personal data might be the principal problem hindering equal participation. Thereby, considering individuals as mere market agents would reduce agency on the economic dimension. On the contrary, framing individuals as digital citizens broadens the concept by taking self-determination in all aspects of online life into account. We thrive for a conceptualization of equal participation in the data economy as an act of data agency of digital citizens, thereby contributing to the ladder's origin in fostering the concept of citizen power. Another inherent assumption of the conceptualization as a ladder is that of a power duality. This indicates that the citizens placed at the bottom of the ladder have less to no power, in dependence to the 'power holders', which are the ultimate decision makers. Thus, reaching one end of the ladder means one of the two 'counterparts' is in charge of the decision process. Since we thrive for collaboration between stakeholders in the data economy (see [17]) we propose reading the ladder from a digital citizen's 'power to' perspective in an upwards direction rather than reading it downwards with a data economic firms' 'power over' perspective in mind. This contributes to the participatory nature of socio-technical design [7], fostering mutual development processes and collaborative thinking. Eventually, we propose a shift to be made when translating the ladder onto the data-economic field by encasing the lowest three rungs of the ladder not with the term 'non-participation' but with 'involuntary participation'. Interacting with data-driven digital services is always a way to be (possibly) and even incautiously participating in the data economy, leaving data traces and therefore opportunities for economic utilization or personal profiling. Thus, being on the bottom end of data economy's ladder does not only mean to be left out in decisions concerning data processes, but also being disregarded about the question when, how and whether to participate at all. Onward, we briefly contemplate on every rung, translating the conceptualization of the different rungs originated in Arnstein's ladder to the data economic context based on the assumptions made above.

Manipulation. At the lowest rung, involuntary participation is forced by firms taking advantages of individual's missing knowledge and misconceptions of how the data economy works. Consequently, the last rung represents firms as power holders in the data economy exploiting users' data and turning it into monetized value without giving individuals a piece of the pie. To exemplify, firms use 'dark privacy patterns' [6] for the interface design of data-driven digital services which lure individuals into contributing more data than they originally intended to just to fulfill a firm's business model goals [13].

Therapy. At this level, communication and participation options are presented through the user interface of the digital service, meaning individuals are highly dependent on how different 'opt-in' or 'opt-out' options are implemented. Those modalities are often found when consent for participation is needed due to regulatory duties like the General Data Protection Regulation, most prominently in the form of so-called 'cookie banners'.

Informing. As firms' data accumulation strategies are mostly hidden processes, or afford a certain amount of technical knowledge to be anticipated, firms are in the responsibility to unveil their data processes in order to offer opportunities to decide on what is happening with one's data. For that reason, we consider all firms to be in duty of proactively revealing all steps of their data processing cycle in a transparent manner. Since the individuals data life cycle is not limited to a one-time touch point, Mortier et al. [20] even advocate for "periodically receiving a 'data statement' indicating by whom our data have been accessed and how they have been used".

Consultation. Consultation is no new concept in the design of digital services and appears often in the form of focus groups, surveys and interviews contributing to a user-centered design process. To avoid being mere market research, in data-economic contexts more sophisticated forms of participation and the willingness of IT designers to be educators of the complex field are needed. One starting point might be finding a common language like ethical values to foster mutual learning processes [18].

Placation. Placation in the original ladder is often demonstrated by having a seat - and thereby a say - in advisory boards. When analyzing which organizational structures match this concept, advisory boards in the data economy are most likely found for privacy issues and are constituted of experts from academia, governments, business and independent organizations. To make this rung of participation attractive for individuals, a promised seat for citizens and discussing privacy issues need to be a matter of concern.

Partnership. On this rung, firms and individuals meet on an equal level. Both sides can profit from exchange, as Mortier et al. states: "The opportunity for data subjects to engage with data systems may enable them to correct and improve the data held and the inferences drawn, improving the overall quality and utility of the applications using our personal data" [20]. Thereby, collaboration between firms and data subjects not only foster a more just ecosystem but can also serve pragmatic ends [17].

Delegated Power. Moving onwards, digital citizens having the dominant decision-making authority are equipped with a counter-veto and can delegate significant powers. We can imagine that auditing and monitoring of data could be delegated to trustworthy specialists or experts that serves as citizen advocates. The World Economic Forum [1], for example, calls for "data intermediaries as a new policy lever" in the data economy.

Citizen Control. On the highest rung digital citizens are in full charge of deciding how and if value is generated and monetized with personal data. Current data activism strategies thrive for a implementation of this distribution of power. It needs to be discussed, whether digital citizen participation at the ladder's partnership level is the more socially sustainable solution.

4 Discussion

We motivated the reframing of the 'Ladder of Citizen Participation' to be a conceptual tool for sustainable socio-technical design of data-driven digital services. To examine its applicability in the field of Human-Computer Interaction, we briefly want to draw links to the work of technology designers. As Mortier et al. [20] point out, technology designers are in the duty of developing ethical systems. This includes to provide individuals with agency and in case of involuntary behavior to support predictability of the systems outcome. Thus, using the ladder as a conceptual lens supports thriving for a design of data-driven digital services that allow digital citizens' fair participation in the data economy and to hinder the development of technology that places individuals at the lowest two rungs of the ladder. Additionally, the ladder may function as a exchange base in the design process for a dialogue between data scientists, interaction designers and business professionals, fostering multidisciplinary negotiation.

Moreover, reframing users of data-driven digital services as digital citizens may shift the focus from solely fulfilling business goals [17] to also centering ethical and democratic aspects of interaction design in the data economy.

Since the presented work is a first introduction of the re-conceptualization of the 'Ladder of Citizen Participation' in the data-economic context, further elaboration of the different rungs is needed. Currently, the formulation of the rungs is still on a very abstract level, consisting of a mixture of the description of ecosystem phenomena and Utopian imaginations from data activism's [17] perspective. Last but not least, a full composition of the concept of *citizen control* and its implications for the data economy is needed. This could possibly result in a general reformulation of a more transparent and regulated data economy and entail the necessity of individuals to be properly educated about IT and data in order to be self-determined digital citizens.

5 Conclusion

Our transfer of the 'Ladder of Citizen Participation' to the field of the data economy aimed at offering a conceptual tool that may aid socio-technical design processes of data-driven digital services. We formulated assumptions derived from the application's ecosystem, like the data economy's prevalent occurrence of involuntary participation. The eight rungs of Arnstein's original ladder were translated to the data economy through examples and design affordances. Moreover, we shortly contemplated on implications for socio-technical design that result from the re-conceptualization of the 'ladder'. Future work could apply the new typology to analyze existing phenomena in the data economy and, moreover, develop possible design solutions to exemplify further elaborating on the rungs.

References

1. Advancing digital agency: The power of data intermediaries. https://www3. weforum.org/docs/WEF_Advancing_towards_Digital_Agency_2022.pdf   (2022), accessed: 2023-03-16
2. Arnstein, S.R.: A ladder of citizen participation. Journal of the American Institute of planners **35**(4), 216–224 (1969)
3. Bano, M., Zowghi, D.: A systematic review on the relationship between user involvement and system success. Information and software technology **58**, 148–169 (2015)
4. Bødker, K., Kensing, F., Simonsen, J.: Participatory IT design: Designing for business and workplace realities. MIT Press, Cambridge, Mass. and London (2009)
5. Bødker, S., Dindler, C., Iversen, O.S., Smith, R.C.: Participatory design, Synthesis lectures on human centered informatics, vol. 52. Morgan et Claypool Publishers, [San Rafael] (2022)
6. Bösch, C., Erb, B., Kargl, F., Kopp, H., Pfattheicher, S.: Tales from the dark side: privacy dark strategies and privacy dark patterns. Proc. Priv. Enhancing Technol. **2016**(4), 237–254 (2016)
7. Bratteteig, T., Wagner, I.: What is a participatory design result? In: Proceedings of the 14th Participatory Design Conference: Full papers-Volume 1. pp. 141–150 (2016)
8. Carpentier, N.: Beyond the ladder of participation: An analytical toolkit for the critical analysis of participatory media processes. Javnost-The Public **23**(1), 70–88 (2016)
9. Church, J., Saunders, D., Wanke, M., Pong, R., Spooner, C., Dorgan, M.: Citizen participation in health decision-making: past experience and future prospects. Journal of public health policy pp. 12–32 (2002)
10. Gasson, S.: Human-centered vs. user-centered approaches to information system design. Journal of Information Technology Theory and Application (JITTA) 5(2), 5 (2003)
11. Gregory, J.: Scandinavian approaches to participatory design. International Journal of Engineering Education **19**(1), 62–74 (2003)
12. Hess, T., Lamla, J.: Einführung: Die zukunft der datenökonomie. zwischen geschäftsmodell, kollektivgut und verbraucherschutz. Die Zukunft der Datenökonomie: Zwischen Geschäftsmodell, Kollektivgut und Verbraucherschutz pp. 1–7 (2019)
13. Horn, V., Engert, S., Draude, C.: Rethinking business models as sociotechnical intersections in data-economy that should be designed participatively. Mensch und Computer 2022-Workshopband (2022)

14. Hornung, H., Pereira, R., Baranauskas, M.C.C., Liu, K.: Challenges for human-data interaction-a semiotic perspective. In: Human-Computer Interaction: Design and Evaluation: 17th International Conference, HCI International 2015, Los Angeles, CA, USA, August 2–7, 2015, Proceedings, Part I 17. pp. 37–48. Springer (2015)

15. Kujala, S.: User involvement: a review of the benefits and challenges. Behaviour & information technology 22(1), 1–16 (2003)

16. Damodaran, L.: User involvement in the systems design process-a practical guide for users. Behaviour & Information Technology 15(6), 363–377 (1996). https://doi.org/10.1080/014492996120049

17. Lehtiniemi, T., Haapoja, J.: Data agency at stake: Mydata activism and alternative frames of equal participation. New Media Soc. 22(1), 87–104 (2020)

18. Leimstädtner, D., Sörries, P., Müller-Birn, C.: Unfolding values through systematic guidance: Conducting a value-centered participatory workshop for a patient-oriented data donation. In: Proceedings of Mensch und Computer 2022, pp. 477–482 (2022)

19. Mapuva, J., Muyengwa-Mapuva, L.: Arnstein's ladder of participation and citizen participation in zimbabwe. International Journal of African and Asians Studies 11, 1–13 (2015)

20. Mortier, R., Haddadi, H., Henderson, T., McAuley, D., Crowcroft, J.: Human-data interaction: The human face of the data-driven society. arXiv preprint arXiv:1412.6159 (2014)

21. Muller, M.J.: Participatory design: The third space in hci: The human-computer interaction handbook. pp. 1051–1068. L. Erlbaum Associates Inc, Hillsdale, NJ, USA (2003), https://dl.acm.org/citation.cfm?id=772072.772138

22. Mumford, E.: The story of socio-technical design: reflections on its successes, failures and potential. Information Systems Journal 16(4), 317–342 (2006). https://doi.org/10.1111/j.1365-2575.2006.00221.x

23. Nissenbaum, H.: Privacy as contextual integrity. Wash. L. Rev. 79, 119 (2004)

24. Norman, D.A., Draper, S.W.: User Centered System Design. New Perspectives on Human-Computer Interaction. L. Erlbaum Associates Inc, Hillsdale, NJ and USA (1986)

25. Pentland, A.: The data-driven society. Scientific American 309(4), 78–83 (2013)

26. Seffah, A., Gulliksen, J., Desmarais, M.C. (eds.): Human-Centered Software Engineering – Integrating Usability in the Software Development Lifecycle. Springer, Netherlands, Dordrecht (2005)

27. Wilson, S., Bekker, M., Johnson, P., Johnson, H.: Helping and hindering user involvement-a tale of everyday design. In: Proceedings of the ACM SIGCHI Conference on Human factors in computing systems. pp. 178–185 (1997)

28. Wright, M., Block, M., von Unger, H.: Stufen der partizipation in der gesundheitsförderung. Info-Dienst für Gesundheitsförderung 7(3), 4–5 (2007)

29. Zuboff, S.: Big other: surveillance capitalism and the prospects of an information civilization. Journal of information technology 30(1), 75–89 (2015)

All Things Coexist Without Harming Each Other-A Growing Research in Multi-species Intelligent Design

Guanqing Hua$^{(\boxtimes)}$ ⓘ, Tanhao Gao ⓘ, Xiaotong Zhang ⓘ, and Hongtao Zhou ⓘ

College of Design and Innovation, Tongji University, Shanghai, China
2280215@tongji.edu.cn

Abstract. The development of artificial intelligence has broken through the previous assumption that "human is the only actor," and interactive haptic technology has become a new actor, bringing users realistic visual and auditory experiences. However, with the continuous improvement of people's requirements for green and healthy living standards, consumer demand has reflected the characteristics of diversification and high quality. Consumers have more specific requests for product quality, variety, flavor, and a growing environment. They also pay more attention to their experience and the sense of engagement when using PC intelligence. The current human-computer interaction design only focuses on human materiality, human-environment interaction, and barrier-free dimensions. In other words, less attention is paid to the existence of other "non-human" beings and the human-natural world entangled with humans, which probably leads to the fact that multi-species intelligent design has not obtained a specific development space to some extent. Based on the field investigation of two cases, this study tries to rediscover the sustainable energy that has long been forgotten, abandoned, and scattered in marginalized locations since the development of advanced technology. Combined with existing research on human-computer interaction design, it points out that the "non-human" voice, emotion, and power temporarily obscured are not only an essential part of Multimodal human–computer interaction design but also the development of immersive and exploratory and emotional experiences for users. It provides a new space to capture social facts' "authenticity" and "aura" meanings. Meanwhile, the research also points out that introducing human interaction technology can make up for what users cannot perceive and see with their senses. In conclusion, an intelligent design framework for understanding multi-species is put forward, which could be helpful in general design in the domain of human-computer interaction. Also, provide a design dimension for the sustainable development of our society.

Keywords: Human-computer Interaction · Multi-species Intelligent Design · Authenticity · Social Well-being

C. Stephanidis et al. (Eds.): HCII 2023, CCIS 1832, pp. 68–77, 2023.
https://doi.org/10.1007/978-3-031-35989-7_9

1 Introduction

In 1964, the American scholar Susan Sontag argued in her book *Against Interpretation* that the earliest fine art must have been magical and witchcraft [1]. French anthropologist Claude Levi-Strauss also believed that "art is located midway between scientific knowledge and mythical or magical thinking" [2]. Malinowski, a British scholar, also found that in the Australian Aboriginal society, witchcraft played a vital role in the construction of canoes, which was both an everyday craftsmanship and a supernatural force that endowed the product with cultural connotations [3].

However, for a long time, most activities about design, research, and discussion of art, especially craftsmanship, have focused on the research and development of "technology" while ignoring the relative stage of "witchcraft." With the application of computer science and human-computer interaction technology, the importance of "witchcraft" has not been further emphasized and expanded. Conversely, widening gaps between "technology" and "witchcraft" have a negative impact on the growth, preservation, and even transmission of handicrafts. On the other hand, as science and technology advance and green and healthy living become more prevalent, consumer demand is changing dramatically. Urban users now have increasingly diverse and high expectations for the quality, variety, and growth environment of the products they use, and they are more concerned with their own experiences and sense of engagement when using PCs intelligently [4]. Moreover, producers are also eager to explore and develop smart agriculture with the help of new technologies. However, because different users' requirements and design understanding of human interaction are highly different from those of researchers, which brings challenges to practitioners and researchers of Human-computer interaction for development when providing users with general interaction services.

Therefore, the authors of this article have carried out long-term anthropological and design research centered on the production and understanding of "things" by producers and proposed "multi-species intelligent design". This design explored how "living things", not humans, can help humans create new worlds for producers, consumers, HCI and other related fields. The invention also provides a framework for understanding multi-species intelligence, which will help these fields better design human-computer interaction interfaces and further enhance the "authenticity" and social well-being of user immersive experiences.

2 Research Hypothesis and Methods

In the context of "Renaissance" and "Humanism", our research is based on the philosophical concept and practice of "all things arise together without harm and all laws of things running without conflict". With the help of human-computer interaction and criticism perspective, this research adopted participatory observation, semi-structured interviews and video recording. Rongchang Pottery in Chongqing, China, and Liangping people's Pomelo planting technique in Chongqing were studied. This paper focuses on the sustainable energy that has long been neglected and marginalized in mainstream society and discusses the importance of "witchcraft", which is associated with all living beings. Theoretically, "witchcraft" is an essential component of multi-mode human-computer interaction design, according to this study's theory. As a result, we focused especially on local, sustainable energy, including the environment, sunlight, fire, earth, creatures, deities, and other essential elements for the human-computer interaction design of customers/users. These elements ought to be incorporated into human-computer interaction design as targets to enhance the relationship between customers and goods. Researchers like Barath Raghavan emphasize the necessity for HCI communities to address concerns outside of computing, such as ecological constraints and fundamental human needs [5]. In order to take care of ourselves and our environment, Anton Poikolainen Rosén et al. also urge attempts to expand the focus away from humans [6].

To complete the study, we entered two separate field sites in August 2019, and the investigation continued until December. In January 2021, research was interrupted due to the COVID-19 pandemic. We revisited the two sites from December 2022 to January 2023 and updated the data and materials. The whole procedure of this study took seven months. From an empirical perspective, COVID-19 has temporarily slowed down the consumption and mobility of products. Still, it has also further activated users' urgent needs and emotional identification for human-computer interaction services.

3   Related Research on Human-Computer Interaction

Science and technology are the primary productive forces, and the development of new artificial intelligence technology breaks the previous assumption that "human is the only actor". The machine has become a new actor, is widely changing, and affects all aspects of human social life. Researchers have conducted many studies on applying human-computer interaction technology in the industry, agriculture, education, fine art, and other fields. In agriculture, researchers use a software named LabVIEW as the development platform to carry out remote monitoring and data collection on the growing environment (temperature, humidity, rainfall, light) and growth process of crops through the human-computer interaction interface [7]. At the same time, machine vision technology is used to analyze the collected images to explore and identify the disease and provide an adequate decision-making basis for producing and managing agricultural products [8]. But the intelligent Agriculture System, AgriSys, struggled to capture data accurately in the face of constant wind, low humidity, and extreme variations in diurnal temperatures [9]. However, researchers still believe that applying human-computer interaction technology can save the costs of agricultural production and management and better inherit farming culture.

Researchers have also found that human-computer interaction technology can promote the production and creation of interactive installation art and intelligent art [10], and enhance the spatial aesthetic value of artworks, the way of dynamic representation, and the multi-sensory immersive experience of users [11]. But how to improve the human-computer interaction environment, identify which design factors could provide information and examination for design decisions. Thus, narrow technology development applications and goals have become a thorny issue. Some scholars believe that effective human-computer intelligence interaction requires computers to interact with users naturally [12], such as by building human-computer interaction models [13]. Although designing human-computer interaction systems could improve the ability of humans and robots to interact in language and behavior [14], users still need to learn autonomously how to use them. So, this raises a new question: simplifying the minority interaction design process, diversification of interaction modes, and unconscious design has become essential, especially in the face of the old [15], children [16], and other special groups. Zhong Xing, Sun Taiwei et al. argued that promoting users' unconscious interaction does not mean that their thinking and decision-making are entirely unnecessary [17], but reduces the cognitive cost and operational cost of users in the process of human-computer interaction through the mental transformation of users and the simulation of physical feedback. Thus, improving the efficiency of human-computer exchange and enhancing users' immersive experience [18]. Furthermore, the design of human-machine interaction should consider people's subjective emotional responses to objects or events [19]. However, it's worth noting that universal design or accessibility design may result in different path choices depending on the varied emotional expressions across different regions and ethnic groups.

In short, the current research mainly focuses on the interface design of human-computer interaction and the interaction design for special people and particular fields. But research on the aesthetic expression in human-computer exchange, capturing the power of "multi-species intelligence" (animals and plants and gods other than human beings), and the universal multimodal design of humanity-environment perception are relatively few. Therefore, multi-species intelligent design has yet to gain a specific space for development.

4   Research Results and Analysis

Multimodal human-computer interaction has been proven advantageous by researchers and users in practice. Even with some deficiencies and limitations, they can compensate for each other through technology [20]. However, it should be pointed out that human emotion is more challenging to be processed through information technology than cognition. The intervention of cultural factors makes the research more complicated, which requires adding human-computer interaction to the dimension of human-culture interaction [21]. Especially for the human-computer interaction design in immaterial and material culture, cross-cultural collaborative design is increasingly becoming the urgent demand of users. Our case studies focus on pottery-making and fruit-growing techniques (see Fig. 1).

4.1   Interactive Design of Pottery Making and Intangible Culture

Haptic technology in human-computer interaction provides users with realistic visual and auditory experiences. Artists have used virtual reality and human-computer interaction technologies [22] to inherit and develop intangible cultural heritage [23]. However, the embodiment of the craft's system is to ensure that the emotional experience users get during interaction is only a "partial reality", making it more challenging for the interaction system to offer users a "pleasant touch" interface [24]and then further restricting the essence of intangible cultural heritage and the multisensory experience of users [25].

Fig. 1. An overall framework for multi-species intelligent design.

We concluded that pottery production is a technique that combines "technology" and "witchcraft" based on the research in Rongchang, Chongqing. Pottery cannot be completed solely by "artificial" means. The natural rhythm and the cooperation of multiple non-human subjects enable pottery to transform from "clay" to "vessel". Bruno Latour's "Actor-Network Theory" states that actors include humans and instruments, tools, technology, objects, and media as multiple living subjects [26]. Each step-in pottery-making involves the participation of "non-human" forces. Especially in the firing process, potters must carefully prepare offerings such as incense, candles, roosters, and pork to worship the kiln deities.

The potters in Rongchang view worshipping the kiln god as an essential step in obtaining a "aura" for their pottery. This strengthens the pottery's "insurance" value and illustrates the connectedness of all things. Even young potters with modern education follow in the footsteps of kiln worship. However, the ritual practice of younger potters is relatively simplified compared to older potters. The offerings are no longer animal sacrifices but replaced by fruits and food, and the worship ritual is exceptionally devout (see Fig. 2). The addition of the offering ceremony precisely reveals that humans cannot control the kiln's firing as their willingness.

In addition, sunlight, temperature, wind, and fuel such as wood and grass are equally important. The involvement of different powers, such as pine trees, horsetail grass, ferns, and green oak trees, is also seen as help from multiple non-human subject forces to pottery making. The participation of numerous "non-human" parties allows the pottery to transform into a unique color and appearance while maintaining harmony. The interaction between fire and clay adds the element of "nature" to the pottery, creating an individual trace of the pottery's life. Therefore, each pottery the potter completes through firing is not a commodity in the ordinary sense but an artistic work with high aesthetic value.

The results of the field research reproduce the technical and cultural context of pottery makers. The Rongchang potters' belief in the "unity of heaven and man" notion indicates that how humans and nature are interdependent and interrelated. However, the current interactive design of intangible cultural heritage only regards pottery as a "manmade product", Its capture is limited to the visual level while ignoring other forces (kiln deities), life, and sound intertwined with humans. These cultural elements can enrich

Fig. 2. Pottery maker sacrificial ceremony of kiln deities.

the boundaries of multimodal human-computer interaction design and re-find the diverse needs of users. The same problem still occurs in the interactive design of material culture.

4.2 Techniques of Fruit Cultivation and Human-Computer Interaction Design in Material Culture

Food can be mirrored by the interactive design in material culture. With increasing emphasis on ecological agriculture and organic food safety, consuming safe food and engaging in multisensory farming has become a new way of life for the contemporary Chinese urban middle class. Unfortunately, however, the current human-computer interactive design regarding agricultural products needs to be improved. It fails to provide users with more than the fixed values and standards since researchers regard the natural environment as the only growth environment for crops, far from the food's role of spiritual needs and cultural significance in material culture.

In the Liangping District of Chongqing in China, this place is an essential base for fruit production. It established a worldwide reputation for its abundant pomelo production, which is welcomed at home and abroad. Driven by the digital economy, pomelo sales rose annually, especially before the COVID-19 pandemic. The Liangping people attribute this phenomenon to their organic cultivation techniques and their holistic understanding of fruit material culture. For them, cultivation is a labor-intensive and aesthetic practice of building the environment for economic purposes and a horticultural craft. Indigene attaches great importance to the sustainable development of their community, the growing state of the fruit trees and the human-nature environment, without deliberately excluding the animals, plants and weeds entwined with the fruit trees. In their view, these inappropriate interference and intervention endow the fruits with their natural flavor, color, and taste. For researchers, however, cultivators' perception of the cultural environment is undoubtedly a backward concept and an inefficient production method, which can be reflected by the fact that the human-computer interaction design in the agricultural field only monitors the natural environment for plant growth and hence deprived of capturing and analyzing other animals and plants inhabiting in the same space and cultural background as the detection objects. Nonetheless, it must also collect the data to detect objects' behavior.

In the process of field studies, we found that indigene's perception of the multi-species power in the plantation did not fit with our theoretical assumption that animals and plants were "inferior creatures". Farmers in Liangping point out that the appearance of animals and plants will temporarily interrupt, disturb and reorganize the monoculture culture and the rhythm and pulsation of work on the plantation. Still, the contact and exchange of animals and plants in space and material ensure that the plantation is always in a state of change so that the pomelo can fully cooperate with the forces of all things and grow naturally.

According to the farmers in Liangping, animals and plants possess souls and can coexist harmoniously. Within their beliefs, the snails, birds, ants, and bees in the plantation are considered "allies" of the pomelo. When fruit trees require pollination, "ally" bees are called upon for assistance. Similarly, when pest attacks occur, "ally" birds are called upon to clean up and care for the tree's offspring (see Fig. 3). The annual harvest and collection eliminate existing diseases and prevent new ones from breaking out. For the Liangping people, fruit trees are production tools and companions.

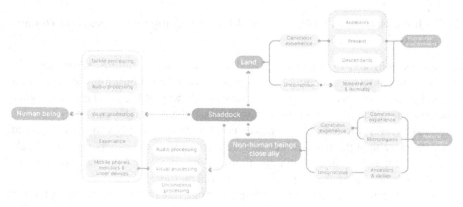

Fig. 3. The skill of fruit cultivation among the Liangping people. In the eyes of these people, the cultural environment, the natural environment, and the relationship between people and the land are all different actors. They believe that these different actors play important roles in fruits' growth and flavor formation process. The collaborative efforts of multiple species precisely shape the unique flavor of fruits.

The Liangping people's farming method emphasizes the interaction and cooperation between plants and their agency on the surface. Still, it goes beyond that to signify a "kinship bond" between the people and the land, as well as between humans and other non-human species in the past, present, and future. Culture and practical rationality are crucial components of plantation economics for the Nuosu minority people. As a result, they have begun to seek technical assistance for caring for their fruit trees, such as using automatic drip irrigation products to provide water to plants and pH test paper to measure soil acidity. Although the primary purposes of remote video monitoring systems in plantations seem to prevent theft and monitor crop growth changes, they have, to some extent, represented the Liangping people's desire to highlight the potential value and demand for showcasing plant intelligence and "primitive" planting techniques through cutting-edge technology or digital services.

5 Conclusions and Prospects

The analysis results of human-computer interaction design literature and case study showed that in addition to improving the robot's speech, emotion and interaction design, some ideas should be considered in the human-computer interaction design category. For example, the sustainable "multi-species" power entangled with human beings and the multi-cultural and natural knowledge long held by the target population. The reproduction and integrated discussion of the two field cases can provide three specific directions for the human-computer interaction design in the future: First, multi-species intelligent design, which could expand the interaction design around the species, and further reveals the existence of harmonious coexistence among all living things rather than being enemies and harms to each other. Second, interactive design of users' emotional motivation, value orientation and multi-cultural needs. In previous interaction designs, local knowledge, culture, and human environment were often excluded. However, field research found that place contains "worldwide elements" and "universal value," which is inherently consistent with current users' design requirements for multimode human-computer interaction. Third, the human-computer interaction design of intangible cultural heritage. With the help of intelligent recognition technology and 3D imaging technology, the auditory, tactile, and visual scenes of "intangible cultural heritage" can be re-displayed to cultivate brilliant cultural translation of intangible cultural heritage and improve the interactive communication of intangible cultural heritage and the multimodal experience of users.

In our future work, we plan to conduct human-machine interaction experiments based on the conclusions drawn from this study at the two research sites. We will use computer devices, visual technology, and sensors to capture the interaction and game between the "multi-species" forces, including things that users cannot perceive through sensory perception or visual observation. This includes the sound of the match between fire, light, wind, wood, and earth during the pottery-making process and the plants in the plantation calling on "allies" to care for insects. To broaden the scope of multimodal human-machine interface design, people explore the world of microorganisms, feel and observe changes in soil moisture, and embrace the emotions of cultivation through their senses. We aim to develop a non-heritage system service platform and expand the research and application of human-machine interaction technology in both material and non-material fields, allowing more users to obtain more excellent social benefits.

We look forward to collaborating with computer science-related teams to explore the boundaries and commonalities between science, technology, and humanities and increase the possibility of interdisciplinary collaboration.

References

1. Sontag, S.: Against Interpretation. Vintage, London, p. 2 (1994)
2. Lévi-Strauss, C.: Wild Thought. Translated by Jeffrey Mehlman and John Leavitt. University of Chicago Press, Chicago, p. 26 (2021)
3. Malinowski, B.: Argonauts of the Western Pacific, pp. 96–97. Routledge, London (1978)
4. Lallemand, C., Gronier, G.: Enhancing user experience during waiting time in HCI: contributions of cognitive psychology. In: Proceedings of the Designing Interactive Systems Conference, pp.751–760 (2012)
5. Raghavan, B., Pargman, D.: Means and ends in human-computer interaction: sustainability through disintermediation. In: Proceedings of the 2017 CHI Conference on Human Factors in Computing Systems, pp.786–796 (2017)
6. Rosén, A.P., Normark, M., Wiberg, M.: Noticing the environment–a design ethnography of urban farming. In: Nordic Human-Computer Interaction Conference, pp.1–13 (2022)
7. Yuan, Y., Li, S., et al.: Application of LabVIEW to remote monitoring system for orchard environment. Trans. CSAE 23(6), 186–188 (2007)
8. Pradeep, F., Boneyfus, N., Theres, S., Gokul, S., Aurelia, S.: Human-computer interaction technique for irrigation and sun tracking solar panel model. In: Paiva, S., Paul, S. (eds.) Convergence of ICT and Smart Devices for Emerging Applications. EICC, pp. 99–118. Springer, Cham (2020). https://doi.org/10.1007/978-3-030-41368-2_5
9. Zhang, P.: Application of Virtual Reality (VR) technology in modern agriculture—take farming cultural experience as an example. Mod. Vocat. Educ. 24, 188–189 (2020)
10. Kortbek, K.J., Grønbæk, K.: Communicating art through interactive technology: new approaches for interaction design in art museums. In: Proceedings of the 5th Nordic Conference on Human-Computer Interaction: Building Bridges, pp. 229–238 (2008)
11. Udsen, L.E., Jørgensen, A.H.: The aesthetic turn: unravelling recent aesthetic approaches to human-computer interaction. Digital Creativity 16(4), 205–216 (2005)
12. Sebe, N., Lew, M.S., Huang, T.S.: The state-of-the-art in human-computer interaction. In: Sebe, N., Lew, M., Huang, T.S. (eds.) CVHCI 2004. LNCS, vol. 3058, pp. 1–6. Springer, Heidelberg (2004). https://doi.org/10.1007/978-3-540-24837-8_1
13. Fischer, G.: User modeling in human-computer interaction. User Model. User-Adap. Inter. 11(1–2), 65–86 (2001)
14. Iwahashi, N.: Language acquisition through a human-robot interface by combining speech, visual, and behavioral information. Inf. Sci. 156(1–2), 109–121 (2003)
15. Wang, S., Zhang, Y., Zhu, B.: On human-computer interaction design of agricultural machine products for elderly users. J. Hunan Univ. Sci. Technol. (Nat. Sci. Ed.) 37(4), 57–65 (2022)
16. Williams, R., Park, H.W., Breazeal, C.: A is for artificial intelligence: the impact of artificial intelligence activities on young children's perceptions of robots. In: Proceedings of the 2019 CHI Conference on Human Factors in Computing Systems, pp.1–11 (2019)
17. Zhong, X., Cao, M., Han, T.: Research on application model of unconsciousness in user interface. In: Ahram, T., Falcão, C. (eds.) AHFE 2019. AISC, vol. 972, pp. 324–332. Springer, Cham (2020). https://doi.org/10.1007/978-3-030-19135-1_32
18. Zhong, X., Sun, T.: On promoting users' unconscious behavior in the process of human-computer interaction. Art Des. (Theor.) 2(1), 90–92 (2023)
19. Moin, A., Aadil, F., Ali, Z., et al.: Emotion recognition framework using multiple modalities for an effective human–computer interaction. J. Supercomputing, 1–30 (2023)
20. Oviatt, S.: Mutual disambiguation of recognition errors in a multimodel architecture. In: Proceedings of the SIGCHI Conference on Human Factors in Computing Systems, pp. 576–583 (1999)

21. Lin, R., Lin, P.-H., Shiao, W.-S., Lin, S.-H.: Cultural aspect of interaction design beyond human-computer interaction. In: Aykin, N. (ed.) IDGD 2009. LNCS, vol. 5623, pp. 49–58. Springer, Heidelberg (2009). https://doi.org/10.1007/978-3-642-02767-3_6
22. Li, W.: Application of virtual reality technology in the inheritance of cultural heritage. J. Phys. Conf. Ser. **1087**(6), 1–6 (2018)
23. Li, T., Chen, Q.: Transmission path of intangible cultural heritage under digital technology. In: Abawajy, J.H., Choo, K.-K., Islam, R., Xu, Z., Atiquzzaman, M. (eds.) ATCI 2019. AISC, vol. 1017, pp. 366–371. Springer, Cham (2020). https://doi.org/10.1007/978-3-030-25128-4_47
24. Laurel, B.: Interface as mimesis. In: Norman, D., Draper, S. (eds.) User Centered System design: New Perspectives on Human-Computer Interaction, pp. 67–86. Lawrence Erlbaum Associates, New Jersey (1986)
25. Giglitto, D., Lazem, S., Preston, A.: In the eye of the student: an intangible cultural heritage experience, with a human-computer interaction twist. In: Proceedings of the 2018 CHI Conference on Human Factors in Computing Systems, pp. 1–12 (2018)
26. Latour, B.: Network theory—networks, societies, spheres: reflections of an actor-network theorist. Int. J. Commun. **5**(1), 796–810 (2011)

Designing for Death: Emerging Technologies for the Process of Dying and the Memorialization of Life

Asad Khan[1,2], Sunzhe Yang[1,2], and Ian Gonsher[1,2]([⊠])

[1] School of Engineering, Brown University, Providence, RI 02912, USA
Ian_Gonsher@brown.edu
[2] Rhode Island School of Design, Providence, RI 02903, USA

Abstract. Death is an inevitable part of life. But the manner in which we mourn death and memorialize life, both in terms of the promise of our own death, and the inevitable death of others, offers designers and artists an opportunity to creatively reimagine the ways emerging technologies might open up new possibilities for understanding and coping with this essential part of life. Our design research begins with a historical critique of various religious and philosophical traditions related to death and dying. This foundation frames our inquiry, as we apply design research methods to better understand how experts working in hospice and the cemetery industry prepare experiences for death and mourning. Drawing on these insights we present a prototype that demonstrates new modalities for memorializing those who have passed through auditory media eventually proposing future work based on these initial prototypes utilizing a mixed reality experience.

Keywords: Death · Mixed Reality · Virtual reality · VR memorials · Experience design · Interaction Design · History · Memorials

1 Introduction

Despite being a universal experience, there is a remarkable dearth of technologies that address the ways we memorialize death. This may be due in part to the sensitive and often personal nature of death, as well as cultural taboos and stigmas surrounding the topic. It may be due to the inertia of cultural and religious traditions about death. But the proliferation of technologies in which we document our lives, from social media to the high-quality cameras we all now carry with us, offer us new opportunities to consider the ways in which we remember.

Death has a number of significant aspects. It marks the end of a person's physical existence and the end of one's time on earth. It is often accompanied by grief and loss, as those left behind must cope with the absence of the deceased. Death can also have a spiritual or religious significance, depending on an individual's belief system. For example, in many religions, death is seen as a transition to an afterlife or a spiritual realm. In other belief systems, death is simply the end of an individual's consciousness and there is no afterlife. Some societies may have traditional rituals or ceremonies to

C. Stephanidis et al. (Eds.): HCII 2023, CCIS 1832, pp. 78–92, 2023.
https://doi.org/10.1007/978-3-031-35989-7_10

mark the passing of a loved one, while others may have more modern approaches. In many societies, the body of the deceased is typically cremated or buried, and a funeral or memorial service is held to honor the person's life. Despite its finality and the sadness it can bring, death is also a reminder of the preciousness and fragility of life. It can inspire people to live their lives to the fullest and make the most of their time on earth.

Our prototype emerged from these concerns. We asked how we might apply emerging technologies in mixed reality towards a reimagining of the mourning experience. We asked: How might we remember? How might others remember us? By asking these questions we arrived at a design that can be installed at the grave noninvasively, yet in perpetuity. We asked how we might overlay memories onto one's lived experience, producing a mixed reality between life and death.

2 Brief History of Memorializing Death

During the Middle Ages, death and funerary practices were more openly acknowledged and integrated into daily life [1]. Many children didn't survive it to adulthood. Disease and war could bring death at any moment, and without warning. Cemeteries were often located in the center of towns near churches, and were not considered separate or hidden spaces. They were also sometimes used for public gatherings and markets. This contrasts modern sensibilities about death, where representations of death are often seen as taboo, and cemeteries are typically hidden outside of urban areas where people live.

The Black Death, which eradicated almost 60% of the population in Europe in the mid-14th century, had a profound impact on medieval society [2]. This event, along with the vicissitudes of medieval life, brought to immediate consciousness the fragility of life, and informed people's attitudes about death and funerary practices.

"The Triumph of Death" by Pieter Bruegel the Elder (Fig. 1) is a powerful illustration of how death was understood by the medieval mind. It was painted at a time when the understanding of death was transitioning from a medieval paradigm; when death was associated with pernicious demons, to an early modern conception of death taking root with the emergence of science in the 16th and 17th centuries. Bruegel's painting features the indiscriminate nature of death and the acceptance of its inevitability. Death, as it is depicted by Bruegel, represents an uncontrollable force. This will contrast with representations in the 17th-19th century that depict death, and nature more generally, as a controllable and manageable force.

Art is a potent technology for memorializing and mourning. Representation is memory made manifest. The art that emerged in the 17th–19th century expressed a tension between the medieval conception of death and the changing attitudes of the Scientific Revolution and Enlightenment. This can be seen in the popularization of the Memento Mori during the 17th century in Western Europe (Fig. 2), which drew on older traditions. It reminded us that despite the material wealth and improvement of living standards occurring in Western Europe at the time, death was still inevitable, which the wonders of living cannot ultimately protect us from. It was a reminder to live a meaningful life. As Socrates says in Plato's Phaedo, "The one aim of those who practice philosophy in the proper manner is to practice for dying and death" [3].

Against the medieval notions of death, with its personifications of demons and monsters, shrouded in fear and uncertainty, the Enlightenment established new perspectives

Fig. 1. 'The Triumph of Death' (1562). Pieter Bruegel the Elder. Painting. Image: Museo del Prado, Madrid.

Fig. 2. 'Vanitas' (1646). Philippe de Champaigne. Pictures. Image: Musée de Tessé.

from which to understand death. This scientific approach was characterized by the application of reason and a desire to better understand the processes that produced death. Rather than an inchoate miasma, or the machinations of demons that bring death, it was possible to see death in the context of germ theory and other emerging modern conceptions of disease. Death could be understood as a function of the body, which was objectified and studied. This shift in understanding, like other natural processes, provided the hope that death could be controlled, at least to some degree.

The idea that science can conquer, or at least control death through rational understanding can be seen in "The Anatomy Lesson of Dr. Deijman" by Rembrandt (Fig. 3).

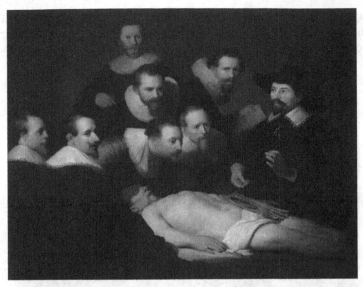

Fig. 3. 'The Anatomy Lesson of Dr. Nicolaes Tulp' (1632). Rembrandt. Painting. Image: Mauritshuis, The Hague.

This 17th century painting shows a group of anatomists and students examining a cadaver in order to understand human anatomy and bodily functions. It reflects the scientific approach to death and the body in the emerging Enlightenment, highlighting the quest for knowledge and reason as a way to overcome the fear of death. Here we find death presented in a very straight forward manner, as a function of the body, as a problem to be solved, or a machine to be fixed, and not as a demon to be cast out or a devil to be exorcised.

In the 18th century this trend continues, as can be seen in the painting "An Experiment on a Bird in the Air Pump" (Fig. 4), which is a depiction of a scientific experiment in which a bird is placed in a glass bottle and air is pumped out. Here the scientist is represented as the agent of death, a role which allows him to understand its mechanisms of dying, as the girls look on with discomfort. The painting depicts people of the period grappling with the horror and hope of such an approach. The painting dramatically depicts the struggle between scientific progress, characterized by an impulse to control the processes of life, and an understanding and acceptance of the inevitability of our mortality.

In contemporary society, there is a strong emphasis on materialism, which often emphasizes the scientific processes of life. This is especially apparent when contrasting the miracles of modern medicine against the concerns of a spiritual life, and by extension, of a spiritual death. The trends of the Enlightenment might have given our species remarkable tools for extending the human lifespan and enhancing the quality of that life, but it may also have inhibited our ability to fully give meaning to that life, and the role death plays in that process [4]. People in modern society may be more anxious about their mortality than they once were, but also less inclined to think about or discuss death. As a result, there may be less urgency to remember, to memorialize, and to mourn in healthy ways that see death and life as a natural part of the same processes that produce life. It is in this historical moment that we might ask how emerging technologies, such as mixed reality, might offer new paradigms for understanding our mortality more fully, and give deeper meaning to our lives, if not our deaths.

Fig. 4. 'An Experiment on a Bird in the Air Pump' (1768). Joseph Wright of Derby. Painting. Image: National Gallery, London.

3 Precedent Work

From the time of the pyramids up until the emergence of the modern $22 billion-dollar funeral industry, attitudes about death and mourning change as technology changes [5]. The ways in which we mourn and memorialize the dead are constrained both by precedents of ritual and custom, as well as by what technology makes possible. Digital death has received a lot of attention in recent years [6–9]. The idea of preserving a person's digital legacy after they have died is a particularly appealing one for many people. Even big tech companies are offering products that preserve users' digital legacies, including social media accounts, online profiles and virtual assets [6, 8]. For example, the "Digital Legacy" program by Apple allows individuals to designate up to five trusted contacts as their "Legacy Contacts". These contacts will have the ability to inherit the deceased person's Apple ID and all its associated data, including passwords, photos, files, text messages, etc. [10] It acts as a way to allow you to keep your digital afterlife if you wish.

There are now a variety of services and tools available that can help people manage their digital assets and ensure that they are properly transferred to designated heirs or deleted after death [8, 9, 11, 12]. Other technologies that are being developed in the realm of death include virtual reality funerals, which allow people to attend a funeral remotely, and biodegradable or compostable burial options, which aim to minimize the environmental impact of traditional burial practices [13, 14]. You can see these new approaches to death in contemporary speculative fiction, too. For example, the Black Mirror episode San Junipero, features a kind of virtual heaven, where a digital copy of the deceased is uploaded to a kind of computer-generated Elysian field [15].

Through such methods and stories, we have imagined new ways of understanding the metaphysics of death. We are always speculating how we might die and be remembered in the future. We remember the past to look for insights about the anxieties of not just death itself, but of being forgotten, which is a second death.

To address some of these issue that Hospice industry has played a very significant role in providing support to people so that they can live a comfortable and dignified experience at their end of lives [14, 16–20]. They also play a crucial role in preparing experiences for death and mourning for their loved ones. Experts use a variety of approaches to improve the quality of life for those who are dying and for those who are left behind [16, 21]. In this way, even though modern technology may not be able to fully understand death, there are still individuals and organizations dedicated to providing support and comfort to those affected by loss. We examined some of the experiences of these industries in an attempt to find out why they are able to make those individuals at the end of life and the loved ones mourning them as comfortable and dignified as possible.

In the hospice setting, the focus is on providing comfort and symptom management for individuals who are nearing the end of their lives, rather than trying to cure their illness. Hospice care teams, which typically include doctors, nurses, social workers, and chaplains, work together to provide physical, emotional, and spiritual support for the patient and their family. Whereas the cemetery industry plays a role in only supporting families during the mourning process [22]. Many cemeteries offer services such as pre-planning, burial or cremation options, and memorialization options [23, 24]. They also may offer emotional support through grief support resources and counseling services.

A great example in popular culture is the documentary film "End Game" by Rob Epstein and Jeffrey Friedman, in which Friedman demonstrates how human knowledge and advances can be used to manage or mitigate death and provide comfort and support to those facing the end of life [25]. It follows the work of a group of hospice specialists who provide end-of-life care to terminally ill patients. It features interviews with doctors, nurses, social workers and patients' families, the film explores the difficult decisions faced by patients, their families and the medical team as they deal with the emotional and ethical issues surrounding death and dying. It offers an intimate look at the experience of death while also exploring the ethical and philosophical issues that arise in the context of hospice care [26]. Overall, hospice care embodies the Enlightenment ideal of valuing human dignity and promoting human well-being, even in the face of death. It is also worth noting that it is one of the biggest industries in the overall death care services in the US in terms of total revenue. According to the National Hospice and Palliative Care Organization (NHPCO), in 2020, the hospice care industry in the United States generated approximately $32.1 billion in revenue [20]. In contrast, the death care industry generated approximately $21.1 billion in revenue, according to the National Funeral Directors Association. While the two industries are related in that they both deal with end-of-life care, they serve different purposes and operate under different regulations [27].

This will be even more accentuated since, by 2060, an estimated 48 million people (47% of all deaths globally) will die from serious health-related suffering, which represents an 87% increase from 26 million people in 2016 [28]. With the highest proportional increase in serious-related suffering will be dementia [28], which is the largest population group receiving hospice care in the United States [20].

4 Emerging Technologies for Death

The methods by which we commemorate the existence of deceased individuals comprise the framework through which we ascribe significance to life, particularly to our own, and therefore, remembrance or memories constitute a crucial component of the grieving process. Since time immemorial, from the humblest grave markers to the conspicuous pyramids and mausoleums of ancient kings and queens, memory has always been one of the most important strategies humankind has had for transcending the catastrophe of death. In the names and monuments of the past, the memory of the dead produces a living history. And with the advent of modern technology, we now live in an age of memory. Our lives are perpetually documented by the digital devices we use [6, 8]. They do not forget. This offers new opportunities to consider how we can ritualize and memorialize death.

In recent years, new forms of memorial practices have emerged that are less bound to institutions such as the church, and more meaningfully connected with individuals and communities [29]. Alternative commemorative practices like roadside memorials and woodland burials have blurred the boundaries between tradition and modernity, religion and secularity, the old and the new, to create a new type of memorials that connect meaningfully to the contemporary lived experiences of individuals and communities [30]. Even at grander scales, symbols of national identity and cultural significance have connected the idea of memory and pride to death through mausoleums [31] and are using it as a means of bringing people together, for example Lenin's Mausoleum in Moscow.

But the death care industry is now becoming a much more complex and evolving field, with a variety of trends and developments taking place. As people are living longer, there is a growing interest in end-of-life planning. This includes pre-planning funerals, making advanced healthcare directives, and other preparations that can help make the end-of-life experience more comfortable and less stressful for both the individual and their loved ones. Personalization is becoming more important for people and they are looking for ways to create unique and meaningful memorials. Virtual reality, telemedicine, smart funeral homes, cryptocurrency, blockchain, artificial intelligence, and digital afterlife services are some of the new technologies that are being used. An interesting example is Hereafter.ai [13] which is a virtual memorial application that allows users to preserve their memories and share life stories with their loved ones through an AI-powered chat interface. This type of application trains language models to generate virtual representations of the user based on the information they provide, allowing their loved ones to talk to a virtual version of them even after they have passed away.

5 People Die Twice

While examining philosophical and artistic perspectives on the topic of mortality, we observed that many individuals utilize unassuming yet consequential items as a vehicle for creative expression. These ubiquitous objects, frequently disregarded in everyday life, possess a wealth of personal recollections and possess the ability to evoke shared memories that resonate deeply within a collective consciousness. This led us to further investigate the role of collective memory.

The tangibility of memory, which simultaneously exists and eludes us within the confines of our minds, represents a key facet of remembrance, while the inherent instability of personal recollections, susceptible to alteration through social interactions, further underscores the complex nature of memory [32]. Its influence on the grieving/dying process can be summarized by this Chinese proverb – "People die twice, first when they die. Then when they are forgotten."

Hiroshi Ishii addressed the issue of the vast, emotional distance caused by bereavement and the inability to receive a response from a loved one. He uses illusionary communication channels to connect with those no longer with us. Using tangible objects like telephones, pianos and brushes, that were once touched by the hand of a loved one [33].

Based on his personal experience and knowledge gained through decades of working with grievers, Psychologist David Kessler introduced a critical sixth stage – meaning, to the classic five stages of grief [34]. Throughout his book he makes several references to the role of collective memory in being able to help those who have experienced loss. Maurice Halbwachs introduced the concept of collective memory to separate it from individual memory [35]. Just as individuals are able to have individual memories in a situation, a group of people is given shared memories. Collective memory is understood as the framework of such a group: it forms the basis of group-specific behavior among members because it allows individuals to present commonalities. Early researchers focused more on the social functions and roles of collective memory, but as research has progressed, more researchers have begun to focus on how collective memories are constructed. In comparison, the former emphasizes the carrying and transmission of collective memories, while the latter highlights the changes in collective memories over time, but both need to be considered, and only from both perspectives can we find a better solution to the problem of finding collective memories shaped by people in each country or culture. Therefore, finding the right collective memories and evoking people's emotions through them is an important aspect of our study. Employing the concept of collective memory, we aim to aid individuals in navigating the various stages of bereavement, facilitating a shift from mourning and distress towards meaning through the different stages of grief.

Interestingly, most people have the natural ability to heal from grief, loss and bereavement on their own [36], by seeking solace with family members, community members, and/or spiritual leaders/clergy. Unresolved and nonintegrated bereavement can lead to chronic depression in approximately 10–15% of individuals [37]. In addition, if individuals do not find relief, they may develop a clinically significant syndrome known as complicated grief, traumatic grief, or prolonged grief disorder which differs from major depressive disorder and involves a heightened risk of distress and dysfunction [38]. In contrast to psychotherapeutic and pharmaceutical therapies, non-traditional interventions and experiences have been repeatedly demonstrated to positively and dramatically impact grief in individuals after the death of a loved one [39].

6 Sensory Experience in Mixed Reality – Why a Voice Device?

As mentioned above, during our research we found that common and unobtrusive objects, often overlooked in daily life, represent a particularly apt medium for creative expression. These commonplace items, integral to our daily routines, harbor a wealth of personal memories and hold the potential to evoke powerful emotions and associations. We have categorized these unassuming items as "neglected memories" which, when activated, serve to elicit collective memories and evoke deep emotional responses. It is important to note that such memories do not represent current reality but rather exist in the realm of imagination within our minds. In our investigation of the profound impact of these memories, we have found that they are closely linked to the notion of boundaries. Indeed, the boundary between the virtual and the real bears a resemblance to that which separates life and death, as both coexist in close proximity, yet remain fundamentally separate and distinct.

Fig. 5. 'Ghost (Rally sports challenge)' (2002). Electronic Arts. Image: VIMEO JOHN WIKSTRØM.

An interesting example is from the video game "Rally Sports Challenge" (Fig. 5), in which players are able to compete against ghost racers which are basically recordings of previous high scorer's laps. The story is of a young boy who comes into possession of his late father's gaming console and discovers his father's high score in the game. The boy spends several days attempting to surpass his father's ghost, ultimately succeeding in doing so. However, rather than breaking his father's record, the boy opts to wait at the finish line, thus preserving his father's memory and perpetuating their connection in a new, imaginative form.

A further example can be found in W. Dewi Rees's 1971 study, which examined the experiences of 293 widows and widowers residing in a specific region of mid-Wales

[40]. The study's objective was to investigate the incidence of auditory hallucinations among the bereaved population, and the findings revealed that approximately 13.3% of participants reported having heard the voice of their deceased spouse subsequent to their passing. This research provides a compelling illustration of the capacity of memory to establish and maintain connections between deceased individuals and those who loved them, specifically through the medium of voice.

7 Prototyping for Memory and Mourning

Consider the following scenario: You arrive at the cemetery. Maybe you pick up a stone. Maybe you brought flowers. You walk towards the grave to make your visit. And just as you approach the headstone, you hear their disembodied voice, as if they were there. Perhaps they are talking about their childhood. Perhaps they are describing the love of their life. You hear their voice, and perhaps you feel their presence.

Fig. 6. 'Prototype' (2023). Photograph. Image: Sunzhe Yang.

The device itself has a long stake that anchors it in front of the headstone (Fig. 6). A solar panel, about 5 by 7 inches, protrudes just above the grassy surface. It faces the sun in perpetuity (Fig. 7). Below it: a battery, an Arduino, a speaker, and a distance sensor, all enclosed in a waterproof case (Fig. 8). As the visitor approaches, the distance sensor triggers a sound file that contains the voice of the deceased, and they encounter the technology of ghosts.

Hearing the voice of a deceased loved one can bring comfort and closure to those grieving. This content can be directly recorded by the individual in the last stages of life, or it can be scraped from social media and other documentation that the deceased amassed while alive. The experience can also be disquieting, but it is in these moments

Fig. 7. 'Prototype' (2023). Photograph. Image: Sunzhe Yang.

that we come to discover the power of a memory most fully. It is in these moments, with the voice of the departed, that we most fully appreciate what is loss and the precocious value of time. Recorded speech of someone no longer living can serve as a reminder of their enduring presence, and help mourners process their feelings in a more concrete manner. Our experience of the deceased, and the emotional response that evokes, keeps the dead alive.

We considered several questions as we applied mixed reality to the cemetery environment.

1. Does the prototype provide comfort? How might mixed reality invoke a recognition of absence through the presence in the deceased voice? How might this awareness give deeper meaning to the attendant feelings of loss?
2. Does the prototype help the mourner to remember? To remember implies that there is also the risk of forgetting. How might mixed reality help to memorialize the dead?
3. Does the prototype occasion reflection on one's own life? How might mixed reality blend the experiences of the virtual and the physical, of death and life, and in the contrast, give deeper meaning to both?

Initial reactions elicited a range of responses, from unsettling to contemplative. Some people encountered these mixed reality ghosts, such as they are, with discomfort, while others welcomed the opportunity to more fully immerse oneself in the memories of loved ones. And while a more formal evaluation of such a device is warranted, these initial reactions indicate that our anxieties about death are complex, both in terms of our own mortality and the mortality of those we love.

Fig. 8. 'Components'. Photograph. Image: Asad Khan.

8 Discussion

The memories we collect throughout our lives constitute a tapestry of experiences and interactions that shape our identities. While we have agency in recalling our own personal histories, our posthumous remembrance is entirely contingent upon others' recollections. In this vein, the question of how we may both remember and be remembered is an age-old inquiry. Hearing the voice of a deceased loved one can be a powerful experience in how it triggers the memory of that person. In the context of the cemetery, the experience further blurs the distinction between the deceased and the living, between the virtual and the physical.

Inspired by the research and examples, we hope to build upon these initial prototypes, in order to create more immersive mixed reality experiences that evoke memory. This can be a powerful way to help people process their grief and emotions. To achieve this, we plan to create an immersive mourning space in a cemetery. By collecting information from public platforms such as social media, including photos, videos, and voices, we will use authorized user content to build personalized memory scenes. These memory scenes will be brought to life through a sensory experience designed to allow loved ones to communicate and mourn with the deceased in an immersive way, as if stepping into their memories.

Advances in technology, specifically the emergence of mixed reality, offer fresh perspectives on this inquiry. Mixed reality's capacity to intermingle the virtual and the physical realms enables the living and the dead to intersect, thus creating a novel paradigm of "ghosts" in the digital landscape. Through mixed reality, innovative modalities of mourning and memorialization may be forged and explored.

References

1. Korpiola, M., Lahtinen, A. (eds.): Cultures of Death and Dying in Medieval and Early Modern Europe. Helsinki Collegium for Advanced Studies, University of Helsinki
2. World Health Organization. Plague Fact sheet N°267 (2014). Archived from the original on 24 April 2015
3. Plato. Plato's Phaedo. Clarendon Press, Oxford (1911)
4. Roser, M., Ortiz-Ospina, E., Ritchie, H.: Life Expectancy (2013). https://ourworldindata.org/life-expectancy
5. Research and Markets. Death Care Services – 2023 U.S. Market Research Report with Updated Recession Forecasts. Research and Markets – Market Research Reports – Welcome, Research and Markets (2023). https://www.researchandmarkets.com/reports/5695995/death-care-services-2023-u-s-market-research
6. Edwards, L., Harbinja, E.: What happens to my Facebook profile when I die? Legal issues around transmission of digital assets on death. In: Maciel, C., Pereira, V.C. (eds.) Digital Legacy and Interaction: Post-Mortem Issues, pp. 115–144. Springer International Publishing, Cham (2013). https://doi.org/10.1007/978-3-319-01631-3_7
7. Thomas, L., Briggs. P.: An older adult perspective on digital legacy. In: Proceedings of the 8th Nordic Conference on Human-Computer Interaction: Fun, Fast, Foundational (NordiCHI 2014), pp. 237–246. Association for Computing Machinery, New York, NY, USA (2014). https://doi.org/10.1145/2639189.2639485
8. Gulotta, R., Odom, W., Forlizzi, J., Faste, H.: Digital artifacts as legacy: exploring the lifespan and value of digital data. In: Conference on Human Factors in Computing Systems – Proceedings, pp. 1813–1822 (2013). https://doi.org/10.1145/2470654.2466240
9. Gulotta, R., Kelliher, A., Forlizzi, J.: Digital Systems and the Experience of Legacy, pp. 663–674 (2017). https://doi.org/10.1145/3064663.3064731
10. Stern, J.: The IPhone Feature to Turn on Before You Die. The Wall Street Journal, Dow Jones & Company (2021). https://www.wsj.com/articles/ios-15-digital-legacy-iphone-11639488636
11. Pereira, F., Prates, R.: A Conceptual Framework to Design Users Digital Legacy Management Systems, pp. 1–10 (2017). https://doi.org/10.1145/3160504.3160508
12. Yamauchi, E., Maciel, C., Mendes, F., Ueda, G., Pereira, V.: Digital legacy management systems: theoretical, systemic and user's perspective. 41–53 (2021). https://doi.org/10.5220/0010449800410053
13. Hereafter AI – Interactive Memory App – Try Free. HereAfter AI – Interactive Memory App – Try Free, HereAfter AI (2022). https://www.hereafter.ai/
14. Hancock, S., Preston, N., Jones, H., et al.: Telehealth in palliative care is being described but not evaluated: a systematic review. BMC Palliat. Care 18, 114 (2019). https://doi.org/10.1186/s12904-019-0495-5
15. Johnson, D.K.: Death in Black Mirror. How Should We Deal with Our Mortality?, pp. 292–300. John Wiley & Sons, Ltd (2019)
16. Mahon, M.M.: Technology in hospice: is it a contradiction? Home Healthcare Nurse J. Home Care Hospice Prof. 24(8), 527–531 (2006)
17. Oechsle, K.: current advances in palliative & hospice care: problems and needs of relatives and family caregivers during palliative and hospice care-an overview of current literature. Med. Sci. (Basel) 7(3), 43 (2019). https://doi.org/10.3390/medsci7030043
18. Garcia, M., Cláudia, A., Domingues Silva, B., da Silva, O., Cristine, L., Mills, J.: Self-compassion in hospice and palliative care: a systematic integrative review. J. Hospice Palliative Nurs. 23(2), 145–154 (2021). https://doi.org/10.1097/NJH.0000000000000727

19. Boyden, J.Y., Feudtner, C., Deatrick, J.A., et al.: Developing a family-reported measure of experiences with home-based pediatric palliative and hospice care: a multi-method, multi-stakeholder approach. BMC Palliat. Care **20**, 17 (2021). https://doi.org/10.1186/s12904-020-00703-0

20. National Hospice and Palliative Care Organization. NHPCO Facts and Figures: Hospice Care in America (2021). https://www.nhpco.org/wp-content/uploads/2021/01/2020-NHPCO-Facts-Figures.pdf

21. Alvariza, A., Mjörnberg, M., Goliath, I.: Palliative care nurses' strategies when working in private homes—a photo-elicitation study. J. Clin. Nurs. **29**(1–2), 139–151 (2019). https://doi.org/10.1111/jocn.15072

22. Colombo, A.D., Vlach, E.: Why do we go to the cemetery? Religion, civicness, and the cult of the dead in twenty-first century Italy. Rev. Relig. Res. **63**(2), 217–243 (2021). https://doi.org/10.1007/s13644-021-00454-1

23. Grabalov, P., Nordh, H.: The future of urban cemeteries as public spaces: insights from Oslo and Copenhagen. Plan. Theory Pract. **23**(1), 81–98 (2022). https://doi.org/10.1080/14649357.2021.1993973

24. Deering, A.: Over Their Dead Bodies: A Study of Leisure and Spatiality in Cemeteries, Doctoral Dissertation. University of Brighton (2012)

25. Epstein, R., Friedman, J.: End Game. Telling Pictures Production Company, Documentary (2006)

26. Hasson, F., Nicholson, E., Muldrew, D., et al.: International palliative care research priorities: a systematic review. BMC Palliat. Care **19**, 16 (2020). https://doi.org/10.1186/s12904-020-0520-8

27. National Funeral Directors Association. The 2020 NFDA Cremation and Burial Report: Research, Statistics and Insights for Funeral Professionals (2021). https://www.nfda.org/news/in-the-news/nfda-news/id/4688/the-2020-nfda-cremation-and-burial-report-research-statistics-and-insights-for-funeral-professionals

28. Sleeman, K.E., et al.: The escalating global burden of serious health-related suffering: projections to 2060 by world regions, age groups, and health conditions. Lancet Global Health **7**(7) (2019). https://doi.org/10.1016/s2214-109x(19)30172-x

29. Wouters, C.: The quest for new rituals in dying and mourning: changes in the We-I balance. Body Soc. **8**(1), 1–27 (2002)

30. Gibbs, M.R., Mori, J., Arnold, M., Kohn, T.: Tombstones, uncanny monuments and epic quests: memorials in world of Warcraft. Game Stud. **12**(1) (2012)

31. Bogorov, V.: In the Temple of Sacred Motherland: Representations of National Identity in the Soviet and Russian WWII Memorials. http://www.dartmouth.edu/ɕrn/groups/geographiers_group_papers/Finalpapers/Bogorov02.pdf. Accessed 20 Sep 2008

32. Van Vree, F.: Absent memories. Cult. Anal. **12**, 1–12 (2013)

33. Ishii, H.: TeleAbsence. https://www.media.mit.edu/projects/Tangible-Media_Garden-CAMBRIDGE_Ars-Electronica-2021/overview/

34. Kessler, D.: Finding Meaning: The Sixth Stage of Grief. First Scribner Hardcover Edition. Scribner, New York, NY (2019)

35. Halbwachs, M., Coser, L.A.: On Collective Memory. University of Chicago Press, Chicago (1992). https://doi.org/10.7208/chicago/9780226774497.001.0001

36. Jordan, J., Neimeyer, R.: Does grief counseling work? Death Stud. **27**, 765–786 (2003). https://doi.org/10.1080/713842360

37. Hensley, P.L.: Treatment of bereavement-related depression and traumatic grief. J. Affect. Disord. **92**(1), 117–124 (2006). https://doi.org/10.1016/j.jad.2005.12.041

38. Prigerson, H.G., Horowitz, M.J., Jacobs, S.C., Parkes, C.M., Aslan, M., et al.: Prolonged grief disorder: psychometric validation of criteria proposed for DSM-V and ICD-11. PLoS Med. **6**(8), e1000121 (2009). https://doi.org/10.1371/journal.pmed.1000121

39. Beischel, J., Mosher, C., Boccuzzi, M.: The possible effects on bereavement of assisted after-death communication during readings with psychic mediums: a continuing bonds perspective. Omega (Westport) **70**(2), 169–194 (2014). https://doi.org/10.2190/OM.70.2.b
40. Dewi, R.W.: The hallucinations of widowhood. Br. Med. J. **4**(5778), 37–41 (1971). https://doi.org/10.1136/bmj.4.5778.37

Requirements for Designing a Collaborative Human-Robot Workstation for Composite Part Production

Johanna Lauwigi[1]([✉]) [iD], Samira Khodaei[1] [iD], Hannah Dammers[2] [iD],
Anas Abdelrazeq[1] [iD], and Ingrid Isenhardt[1] [iD]

[1] WZL-MQ/IMA of RWTH Aachen University, Dennewartstr. 27,
52068 Aachen, Germany
johanna.lauwigi@ima.rwth-aachen.de

[2] ITA of RWTH Aachen University, Otto-Blumenthal-Str. 1, 52074 Aachen, Germany
https://cybernetics-lab.de, https://www.ita.rwth-aachen.de

Abstract. Small and middle-sized companies in the composite part production struggle with a lack of skilled workers while they cannot meet the demands of the market. For these companies, a full automation of the process is usually not economically feasible due to high implementation costs and small batch sizes. One solution for this challenge can be the introduction of a collaborative robot to the process that supports the worker. To design a collaborative human-robot workstation, it is essential to define requirements that include the human as the user of the system. Therefore, we conducted a qualitative study based on a mixed method approach. With a focus group, expert interviews, and observational studies we derived a first set of chances and risks of a collaborative workstation in the composite part production and potential manufacturing steps the robot could take over. These results are the basis for the definition of the requirements for designing a collaborative workstation in the composite part production.

Keywords: composite part production · human-robot-collaboration · human-machine-collaboration · requirements analysis · mixed methods

1 Introduction

The composite industry is dominated by small and medium-sized enterprises (SMEs). They produce small series to a large extent and can react flexibly to changes in the market due to a high proportion of manual work. A survey from Composites World showed that about 60% of the companies use manual processes in composite part production [13]. Due to demographic change, experts retiring, and less experts following, companies struggle with hiring skilled workers to meet the demand of the market [3]. Thus, the fully manual approach is reaching it's limits while a full automation is not feasible for SMEs due to high investment costs and a loss of flexibility.

In order to address the previously mentioned constraints, we suggest a hybrid solution that involves a collaboration between a human and a collaborative robot (cobot). The setup will be implemented in form of a workstation focusing on the lay-up process in which a limp reinforcement textile is shaped into the 3D geometry of the final composite part. The research project RaCPro (Robot-assisted Composite Production) aims to analyse, design, implement and evaluate the interaction between human and cobot at a collaborative workstation. The success of such a workstation depends on the collaboration with the worker. Thus, it is essential to include the human in the design process to develop a system that supports the worker. Therefore, we analyzed the manual lay-up process including the human point of view to define the requirements for designing a collaborative workstation for composite part production. Therefore, we conducted a qualitative study using a mixed method approach. The paper, gives an overview about the previous work, including the composite part production and the analysis of the production, followed by the study design, the results, and a discussion.

2   Previous Work

A study by Dammers et al. investigated the chances and risks of a human-robot collaboration in the composite part production industry focusing on preforming. It showed that the introduction of a cobot to the process can bring advantages like an increased efficiency and elimination of specific tasks. However, the paper also points out that a collaboration does not work for all lot sizes and complexities and might have too high costs. [3] Another study presents five human-robot interaction modes for processing of reinforcement textiles, concentrating on big plies for aviation or boating goods [5]. Furthermore, a user study with collaboration types for the lay-up process showed that the cobot is considered as a technical assistant that does a good job in the lay-up process [4].

The described research gives an overview about the possibilities of a cobot in a lay-up workspace. However, it is missing concrete requirements for the design of such a workstation considering the human as the collaborator for the robot.

For the analysis, it is crucial to understand the manual composite production process. Composite materials are used to produce high-performance parts with low weight. The combination of a polymer matrix material (e.g., epoxy resin) with textile reinforcement (e.g., carbon or glass fibre) can achieve very good mechanical properties. Thus, the material is used in different applications including aviation, automotive, wind energy and sporting goods. [8] The process steps for manufacturing a composite part by preforming can be summarized in the following basic steps: cutting the textiles to near-net-shape, pick and place, joining the layers, and forming into the desired three-dimensional shape. Even the most experienced workers manually perform the process differently every time, as they respond to the textiles' behavior with their haptic and visual abilities. Currently, such an online control loop cannot be implemented with robots. [5,6]

3   Study Design

The requirements for designing the collaborative human-robot workstation can be derived from the answers to the following research questions:

1. What opportunities and risks must be considered in the development and design of a collaborative workstation for composite part production?
2. Which manufacturing steps in the lay-up process would provide relief for workers if they were done by a cobot?

To identify the first results for the previously mentioned questions, we conducted a study with a mixed method approach [9]. This approach consisted of a focus group with the management level [11,12], expert interviews with workers for the composite part production [2] (evaluated with qualitative content analysis [1]), and an observational study with thinking aloud method [7].

Table 1. Study Design

Method	Participants	Approach
Focus group	Management Level (n = 12) representing all stakeholders from automation, composite industry, and research	1) SWOT analysis 2) Persona creation 3) Discussion
Expert interviews	Workers (n = 3) from composite production	Deductive approach
Observational study	Workers (n = 3) from composite production	Openly and passively Thinking aloud method

To investigate the first research question, we evaluated the chances and risks in the development of a collaborative lay-up workstation in cooperation with the management level (Table 1). The participants were from SMEs and research institutions in Germany. Starting with a SWOT analysis (strengths, weaknesses, opportunities, and threats), the twelve participants envisioned the collaborative workstation. After a discussion, the participants created a persona that describes the person that will be working with the cobot at the collaborative lay-up station. With this approach, we got a closer view of how the management level imagines how the workers feel and act, as well as their estimation of the workers' pains and gains. In a final step, the results were presented and discussed.

The focus group results were used in a following comparison with the workers' point of view, concentrating on the evaluation of chances and risks in the lay-up process itself. Therefore, we conducted expert interviews with workers (n = 3) from three composite production companies. The expert interviews followed a deductive approach in which the categories were defined before the interview based on the literature and the results of the focus group (see Table 2) [10]. The interviews also gave an overview of the lay-up process and the corresponding tasks.

Table 2. Main-categories and sub-categories of first order for the deductive approach in the expert interviews (n = 3)

Main-categories	Sub-categories of first order
Expertise	Professional socialization
	Experience in professional field
	Experience in current job
	Assessment of own abilities
Tasks	General tasks
	Lay-up process
	Parts to be produced
	Time
Future perspective	Support by cobot
	Sustainability of the job

To evaluate the findings from the interviews and discover hidden knowledge, the interviews were followed by an observational study. The observation was conducted openly and passively. Thus, the workers could see the observers but the observers did not interfere with the working process. The workers were asked to think aloud during the process. The combination of the interviews and the observation allowed an approximation of mental models for the composite production processes in the three companies. These mental models helped to identify first hints about the kind of tasks the cobot could do to support the human (research question two).

All participants of the study took part voluntarily. It was made sure that the interviews and the observational studies were anonymized.

4   Results

4.1   Focus Group

In the focus group, it was possible to identify a first overview about chances and risks of a collaborative workstation for composite part production. While the SWOT-Analysis revealed mainly economic factors, the discussion about the Personas covered more social factors. Due to the influence of some economic and social factors on each other, the results are combined in the following.

The participants of the focus group saw potentials in the collaborative workstation. Especially the possibility to avoid health issues of the workers was pointed out, e.g., cuts from sharp tools or issues due to exposure to chemical substances. Additionally, they identified the possibility in a reduction of production time while keeping a high process reliability. This combination enables a more cost-efficient production and allows to follow market demands without pushing the pressure to the workers. All in all, the focus group could see relevant chances in introducing a cobot.

However, the participants also detected risks. They pointed out that some workers might not want to change their way of working by introducing a cobot. Also, they saw a risk in the programming of the cobot, as it might be too time-consuming to ease the working situation. In that case, the above-mentioned chances would not be met. In conclusion, the focus group saw advantages for workers and companies in the introduction of a cobot to composite production if it is easy to use and program, and the acceptance of the workers is considered.

4.2 Expert Interviews

The interviewed experts show common characteristics but also differences in all main categories according to the categories in Table 2. Common characteristics are that all three experts

- originally pursued a different career than composite part production.
- went through training on top of their original education.
- find satisfaction in their jobs through challenges and high variety in tasks.
- work by themselves or with coworkers dependent on the task.
- describe the relevance of experience, visual judgment, and feeling of the material.
- rather like to show the process than explain it.
- do not describe any stress or urgency in their jobs.
- assume that they can do their job until retirement.
- consider their jobs as safe.

The differences especially cover the future perspective of the job. Each expert named different aspects to improve the working environment and make the job fit for the future. The topics range from digitization and support systems up to automation of tasks like cutting. In regards to the support by a cobot, the experts expressed positive as well as skeptical opinions. One expert pointed out that the robot needs to be easy to program and make the work easier instead of harder. All in all, the experts have different ideas on how and where a robot can be helpful in their jobs in the future.

4.3 Observational Study

The observational study enabled us to validate the findings from the expert interviews and to define mental models for the lay-up process in the composite production.

All processes can roughly be divided into three main parts: 1) Preparation (of the workstation and the material), 2) Lay-up process, and 3) Post-processing (incl. quality management). In detail, the processes differed in all three cases so we derived one mental model per company. The differences are reasoned by different complexities of the geometry of the part and different batch sizes.

In all cases, the main part is the lay-up process, which takes most of the time as it is done layer-wise. In some cases, the workers switched between the

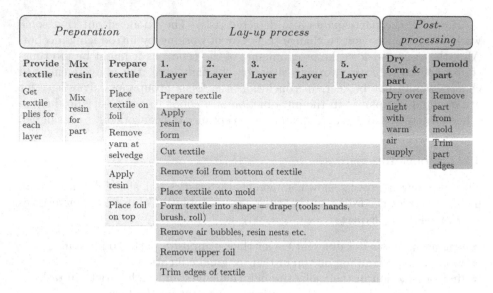

Fig. 1. Mental model for laying-up composites derived from one observation

preparation and the draping process because preparations had to be done for each layer. An example for such a process shows the mental model in Fig. 1.

While the lay-up process was very similar in all three companies, the preparation and the post-processing differed more. In one company, for example, the cutting of the textile was done automatically so that the workers only had to sort the material for the lay-up process. Despite the differences, the following steps could be observed in all cases: Cutting textile, Providing textile at work station, Placing material onto the mold, Removing foil from the textile, Bringing textile into shape (draping); Trimming edges, Curing part.

5   Requirements and Discussion

Based on the results of the study, we discovered the first answers to the research questions defined in Sect. 3. Chances and risks (research question one) can be drawn directly from the focus group. The results from the expert interviews and the observational study need to be further analyzed to identify which manufacturing steps could be taken over by a cobot (research question 2).

As all workers who participated in the study enjoy their work, it is important not to take away interesting, challenging, and various tasks. Hence, the cobot should rather take over tiring and repetitive tasks. Considering the safety issues of the management level, the cobot should not create further safety risks (e.g. by using sharp tools like knives). In combination with the common characteristics of the mental models, possible tasks for a cobot human-robot collaborative workstation could be:

- Providing textile at work station
- Placing material onto the mold
- Removing foil from the textile
- Forming textile into 3D shape (draping) for large, flat, and simple geometries

These results show first hints that the cobot could support in different areas of the composite production so that it can provide relief for the workers. However, the cobot should not take over more than one or two tasks so that the worker is still in control of the process. Also, the work still has a high variety while the worker has more capacity to focus on challenging tasks.

Based on the findings regarding chances and risks as well as the potential tasks for the cobot, we derived a first set of requirements for designing a collaborative workstation.

The cobot is required to have specific abilities to handle the previously described tasks:

- Mobility to cover rather big workspaces (cobot plus mobile platform)
- Autonomous movement of the cobot to move to the requested position
- Sensitivity to the environment so that the cobot does not disturb the worker
- Ability to handle the requested material with a suitable robotic end-effector (e.g. gripper, suction head, draping tool)
- Flexibility in the programming to adapt to different work situations

Additionally, the collaborative workstation should be included in the composite part production in a way that chances are used and risks are avoided. This brings additional requirements to the workstation.

One risk mentioned in the study was additional work and cost. To avoid this risk, the cobot needs to be programmed easily and quickly. In all cases, the estimated return on investment should be calculated and economic issues should be taken into account. This is especially challenging as profits through factors such as increased ergonomics or well-being are hard to calculate. In addition to the economic risks, the workers also need to learn how to use the cobot and like to use it. Thus, the workers need to be trained and introduced to the cobot's capabilities. Furthermore, an interface between human and robot could help to make the cobot and its movements understandable to the worker.

The results show that the presented mixed method approach is a suitable method to define requirements for designing a collaborative workstation. Due to the small number of participants in the expert interviews and the observational study, the outcome needs to be validated with further experts from the composite part production.

The requirements defined in the proposed method, can help to design a collaborative workstation for composite part production. When a collaborative workstation is developed, it can be evaluated and compared to the results from the presented study. Therefore, three parts of the workstation are being developed: a human-robot interface, the robotic end-effector and the mobile cobot including easy programming.

Acknowledgements. This publication is part of the project "RaCPro: Robot-assisted Composite Production" (IGF project number: 22611 N/1), funded by the Federal Ministry of Economics and Climate Protection according to a resolution of the German Parliament.

References

1. Boehm, A. (ed.): Texte verstehen: Konzepte, Methoden, Werkzeuge, Schriften zur Informationswissenschaft, vol. 14. Univ.-Verl. Konstanz, Konstanz (1994)
2. Bogner, A., Littig, B., Menz, W.: Interviews mit Experten. QS, Springer, Wiesbaden (2014). https://doi.org/10.1007/978-3-531-19416-5
3. Dammers, H., Lennartz, M., Gries, T., Greb, C.: Human-robot collaboration in composite preforming: chances and challenges (2021)
4. Dammers, H., Vervier, L., Mittelviefhaus, L., Brauner, P., Ziefle, M., Gries, T.: Usability of human-robot interaction within textile production: Insights into the acceptance of different collaboration types. In: Usability and User Experience. AHFE International, AHFE International (2022). https://doi.org/10.54941/ahfe1001710
5. Eitzinger, C., Frommel, C., Ghidoni, S., Villagrossi, E.: System concept for human-robot collaborative draping (2021)
6. Elkington, M., Bloom, D., Ward, C., Chatzimichali, A., Potter, K.: Hand layup: understanding the manual process. Adv. Manuf. Polymer Compos. Sci. **1**(3), 138–151 (2015). https://doi.org/10.1080/20550340.2015.1114801
7. Ericsson, K.A., Simon, H.: Protocol analysis: Verbal reports as data (1984)
8. Fleischer, J., Teti, R., Lanza, G., Mativenga, P., Möhring, H.C., Caggiano, A.: Composite materials parts manufacturing. CIRP Ann. **67**(2), 603–626 (2018). https://doi.org/10.1016/j.cirp.2018.05.005
9. Langley, A., Abdallah, C.: Templates and turns in qualitative studies of strategy and management. In: Bergh, D.D., Ketchen, D.J. (eds.) Building methodological bridges, Research Methodology in Strategy and Management, vol. 6, pp. 201–235. Emerald, Bingley (2011). https://doi.org/10.1108/S1479-8387(2011)0000006007
10. Mayring, P.: Qualitative inhaltsanalyse - abgrenzungen, spielarten, weiterentwicklungen: Forum qualitative sozialforschung/forum: Qualitative social research, vol. 20, no 3 (2019). Qualitative content analysis i (2019). https://doi.org/10.17169/FQS-20.3.3343
11. Schulz, M.: Quick and easy!? fokusgruppen in der angewandten sozialwissenschaft. In: Schulz, M., Mack, B., Renn, O. (eds.) Fokusgruppen in der empirischen Sozialwissenschaft, pp. 9–22. Springer VS, Wiesbaden (2012). https://doi.org/10.1007/978-3-531-19397-7_1
12. Schulz, M., Mack, B., Renn, O. (eds.): Fokusgruppen in der empirischen Sozialwissenschaft: Von der Konzeption bis zur Auswertung. Springer VS, Wiesbaden (2012). https://ebooks.ciando.com/book/index.cfm/bok_id/328734
13. Sloan, J.: Compositesworld 2018 operations report (2018). https://www.compositesworld.com/articles/compositesworld-2018-operations-report

Research on Emotional Design Strategies of Voice Interaction on Smartphones: A Case Study of College Students' Use of Smart Phones

Lin Li and Meiyu Zhou(✉)

East China University of Science and Technology, No. 130 Meilong Road, Xuhui District, Shanghai, China
zhoutc_2003@163.com

Abstract. Through studying the use of mobile phone voice interaction function in the daily life of college students, summarizing the current situation of its use and future improvement suggestions, the study finds that the current college student group does not use the voice interaction function that comes with the mobile phone very frequently at present, how to make the language interaction function better facilitate the life of college students and improve the emotional experience of voice interaction of the college student group will become the problem to be solved in this study; this study Based on the three-level theory of emotional design proposed by Donald A. Norma, the emotional design strategies of voice interaction for future smartphones are proposed to provide theoretical guidance for the innovation of intelligent voice product design; in the context of smartphones, the competitiveness and influence of smartphones can be enhanced by improving the voice interaction experience of smartphones.

Keywords: Voice interaction · Emotional design strategies · Smartphones · University student

1 Introduction

With the rapid development of technology, more and more intelligent voice interaction technology has been further improved and gradually put into the market, a large number of voice interaction products are active in people's vision. The most frequently used smart product in our daily life – mobile phone contains the function of voice interaction, intelligent voice interaction relies on algorithms and data, the rapid development of these technologies also promote the development of intelligent voice interaction, but it still has the problems of insufficient data, insufficient logical processing and insufficient emotional expression. In the context of the rapid development of smartphones and the commitment to enhance the competitiveness of the smartphone market, relevant companies should start from the needs of consumers and form a good brand effect; and in today's era of increasing attention to user experience, the above problems should be solved so as to enhance user experience more effectively in the future.

C. Stephanidis et al. (Eds.): HCII 2023, CCIS 1832, pp. 101–108, 2023.
https://doi.org/10.1007/978-3-031-35989-7_12

Studies have shown that human-computer interaction products pay more attention to the two aspects of "user-friendly" and "human-computer symbiosis", and the research of emotional design has injected new vitality into human-computer interaction product design [1]. So if the system wants to become more kind and warm, it should combine emotion with creativity [2]. At the same time, the expression of emotion in design has a lot to do with brand innovation, and highly innovative brands generally convey deeper emotions [3].

Therefore, future research will focus on strengthening the human-computer relationship and improving the user's interaction experience. Therefore, based on this, this study was conducted among the most frequent users of mobile phones – university students, and combined with the basic characteristics of university students, to study how to improve their emotional experience in terms of voice interaction when using mobile phones, which can also provide some new ideas for smartphone voice interaction development, and also help to improve brand innovation.

1.1 Overview of Voice Interaction

Voice interaction is the acquisition, recognition and feedback of language by a product, so that users can interact with the product more naturally and efficiently [4]. In some specific scenarios, simpler and more natural voice interaction will occur in the interaction between people and computers, voice interaction will slowly become mainstream in some scenarios where the accuracy requirements are not very high, and in some scenarios will better assist touch interaction to meet people's needs.

The advantages of voice interaction are that it is highly relevant to people's lives, fast and low threshold, and it has been used in various scenarios [5]; however, some studies show that the effectiveness of voice interaction is not maximized in consumers due to technical limitations and the solidification of user habits, and the intelligent voice industry is also facing questions and dilemmas such as "non-interactive rigid demand", "only a middleware for other smart products", and "voice information security hazards" [6]. The smart voice industry also faces questions and dilemmas such as "non-interactive rigidity", "only a middleware for other smart products", and "voice information security concerns" [6]. Most of the existing research on voice interaction in smartphones is focused on the technical aspect of "usability", focusing on the solution of different stages of voice interaction technologies, such as speech recognition and speech synthesis, etc., while little research has been conducted on "usability" indicators such as user experience satisfaction.

1.2 Overview of Voice Interaction

In his book "Emotional Design", Donald A. Norman introduced the term 'emotional design', which aims to attract the consumer's attention and lead to a positive emotional response, conscious or unconscious, in order to increase their purchasing behaviour. Research has found that modernist products focus more on functionality and neglect the emotional aspects of human needs, emotional product design is therefore proposed. It has also been suggested that emotional product design should focus on the human being at the core, always thinking from a human perspective rather than the traditional product as the main starting point [7].

In the book "Emotional Design", emotional design is divided into three levels: the instinctual level is an immediate feedback that people give to what is happening in the moment, such as the shape and design of a product, the tactile sensation it gives, etc. [8]. The behavioural level is the part that is controlled by the brain. The behavioural level is not conscious and is a subconscious response along with the instinctual level. The user's operational feelings when using voice interaction are what the behavioural level is concerned with. The reflective level is the part of the brain that thinks and focuses on the symbolic and social value of the product, shaping the user's self-image and maintaining his or her social status so that the user's emotional needs are met. This level focuses on the interaction with the user and the post-care, so that the machine truly understands the human being and allows a two-way communication between the human and the machine to improve people's productivity or soothe their emotions [9, 10].

As previous research has shown: only when designers deal with the correspondence between emotion and design features at the emotion injection stage can they accurately express emotion [11]. Based on the theory of emotional design, this study corresponds the design features of smartphone voice interaction with emotional vocabulary, explores the emotional experience from the perspective of design features, and enhances the emotional experience of user interaction.

To facilitate the study, a number of emotion words were selected after expert panel discussions. In this study, emotion words were used as direct expressions of feature emotions, which were assigned to different levels according to their primary meaning. The correspondence between speech interaction design features and emotions is shown in the Fig. 1.

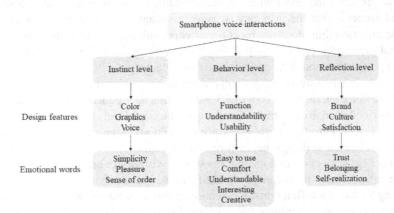

Fig. 1. The relationship between voice interaction design features and emotion

2 Experiment

The voice interaction of smartphones is mainly reflected in voice assistants, the research object is college students, according to the network data collection and collation found: China's "2022 National Depression Blue Book" shows: 50% of depression patients are school students, many parents only see their children's behavioural performance, but cannot see the emotional and spiritual factors behind, in the long run, their road to depression The road is "long and difficult"; and the increasing dependence of university students on smartphones is actually due to the lack of emotions behind it. In order to care more about the emotional needs and spiritual comfort of users, we first conducted a research on the current situation of university students using smartphones for voice interaction.

The survey was conducted using the self-designed "Mobile Phone Voice Assistant Questionnaire", which mainly included personal information research and information about the use and feedback of mobile phone voice assistants. Online questionnaires were distributed due to the epidemic, and the groups targeted were mainly undergraduate and postgraduate students, and 156 valid questionnaires were finally collected for this study.

3 Survey Results and Analysis

The survey found that nearly half of the population hardly uses the voice assistant; the voice assistant is still a service-oriented machine, so university users generally use the voice assistant to complete quick operations, but at the same time the data shows that more than a third of the population will chat with the voice assistant, which is an indication that their interaction needs with the voice assistant are increasing. Figure 2 shows the problems that exist when university students use voice assistants: firstly, the technical aspect is that the accuracy of voice assistants' recognition is low and their semantic understanding does not meet users' expectations; secondly, there is a lack of emotional interaction and it is hoped that voice assistants will be more humane, and future improvements should focus on these two aspects.

In this study, users are asked to select the emotional words represented by the current smartphone voice interaction. From Fig. 3, we find that the frequency of emotional words being described decreases from the first level to the third level, which also reflects that the emotion of the current smartphone voice interaction design stays at a low level, and the high-level emotion design needs further exploration. As shown in the word cloud diagram in Fig. 4, most users hope that the voice assistant can become more intelligent and humanized, wake it up quickly, identify its needs accurately, and provide more interesting feedback and functions. As mentioned above, according to the corresponding relationship between smartphone voice interaction features and emotional vocabulary, we can transfer the study of emotional experiences to their design features, and finally produce high-level emotional interaction experience.

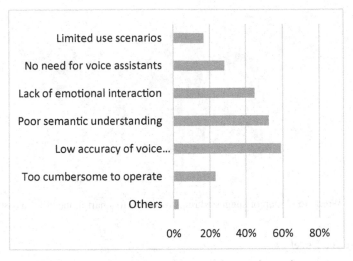

Fig. 2. The main problem with smartphone voice assistants

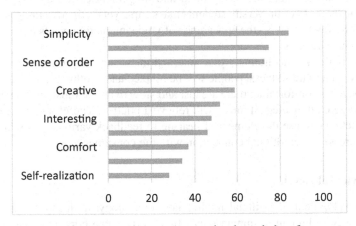

Fig. 3. Smartphone voice assistant emotional vocabulary frequency

4 Emotional Design Strategies for Voice Interaction in Smartphones

Today's university students have the following characteristics: they are under pressure in their studies and life, they are more receptive to new things and technologies, they have the most cutting-edge knowledge in life and consumption; they have a strong reliance on smart products and tend to prefer personalised and fun products, as distinctive interactions can appear more unique to them. This study then proposes strategies to improve the design of smartphone voice interaction based on the findings and the characteristics of university students.

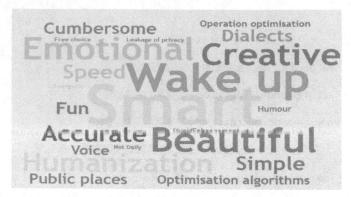

Fig. 4. Word cloud map of suggested improvements to smartphone voice assistants

4.1 Instinctive Level

Visual aesthetics are the most fundamental for users to interact with voice. Products that match the consumer's age, life background and judgement of beauty are what are in demand. The majority of university students like simple yet distinctive images, and their preferences follow trends. So the appearance of voice interaction needs to be constantly pushed into new designs.

Hearing is the key to human voice interaction, sound can control the change of people's joy, anger and sadness, people will be relaxed and soothing music, let the body and mind become comfortable; there are fast and slow dynamic music will make people become energetic; then elegant music will relieve anxiety... Therefore, in the design of voice interaction can use the element of hearing to feedback various information to the user and increase the emotional connection with the consumer.

4.2 Behavioural Levels

With the development of artificial intelligence technology, multimodal interaction is the closest way to human-to-human interaction, and human-computer interaction has become more natural and easy [12]. College students like novel and interesting products, and on the basis of ease of use, interesting voice interaction can allow users to find a little pleasure in hunting things even under heavy work pressure. Therefore, voice interaction products can combine interaction modes such as sound, smell, vision, and gestures with scenes to keep pace with the times, and will not make users feel that this is just a blunt exchange of information, but allow users to experience a more entertaining lifestyle.

4.3 Reflective Levels

For product design, it is not enough that the material functions of the product are perfect, but requires more consideration of people's emotional appeals and inner feelings when using or buying the product [13], thus the reflective level can create a brand culture and convey chic ideas to users, so that they will be reminded of their previous experiences and create memories during and after use.

For example, Chat GPT, a recently emerged artificial intelligence chatbot program, its greater value lies in having powerful natural language understanding and communication capabilities; future intelligent conversations can be based on speech recognition and natural language analysis technology, after recognising the voice content and user relationship and emotion, based on the content to carry out a comprehensive analysis of user status, emotion and other multi-dimensional information, so as to feedback information more in line with the state of human-human communication, which can also generate a high-level emotional experience.

Voice interaction products for university students need to accurately analyse emotions and detect emotions, so we can guide university students to reveal their true emotions through a gentle and seductive approach. We can also adjust the output performance of voice interaction according to the different emotional states of university students, for example, by expressing empathy and emotion through tone of voice, intonation and timbre, to build up a story between university students and the voice assistant and gain their trust.

5 Conclusion

Based on the background of smart phones, this study starts from the user group of college students, provides new ideas for smart phone voice interaction design from the perspective of emotion, and provides theoretical guidance for the innovation of intelligent voice product design, which aims to deepen the emotional communication between users and voice assistants and thus improve the user's voice interaction experience, and enhance the competitiveness of smart phone brands.

References

1. Jeon, M.: Chapter 1 – Emotions and Affect in Human Factors and Human-Computer Interaction: Taxonomy, Theories, Approaches, and Methods. In: Jeon, M. (ed.) Emotions and Affect in Human Factors and Human-Computer Interaction, pp. 3–26. Academic Press, San Diego (2017)
2. Zhang, C., Gu, Y.: Emotional interaction design of an artificial intelligence voice 648–652 (2022)
3. Demirbag Kaplan, M.: The relationship between perceived innovativeness and emotional product responses: a brand oriented approach. Innov. Mark. 5, 42–50 (2009)
4. Kostov, V., Fukuda, S.: Emotion in user interface, voice interaction system. In: SMC 2000 Conference Proceedings. 2000 IEEE International Conference on Systems, Man and Cybernetics. "Cybernetics Evolving to Systems, Humans, Organizations, and their Complex Interactions" (Cat. No. 00CH37166), pp. 798–803. IEEE, Nashville, TN, USA (2000)
5. Poushneh, A.: Humanizing voice assistant: the impact of voice assistant personality on consumers' attitudes and behaviors. J. Retail. Consum. Serv. 58, 102283 (2021)
6. Murad, C., Munteanu, C., Cowan, B.R., Clark, L.: Revolution or evolution? Speech interaction and HCI design guidelines. IEEE Pervasive Comput. 18, 33–45 (2019)
7. Ho, A.G., Siu, K.W.M.G.: Emotion design, emotional design, emotionalize design: a review on their relationships from a new perspective. Des. J. 15, 9–32 (2012)

8. Sun, W., Sun, P.: The research on emotional design. In: Pan, Y. (ed.) 9th International Conference on Computer-Aided Industrial Design & Conceptual Design, vols. 1 and 2: Multicultural Creation and Design – Caid & Cd 2008, p. 105. IEEE, New York (2008)

9. Zhang, S., Wang, H., Li, J., Bao, J., Zhu, Q.: Research on emotional design of electric power products in experience economy era. In: Ahram, T., Falcão, C. (eds.) Advances in Usability and User Experience, pp. 571–580. Springer, Cham (2020). https://doi.org/10.1007/978-3-030-19135-1_56

10. Wang, Y., Ge, Q.: The user's emotional elements research of mobile network products development guided by user experience. In: Rau, P.L.P. (ed.) Internationalization, Design and Global Development. LNCS, vol. 6775, pp. 332–340. Springer, Heidelberg (2011). https://doi.org/10.1007/978-3-642-21660-2_37

11. Zhao, T., Zhu, T.: Exploration of product design emotion based on three-level theory of emotional design. In: Ahram, T., Taiar, R., Colson, S., Choplin, A. (eds.) Human Interaction and Emerging Technologies, pp. 169–175. Springer, Cham (2020). https://doi.org/10.1007/978-3-030-25629-6_27

12. Esau, M., Krauß, V., Lawo, D., Stevens, G.: Losing its touch: understanding user perception of multimodal interaction and smart assistance. In: Designing Interactive Systems Conference, pp. 1288–1299. Association for Computing Machinery, New York, NY, USA (2022)

13. Zhou, M.Y.: Emotional Design. Shanghai Scientific & Technical Publishers, Shanghai (2011)

Future Visions for a Decolonized Future of HCI

Thick Descriptions of a Survey Interaction to Discuss the Colonization of Imagination

Elen Nas[1]([✉]) [iD], Fernando Longhi[1] [iD], Luciana Terceiro[1] [iD], Telma Azevedo[1] [iD], and Tânia Valente[1,2] [iD]

[1] Universidade de São Paulo, São Paulo, SP 05508-060, Brazil
elennas@usp.br
[2] Universidade Federal do Estado do Rio de Janeiro, Rio de Janeiro, RJ 20271-062, Brazil

Abstract. A forecast of a high-tech society often represents the visions of industry. The possible technological developments and innovations presented by tech companies promise a bright future, supposedly offering all a better quality of life. However, the ideas give protagonism of a particular style of life and reveal privileges that do not match the environmental and socio-economic tensions from the global south. We started an experiment among us to analyze historical visions of the future commonly presented by companies. We created a questionnaire with an additional form to allow participants to proactively propose alternate concepts by sending images. From this experience, we offer a thick description of the perspectives and feelings related to the questions submitted. This ethnography is a ground for future work where we aim to investigate how HCI literacy and knowledge of cultural studies impact the identification of biased content. Also, collecting data through questionnaires and forms can help participants increase awareness of image content on the internet and motivate them to present their voices proactively. In our interactions with other researchers, as we give this work, we invite others to volunteer to answer the questions and offer alternate views from the ones on the questionnaire through AI images. This is a primary step of qualitative research. For further actions, we aim to develop a platform able to provide quantitative data with diverse aesthetics for future visions, capable of adding diversity to the digital ecosystem.

Keywords: hci · cultural diversity · AI decolonization

1 Introduction

We are Brazilian researchers from diverse backgrounds. Our group comprises white, black, urban citizens, some with indigenous origins and from different ages. The preliminary information in this paper results from one of the topics covered in the studies of the decolonization of AI.

Methodology. As the research leader, the first author invited participants to answer questions organized on a digital platform embedded in the project's main website [1].

C. Stephanidis et al. (Eds.): HCII 2023, CCIS 1832, pp. 109–116, 2023.
https://doi.org/10.1007/978-3-031-35989-7_13

After answering the questions, participants were asked to send data representing their visions for the city's future, health, arts, food, communication, education, housing, transport, tools, and trade [2]. The broad coverage follows the patterns of the futuristic views the tech industry offers through propaganda films. As additional data, the participants provide images and 'thick descriptions' to complete the case study ethnography [3]. Because producing images in a short period is challenging, participants without specific drawing skills made pictures with an AI or searched for them on the web. A conflict between an imagined scenario and what is available as an outcome presented by a web search of images or an AI is expected. Thick descriptions situate the possible gaps, while further analysis can identify patterns of the framing of imagination by recurrent results.

2 Thick Description#1: Elen Nas

As a result of previous investigations related to HCI [4] and the teaching of Design classes about emerging technologies, I found images and videos like "Cool Town HP" [5], IBM RFID [6], Microsoft Future Vision 2020 [7], Siemens [8] and Virgin Media [9], among others. When I opened the discussion with the students, I realized that even well-informed and wealthy individuals considered such visions 'pretentious as the type of life mediated by such technologies did not seem to take into consideration poverty, people without jobs, houses, access to education, food, and so on.

I then realized the importance of contextualizing ideas and ideals. Tech companies' visions of the future were connected to notions of the global north and from countries that don't know the realities of big cities like Rio de Janeiro and São Paulo.

The quiz was created for a group of informed people. Still, because of the excessive specialization of research topics, most did not know the information provided in the questionnaire.

Thus, the first objective of the illustrated questions was to provoke reflections about the cultural perspectives that might be over-represented in digital content, resulting in the colonization of imagination.

The 'Discussion' will explore the first outcomes of the proposed ongoing debate.

3 Thick Description#2: Fernando Longhi

As an Architect, I have always thought more about spaces than people. I believe that the two future visions (Fig. 1a,b) I have created with Dall-e 2 [10] to answer the quiz [1] can best illustrate my journey through the profession and individual beliefs. Designing spaces in the real world made me increasingly aware of how influential the built environment can be to people's perceptions, emotions, and experiences.

Kevin Lynch's "The Image of the City" [11] shows how different urban structures and elements can create mental images that impact and constitute these social spaces. Today, I question if the images we constantly consume through multiple screens – from tablets to smartphones and others – can also play an essential part in these social spaces, including the imaginaries we create and collect.

a

b

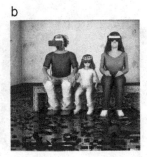

Fig. 1. a, b. Images produced with Dall-e 2. 2a shows the answer for the "future of cities" while 2b shows the answer for the "future of housing". Produced November 3rd, 2022, by Fernando Longhi with Dall-e 2.

To create an image to symbolize the future of the city (Fig. 1a), divided into two mental scenarios: a positive one and a negative one. On the one hand, a promising future for the city and its citizens would represent an inclusive and environmentally aware. But with the countless difficulties in the urban realm as social segregation, the housing crisis, and climate change, the first image that came to me was a post-apocalyptical cyberpunk city.

A romantic approach as the Garden City [12] mixed with the Stanford Torus [13] represents a surgical urbanism, a naïve and hygienist angle for the future, perhaps lacking humanity. This monumental uninhabited city image triggered discomfort and made me question my reality again. My choice of the future of housing was critical and skeptical (Fig. 1b). Considering the extreme social stratification in Latin America, I imagined a family in a vulnerable environment where all interactions were performed virtually. In contrast, the built environment was just a ruined shelter neglecting materiality that needed to be forgotten.

This survey interaction felt like a conversation. I was influenced by the set of images Dall-e asked me to choose, which reminded me of Vilém Flusser's "programmed freedom" [14]. Is there freedom and free will in a programmed world?

4 Thick Description#3: Luciana Terceiro

The stimulus to think of future visions reminded me of all the science fiction movies and their inaccurate forecasts. As Loewenstein and Angner [15] pointed out, the projection bias may be one of the factors responsible for projecting the present into the future, leading humans to imagine a tomorrow limited by today's knowledge. Although I would probably step into the same misconceptions and biases, I decided to board into the imaginative exercise and take my chances on creating my visions of the future.

First, the chosen videos and pictures in the questionnaire amused me. The past perspectives of the future presented an optimistic view of the tomorrow, created within white Western, Global North references. I guess this is the desired future in my subconscious. The videos produced by large tech corporations showed cheerful families enjoying the best life that emerging technologies could offer. Who would not love that?

a  b

Fig. 2. a, b. Images that describe future urban spaces and art

My future visions [16] were collected with Google Images from several keyword combinations to describe what I envisioned for education, communication, food, tools, urban spaces, health, transport, retail, arts, and living. I am a Brazilian citizen based in Sweden, and I did the research using English keywords. I am aware that geographical location and language affect search results. Thus, my experience projecting the future tends to be disconnected from my origins.

For the future of Cities (Fig. 2a), Transportation, and Living, I desired environments in balance with nature, envisioning a place where technical advances could provide a green, ecological space for humanity. However, these verdant and high-tech settings were not so far-fetched for Scandinavian countries; they tend to be pure science fiction for other realities.

For Education [17], my keywords expressed wishes to encourage the learning of collaboration more than the technology itself. Technology may be a powerful tool to facilitate access to information and promote knowledge. Still, without observing the aspects of diversity and inclusion, it will not lead to significant and democratic changes. And when thinking about Art, I looked for images that could have the potential for various interpretations (Fig. 2b). Art, like the future, is still open to many possibilities.

5   Thick Description #4: Telma Azevedo

My imagination about the future corresponds to identifying contrasts between the global north and south. The north, to my perception, represents too many generic buildings, with transitory or passing ambiance, with sumptuous volumes loaded in chrome, glass, or fiberglass and very cold – to the molds of the cities-scenery as Las Vegas – with artificial plants that do not dirty and are efficient in mimicking an instagrammable well-being. In these places, resources and technology are concentrated, and everyone complies with the standards accepted there, acting so that the accumulation intensifies [18]. The south not only refers to the southern region of the consensual political representation of the globe but to the diverse souths that exist and are the counterpoint to the accumulation of the global north. In these places, aridity by the subtraction of natural resources and the lack of basic sanitation and dignified subsistence, precariousness, and attempts to erase its importance only find loopholes when cultural expression and creativity are co-opted

a

b
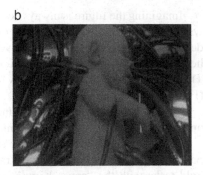

Fig. 3. a, b. "Marina Bay Sands", Singapore. (a) "The Matrix" (1999) movie frame. (b)

to give an air of relevance and personal sense to the increasingly fetishized goods of the global north (Fig. 3).

My images of the future are also metaphorical due to the lack of correspondence with the existing material. Often specific scenarios have become a shared future, such as the education of the future is an existing space of a first-world country in a constructivist school with elements of Waldorphian pedagogy, for example. That is, this school exists somewhere on the globe.

I answered the questionnaire in São Paulo, a central neighborhood, Consolação, where the amount of people on the streets and socially vulnerable grows by the window of my apartment. As I look out the window, I see myself and don't see myself in the giddiness of an echo. Many delivery men have their motorcycles stopped, which gives me the perspective of effective social transformation mediated by technology. This change has sound, color, substance, and feeling.

Along the lines of Rolnik's [19] thinking, these visible and not-so-obvious environments that cover cities, and more intimately the environments, carry textures and ontologies that permeate meanings and modes of existence.

6   Thick Description #4: Tânia Valente

a

b

Fig. 4. a shows "Blade Runner movie vision" and 4b shows "Elysium movie vision" in a collapsed world. Searched December 5th, 2022, by Tania Valente with Google Images.

Imagining the future is always complicated, even more so for someone like me who was born in the 1950s and has lived in a changing world. Artificial Intelligence and its developments brought (and will get) very significant changes to human beings regarding health, food, transport, communication, education, and commerce, among other fields. The questionnaire clearly shows how today's world was unimaginable for my ancestors (Fig. 4).

Since I belong to a time of exclusive face-to-face relationships, my concern is if humanity will lose its psychic and emotional reference when dealing with technology.

The questionnaire brought some elements that present a much easier life with the presence of AI: autonomous cars, ultra-fast communication, less time wasted on household tasks with the "smart home," changes in commercial relationships, and access to information, among others. But I can't stop thinking that this will not be distributed equally. It would be a utopia to think this way. Humanity is increasingly divided between those with easy access to such resources and those far from these privileges. The image I found and chose on the web about the art of the future did not represent what I would like to see. I expected a more interactive and decolonized perspective that was not available.

The images I chose to insert in the answers [20] presented a predominantly pessimistic vision of the future. The photos that caught my attention among those offered by Google Images reflected a dystopic vision, either uninhabited or with a few humans.

7 Discussion

A performative aspect of shaping the future through ideas expressed in pictures and films shows that 'envisioning a future' is like preparing public opinion to embrace an agenda of a technological future in which the industry is willing to invest. Yet, representing specific types of futures in particular ways [21] has politics embedded. Most images illustrate that the target public of those products is middle to upper-class whites, mainly citizens of the Global North (including the British in Oceania).

Images from the beginning of the twenty century and other moments of 'futurist waves' in the 60s, 80s, and 90s reflect that the promised technological advancements claim a better future for all. Still, Including people of color in the new films does not change that they represent populations excluded from enjoying many technological facilities. It creates tensions, confusion, and identity conflicts as the vision of the future are colonization by other means.

AI often presents white as a default for people, and to get images showing diverse ethnicities is necessary to specify. When we discuss data, this logic continues to other contexts where a 'cultural supremacy' occurs in practice by repeating the invisibility of otherness.

When participants looked for content to present their vision of the future with a Google search or an AI, the results represented the hegemonic aesthetics present in future images. It indirectly obstructed their imagination to think about a decolonized future that would dialogue with our culture and social, economic, and environmental conditions.

All participants saw the art of the future mediated by high technology, with the invisibility of other ways of artistic expression as body performance and low-tech inventions.

The hypothesis to justify a lack of diversity in future visions is because of the focus on extraordinary technological solutions. Nevertheless, if humanity has a future, it will be by valuing the traits where humans can be unique.

8 To Be Continued

This discussion further with more qualitative research until it touches the infrastructures, where quantitative data is transformed into computable knowledge. The cultural aspects of monoculture by colonization dissipate and become trends, beauty, and shared visions. Technical discussions involving ontologies in HCI [22] and the semantic web [23] should consider multiculturalism to find better solutions for our interactions with algorithms, APPs, software, and devices.

One of the challenges is that the data available on the internet and which fed machine and deep learning reinforce that the future is related to spectacular technological advancements or, if not, a dystopia where human lives with destruction. In paradise or purgatory, the protagonists are few. Therefore, the idea of a community acting together is rarely present in those images.

The future mediated by 'high' technologies seems effortless to only a few, potentially influencing everyone to pursue the same goal, which can be stressful for those without such resources. Therefore, such ideas for the future are not dialoguing with everyone's realities. It gives a false sense that society is homogeneous within pervasive global aesthetics.

Decolonization in human-computer interaction proposes investigating all the implicit biases we might have due to this politics of anticipation when interacting with the web, devices, and apps and finding creative ways to deconstruct that forced monoculture.

Acknowledgments. Thanks to the Brazilian Committee for Internet Management (CGI.BR) for supporting our research with the Institute for Advanced Studies of the University of São Paulo (IEA/USP) under the lead of Professor Virgilio de Almeida at Cátedra Oscar Sala.

References

1. Cátedra Oscar Sala. DecolonizAI. https://www.decolonizai.com/visoes-sobre-o-futuro/. Accessed 06 Mar 2023
2. Cátedra Oscar Sala. Visões de Futuro – Imagens. Decolonizai. https://www.decolonizai.com/visoes-de-futuro-imagens/. Accessed 14 Mar 2023
3. Cátedra Oscar Sala. Future Visions – Thick Descriptions. Decolonizai. https://www.decolonizai.com/visoes-de-futuro-artigo/. Accessed 14 Mar 2023
4. Nas, E., Lopes, J.: Interface design for ludic experiences with new technologies: the case of open-source software reactivision in sound interactions. In: 12° Congresso Brasileiro de Pesquisa e Desenvolvimento em Design. Blucher Design Proceedings. Vol. 2(9), pp. 4960–4970. Belo Horizonte (2016)
5. Acsofficesolutions. HP Cool Town from 2000. Youtube. https://youtu.be/U2AkkuIVV-I last accessed 2023/03/06
6. Preece, D.: IBM RFID Commercial – The Future Supermarket. Youtube. https://www.youtube.com/watch?v=wzFhBGKU6HA. Accessed 06 Mar 2023

7. Cosmo 365. Microsoft's Concept – Future Vision 2020. Youtube. https://youtu.be/dhmWsE U5KXE. Accessed 06 Mar 2023
8. Siemens. The Crystal Future Life. YouTube. https://youtu.be/zuPIyqUc9oA. Accessed 06 Mar 2023
9. Virgin Media Business. Generation IP: 2025. YouTube. https://youtu.be/yEXEonTlfT0. Accessed 06 Mar 2023
10. OpenAI. Dall-e 2 (2022). https://openai.com/dall-e-2/. Accessed 10 Dec 2022
11. Lynch, K.: The Image of the City. The MIT Press (1960)
12. Howard, E.: Garden Cities of To-Morrow. Faber and Faber (1946)
13. Johnson, R.D., Holbrow, C.: Space Settlements: A Design Study. U.S. National Aeronautics and Space Administration, NASA SP-413 (1976)
14. Flusser, V.: The Shape of Things: A Philosophy of Design. Reaktion (1999)
15. Loewenstein, G.: Angner, E.: Predicting and indulging changing preferences. In: Loewenstein, G., Read, D., Baumeister, R. (eds.) Time and Decision: Economic and Psychological Perspectives on Intertemporal Choice, vol. 12, pp. 351–391. Russell Sage Foundation (2003)
16. Cátedra Oscar Sala. Future Visions – Thick Descriptions: Descrição densa #2 – Luciana Terceiro. Decolonizai. https://www.decolonizai.com/visoes-de-futuro-artigo/. Accessed 14 Mar 2023
17. Cátedra Oscar Sala. Visões de Futuro – Imagens: Figure 4b. Decolonizai. https://www.decolonizai.com/visoes-de-futuro-imagens/. Accessed 14 Mar 2023
18. Huyssen, A.: Culturas do passado-presente: modernismos, artes visuais, políticas da memória. Trad. Vera Ribeiro. 1. ed. Contraponto; Museu de Arte do Rio, Rio de Janeiro (2014)
19. Rolnik, S.: Desvendando futuros. ComCiência, Campinas, n. 99 (2008)
20. Images 1d; 2d; 3d; 4d; 5d; 6d; 7d; 8d; 9d; 10d. https://drive.google.com/file/d/1U7Da9djbxzx 6oLlFQPr7psAv4-AKvBnA/view?usp=sharing
21. Kinsley, S.: Representing 'things to come': feeling the visions of future technologies. Environ. Plan. A **42**(11), 2771–2790 (2010)
22. Costa, S.D., Barcellos, M.P., Falbo, R.D.A.: Ontologies in human–computer interaction: a systematic literature review. Appl. Ontol. (Preprint), 1–32 (2021)
23. Dobson, G., Sawyer, P.: Revisiting ontology-based requirements engineering in the age of the semantic web. In: Proceedings of the International Seminar on Dependable Requirements Engineering of Computerised Systems at NPPs, pp. 27–29 (2006)

The Game Beyond the Game: The Concept of Metagame and Its Use for Interaction Design

Gabriel Patrocinio(✉) 📷

Universidade de Évora, Évora, Portugal
patrocinio.design@gmail.com

Abstract. The purpose of the article is an comes from our Doctoral research, it investigates an authorial project named Halag, an e-learning platform for game development that uses gamification as a tool for motivation, engagement and to improve the user experience for those students with the platform. As one of the main characteristics of this project, users who consume the platform's educational content is invited to participate in the production of a game, where the game design elements themselves will be created and selected by the participants, in a collaborative, democratic and sustainable and free ecosystem. We intend to expand our research and concepts seen during our research, for now a concept called Metagame. The word of Greek origin, meta is a prefix that can be interpreted in addition to, on the way to, that when united with a noun, another reflective and conceptual interpretation originates that can discuss various points of the sciences. The use of the meta, being something already understood in the academic environment to describe proposals that scientifically expand the research in question, for example in concepts about metalanguage, metapolitics, metadata, metaphysics, metaverse, among others. In our research, we rely on metadesign research by the authors Maturana (1997) Vassão (2010), Giaccardi (2003) and other authors, to discuss the concept of Metagame, bringing it closer to our research object, framed in a "game produced by game methodologies and created by gamers."

Keywords: Metagame · Interaction Design · Concept

1 Introduction

In the contemporary world, theories and interactive methods coexisting between man and machine become more complex in the face of new demands, needs and updates to society's needs, mainly information and communication. Thus, new paradigms emerge that influence the principles and practices of Design with the responsibility of designing intelligent and functional solutions for certain target audiences, in a sphere where cultural, material, economic, marketing, emotional guidelines are considered […] method of project.

Faced with so many opportunities to meet certain objectives that dialogue with the desires of users, a range of variations of design project possibilities is available to meet the known product differential. This differential not only brings benefits to the

C. Stephanidis et al. (Eds.): HCII 2023, CCIS 1832, pp. 117–122, 2023.
https://doi.org/10.1007/978-3-031-35989-7_14

user, but also affects the entire production chain of the product or service, seeking the most effective solution for the user in a holistic analysis of the issue, bringing together environmental, health, and social aspects and thus permeating in search for opportunities for improvement and value to the business.

Therefore, it is up to the user to choose the product or service available for that context, within the spectrum of everyone's reality, and thus conclude what made him seek that solution. In a process of human-object interaction, an evolutionary coo environment is built that accompanies and interferes with the changes and transformations of the contemporary world.

Following this line of reasoning, where new paradigms of design in the design process are adequately dedicated to this increase in invitations among the agents involved, other methodologies and organizational modus operandi arise with the objective of aligning and including these proposals in the scope of the product, where it is necessary a look at the process and methodological context that design is designed, exploring the dynamism and fluidity of how design acts on complexity.

This complexity, according to Dolzan [2] is not a theory, but a fact of contemporary society, without reductionist, simplistic explanations, or closed schemes, but on the contrary, it is understood in open, comprehensive, and flexible systems. Therefore, this so-called complexity singles out the limits and scope of design and tangible human interactions through technology and reflections of society, as an opportunity for innovative and multidisciplinary processes, seeking to transform this form of creation and sociability.

This reflection is called Metadesign, a critical reflective current before these new paradigms that the design culture emerges from this complexity of information and data that are part of the strategic planning of the product. Therefore, according to Giaccardi [3], we can adapt this concept translated as "the design of the design process". Metadesign is presented as a transdisciplinary approach mechanism, where the proposal is to simplify complexity. A project and creation method with the interest in proposing a radical innovation and mainly, acting and manipulating what we consider as reality.

In our article, we have as an initial starting point to review some research related to the concept or philosophy about Metadesign, its elaborations and proposals on how this current of design acts on the design project itself, on the creator, and on the final consumer user. This space will be important for our conceptual idealization of Metagame, the main argument of this article.

2 Methodology

Our method applied in this research is assumed mainly in the referential theoretical review, of researchers who traced the concept of Metadesign and their reflections from this terminology and relevance to our subject. In sequence, we will present a brief description of our research object, the Halag project and its foundations of design and gamification. This project was the starting point of reflection where our inquiry about the concept of Metagame emerges, where we will present our connections with the theoretical basis and this proposal of thought and methodology design of interaction design and game design components, extracting this essence that tends to be resulting in a fun and stimulating experience for users.

3 Investigations and Research on Metadesign

It is pertinent to mention at this point in the article, in addition to research related to Metadesign, the prefix of the word Meta. Consulting the Oxford, Cambridge, and Online Etymology dictionaries, this word of Greek origin, meta is a prefix that can be interpreted as between, with, after, in addition to, on the way to, through [...]. In Modern Latin, the adoption of the goal prefixed to a noun, describes something that is written or performed, referring to itself or something of its own essence, thus developing other philosophical, conceptual interpretations that can be discussed at various points in the science.

In its most common usage, meta describes a subject in a way that transcends its original limits, considering the subject itself as an object of reflection. Simply put, Metalanguage means a specialized form of language used to describe a language itself. Metatheory, is a theory about the theory; Metacriticism is the critique of how a work of art in general is criticized; metafiction is fiction in which the author takes steps to recognize the artifice of writing fiction; Metadata is data that helps analyze other data, such as the number of searches that have been performed on a particular topic; Metaphysics is what is beyond physics, and a philosophical current that seeks knowledge of the essence of things.

To contextualize one of the most relevant topics for this article, we investigated some references that describe the concept of Metadesign. Although we have already introduced this nomenclature, it is pertinent and respectable to cite some research already carried out on some reflections about the mental model of analyzing the project, looking at the project itself, and not with a historical approach, but linking the concepts arising from investigations to help our object of study.

According to author Almeida [1] the term Metadesign was used for the first time in 1960 by the researcher Van Onck, as the denomination of a university project discipline. Subsequently, Onck cites Metadesign as a more abstract feature of design, treating it as a connection that precedes the project itself, and resulting in multiple possibilities of possible solutions, making the design process more fluid and not directly interconnected only to the creator.

Giannetti [4] addresses Metadesign and the professional Metadesigner from the perspective of the author Youngblood [8] during the 1980s, craftsman as a director, IT technician as a technician, designer as a designer), where the Metadesigner can work in different fields, from the museum and the gallery to the means of communication and telematics networks. Complementing the reading of Youngblood, the author Giaccardi [3] presents the conception of the approximation of art and communication, where telecommunication and computer networks allow Metadesigners to appropriate electronic and digital artifices, becoming capable of controlling and manipulating meaning and context, thus altering the medium of creativity.

From the perspective of biologist Maturana [5] Metadesign is a dynamic work of art, where an aesthetic and experience of the world is produced, which is intertwined with the current technological environment, enabling an expansion on design and the nature of human existence itself, proposing a new way of epistemologically and ethically rethinking the relationship between humans and technology. Like art, Metadesign has the potential to expand related new dimensions and create an alternate reality throughout human history.

In this article, our intention is not to list all the concepts and investigations that were prefixed with Meta, or even to make a complete grammatical, historical, or reflexive review about them. There are several fields that are increasingly explored, since the fourth century with Aristotle analyzing Metaphysics, or even the contemporary concept, from the cybernetic world called Metaverse. This last one approaches the desire to add the sensation of reality in a virtual environment, that is, to create a structure in the real world capable of offering an immersive experience mediated by computer.

Dialoguing directly with the design project and an immersive environment, we have our research object of our PhD, entitled Halag. Therefore, it is pertinent to approach in a synthetic way what this project represents to follow our investigation of the text and thus reach the foundations and conceptual characteristics of the Metagame. It is pertinent to mention that, in tenuous lines, users transited their collaborations, at times assuming their roles as students, and others as players.

4 Halag and Halag: Open Game

The object of study of our project, entitled Halag [6], was developed at the Universiade de Évora, in Portugal, to obtain a doctorate in Visual Arts with a research line in Design and Metamidia. Halag is an online teaching and learning platform for technical knowledge in the field of game design. Managers of some cross-sectional areas of game development, developer, script, visual, sound design, level design, etc., could share materials, which teach the process of creating digital games.

In our case, we created some limitations of the addressed software, programming language, graphic and artistic style, considering the soundtrack and sound design, and the creative process on narration and storytelling. One of our interface and interaction design project methodologies was to apply Gamification on our platform, where for each material consumed by the students, the same would have to go through more beginner levels to gradually evolve according to the complexity and execution time and knowledge with each tool. The basic concepts used by interface design with gamification methodology such as awards, scores, ranking, and challenges were applied to our Halag platform.

In this path, Halag: Open Game emerged, a fully collaborative game, built, developed, and idealized by the users themselves, according to the area of interest and skill affinity within the game design process. The game with the alpha version pre-defined by the managers, that is, initial plot, mechanics, visual design, gameplay are presented to the players, but only a primary version, which illustrates what the collaboration of the users will result.

Briefly, a practical example could be: One of the platform managers responsible for programming proposes an intermediate level activity, with the objective of creating a collision course between the object and the character inserted in the scene. The material explaining the statement of the creation of these codes, are made available on the platform, where the student after learning has the possibility to send this code as an official version that will be inserted for that function in the game Halag: Open Game.

All material pre-ordered by the platform and prepared by the managers are open and inviting to user participation. The criteria for using these materials in the game itself are chosen in a democratic way, moving between voting, considering adequacy to the theme, production time, creativity, among others. In this process, we can see that the game Halag: Open game transcended the rules of game production, whereby individual choice, the collective is rewarded with what makes the most sense to the players at that moment. In this process, the role of the educator or manager is based on observation and guidance, while the players themselves provide support, material, and stimuli among the community for the development of the collaborative game. Produce a game, within the game itself, or we call can it a Metagame.

5 Metagame

Therefore, in the writing methodology for this article, we trace this investigative path in references about Metadesign and its multiplicities that involve the designer, technology, and the consumer. After that, it was pertinent to present our object of doctoral study, the Halag platform, a proposal where we inquire into the possibility of applying and researching this Metagame nomenclature. This nomenclature is not something entirely new. Several types of games, whether online, digital, card games, among others, use Metagame as a synonym for what works and is at a higher level of victory, rules, and trends in the gaming world. In this text, we intended to add this debate with another perspective on this approach of transcending the game environment, in the nature of the game itself.

We realized that, in an embryonic way, we started this study to collaborate for future discussions. With a secure bibliographical review of references on Metadesign to contextualize the nomenclature and thinking about the Metagame, we evaluate this relevant research in projects that involve several users when carrying out a collaborative work, adding knowledge in favor of a project, offering a universe derived from culture of games. In this specific situation, users try to act in the game itself, where involved by the playful environment, they receive visual, mechanical, and social stimulus to proceed with our project proposal, to produce a digital game with the knowledge acquired on our platform.

Engaging users in an education environment, with game mechanics to build a game, that is, the game (Halag) for game development (Halag: Open Game) with game mechanics (gamification), can have the approximation of imprint in Metagame. Analyzing this concept from the perspective of interaction design, adds value to the project and if one of the objectives, in addition to engagement and user experience in completing tasks, add fun and social parts transform the environment into something beyond the primary utility, and offer users other layers that the product has to offer, based on the uses, in our case, of game development elements as a design project methodology.

The transdisciplinarity present in the Halag platform may have been one of the factors that contributed to creating this interactive and stimulating environment for players. In this process, users with different trajectories and personal knowledge and experience prior to joining the platform, create an environment of coexistence, community, and socialization, where in a way the sense of collaborative production is stimulated to produce a final game, each one with your individual contribution, considering the macro perspective. Vassão [7], Metadesign processes and structures are something fluid, liquid, non-prescriptive and related to the more reflective and collaborative practice of design.

The prerequisite for launching the game is the spirit of unity and teamwork. With this motivating purpose, the sense of dispute between the players is put in the background, where the victory and conquest of the users are transformed into propellants for the objective of intrinsic and extrinsic achievement, materializes in Halag: Open Game, where the system de Metagame creates an interactive environment with those involved in the process, where the pre-established rules are relaxed according to the freedom of the players to choose the form of collaboration in this environment, which, in a stimulating way, results in good and fun experiences and products.

References

1. Almeida, C.: O conceito de Metadesign: O Colloquium on Metadesign, na Universidade Goldsmiths em Londres, pp. 62–66 (2014). https://doi.org/10.5151/despro-sigradi2014-0008
2. Dolzan, J.E.: Design e Complexidade: As dimensões do Humano nos Processos de Design. Universidade Federal de Santa Catarina, Centro de Comunicação e Expressão, Programa de Pós-Graduação em Design, Florianópolis (2018)
3. Giaccardi, E.: Metadesign as an emergent design culture. Leonardo 38, 342–349 (2005). https://doi.org/10.1162/0024094054762098
4. Giannetti, C.: Interface: Arte & Digital na Era Digital. Revista Arte y Parte, Madrid (1988)
5. Humberto, M.R.: Cognição, ciência e vida cotidiana. Ed. UFMG, Belo Horizonte (2001)
6. Gabriel da Costa, P.: Halag: A gamificação como metodologia para plataforma colaborativa on-line de produção de jogos digitais. Universidade de Évora, Portugal (2022). http://hdl.handle.net/10174/32813
7. Vassão, C.A.: Metadesign: ferramentas, estratégias e ética para a complexidade. Blucher, São Paulo (2010)
8. Youngblood, G.: Metadesign: Toward a Postmodernism of Reconstruction in Ars Electronica Catalog (1986)

Multimodal Analysis of Joint Attention in Remote Co-creative Design Process

Rui Sakaida(✉) and Nam-Gyu Kang

Future University Hakodate, 116-2 Kamedanakano, Hakodate 041-8655, Hokkaido, Japan
sakaida@fun.ac.jp

Abstract. We investigated how empathy for co-creative communication is achieved in the remote co-creative design process. We analyzed interactions occurring during a remote co-creative design process involving the KJ method and Miro, which is a remote working tool. In particular, we used multimodal conversation analysis to evaluate the interactions, focusing on each participant's mouse cursor movements and how they achieved joint attention to the same object on the screen. We observed two methods of using a mouse cursor to jointly attend to something: using the cursor to produce a pointing gesture, thereby drawing others' attention, and using it to indicate that the person is attending to others' pointing. A participant who wants to achieve joint attention with others to a particular object in the Miro environment draws their attention by hovering the mouse cursor over the object. Other participants who are instructed to pay attention demonstrate that they are doing so by moving their mouse cursors closer to the object. This transition to joint attention is visualized on the screen in real-time, which makes it clear whether or not joint attention has been achieved. The results suggest that teleworking environments, such as Miro, provide a unique means of establishing common ground, and that these environments may create a sense of "co-presence" that is different from face-to-face conversations.

Keywords: Joint Attention · Co-creative Design · Multimodal Analysis

1 Introduction

In the current era, it is essential to adapt to drastic changes, possess thinking skills allowing the application of knowledge and experience, and make judgments to solve problems without obvious answers [1]. A co-creative design process allows one to solve problems through empathizing with others with diverse knowledge, experiences or characteristics. Tada [2] emphasized that co-creative dialogue is essential for collaborative problem-solving. Co-creative dialogue is increasingly being used in various contexts. However, due to the COVID-19 pandemic, conducting face-to-face trials using co-creative communication is challenging. We assessed the potential utility of a newly developed remote co-creative design process in 2020. However, the use of remote co-creation communication has not been investigated in detail.

© The Author(s), under exclusive license to Springer Nature Switzerland AG 2023
C. Stephanidis et al. (Eds.): HCII 2023, CCIS 1832, pp. 123–129, 2023.
https://doi.org/10.1007/978-3-031-35989-7_15

We evaluated the remote co-creative design process and characteristics of remote co-creation communication. To explore the empathy that emerges from co-creation communication arising during the remote co-creative design process, we evaluated the characteristics of interactions occurring in the remote work environment when applying the KJ method and Miro, which is a remote working tool. In particular, we examined how participants achieve joint attention to the same object [3]. The findings suggest that joint attention may create a sense of "co-presence," which is necessary for empathy in the remote work environment.

2 Data and Methods

We analyzed video data of multimodal interactions [4] occurring during use of the KJ method and Miro. Specifically, we analyzed the use of the KJ method by seven university students. Data are in Japanese with English translation.

3 Analysis

When using Miro, a mouse cursor with each participant's name is displayed on the screen. The mouse cursor is used to manipulate objects, such as by dragging them on the screen; each participant can see who else is manipulating objects. However, an analysis of the group interactions occurring during the use of Miro showed that the mouse cursor is used for two additional purposes.

First, the cursor may be used for pointing. In real space, pointing is sometimes used to draw the attention of others to a specific person or object, thus achieving joint attention [5]. However, in remote conversations it is impossible to physically point to an object that appears on the screen. Therefore, a participant using Miro often encourages others to pay attention to an object by placing the mouse cursor on it. For example, in excerpt 1 below, participant A is about to discuss two groups of pictures shown on Miro.

Excerpt 1

1 A ((wiggling the mouse cursor)) *kono, #koko no futatsu tte waketeru imi attakke?*
            "This, here are two ((groups)), was there any reason
            to separate ((them))?"
            #fig.1

Participant A places the mouse cursor in the middle of the two groups of pictures in the lower right corner of the screen, wiggles the cursor (Fig. 1), and says, "This, here are two ((groups)), was there any reason to separate ((them))?" In this way, participant A points draws attention to a specific object in virtual space using the mouse cursor. As stated above, each cursor is labeled with the user's name, so that other participants know who is pointing at the object. However, because the mouse cursors of all participants are always visible on the screen when using Miro, other users may not be able to find the cursor instantly. Therefore, participant A emphasizes where they are pointing through small movements of the mouse cursor.

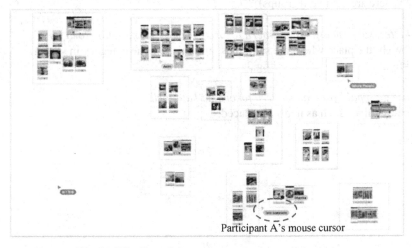

Participant A's mouse cursor

Fig. 1. Wiggling of the mouse cursor by participant A.

The mouse cursor can also be used to indicate where one's attention is focused. In real space, attention to a specific location is generally communicated by gaze [6]. For example, a person trying to attract another person's attention by pointing often indicates where their attention is directed by looking at the object. However, because the gaze is directed toward the screen in general during a teleconference, it is not possible to show which specific part of the screen is being focused on through gaze alone. In the KJ method, the user can indicate the specific location that they are focusing on by moving their mouse cursor to that location. The following excerpt is a continuation of Excerpt 1.

Excerpt 1'

1 A ((wiggling the mouse cursor)) *kono, #koko no futatsu tte waketeru imi attakke?*
                            "This, here are two ((groups)), was there any reason
                            to separate ((them))?"
                            #fig.1

2   (1.2)

3 B *doko da? futatsu*
     "Where are the two ((groups))?"

4 A *#etto:, sakuramasu ga hai#tteru tokoro to kono:, ano:, nattoo toka no*
     "Well, the place where the salmon is, and this, uh, the category in which
     #fig.2   #fig.3

5   *are ga ippai byatte naranderu tokoro no kategorii?*
     many things such as natto are placed."

Fig. 2. The mouse cursors of other participants gradually gather round that of participant A.

Responding to participant A, who said, "Here are two ((groups)), was there any reason to separate ((them))?" (line 1), the other participants' mouse cursors (Fig. 1), which were previously scattered, gradually gather round that of participant A (Fig. 2). Participant B did not identify where participant A was pointing and thus asked, "Where are the two groups?" Then, participant A explained the location of the salmon, saying, "Well, the place where the salmon is." (line 4). Thereafter, the mouse cursors of almost all participants gathered round that of participant A (Fig. 3), indicating that the participants directed their attention to the object pointed at by participant A's cursor, i.e., the two groups of pictures in the lower right corner of the screen.

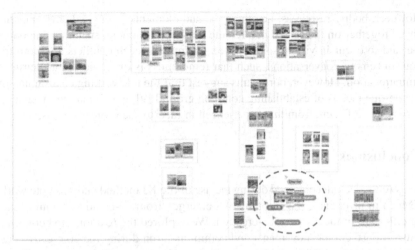

Fig. 3. The cursors of almost all participants are gathered round that of participant A.

The above shows that a participant trying to achieve joint attention with others to a particular object in the Miro environment attracts the attention of others by hovering the mouse cursor over the object and moving it incrementally by small amounts. Other participants who have been instructed to pay joint attention show that they are doing so by moving their mouse cursors closer to the object. The transition to joint attention is visualized on the screen in real-time, and it thus becomes clear whether or not joint attention is achieved.

4 Discussion

With the KJ method, a large piece of paper and sticky notes are used in real space. Participants often point to the sticky notes to achieve joint attention [5]; however, they do not always know which sticky note another participant is paying attention to at any given time because it is difficult to determine others' gaze direction in this scenario.

In contrast, when using the teleworking tool Miro, a cursor with each participant's name is always visible on the screen. Although each participant primarily places the cursor where they want to operate, they can also use the cursor to attract the attention of others or indicate the area of the screen to which they are paying attention. With Miro, information about the object of interest, including who is currently paying attention to it, is easily visualized. For participants who want to establish joint attention with others, such as participant A in excerpt 1 in this study, it is obviously crucial to ascertain whether or not the attention of others has been successfully secured.

Visualization on the screen of a state of joint attention among several participants may promote a sense of "co-presence" [7] that is specific to teleworking tools. Co-presence refers to a state in which participants feel close to each other through mutual perception [8]. In collaborative work using teleworking tools, participants cannot easily display their gestures and postures to others, and are not aware of the gaze directions of others. In such a situation, "embodiment" is generally considered to be limited.

However, bodily resources, i.e., the eyes, and elements of the real environment are displayed together on the screen in a remote work environment, such that embodiment can be said to occur in virtual space. As an example, speech conflicts are more likely to occur in remote conversations, such that remoteness is often viewed as detrimental to communication. However, our results suggest that the teleworking environment provides a unique means of establishing common ground [9], which may produce a sense of co-presence different from that experienced in face-to-face conversations.

5 Conclusions

We analyzed video data obtained during the use of the KJ method and a remote working tool (Miro) to investigate the empathy that emerges from co-creation communication, which differs from face-to-face co-creation. We explored the relationship between participants' mouse cursor movements and communication during the co-creative design process. We suggest that a sense of co-presence is a particular feature of joint attention arising during the remote co-creative design process.

The participants engaged in the remote co-creative design process in this study attempted to develop a sense of co-presence and show empathy to others, which may be analogous to body movements such as eye contact and finger-pointing occurring in face-to-face interactions (and which serve to enhance empathy).

Future studies should evaluate features other than the mouse cursor. By comparing face-to-face and remote co-creative design processes using the same task employed herein in future studies, the mechanisms underlying empathy in the remote co-creative design process may be elucidated. In addition, we plan to perform a qualitative analysis of a remote international design workshop using the evaluation grid method, and to comprehensively analyze the mechanisms through which empathy arises during the remote co-creative design process.

Acknowledgement. This research was supported by JSPS KAKENHI Grant Number 21K12564.

References

1. Matsuo, T.: Nijūisseiki-gata sukiru towa nani ka: konpitenshī ni motozuku kyōiku kaikaku no kokusai hikaku (What are 21st century skills: an international comparison of competency-based educational reforms). Akashi Shoten, Tokyo (2015) (in Japanese)
2. Tada, T.: Gurōbaru jidai no taiwa-gata jugyō no kenkyū: Jissen no tame no jūni no yōken (Research on interactive teaching in the global age: 12 requirements for practice). Toshindo, Tokyo (2017) (in Japanese)
3. Takanashi, K., Sakaida, R.: Nichijō seikatsu bamen no sōgokōi bunseki (Interaction analysis in daily life situations). In: Suzuki, H. (ed.) Ninchi-kagaku kōza 3: Kokoro to shakai (The Lecture Series of Cognitive Science, Vol. 3: Mind and Society), pp. 103–140. University of Tokyo Press, Tokyo (2022) (in Japanese)
4. Mondada, L.: Multiple temporalities of language and body in interaction: challenges for transcribing multimodality. Res. Lang. Soc. Interact. **51**, 85–106 (2018)

5. Goodwin, C.: Pointing as situated practice. In: Kita, S. (ed.) Pointing: Where Language, Culture and Cognition Meet, pp. 217–241. Lawrence Erlbaum, NJ (2003)
6. Goodwin, C.: Conversational Organization: Interaction Between Speakers and Hearers. Academic Press, MA (1981)
7. Kimura, D.: Kyōzai kankaku: Afurika no futatsu no shakai ni okeru gengo-teki sōgokōi kara (The Sense of Co-presence: From Linguistic Interactions in Two African Societies). Kyoto University Press, Kyoto (2003). (in Japanese)
8. Goffman, E.: Behavior in Public Places: Notes on the Social Organization of Gatherings. Free Press, New York (1963)
9. Clark, H.H.: Using Language. Cambridge University Press, Cambridge (1996)

Design & Futures – A Process Model Integrating Design Thinking and Strategic Foresight

Jeffrey David Serio$^{(\boxtimes)}$ (iD)

Business Academy Aarhus, Viby J 8260, Aarhus, Denmark
jds@eaaa.dk

Abstract. The paper presents a practical process model that integrates design thinking and strategic foresight. The model is proposed by comparing different design thinking and strategic foresight processes, with the methods required to undertake the process presented. Each phase of the model is described, along with the benefits of their integration. Finally, the model is applied, and benefits of an integrated process reflected upon through expert interviews and co-creation workshops with companies developing new product or service innovations.

Keywords: Design Thinking · Strategic Foresight · Design Process

1 Introduction

In today's turbulent landscape, companies face diverse challenges such as changing customer demands, rising competition, technological advancements, and digitalization [1]. Companies find it difficult to determine the direction of their innovation efforts and what new products or services to develop or markets to enter, creating uncertainty [2]. While design thinking can help companies focus on their customers' needs and pain points, users may struggle to imagine or provide feedback on non-existent solutions, and observing users alone may not reveal future changes in their needs [3].

These factors make it increasingly difficult for organizations to plan since they do not know what is to come. Traditional approaches like design thinking alone may not suffice in accounting for the rapidly changing world, leading to a gap between identifying current needs and their relevance at the time of release as well as the higher-order implications of an innovation. To bridge these gaps, this paper proposes an integrated model of strategic foresight and design thinking and presents its benefits along with expert interviews and co-creative workshops with three companies where the integrated approach is applied.

2 Designing with Foresight

2.1 Contributions of Strategic Foresight to Design Thinking

We are all concerned about the future, companies too, however in different ways. Companies can think about the future in three ways: the future as given, the future as uncertain, and lastly the future as created [4]. The future as created recognizes that we play an active role in defining and realizing a desired future through visioning and creating. While design takes a point of departure in user needs, aesthetics, form, and function, it too ends in the creation of an intervention that makes change and has a positive impact on the world [5]. It is evident that both design and strategic foresight are concerned with the future and the results of both to create a more desirable future. The mutual attention to the future can be seen by the different design thinking approaches lending from strategic foresight of recent. Dune and Raby began to bring the two practices together through a speculative approach. Creating provocative prototypes as representations of artefacts set to exist in and describe alternative futures [6]. With the artefacts intended purpose to critique current issues. A speculative approach than lays more emphasis on alternative futures and raising discussions than the creation of a more desirable or better future. Alternatively, Bespoke, a futures design studio, works with and presents their futures design framework, applying design and cocreation to a process of foresight, emphasizing the imaging and iterating of futures [7]. However, there is still a concern for a more specific and practical integration of the two processes.

2.2   Proposals for Design Thinking & Strategic Foresight

Other authors continue to propose a more integrated approach through the analysis of the benefits of practicing foresight in innovation processes. At the beginning of projects foresight can initiate an innovative process by identifying new needs, technologies, competitive concepts, critique the process by challenging basic assumptions in customer needs, technological developments or political, or cultural issues, and lastly, enhance the overall strategic guidance through the creation of visions, consolidating opinions, and assessing the innovation [8]. Being more specific to design thinking as an innovative process, a comparison is presented between two processes: the Stanford D. School's design thinking process and Rohrbeck and Kum's 3Ps of Perceiving, Prospecting, and Probing [9]. The proposed solution is a strategic foresight-informed design thinking process and outlines the necessary stages to achieve it and their importance. Ensuring the same benefits of strategic foresight in innovation processes previously introduced but specific to design thinking. The proposal gives a theoretical look at how the stages could be aligned; however, the subsequent methods of each process need to be defined, their interdependence considered and combined to be actualized in practice and reflected over.

3   A Practicable Model

To illuminate how strategic foresight and design thinking can be integrated different strategic foresight processes and design thinking processes are presented. The results of each are a set of common methods and a three-phase process with number of phases decided from the start. This is selected based on ensuring commonality across all the different processes and keeping the feasibility of the model in mind which is to be applied in co-creation workshops. The strategic foresight and design thinking phases will be presented and then combined to define the resultant model which is then described in detail.

3.1 Strategic Foresight Processes

The table below presents a strategic foresight process consisting of three phases, and the methods for each arrived at from a side-by-side comparison of different foresight processes [10]. Following the table is a description of the purpose of each phase and the corresponding methods to be integrated.

Table 1. Strategic Foresight Phases & Methods.

Phase	Methods
Sense	Scope Wheel, Stakeholder Analysis, Scanning Hits/Scan Cards
Orient	Future Wheel, Future Cone, Storytelling, Scenarios
Act	Backcasting, Capacity Building, Product Roadmapping

In the Sense phase, one identifies main issues and stakeholders, uncovers biases, and establishes a baseline of current knowledge. The Orient phase involves using signals of change to create visions of future worlds and evaluating the implications using methods like the future wheel. In the Act phase, the company prioritizes potential scenarios, creates a roadmap, and takes necessary actions to achieve the desired future state.

3.2 Design Thinking Processes

Various models of design thinking exist to capture the creative problem-solving process, reflecting the approaches of designers. The phases of these models are often generalizations of different designers' work and not starting or stopping points [11]. To make the models more accessible the table below presents a synthesis of design thinking processes, including the phases and their corresponding methods [10].

Table 2. Design Thinking Phases & Methods.

Phases	Methods
Observe	Observation and registration of place, mind maps, information maps, personas, empathy
Ideate	Brainwriting and brainsketching, sketching, visual & semantic confrontations, HMW
Make	Storyboards, rapid prototyping, Storytelling and learning experiences for testing like role playing

The design thinking process presented includes three phases: Observe, Ideate, and Make. Observe involves using methods such as mind maps, information maps, personas empathy maps, and ecosystem maps to understand the existing situation. Ideate uses diagrams, mappings, brainwriting, sketching, visual and semantic confrontations, and

HMW questions to generate solutions. Make involves using methods like 2D and 3D renderings, rapid prototypes, storyboarding, storytelling, role playing, and experimentation to prototype and create solutions.

3.3   The Model

Having presented both design thinking and strategic foresight, it can be seen how to combine them in an innovation process and the benefit of doing so. This is achieved in the Table 3, integrating strategic foresight from Table 1 with design thinking from Table 2. The integrated process model is presented and its impact on different phases and the methods to be used described. Finally, the purpose and outcomes of using these methods during each phase is discussed.

Table 3. An Integrated Model

Strategic Foresight	Design Thinking	Integrated Description
Sense	Observe	Understand users' problems empathetically, recognize personal biases and knowledge gaps, broaden the search area by scanning for potential changes, and interpret insights from both the user's and macro perspectives
Orient	Ideate	Explore future possibilities by envisioning potential futures and crafting alternative narratives. Use scenarios or future worlds to ideate on product or service solutions that consider both problems and opportunities. Evaluate the desirability of each scenario by understanding the potential implications and iterate on conceptual ideas accordingly
Act	Make	Prioritize desirable futures by selecting different scenarios and backcast to determine the requirements and capacities needed for the product or service. Prototype and visualize high fidelity 2D or 3D concepts to be tested and improved before entering the market

By setting the two processes side by side, one can see how strategic foresight can be worked with in an innovation process of design thinking. In doing so, it changes the activities taking place and hence the mindset and expected outcome of a design thinking processes itself.

The subsequent phases of an integrated approach then become:

Sense & Observe. Sensing and observing to understand limitations and potential shifts in knowledge that can occur from changes in the macro environment, as well as gain empathetic understanding of individuals and identify weak signals of change to broaden the perspective. These can indicate new emerging needs or technological advancements that become not only problems, but opportunities not identified otherwise. The outcome of the phase Sense & Observe is to have observed and gained empathy on individuals, to have discovered signals of change, and have interpreted them to be used in the next phase.

Orient & Ideate. Create visions of different futures from the investigations conducted in the Sense & Observe that include both the problems faced today but potential opportunities of tomorrow. Use these to inspire and ideate on products and services that will contribute to this future and evaluate their desirability. Understand the larger consequences the different futures and the products and services hold. Continue to ideate and iterate based off the implications to better aid in the decision-making process. The outcome of Orient & Ideate, is then building worlds, to have explored and envisioned different alternative scenarios, and created stories surrounding the world in which these are taking place.

Act & Make. Prioritize desirable futures from scenario exploration and narrow down product and service ideas. Create a roadmap by backcasting the future state and the experiential and functional requirements of chosen products or services. These will be the steps the company will have to take to bring the product or service to life. Evaluate whether the company has the capacity to do so or whether external changes to the world are also necessary for this to be implemented. Create prototypes and test them with potential users to continue to iterate on the experience and functionality. Keep track of the signals of change that might indicate that the external macroenvironment does not move against the experience or functional requirements for the product and service. Lastly, the outcome is to make change, having acted and made the products and services and changes in the world necessary to move that future closer to fruition.

4   Expert Interviews & Co-creation Workshops

4.1   Methodology

The following section introduces the key findings from a set of interviews and co-creation workshops. Conducting the interviews and workshops based off the model allowed for a triangulation connecting the findings of all three [12]. Four interviews were held from May to October of 2021 and were approached in a semistructured manner allowing for specific questions and an open dialogue where the interviewees were selected based upon their qualifications and professional experience in their approach of combining strategic foresight and design at global design studios [13]. The co-creation workshops were conducted between May and November of 2021 with one startup developing novel IoT equipment, and two innovating on their product and service offerings where the model was applied [14].

Findings from the interviews showed several different perspective shifts when working with a combined strategic foresight and design thinking process.

4.2 Interviews

The results of the interviews are presented as themes, synthesized from found patterns in the interview data:

Trends as Tangible Material. The combination of design and foresight turned the discovery of trends in a foresight process to viewing trends as material that designers could use in a process of understanding and discovery. What could come about and be created by thinking of trends as a material to shape futures through their unique combination.

Bottom-Up and Outside-In. Design and foresight together end up combining bottom-up and outside-in approaches. Avoiding a top-down deterministic approach by using both user insights and external signals such as new technologies or market perspectives. Resulting in a broader foundation of knowledge for defining related user insights and trends creatively.

Challenging Belief Systems. Discovering insights during the design process situates efforts to a specific context and domain. But by incorporating strategic foresight, designers can explore new domains and challenge their assumptions and biases opening the space of exploration to include domain areas not known before. To do this, designers must use strategic foresight methods to challenge their mental models of the future.

Evidence, Patterns, and the Evolution of Trends. Recognizing that the world changes requires the revisiting of the origins of the evidence and evolving them if they have changed creating a continuous process. Not done in a needing finding process, as the need would no longer exist if the resultant solution addressed it.

Responsibility and Implications for Decision Making. Design thinking involves engaging with users to gain empathy, and strategic foresight extends this process by considering a broader range of stakeholders, including the environment, privacy, and other issues. These complex problems are often called wicked problems and have no simple solutions. By using strategic foresight methods like the future wheel, designers can explore the implications including the higher order implications of their choices and take responsibility for the product or services they create.

Common Ground in Shared Futures. Manifesting different futures requires change within an organization or team. Design and strategic foresight offer collaborative methods to co-create and illuminate implications for future scenarios. However, designing for a better future means different things to different people. The role of the designer then shifts to being one of a facilitator to uncover the different elements that stakeholders agree upon as being desirable.

4.3 Co-creative Workshops

The different projects with companies implemented the model to address their challenges in developing new digital products or services. The collaboration began with an introductory meeting to understand each company's values, current activities, and market environment. The integrated design and foresight model was presented with expected benefits and alignment of expectations. Multiple workshops were held with a few weeks in between for material preparation and planning.

The initial workshop focused on the Sense & Observe and Orient & Ideate phases as the activities within them are quite similar, including discussions, presentations, and brainstorming ideas. The goal being the exploration of different possible futures relevant to the companies and undertaking the methods from the first two phases.The second workshop was then dedicated to the final phase of the model Act & Make, as the activities then changed focus to more concrete exercises involving decision making, road mapping, creation, and making the ideas tangible through sketching and prototyping.

4.4 Examining the Model in Practice

Reflecting over the model from Table 3 used in the workshops revealed some surprising results specific to each individual workshop and company highlighted here.

The Business. The model aimed to create a new product or service, but during scenario building, it revealed challenges to the current business model. This led to testing the business model with the future world, which encouraged the company to develop new offerings.

Workshop outcomes suggested the following expansions:

- Stress testing the existing business model against the future world in the form of a scenarios.
- Entirely new products, services, or combination of products and services.
- Further development of existing products and or services through new functionality.
- New business opportunities, leveraging either a new or further developed product or service.

Whose Future Are We Design For? While working with the model in the Orient & Ideate phase of the workshop the method How Might We…?, used to explore solutions brought up a challenge [15]. Whose perspective are we seeing the future from? It became important to decide this. Now that we know that for instance a challenge of saving time, together with the potential of artificial intelligence, can have the purpose of relieving work through the automation of a process, the question of perspective remains.

From the perspective of a salesperson, the product would be different from that of a user or a client. So first it was decided which stakeholders' point of view this would be seen from, and then continue.

Being Proactive Through Structure and Rigor. The workshops further revealed how working through the model provided a needed structure. The model helped to collect and synthesize the different ways the participants had been on their own considering the future and then document it.

This can impact a company greatly enabling activation of already existing knowledge. So, being proactive means not only thinking about the future and returning to delivering the assignments or tasks of the day to day. But provide a process to synthesize them and make them tangible.

How Radial Are They? When using the future wheel method to explore the implications of articulated trends it was found that some trends didn't bring enough change to justify further exploration. Allowing for a more iterative approach taking on other trends or returning to discover and articulate more impactful ones.

5 Discussion

Reflecting over the model put into practice through workshops together with companies revealed different considerations ranging from the model itself, to facilitating the process of working with it and lastly, to interpreting and acting on the results. As the model intends to actualize a product or service and hence manifest a future the workshops alone would not be able to accomplish such a task. A larger project initiative followed to product completion and not prototype would have to be undertaken. The model also was put to work from a more design thinking approach orienting the discussions. However, having practiced the model through workshops it can provide a point of departure and a set of steps to follow for companies who wish to begin to work with an integrated approach. It has been found that the model can help companies recognize change around them and subsequently be better prepared. And the structured approach from the model can formalize and articulate what were previously implicit thoughts or knowledge. It can help find common ground amongst stakeholders, help make decisions, and challenge one's beliefs. Hence a company can be more proactive in creating a desired future.

References

1. Buehring, J., Bishop, P.C.: Foresight and design: new support for strategic decision making. She Ji J. Des. Econ. Innov. **6**(3), 408–432 (2020)
2. Dore, F., Kouyoumjian, G., Sarrazin, H., Sheppard, B.: The Business Value of Design. McKinsey & Company (2018)
3. Reeves, M., Deimler, M.: Adaptability: the new competitive advantage. Harv. Bus. Rev. **89**(7/8), 134–141 (2011)
4. Svendsen, S., Olsen, S., Mac, A.: Forandringsforståelse. In: Mac, A., Madsen, S. (eds.) Samfundslitteratur (2018)
5. Cary, J.: Design for Good: A New Era of Architecture for Everyone. Island Press/Center for Resource Economics, Washington, DC (2017). https://doi.org/10.5822/978-1-61091-794-0
6. Dunne, A., Raby, F.: Speculative Everything: Design, Fiction, and Social Dreaming. The MIT Press (2013)
7. Dyrman, M., et al.: Book of Futures, 3rd edn. Bespoke (2018)
8. Rohrbeck, R., Gemünden, H.G.: Corporate foresight: its three roles in enhancing the innovation capacity of a firm. Technol. Forecast. Soc. Change **78**(2), 231–243 (2011)
9. Gordon, A., Rohrbeck, R., Schwarz, J.: Escaping the 'faster horses' trap: bridging strategic foresight and design-based innovation. Technol. Innov. Manage. Rev. **9**(8), 30–42 (2019)
10. Serio, J.: Hello Future. Business Academy Aarhus, Department of Research and Innovation (2022)

11. Brown, T., Wyatt, J.: Design thinking for social innovation. Stanf. Soc. Innov. Rev. **8**(1), 31–35 (2009)
12. Eisenhardt, K.M.: Building theories from case study research. In: Huberman, M., Miles, M.B. (eds.) The Qualitative Researchers' Companion, pp. 5–36. SAGE Publications (2002)
13. Bryman, A.: Research Methods and Organization Studies. Routledge (2003)
14. Sanders, E., Stappers, P.J.: Probes, toolkits and prototypes: three approaches to making in codesigning. CoDesign **10**, 5–14 (2014)
15. Stickdorn, M., Hormess, M., Lawrence, A., Schneider, J.: This is Service Design Doing. O'Reilly Media Inc. (2018)

Insights from the Practical Application of a Human-Centered Design Process for the Digitalization of Maintenance in Food Industry

Hendrik Stern[1]([✉]) [ID], Moritz Quandt[2] [ID], Julien Mensing[1],
and Michael Freitag[1,2] [ID]

[1] Faculty of Production Engineering, University of Bremen, Bremen, Germany
hstern@uni-bremen.de

[2] BIBA - Bremer Institut für Produktion und Logistik at the University of Bremen,
Bremen, Germany

Abstract. This paper focuses on the practical application of a human-centered design (HCD) process to redesign processes for need-based use of technological possibilities, such as intelligent assistance systems. HCD is a resource-intensive approach which requires repeated development and evaluation of design prototypes with active involvement from people. The paper provides insights from a case study on the digitalization of processes within the maintenance of production machines in the food industry, intending to develop an information platform that supports maintenance workers. Various methods were used during the platform's development, including personas and user studies. The lessons learned from the practical application of HCD can aid future applications in an industrial work context, including using different user-centered methods, observed effects on workers, and challenges that emerged due to the HCD approach.

Keywords: Human-Centered Design · Digitalization · User Experience · Cognitive Assistance

1 Introduction

Companies face the challenge of redesigning their processes for a need-based use of technological possibilities, e.g., through cognitive assistance systems. Successful implementation of such changes can be promoted by using a human-centered design (HCD) process, as the active involvement of people can improve the usability of the systems as well as their acceptance [4, 10]. In projects where this framework was used, a high acceptance by the prospective users could be observed, and the designed system was rated as suitable for practical use [3, 11, 16]. However, this approach is resource-intensive. Since, for example, design prototypes have to be repeatedly developed and evaluated with users. In particular, small and medium-sized companies must carefully consider how such an approach can be used. Consequently, among others, current research in this area deals with a fostering of low-effort work design research (e.g., at [18]) or with the development of UI guidelines

© The Author(s), under exclusive license to Springer Nature Switzerland AG 2023
C. Stephanidis et al. (Eds.): HCII 2023, CCIS 1832, pp. 139–146, 2023.
https://doi.org/10.1007/978-3-031-35989-7_17

in cyber-physical manufacturing and logistics systems (e.g., at [19]), which both could lead to less iterations during an HCD process.

This paper deals with insights gained from the practical application of an HCD process. An HCD approach was applied to the use case of the digitalization of processes in the food industry's maintenance of production machines. The various phases of the procedure model for the human-centered design of interactive systems were iterated according to DIN EN ISO 9241-210 [8]. The objective here is to develop an information platform that supports maintenance workers, e.g., for access to instructions, documentation, or responsibilities.

Various methods were used during the platform's development, e.g., personas, to determine user requirements [15]. The people involved actively participated in the design process in several ways, e.g., via oral or paper surveys, collaborative tools, or as participants in user studies. From this, lessons learned can aid future applications of an HCD process in an industrial context. This includes the findings on using different methods, observed effects on workers, and challenges and experiences that have emerged due to the practical application of HCD.

2   Exemplary Application of HCD at a Production Facility in Food Industry

Human-centered design (HCD) describes an approach that places humans as users at the very center of design and development processes [12], but can be also used during the entire product life cycle [16]. This way, humans are brought into focus and the activities and systems to be integrated are adapted to human requirements and needs [4]. The entire HCD process, according to DIN EN ISO 9241-210, consists of four phases that are passed through iteratively. The design process ends after an evaluation shows that the identified usability requirements have been met [8,13].

The present use case concerns the maintenance of production machines in a production site in food industry. It includes various maintenance activities at the production machines, both in the context of scheduled maintenance and due to malfunctions. Due to the large number of machines for processing, transporting, and packaging the products, a high level of expertise of the workers is required for troubleshooting. The project aims to develop a cognitive assistance system that supports operators in their tasks and contributes to improved working conditions and a decreased error rate. This shall be accomplished following the HCD process of DIN EN ISO 9241-210.

At the outset of the use case, the maintenance staff faces various problems. First, there are difficulties in planning and preparing the maintenance operations to be carried out. Here, the identification of experts for the current malfunction or the affected type of machinery is often unclear. Second, there is a lack of communication between the workers or the shifts, which leads to unnecessary duplication of specific tasks. In addition, errors occasionally occur in the execution of tasks, e.g., based on an incorrect error analysis, an unsuitable action is carried out to solve the malfunction. This led to the goal of establishing an interactive information and knowledge platform for workers. This platform is intended to bundle relevant information for maintenance workers and thus counteract the abovementioned problems.

2.1 Planning the Human-Centered Design Process

First, the identification of suitable tools and methods for HCD in the present case study was carried out, and their integration into the subsequent process steps was planned. Existing documents on the work environment and work activities shall be evaluated to obtain an overview of the use case (document analysis). Workers shall be consulted throughout the process to ensure that many different and frequent opinions can be expressed (workshops, questionnaires, and interviews). Here, illustrative visualizations of the requirements of different user groups shall be used to guide the requirements assessment (personas). Through interactive mock-ups, evaluations shall be carried out to gather feedback without the effort of actual implementation (prototyping). A standardized questionnaire to evaluate the user experience of a functional prototype shall be used (meCUE 2.0).

Furthermore, the planned information and knowledge platform stakeholders were identified (stakeholder analysis) [2]. For the use case, the maintenance department's managers and staff members for preventive maintenance and malfunction-induced maintenance were identified as the most important stakeholders.

2.2 Phase 1: Understanding and Describing the Context of Use

Based on the stakeholder analysis in phase 0, the respective attributes of the users of the information and knowledge platform were determined, and their goals and tasks were identified. This was initially based on a document analysis, including organizational charts of maintenance, job descriptions, maintenance rules and regulations, and the layout of the work environment. In one-on-one interviews with the stakeholders and utilizing a questionnaire, the characteristics of the users concerning responsibility, age distribution, and professional experience were collected.

The used questionnaire was adapted from the Job Diagnostics Survey (JDS) and the Work Design Questionnaire (WDQ) to increase the fit to the present use case. The JDS is a standardized survey instrument for diagnosing significant task and activity characteristics and their effect and evaluation of work design actions to change these characteristics [5,9]. The Work Design Questionnaire (WDQ), according to Stegmann et al. [17], pursues the goal of evaluating an entire workplace. The assessment led to the following results: Out of 25 workers, 6 are assigned to preventive maintenance, 7 to malfunction-induced maintenance, and 9 to administration. In addition, the workers are predominantly between 26 and 45 years old (18/25) and have more than 6 years of work experience (21/25). The following work tasks account for the largest share of work: planned maintenance activities, unplanned maintenance activities, optimizations, and fault diagnosis and analysis.

2.3   Phase 2: Specify the Usage Requirements

In workshops, we gathered the workers' needs for a knowledge and information platform. Among others, the following points were mentioned:

- Incorrect execution of activities due to outdated information
- Informal information sharing, both within the team and across departments, especially during shift handovers
- Decisions "by heart"
- Individual differences in the parameter settings, resulting in a following shift interpreting them as erroneous
- Duplication of actions due to unclear distribution of tasks
- Incorrect fault analyses leading to incorrect measures

In order to derive the goals and requirements of the workers from these needs, three personas were developed as fictitious characters that represent real workers, e.g., a staff member of the maintenance team, who mainly wants to establish an efficient process to get the work done, or a member of the management team, who's predominant goal is to optimize the overall system performance. This resulted in the following usage requirements:

- The user must be able to display up-to-date technical manuals
- The user must be able to link the technical manuals to the systems
- The user must be able to retrieve the current production plan of an area
- The user must be able to find all information intuitively in the system

These requirements were intended to serve as an essential basis for the design drafts. The requirements were additionally supplemented by existing design guidelines, e.g., the interaction principles according to DIN EN ISO 9241-110 [6] and the principles of information presentation DIN EN ISO 9241-112 [7].

2.4   Phase 3: Develop Design Solutions that Meet the Requirements of the Use

A total of three prototypes were developed. After the first two designs, a further iteration loop was required in each case because the evaluation had not led to satisfactory results, e.g., because initial layout proposals did not match the requirements or buttons could not be easily operated. The three design solutions are referred to hereafter as early design, refined design, and concretized design.

Based on the usage requirements, we developed initial solution ideas. This resulted in the following functions for the information and knowledge platform to be developed:

- Clear clustering of relevant information for maintenance staff in order to minimize search efforts
- Support in the information provision procedure
- Support for internal communication.

The early design was primarily used to develop the information architecture and the interaction design. In contrast, the refined design was responsible for the design of the page structures and the user interface (each based on interactive mock-ups). Finally, the concretized design also included a functional prototype. Evaluation tests accompanied the entire prototyping process. While the first two designs were evaluated based on feedback gathered at workshops, a user experience evaluation took place for the third design. User experience describes all aspects that result from using an interactive system for the users, e.g., feelings, emotions, usability, and fit [1]. For this purpose, the meCUE 2.0 questionnaire was used, which allows a modular collection of user-centered assessments in the experience of interactive technical products [14]. Figure 1 shows the refined design.

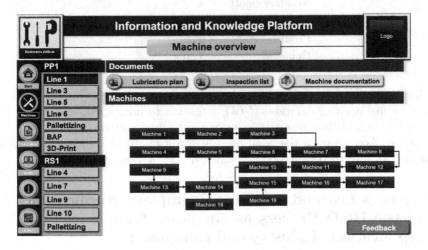

Fig. 1. Screenshot of the refined design

2.5   Phase 4: Evaluate from the User Perspective

In the final evaluation, the workers tested the user interface, the interaction, and the functionalities included in the concretized design on a task basis. Workers were first asked to interact freely with the system during a five-minute interaction phase before they completed the tasks which led them through the entire system.

To gather feedback, users were asked to share their impressions and wishes by thinking aloud, followed by a short interview. After performing the tasks, the user experience was surveyed using an adapted version of the "meCUE 2.0 questionnaire" developed by Minge [14]. The questionnaire has a modular structure consisting of central aspects of user experience. The users rate the statements on a Likert scale from 1 (completely disagree) to 7 (completely agree). The statements allowed to draw conclusions about usefulness, usability, visual aesthetics, perceived emotions of the users in positive and negative terms, system loyalty, and intention to use. Finally, users are asked to give an overall assessment of the system on a scale ranging from "−5" to "5" [14]. Fifteen maintenance workers took part in the evaluation. This resulted in the following ratings (Table 1):

Table 1. Assessment of the user experience according to meCUE 2.0

Dimension	Average rating
Usability	6.33
Usefulness	6.50
Visual aesthetics	6.06
Positive emotions	5.61
Negative emotions	1.42
Intention to use	5.78
Product loyalty	6.06
Cumulative	4.30

Good ratings were obtained for usability (6.33), usefulness (6.50), visual aesthetics (6.06), positive emotions (5.61), intention to use (5.78), and system loyalty (6.06). In addition, negative emotions were predominantly denied to occur during use. According to the good overall rating (4.30) as well as the feedback expressed around the evaluation, we finished the HCD process.

3 Lessons Learned from the Exemplary Application of the HCD Process as Guidance for Future Applications Industry and Conclusion

Applying the human-centered design process has also resulted in various lessons learned for the authors. They will be described in the following.

Throughout the HCD process, a change in the workers' opinion regarding the approach itself was discernible. It was perceived as abstract when it was first presented, but after a detailed explanation and providing examples of the process and possible results, the skepticism and passivity changed to acceptance and active participation.

– *Lesson 1:* Initial explanation of the HCD approach and associated goals leads to acceptance and participation.

During phases 1 and 2 of the HCD, workers were asked to complete two questionnaires. The first questionnaire had a high response rate (92%). The second questionnaire, on the other hand, had a much lower response rate (56%). After conversations with the workers, it turned out that the time needed to complete the first questionnaire was perceived as too long, so some of them refused to participate in the second questionnaire. A perceptible change in acceptance and cooperation could also be observed in the definition of the usage requirements. Workers showed increased participation by focusing on concrete scenarios from their everyday work.

- *Lesson 2:* An inappropriate level of frequency or duration of the surveys leads to less participation.
- *Lesson 3:* Orientation of the surveys close to the actual use case leads to acceptance and participation.

At the beginning of the HCD, many workers feared the consequences of giving honest feedback. There was an explicit fear that individual opinions on specific topics would be brought directly to the attention of supervisors and that this would lead to negative consequences.

- *Lesson 4:* A central prerequisite is removing workers' fear of expressing their opinions, leading to participation.

Due to availability issues of the workers, an intensive participation of the workers was challenging to implement. Besides, the required release from their regular work should be settled in advance with the team leaders. A successful human-centered design presupposes that workers are willing to participate actively. Accordingly, it should be clarified in advance to what extent it makes sense to involve which workers.

- *Lesson 5:* Provide careful resource planning in advance to ensure workers to participate, as cancellations at short notice are to be expected.
- *Lesson 6:* Select workers on a voluntary basis to ensure that they are willing to participate actively.

In conclusion, we can state that the theoretical potentials of HCD were also recognizable in the practical application case. At the same time, however, sensible use of the method is essential to balance the costs and effort associated with its application and the resulting benefits. This is reflected in the lessons learned recorded. Such lessons learned appear to be helpful for users of an HCD, as usually no specific implementation recommendations are given. This is where the present work can make a significant contribution. Its limitations lie primarily in considering only a single application example and, consequently, the low variety of the methods used. For future applications, we aim to further focus on the research question of an adequate fit of specific methods for specific phases and user groups of the HCD to enhance the quality of its results.

Acknowledgements. The authors would like to thank the University of Bremen for funding the independent postdoc project "Human Factors in Hybrid Cyber-Physical Production Systems" by the University of Bremen's Central Research Development Fund.

References

1. Alben, L.: Quality of experience: defining the criteria for effective interaction design. Interactions. **3**(3), 11–15 (1996)
2. Becker, T.: Prozesse in Produktion und Supply Chain optimieren. Springer, Berlin; Heidelberg (2005). https://doi.org/10.1007/978-3-540-77556-0
3. Birtel, M., Ruskowski, M.: Developing and implementing human-centered information services in a modular production environment. Proc. Manuf. **51**, 592–597 (2020). https://doi.org/10.1016/j.promfg.2020.10.083
4. Boy, G.A.: The Handbook of Human-machine Interaction. Ashgate, Farnham Surrey England; Burlington VT (2011)
5. Dieninghoff, M.: Der Job Diagnostics Survey (JDS). In: Zur Berücksichtigung motivationaler Faktoren im Qualitätsmanagement, pp. 71–81. Springer, Wiesbaden (2014). https://doi.org/10.1007/978-3-658-06290-3_5
6. DIN 9241–110: DIN EN ISO 9241–110 Ergonomics of human-system interaction - Part 110: Interaction principles (ISO 9241–110:2020) (2020)
7. DIN 9241–112: DIN EN ISO 9241–110 Ergonomics of human-system interaction - Part 112: Principles for the presentation of information (ISO 9241–112:2017) (2017)
8. DIN 9241–210: DIN EN ISO 9241–210 Ergonomics of human-system interaction - Part 210: Human-centred design for interactive systems (ISO 9241–210:2010) (2010)
9. Hackman, J.R., Oldham, G.R.: Development of the job diagnostic survey. J. Appl. Psychol. **60**(2), 159 (1975)
10. Heinecke, A.M.: Mensch-Computer-Interaktion. Springer, Heidelberg (2012). https://doi.org/10.1007/978-3-642-13507-1
11. Koenig, C.: Analyse und Anwendung eines menschzentrierten Gestaltungsprozesses zur Entwicklung von Human-Machine-Interfaces im Arbeitskontext am Beispiel Flugsicherung. Dissertation, Technische Universität Darmstadt, Darmstadt (2012)
12. Kurosu, M. (ed.): HCD 2011. LNCS, vol. 6776. Springer, Heidelberg (2011). https://doi.org/10.1007/978-3-642-21753-1
13. Merkel, L.A.: Einführung kognitiver Assistenzsysteme in der manuellen Montage. Dissertation, Technische Universität München, München (2021)
14. Minge, M., Thüring, M., Wagner, I.: Developing and validating an English version of the meCUE questionnaire for measuring user experience. Proc. Human Factors Ergon. Soc. Ann. Meet. **60**(1), 2063–2067 (2016)
15. Pruitt, J., Grudin, J.: Personas: practice and theory. In: Proceedings of the 2003 Conference on Designing For User Experiences, pp. 1–15 (2003)
16. Quandt, M., Stern, H., Zeitler, W., Freitag, M.: Human-centered design of cognitive assistance systems for industrial work. Procedia CIRP **107**, 233–238 (2022). https://doi.org/10.1016/j.procir.2022.04.039
17. Stegmann, S., et al.: Der Work Design Questionnaire. Zeitschrift für Arbeits- und Organisationspsychologie A&O **54**(1), 1–28 (2010). https://doi.org/10.1026/0932-4089/a000002
18. Stern, H., Becker, T.: A variable low-cost platform for conducting work design experiments. In: CEUR Workshop Proceedings, vol. 2009, pp. 126–130 (2017)
19. Stern, H., Becker, T.: Influence of work design elements on work performance and work perception - an experimental investigation. Proc. CIRP **72**, 1233–1238 (2018). https://doi.org/10.1016/J.PROCIR.2018.03.077

A Study on Mobile APP Icon Design Based on the Hamilton's Principle

Jungho Suh[✉]

Gachon University, Seongnam-Daero 1332, Republic of Korea
hoseo@gachon.ac.kr

Abstract. Hamilton's principle, also known as the principle of least action, states that natural systems composed of moving particles, as studied in classical mechanics, move in a direction that minimizes their Kinetic Energy (KE) and Potential Energy (PE). In other words, natural systems move along the shortest path. Icon designs in mobile game APPs with a high degree of physical activity depict objects descriptively and disrupt the balance of vertical and horizontal lines to convey incomplete Kinetic Energy. Conversely, icon designs in social media APPs use simple shapes and colors to convey a company's symbolic energy while maintaining a precise balance of vertical and horizontal lines. This study aims to classify types of action-inducing icon designs based on Hamilton's principle, distinguishing them by Kinetic Energy (KE) and Potential Energy (PE), and deriving Symbolic Energy (SE) as a new axis, to propose a design strategy for application icons that trigger users' optimized behavior. The study found that game APP icons more strongly represent incomplete Kinetic Energy elements compared to social media APP icons. As a result, game APP icons strongly express movement through the game player's appearance and incomplete Kinetic Energy, while social media APP icons strongly express the company's symbolism through logos, colors and shapes and complete Potential Energy as Symbolic Energy.

Keywords: Hamilton's Principle · Mobile APP Icon Design · Lagrange Equation Design · Symbolic Energy

1 Introduction

This study proposes that by using Hamilton's principle as a framework for designing Affordance icons, more intuitive and effective interfaces can be created for users. Hamilton's principle is one of the principles used in physics, which refers to a system moving along a Hamilton's path following the principle of least action. [1] Action refers to the quantity associated with the momentum of an object moving for a fixed time and is used to describe the motion state of a physical object. This principle is generally referred to as the principle of least action or the Hamilton-Jacobi equation. [2] Hamilton's principle is an important concept applied in various fields of physics. For example, in classical mechanics, Hamilton's principle can be used to predict the motion of objects, and in quantum mechanics, it can be used to describe the changes in the wave function over

C. Stephanidis et al. (Eds.): HCII 2023, CCIS 1832, pp. 147–153, 2023.
https://doi.org/10.1007/978-3-031-35989-7_18

time. In computer science, Hamilton's principle is used to find solutions to optimization problems through the brute-force method of the Hamilton's algorithm. Thus, Hamilton's principle is an important concept not only in physics but also in various academic fields.

In this paper, I tried to apply Hamilton's principle to smartphone APP icon design to research methods of improving efficiency and intuitiveness in interface design. Hamilton's principle is a concept used in physics to explain motion, which calculates movement based on the position and momentum of objects. If applied to APP design, it can be used to design interfaces based on the dynamic changes caused by movement and the size and position of interface elements. [3] In this study, I explored APP icon designs that applied imperfect movement with tilted incomplete elements of Kinetic Energy in game icons and symbolic elements of positional energy in general APP icons. I propose principles for efficient and intuitive mobile APP icon design through our research.

2   Theoretical Background

The Hamilton's principle, following the Lagrangian equation, explains the motion of an object based on the conservation of momentum and energy. [4] It uses a generalized coordinate system that represents the object's motion state and induces the object's motion using two types of energy: Kinetic Energy and Potential Energy, which represent the object's motion state. [5].

First, Kinetic Energy is the energy that an object possesses while in motion. It is proportional to the object's mass and velocity. In other words, the more massive the object, the more Kinetic Energy it has, and the faster the object moves, the more Kinetic Energy it has. According to the Hamilton's principle, the object's Kinetic Energy can be expressed as a function of its momentum (p) and velocity (v). Therefore, the object's Kinetic Energy can be expressed as follows: Here, E_k is Kinetic Energy, p is momentum, m is the object's mass, and v is the object's velocity.

$$E\_k = (1/2) * p^2/m = (1/2) * m*v^2$$

On the other hand, Potential Energy is the energy that an object possesses by virtue of its position. It is related to the object's position, and Potential Energy varies depending on how high the object is positioned or how much mechanical tension it possesses. For example, the higher an object is positioned, the greater its Potential Energy, and if an object expands due to a constant mechanical tension, its Potential Energy also increases. According to the Hamilton's principle, the Potential Energy of an object can be expressed as a kind of potential function related to the object's position. Therefore, the Potential Energy of an object can be expressed as follows, where E_p is the Potential Energy, V is the potential function related to the object's position, and x is the object's position.

$$E\_p = V(x)$$

Therefore, the total energy of an object can be expressed as the sum of its Kinetic Energy and Potential Energy, $E = E\_k + E\_p = (1/2) * p^2 / m + V(x)$. Generally, when the state of a system changes, there is a mutual transformation between Kinetic Energy and Potential Energy, and the sum of the two remains constant. Based on this principle, the visual representation of smartphone icons also creates a balance between kinetic and Potential Energy, inducing an aesthetic tension between incompleteness and completeness. For example, the game APP icon with high Kinetic Energy generates incomplete Kinetic Energy and induces physical behavioral interaction of users. In contrast, the social media APP icon eliminates incomplete kinetic elements and stimulates the formation of users' psychological image by utilizing Potential Energy of symbolic elements.

3 Method

Mobile APP Download Data Collection. Using Data.AI[1], I collect APP download ranking data for global users who use AOS and IOS from January 1, 2023 to February 28, 2023 for two months. The collected data is categorized into game APPs and general APPs, and the top 10 APPs in each category are derived.

Mobile APP Icon Image Analysis. The image analysis utilizes Google's Vision AI technology[2], which applies Vertex AI Vision algorithms. This technology can analyze image attributes through pre-trained APIs using automatic Machine Learning (AutoML) trained by Google. The Vertex Vision AI algorithms include various pre-built models, such as image classification, object detection, and semantic segmentation. These models are trained on large datasets and use deep learning techniques such as convolutional neural networks (CNNs) to automatically recognize and categorize visual patterns within images. Using Vision AI, I analyze the top 10 icon designs that are categorized into game APPs and general APPs (Mainly composed of social media APPs.). to objectively extract individual attributes.

Mobile APP Icon Geometry Analysis. To assess the balance of game APPs and social media APPs icon graphics, an analysis of their vertical and horizontal alignments is performed. Typically, deviations from vertical and horizontal alignments generate high Kinetic Energy, which, according to Hamilton's principle, yields incomplete Kinetic Energy and imbues objects with a sense of motion. Such incomplete Kinetic Energy enhances the total Kinetic Energy of the equilibrium system combining Potential Energy, thereby inducing intuitive user behavior. To evaluate the balance of mobile APP icons, the inclination of each graphic depicted in the icon is measured.

4 Results

From January 1st to February 28th, 2023, the top 10 downloaded APPs among global users using AOS and IOS for two months were as follows. The icons on the left of the image below are the top 10 mobile game APPs. The icons on the right are the top 10 downloaded APPs worldwide, excluding games, and it is noteworthy that most of the APPs are social media. Therefore, in this study, I decided to refer to them as game APP icons and social media APP icons, respectively.

---

[1] Data.AI. Adopted by https://www.data.ai, Accessed 18 Mar 2023.

[2] Cloud Vision API. Adopted by https://cloud.google.com/vision/docs/drag-and-drop, Accessed 18 Mar 2023.

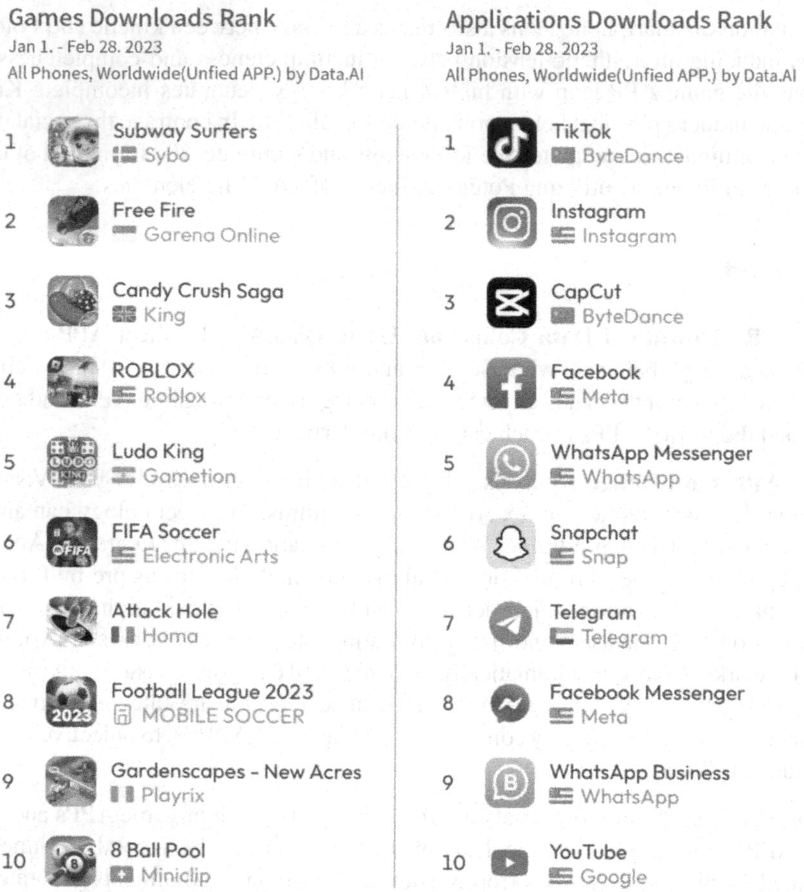

Games Downloads Rank
Jan 1. - Feb 28. 2023
All Phones, Worldwide(Unfied APP.) by Data.AI

1		Subway Surfers Sybo
2		Free Fire Garena Online
3		Candy Crush Saga King
4		ROBLOX Roblox
5		Ludo King Gametion
6		FIFA Soccer Electronic Arts
7		Attack Hole Homa
8		Football League 2023 MOBILE SOCCER
9		Gardenscapes - New Acres Playrix
10		8 Ball Pool Miniclip

Applications Downloads Rank
Jan 1. - Feb 28. 2023
All Phones, Worldwide(Unfied APP.) by Data.AI

1		TikTok ByteDance
2		Instagram Instagram
3		CapCut ByteDance
4		Facebook Meta
5		WhatsApp Messenger WhatsApp
6		Snapchat Snap
7		Telegram Telegram
8		Facebook Messenger Meta
9		WhatsApp Business WhatsApp
10		YouTube Google

Fig. 1. Screen of data collection of download rankings for 2 months using DATA.AI.

Based on this, I used Google Vision AI to analyze the labels of the game APP icons and social media APP icons. In the label analysis of game APP icons, except for Ludo King, many of them directly described nature and objects such as food, hoods, capsules, sports, football, clouds, and people in nature. On the other hand, the APPs composed of social media had many labels describing the symbols of the company, such as font, color, and shape (Table 1).

The next analysis was on the vertical and horizontal arrangement of the icons. Except for Ludo King, the top 9 game APP icons caused incomplete Kinetic Energy by deviating from the vertical and horizontal standards. On the other hand, most of the social media APP icons, except for WhatsApp and Telegram, did not deviate from the vertical and horizontal standards. Furthermore, WhatsApp and Telegram maintained geometric balance at 45 degrees and -45 degrees, respectively.

Using radar charts, I visualized the slope of each group. Overall, it was found that game APP icons had higher slope values compared to social media APP icons.

Table 1. Icon label analysis result of each APP groups.

APP	Title	Label analysis
Games	Subway Surfers	Vertebrate 92%, Blue 91%, Mammal 85%
	Free Fire	Hood 92%, Automotive Tire 91%, Automotive Lighting
	Candy Crush Saga	89%
	ROBLOX	Food 86%, Font 79%, Cloud 78%
	Ludo King	Cloud 95%, Photograph 94%, Sky 94%
	FIFA Soccer	Font 83%, Rectangle 83%, Symbol 72%
	Attack Hole	Sports Equipment 92%, Sports Uniform 91%, Jersey
	Football League	90%
	Gardenscapes	Capsule 95%, Paint 82%, Drinkware 81%
	8 Ball Pool	Sports Equipment 94%, Soccer 94%, Football 92%
		Toy 87%, Leisure 76%, People in Nature 75%
		Billiard Ball 97%, Pool 94%, Sports Equipment 93%
Non-Games (SNS)	TikTok	Font 84%, Electric Blue 75%, Magenta 75%
	Instagram	Rectangle 88%, Font 82%, Magenta 77%
	CapCut	Symbol 75%, Logo 71%, Triangle 66%
	Facebook	Blue 91%, Font 78%, Cross 78%
	WhatsApp Messenger	Rectangle 84%, Font 81%, Symbol 75%
	Snapchat	Yellow 85%, Symbol 71%, Circle 63%
	Telegram	Azure 90%, Electric Blue 76%, Parallel 70%
	Facebook Messenger	Symbol 77%, Magenta 74%, Sign 63%
	WhatsApp Business	Font 80%, Symbol 76%, Signage 71%
	YouTube	Rectangle 77%, Logo 68%, Magenta 67%

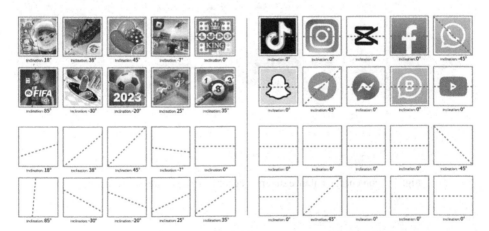

Fig. 2. A vertical and horizontal arrangement analysis of APPs.

The game APP icon designs, which embody physical activity, mostly express high Kinetic Energy (KE) through incomplete slopes, while social media APP icon designs are expressed through energy that emphasizes the corporate identity, such as shape and color. The icon designs represented in social media APPs have a Symbolic Energy (SE)

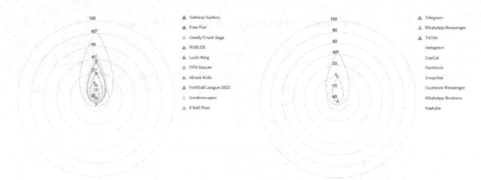

Fig. 3. Vertical and horizontal arrangement analysis of APPs using radial chart.

that includes Potential Energy (PE), as shown in Fig. 4, which is added while moving from T1 to T2.

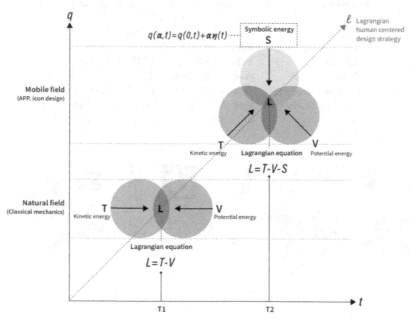

Fig. 4. Icon energy balance diagram according to Hamilton's principle.

5 Conclusion

In a study on smartphone APP design using the Hamilton's principle, it was found that designing icons by considering both Kinetic Energy and Potential Energy is important. Specifically, the study surveyed icon design for game APPs and social media APPs, which were categorized by their global mobile APP download rankings.

The study found that game APP icons more strongly represent incomplete Kinetic Energy elements compared to social media APP icons. This design approach, which considers both Kinetic and Potential Energy, is in accordance with the Hamilton's principle. Game APP icons strongly express movement through the game player's appearance and incomplete Kinetic Energy (KE), while social media APP icons strongly express the company's symbolism through logos, colors, shapes and complete Potential Energy (PE) as Symbolic Energy (SE).

Therefore, designing icons using the Lagrangian equation based on the Hamilton's principle is a more fundamental approach to reaching users' psychology. These research results are expected to contribute to the understanding and improvement of smartphone APP design.

References

1. Hamilton, W.R.: On a General Method in Dynamics. Richard Taylor, United Kingdom (1834)
2. Jacobi, C.G.J.: CGJ Jacobi's Vorlesungen über Dynamik. G. Reimer (1884)
3. Jungho, S., Soonkyu, J., Soojin, J.: A study on user engagement through improving UX·UI design for Tip-offs news service on mobile. J. Commun. Des. **67**, 88–98 (2019)
4. Lagrange, J.L.: Mécanique Analytique. Vol. 1. Mallet-Bachelier, 3 (1853)
5. Lagrange, J.L.: Mécanique analytique. Vol. 2. Mallet-Bachelier, 5–6 (1855)

Automated Tools Recommendation System for Computing Workshops

Ya-Chi Tien[✉], Teng-Wen Chang, and Shih-Ting Tsai

National Yunlin University of Science and Technology, Yunlin, Taiwan
doristien1208@gmail.com

Abstract. Workshops are a very common mode of interaction for team learning, and depending on the type of workshop, there are different ways of interaction and questions. In digital media workshops, design and computation coexist, but the logical conflict between them is always difficult for designers to understand and master. In the research team's previous study, we found that designers often had difficulty combining their imagination with the computational tools we were given at the time of the workshop, or not sure what tools could help them. In a multi-person workshop, it is difficult for the facilitator to take care of both the activity and the participants, resulting in an increased burden on the facilitator and a decrease in the participants' willingness and self-confidence to engage in computation.

In the previous study, we tested and adjusted the interaction process of the workshop and developed a new workshop process. In this study, we took the role of the facilitator as the main part, the scenario as the computing workshop, and the user as the designer. The process of the previous study was used as the base concept for the next iteration of the system, for which we designed a model of the workshop support system.

After the participants have gone through the design thinking process, they put their design ideas into the system, and after a set of natural language processing, the system can suggest the participants' computational tools based on the data, and provide them with the direction to choose the right tools for their ideas.

The system should also be able to make iterative corrections and learn from the iterative corrections in the original prescribed route to generate new answers. Through machine learning, the system can automatically learn and update, and can switch between different computational workshops more freely, so that the results can be more flexible.

Keywords: Workshop System · Machine Learning · Design Computing · Computing Thinking

1 Background

1.1 Digital Workshop for Designers

In the field of digital media design, the relationship between computation and design is inseparable, and interdisciplinary collaboration and learning are common. However, for designers, it is more difficult to analyze problems and tasks using computational methods

© The Author(s), under exclusive license to Springer Nature Switzerland AG 2023
C. Stephanidis et al. (Eds.): HCII 2023, CCIS 1832, pp. 154–161, 2023.
https://doi.org/10.1007/978-3-031-35989-7_19

due to a lack of information-related knowledge. We have organized many workshops related to computational themes, which can promote communication and mutual learning among participants. By using workshops that combine digital media, participants can experience how computational technology can accelerate and assist designers in creating and developing [1]. However, the logic between design and computation is different, and in such conflicts, designers are easily confused and unsure of how to understand or approach the problem from a computational perspective.

1.2 The Predicament for Facilitator

In the computation workshops we have conducted, the participants are mainly students in the field of digital media design, with their main abilities being design-related, and their understanding of computation varying in depth. This is difficult for the workshop leader to control as we cannot immediately grasp the difficulties and ideas of all participants while also controlling the overall process execution. When faced with questions from multiple participants, it may be difficult for the workshop leader to answer every question, especially when there is only one workshop leader, resulting in uneven resource allocation for each participant, which can affect their learning.

1.3 AI and Workshop

Machine learning can be used to mimic human intelligence and behavior patterns [2], and can be used to predict outcomes and help users find answers. In the research of GObot [3], it is also mentioned that using AI to develop brainstorming workshops can enable more effective communication among participants, as well as establish unresolved issues and propose methods and techniques for participants who are also designers. In workshops, many data are generated, including environmental factors, objects, and human reactions, and AI can assist in analyzing this data to help facilitators and participants make decisions. Through AI's continuous learning ability and the experience data gathered from each workshop, we can try to provide participants with more answers and decisions in the context of the workshop.

2 Literature Review and Related Works

2.1 Computing Thinking

Design and computation are two different thought processes. Among the many ideas generated by designers, they are equivalent to producing a large amount of data. Computation can assist designers in summarizing this vast amount of data, allowing designers to describe the content more clearly [4].

At first glance, computational thinking may seem only important for computer science professionals, but it is more about thinking than computation [5]. The key is how to efficiently process the project. Computational thinking is a problem-solving approach that involves breaking down complex problems into smaller, more manageable pieces and can be applied to a wide range of problems in everyday life. It is an important skill that can help individuals approach complex problems with a structured and logical approach, leading to more effective decision-making.

2.2 AI Drawing

AI drawing is the ability to draw images based on the sentences provided by the user. After undergoing natural language processing, these data are used to draw corresponding images. AI drawing allows users to collaborate with AI, such as Storydrawer [6], which can transform the stories described by users into drawings, and generate abstract sketches that have semantic similarity with existing story content. This promotes participants' creativity and detailed ideas, and creates an engaging visual narrative experience.

In addition to drawing, designers can also use this tool to quickly produce the desired appearance (Fig. 1), allowing the imagined textual description to be presented as an image. This makes communication more convenient and effectively speeds up the communication and correction process.

Fig. 1. Designers use the AI drawing tool Midjourney to help them present their ideas as images by transforming them from text to visual representations.

2.3 ChatGPT

ChatGPT (Fig. 2) is an artificial intelligence language model created by OpenAI, based on the GPT-3.5 architecture. Through extensive database training, ChatGPT has acquired a wide range of knowledge. It provides a language interface with outstanding conversational and reasoning abilities across multiple domains, making it attractive to various fields [7]. It significantly enhances productivity and offers advantages in many fields [8].

According to Baki Kocaballi's research [9], ChatGPT effectively performs tasks assigned to it as a designer, user, or product, providing the most appropriate response. ChatGPT can provide various assistance to designers from conception to development, such as providing concepts and inspiration, assisting in data analysis, content creation, and helping to accelerate the development and testing process while making the process more automated.

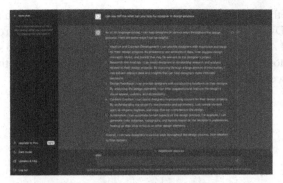

Fig. 2. ChatGPT.

3 Literature Review and Related Works

3.1 Research Methods

In the preliminary research, we developed a new workshop process (Fig. 3) through personas and user journey mapping. The process is divided into three parts: design ideation, technology integration, and implementation and testing. Each part has different AI systems for assistance, and although information flows between them, they do not interfere with each other.

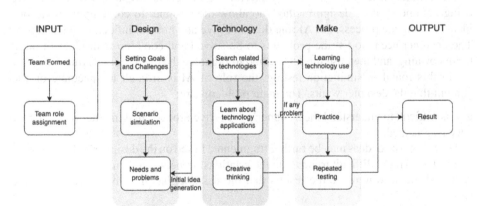

Fig. 3. DTM (Design, Technology and Make) Workshop System flow design.

In this study, we focused on how designers can use AI to assist them in developing strategies and feasible technologies or tools during the design ideation stage. This will serve as a method for our workshop support system, starting from the design perspective, using different design methods as references, and moving towards computational thinking to find a balance point.

We simulated three different methods (Fig. 4) in this study: (a) Brainstorm & KJ (b) Short answer (c) Dismantling & Reassembly, with information background researchers playing the role of AI systems. We attempted to help designers develop strategies, model presentations, or tools based on the ideas provided by designers and the conditions set in the workshop scenario.

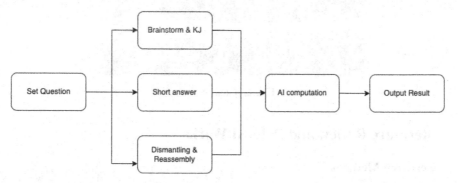

Fig. 4. Three different methods flow.

3.2 Initial Thoughts of Workshop Support Tool: Brainstorm and KJ

In the simulation test, we first set a topic for the designer, and started brainstorming using commonly used design methods to allow the designer to come up with various ideas. During the process, the AI role does not give any hints to influence the designer. The designer needs to list the problems to be solved and come up with ideas through brainstorming, and then use the KJ method to organize the divergent information.

In this round of simulation testing, the role of AI is difficult to speculate on the content that the designer wants. The main problems are:

a. It is difficult to understand the designer's deductive process, making the words appear very fragmented.
b. The categorized ideas may be further fragmented based on the designer's classification method, making it difficult to imagine the relationship between them.
c. It is difficult to imagine the results that the designer has in mind based on simple words.

Since this method allows the designer to constantly diverge and then organize, if the designer's thinking process is not clear, it may be difficult to connect the points together. However, this method is not completely without advantages. When the designer performs KJ organization, some redundant information will be cleared, which can reduce the interference of useless data.

3.3 Short Answer Question

In order to increase the amount of data that can be calculated, in the second round of testing, we adopted the method of brainstorming. This time, we asked designers to describe their ideas in simple sentences to replace short words. Designers proposed solutions to various problems, but because the sentences were too brief, it was still difficult to understand their thinking when trying to break them down. In addition, when the description was ambiguous, it was difficult for the engineering team to come up with ideas, and more questions and answers were needed to deduce the answers. Compared to the first approach, we obtained more data and were better able to generate imagination.

3.4 Dismantling and Reassembly

From the previous section's use of simple sentence descriptions, we found that this method was able to better capture the designer's ideas because there was a clear description. Therefore, in this round, we asked the designers to describe using a puzzle approach. For one of the questions, they imagined it as putting together a puzzle and broke it down into individual puzzle pieces, describing each step. After going through these steps, they could achieve the result that the designer had imagined. (Fig. 5).

Fig. 5. We try to have designers break down their ideas into individual steps and write them down.

This method not only provides more design details, but also helps designers present their ideas clearly and think through them by breaking them down into modules, streamlining the process, and ensuring that the final design result meets expectations. In addition, this way of thinking can also help designers communicate more effectively with the team, improve team collaboration efficiency, and achieve better design results.

During the breakdown process, we also found that the designers would produce unnecessary content, and filtering this content made the overall content more organized. Therefore, we have summarized the process of this approach based on the above (Fig. 6).

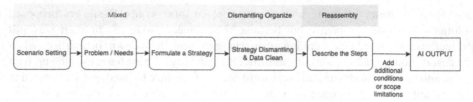

Fig. 6. The workshop flow what designer do in design part.

4 Conclusion

In design work, both computational thinking and design thinking are essential. Computational thinking refers to using logical, analytical, and reasoning methods to solve problems, while design thinking refers to using creative methods to solve problems. Both of these thinking methods are crucial because designers need to consider multiple factors such as user needs, design functionality, and aesthetics when working on a design project. Integrating computational and design thinking can help designers solve complex problems in their work.

One effective way to integrate these thinking methods is through the use of a "puzzle" design approach. This approach involves breaking down the design process into specific steps, with each step represented as a puzzle piece. By piecing together these steps, the designer can gradually build the final design outcome.

This puzzle design method offers several advantages. Firstly, it provides more design details, ensuring that designers can consider problems from different perspectives. Secondly, by breaking down the design process into modules, designers can streamline the process and ensure that the final design outcome meets expectations.

References

1. Neiman, B., Bermudez, J.: Between digital and analog civilizations: the spatial manipulation media workshop. In: Proceedings of ACADIA (1997)
2. Cakmak, M., et al.: Exploiting social partners in robot learning. Auton. Robot. **29**, 309–329 (2010)
3. Chang, C.-C., Chang, T.-W.: Ontology extraction and generation for supporting affinity diagram workshops: GObot. In: The 2022 International Conference on Taiwan Institute of Kansei and Taiwan Association of Digital Media Design, pp. 141–149. National Taitung University, Taitung, Taiwan (2022)
4. Liao, H.-T., Chang, T.W., Lai, I.-C.: Storytelling: a computational approach for convergent thinking (2010)
5. Li, Y., et al.: Computational thinking is more about thinking than computing, pp. 1–18. Springer (2020)
6. Zhang, C., et al.: StoryDrawer: a child–AI collaborative drawing system to support children's creative visual storytelling. In: Proceedings of the 2022 CHI Conference on Human Factors in Computing Systems (2022)
7. Wu, C., et al.: Visual ChatGPT: Talking, Drawing and Editing with Visual Foundation Models. arXiv preprint arXiv:2303.04671 (2023)

8. Dwivedi, Y.K., et al.: "So what if ChatGPT wrote it?" Multidisciplinary perspectives on opportunities, challenges and implications of generative conversational AI for research, practice and policy. Int. J. Inf. Manage. **71**, 102642 (2023)
9. Kocaballi, A.B.: Conversational AI-Powered Design: ChatGPT as Designer, User, and Product. arXiv preprint arXiv:2302.07406 (2023)

Empower Product Designers in Enterprises to Leverage Data as Creative Compass to Drive Innovation

Kratika Varma[✉]

ServiceNow BV, Amsterdam, Netherlands
kratika.varma@servicenow.com

Abstract. Large-scale user experience evaluation faces new obstacles as ServiceNow continues to roll out new platform services while enhancing data-informed product decision-making, but it also has new opportunities. Enterprise applications have a significant demand for user-centered metrics that may be used to track development toward key goals and inform product choices. A Design Thinking workshop, generative interviews, and naturalistic observation with a wide range of user profiles were utilized to blend outcome-based goals with a process that is based on carrying out experiments. A UII framework for user-centered metrics and a way for connecting product goals to metrics on contextual dashboards were conceptualized to emphasize the impact of user experience on product strategy.

Keywords: Metrics · Platform Analysis · Enterprise Products · Data Informed Decision · Human Centered Design Process

1 Introduction

To manage the complexity of enterprise product usecases, it is difficult for product designers to advocate for their creative design choices. Subjectivity and personal biases introduced early in the design process result in a creative "value gap" [1] and an ill-defined measure of the designer's contribution to the company's vision and product strategy.

ServiceNow was eager to invest in a scalable solution to streamline business operations and provide its product teams more power by enabling them to work more effectively while making data-driven product decisions. In close collaboration with internal stakeholders, pilot research utilizing human-centered methodologies was carried out to re-define the key business metrics [2] harmonizing with corporate strategies. To further test the theory with personas involved in product decision-making, an analytical dashboard was created. This made it easier to comprehend how each persona uses data insights to validate creative ideas, gauge the effectiveness of their work, improve results, analyze customer behavior, and develop greater intelligence. The "context of use" was recognized as a crucial driver for product designers to close the "value gap" to successfully utilize the usage data. As an outcome, a framework was designed, as a toolkit to

C. Stephanidis et al. (Eds.): HCII 2023, CCIS 1832, pp. 162–168, 2023.
https://doi.org/10.1007/978-3-031-35989-7_20

guide product designers to use three data measures – 'point of inquiry', 'design metric' and 'variable of visualization' to create contextual dashboards to reflect the impact of user experience on product strategy.

2 Research Methodology and Frameworks

To raise awareness about product usage analysis, the product development team had first conversations over remote calls with internal business stakeholders, product managers, product designers, engineers, and data scientists. Discussions about internal procedures, difficulties, the desired state, and high-level end user touch points were sparked by this. They were documented as the basic business process flow and the initial user journey (see Fig. 1). While this made it easier to get a head start on the issue, the personas, models for collaboration, duties, and difficulties were still not well understood. Due to this, a 3-day in-person design thinking workshop [3] was organized and carried out, which involved brainstorming, group discussions, and naturalistic observation [4] with product managers, business executives, and leadership. An analytical dashboard was designed to further test the notion with personas involved in product decision-making (see Fig. 2).

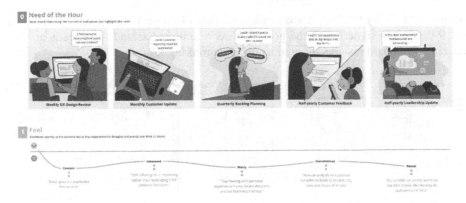

Fig. 1. User journey

Fig. 2. Analytical dashboard

2.1 Testing Procedure and Results

Formative usability testing [5] was conducted with 14 product managers, 5 developers and 9 product designers with the goal to observe and understand their needs around utilizing dashboard insights for product decision making (Fig. 3).

	Home	Search Metric	Export	Metric Detail	Metric Analysis	Dashboard: Overview	Dashboard: Key features	Dashboard: Events
Deepta	1	3	1	2	2	3	3	3
Ram	1	3	1	2	2	2	2	2
Daniel	1	3	1	3	3	3	2	2
Stefano	1	3	1	3	2	2	1	2
Olga	1	2	1	2	2	2	2	2
Chiarng	1	2	1	2	2	2	1	2
SUM	6	16	6	14	13	14	11	13

3: User can perform task quickly and met the needs   >12 Worked as expected
2: User can perform task with probe and suggests minor enhancements   8–12 Can be enhanced
1: User can perform task, but has some struggles or other expectations   < 8 Needs attention

Fig. 3. Task completion matrix based on value, context relevance and intuitiveness.

2.2 Overall Outcome

The significance of self-configured dashboards as a result to show the influence of product/feature performance dependent on context of use (see Fig. 4). Was the key insight to consider for next steps. The need for a technique that combines qualitative and quantitative measures to study user experience of a feature or product to represent the impact of user experience on product strategy was felt by product designers (Table 1).

Table 1. End user research learnings

Themes	Learnings
Context of use	A customized strategy based on the collaboration model was required to increase user engagement
Self service	Data on consumption based on objectives for user-specific collaboration
Adaptive insights	Persona based insights, relevant to the context of use, providing relevant adaptive insights as the point of inquiry

Usage patterns and metrics were analyzed, and inferences were made to put these discoveries into a framework that would help design teams put the ideas into practice as they transition through different phases of design process.

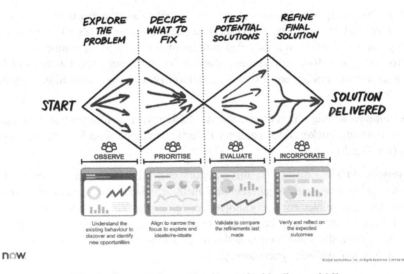

Fig. 4. Context of use mapping on double diamond [6]

3   UII Framework

Usability, Intuitiveness, and Investment, or UII, is a design metric framework that was conceptualized as a toolkit to help product designers assess the quality of the user experience and offer data that can be used to take appropriate action. These three categories are available for design teams to choose from and mix to spark their creativity and get ready to develop their contextual dashboards. To expedite the conceptual stage of dashboard creation, each bucket includes "design measures," "visualization functions," and "point of inquiry". To align business impact, each "design measure" is mapped to the identified key business metrics, suggestive visualization function. It is not always suitable to use metrics from every bucket, but using the framework as a guide can help designers decide explicitly whether to include or exclude a certain measure.

A straightforward approach was created that guides design teams through defining the objectives of a product, feature, or service, identifying the signs of success, and then creating precise metrics to monitor on a contextual dashboard.

3.1 Design Measures

Unless a measure explicitly links to an outcome that drives business result and can be used to track progress towards that objective, it is unlikely to be useful, regardless of how user-centered it may be. Finding the product's or feature's objectives is the first step, particularly in terms of user experience. What duties must users carry out? What aims does the design hope to accomplish? Utilize the "design measures" to promote the articulation of outcomes (e.g. is it more crucial to draw in new users or to motivate current ones to engage with your content more?).

Usability. Product quality for this category is described as "the extent to which a product or feature can be used by specified users to achieve specified goals with effectiveness, efficiency and satisfaction in a specified context of use" [7]. To operationalize it, suitability for the task, self-descriptiveness, conformity with user expectations, suitability for learning, controllability, error tolerance, suitability for individualization [8] needs to be considered.

UII framework categorizes effectiveness, efficiency, error tolerance and ease of use as part of usability bucket. Each category is further mapped with key business impact metrics (see Fig. 5).

Intuitiveness. Product quality for this category can fulfil human needs and motivate human beings since aesthetic objects contain intrinsic value that is higher than functional value [9]. They are related to purely subjective elements of the user experience, such as satisfaction, aesthetic appeal, likelihood of recommendation, and perceived usability. It is possible to track the same measures throughout time to see progress as changes are made with a broad, well-designed survey.

UII framework categorizes attitude, emotion, and aesthetics as part of usability bucket. Each category is further mapped with key business impact metrics (see Fig. 5).

Investment. Product quality for this category is described as "is the question of whether the functionality of the system in principle can do what is needed" [8, p. 25]. Operation aspects can cater to identity management, relationship management and information management [10].

UII framework categorizes utility, engagement, acquisition, and satisfaction as part of investment bucket. Each category is further mapped with key business impact metrics (see Fig. 5).

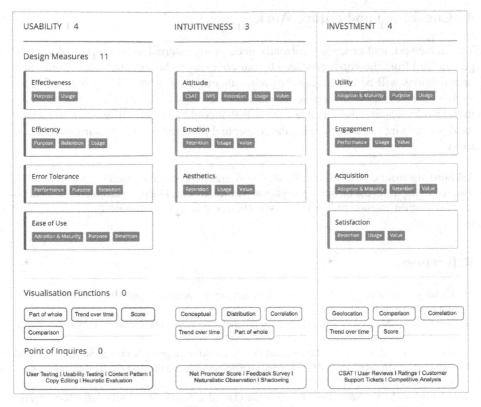

Fig. 5. UII framework

3.2 Visualization Functions

Data visualizations are an essential component of a data analysis since they can efficiently summarize vast volumes of data in a graphical format. One of the most challenging tasks in the analytical process is choosing the proper representation to employ for your data. Certain types of functional measures are matched with each bucket to help designers make an easy choice. The style of data visualization required to describe the product, feature, or functional usage for a given usecase on a contextual dashboard might be driven by these pertinent criteria (see Fig. 5).

3.3 Point of Inquiry

Cross-functional teamwork is crucial to the role of the product designer as they go from one design phase to the next. To achieve a certain outcome, a specific activity must be aligned with each engagement with a stakeholder. This is a "point of inquiry," according to UII. It is advised to combine "design measure" and "Visualization Function" for each framework bucket to create a contextual dashboard with research related to the "point of inquiry" (see Fig. 5).

4   Conclusion and Future Work

The framework and procedure currently undergoing internal testing to be sufficiently generalized from the goods produced by our company to be sure that teams from other organizations will be able to reuse or adapt them. We also intend to promote further study of metrics based on massive amounts of behavioral data. There are a few concepts in the works that are also tangible cue cards that could strategically assist in triggering the designer's mental model during the conceptual phase of product, feature, or function study.

Acknowledgements. Aida Rikovic Tabak, Giu Vicente, Robert-Jan Barmentloo, and other advisors, leadership from the Platform Analytics at ServiceNow [11] helped establish the foundation of data informed decision-making culture via self-served contextual dashboards.

References

1. Closing the value gap. https://www.accenture.com/_acnmedia/pdf-108/accenture-closing-data-value-gap-fixed.pdf
2. KeyBusinessMetrics. https://discover.mixpanel.com/rs/461OYV624/images/Guidetoproductmetrics-Mixpanel.pdf
3. Thoring, K., Muller, R.M.: Understand design thinking: a process model based on method engineering. In:International Conference on Engineering and Product Design Education, City University, London, UK (2011)
4. Angrosino, M.V.: Naturalistic Observation (1st ed.). Routledge (2007). https://doi.org/10.4324/9781315423616
5. Jos, N.: Formative Evaluation of Software Usability: A case study, 5th International Conference on ICT Applications (AICTTRA). https://www.researchgate.net/publication/323259268_Formative_Evaluation_of_Software_Usability_A_case_study
6. Double Diamond. https://www.designcouncil.org.uk/our-work/skills-learning/the-double-diamond/
7. ISO 9241-11, E.: Ergonomische Anforderungen für Bürotätigkeiten mit Bildschirmgeräten - Teil 11: Anforderungen an die Gebrauchstauglichkeit. Leitsätze. Beuth Verlag, Berlin (1998)
8. Nielsen, J.: Usability Engineering. Morgan Kaufmann (1993)
9. Tractinsky, N.: Does Aesthetics Matter in Human-Computer Interaction? Mensch and Computer 2005: Kunst und Wissenschaft – Grenzüberschreitung der interaktiven Art, pp. 29–42. Oldenbourg Verlag, Seiten, München (2005)
10. Zerfaß, A., Welker, M., Schmidt, J.: Kommunikation. Halem Verlag, Partizipation und Wirkungen im Social Web (2008)
11. https://www.servicenow.com/products/performance-analytics.html

The Scope and Analysis of Design Methodologies for User Experience in Interaction Design

Yichen Wu[✉]

China Academy of Art, Hangzhou 310025, People's Republic of China
wuyc@caa.edu.cn

Abstract. The era of the digital revolution promotes the new need for design in HCI to optimize the user experience in virtual or physical products. Therefore, the development of methods for how to design these intelligent products is an emerging issue. This paper focuses on the methodologies for user experience in interaction design, and it is the research part for generating new design methodologies for digital products. In order to extract the feature of potential design methodologies, the research illustrates the traditional approach, which includes Interaction Design and User Experience Design with the interpretation of the specific process, and methods, to have a sound understanding of them and the state of the art. Meanwhile, from the point of view of business, the emerging markets and users lead to the new form of design methodologies is the significant evolution in the design field, including Agile, Lean UX and design sprint. They are another critical part of this research.

Keywords: Design methodology · Digital Products · User experience

1 The Overview of Design Methodology

1.1 Problem-Guided Design Methodology

The design methodology is a wide-ranging concept, Nigel Cross defined it is the study of the principles, practices and procedures of design in a rather broad and general sense, it includes the study of how designers work and think; the establishment of appropriate structures for the design process; the development and application of new design methods, techniques, and procedures; and reflection on the nature and extent of design knowledge and its application to design problems [1]. It emphasizes the design process, and its primary focus is to develop a deep and practical understanding of the design process and how this process can be modified, made more effective and transparent and be managed to achieve sustainable design outcomes [2]. Hence, the design methodology is focusing on the process, methods and tools in the design.

1.2 Design Methodology in Digital Era

Meanwhile, the design methodology is a general term, and it could be referred by any design field, such as Architectural Design, Engineering Design, Industrial Design, and so

C. Stephanidis et al. (Eds.): HCII 2023, CCIS 1832, pp. 169–175, 2023.
https://doi.org/10.1007/978-3-031-35989-7_21

on, there is should be an entry point to begin the study of design methodology entirely and efficiently. With the Computer Revolution since the 1970s, GUI which is the interface of the software, it appeared as the new object for designers, and designers walked into a new field and played more critical roles since that era. Interaction designers sought inspiration and expertise not only from traditional design fields but from psychology, sociology, communication studies, and computer science.

Since the Internet appeared in the 1980s, the design methodology faced the problem of the consequence by the new technology, designers thought about the methods and tools for understanding the customers or users. In the contemporary era, with the enormous progress of information technology, the design methodology is developing into the third generation. It treats design as a "new" research discipline, which is becoming from one discipline to an interdisciplinary subject, and new design methodologies are emerging from the technology-related area, such as software development.

2 The Typical Design Methodologies for User Experience

2.1 The UCD Design Methodology

UCD is the short term of User-Centered Design, it originated by Donald Norman in 1980s, and he recognizes the needs and the interests of the user and focuses on the usability of the design [3]. From the name of UCD, the user is a critical element in it. A core component of the user-centered design process is exploring practical ways to communicate with users. UX is one of the many focuses of UCD; it includes physical and emotional reactions in the user's entire experience of the product. UCD calls for involving users throughout the design process via a variety of research and design techniques to create highly usable and accessible products for them. It is a methodology used by developers and designers to ensure they are creating products that meet users' needs by concerning the UX in each phase of the design process, and it involves much more than making applications aesthetically pleasing [4].

In the UCD, there are no strict rules to limit the number and the way of employing the methods by practitioners. The user is the research object, the process and methods are adopted for better understanding the user by collecting the information, opinions and feedback from the user. The specific adoption and organization of diverse methods in the process have to depend on the project. It makes the designer have a deeper understanding the physiology, psychology, communication of the user when they are using the technology products. UCD involves the user into every stage in the design process. Generally, the methods of UCD include personas, scenarios, use cases, focus groups, usability testing, card sorting, participatory design, questionnaires, interviews and prototyping.

2.2 The GDD Design Methodology

GDD (Goal-Directed Design) was developed by Alan Cooper et al. in later of the 20th century. It is a kind of behavior-oriented design, providing a complete process for understanding users' goals, needs, and motivations [5]. It intends to answer the questions in the interaction design, such as how people use products, especially the products with user behaviors; and making more efficiency in translating research results into design solutions. Alan Cooper describes the GDD seeks to bridge the gap that currently exists in the digital product development process-the gap between user research and design through a combination of new techniques and known methods brought together in more effective ways.

In terms of design process and methods, GDD is a more complex and complete methodology than UCD. It takes a long term and requires resources to understand the users thoroughly and find the connection between users and products by diverse investigate activities. GDD employs both fictitious and actual user model construction methods, e.g., personas and ethnography. GDD asks why the user must perform those tasks or activities, to understand what value, purpose, or meaning the tasks or activities have for the user [6]. The main purpose of practitioners to adopt the GDD understands the motivation and objective of the user, thereby to find the best solution from several possibilities. The final solution should create the user experience to fit for the user's behavior and habit by concerning the context, environment and scenario. Goal-directed design commitment to user goals, to achieve user objectives and meet customer needs, not contradictory [7].

3   The Emerging Design Methodologies

With the popularity of interaction design and the research of user experience, the user desire of the innovative products' features, functions changing into a new level, it is speeding up the frequency of the product iteration to satisfy the market requirements immediately. Therefore, the new form of design methodologies is the significant evolution in the design field, especially the user experience and interaction design. There are several methodologies and approaches which could represent the new generation of design methodology, including the Agile, Lean UX and design sprint. They are related to the design process, project management or company organizations, to solve the problem such as financial constraint, resource shortage or time press.

3.1   Agile

Agile is the short name of Agile software development, as the name implies, it is a professional terminology in the software development field. In brief, it is a human-centered, iterative, step-by-step development approach, and it is a flexible process that allows developers to change direction during the project and quickly respond to changing circumstances. The Agile methodology looks for a form that contributes more value to the processes and decision making in the development. In Agile development, the construction of the software project is divided into several sub-projects, and the outcomes of each sub-project will be tested, with integrated and operational features.

Agile development does not pursue the perfect design and coding in the initial stage. Instead, it strives to develop out the core functions of the product in a short period and release the available version as soon as possible. Then, iteratively upgrades and improves the products according to the requirements in the subsequent production period.

The Agile emphasize the solid object, testable MVPs (Minimum Viable Products) are required from the beginning to the end. It could make the developers find the shortages of the design in time, thereby to take actions to generate solutions immediately, thus to make the product better and better. Additionally, compared to the waterfall approaches in software development, the Agile makes the process into a procedure with sequential sprints, the iteration is continuously conducting. This feature of the principles makes the process more efficient to test with less risk, and the practitioner could calmly deal with the uncertainties in the entire approaches. Through the analysis of these two main features and comparing to the Agile, the shortcoming of the traditional process is obviously, the evaluation and testing are usually in the final stage of the design process. It causes the problem finding in the last stages either, which possibly makes all the uncertainties together, it makes the project have risks in the final period, to impact the efficiency. However, time and resource are the most crucial issues for a project.

Although the Agile is a methodology for software development and design, software and physical products have a difference in mass production and marketing, it related to the connected object design, since the software is part of these smart products and the interaction is the primary factor as well as the user experience. Consequently, the Agile has the reference value for the connected object design methodologies. Meanwhile, Agile is the basic and component of some emerging methodologies, such as lean UX and design sprint.

3.2 Lean UX

By the development of Agile, there is a terminology named "Lean" to address the relevant approaches, and Lean UX is the name for a set of principles worked in lean start-ups, where the companies apply the Agile as the methodology in their projects. Instead of thinking of a product as a series of features to be built, Lean UX looks at a product as a set of hypotheses to be validated. In other words, we don't assume that we know what the user wants [8]. For instance, the Leaner conduct customer interviews and research to develop a hypothesis about what a customer might want, and then they test that hypothesis in various ways, especially MVPs to see if they were right. Moreover, they keep doing that every time we make a change to the product.

Meanwhile, comparing to traditional UX, Lean UX is more practical; it focused on the experience under design instead of deliverable documents. Lean UX is the practice of bringing the true nature of a product to light faster, in a collaborative, cross-functional way that reduces the emphasis on thorough documentation while increasing the focus on building a shared understanding of the actual product experience being designed [9]. It emphasized to obtain feedback from users and to make quick decisions as early as possible. The nature of Agile development is to work in rapid, iterative cycles and Lean UX mimics these cycles to ensure that data generated can be used in each iteration.

By the research of Lean UX, we can find the Lean UX is an efficient methodology to design a product compares to traditional design methodologies, such as the UCD, GDD, although it produces for the software development at the beginning. Time-consuming and design waste are the primary argument between Lean UX and traditional UX. Lean UX shorten the traditional design process which based on many deliverables by MVPs, to create a minimum complete product, and use it to collect the feedback, then to iterate and so on. Furthermore, Lean UX is focused on using assumption and validating hypotheses to know the users, thus to refine the product and to improve it.

In conclusion, Lean UX is a methodology for designers and developers to adapt to the rapidly developed market and the growing need of users. What will happen if we apply it for connected objects design?

3.3 Design Sprint

Like Lean UX, Design Sprint is another extension of Agile. A design sprint is a flexible product design framework that serves to maximize the chances of making something people want. It is an intense effort conducted by a small team where the results will set the direction for a product or service [10]. It generated by GV (Google Venture) almost around one decade ago, it is also a methodology for efficient design. More specific, the sprint is GV's unique five-day process for answering crucial questions through designing, prototyping and testing ideas with customers as little investment as possible in as real an environment as possible. It's a "greatest hit" of business strategy, innovation, behavioral science, design, and more—packaged into a step-by-step process that any team can use [11]. Besides software design, the Design Sprint also come from the industrial design, especially by the emergence of digital product design that desires immediate refinement to test and iterations to release follow the need of users. By the definition of Design Sprint by GV, in a sprint process, the designers can shortcut the endless-debate cycle and compress months into five days, almost a single week. In these days, designers can find out the future product situation and the users' reactions in such short time by prototypes, instead of using Idea-Build-Launch-Learn process, which is time consuming and resource waste.

Through the understanding of the process, we can find it is a simple approach from the perspective of phase and activity numbers. It is also could be a methodology to solve business problems through design. With the sprint feature, it helps the companies reduces risk, such as the time, financial resource, which used to refine the process to get them thinking from users, which is an expensive and complicated phase before developing a new product by usual approaches, after all, it just cost five or six days.

By the testing of prototypes, designers can get the first-hand knowledge of real users or customers, and the feedback is valuable not only because of the facticity but also for the timeliness. Above all, data is valuable in this era, especially for emergency service and production industry, such as technology and the Internet; experts from diverse disciplines compose the team of Design Sprint, it makes all the activities and process are running completely, designers, engineers, users, operators etc. advise from diverse perspectives to generate a considerate product, despite it is just in the initial phases concerning the entire product development process.

The Design Sprint promotes business issues. The Design Sprint is an agile and fast methodology for designers can validate the business idea or product functionality, which depends on the inspiration from the experts. Once the Design Sprint methodology is internalised, it can be used and coordinated with other processes that have already been established in projects or businesses.

4   The Scope of Design Methodologies for Interaction Design

4.1   The Classic of Traditional Design Methodologies

UCD and GDD are the standard design methodology in the design field, both of them developed around two decades, and the Industrial Design developed almost one century. With the feature of connected objects, the technology promotes the changing of products' forms and functions, and it pushes the user to the center of the design. As a design methodology, UCD more like a guideline for other approaches when concerning the user study, while GDD is the complete methodologies in terms of the process and methods. UCD should be the guiding principle in the research stage. That design should be in the overall use of goal-directed design. In the early research stage, using UCD concepts can be more objective and accurate.

Meanwhile, as the consequence of the bloom of IoT, the requirements and context for designers and producers are evolving. Time, resource, policies, such factors are becoming dynamic and valuable for companies in the competitive market and industrial environment, thereby, the efficiency and effect of the design methodology are put into a higher level at present. In order to satisfy these new requirements, several new design methodologies emerged for IxD and UX design-related products from the software development field. They emphasize the efficiency by using high-frequency iterations and rapidly assumptions and verification process. However, with the virtual feature of the software, it cannot be adopted to the design of connected objects directly since it is a physical product which cannot be iterated in several days. Therefore, the design methodology of connected objects should combine the advantages of both the traditional and emerging design methodologies, to concern the user, the physical product, the digital service and the efficiency of the design process.

Innovation is the driven force for the world at present and future, not only for the great purpose, such as society or human wellbeing but also for the more practical goals, the benefit of the company, the satisfaction of the human needs. The digital service, intelligent products are the crossroad to creating new kind of products and also concern the users and commercial value. Building innovative products, processes, and business models requires a new approach to management in general and project management in particular [12]. For instance, when designers employ the standard design methodologies such as UCD to design an interactive product, its design process divides the develop period into several phases, in which the interface design and its implementation are in a settled sequence.

4.2   The Appropriate Employment of Emerging Design Methodologies

Besides the standard methods which from traditional design methodologies, in the emerging design methodologies, Agile, Lean UX and Design Sprint presents some particular features, which could be referred to the design of interaction and user experience. Firstly, these new approaches employ fewer methods in their process to reduce the time, and they usually combine methods to create an efficient methodology and to achieve the goals, they pursue time-saving in the process. Thus, they generate some efficient methods, such as the Crazy 8's, the core method of Design Sprint to push participators sketching eight ideas in eight minutes.

Secondly, all of the emerging methodologies those I mentioned were originated from Agile; they focus on using the sprints to iterate the product from a rough one to a complete one. Therefore, the methods of testing phase should have the capability to make the user engage every time but easy to carry out, such as A/B testing, it is a way to collect the users' interactive data gradually.

Thirdly, the Agile related methodologies involve different roles for a product; usually, the team will include but no limit the experts from design, develop, business, technology, marketing, and so on. Compare to traditional approaches, the business has unprecedented engagement, and it participates the process in the very beginning phase. For instance, business model canvas, the golden path, future press release, these methods are employed to conduct the design from the perspective of the business. The initial participation of business makes the product more practical to survival in the market competition, and it also could lead the entire team concerning the success factor of business.

References

1. Cross, N.: Developments in Design Methodology. Wiley (1984)
2. Green, L.N., Bonollo, E.: The importance of design methods to student industrial designers. Global J. of Engng. Educ **8**(2), 175–182 (2004)
3. Abras, C., Maloney-Krichmar, D., Preece, J.: User-centered design. W. Encyclopedia of Human-Computer Interaction. Sage Publications, Thousand Oaks, Bainbridge **37**(4), 445–456 (2004)
4. Lowdermilk, T.: User-Centered Design: a Developer's Guide to Building User-Friendly Applications. O'Reilly Media, Inc. (2013)
5. Cooper, A., Reimann, R., Cronin, D.: About face 3: the Essentials of Interaction Design. John Wiley & Sons (2007)
6. Williams, A.: User-centered design, activity-centered design, and goal-directed design: a review of three methods for designing web applications. In: Proceedings of the 27th ACM international conference on Design of communication, pp. 1–8. ACM (2009)
7. Wei, C., Xing, F.: The comparison of user-centered design and goal-directed design. In: 2010 IEEE 11th International Conference on Computer-Aided Industrial Design & Conceptual Design 1, vol. 1, pp. 359–360. IEEE (2010)
8. Klein, L.: UX for Lean Startups: Faster, Smarter User Experience Research and Design. O'Reilly Media, Inc. (2013)
9. Gothelf, J.: Lean UX: Applying Lean Principles to Improve User Experience. O'Reilly Media, Inc. (2013)
10. Banfield, R., Lombardo, C.T., Wax, T.: Design Sprint: a Practical Guidebook for Building Great Digital Products. O'Reilly Media, Inc. (2015)
11. Knapp, J., Zeratsky, J., Kowitz, B.: Sprint: How to Solve Big Problems and Test New Ideas in Just Five Days. Simon and Schuster (2016)
12. Highsmith, J.R.: Agile Project Management: Creating Innovative Products. Pearson Education (2009)

Children's Ideal Nature-Related Digital Tools: A Co-design Experiment

Shengchen Yin[1]([envelope]), Dena Kasraian[1], Gubing Wang[2], Suzan Evers[1],
and Pieter van Wesemael[1]

[1] Department of the Built Environment, Eindhoven University of Technology, P.O. Box 513,
5600 MB Eindhoven, The Netherlands
s.yin@tue.nl

[2] Department of Medical and Clinical Psychology, School of Social and Behavioral Sciences,
Tilburg University, Warandelaan 2, 5037 AB Tilburg, The Netherlands

Abstract. Children living in cities are interacting less and less with their surrounding green spaces. It is argued that, while online digital games can decrease children's outdoor play, emerging digital technologies have the potential to motivate children's interaction with nature. However, children, who are the end-users of such tools, are hardly involved in their design process. Over the past two decades, children are increasingly being involved in urban and technological design, yet their participation in the design process has been rather passive. To address this gap, we explore the desired characteristics of digital tools for an ideal interaction with nature, from the perspective of children. We conducted an outdoor activity and a co-design workshop with 23 children aged 12–14 years from a secondary school in the Netherlands. The findings of this participatory design process indicate the design characteristics, requirements, functions, and usage of children's ideal digital tools that can increase their interaction with nature. Our findings are not only relevant for investigating the role of children as co-designers in the whole participatory technology design process, but also helpful for urban or digital intervention designers to improve child-friendly digital tools for ideal interaction with nature.

Keywords: Children · Co-design · Participatory design · Nature-related digital tools · Children-nature interaction

1 Introduction

Children and teenagers in cities are interacting less and less with nature and this is bad for their health. Meanwhile, the pervasiveness of digital technology has resulted in the emergence of various digital tools designed for children's interaction with nature [1]. Children are using interactive technology more frequently in the digital age. Besides, over the past two decades, the field of design research has shifted closer to the users, and children have more recently been involved in the design process since designers have grown more conscious of the significant insights and firsthand knowledge that children

C. Stephanidis et al. (Eds.): HCII 2023, CCIS 1832, pp. 176–181, 2023.
https://doi.org/10.1007/978-3-031-35989-7_22

can contribute to the design process [2]. Even though there is a growing interest in engaging children in the design of interactive technology, children are often involved only passively in the process [3].

The aim of this work is to explore the characteristics of children's ideal nature-related digital tools. Our research questions are:

- What are the potential design characteristics, requirements, and functions of an attractive digital tool that children think can motivate their interaction with nature?
- According to children's designs, how will children use their ideal nature-related digital tools in nature?

Here, nature-related digital tools are digital devices that support interaction with nature for children or adults, such as QR codes that can be scanned in nature or mobile applications that provide natural information in nature. Besides, design characteristics refer to the general traits and qualities that should be there to provide a good user experience; design requirements mean the specific needs and expectations that must be met; and design functions refer to specific purposes or uses that are designed to serve. In this study, we used the component of the COM-B model [4] and the model of children-UGI interaction (i.e., children's interaction with urban green infrastructure) [5] to structure children's designs in the co-design workshop.

2 Methods

We undertook two-day activities with a class from a secondary school in Rotterdam, the Netherlands. This study was approved by the Human Research Ethics Committee of the Eindhoven University of Technology. Child participants were recruited with their parents' consent as well as their own. All participants were informed about their data collection process, their participation, and their possibility to withdraw from the study at any time desired. In the end, a total of 23 children participated in the activities.

2.1 Procedure

On the 6th of March 2023, outdoor activity in nature was conducted. Children were invited to experience nature by using one of the existing digital tools for interacting with nature. After an-hour experience in nature, we gave them assignments and asked them to bring back for the next-day workshop. The aim of the assignment is to motivate children to reflect on their experience and prepare some ideas ahead of time. The assignment includes reflective questions about their experience of using this digital tool in nature and their opinions on whether this digital tool changes any of their abilities, opportunities, and motivation to interact with nature.

Then, on 7th March 2023, we conducted a co-design workshop with children to design prototypes for children's ideal nature-related digital tools. We organized this at the school, to ensure a familiar and safe environment. The design team consisted of 23 children. At the start, children were randomly divided into five teams of 4–5 participants, while two researchers and a teacher moved among groups.

The workshop started with a brief introduction to explain its aim and tasks. Children were then invited to design models for a digital tool in subgroups within approximately an hour. On each table, we provided children with four A3 or A2 papers to guide them to express, develop and document their ideas for a natural-related digital tool. The aim and slogan on the first page let children have an overview of their designed tools. On the second page, we asked the students to describe their tool's design characteristics, requirements, and functions. Besides, children were also invited to create interfaces of how their ideal nature-related digital devices communicate with them on page 3. Then on the last page of the paper, children can draw scenarios and rough sketches on a storyboard to describe their use of any type of digital device that interacts with nature. We invited children to use rough sketches to describe their ideal tools. Each team was also provided with pens, colored pencils, crayons, erasers, sticky notes, and plasticine for building their ideal models. Children could choose their preferred materials to express their thoughts. In the end, each group was asked to share and present their group ideas of their designs and prototypes in a three-minute presentation.

2.2 Data

Data collected from the co-design workshop included recordings of each group's presentation and the design output produced by the children. The recordings were translated and transcribed from Dutch to English in detail. Children's designed models, images, and texts were analyzed based on the COM-B framework [4] and the model of children-UGI interaction [5] to better understand the attractive digital tools that children think can motivate their interaction with nature. Here, the COM-B model is a behavior change framework with three behavior components which are capability, opportunity and motivation. Besides, the model of children-UGI interaction is a new model that captures a wide range of determinants related to children's behavior in nature (i.e., ability to independently move or play in nature, ability to understand or remember the natural environment, desire to interact with nature, feelings about decision making to interact with nature, and both social and physical opportunities to interact with nature). We used these two models to structure the co-design workshop and the findings.

3 Results

We transcribed the recorded group presentations to illustrate the ideas of children's designed tools. We also reported photo content analysis results as an added finding of the direction of their designed tools.

3.1 Design Characteristics, Requirements, and Functions

From these five groups' designs, all groups proposed that the aim of their designed tools was mainly focused on encouraging children and teenagers to go outside with a digital tool. The designs of their ideal tools were expressed from six aspects based on the COM-B model and the model of children-UGI interaction. The following Table 1 shows the

Table 1. Children's suggestions based on the COM-B model [4] and the model of children-UGI interaction [5].

The components of the COM-B model		Specific aspects of the model of children-UGI interaction	Suggestions from children
Capability	Physical capability	Ability to independently move or play in nature	· Emphasizing the importance of gamification in the form of awards or prizes to improve their independent ability (e.g., collecting points to move up to the rankings) · Adding safe and playful functions when using digital tools in nature
	Psychological capability	Ability to understand or remember the natural environment	· Showing digital stories, images, questions, and QR codes to provide information about nature
Motivation	Automatic motivation	Desires to interact with nature	· Adding interesting questions about nature · Helping to discover new things through digital tools
	Reflective motivation	How I feel about my decision-making to interact with nature	· Adding explanations about extinct plants or animals to the digital tools
Opportunity	Social-cultural environment	Social opportunities to interact with nature (e.g., social interaction with families, friends, and peers to play with in nature)	· Emphasizing the importance of competing with peers or family members in groups because they could share interesting information about nature
	Physical environment	Physical opportunities to interact with nature, such as natural features (e.g., it influences the access to nature, playing equipment and places for natural activities)	· Being notified of the questions when approaching a playground or any other play equipment

suggestions from the children about their designed tools' characteristics, requirements and functions based on these two models.

Children in groups gave more suggestions in terms of the ability to independently move or play in nature and desire to interact with nature, while children's suggestions were more singular and consistent in the other four aspects.

3.2 The Usage of Children's Ideal Nature-Related Digital Tools

Taking into account these design purposes, characteristics, requirements, and functions, each group created the potential interfaces for the tools and how they would use their designed tools in nature. Children's designs showed that the most frequently discussed topics are nature conservation, social opportunities, and incentives. One group emphasized the theme of nature protection in specific. They suggested middle interfaces with a search function to show the length of the journey, the difficulty of the process, and the current location on the map. Then they also demonstrated the final interface with questions about environmental conservation to encourage individuals to take the necessary actions to preserve nature. Additionally, some groups focused on mechanisms to share nature-related information with friends or families. One group drew a typical scenario, which showed that children could use their designed tools to share natural elements with others in an open chat. Another impressive point in their design was the reward mechanism. One group designed the points earned by using tools to complete a number of tasks in nature that could be redeemed at the end of their natural experience in a real point store. In general, children in groups generated interesting ideas and imaginations in designing tools for their activities in nature.

4 Discussion and Conclusion

This work explores the design characteristics, requirements, functions and usage of children's ideal nature-related digital tools. It outlines our vision of using digital technologies for encouraging children to explore nature outdoors.

In a technology design process, children can be involved in the design process in distinct roles, including a user, a tester, an informant, a design partner [6], or even a protagonist [7], a co-researcher [8], and a co-designer [9–11]. These roles can influence the creation of technologies. More specifically, the child is 'a user' when given a passive role in the design process or 'a tester' of initiative ideas when adults observe and learn from children's experiences. On the other hand, the child is 'an informant' when providing feedback at various points in the design process. Besides, a child is 'a design partner' when he or she is treated as an equal to the designer throughout the entire process. Additionally, treating the child as 'a protagonist' develops their capacity for introspection and makes them the main agents guiding the entire design process. Conversely, treating the child as 'a design partner' give the child an important role to play in collaborating with designers to create new technologies. Besides a co-designer's role, children's role in a design process can also be regarded as 'a co-researcher', which is developed to overlap researchers' and users' aspects. However, there is a relationship between co-researchers and co-designers. Children as co-researchers focus on more fundamental aspects of the research process (e.g., research question development, data collection and analysis) [8]. Compared to co-researchers, children as co-designers are centered on collaborating with participants to create a specific method or experiment [10]. In this co-design workshop, students were engaged in the technology design process mainly as co-designers, and we gave the children themselves the ownership of the design activities. This study showed that children were better involved in the entire technology design process.

There are several limitations to this study. First, this study was carried out in the context of the Netherlands. We obtained contextualized findings from children in the Netherlands, but it has not been generalized to all children worldwide. Therefore, more relevant research should be conducted. Another limitation of this study was the limited time available for the co-design workshop. When probed, all children expressed a desire to continue playing, designing, and brainstorming with group members. Thus, more time should have been given to the children in the design.

Overall, the objective of our study is to contribute to a child-friendly approach to children's interaction with nature. It will help urban or digital intervention designers to improve nature-related tools for children.

References

1. Wang, J., Komlodi, A.: Children's formal and informal definition of technology. In: ACM International Conference Proceeding Series, pp. 587–588. ACM Digital Library (2012)
2. Dudek, M.: Children's Spaces. Routledge (2005)
3. Palaigeorgiou, G., Sidiropoulou, V.: Can elementary students co-design the learning content of educational apps: the we! design!fractions participatory design approach. In: Auer, M.E., Tsiatsos, T. (eds.) CONFERENCE 2021, AISC, vol. 1192, pp. 202–214. Springer, Switzerland (2021)
4. Michie, S., van Stralen, M.M., West, R.: The behaviour change wheel: a new method for characterising and designing behaviour change interventions. Implement. Sci. **6**(1), 1–12 (2011)
5. Yin, S., Kasraian, D., van Wesemael, P.: Children and urban green infrastructure in the digital age: a systematic literature review. Int. J. Environ. Res. Public Health **19**(10), 5906 (2022)
6. Druin, A.: The role of children in the design of new technology. Behav. Inf. Technol. **21**(1), 1–25 (2002)
7. Iversen, O.S., Smith, R.C., Dindler, C.: Child as protagonist: expanding the role of children in participatory design. In: ACM International Conference Proceeding Series, pp. 27–37. ACM Digital Library (2017)
8. Spriggs, M., Gillam, L.: Ethical complexities in child co-research. Res. Ethics **15**(1), 1–16 (2019)
9. Stålberg, A., Sandberg, A., Söderbäck, M., Larsson, T.: The child's perspective as a guiding principle: young children as co-designers in the design of an interactive application meant to facilitate participation in healthcare situations. J. Biomed. Inform. **61**, 149–158 (2016)
10. Clark, A.T., Ahmed, I., Metzger, S., Walker, E., Wylie, R.: Moving from co-design to co-research: engaging youth participation in guided qualitative inquiry. Int. J. Qual. Methods **21**, 1–14 (2022)
11. Hjorth, M., Smith, R.C., Loi, D., Iversen, O.S., Christensen, K.S.: Educating the reflective educator: design processes and digital fabrication for the classroom. In: Proceedings of the 6th Annual Conference on Creativity and Fabrication in Education, pp. 26–33 (2016)

Technological Project Management Proposal for Designing a Social Robot

Mireya Zapata[1]([⊠]) [iD], Jorge Alvarez-Tello[2,3] [iD], and Hugo Arias-Flores[1] [iD]

[1] Centro de Investigación de Mecatrónica y Sistemas Interactivos - MIST, Universidad Indoamérica, Av. Machala y Sabanilla, Quito 170103, Ecuador
{mireyazapata,hugoarias}@uti.edu.ec
[2] Escuela Superior de Ingeniería, Tecnología y Diseño, Universidad Internacional de la Rioja (UNIR), Logroño, Spain
[3] Centro de Innovación Social y Desarrollo (CISDE), Quito, Ecuador
jorge.alvarez@cisde-ec.com

Abstract. Introduction: Social robotics is integrated into everyday activities, addressing social interactions with diverse groups of people. Therefore, the development of Autonomous Social Robot for Ecuadorian Universities (ASREU), an evolutionary social robotic platform in hardware and software that allows the exploratory research of social, technological, and energetic variables for the generation of social robotics prototypes. **Method:** To improve the management of the project, the structures for the development of technological projects are analyzed from the administrative management of the project, as well as the execution and technological implementation of the **Results:** A diagram is obtained to identify the interaction of technical, engineering and scientific working groups and the interaction with the project management, as well as a roadmap for the development of technological products defining the systems, the type of prototyping and the intellectual property protection, in addition to the circular strategy for the integration from and for society in the area of social robotics and the identification with the evolution of the prototype with the corresponding intellectual property protection for feasible results to **Conclusion:** Currently the development of technological projects lead mostly software developments in social robotics, when integrated with physical systems (mechanical, electrical and electronic), there is planning from traditional environments and agile environments, which need a coexistence to jump from one to another environment.

Finally, guidelines and tools have been developed to facilitate the management and design of social robots, in the case of ASREU, a 6 DoF and autonomous mobile robot (AMR).

Keywords: V-Model · Social Robotics · TRL · Intellectual Property · Technological Project Management

1 Introduction

Social robotics (SR) is integrated into everyday activities, addressing social interactions with various groups of people in rehabilitation, assistance, construction; concepts for social robots can be developed from prospective based on comics and define intelligent architectures oriented for fields such as autism, among others [1–4]. It also raises

C. Stephanidis et al. (Eds.): HCII 2023, CCIS 1832, pp. 182–188, 2023.
https://doi.org/10.1007/978-3-031-35989-7_23

human-machine co-innovation environments has a gradual evolution depending on the growth of machines and the adoption of management models, with intelligent systems that will allow it to replace various professions in complex environments. Creative capabilities will accelerate the functioning of innovation systems in the future between AI and innovation [5]. This calls for project manager profiles with specializations suited not only to technology with issues such as applications of cyber-physical systems, big data, artificial intelligence, and intelligent robotics in the management of time, cost, and quality of projects, but also to project management, progress tracking, real-time monitoring, and schedule estimation [6]. In the meantime, proposals are being developed that link information technology and security in projects to minimize inefficiencies and eliminate dangerous and unpleasant aspects by equipping workstations with technology [7]. At the same time, it must be established that in R&D departments whether in academia or industry, the activities done in this area can be of great use for future commercial projects such as education among others, giving a technological boost, so that adequate resource management can be an excellent tool for efficient and effective R&D management [8]. In addition, the joint development of industry and academia can transform the objectives of innovation with the transfer of knowledge and technologies leading to sustainable industry in the region and the possibility of jobs, as well as better education in technology at universities and increased social development [9]. There are other fundamental methodological aspects on which the design and development of mechatronic systems are based, the V model according to the VDI 2206 guideline, represents a logical sequence of tasks that relates the integration of systems for the management of agile or classic projects, where the integration of requirements engineering is explained in detail, which is very important for the correct definition of the project [10]. Similarly, technology transits between different areas of academia and industry at different times in the maturation from idea to prototype and then to product, so that depending on the technological maturation according to Technology Readiness Level (TRL), the information can be used to have better approaches to project management based on the preparation of technologies [11].

Therefore, the development of the Autonomous Social Robot for Ecuadorian Universities (ASREU) is proposed, an evolutionary social robotic platform in hardware and software that allows the exploratory research of social, technological, and energetic variables for the generation of knowledge. The interaction in the development of different methodologies is an important problem when hardware and software must be integrated in social environments, increasing development costs and the use of material or intangible resources in the materiality of this. Project research in robotic technologies is generally framed in terms of cost and quality and time management.

In addition to the management of technological projects from the planning phase, which in many cases are carried out with traditional methods and for the execution agile methodologies are used, where the definition is important to obtain the projected product. The whole project management is reduced to answer the following questions: How to have the design of the social robot planning from the concept as a starting point, with the considerations of prototype and evolution to product, for its corresponding intellectual protection and scientific innovation? How to integrate different methodologies to develop a framework that allows to have the global vision of the technological project in social robotics?

2 Method

Based on the bibliographic analysis by means of a systematic search in SCOPUS, details of improvements in the management of technological projects are identified, where the structures for the development of technological projects are analyzed from the administrative management of the project, as well as the execution and technological implementation of the project and its design. Then, the organization of the project is planned, using the V-model according to VDI 2206 as a methodological framework for mechatronic products, the technological maturity according to the Technology Readiness Level (TRL) scale for the design of non-destructive experiments (DoE) and the generation of controlled spaces in academic or research laboratories, as well as the experimental evaluation with social tests in public spaces that allow the generation of new knowledge applied to services that can be developed in social interaction with people. For the project management framework, good project management practices (PMBOK) and agile SCRUM projects (S-BOK) are merged, determining an initial planning for the development of technological projects in social robotics. Based on these tools, a roadmap is drawn up for the definition of work packages for the development of the technological project. With the TRL and V-Model scales, a graph is drawn up to identify the technological maturity of the prototype from proof of concept to manufacturing and market implementation. In addition, the issue of intellectual property and its management is also considered, without losing the novelty and originality.

3 Results

A simplified and more detailed diagram is obtained (see Fig. 1) to identify the interaction of the technical, engineering and scientific working groups and the inter-action with the project management, as well as a roadmap for the development of technological products defining the systems, the type of prototyping and intellectual property protection, as well as the circular strategy for integration from and for society in the field of social robotics and the identification with the evolution of the prototype with the corresponding intellectual property protection for feasible results of further innovation for the corresponding technology transfer to society.

The conceptual model with the technical and mechanical characteristics of the robot is also presented, as well as the reference schemes of the social characteristics of communication and gestures. People project qualities onto robots that are ethical issues of use and politics. When there is anthropomorphizing of the robot there are qualities for acceptance or not and the framing in certain contexts must be evaluated [12]. Strategies for the development of digital twins are integrated for both the logical and physical part. For the development of a cyber-physical model, data from a physical process and from psychology is used in the prediction or reflection in a cybernetic model. From this interaction we can improve the integration of the use of technology in the design of integrated modular construction with application in various sectors [13].

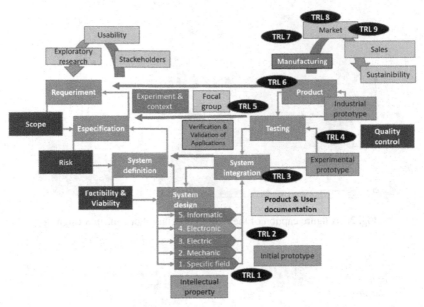

Fig. 1. A figure caption of the V-Model & TRL & IP for SR

The IT integration of the platform is shown in a general way for future implementation in the project. The conceptual model (see Fig. 2) has 3 DoFs for mobility, 3 DoFs for the positioning of the kinematic chains of the head that facilitate communication with people in the environment. Through the reproduction of biomechanical systems, it is possible to achieve systems that emulate anthropomorphic behavior in gestural communication for human-robot and robot-robot interaction [14], as well, The prototype requires meta-modelling to generate the CAD prototype and 3D printing of components that allow the head to be set up as a whole to facilitate non-verbal communication with different stakeholders [15]. Also on the platform, the integration of technology through the emulation interfaces helps for pattern recognition in people with disabilities in a bidirectional sense between human and robot [16] or apply literacy assessment tools proposed by the T.A.L.E. test, among others [17].

Additionally, there is the configuration of a chart for the evaluation of the technology evolution of the project, state of the development of knowledge and research, development and innovation that serves to identify the maturity of the prototype.

Below is also a summary of the planning in project management that will serve as a basis for the development of the project (see Fig. 3) [18]. Through technology assessment with focus groups, it is possible to determine the evolution of the technology from laboratory to commercial transition as in the case of SR Peper which has a TRL 6 and is currently commercialized, with a development of technology transfer for the transition from academia to industry [19].

In order to have a more accurate assessment of the TRL scale, it is necessary to consider the short- and medium-term generality levels for the IA integrating the robot systems [20].

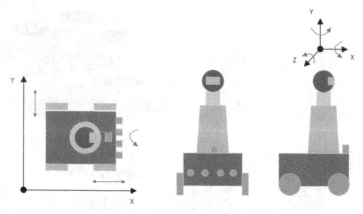

Fig. 2. A figure caption of the ASREU social robot concept design

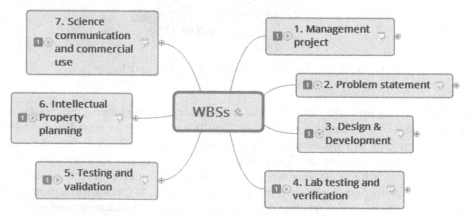

Fig. 3. A figure caption of the WBS for the social robot ASREU.

4   Conclusion

Currently, the development of technological projects mostly leads software developments in social robotics, when integrated with physical systems (mechanical, electrical and electronic), there is a planning from traditional environments and agile environments, which require coexistence to jump from one environment to another. Limitations have been given around the qualification of development teams to re-perform verification tests from the concept to the development of virtual prototypes with different types of organization, file nomination, versioning that do not facilitate the traceability of the product, among others.

A diagram analogous to the V-model has also been developed, which integrates different methodologies and serves as a trigger for processes that are integrated in the execution or implementation of a technological project in agile environments and which allows for an overview of its development, with the advantage of being able to better plan costs and the appropriate use of resources.

Finally, guides and tools have been developed to facilitate the management and design of social robots, in the case of ASREU, a robot with 6 DoF and autonomous navigation.

It is important to maintain as a minimum the definition of the problem and the context of application, as well as the impact on society. Technical requirements include the development of both hardware and software and the articulation of sensors and actuators with algorithms and software architectures. Ethical and societal implications must also be considered. Very important is the collaboration and strategic alliances both for the formation of multidisciplinary agile development groups, as well as laboratory and field test environments and even future investors.

Finally, a framework has been developed as a proposal for the development of social robots where the application of specialties with expertise in different fields, artificial intelligence, psychology, sociology, and human-computer interaction can be deployed, integrating the minimum conditions of development, intellectual property, and technological maturation for the development of the social robot. This research serves as a basis for further deepening in this field of social robotics and mechatronic system developments.

References

1. Dautenhahn, K.: Design spaces and niche spaces of believable social robots. In: Proceedings - IEEE International Workshop on Robot and Human Interactive Communication, pp. 192–197 (2002)
2. Šabanović, S., Chang, W.-L., Bennett, C.C., Piatt, J.A., Hakken, D.: A robot of my own: participatory design of socially assistive robots for independently living older adults diagnosed with depression. In: Zhou, J., Salvendy, G. (eds.) ITAP 2015. LNCS, vol. 9193, pp. 104–114. Springer, Cham (2015). https://doi.org/10.1007/978-3-319-20892-3_11
3. Fan, J., et al.: A robotic coach architecture for elder care (ROCARE) based on multi-user engagement models. IEEE Trans. Neural Syst. Rehabil. Eng. 25(8), 1153–1163 (2017)
4. Robins, B., et al.: Human-centred design methods: developing scenarios for robot assisted play informed by user panels and field trials. Int. J. Hum. Comput. Stud. 68(12), 873–898 (2010)
5. Botha, A.: A mind model for intelligent machine innovation using future thinking principles. J. Manuf. Technol. Manag. 30(8), 1250–1264 (2019)
6. Zhu, H., Hwang, B., Ngo, J., et al.: Applications of smart technologies in construction project management. J. Constr. Eng. Manag. 148(4), 04022010 (2022)
7. Yamamoto, H., Uesaka, K., Ishimatsu, Y., et al.: Introduction to the general technology development project: research and development of advanced execution technology by remote control robot and information technology. In: 2006 Proceedings of the 23rd International Symposium on Robotics and Automation in Construction, ISARC, pp. 24–29 (2006)
8. Mankins, J.: Three views of technology management: pull, push and strategic. In: International Astronautical Federation - 59th International Astronautical Congress 2008, IAC 2008, vol. 12, pp. 8001–8004 (2008)
9. Cox, D., Schönning, A.: Engineering education via robotics, mechatronics, and automation projects. In: 2006 World Automation Congress, WAC 2006 (2006)
10. Graessler, I., Hentze, J.: The new V-Model of VDI 2206 and its validation das Neue V-Modell der VDI 2206 und seine Validierung. At-Automatisierungstechnik 68(5), 312–324 (2020)

11. Ilas, C.: Technology readiness impact on high-tech R&D projects. UPB Sci. Bull. Ser. D: Mech. Eng. **75**(2), 241–250 (2013)
12. Darling, K.: Who's Johnny?. Anthropomorphic framing in human-robot: interaction, integration, and policy (2017)
13. Xie, M., Pan, W.: Opportunities and challenges of digital twin applications in modular integrated construction. In: Proceedings of the 37th International Symposium on Automation and Robotics in Construction, ISARC 2020: From Demonstration to Practical Use - To New Stage of Construction Robot, pp. 278–284 (2020)
14. Alvarez, J., Zapata, M., Paillacho, D.: Mechanical design of a spatial mechanism for the robot head configuration in social robotics. In: Ahram, T., Karwowski, W., Pickl, S., Taiar, R. (eds.) IHSED 2019. AISC, vol. 1026, pp. 160–165. Springer, Cham (2020). https://doi.org/10.1007/978-3-030-27928-8_25
15. Tello, J.A., Zapata, M., Paillacho, D.: Kinematic optimization of the robot head movements for the evaluation of human-robot interaction in social robotics. In: Di Nicolantonio, M., Rossi, E., Alexander, T. (eds.) AHFE 2019. AISC, vol. 975, pp. 108–118. Springer, Cham (2020). https://doi.org/10.1007/978-3-030-20216-3_11
16. Ramos, P., Zapata, M., Valencia, K., Vargas, V., Ramos-Galarza, C.: Low-cost human–machine interface for computer control with facial landmark detection and voice commands. Sensors **22**(23), 9279 (2022)
17. Zapata, M., Gordón, J., Caicedo, A., Alvarez-Tello, J.: Social robotic platform to strengthen literacy skills. In: Zallio, M., Raymundo Ibañez, C., Hernandez, J.H. (eds.) AHFE 2021. LNNS, vol. 268, pp. 143–149. Springer, Cham (2021). https://doi.org/10.1007/978-3-030-79997-7_18
18. Negrello, F., Stuart, H., Catalano, M.G.: Hands in the real world. Front. Robot. AI **6**, Article ID 147 (2020)
19. Fattal, C., Cossini, I., Pain, F., et al.: Perspectives on usability and accessibility of an autonomous humanoid robot living with elderly people. Disabil. Rehabil.: Assistive Technol. **17**, 1–13 (2020)
20. Martínez-Plumed, F., Gómez, E., Hernández-Orallo, J.: Futures of artificial intelligence through technology readiness levels. Telematics Inform. **58**, 101525 (2021)

Chaotic Customer Centricity

Benjamin Zierock[1]([⊠]), Asmar Jungblut[2], and Nicola Senn[1]

[1] SRH University Heidelberg, Ludwig-Guttmann-Straße 6, 69123 Heidelberg, Germany
benjamin.zierock@srh.de
[2] Asmaros GmbH, Carl-Friedrich-Gauß-Ring 5, 69124 Heidelberg, Germany

Abstract. Implementing innovative projects is critical for businesses to stay competitive and meet customers' changing needs. However, understanding and incorporating customer needs into the design process can be challenging using traditional methods. This has led to the emergence of new approaches, such as design thinking, which focuses on understanding customer needs and incorporating them into the innovation process. To overcome the limitations of traditional approaches and integrate unstructured information, the concept of "cluttered client orientation" has emerged. This paper examines how an iterative approach and customer journey mapping can achieve chaotic customer centricity and create successful innovations. The paper emphasizes the importance of incorporating customer needs into the innovation process and introduces the concept of "chaotic customer centricity" as a way to create successful innovations by using unstructured information.

Keywords: customer centricity · agile · design thinking · stacey matrix · story telling

1 Introduction

The challenge of implementing innovative projects lies in the generation of ideas and the development of concepts as well as their implementation. It is often difficult to understand the needs and expectations of users or customers and incorporate them into the design of a product or service. The design thinking approach is gaining in importance as it provides a way to better understand customer needs and take them into account in the innovation process.

In this context, the idea of "chaotic customer centricity" has emerged. The idea is based on the fact that user needs do not always fit into a rigid structure and that it may be necessary to use unstructured information to create successful innovations. To achieve this, the iterative approach can be used to create a customer journey to better understand the needs and wants of customers and integrate them into the innovation process [12].

2 Literature Review

Motivation of Our Work. This paper aims to explore innovative processes for the implementation of unresolved, chaotic projects that focus on user problem solving. It examines the relationship between the Stacey Matrix, the process of Design Thinking, the Hero's journey and customer centricity. Motivated users are often seen as a key success factor because they are more productive and engaged.

Identification and direct approach are often seen as critical success factors. This identification of factors requires a structure to be successfully implemented. Customer Centricity is a philosophy that encourages putting user needs and wants at the centre of your strategy [5].

The process of design thinking, on the other hand, is an approach that aims to solve complex problems by creating solutions that are focused on user needs [9]. An important method in this approach is the Customer Journey Map, which provides a detailed representation of the customer journey from start to finish. This type of map highlights important touchpoints between users and providers and helps identify potential problems and opportunities. By combining Customer Centricity and Design Thinking, projects can create a purposeful culture of innovation that enables them to develop innovative products and services tailored to their customers' needs [7, 10].

Method. This paper has been compiled through a systematic selection and analysis of relevant articles and other sources and aims to identify gaps, inconsistencies and areas for future research.

Literature review based on:

1. Planning the review: For this paper, a literature review will be conducted to analyze a set of articles related to the topic at hand. The literature review will follow a three-step process: planning, conducting, and summarizing. In the planning stage, the research question and objectives will be defined, relevant keywords and databases will be identified, and inclusion and exclusion criteria will be established.
2. Conducting the review: The conducting stage will involve a systematic search of the selected databases, screening of the identified articles based on the inclusion criteria, and data extraction from the included articles.
3. Summarizing the review: In the summarizing stage, the extracted data will be analyzed and synthesized to identify key themes, patterns, and insights across the selected articles. This literature review process will help to provide a comprehensive overview of the existing literature on the topic, and any gaps or inconsistencies in the research will be identified, as well as practical recommendations for future research in this area will be provided.
4. Creating graphics: Finally, with the creation of infographics based on the analyzed and synthesized data, the research findings can be effectively communicated to a broader audience, including policymakers, practitioners, and the general public. This will help to ensure that the research has a greater impact and contributes to the advancement of knowledge in the field (Tables 1 and 2).

Table 1. Inclusion and exclusion criteria.

Inclusion criteria	Exclusion criteria
Full text	Blogs, Website
Published	Non-published
Academic journals, books	Duplicates papers
Date published: 2015–2020	Date published: before 2015
Language: English, German	Language: other languages

Table 2. List of papers and sources.

Author	Title	Objective of study
Sowa, A. F., & Paauwe, J. (2015)	Sensemaking in strategic change: The Stacey matrix as a tool for understanding change processes. Journal of Change Management, 15(1), 21–37	The paper is concerned with the application of the Stacey matrix as a tool for improving understanding of change processes. The authors argue that the Stacey matrix helps to consider different perspectives and levels of complexity and thus provides a better basis for decision-making and action
Hopp, C., & Vargo, S. L. (2019)	The Stacey matrix and service ecosystems: insights and opportunities. Journal of Service Management, 30(4), 444–459	The paper explores how the Stacey matrix can be used to analyse and design service ecosystems. The authors argue that the Stacey matrix can help to understand the complexity of service ecosystems and take targeted action to improve performance. They use case studies to show how the matrix can be used in practice
Nicolini, D., & Monteiro, P. (2016)	The practice approach to hierarchy and heterarchy in organisation studies: A critical review and a way forward. Academy of Management Annals, 10(1), 237–274	The paper addresses the question of how hierarchies and heterarchies can be implemented in agile organisations at a practical level. The authors argue that the practice perspective is an appropriate concept for exploring hierarchies and heterarchies in organisations and offer a critical review of the existing literature on the subject

(*continued*)

Table 2. (*continued*)

Author	Title	Objective of study
Verhoef, P. C., Lemon, K. N., Parasuraman, A., Roggeveen, A., Tsiros, M., & Schlesinger, L. A. (2015)	Customer experience creation: Determinants, dynamics and management strategies. Journal of Retailing, 91(2), 253–270	The paper examines how customer experience is influenced by different elements, such as personnel, interaction and emotions. The authors also identify factors that can create a successful customer experience and provide recommendations for management
Lemon, K. N., & Verhoef, P. C. (2016)	Understanding customer experience throughout the customer journey. Journal of Marketing, 80(6), 69–96	The paper explores how to design the customer experience throughout the customer journey. The authors present various elements that can contribute to the design of a positive customer experience and provide recommendations for management
Parthasarathy, M., & Sohoni, M. G. (2018)	The impact of speed on customer satisfaction in e-commerce last-mile delivery. Production and Operations Management, 27(5), 959–976	The paper investigates how speed of delivery affects customer satisfaction in e-commerce. The authors show that fast deliveries can lead to higher customer satisfaction and provide recommendations on how companies can optimise their delivery processes to create a better customer experience
Vargo, S. L., & Lusch, R. F. (2017)	Service-dominant logic 2025. International Journal of Research in Marketing, 34(1), 46–67	The paper looks at the future of the service-dominant logic approach and shows how technologies such as artificial intelligence and the Internet of Things will change the customer experience. The authors argue that companies should align their technology strategy to create a personalised and individualised customer experience
Hommel, D., Goll, J. (2015)	Mit Scrum zum gewünschten System. Deutschland: Springer Fachmedien Wiesbaden	The book is a guide to using Scrum methodology for software development projects. The authors provide a step-by-step approach to implementing Scrum with the roles and responsibilities of the Scrum team, the Scrum events, and the artifacts used in Scrum

(*continued*)

Table 2. (*continued*)

Author	Title	Objective of study
Vogler, C. (2020)	The Writer's Journey: Mythic Structure for Writers (3rd ed.). Michael Wiese Productions	The book is a guide for writers to use the hero's journey, a storytelling framework popularized by Joseph Campbell, to craft engaging and effective stories. It explains the various stages and archetypes of the hero's journey, provides examples from popular films and literature
Kim, S. (2019)	An integrated approach of design thinking and customer centricity for organizational innovation. Journal of Open Innovation: Technology, Market, and Complexity, 5(3), 56	The paper explores the integration of customer-centricity and design thinking to promote organizational innovation
Michael Lewrick (2018)	Das Design Thinking Playbook: Mit traditionellen, aktuellen und zukünftigen Erfolgsfaktoren. Deutschland: Vahlen	The book provides an overview of the design thinking approach, which is a human-centered approach to problem-solving and innovation. It presents a step-by-step guide to applying design thinking in various contexts, such as product design, service design, and business model innovation

3   Conclusion and Future Work

3.1   Overall Result Evaluation of the Research

Chaotic structures are systems or organizations that are highly complex and uncertain, with a high level of complexity and uncertainty. Analyzing a chaotic structure can be a challenging task, as it involves understanding the various factors that contribute to the complexity and uncertainty of the system.

Here are some steps that can be taken to analyze a chaotic structure:

1. Identify the key components: The first step in analyzing a chaotic structure is to identify the key components of the system, such as people, processes, technologies, and other factors. This can help to better understand the interactions and dynamics within the system [4].
2. Gather data: Collecting data on the key components of the system can help to understand their behavior and how they contribute to the overall complexity and uncertainty of the system. This can include things like performance data, customer feedback, and other relevant information.
3. Map the system: Creating a map or visual representation of the chaotic structure can help to understand the relationships and interdependencies between the different components of the system. This can include things like process flow diagrams, network diagrams, or other types of visualizations.
4. Analyze the data: Once the data has been collected and the system has been mapped, it is important to analyze the data to identify trends, patterns, and opportunities for

improvement [6]. This can involve using statistical analysis or other data analysis techniques to better understand the system [4].

5. Develop strategies: Based on the analysis of the chaotic structure, it is important to develop strategies for addressing the complexity and uncertainty of the system. This can involve things like improving processes, introducing new technologies, or making organizational changes to better manage the complexity and uncertainty of the system [4].

Overall, analyzing a chaotic structure involves understanding the key components of the system, gathering and analyzing data, mapping the system, and developing strategies for addressing the complexity and uncertainty of the system. By following these steps, it is possible to better understand and manage a chaotic structure.

The Stacey Matrix. The Stacey matrix is a tool used to help decision-makers understand the complexity and uncertainty of a situation and to identify appropriate strategies for dealing with it. It was developed by Dr. Martin Stacey and is based on the idea that different situations require different approaches and that there is no one-size-fits-all solution [1, 2, 11] (Fig. 1).

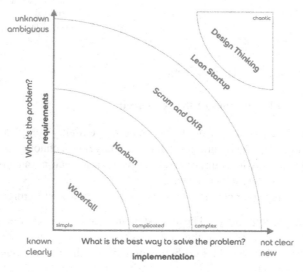

Fig. 1. The Stacey matrix to represent different levels of complexity

The Stacey matrix consists of four quadrants that represent different levels of complexity and uncertainty:

1. Simple: This quadrant represents situations that are relatively simple and predictable, with low complexity and low uncertainty. In these situations, a rule-based approach is often appropriate.
2. Complicated: This quadrant represents situations that are more complex and less predictable, with high complexity and low uncertainty. In these situations, a analytical approach is often appropriate.

3. Complex: This quadrant represents situations that are highly complex and uncertain, with high complexity and high uncertainty. In these situations, a trial-and-error approach is often appropriate.
4. Chaotic: This quadrant represents situations that are highly complex and highly uncertain, with high complexity and high uncertainty. In these situations, an intuitive or improvisational approach is often appropriate.

The Stacey matrix can be used within the design thinking process to help decision-makers understand the complexity and uncertainty of a problem and to identify appropriate strategies for addressing it. By considering the complexity and uncertainty of a problem, decision-makers can better understand the risks and challenges involved and can choose strategies that are most likely to succeed.

Design Thinking. Design thinking is a process that involves a structured and iterative approach to problem-solving and innovation. It is focused on understanding and empathizing with the needs and preferences of the end user, and on creating solutions that are both functional and desirable [7, 12].

Customer centricity is the practice of putting the needs and preferences of the customer at the center of all business decisions and actions. It involves designing products, services, and processes with the customer in mind and continuously seeking to understand and meet their needs [8, 12].

There is a strong connection between design thinking and customer centricity, as both approaches are focused on understanding and meeting the needs of the end user. By applying design thinking principles to customer centricity, businesses can create solutions that are tailored to the specific needs and preferences of their customers, leading to improved customer satisfaction and loyalty [8, 9] (Fig. 2).

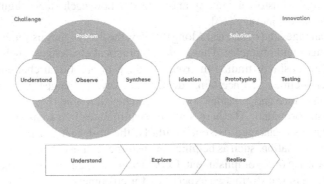

Fig. 2. The Design thinking process to customer centricity ideation

Some specific ways in which Design thinking [12] can be applied to customer centricity include:

1. Emphasizing empathy: Design thinking emphasizes the importance of understanding and empathizing with the end user, which is also a key component of customer centricity. By taking the time to truly understand the needs and preferences of your customers, you can design solutions that better meet their needs.

2. Focusing on co-creation: Design thinking often involves co-creation, or working closely with end users to create solutions that meet their needs. This same approach can be applied to customer centricity, by involving customers in the design process and seeking their input and feedback.
3. Iterating and testing: Design thinking involves an iterative and testing process, which can also be applied to customer centricity. By continuously testing and refining solutions based on customer feedback, businesses can improve their products and services and better meet the needs of their customers.

Design thinking and customer centricity are closely connected approaches that both prioritize the needs and preferences of the end user. By applying design thinking principles to customer centricity, businesses can create solutions that are tailored to the specific needs of their customers, leading to improved customer satisfaction and loyalty.

The Hero's Journey and Story Telling. The hero's journey is a narrative framework that describes the journey of a hero as they embark on a quest, face challenges and obstacles, and ultimately emerge as a changed person. It is a common theme in literature and storytelling, and it can also be applied to the customer journey to create a more immersive and meaningful experience [13, 14].

Here are some steps for developing a customer journey map using the hero's journey framework:

1. Identify the hero: The hero of the customer journey is the customer themselves. It is important to understand their motivations, needs, and goals as they embark on their journey.
2. Map the journey: The hero's journey typically consists of several distinct stages, including the call to adventure, the journey itself, and the return home. Map out the key stages of the customer journey and consider how each stage aligns with these stages of the hero's journey [13].
3. Identify challenges and obstacles: Along the way, the hero of the customer journey will face challenges and obstacles. These may be practical challenges, such as difficulty navigating a website or finding the right product, or emotional challenges, such as feeling overwhelmed or uncertain. Identify the key challenges and obstacles that customers may face and consider how they can be overcome [13, 14].
4. Create a transformation: The hero's journey culminates in a transformation, as the hero emerges as a changed person. Similarly, the customer journey should aim to create a transformation, such as helping the customer achieve their goals or providing them with a sense of accomplishment. Consider how the customer journey can create a meaningful and transformative experience for customers.
5. Test and refine: Once the customer journey map has been developed, it is important to test and refine it to ensure that it meets the needs and expectations of customers. This can involve gathering feedback from customers and iterating on the journey map to improve the overall customer experience.

Summarised, the hero's journey framework can be a useful tool for creating a more immersive and meaningful customer journey. By mapping out the key stages of the customer journey and identifying challenges and opportunities for transformation, businesses can create a customer experience that is both functional and engaging (Fig. 3).

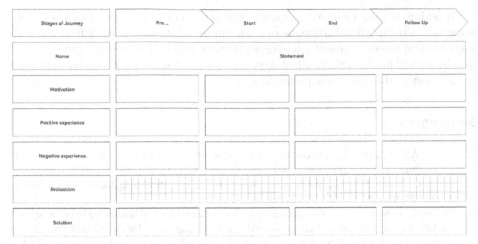

Fig. 3. The Customer Journey Map is a visual representation of all interactions with a brand within the framework of its purchasing process. The aim of a customer journey is to capture the wishes of the customer at each station or touchpoint of the process in order to use the most suitable and individual communication channel.

Future Work. How can a customer-centric approach be implemented in both Agile and Waterfall methodologies to prioritize customer involvement, feedback, and validation throughout the project lifecycle?

A customer-centric approach can be applied to both Agile and Waterfall methodologies by emphasizing customer involvement, feedback, and validation throughout the project lifecycle.

In Agile project management, customer feedback and involvement are crucial components for success. Agile teams work closely with customers to understand their needs and preferences and to prioritize requirements accordingly. This approach is aligned with the customer-centric mindset, which focuses on putting the customer at the center of all decision-making [11].

Previous research on hierarchy and heterarchy has been limited by a narrow focus on formal structures and relationships, and a failure to take into account the complexity and fluidity of organizational practices. They propose a practice approach that emphasizes the importance of studying the everyday practices of organizations and the relationships and networks that emerge from those practices [3].

In Waterfall methodologies, customer needs and preferences are typically defined upfront during the requirements gathering phase. However, a customer-centric approach can still be applied by ensuring that the requirements are validated throughout the project lifecycle. This can be achieved by regularly reviewing the requirements with the customer, and ensuring that the final product meets their needs.

Both Agile and Waterfall methodologies can benefit from incorporating customer feedback through user testing and validation. This can help to ensure that the product is meeting the customer's needs and expectations, and can help to identify any issues early in the project lifecycle.

In addition, Agile methodologies often emphasize continuous improvement and iteration, which is aligned with a customer-centric mindset that values ongoing feedback and improvement based on customer needs and preferences [11]. This iterative approach can also be applied in a Waterfall methodology by ensuring that feedback from the customer is incorporated throughout the project lifecycle.

References

1. Sowa, A.F., Paauwe, J.: Sensemaking in strategic change: the Stacey matrix as a tool for understanding change processes. J. Change Manag. **15**(1), 21–37 (2015)
2. Hopp, C., Vargo, S.L.: The Stacey matrix and service ecosystems: insights and opportunities. J. Serv. Manag. **30**(4), 444–459 (2019)
3. Nicolini, D., Monteiro, P.: The practice approach to hierarchy and heterarchy in organisation studies: a critical review and a way forward. Acad. Manag. Ann. **10**(1), 237–274 (2016)
4. Verhoef, P.C., Lemon, K.N., Parasuraman, A., Roggeveen, A., Tsiros, M., Schlesinger, L.A.: Customer experience creation: determinants, dynamics and management strategies. J. Retail. **91**(2), 253–270 (2015)
5. Meuter, M.L., Bitner, M.J., Ostrom, A.L., Brown, S.W.: Choosing among alternative service delivery modes: an investigation of customer trial of self-service technologies. J. Mark. **79**(2), 83–98 (2015)
6. Lemon, K.N., Verhoef, P.C.: Understanding customer experience throughout the customer journey. J. Mark. **80**(6), 69–96 (2016)
7. Kim, S.: An integrated approach of design thinking and customer centricity for organizational innovation. J. Open Innov.: Technol. Mark. Complex. **5**(3), 56 (2019)
8. Parthasarathy, M., Sohoni, M.G.: The impact of speed on customer satisfaction in e-commerce last-mile delivery. Prod. Oper. Manag. **27**(5), 959–976 (2018)
9. Brown, T.: Design thinking. Harvard Bus. Rev. **86**, 86–92 (2018)
10. Vargo, S.L., Lusch, R.F.: Service-dominant logic 2025. Int. J. Res. Mark. **34**(1), 46–67 (2017)
11. Hommel, D., Goll, J.: Mit Scrum zum gewünschten System. Springer, Deutschland (2015). https://doi.org/10.1007/978-3-658-10721-5
12. Das Design Thinking Playbook: Mit traditionellen, aktuellen und zukünftigen Erfolgsfaktoren. Vahlen, Deutschland (2018)
13. Vogler, C.: The Writer's Journey: Mythic Structure for Writers, 3rd edn. Michael Wiese Productions, Los Angeles (2020)
14. Marguerite, A.S., Rață, C.: The hero's journey: a framework for creating memorable customer experiences. Manag. Dyn. Knowl. Econ. **7**(4), 545–559 (2019)

The Co-design Process for Interactive Tools for Predicting Polygenic Risk Scores

Amaan Zubairi[1,3], Dalal AlDossary[1,3], Mariam M. AlEissa[2,3], and Areej Al-Wabil[1,3(✉)]

[1] Software Engineering Department, Alfaisal University, Riyadh, Saudi Arabia
{azubairi,daldossary,awabil}@alfaisal.edu
[2] Molecular Genetics Laboratory, Public Health Authority, Riyadh, Saudi Arabia
mmeissa@CDC.gov.sa
[3] Artificial Intelligence Research Center, Alfaisal University, Riyadh, Saudi Arabia

Abstract. This paper describes several strategies for engaging bioinformaticians in the software design process for Bioinformatics tools. These tools and co-design processes are intended to support and enhance their profession within a web-based context by discussing artifacts and databases, reacting to scenarios, customizing prototypes, and identifying user journeys. Using design artifacts and documents of scientists' reflections, an illustration of how these techniques were applied in the context of PRS prediction tools for Bioinformatics. This further includes discussing design implications for Bioinformatics tools.

Keywords: Prediction Tool · Participatory Design · Preventive Medicine · Complex Genetics · Bioinformatics · Computational Genomics

1 Introduction

With the ever-increasing technological advancements comes the age of virtual twins, also known as Digital Twins. The concept of Digital Twins is often considered in the context of healthcare to assess the diagnosis and treatment of specific conditions, such as orthopedics, cardiovascular disease, and precision medicine [1]. Real-time data monitoring using Artificial Intelligence (AI) provides assessment for diagnostics and treatments; it can also help predict disease predisposition [2].

Such technology facilitates the creation of a virtual copy of a person using their genetic code, thus [1]. Some companies use Digital Twins to trace a person's ancestry and the potential risk of developing certain diseases that might have been found within their DNA [2]. The concept also allowed for remote healthcare, where healthcare professionals would monitor and assess patients through their digital twin for certain complications and illnesses. Further, the concept of the digital twin expands its reach above simple ancestry, it is also widely used to create virtual copies of machinery and products and even simulate the inner workings of different species before real-life experimentation [3]. Allowing such simulations contributes toward preventing any unnecessary danger or potential hazards (e.g. from chemicals or potential heavy machinery). It also paves

C. Stephanidis et al. (Eds.): HCII 2023, CCIS 1832, pp. 199–206, 2023.
https://doi.org/10.1007/978-3-031-35989-7_25

the way for using fewer resources during testing and ensuring product safety before commercial releases as noted in [1].

Moreover, digital twin technology has been integrated into the healthcare sector to facilitate some medical practices such as diagnostics, prevention, and detection of diseases. Such technology has been adjusted and improved (or altered) to fit the specific needs of medical personnel. One such addition is the Polygenic Risk Score (PRS), which refers to the likelihood of developing a certain disease based on statistical analyses conducted on the patient's genomic code [4]. Integrating these calculations contributes towards interventions that aim to prevent diseases they might develop by changing their lifestyle [5]. It is also used in finding the root cause of patients' issues and beginning the correct course of action rather than going through trial and error until the correct diagnosis is reached [6]. However, it is important to note that the PRS' calculation is only used for prediction as its accuracy depends on the sample size of studies and widely available disease variant data. Research has shown that different factors also play a role in the calculation of the PRS, such factors include culture, ethnicity, gender, and family relations (if any are present) [7].

Furthermore, software companies often merge the two concepts to investigate various issues such as non-communicable diseases (e.g. diabetes, cardiovascular disease) and complex diseases (e.g. Alzheimers, Parkinsons). This approach has led to the recent commercialization of DNA testing and genomic analysis that has been shown to reveal various elements including a person's ancestry to their risk of developing hereditary cancer [8]. More often than not, these companies will be fairly expensive due to the costs of lab-based work and testing, contributing to factors that hinder the scalability and accessibility of these services [9]. Fundamentally, this type of service will not be available to a large portion of the general public as expenses can be hard to cover [9]. They will also depend on their databases and previously collected customer data to conduct their computations [2]. Although some companies have made tools that address physical ailments such as heart disease and some chronic illnesses, many do not discuss alternate aspects of non-communicable diseases [9]. Additionally, service providers often present the data in a report format rather than diagrams, which is a noticeably less user-friendly and digestible visual. Thus, it is a new approach that has not been undertaken at length [4].

This paper describes the co-design process for tools designed and developed to simplify the prediction process using software that takes the DNA seq as input and gets a prediction score for that disease. Leveraging the accessibility of big data, tools can be designed to access millions of variants for diseases and more statistical data from research studies in the applied health domains. The workflow starts with variant matching, followed by querying which is done through the data found in previous research to get its effect size (beta/OR) value. This is then used to calculate the PRS for that disease. The value is not 100% accurate but narrows the scope, making it easier to analyze knowing the exact variants associated with specific diseases. The expected or foreseen contribution of such technology is twofold; cost reduction and accessibility to a wider target population.

2 Co-design Process for PRS

Bioinformatic tools are most effective when aligned with scientists' goals and expectations [14]. Participatory methods, which involve scientists (such as bioinformaticians or domain experts) closely in the co-design process, are widely recommended for establishing precise design requirements that address users' needs. In this section, the co-design process in the ideation phase is described at length. The process involved the creation of diagrams such as influence diagrams, stakeholder maps, and design signatures. These diagrams helped identify the functional and non-functional requirements and visualize and understand the relationships and interactions between the different components and stakeholders in the system. They further allowed the team to identify potential improvement areas and make informed decisions about the design. The diagrams also facilitated communication and collaboration between team members, enabling them to work together more effectively. Overall, using these diagrams contributed to creating a more comprehensive and accurate genomic digital twin.

2.1 Influence Diagram

The process of drafting the influence diagram aimed to identify the key relationships among the parameters involved in PRS prediction and possible causes that provide additional insights into the process behavior. The graphical representation depicts the connection between the outcomes and/or processes along with the key features or factors that can exert any type of influence. The co-design activity involved collaborating with subject matter experts and exploring the field of genetics through a guided learning program. This co-design helped build upon prior genetics and software development knowledge, further merging the two fields (Fig. 1).

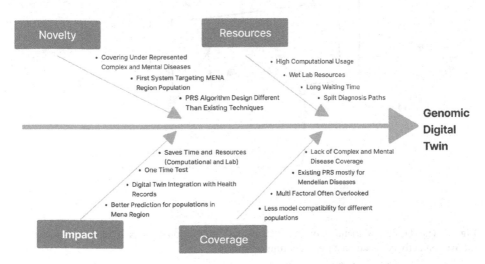

Fig. 1. Influence diagram for the PRS disease prediction tool

The influence diagram aided in building a digital genomic twin by visually displaying the relationships between key variables and objectives [13]. The process of co-design helped the team identify crucial factors and potential areas for improvement while ensuring non-functional requirements are aligned with stakeholders' needs.

2.2 Design Signatures

The co-design process used a Design Innovation (DI) framework [10] which is built, in part, on the UK Council's '4D' design scheme of four phases; namely the "Discover", "Define", "Develop", and "Deliver" phases. In our pursuit of reflecting on the co-design process across different applied computing domains, modeling and consequently analyzing design processes is a critical endeavor. The Design Signature in Fig. 2 is an illustration of design activities across the four phases (i.e. Discover, Define, Develop, Deliver), which can be used to plan and manage innovation teams and activities, and to identify critical features for reflection, for clarification, and further analysis.

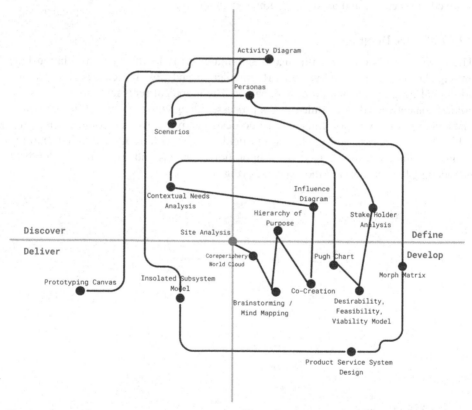

Fig. 2. The Design Signature for the PRS disease prediction tool is a stage-based map of innovation activity based on a polar coordinate system.

Design signatures helped represent the patterns and processes of design innovation in a graphical form [10]. They can be used to analyze, compare, and communicate different design approaches and outcomes. The design activities in Fig. 2's illustration are linked chronologically, starting at the origin, and plotted based on their codified 'D' quadrant. Table 1 describes the mapping that is used in the Design Signature to model the software development processes as co-designers and developers progress through the design process to the delivery of incremental functional prototypes. It also readily reveals insights into the project's iterative design process.

Table 1. The Design Innovation (DI) Scheme for processes and Mindsets.

	Discover	Develop	Define	Deliver
Mindset	Empathy	Visual	Cognitive	Active
Focus	Needs and Requirements	Reframing Opportunities	Idea/Concept Generation	Building and Testing
DI Modules	Scenarios	Personas	Pugh Chart	Prototyping Canvas
	Contextual Needs Analysis	Activity Diagram	Morph Matrix	
		Influence Diagram	Mindmapping	Insolated Subsystem Model
	Site Analysis	Stakeholder Map	Co-Creation	
		Hierarchy of Purpose	DVF Model	

The presence of back and forth movement between the "Define" and "Develop" quadrants and the "Discover" and "Define" quadrants highlight key iterations between these phases, as substantial focus on the user experience drove the design process. The mapping of the DI activities was conducted retrospectively once the project completed its first development cycle [12]. The DI Modules were selected in alignment with the participatory design recommendations in each phase. The iterations can be attributed to multiple design review sessions requested by the stakeholder or subject-matter experts as well as the built-in cost, performance, and schedule flexibility in the project. The site analysis and scenarios were key to establishing a common understanding of the state-of-the-art and the technology limitations. The "Develop" phase's diagrams, along with the Stakeholder map were essential communication tools among key participants in the design processes. The stakeholder analysis, such as creating a stakeholder map, helped prioritize stakeholders by their level of impact and interest as noted in [12]. By focusing on primary stakeholders and conducting interactions, such as interviews, the developers were able to tailor the requirements to the stakeholders' needs and contextual requirements, ensuring alignment and key stakeholders' satisfaction and engagement in its success [12].

3 Conceptual Design

The software development project aimed to develop a tool to predict the PRS for complex diseases such as Bipolar Disorder (BD) and Alzheimer's Disease using genomic data from sources such as the National Center for Biotechnology Information (NCBI), University of California, Santa Cruz (UCSC) genome browser, and Ensembl. The pathogenic variant list for different diseases was obtained from The Polygenic Score (PGS) Catalog. The data was further investigated to obtain beta values for each allele, wherein the effect weight was used for PRS calculation. Variants for the diseases were identified using the rsID/Chr position. This located the variants within the DNA sequence FASTA file obtained from the medical professional.

Moreover, The quality score of the DNA sequence is directly proportional to the PRS calculation. Using the PGS' variant data file (containing the variant change), allele positions and chromosome numbers were identified to determine if there is a mutation. Expanding further, the mutation was categorized as benign or pathogenic. Finally, each variant change is weighted, presenting its overall effect on the score. The calculation then considers the effect weight and the number of variants to find the PRS. For example, calculating the PRS for BD would require the number of variants and their effect weights. The number of variants refers to the number of mutations perceived in the DNA sequence. The effect weight is a statistically calculated constant taken from the Genome-Wide Association Study (GWAS), representing a measure of strength between the variant and the disease. Plugging in these two values will result in the PRS score for that person, effectively predicting their risk of developing the disease.

Similarly, Color is a health technology company that provides genome-wide polygenic scores (GPS) for various traits and diseases [12]. GPS are numbers that summarize the estimated effect of many genetic variants on an individual's phenotype. Color uses a low-pass whole genome sequencing (WGS) assay to generate genotype data for each individual and a bioinformatics pipeline to align the reads and call variants [12]. Furthermore, they use a curated list of traits and diseases with high-quality GWAS data (publicly available) that is relevant for clinical and preventive care. Color uses a standardized framework to select SNPs (Single nucleotide polymorphisms), estimate effect sizes, standardize weights, and compute GPS across different traits and diseases. They validate the GPS using external data sources such as UK Biobank, FinnGen, and gnomAD. Also, they compare their GPS with other existing GPS methods, such as PRSice2 and LDpred2. Finally, they interpret their GPS using percentile ranks based on empirical distributions from large cohorts [12].

On the other hand, 23andMe's PRS methodology involves collecting genotype and phenotype data from its customers [8]. Using a custom-designed genotyping chip that covers over 600,000 SNPs across the genome. The genotyping data were combined with self-reported surveys that asked about their health conditions, wellness traits, and lifestyle factors. The company then uses a machine learning approach to create PRS models for different phenotypes based on a subset of customers' genotype and phenotype data [8]. The models are trained to predict the phenotype status or value based on the genotype data of each customer. Different algorithms and methods are used depending on the type of phenotype, and the most relevant SNPs are selected using techniques such as p-value thresholding or LASSO regularization [8]. The accuracy and performance of each PRS model are evaluated using an independent subset of customers who were not used during the model's creation [8].

All the aforementioned approaches have advantages and limitations. Their suitability depends on the specific application, context, and use case. It is important to note that genetic testing and interpretation should be made cautiously and in consultation with a healthcare professional. The DI modules coupled with the graphical approaches to process modeling, such as the PRS Design Signature that was described in Sect. 2.2, can be easily understood by individuals with varying backgrounds and remain flexible enough for a model to be incrementally constructed at different levels of granularity and formality according to the stakeholder's or team members' needs and preferences.

4 Conclusion

Design techniques play a crucial role in developing effective and accurate tools for predicting genetic risk scores. Using design signatures, influence diagrams, and stakeholder maps, researchers and designers can consider a broad range of design activities to facilitate eliciting requirements related to identifying the most relevant genetic variants for each phenotype and estimating their effect size. The design of tools for predicting genetic risk scores can vary widely, from low-pass whole-genome sequencing to custom-designed genotyping chips. Each approach has its strengths and limitations, and the choice will depend on factors such as the cohort's size, the phenotype's complexity, and the availability of high-quality genomic data. Overall, a combination of design techniques, including stakeholder maps and influence diagrams, can help researchers and companies to develop effective and accurate tools for predicting genetic risk scores, which can have significant implications for clinical and preventive care.

Acknowledgment. We would like to acknowledge the Artificial Intelligence Center and the College of Engineering at Alfaisal University for supporting this project. The appreciation is also extended to the Molecular Genetics Laboratory at the Public Health Authority for the co-design, knowledge support, and guidance through this project.

References

1. Boschert, S., Rosen, R.: Digital twin—The simulation aspect. In: Hehenberger, P., Bradley, D. (eds.) Mechatronic Futures, pp. 59–74. Springer, Cham (2016). https://doi.org/10.1007/978-3-319-32156-1_5
2. Berger, M.J., et al.: Color Data v2: a user-friendly, open-access database with hereditary cancer and hereditary cardiovascular conditions datasets (2020)
3. Haag, S., Anderl, R.: Digital twin – proof of concept. Manuf. Lett. **15**, 64–66 (2018). https://doi.org/10.1016/j.mfglet.2018.02.006
4. Adeyemo, A., et al.: Responsible use of polygenic risk scores in the clinic: potential benefits, risks and gaps. Nat. Med. **27**, 1876–1884 (2021)
5. O'Mara, T., Crosbie, E.: Polygenic risk score opportunities for early detection and prevention strategies in endometrial cancer. BJC—Br. J. Cancer **123**, 1045–1046 (2020). https://doi.org/10.1038/s41416-020-0959-7

6. Hadley, T.D., Agha, A.M., Ballantyne, C.M.: How do we incorporate polygenic risk scores in cardiovascular disease risk assessment and management? Curr. Atheroscler. Rep. **23**(28), 1–7 (2021). https://doi.org/10.1007/s11883-021-00915-6

7. Duncan, L., et al.: Analysis of polygenic risk score usage and performance in diverse human populations. Nat. Commun. **10**, 3328 (2019). https://doi.org/10.1038/s41467-019-11112-0

8. Ashenhurst, J., et al.: A Generalized Method for the Creation and Evaluation of Polygenic Scores. 23andMe (n.d.). https://medical.23andme.com/wp-content/uploads/2020/06/23_21-PRSMethodology_May2020.pdf

9. Wilde, A., Meiser, B., Mitchell, P., Scholfield, P.: Public interest in predictive genetic testing, including direct-to-consumer testing, for susceptibility to major depression: preliminary findings. Eur. J. Hum. Genetics **18**, 47–51 (2010). https://doi.org/10.1038/ejhg.2009.138

10. Seow, O., et al.: Design signatures: mapping design innovation processes. In: Technical Conferences and Computers and Information in Engineering Conference (2018)

11. Chinyio, E., Olomolaiye, P.: Construction Stakeholder Management - Mapping Stakeholders, pp. 99–120. Wiley-Blackwell, Hoboken (2010)

12. Color Health Inc.: Color Genome-wide Polygenic Score, vol. 1 (2021)

13. Ronald, A., Matheson, J.E.: Influence diagrams. Decis. Anal. **2**(3), 127–143 (2005). https://doi.org/10.1287/deca.1050.0020

14. Al-Ageel, N., Al-Wabil, A., Badr, G., AlOmar, N.: Human factors in the design and evaluation of bioinformatics tools. Proc. Manuf. **3**, 2003–2010 (2015). https://doi.org/10.1016/j.promfg.2015.07.247

Multimodality and Novel Interaction Techniques and Devices

Understanding the Pushbutton Revisited: From on and off to Input and Output

Heidi Bråthen(✉) and Jo Herstad

University of Oslo, Oslo, Norway
heibr@ifi.uio.no

Abstract. The button is a familiar technology that is used to control and regulate things and machines in our everyday lives. With the digitalization of the button, many possibilities for novel and innovative functions have been invented and implemented. The use of digital buttons comes with some challenges that are explored in this paper. We describe the transition between the mechanical switch to the digital switch, and specifically use the concept of familiarity to find out more about the use of digital switches in a case study of indoor lighting. The contribution of the paper is to open for the transition between mechanical buttons and digital buttons and point to some challenges that arise in everyday use.

Keywords: Interface · Understanding · Pushbuttons

1 Introduction

The concept of the button is familiar to users of technology. Over the last decades, however, the button has developed from mechanical buttons to digital buttons, adding complex programmable possibilities to their application and use. We therefore ask how users make sense of the familiar buttons featuring new possibilities for interaction.

Rachel Plotnick [1] shows that the understanding of pushbuttons was already a subject to societal concern at its introduction in the late 19th century. Advertisers, producers, journalists, and educators participated in a debate encompassing many different perspectives on how users, or consumers, could best understand the pushbutton in the time from 1880 to 1915. Perspectives ranged from those who believed that creative interrogations of pushbuttons should serve as an introduction to a broader electrical education, to those who argued for the ability of the pushbutton to make use effortless [1]. From 1915, however, the consumers familiarity with the pushbutton led to the interface design to stabilize and the pushbutton became "black boxes", resulting in less need for understanding the workings of the pushbutton [1].

While users' familiarity with the button was established more than a century ago, the added possibilities offered by programming of buttons now make electrical and digital buttons more complex to both use and understand [2]. We therefore revisit the discussion on how users understand buttons in the context of interaction design and HCI.

© The Author(s), under exclusive license to Springer Nature Switzerland AG 2023
C. Stephanidis et al. (Eds.): HCII 2023, CCIS 1832, pp. 209–215, 2023.
https://doi.org/10.1007/978-3-031-35989-7_26

To illuminate changes and new challenges in designing for interactions with new and emergent technologies such as autonomous technologies.

The Guiding Question. That we address in this paper is comprised of two parts. First, we ask what the transition between the mechanical button to the digital button entail? What exactly is it that have changed as the mechanical pushbutton has developed to digital buttons? Secondly, we ask what challenges that evolve with the transition and how this affects users understanding of buttons.

Layout and Objectives. The rest of the poster is organized in the following way. We first describe the development of the pushbutton to examine the transition from the mechanical to the digital button. We apply a model to illustrate an important new feature of the digital button as input to a system. Then we describe the concept of familiarity to discuss the implications of emerging challenges. After this, we examine a case of the basic operations of switching lights on and off with digital buttons to explore the challenges and opportunities that buttons introduce in use situations. Finally, we discuss our findings and conclude by identify implications and areas of concern for further research into the understanding of technology in design and use.

2   The Development of the Pushbutton

The pushbutton as a switch for electricity was developed in the last twenty years of the nineteenth century. They were increasingly built into household items like lamps and doorbells from the beginning of the 20th century and developed to represent instantaneous control of electrical devices [1]. We will name these early electrical buttons as "mechanical" buttons, in that they are mechanical devises that works by breaking or closing an electrical circuit [2]. They usually represent their own state by their position, for example by latching in a lowered position and then released, or a knob turning to a horizontal or vertical position [2]. The possible states of mechanical buttons are thereby limited, and their states are observable by human users. The button typically offers two states, that is "on" and "off".

A century later buttons still come in many different sorts and shapes, as examined elegantly by [2]. Where mechanical buttons worked by closing or breaking an electrical circuit, new digital buttons can be in the form of physical buttons or graphic buttons on screens and work by submitting a signal as input to a computer for processing. Still, they often utilize the same feedback mechanisms which are inherent consequences of the construction of the mechanical button, such as clicks and latched positions [2].

A Model of Input and Output. To illustrate the new functionality of digital buttons, we apply a model of interactive artefacts that has been applied in robotics, electronics DIY communities [3], and in interaction design materiality studies [4]. This model describes the structure or anatomy of a digital artefact as consisting of three main components: sensors, processing unit and actuators (Fig. 1). Sensors are components that take in information about its surroundings, or "read" the environment. The button is such a sensor that senses the push from its environment, for example embedded in the mouse and keyboard of a PC. The signals are processed and transformed by a processing unit, like the processor of a PC. Actuators are components that actuate the signals from the processing unit, they can "act" or "write" on its surroundings, like computer screens and light bulbs.

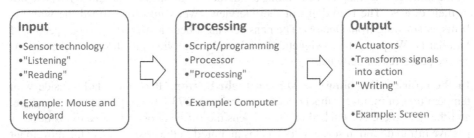

Fig. 1. The model of Interactive Things

3   Familiarity – A Way to Understand the Use of Buttons

What does it mean to understand buttons, use or technology? We will approach understanding as a part of the concept of familiarity, a concept that has previously been applied within HCI. Phil Turner makes references to philosophy, and especially the early Heidegger to explore the phenomenon familiarity [5, 6]. Heidegger claims that the basis for understanding our being-in-the-world lies in the everyday lives that we all live [7, 8]. He discusses three underlying concepts that are based upon our familiarity with the world. First, the idea of involvement or engagement, which Heidegger simply expresses as "being-in-the-world". Second, we relate to our world based upon understanding. This understanding is based or embedded in our activities and this understanding shows up in the activities we are engaged in. Understanding is essentially a skill, or a capacity to do something, according to Heidegger. Third, self and world are not primordially two distinct entities, like a subject relating with an object, but a unity of person-world. This unity is based upon the involvement and understanding in the world, as described for example in [8].

Within HCI, there are also various other lines of thoughts and analytic concepts that have evolved from our understanding of the everyday world. Norman [9] has been advocating using our everyday world, doorknobs, and light switches for example, as inspiration and sources for guiding how interaction and interfaces to computers can be designed. Ehn [10], referring Wittgenstein, introduced family resemblance, to promote the involvement of the user in the design of interfaces for new typesetting systems. This concept has been further developed by Mørch [11], in the context of tailorable systems and adaptive evolutionary systems. From the perspective of Tangible and embodied Interaction, Dourish points out that while familiarity is subjective, outcomes of interaction, such as i.e., easiness, success, or performance can be understood observable signs of familiarity [12].

4   A Case of Programmable Light Switches

Method. Our case is a system providing automated lights, blinds, and heating in a $10\,000\,\text{m}^2$ office building that is ten years old. We have conducted two in-depth interviews with employees working in the building about their relationship with the lights switches in their offices. The recordings of the interviews were auto transcribed the with the Whisper software from OpenAI. Their answers have been analyzed in the perspective of familiarity. We present two vignettes based on the interviews to show how the buttons can be perceived of daily users.

In the Office – Disabling the Manual Light Button. It is pitch dark outside with temperatures of minus 5C this December morning at 0730. Harold is entering his office, and the light there is switched on as he opens the office door and move to his desk. A passive infrared motion sensor (PIR) that is mounted in the ceiling detect the movement in the room, and signals to the system that the light is to be switched on.

Fig. 2. Left: Motion sensor mounted in the ceiling of the offices. Right: Button disabled with gaffe tape.

During an ordinary office day, many people pop into Harold's office to get advice, and to pick up parcels. He noticed that some colleagues pressed the button at the door when they went out from his office, especially when he was not there. Harold have noted that when the light is switched off manually, information from the PIR sensor is disabled for 30 min (Fig. 2). Since this was frustrating, he decided to disable the button at the door. This he did by a strip of gaffe tape that simply locked the button to one position (Fig. 2). By this, he can always enjoy a fully lit office.

In the Office – Disabling the PIR Motion Sensor. Hanna likes indirect lighting in her office. She has two light sources that lights up the desk, and the shelves in the office. She works better when the light sources are this way as compared to a fully lit office from the standard ceiling light. When moving into the office, Hanna used to turn the light off manually by pressing the button at the side of the door. However, the ceiling light turned on after approximately 45 min in the room because of her movements. She then had to walk over to the button to press the button again. After a few weeks with this routine, she decided to cover the PIR sensor in the ceiling by attaching an A4 sheet of paper in the ceiling with two pushpins. This worked fine for Hanna, as the sensor was disabled and did not register any movement in the room.

5 Results and Discussion

Our findings from the case highlight some of the changes of the button from its introduction in the 1890's. The light switches in the building have kept their two-state form, while they are performing more complex temporal light control and dimming.

In each office, the button has become distributed and now consist of minimum two entry points; the light switch in its traditional form in the form of a two-state switch, and an added PIR sensor mounted in the ceiling that measures movement in the lighted area. The introduction of emerging interaction mechanisms like movement control is also introduced in addition to physical button control may challenge the understanding of the user interface. Further, the temporal programming that controls lights overrides the input that the user has given to the system in form of pressing buttons. This may pose challenges to the user's understanding of the system. It may also indicate that the end user is not the intended user. The owner of the building and the environment may benefit from timing lights and making sure someone is present to enjoy the light. This points to a new and emerging challenge raised by programmable, autonomous systems like in our case study.

Hanna and Harold demonstrate that they have become familiar with the workings of these buttons and their added points of input in their offices and understands how they function by countering and partly disabling them through applying appropriations. Other people visiting Harold, however, demonstrate unfamiliarity with the button. They may assume that the light switch button is an analogue button and make sure to turn the light off as they leave. But it has a programmed delay of 45 min programmed into it that is unfamiliar to the visitor, an *invisible and temporal* feature. This can be understood as an example of the familiar acting in unfamiliar ways. When the digital button looks and feels like an analogue button, users expect it to work as an analogue button. We use our familiarity with the old to understand the new. When the feedback to the user from digital buttons is different from that of analogue buttons, challenges with understanding feedback may arise.

Even if Hanna and Harold demonstrate familiarity and understanding of the buttons, they can't control and adapt the mechanisms to their needs. We found that both have created appropriations to their light switches. While originally being introduced as a means of instant control over electrical devices, the functionality of the light switch button is outside of their control and partly inaccessible due to the added motion sensor that will detect movement regardless of their need for light, and the programmed timer. The effect is that they have effectively broken their relationship with the buttons by disabling them.

6 Conclusion and Future Work

This study contributes by unpacking some issues with the use of digital buttons today. From our examination of the transition from the mechanical to the digital button, we understand the main difference to be that whereas the mechanical button is giving a causal, direct impact of the thing that is switched on or off, a digital button is an input to a computer system. The signals that are sent into the computer can be used to do countless different things, challenging the users understanding of the interaction on several levels. Our preliminary findings indicate that areas of concern include insufficient control for end users, challenges to users understanding of the interface and of the wider system because of the complexity introduced by the programming of digital buttons.

Implications for Further Research. We round off this poster by identifying a few implications and areas of concern for our further research into the understanding of technology in design and use of new and emerging technologies.

Understanding as a Skill. Approaching understanding as an ability that builds on existing competence points to the importance of drawing on designers and users existing competence. However, in many use cases, the familiarity many users have with mechanical buttons cannot be successfully invoked with digital buttons. The button therefore lends itself as a good example technology for further experiments to illuminate some of the challenges with understanding design and use of new and emerging technologies through building on the familiar.

From Off and On to Input and Output. Users who are familiar with mechanical buttons are used to see the status of the system by observing the button. This however is not always the case with digital buttons and might be challenging users understanding of the interface and the consequences of their actions in the system. However, our case suggests that challenges to understanding are not confined to the surface of the interface but concern the understanding of systems as well. Inspired by the long tradition of creative interrogations of the pushbutton as educational for understanding electrical devices, conceptualizing the digital pushbutton as input in the digital artefact model could serve as foundation for engaging users with digital pushbuttons to provide insights on autonomous systems through the interactive things model.

From Single Point of Control to Distributed Control. When digital buttons are used in concert with sensors in the environment of the users, user control are challenged. We would like to investigate how users can regain the control in such distributed systems.

Local and Remote. When digital switches can be programmed and reprogrammed without changes to the hardware, control and overview are removed from the end user, who is not necessarily the intended user.

Acknowledgement. We thank the enthusiastic participants in this study and our colleagues at the Design group for helpful feedback on our project.

References

1. Plotnick, R.: At the interface: the case of the electric push button, 1880–1923. Technol. Cult. **53**(4), 815–845 (2012)
2. Janlert, L.-E.: The ubiquitous button. Interactions **21**(3), 26–33 (2014). https://doi.org/10.1145/2592234
3. Severance, C.: Massimo Banzi: building Arduino. Computer **47**(1), 11–12 (2014). https://doi.org/10.1109/MC.2014.19
4. Wiberg, M.: The Materiality of Interaction: Notes on the Materials of Interaction Design. The MIT Press, Cambridge, Massachusetts (2017)
5. Turner, P.: Being-with: a study of familiarity. Interact. Comput. **20**(4–5), 447–454 (2008). https://doi.org/10.1016/j.intcom.2008.04.002
6. Turner, P., Van de Walle, G.: Familiarity as a basis for universal design. J. Gerontechnol. **5**(3), 150–159 (2006). https://doi.org/10.4017/gt.2006.05.03.004.00
7. Heidegger, M.: The Basic Problems of Phenomenology, Rev. edn. Indiana University Press, Bloomington (1982)
8. Stambaugh, J., Schmidt, D.J.: Being and Time: A Revised Edition of the Stambaugh Translation. State University of New York Press, Albany (2010)
9. Norman, D.A.: The Design of Everyday Things, Revised and Expanded edn. Basic Books, New York (2013)
10. Ehn, P.: Work-oriented design of computer artifacts (1988). http://urn.kb.se/resolve?urn=urn:nbn:se:umu:diva-62913. Accessed 17 Mar 2023
11. Morch, A.I.: Evolutionary Growth and Control in User Tailorable Systems. Adaptive Evolutionary Information Systems (2003). https://www.igi-global.com/chapter/adaptive-evolutionary-information-systems/www.igi-global.com/chapter/adaptive-evolutionary-information-systems/4213. Accessed 17 Mar 2023
12. Dourish, P.: Where the Action Is: The Foundations of Embodied Interaction. MIT Press, Cambridge, Mass (2001)

Pressure Tactile Feedback Pin Pad Module Application: Reduce Shoulder Surfing Success Rate

Hsu Feng Chang[✉] and Shyang Jye Chang[✉]

Department of Mechanical Engineering, National Yunlin University of Science and Technology, Douliu 64002, Yunlin, Taiwan (ROC)

Phd.hfchang@gmail.com, changjye@yuntech.edu.tw

Abstract. Automated teller machines (ATMs), self-service payment terminals, and other devices that use PIN passwords for user authentication are susceptible to various forms of tampering or attacks in unattended settings. One such attack is shoulder surfing, where an attacker observes the sequence of key presses or steals the password through the use of cameras or peeping methods. To address this issue, this study proposes a design of a pressure sensing matrix combined with a PIN pad that can detect the amount of force applied during key presses, while providing real-time tactile roughness feedback.

Using the high elasticity properties of polydimethylsiloxane (PDMS), the device prototype was designed by defining the required force intervals for key presses and assembling the upper electrode elastic layer, spacer, and lower electrode PCB board.

The input accuracy using the tactile feedback method reached 70.83%, which was significantly higher than the 56.00% accuracy achieved without providing tactile feedback. Moreover, in the case of shoulder surfing, the defense rate of numeric passwords was only 8%, while the defense rate for pressure passwords was 40%, proving effective in protecting passwords.

Keywords: Pressure sensing pin pad · prevent shoulder surfing · Roughness Haptic Feedback

1 Introduction

Protecting and using personal data has become an integral part of daily life. Traditional physical keypads, such as pin pad, are often used to verify identity information and are commonly used in devices such as ATMs, automated payment systems, and security systems. PIN codes are one of the methods used for identity verification. However, these automated devices are often set up in unattended stores or open spaces that remain open for extended periods, and they are fixed and cannot be moved. These devices are vulnerable to various forms of tampering or attack in unattended settings.

The method of using a fake keypad overlaid on a real pin pad and a fake card reader device overlaid on a real card reader device to obtain card and password information is

© The Author(s), under exclusive license to Springer Nature Switzerland AG 2023
C. Stephanidis et al. (Eds.): HCII 2023, CCIS 1832, pp. 216–223, 2023.
https://doi.org/10.1007/978-3-031-35989-7_27

known as a skimming device attack [1]. These attacks often occur in unattended or poorly monitored environments, where automated devices such as ATM machines and other payment terminals are located. The skimming devices are designed to blend in with the legitimate equipment and are often difficult to detect, making them a popular method for stealing sensitive information. In addition, there is also a type of attack called "shoulder surfing," where attackers use a camera or spy on the user to observe the order in which the PIN is entered, in order to obtain the password [2], Methods such as skimming devices and shoulder surfing are common and quick ways to carry out attacks that are difficult to prevent. With the advancement and development of technology, thermal attacks have become a new method of attack, which involves guessing password information from the residual heat left on the pin pad after the user presses the keys. This method can still be used to determine the password information for a period of time after the user has left, making it one of the most energy-efficient attack methods available. Therefore, attackers can wait until the user has left before starting the thermal imaging attack.

It is difficult for ordinary people to quickly and accurately determine whether a machine has been tampered with or is in normal condition, making it challenging to effectively prevent or solve pin pad tampering or attacks. To address this issue, we have found that increasing the difficulty of verification can effectively reduce the likelihood of successful attacks. Using a virtual keyboard [3] or AR projection [4] to change the presentation of the pin pad or display randomized digits can effectively reduce the success rate of shoulder surfing attacks.

Currently, most defense mechanisms are designed with multiple sensor collaboration to reduce the success rate of attacks. However, this is not an intuitive input method and requires users to undergo a learning process to effectively defend against attacks. The most intuitive design is to expand the design in a way that does not change the user's original perception of pressing the pin pad. This study proposes a design matrix-style pressure sensor overlay on the pin pad to create a device that can distinguish the size of pressure applied while entering the password, and provide real-time tactile roughness feedback during the pressing process. This method is expected to increase the difficulty of identifying shoulder surfing and thermal imaging attacks.

2 Design Approach

In the design, the user's cognitive process of entering a password is extended and augmented to the design of the password keypad press mechanism in this study. During the pressing process, in addition to the normal password input, hereafter referred to as the clear code, the pressure password, hereafter referred to as the dark code, is simultaneously pressed. By simultaneously pressing the clear code and dark code, the success rate of password attacks can be effectively reduced. Simultaneously entering both clear and obscure passwords effectively reduce the success rate of password attacks. Typically, clear passwords are vulnerable to visual recognition attacks such as shoulder surfing [2, 5] and thermal imaging attacks [6] that can identify the sequence and location of password inputs. However, obscure passwords based on pressure sensors are not easily attacked because pressure information cannot be easily recognized visually. By integrating a tactile feedback mechanism, different vibration sensations are provided to users based on the pressure applied when entering obscure passwords, distinguishing between light and heavy pressure, and indicating the interval of the password being input. To achieve this, it is necessary to understand the parameters of the pressure required for each key, with light pressure being 1–10 kPa [7], medium pressure being 10–50 kPa, and heavy pressure being greater than 50 kPa [8].

The vibration frequency range that humans can perceive is between 10 Hz to 200 Hz [9], and the lower the vibration frequency, the coarser the perceived vibration feedback [10]. For the light pressure range (1 kPa to 10 kPa), a 50 Hz vibration frequency will be used to generate a coarser tactile feedback. On the other hand, for the heavy pressure range (10 kPa to 50 kPa), a vibration frequency of 150 Hz will be used to provide finer tactile feedback.

2.1 Sensor Architecture

A capacitive pressure sensor is composed of two electrodes and a dielectric layer over-laid together. In the application scenario of pressure sensing, the capacitance can be changed by altering the relative distance between the two electrode plates. To realize the characteristics of a capacitive sensor, the upper and lower electrode plates need to be designed as a fixed and controllable mechanical structure. The upper electrode plate is made into an elastic layer by bonding it with PDMS, taking advantage of the high elasticity of PDMS. The lower electrode plate is implemented using a PCB circuit board and is separated and maintained at a distance from the upper electrode plate by a spacer. After stacking the upper electrode elastic layer, spacer, and lower electrode PCB board together, the prototype of the capacitive pressure sensor is completed (see Fig. 1 Fig. 2).

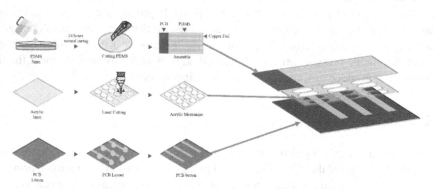

Fig. 1. Process Flow for Manufacturing a Pressure Sensing Pin pad with Bonded Soft Layer and Integrated Circuits

When pressure is applied by the finger on the elastic layer, the deformation of the upper electrode layer causes a change in capacitance by bringing the upper and lower electrode plates closer together. The capacitance value is then detected and analyzed by the driving and sensing circuits to determine the corresponding pressure range (see Fig. 2).

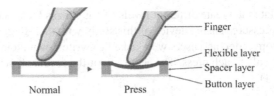

Fig. 2. When an external force is applied to the soft layer, it results in a deformation that alters the sensing capacitance.

2.2 Sensor Circuit Design

A square wave signal is generated by a high-frequency signal generator and transmitted to the upper electrode elastic layer through an array scanning method. The voltage values of each key are sequentially received by the lower electrode. When the signal passes through the capacitive pressure sensor, there will be a certain amount of signal loss. Therefore, the signal voltage needs to be preliminarily amplified and filtered by an OPA amplifier. The amplified square wave signal is then converted to a DC voltage signal by an RMS-to-DC converter. The voltage is then read by an ADC IC, and the Arduino determines the pressing force and provides corresponding vibration tactile feedback (see Fig. 3).

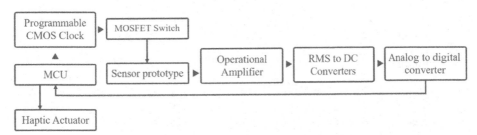

Fig. 3. Diagram of Circuit Control Architecture for Electronic System

3 Results

In order to provide real-time feedback on the force of the user's finger pressing, the pressing force in this experiment was divided into light and heavy pressures. During the light pressure process, a low-frequency vibration of 50 Hz was used to remind the user, with a coarser texture. However, during heavy pressure, a high-frequency vibration of 150 Hz was used to remind the user, with a finer texture. In this way, the user is reminded of the current pressure level. Ten subjects will be recruited for this experiment, and three experiments will be conducted.

3.1 Roughness Perception Experiment

To verify users' acceptance of the roughness feedback, various frequencies were tested to determine their effect on users' perception of roughness. Vibrations at 50 Hz, 100 Hz, and

150 Hz were simulated to create different levels of roughness feedback, and users were asked to press the pressure sensing device of this study with their fingers. The vibrations were given in random order, and users were asked to write down their perception of the roughness feedback after each press. The accuracy of the feedback perception was then analyzed (see Fig. 4).

Fig. 4. Testing Vibration and Roughness Simulation on Pressure Sensing Pin pad

The user's accuracy rate in distinguishing three different levels of roughness was 46%, indicating that the roughness can be perceived but the recognition effect was not significant (see Fig. 5).

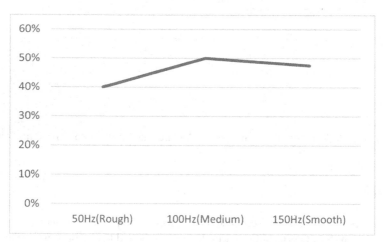

Fig. 5. User Accuracy in Identifying Three Different Roughness Identifications on Pressure Sensing Pin pad: Results and Implications

3.2 Password Accuracy Experiment

This experiment aims to investigate the success rate of entering both a numeric and a pressure password when there is or is not tactile feedback. Participants will be given a set of numeric and pressure passwords and will use their fingers to press the pressure sensor device according to the instructions on the password sheet. When there is tactile feedback, the vibration motor will provide different levels of roughness feedback for different pressure levels during the password input process, which can be perceived through the linear vibration motor in the finger (see Fig. 6 Fig. 7).

Fig. 6. Testing Password Accuracy using Pressure Sensing Keyboard with and without Tactile Roughness Feedback

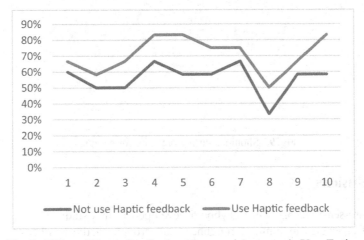

Fig. 7. Effect of Haptic Feedback on Password Accuracy in User Testing

3.3 Shoulder Surfing Experiment

This experiment involves two participants simultaneously testing. One user uses the pressure sensing device of this study to input both the number password and the force password with their fingers according to the password list. Meanwhile, the shoulder surfer observes the pressing process by using shoulder surfing attack and answers the contents of the number and force passwords (see Fig. 8 Fig. 9).

Fig. 8. Protecting Pin pad Passwords from Shoulder Surfing Attacks: Rear and Side Placement of Pressure Sensing Pin pad.

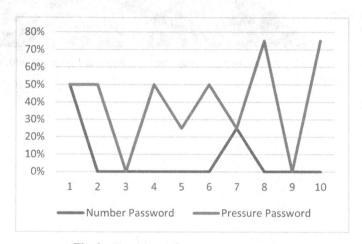

Fig. 9. Shoulder surfing prevents correct rate

4 Conclusions

The pressure-sensitive password keyboard developed in this study provides different vibration frequencies to simulate roughness and provide tactile feedback. Users can use the tactile feedback mechanism to distinguish the strength of the pressure applied, allowing them to clearly understand the intensity of the pressure during password entry. With tactile feedback, the input accuracy reached 70.83%, which is much higher than the 56.00% accuracy achieved without tactile feedback. In addition, under the condition of shoulder surfing, the defense rate of the numeric password was only 8%, while the defense rate of the pressure password was 40%, proving its effectiveness in achieving password protection.

References

1. Rizqi, M.R., Waluyo, A., Edgy, G.M., Sunaringtyas, S.U.: Enhanced authentication mechanism for Automated Teller Machine (ATM) through implementation of soft two-factor authentication. In: Editor (ed.) Book Enhanced Authentication Mechanism for Automated Teller Machine (ATM) through Implementation of Soft Two-Factor Authentication, pp. 3–7 (2020)

2. Lai, J., AArko, E.: A shoulder-surfing resistant scheme embedded in traditional passwords. In: Proceedings of the Annual Hawaii International Conference on System Sciences, pp. Medium: X (2021)
3. Varma, M., Watson, S., Chan, L., Peiris, R.: VibroAuth: authentication with haptics based non-visual, rearranged keypads to mitigate shoulder surfing attacks. In: Moallem, A. (ed.) HCII 2022. LNCS, vol. 13333, pp. 280–303. Springer, Cham (2022). https://doi.org/10.1007/978-3-031-05563-8_19
4. Düzgün, R., Mayer, P., Volkamer, M.: Shoulder-surfing resistant authentication for augmented reality. In: Editor (ed.) Book Shoulder-Surfing Resistant Authentication for Augmented Reality, pp. 1–13 (2022)
5. Binbeshr, F., Mat Kiah, M.L., Por, L.Y., Zaidan, A.A.: A systematic review of PIN-entry methods resistant to shoulder-surfing attacks. Comput. Secur. **101**, 102116 (2021)
6. Kaczmarek, T., Ozturk, E., Tsudik, G.: Thermanator: thermal residue-based post factum attacks on keyboard data entry. In: Editor (ed.) Book Thermanator: Thermal Residue-Based Post Factum Attacks on Keyboard Data Entry, pp. 586–593 (2019)
7. Mahata, C., Algadi, H., Lee, J., Kim, S., Lee, T.: Biomimetic-inspired micro-nano hierarchical structures for capacitive pressure sensor applications. Measurement **151**, 107095 (2020)
8. Liao, X., Wang, W., Zhong, L., Lai, X., Zheng, Y.: Synergistic sensing of stratified structures enhancing touch recognition for multifunctional interactive electronics. Nano Energy **62**, 410–418 (2019)
9. Ozioko, O., Navaraj, W., Hersh, M., Dahiya, R.: Tacsac: a wearable haptic device with capacitive touch-sensing capability for tactile display. Sensors **20**(17), 4780 (2020)
10. Hassan, A., George, A., Varghese, L., Antony, M., Sherly, K.K.: The biometric cardless transaction with shuffling keypad using proximity sensor, pp. 505–508 (2020)

Grammaticalisation of a Hybrid Interface

Marina Derzho⬤, Alex Shafarenko(✉)⬤, and Mariana Lilley⬤

University of Hertfordshire, College Lane, Hatfield AL10 9AB, UK
{m.derzho,a.shafarenko}@herts.ac.uk

Abstract. This paper presents the next stage in development of the hybrid interface concept, published earlier. Hybrid means a combination of a CLI and a GUI intended to best serve control applications (as opposed to data acquisition and search ones) when operators' familiarity with the application may vary a great deal. We focus on capturing the graphic and command-line behaviour solely by the grammar of the control language, which makes our approach quasi application-independent. Use of an extended BNF grammar overloaded with graphical behaviour is discussed and pros and cons briefly outlined.

Keywords: Graphical User Interface (GUI) · Command Line Interface (CLI) · Hybrid interface · graphicalisation · attribute grammar

1 Introduction

In this article we report work in progress on the project "Hybrid Interface" conducted by the University of Hertfordshire Human-Centred Computing group.

The concept of hybrid interface was defined and discussed in our previous work [1]. We stated that control applications are resistant to the conventional GUI approach for two major reasons:

1. A control application typically has a large number of commands having several optional parameters, of which only a small subset is used frequently, but the rest should still be accessible should the need arise.
2. The choice of commands and their parameters changes infrequently; there is a high degree of repetition.

In such circumstances a pure GUI compels the user to repeat almost without modification a sequence of graphical actions (mouse clicks, control selection etc.) on a hierarchy of unfolding pages, making it a protracted, tedious and error-prone process. The CLI interface, on the other hand, provides a direct access to a finely tuned command as it can be entered by keyboard or fetched from a command script. Having said that, the learning curve of the CLI tends to be steeper than that of the GUI interface as the user has to recall (or be prompted to) various action verbs and command parameters, whereas a typical GUI provides extensive guidance around its graphical controls. We argued in [1] that this challenge can be addressed by taking a hybrid approach: a combination of an active command line supported by continual analysis of the content being entered

© The Author(s), under exclusive license to Springer Nature Switzerland AG 2023
C. Stephanidis et al. (Eds.): HCII 2023, CCIS 1832, pp. 224–229, 2023.
https://doi.org/10.1007/978-3-031-35989-7_28

and a set of GUI controls kept consistent with the state of the line. The user can utilise either part of the hybrid interface at any stage, including right from the beginning. As the user becomes more and more familiar with the command language, we expect that the graphical facilities will be used less often. Also, as the system learns the user's typical behaviour, parts of the command language become graphicalised, offering the user accelerated command-entry opportunities.

The difficulty we immediately discovered in our design efforts was that command languages for large systems (for example, a Linux shell) tend to be extensive: they support hundreds of highly diverse commands, whose parameters can be of a variety of types and forms. The CLI part should validate input and provide useful prompts, which requires a language-specific implementation. Since the GUI part reflects the CLI structures, its implementation must also be language-specific. Furthermore, both parts should be derived from the same language, or more precisely, from the same grammar. We seek an elegant solution whereby the grammar definition is overloaded with the information about the graphics controls, so that not only the CLI's active parser but also the GUI structures can be derived from it (Fig. 1).

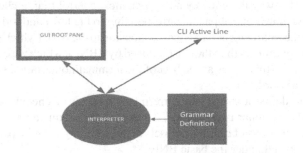

Fig. 1. Grammaticalised hybrid interface.

In the next section we discuss the grammar that we intend to use in our experiments. Section 3 is for related work and there are some conclusions.

2   Grammar

A command-line grammar is typified by the grammar of Linux shell commands, which is not only simple but also regular. This means that it can be defined by a regular expression, for example:

$$<\text{command ls}> = \text{ls } (-(l|a|r))^* [\char`\^-].^*$$

That is, the 'ls' command of Linux starts with a verb ls followed by zero or more options, each specified as a minus '−' followed by a single letter (l, a, or r); and that is followed by a filename that must not begin with '−', and which can be empty. This is a simplified example, since the 'ls' command has many more options and can have more than one filename specified. Also some of the options require a value (e.g., an integer) to follow after a space. Nevertheless, all commands can be described by a regular grammar, albeit an unwieldy one.

This grammar defines the structure of the command precisely, but its graphicalisation would involve a separate description of the GUI part as well as its relationship with parts of the regular expression. The grammar does not define the structure and properties of any GUI that can be constructed to support the same functionality.

We propose to relax the grammatical constraint and ascend to the level of context-free grammars instead. Whereas a regular grammar permits only production rules of the form

    \<nonterminal\> ::= \<terminal\>

    and

    \<nonterminal\> ::= \< terminal\> \<nonterminal\>

which are equivalent in descriptive power to regular expressions, general context-free grammars are an extension of that, allowing the right-hand side to be a sequence of terminals and nonterminals of any length. We require the grammar to be *separable* in that a terminal string in the right-hand-side can only be specified in only one rule of extended BNF. This way the corresponding graphical control (e.g. a checkbox) can be placed inside a definite control panel, corresponding to the left-hand-side nonterminal.

We propose the following metalanguage extension to the BNF (which does not define a broader class of grammars than the one produced by a BNF), which we call *set brackets*:

    $(|e_1, e_2, ..., e_n|)$ (*this codes any subset of the terminal/nonterminal set $e_1, e_2, ..., e_n$ concatenated in any order*)

This helps to define a string that corresponds to a set of checkboxes in the GUI part. As far as the grammar is concerned, the expression is equivalent to the 2^n strings containing concatenations of different subsets of the set $e_1, e_2, ..., e_n$ separated by choice bars, and so is covered under the basic BNF.

3 GUI Controls

Checkbox Panel. We interpret concatenation ',' as *horizontal* between set brackets. A double comma is functionally the same but has a *vertical* GUI interpretation. For example, in our extended EBNF, the following separable rules

```
regimes = (|(* washing modes: *)wash,,(* drying modes: *)dry|)
wash = (|"-d"(* delicate *),"-f"(* fast *),"-e"(* economic *)|)
dry = (|"-s"(* slow *), "-c" (* cool *) |)
```

define regimes of a washing machine as options to a washcommand. For the CLI part this would be equivalent to

$$regimes = (|\,"-d", "-f", "-e", "-s", "-c"\,|)$$

but for the GUI part, a panel with 5 check boxes will be produced, such as this:

```
washing modes:  ☐ delicate (-d)    ☐ fast (-f)    ☐ economic (-e)
drying modes:   ☐ slow (-s)         ☐ cool (-c)
```

EBNF allows nonterminals to consist of more than one word, separated by the space. We use this opportunity to inject graphical meaning. A nonterminal in a command language grammar intended for a hybrid interface may contain an optional second word, defining the nature of the graphical control. If it is not specified, the default control is used. For example, for a nonterminal with a set bracket at the top level of the right-hand side, we assume a checkbox panel to be the graphical version. However, if the suffix menu is used:

```
regimes menu = (|(* washing modes *)wash,,(* drying modes *)dry|)
```

a pull-down menu is produced with the behaviour of menu items conforming to the rules for nonterminals. In this particular case, the menu will have a divider, with the upper part titled "washing modes" and the lower part "drying modes" and the labels that we placed around checkboxes now presented as menu items in the corresponding parts.

Radio Buttons. EBNF contains an operator "|", which is used to define alternatives. We overload it with a graphical meaning as an indication that the corresponding controls are operated as radio buttons with the first one checked by default:

```
temperature = (*70°*)"-hot" | (*70°*)"-warm" | (*70°*)"-cold"
```

```
70°(-hot) ◉    40°(-hot) ○    30°(-warm) ○
```

Naturally the menu suffix applies here and has the same effect (a pull-down menu with alternative choice of menu items). If the group of alternatives is enclosed in the square brackets, which mean 'optional' in EBNF, the default interpretation is radio buttons without a default choice. With the menu suffix none of the items is checked by default. Vertical vs horizontal composition is conveyed by doubling the vertical bars, similar to doubling the comma in the previous case.

Text Parameter. Commands may contain arbitrary textual parameters, delimited by either whitespace or some punctuation. The corresponding GUI control is a text-entry field. ISO 14977 standard [3] for EBNF allows an arbitrary string between two question marks '?' to be used as an externally defined nonterminal. We utilise this facility to allow a regular expression to be specified that defines a set of allowable inputs, for example:

```
filename = ?@[^-].*\.txt@?
```

which is a text string that must not start with a '-' and which ends with '.txt'. The character immediately following the first question mark is interpreted as a new delimiter since a regular expression can contain a question mark in it, which would introduce an ambiguity. On the graphic side, the text-entry field is equipped with a validation facility which checks user input based on the regular expression when the focus moves out of the control.

Recursion. What makes this approach particularly simple is that we eschew recursion, which is inherent in programming language grammar definitions, but typically not in command-line languages. Non-recursive grammars are graphicalised particularly simply as they define a finite hierarchy of containers enclosed in other containers up to and including the whole command, or even the whole command set. However, it is conceivable that some instructions require a recursive structure, for example when some kind of 'expression' is to be entered. There is a conventional approach to recursive structures in GUI, exemplified with the Microsoft Equation Editor [4]. However, the idea here is to approach the grammar top-down, rather than the usual bottom up as per standard shift-reduce parser [5], and that breaks the principle of hybridisation. The operator would have to jump around an expression following a structured pattern; for example in an <exp> + <exp> situation, the '+' would be structurally above the two expressions and would have to be navigated to in a special way. Linear editing of a recursive structure generally destroys that structure, causing, in the case of a hybrid interface, sudden and unexpected changes of the configuration of the graphic controls. Our approach to recursion is to relegate it to unstructured text marked by EBNF extension brackets ?"…"?. The text between the quotes is in fact a nonterminal not reachable from the start symbol of the grammar but which expands to a text string using grammar rules. This way the implementation is fully CLI without a graphical component, but the text can be presented in the form of a text-entry control with input validation on the basis of the nonterminal provided.

Related Work: Piggybacking semantic information on grammar rules has been known for a long time thanks to Knuth's concept of attribute grammars. The way we use them is not for derivation of the language's semantic attributes from terminals to nonterminals of higher and higher levels; we would like to use attributes to define graphic representations of syntactic entities and major features of the layout of the GUI part. If we succeed, we will produce a *generic* hybrid interface configurable by a single configuration entity: a grammar definition.

4   Conclusions

Using context-free grammar (EBNF) enriched with GUI semantics is an elegant and effective way of supporting a hybrid interface. Our analysis shows that behavioural characteristics of GUI controls can be reflected in grammatical structures, e.g. choice bars and set brackets. We have also discovered that hybridisation of recursive grammars is problematic even if techniques exemplified by the MS Equation Editor are used. The reason being that they require explicit top-down parsing of user input, whereas hybridisation needs to maintain correspondence between the command line and GUI controls, which requires bottom up analysis (such as the standard shift-reduce parser).

Future work will focus on the implementation of the hybrid generator, which will produce a parser and a dynamic GUI from a grammar definition in EBNF.

References

1. Derzho, M., Shafarenko, A., Lilley, M.: Controlling an application via a hybrid interface. In: Stephanidis, C., Antona, M., Ntoa, S. (eds.) HCII 2022, pp. 194–200. Springer, Cham (2022). https://doi.org/10.1007/978-3-031-06417-3_26
2. Knuth, D.E.: The genesis of attribute grammars. In: Deransart, P., Jourdan, M. (eds.) Attribute Grammars and their Applications. LNCS, vol. 461, pp. 1–12. Springer, Heidelberg (1990). https://doi.org/10.1007/3-540-53101-7_1
3. BS ISO/IEC 14977:1996: Information technology. Syntactic Metalanguage. Extended BNF (1996)
4. Gebhard, C., Rosenblum, B.: Wrangling math from Microsoft Word into JATS XML workflows. In: The Journal Article Tag Suite Conference (JATS-Con) Proceedings 2016. National Center for Biotechnology Information (US), Bethesda, MD (2016). https://doi-org.ezproxy.herts.ac.uk/ https://doi.org/10.1002/leap.1058
5. Knuth, D.E.: On the translation of languages from left to right. Inf. Control **8**(6), 607–639 (1965)

Tactile Angle Characteristics for Reproduction by Force Sensation

Manabu Ishihara[1][(✉)] and Kazuhiro Owada[2]

[1] National Institute of Technology, Tokyo College, Hachioji 193-0997, Tokyo, Japan
`ishihara@m.ieice.org`
[2] National Institute of Technology, Oyama College, Tochigi 323-0806, Japan

Abstract. In recent years, studies on tactile sensations have been actively conducted. The tactile sense enables people to touch and move objects remotely and feel the weight, shape, and smoothness of the surface of an object. A haptic device is a system that stimulates the deep space of muscles and tendons by applying physical force to the fingers or hands. Moreover, the tactile sensation is sensed by stimulating physical contact. These two senses are not considered to be reciprocal. However, in practice, when we explore the surface condition of an object, we have experienced that this exploration provides a mutual stimulus of tactile and force senses, for example, when writing on Japanese paper with a brush. Therefore, this study evaluated whether tactile stimuli can be reproduced using a force-sensing device.

Keywords: Haptic device · Tactile sensation · Surface condition

1 Introduction

In recent years, studies on tactile sensations have been actively conducted. The tactile sense enables people to touch and move objects remotely and feel the weight, shape, and smoothness of the surface of an object. A haptic device [1–3] is a system that stimulates the deep space of muscles and tendons by applying physical force to the fingers or hands. Moreover, the tactile sensation is sensed by stimulating physical contact. These two senses are not considered to be reciprocal. However, in practice, when we explore the surface condition of an object, we have experienced that this exploration provides a mutual stimulus of tactile and force senses, for example, when writing on Japanese paper with a brush. The advantages of a system that uses virtual reality (VR) are that the software program can be modified to allow different types of technical training to be performed with a single device, and the work environment can be easily changed. Another advantage is that a network can be used to allow multiple users to train at different remote locations [4–6]. Therefore, this study evaluated whether tactile stimuli can be reproduced using a haptic device.

C. Stephanidis et al. (Eds.): HCII 2023, CCIS 1832, pp. 230–238, 2023.
https://doi.org/10.1007/978-3-031-35989-7_29

2 Experimental Apparatus

Sensable's "PHANToM Omni" (hereinafter referred to as PHANToM) was used as a device to reproduce tactile actions through a haptic device. The application to reproduce the tactile actions was developed using "Microsoft Visual C++ 2010" and the 3D graphics library using "OpenGL Utility Toolkit" on a Windows 10 Education © 2018 Microsoft Corporation.

3 Outline of the Experiment

The limit value of the "roughness" sensation a person can feel in a virtual space through a haptic (force-sensing) device was determined in a previous study [7]. In this study, we examined materials to evaluate the roughness interval when the unevenness was placed on the board as a standard. In particular, we investigated the materials that can be used to determine the interval between the roughness and unevenness of the board. In this study, we investigated the state of palpation of the human body. We assumed a palpation sensation on and under the skin. The actual execution screen of the program is shown in Fig. 1(a) and (b).

Fig. 1. **(a)** Haptic device(PHANToM Omni) **(b)** Program execution screen

3.1 Differences in Object Recognition when the Board was Fixed

We measured experimentally the difference in recognizing spaces between bumps using PHANToM. In this experiment, a standard board was created on the screen, objects were placed on it and changed in several patterns of shapes, and the differences due to the shapes were examined. The shape of the object was performed with three patterns: a standard figure, vertex change, and inclination change, as shown in Fig. 2.

Fig. 2. Shape of the objects

The subjects were asked to compare the friction sensation at four different intervals, and the results were calculated as the percentage of correct answers, with "the narrowest" as 1, "the second narrowest" as 2, "the third narrowest" as 3, and "the fourth narrowest" as 4.

Standard Model. We measured whether people could recognize the sensation of unevenness in the case of a standard figure. The shape of the standard figure is shown in Fig. 2. The experimental settings are listed in Table 1.

Table 1. Setting value of Standard Model

Experimental conditions	Setting value
Spacing between objects	0.1, 0.15, 0.2, 0.25 [mm]
Angles	45°
Height	0.345 [mm]
Age of subjects	18 to 22 [Years old] (15 persons)

Vertex Change. We measured whether people could recognize the unevenness sensation when the vertex of an object was changed. The shapes of the objects are shown in Fig. 2. The experimental setup is presented in Table 2.

Table 2. Setting value of Vertex change

Experimental conditions	Setting value
Spacing between objects	0.1, 0.15, 0.2, 0.25 [mm]
Angles	30°
Height	0.345 [mm]
Age of subjects	18 to 22 [Years old] (15 persons)

Variation of Inclination Angles. We measured whether people could recognize the sensation of unevenness when the slope of an object was changed. The shapes of the objects are shown in Fig. 2. The experimental settings are listed in Table 3.

Table 3. Setting value of Variation of inclination angles

Experimental conditions	Setting value
Spacing between objects	0.5, 0.8, 0.9, 1.0, 1.5, 2.0
Ratio of circle radius	1.5
Angles	45 [degree]
Height	0.345 [mm]
Age of subjects	18 to 22 [Years old] (15 persons)

3.2 Determination of Object Recognition Assuming a Realistic Environment

We measured the ability of PHANToM to recognize a real object under the assumption that a real object was present. The experimental setup is presented in Table 4. The program execution screen is shown in Fig. 3. Here, we assume a breast cancer lump. The lump that a person can recognize in a real environment is 1 cm in diameter [8]. Based on this, we gradually decreased the size of the diameter by 1 cm as a standard and measured the minimum value at which the object could be recognized.

Table 4. Variables for experiments on object recognition assuming reality

Experimental conditions	Setting value
Spacing between objects	5.13 and 1.38, 2.3, 3.46, 4.61 [mm]
Angles	30, 45, 60 [Deg]
Height	0.354 [mm]
Age of subjects	18 to 22 [Years old] (15 persons)

Fig. 3. Program execution screen

4 Experimental Results

4.1 Differences in Object Recognition when the Board is Fixed

The experimental 3.1.1 results are presented in Fig. 4 and Table 5. In the standard figure, that is, the triangular prism, the results changed slightly depending on whether the objects were visually observed.

Table 5. Change in sensory volume due to differences in surface model settings

	Percentage of correct answers (%)		
	Standard model	Vertex change	Inclination change
Visual inspection	100	86	100
Not sighted	80	20	60

Visual inspection was defined as the appearance of objects placed on a board. The percentage of correct answers was 80% without visual inspection, which was 20% less than that with the visual inspection.

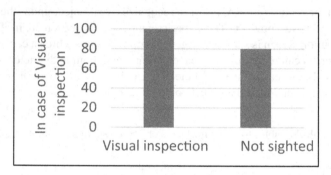

Fig. 4. In case of Visual inspection and not sighted

Vertex Change. The experimental 3.1.2 results are shown in Fig. 5, and the vertex changes are listed in Table 5. For vertex change, the correct response rate was 87% when the subject observed the vertex and 20% when the subject did not observe the vertex. This is because the pen can only trace up to the vertex for the standard stimulus. Moreover, the force to move up the slope is small, as shown in Fig. 6. However, for a vertex change, the tip of the pen is circular; thus, the force to move to the other side of the slope becomes large. Therefore, if the distance between the two slopes is minimal, the pens will jump over the unevenness, and the correct answer rate will be lower because of the misunderstanding that the distance between the two slopes is substantially wide. Thus, the object is prone to be misrecognized when the distance between the two objects is narrow, regardless of whether the object is visually observed. The misrecognition rate of an object is also considered to depend on its shape.

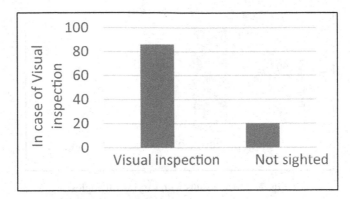

Fig 5. Visual effects of vertex changes

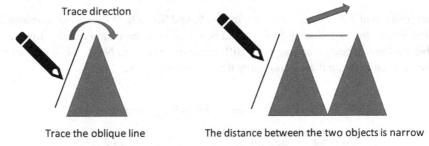

Fig. 6. Single and multiple configurations tracing models

Inclination Change. The experimental 3.1.3 results are shown in Fig. 7, and the tilt variations are presented in Table 4. For example, the percentage of correct responses decreased when the figures were not observed. The percentage of correct responses in the tilt variation was 60%, which was 20% lower than 80% for the standard figure. This is because the shape of the object affects people's recognition of it because the correct response rate decreases when the distance between the objects narrows. The above three experiments showed that the percentage of correct responses decreased when the participants were not observed the object compared to when they observed the object. Therefore, a device providing visual information is required when the force-sensing device is used remotely.

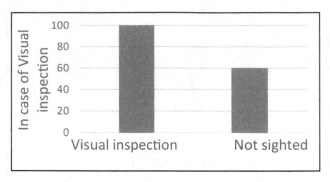

Fig. 7. Model results with varying tilt angles

4.2 Identification of Vertex Distance Changes in Standard Shapes

The experimental 3.2 results are shown in Fig. 8, and Table 6. If the device contains an internal inertia, the experimental results will be unstable in the vicinity of the limit value at which a human being can judge the difference in sensation. Next, the senses of the subject are stable when there is no internal inertia of the device.

Table 6. Experimental results of recognition assuming reality

	Minimum value [cm]	Maximum value [cm]
30°	0.1 to 0.15	0.2 to 0.25
45°	0 to 0.1	0.2 to 0.25
60°	0 to 0.1	0.2 to 0.25

In addition, according to the results of the interviews with the subjects, many of them responded that the difference in the unevenness was clear. This suggests that the internal inertia of the device affected the subjects' judgments. In this experiment, the threshold for determining the distance between the vertices of the standard figure did not vary significantly with angle. However, when the minimum value was 30°, there was a significant difference in perception at other angles. It is difficult to detect when the angles of the model are small and the distance between vertices is small. It is also difficult to detect when the angles of the model are large and the vertices are widely spaced. The results for the 1 cm diameter case, used as a standard in this study, showed that all subjects could recognise the object. However, in order to simulate a real environment, it is necessary to adjust the skin sensation. In particular, if we intend to palpate the inside of the human body from the outside.

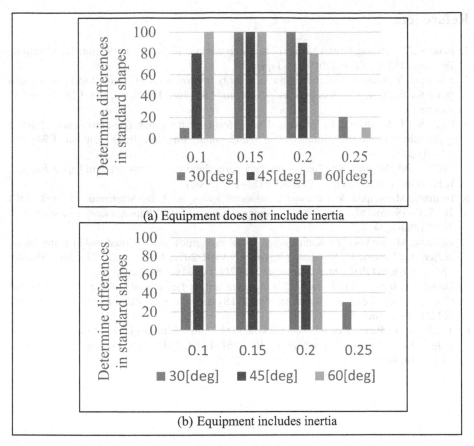

(a) Equipment does not include inertia

(b) Equipment includes inertia

Fig. 8. Inertia effects on equipment by identifying standard shapes

5 Conclusions

In this experiment, we investigated the influence of human vision on object recognition and object recognition in a realistic environment. However, we could not reproduce the real environment through the implemented experimental method.

Experiments have been conducted on the relationship between the manipulation and the reproduction of the force sensing device. The effect of equipment inertia was also found to be important in reproducing surface roughness. The model must be reconstructed to reproduce the surface roughness. The experiment should also consider the spacing of the vertices and the combination of vertex shapes.

Acknowledgments. This work was supported by JSPS KAKENHI Grant Number 21K12186.

References

1. Ishibashi, Y., Huang, P.: Mechanism of haptic communications. J. Inst. Electron. Inf. Commun. Eng. Jpn. **102**(1), 42–46 (2019). (in Japanese)
2. Ishibashi, Y., Huang, P.: Stabilization and quality improvement of remote robot control with force feedback. J. Inst. Electron. Inf. Commun. Eng. Jpn. **J99-B**(10), 911–925 (2016). (in Japanese)
3. Ohnishi, H., Mochizuki, K.: Effect of delay of feedback force on perception of elastic force: a psychophysical approach. Inst. Electron. Inf. Commun. Eng. Jpn. Trans. Commun. **E90-B**(1), 12–20 (2007)
4. Ishihara, M., Negishi, N.: Effect of feedback force delays on the operation of haptic displays. IEEJ Trans. Electr. Electron. Eng. **3**(1), 151–153 (2008)
5. Ishihara, M.: Haptic device using a soldering test system. In: Stephanidis, C. (ed.) HCI 2015. CCIS, vol. 528, pp. 190–195. Springer, Cham (2015). https://doi.org/10.1007/978-3-319-21380-4_34
6. Ishihara, M., Komori, T.: Auditory and visual properties in the virtual reality using haptic device. In: Lackey, S., Shumaker, R. (eds.) VAMR 2016. LNCS, vol. 9740, pp. 135–146. Springer, Cham (2016). https://doi.org/10.1007/978-3-319-39907-2_13
7. Owada, K., Iijima, Y., Ishihara, M.: Tactile characteristic reproduced by force. In: 2022 Annual Conference of Electronics and Information and Systems Society. IEE of Japan, pp. 1391–1392 (2022). (in Japanese)
8. Tsujimoto, F.: Reading comparison between MMG and US images in breast cancer screening. J. Jpn. Assoc. Breast Cancer Screen **23**(1), 161–184 (2014). https://doi.org/10.3804/jjabcs.23.161. (in Japanese)

Portable Transformable Kit

Masaya Ishino and Mitsuharu Matsumoto[✉] [iD]

The University of Electro-Communications, 1-5-1, Chofugaoka, Chofu-shi, Tokyo 182-8585, Japan
mitsuharu.matsumoto@ieee.org

Abstract. In this paper, we describe a portable transformable device composed of shape memory resin. Although many studies on transformable robots focus on their mobility to adapt various environments, few studies pay attention to using transformable robots in our daily life. To solve the problem, we focus on the applications of transformable devices to our daily usage. In previous research, we used a water heater to transform the device by preparing hot water. Although we could show the potential of the device, it is not so convenient for users to use them. In this research, we improved it so that it can be transformed by using a USB connector to overcome the shortcomings of past devices. The developed devices are lightweight and easy to carry. Users can just connect the USB cable from the devices and can easily transform the device and combine them. We show some examples of usage scenario to show the potential of our proposed approach.

Keywords: Transformable Device · Shape memory resin · Heating by USB

1 Introduction

Transformable robot is a robot that can change its shape. There are many studies on transformable robots in the past. A hybrid robot proposed by Kossett et al. can fly with a helicopter mod and move on the ground with a wheel mode [1]. A robot proposed by Boria also can move and fly [2]. They extend the locomotion possibilities of conventional robots but limit their deformation. Modular robots (MSRs) are other approaches to adapt to various environments [3]. They are composed of many simple robots with a simple structure called modules. The earliest research on MSR started in the 1980s, and various studies have been done [4]. For example, Gilpin et al. have proposed a grid-like modular robot [5]. Kurokawa made several reports on a modular robot called M-TRAN [6]. Yim et al., have developed a modular robot with a different gait form called Pollybot [7]. In these studies, they have succeeded in forming complex robots with various movements from modular robots with simple structures. In the field of research on human-machine coexistence, there are several studies aimed at applying swarm robots to everyday life [8, 9]. In recent years, research on the daily use of sheet-type transforming robots has been proposed by Ishida et al. [10]. Their research demonstrates the applicability of transformable robots to our daily lives. However, their research is considering the application of transforming robots to tableware, and the range of applications is limited. In

© The Author(s), under exclusive license to Springer Nature Switzerland AG 2023
C. Stephanidis et al. (Eds.): HCII 2023, CCIS 1832, pp. 239–243, 2023.
https://doi.org/10.1007/978-3-031-35989-7_30

this research, we follow the idea of modular robots that realize complex shapes with simple structures, and aim to realize various functions by combining deformable devices with simple structures. In this paper, we introduce a portable deformation kit for daily use. It is composed of many stick-shaped devices. In our previous study, the devices are transformed after heating the device by using the water heater [11]. They can be transformed using a battery or USB and can be connected. The device is made of shape memory resin and is lightweight and easy to carry. By combining them, users can create various structure for daily use.

2 Overview of the Proposed Devices

Figure 1 shows the usage scenario of the proposed device. When the user uses it, s/he connect to the battery or USB-C connecter. After the connection, the device is softened. The user can deform it if necessary. By freely deforming the device shape, the user can use the device for various purposes in daily life such as pen stands and hangers. Considering the convenience for actual use, the following conditions were set as the required specifications.

1. The rigidity of the device can be changed as needed.
2. The device is light enough for the user to carry the device.
3. The device can not only change its shape but also expand and contract.

We selected shape memory resin as the material for the device to meet the above specifications. Shape memory resin has the advantage of being light and capable of deforming its shape as many times as necessary. If there is no external force, it will return to its original shape just by immersing it. It was thought that the required specifications 1 and 2 could be satisfied by using a shape memory resin. The requirement specification 3 is solved by devising the shape design of the device as shown in Fig. 2.

3 Examples to Use Devices

We show some examples to clarify the usage scenario of the proposed device. Figure 3 shows a usage example of the device as a hanger (hook). To verify its usability as a hanger, we transformed the device into a hook shape and checked whether we could actually hang an object. The figures on left and right in Fig. 3 show the shape of the actually deformed hanger without and with hanging a backpack, respectively. The prototype is made by combining two devices and is transformed so that it can be hooked on a desk. As shown in Fig. 3, it was confirmed that it can be used as a hook to hang a backpack. Figure 4 shows a usage example of the device as a smartphone stand. The prototype is made by combining three devices and is transformed so that it can be used as a smartphone stand. The figures on left and right in Fig. 4 show the shape of the actually deformed smartphone stand without and with a smartphone, respectively. The first example showed the strength of the device enough for daily use. The second example shows the effect of the combination of the device (Fig. 4).

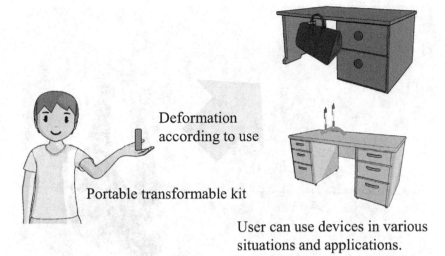

Deformation
according to use

Portable transformable kit

User can use devices in various
situations and applications.

Fig. 1. Application scenario of the proposed device.

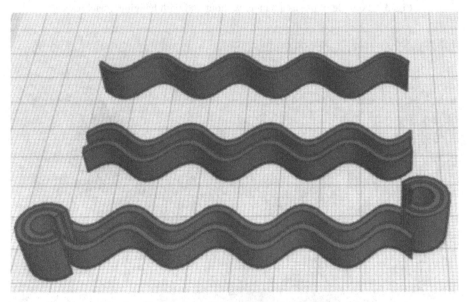

Fig. 2. CAD design of a portable transformable device.

Fig. 3. Example of use as a hanger without and with hanging a backpack.

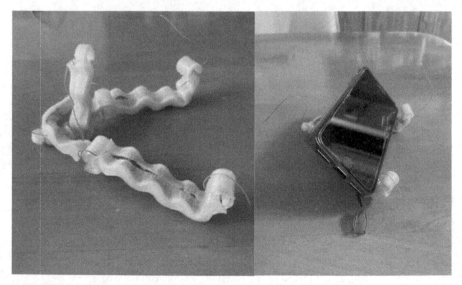

Fig. 4. Example of use as a smartphone stand without and with a smartphone.

4 Conclusion

In this paper, we introduced an improved portable transformable device composed of shape memory resin. Users can easily soften the devices by connecting USB-C connecters unlike previous devices. To show the applicability of the proposed devices, we showed some usage examples.

Although it becomes easier to use the devices by improving them, it should still be improved regarding cooling system. We also would like to apply the proposed devices to educational fields.

Acknowledgements. This research was supported by JSPS KAKENHI Grant Number JP20H02412.

References

1. Kosett, A., Papanikolopoulos, N.: A robust miniature robot design for land/air hybrid loco-motion. In: Proceedings of 2011 International Conference on Robotics and Automation, pp. 4595–4600 (2011)
2. Boria, F., Bachmann, R., Ifju, P., Quinn, R., Vaidyanathan, R., Perry, C.: A sensor platform capable of aerial and terrestrial locomotion. In: Proceedings of 2005 IEEE/RSJ International Conference on Intelligent Robots and Systems, pp. 3959–3964 (2005)
3. Yim, M., et al.: Modular self-reconfigurable robot systems. IEEE Robot. Autom. Mag. **14**(1), 43–52 (2007)
4. Fukuda, T., Nakagawa, S.: Dynamically reconfigurable robotic system. In: Proceedings of IEEE International Conference on Robotics and Automation, pp. 1581–1586 (1988)
5. Gilpin, K., Kotay, K., Rus, D., Vasilescu, I.: Miche: modular shape formation by self-disassembly. Int. J. Robot. Res. **27**(3–4), 345–372 (2008)
6. Kurokawa, H., Tomita, K., Kamimura, A., Hasuo, T., Murata, S.: Distributed self-reconfiguration of M-TRAN III modular robotic system. Int. J. Robot. Res. **27**(3–4), 373–378 (2008)
7. Yim, M.: New locomotion gaits. In: Proceedings of IEEE International Conference on Robotics and Automation, pp. 2508–2514 (1994)
8. Goc, M.L., et al.: Zooids: building blocks for swarm user interfaces. In: Proceedings of the 29th Annual Symposium on User Interface Software and Technology (2016)
9. Suzuki, R., et al.: ShapeBots: shape-changing swarm robots. In: Proceedings of the 32nd Annual ACM Symposium on User Interface Software and Technology (2019)
10. Ishida, Y., Matsumoto, M.: Sheet type transformable plate ware. IEEE Access **7**, 91593–91601 (2019)
11. Ishino, M., Matsumoto, M.: A portable transformable device. IEEJ Trans. Electr. Electron. Eng. **18**(1), 153–155 (2023)

Multimodal Expressive Embodied Conversational Agent Design

Simon Jolibois[✉], Akinori Ito, and Takashi Nose

Ito-Nose Lab, Graduate School of Engineering, Tohoku University, Sendai, Japan
jolibois.simon.christophe.t1@dc.tohoku.ac.jp, {aito.spcom,
nose}@tohoku.ac.jp

Abstract. Embodied Conversational Agent (ECA) is a term encompassing virtual agents designed to converse with a human user, with a physical representation in its virtual environment. Other types of conversational agents like chatbots feature other functionalities like an image for text-based communication. However, nothing has been proposed to exploit a media such as an image, in the case of Embodied Conversational Agents, which would emphasize said media in the dialogue with an embodied character that can react to its content and display emotions. We propose a design for an Embodied Conversational Agent with multi-modal perception, able to express emotions, with which the conversation revolves around a media available to both the agent and the user. Using a BERT-based model, emotion classification of the user's words and of his/her facial expressions captured through a webcam are combined to select an expression and an answer on a turn-based basis. The agent features both real-time lip-syncing and expression animation. The application case for the study is a discussion revolving around images of paintings, where the user wants to know more details about the artwork.

Keywords: Interactive Embodied Conversational Agent · Facial Expression · Multimodal interface · Multimedia

1 Introduction

Embodied Conversational Agents (ECA) are autonomous interaction interfaces designed to communicate with a human user. Based on Human-Human Interaction, ECAs often have a human-like appearance and entail some human characteristics. Avatars can move their head, facial parts, and body to mimic the user's movement, and display the ability to speak. ECAs have been developed for more than 30 years, and much has been discussed, from their conversation skills [4], to the naturalness of their facial and body movements [10], passing by the design of affective states [5] and the correct metrics to evaluate them [3].

Meanwhile, some text-based chatbots feature functionalities such as image recognition and captioning [15]. These chatbots behave depending on the image content provided by the user. However, in the case of ECA, no system has included a multimedia source as a core component of a design.

© The Author(s), under exclusive license to Springer Nature Switzerland AG 2023
C. Stephanidis et al. (Eds.): HCII 2023, CCIS 1832, pp. 244–249, 2023.
https://doi.org/10.1007/978-3-031-35989-7_31

In this paper, we present our design of expressive ECA with multimodal perception, with media (image, video, audio) at the core of the conversation with the user. The ECA can express emotions in real-time, both visually through facial animation and lip-syncing, and orally with Text-To-Speech (TTS). The user's speech and facial features are synchronously used in a BERT-based emotion classification model. According to the design strategy, we developed a system where the agent talks with a user about artwork images.

2 Related Work

Conversational Agents appeared in the first half of the 20th century, with text-based conversational systems such as Eliza [2] and Alice [12]. These agents were designed to converse with humans through natural language. Social chatbots are an evolution of these systems, focusing on the relationship between the user and the conversational agent, with a long-term memory of each other's actions and profiles.

Visual and audio cues play an important role in human-to-human conversations, through micro-expressions, body language (non-verbal communication), or intonation and pitch and emphasis (paraverbal) [7]. The expressivity of the agent can be conveyed through facial expressions, gazes, and gestures. C. Pelachaud developed Greta, a multimodal expressive ECA, with a markup language called "Affective Presentation Markup Language" (APML) to control the intensity of the actions of Greta's body and facial animation [5]. The MMD-Agent dialogue system raises events and transitions between states in a finite-state transducer [9].

Besides a text-based conversation, ECA incorporated multimodal data integration such as Text-to-Speech, Speech-to-Text, and facial expression detection. Thus, the dialogue with the ECA evolved with the appearance of multimodal perception ECA, approaching the dynamics of a genuine conversation between two humans. Other inputs like audio, images, and videos have been successfully integrated in the text-based social chatbot XiaoIce [4], where image recognition and captioning are used to activate specific modules of the chatbot. When given a video, Video ChatBot [14] looks for similar videos and answers based on associated comments.

3 Embodied Conversational Agent Design

Figure 1 describes the framework of the ECA. The conversation progresses turn-by-turn, where the user asks orally a question, which is processed to create an answer with the data collected from the content. Both the question and the answer are classified into one of several emotions. In conjunction with the user's facial expression emotion classification, an expression is chosen to be displayed on the 3D character's face. The audio of the answer and corresponding lip-syncing animation are created during runtime, to be played back when appropriate for the ECA. A video of the system is available at: https://youtu.be/Z8aNFFNfnSQ.

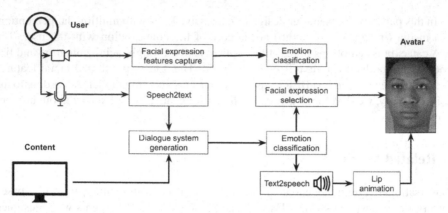

Fig. 1. System architecture

3.1 User Input

Facial Expression. The user's facial features are detected with a webcam and the Openface software [11]. Based on Ekman's Facial Actions Coding System (FACS), the deformation of the face is described by a set of Action Units that express the contraction or relaxation of a group of muscles. This system is also exploited for the animation of human 3D characters. The software captures 17 of the AU on the face of the user.

Speech. The user mainly uses his voice to chat with the agent. His voice is converted to text using Microsoft Azure's Speech-to-Text. The text is then exploited as input in an emotion classification model.

3.2 Emotion Classification Models

AU Classification Model. Each time the user speaks, the average AU data from the last 10 frames is used to classify the user's expression. A 4-layer Multilayer Perceptron with RELU activation function sorts the AU list as *neutral* or among seven emotions: *anger, contempt, disgust, fear, happy, sadness*, and *surprise*.

The model was trained using the CK+ dataset [13], which consists of 593 sequences of images from 123 subjects. 327 out of these sequences have emotion labeling, as they fit the stereotypical definition of said emotion. Each sequence ranged from a neutral expression to a high-intensity expression and was manually labeled among the same eight emotions. As a result, the model achieves an average accuracy of 85%.

Text Classification Model. Demszky et al. [6] proposed the GoEmotions dataset, a collection of 58k Reddit comments labeled as one or more of 27 emotions or *neutral*. A BERT-based model was fine-tuned on a subset of 14 emotions of the GoEmotions dataset: *anger, annoyance, confusion, curiosity, disgust, embarrassment, excitement, fear, grief, joy, nervousness, pride, sadness*, and *surprise*. The choice of reducing the number of emotions is mainly due to the difficulties in clearly distinguishing between the expressions associated to the emotions, but also in order to improve the performances of the classification model. The model achieves a weighted macro-average precision of 45%.

Expression Selection. A ruled-based selection takes as input the user's facial expression, the emotion prediction results of the model's current and previous responses, and their confidence values. The predicted emotion is selected if the confidence value is sufficiently high; otherwise, the previous state is retained. Nevertheless, in the case of a neutral prediction, the user's expression is mirrored. The interactivity of the agent comes from its ability to react to the user, and mirroring is an integral part of how humans behave in a normal conversation. Navarretta [8] shows that smile, laugh, and raised eyebrows are likely mirrored in human-to-human conversations.

3.3 Dialogue System

The dialogue system makes the interface between the user's sentence and the ECA's answer. At launch, the user selects the media file that will be the topic of the conversation, and the corresponding data is loaded. The system finds the closest sentence for each user utterance in a custom database of matching sets of input-output sentences. The database input sentences are encoded into vectors, for which the cosine similarity with the encoded user's question is calculated. A matching output sentence is then randomly selected. The generic database contains markers replaced by relevant data from the artwork data. In the artwork case study, the data is stored in a JSON file and consists of the name, creation date and location, and dimensions of the artwork, but also a visual description, the historical context in which the artwork was created, and the intent of the author.

3.4 Generation of the Agent's Behavior

Speech Synthesis. A reply to the user's speech is produced with Microsoft Azure's Text-to-Speech. Speech Synthesis Markup Language (SSML) provides the language, voice, and pronunciation characteristics, notably an emotional specification. Both the resulting audio file and the associated viseme data are outputted and sent to the animation software, where a lip-syncing animation is produced from the viseme data.

Facial Animation. In the animation software, the animation processed is subdivided into four parts. The first handles the user input on the screen for fine-tuning and debugging purposes, while the second is a Transmission Control Protocol (TCP) client that receives messages from the main script. The third part stores all variables relating to the dialogue and the character's state and animation. The last is the animation graph, changing the animations according to the previous part's variables (Fig. 2).

Fig. 2. Interface of the ECA in the animation software (Unreal Engine 5). On the left, the debugging panel to manipulate the expression. On the right, the image of the painting. The upper-right part can be used to display the ECA answers.

4 Discussion and Future Work

The design has been implemented, with each block working successfully together. Future research will focus on improving each part separately and the overall performance. We present here the limitations of the current framework and some directions in which research can be pursued.

In the study case of artworks, both the data relating to each artwork and the sentence database were built manually. The sentence database, in particular, restrains the conversation to a limited number of topics relative to the artwork. A proper language model will improve answer's naturalness in quality and quantity. Meanwhile, image recognition and online scraping could be added to automate the data-gathering step for image media.

The current study case focused only on images. Other media and applications examples could be explored, such as the agent and the user watching together and commenting a video or listening to a music together.

The interactivity can be further expressed through nonverbal communication, as described by Vinayagamoorthy [1], like body animation, the amplitude of the movements, emotional decay, and personality. Switching from a turn-based conversation to a free-flowing one would allow the ECA to react to the user's actions without waiting for his/her speech.

A more in-depth analysis of the selection of emotions for each model and animation will be conducted, as some may be currently too prevalent or underrepresented. Reevaluating the emotions to Plutchik's eight basic emotions would also homogenize the framework.

References

1. Vinayagamoorthy, V., et al.: Building Expression into virtual characters. In: Eurographics 2006, Vienna, Austria, 04–08 September 2006 (2006)
2. Weizenbaum, J.: ELIZA—A computer program for the study of natural language communication between man and machine. Commun. ACM. **9**, 36–45 (1966). https://doi.org/10.1145/365153.365168
3. Ruttkay, Z., Pelachaud, C. (eds.): From Brows to Trust: Evaluating Embodied Conversational Agents. Kluwer Academic Publishers, USA (2004)
4. Shum, H., He, X., Li, D.: From Eliza to XiaoIce: challenges and opportunities with social chatbots. Front. Inf. Technol. Electron. Eng. **19**, 10–26 (2018). https://doi.org/10.1631/FITEE.1700826
5. de Rosis, F., Pelachaud, C., Poggi, I., Carofiglio, V., Carolis, B.D.: From Greta's mind to her face: modelling the dynamics of affective states in a conversational embodied agent. Int. J. Hum Comput Stud. **59**, 81–118 (2003). https://doi.org/10.1016/S1071-5819(03)00020-X
6. Demszky, D., Movshovitz-Attias, D., Ko, J., Cowen, A., Nemade, G., Ravi, S.: GoEmotions: a dataset of fine-grained emotions. In: Proceedings of the 58th Annual Meeting of the Association for Computational Linguistics, pp. 4040–4054. Association for Computational Linguistics (2020, online). https://doi.org/10.18653/v1/2020.acl-main.372
7. DeVito, J., O'Rourke, S., O'Neill, L.: Human Communication: The Basic Course. Longman, New York (2000)
8. Navarretta, C.: Mirroring facial expressions and emotions in dyadic conversations. In: Proceedings of the Tenth International Conference on Language Resources and Evaluation (LREC 2016), pp. 469–474. European Language Resources Association (ELRA), Portorož, Slovenia (2016)
9. Lee, A., Oura, K., Tokuda, K.: MMDAgent—A fully open-source toolkit for voice interaction systems. In: 2013 IEEE International Conference on Acoustics, Speech and Signal Processing, pp. 8382–8385 (2013). https://doi.org/10.1109/ICASSP.2013.6639300
10. Pelachaud, C.: Multimodal expressive embodied conversational agents. In: Proceedings of the 13th Annual ACM International Conference on Multimedia, pp. 683–689. Association for Computing Machinery, New York (2005). https://doi.org/10.1145/1101149.1101301
11. Baltrusaitis, T., Zadeh, A., Lim, Y.C., Morency, L.-P.: OpenFace 2.0: facial behavior analysis toolkit. In: 2018 13th IEEE International Conference on Automatic Face & Gesture Recognition (FG 2018), pp. 59–66 (2018). https://doi.org/10.1109/FG.2018.00019
12. Wallace, R.S.: The anatomy of A.L.I.C.E. In: Epstein, R., Roberts, G., Beber, G. (eds.) Parsing the Turing Test, pp. 181–210. Springer, Dordrecht (2009). https://doi.org/10.1007/978-1-4020-6710-5_13
13. Lucey, P., Cohn, J.F., Kanade, T., Saragih, J., Ambadar, Z., Matthews, I.: The extended Cohn-Kanade dataset (CK+): a complete dataset for action unit and emotion-specified expression. In: 2010 IEEE Computer Society Conference on Computer Vision and Pattern Recognition – Workshops, pp. 94–101 (2010). https://doi.org/10.1109/CVPRW.2010.5543262
14. Li, Y., Yao, T., Hu, R., Mei, T., Rui, Y.: Video ChatBot: triggering live social interactions by automatic video commenting. In: Proceedings of the 24th ACM International Conference on Multimedia, pp. 757–758. Association for Computing Machinery, New York (2016). https://doi.org/10.1145/2964284.2973835
15. Das, A., et al.: Visual dialog. In: Proceedings of the IEEE Conference on Computer Vision and Pattern Recognition, pp. 326–335 (2017)

Real-Time Multi-view 3D Pose Estimation System with Constant Frame Speed

Minjoon Kim[(✉)] and Taemin Hwang

Korea Electronics Technology Institute, Seongnam, South Korea
{mjoon,taemin.hwang}@keti.re.kr

Abstract. Vision-based 3D human pose estimation is a key technique in recognizing human behavior and is widely applied to various fields dealing with human-computer interactions. In particular, the multi-view-based 3D pose recognition method is a method of predicting hypothetical accurate 3D poses that solve problems such as rotation and obscuration by compensating for the shortcomings of viewpoint-dependent 2D pose recognition method and single-view-based 3D pose recognition method. The multi-view-based 3D pose recognition method has excellent prediction performance, but there are difficulties that come because it uses multiple cameras. It is a difficulty in synchronization to simultaneously control an excessive amount of computation at the central server and multiple cameras. In this paper, we propose a distributed real-time 3D pose estimation framework based on asynchronous multi-cameras. The proposed framework consists of a central server and a number of edge devices, which utilize timestamp techniques to output 3d pose estimation results at constant frame speed. Finally, we implement and demonstrate that we successfully estimate a 3D human pose of 30 fps in real time by constructing the proposed framework as a demo platform.

Keywords: 3D Pose Estimation · Human Pose Estimation · Human-Computer Interaction · Real-time Application · Asynchronous Edge Processing

1 Introduction

As the performance of computer vision technology improves with the development of artificial intelligence, human posture estimation is widely applied in real life through many studies [1]. In the past, marker-based motion capture systems have been used to continuously track human poses in the field of gaming and entertainment. However, marker-based systems have limitations by wearing a marker suit with sensors attached or by using a special camera so that the system can capture motion. Recently, technologies using deep learning technologies such as CNN through simple RGB cameras have become popular in human pose estimation, and human pose estimation has been researched and commercialized in many fields to achieve very high performance in a single image [2, 3]. Furthermore, in recent years, 3D pose estimation, which is a three-dimensional position, has been widely studied as more precise pose estimation performance is required [4–6].

© The Author(s), under exclusive license to Springer Nature Switzerland AG 2023
C. Stephanidis et al. (Eds.): HCII 2023, CCIS 1832, pp. 250–255, 2023.
https://doi.org/10.1007/978-3-031-35989-7_32

3D human posture estimation methods are largely divided into multi-view models and single-view models. As shown in Fig. 1, the multi-view model that uses images from multiple camera points of view as input is capable of more accurate posture estimation than a single-view model that uses only one camera [7–9]. This is because the multi-point model can learn from multi-point images that are robust to depth ambiguity problems and occlusion problems depending on image time points in estimating three-dimensional human posture. However, the multi-view model makes it difficult to construct the system in that it needs to perform operations on multiple images and synchronization on multiple cameras [10, 11].

In this paper, based on a number of asynchronous cameras, we propose a real-time 3D pose estimation system that performs deep learning operations on each edge device. We propose a real-time multi-view 3D pose estimation algorithm with a fixed output power rate in the proposed system and verify its performance by demonstrating the system.

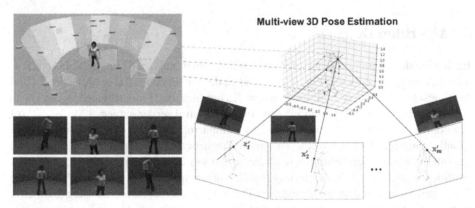

Multi-view 3D Pose Estimation

Fig. 1. Description of multi-view 3D pose estimation method.

2   System Configuration

In general, configuring a multi-view 3D pose estimation system requires a number of synchronized cameras, a central server with excellent computational power, and a media network for transmitting and receiving multi-channel images. To address these barriers to entry, we propose a distributed framework consisting of asynchronous multi-cameras and edge devices, and Ethernet-based lightweight servers as shown in Fig. 2. First, each multi-edge device connected to multiple cameras estimates a 2D human pose from the acquired RGB image and transmits it to the central server, respectively. At this time, only the result of pose extraction, not the media, is transmitted, so only a network of tens of Kbps is generally required. The central server sorts the received 2D human pose data based on the timestamp, and reconstructs the 3D human pose using geometric triangulation. Compared to the existing system, the proposed system is much more advantageous for real-time applications as the deep learning operation of the central server is distributed to each edge device and network traffic is reduced by about tens of times.

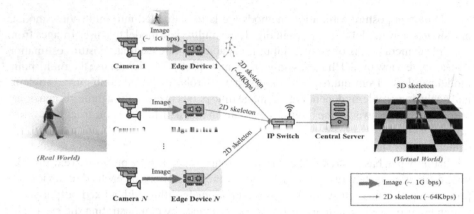

Fig. 2. Distributed Real-time Multi-view 3D Pose Estimation System.

3 Algorithm Design

Each edge device independently detects the 2D human pose in the image and sends it to a central server as shown in Fig. 3. The ith edge device transmits 2D coordinates $\mathbb{X}_i$ and the timestamp t_i to the central server, where $\mathbb{X}_n$ denotes the 2D coordinates $\{u_n, v_n\}$ with the confidence score $\{c_n\}$ from n^{th} camera. The central server gathers $\{\mathbb{X}'_1, ..., \mathbb{X}'_m\}$ of 2D coordinate group that are arranged by comparing the corresponding timestamps. Finally, the central server synthesizes and reconstructs a 3D human pose $\mathbb{X}$ using the 2D human pose group, where $\mathbb{X}$ denotes the 3D world coordinates $\{x_w, y_w, z_w\}$ with confidence score $\{c_w\}$. For detecting the 2D human pose, we need to synchronize the 2D human pose based on the timestamp. The 3D pose is reconstructed using geometric triangulation techniques with a set of 2D human poses using the direct linear transform (DLT) method [11].

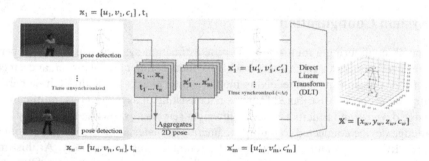

Fig. 3. 3D Pose Reconstruction using DLT method

The 2D human poses coming from each edge device must be synchronized based on the timestamp stored together. However, since it is generally impossible to obtain exactly the same amount of time from different devices, the data within that error is defined as the same time with an error range. For the error range Δt, it can be expressed in a grid form as shown on the left side of Fig. 4, green if data is sent at the corresponding time of each device, and red if not. In the case of the DLT method, more than two pieces of information are required, so if less than two pieces of data are received, the value of the front frame will be used, but this will rarely occur as the number of edge devices in the proposed distributed system increases.

To evaluate the performance of the proposed time synchronization algorithm, we used the following detected joint ratio (PDJ) as an evaluation indicator [2].

$$PDJ^{\alpha}(\%) = \frac{\sum_{i=1}^{k} \mathrm{B}(d_i < \alpha D)}{k} \times 100, \tag{1}$$

where d_i is the Euclidean distance between the ith predicted and ground-truth keypoints, D is the Euclidean distance of the 3D bounding box of the human body from the edge devices, and α is a certain distance threshold to verify the accuracy of the estimation. In addition, k is the number of keypoints on the human body, and $\mathrm{B}(\cdot)$ is a boolean function that returns one if the condition is true and zero if it is false.

An appropriate Δt can be set through the computer simulation results shown on the right side of Fig. 4. The corresponding result showed the PDJ figure for Δt for 8 edge devices, and the detection requirement performance was adjusted through α. Simulation results show that having Δt near about 33 ms for fixed 30 fps provision shows about 80% PDJ. In addition, it can be seen that about 20 ms for 60 fps provision shows performance close to 90%. For field application, the output speed, Δt, must be set based on the number of cameras and edge devices, the edge processing speed, network environment, and so on.

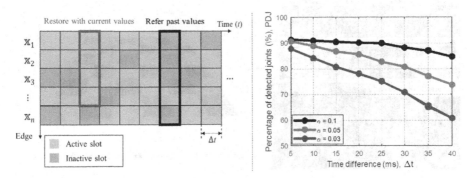

Fig. 4. Data from asynchronous multi-devices and PDJ evaluation results.

4   Real-Time Demonstration

We implemented a prototype to demonstrate that the proposed system can support constant 30 fps estimation in real time. As shown in Fig. 5, a demonstration environment was constructed and experimented so that real-time 3D pose estimation results could be viewed directly on the screen. Six RGB cameras were connected to three NVIDIA

Jetson TX2 and three Jetson AGXs, respectively, as edge devices. Each edge device performs 2D pose estimation on the single-view RGB image and outputs the result with timestamp. All edge devices are connected to the server through an IP switch, and an ethernet network has been established. Since image data is not communicated, network traffic occurs within hundreds of kbps. As a result of the experiment, it was confirmed that 2D pose estimation results of about 19 fps for Jetson TX2 and 27 fps for Jetson AGX were output. The server synthesized the collected 2d pose data and performed a fixed 3d pose estimation at 30 fps, which was confirmed in the field through the GUI S/W. The delay time between the actual scene and the GUI S/W was about 200 ms, which was sufficient to feel the real-time interaction.

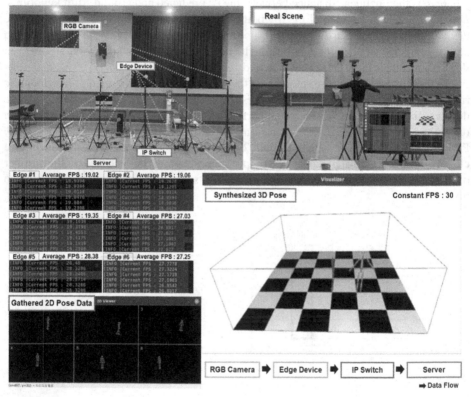

Fig. 5. Demo platform for real-time 3D pose estimation system with constant 30 fps.

5 Conclusion

In this paper, a distributed real-time 3D pose estimation framework is proposed and implemented to facilitate real-time implementation of a multi-view-based 3D pose estimation system. The proposed framework consists of a central server and a number of edge devices, leveraging timestamp techniques to output 3D pose estimation results at constant frame rates. We demonstrate that we successfully estimate 3D human poses at 30 fps in real time by implementing the proposed framework as a demo platform.

Acknowledgments. This research is supported by Ministry of Culture, Sports and Tourism and Korea Creative Content Agency (Project number: R2021040128).

References

1. Kumar, P., Chauhan, S., Awasthi, L.K.: Human pose estimation using deep learning: review, methodologies, progress and future research directions. Int. J. Multimed. Inf. Retrieval **11**, 489–521 (2022)
2. Toshev, A., Szegedy, C.: DeepPose: human pose estimation via deep neural networks. In: Proceedings of IEEE Conference on Computer Vision and Pattern Recognition (CVPR), USA (2014)
3. Kiefel, M., Gehler, P.V.: Human pose estimation with fields of parts. In: Fleet, D., Pajdla, T., Schiele, B., Tuytelaars, T. (eds.) ECCV 2014. LNCS, vol. 8693, pp. 331–346. Springer, Cham (2014). https://doi.org/10.1007/978-3-319-10602-1_22
4. Pavlakos, G., Zhou, X., Derpanis, K.G., Daniilidis, K.: Coarse-to-fine volumetric prediction for single-image 3D human pose. In: Proceedings of IEEE Conference on Computer Vision and Pattern Recognition (CVPR), USA (2017)
5. Martinez, J., Hossain, R., Romero, J., Little, J.J.: A simple yet effective baseline for 3D human pose estimation. In: Proceedings of IEEE Conference on Computer Vision and Pattern Recognition (CVPR), USA (2017)
6. Zhou, K., Han, X., Jiang, N., Jia, K., Lu, J.: HEMlets pose: learning part-centric heatmap triplets for accurate 3D human pose estimation. In: Proceedings of IEEE International Conference on Computer Vision (ICCV), Korea (2019)
7. Belagiannis, V., Amin, S., Andriluka, M., Schiele, B., Navab, N., Ilic, S.: 3D pictorial structures for multiple human pose estimation. In: Proceedings of IEEE Conference on Computer Vision and Pattern Recognition (CVPR), USA (2014)
8. Qiu, H., Wang, C., Wang, J., Wang, N., Zeng, W.: Cross view fusion for 3D human pose estimation. In: Proceedings of the IEEE International Conference on Computer Vision (ICCV), Korea (2019)
9. Elmi, A., Mazzini, D., Tortella, P.: Light3DPose: real-time multi-person 3D pose estimation from multiple views. In: Proceedings of IEEE International Conference on Pattern Recognition (ICPR), Italy (2020)
10. Remelli, E., Han, S., Honari, S., Fua, P., Wang, R.: Lightweight multi-view 3D pose estimation through camera-disentangled representation. In: Proceedings of IEEE Conference on Computer Vision and Pattern Recognition (CVPR), USA (2020)
11. Dong, J., et al.: Fast and robust multi-person 3D pose estimation and tracking from multiple views. IEEE Trans. Pattern Anal. Mach. Intell. **44**(10), 6981–6992 (2022)

Textile Circularity Through Iot Innovation: An Approach to Wearable Wireless-Sensor-Based Textiles

Sharon Koshy[1], G. Sandhya[1(✉)], and Shanthni Veetaputhiran[2]

[1] Department of Management, Amrita Vishwa Vidyapeetham, Kochi, India
ek_sharon@asb.kh.students.amrita.edu,
g_sandhya@asb.kochi.amrita.edu
[2] Department of Computer and Systems Science, Stockholm University, Stockholm, Sweden
shve7795@student.su.se

Abstract. The investigation of Circular Economy (CE) and the Internet of Things (IoT) has grown in popularity in the past few decades due to their potential to link innovative technologies with novel circular industry production and business models. Although numerous scientific studies have emphasized the potential of the Internet of Things (IoT) in advancing Circular Economy (CE), further research is required to establish systematic IoT approaches for promoting circular practices. The study develops a comprehensive framework for efficient circular textile economy practices using insights from data acquired through the triangulation approach. The proposed model, built on non-intrusive and wearable textile-based communicative sensors, enables efficient textile circular economy recall practices in any business setting and fosters Circular Economy evolution and sustainability transition in any business setting. The proposed wearable framework for unobtrusive textile life cycle analysis addresses circular economy implementation best practices, promotes sustainability, and mitigates long-term environmental, social, and economic consequences. As a crucial enabler, this innovative network investigates textile life cycle analysis to enhance resource efficiency, extend textile lifespan, and narrow the material loop. Integrating IoT technology with a low-cost, scalable network of intelligent sensors enables real-time traceability throughout the textile value chain, replacing take-make-waste textiles with wireless sensor networks to provide reliable data for every lifecycle phase. The results can contribute to future research by inspiring and concretizing the design facets of proposed IoT-supported wearable communication textile-based sensors and actuators to demonstrate their effectiveness in real-time textile life cycle analysis.

Keywords: Internet of Things (IoT) · Textile-based wearable system · Circular Economy (CE) · Sustainable business models · Wearable textile sensor

1 Introduction

Recent years have witnessed a surge of initiatives fostering a paradigm shift in business practices, substituting conventional linear approaches with renewed production strategies designed to minimize environmental impact, develop innovative eco-sustainable

C. Stephanidis et al. (Eds.): HCII 2023, CCIS 1832, pp. 256–263, 2023.
https://doi.org/10.1007/978-3-031-35989-7_33

products, and overhaul business models accordingly [1]. Since then, a plethora of research has been conducted to explore the use of technologies and strategies by businesses for sustainably optimizing their product and service delivery [2–5]. Many industry sectors have adopted intelligent technologies like the Internet of Things (IoT) and blockchain to revamp their conventional linear methodologies in the pursuit of sustainable practises [6, 7]. Implementing such intelligent technologies in industries focuses on organizational and environmental performance; however, the emphasis on mitigating risks and maximizing social returns has received limited attention despite extensive literature on sustainable waste management practices [8].

The United Nations Environment Programme (UNEP) estimates that 92 million tonnes of textile waste is generated annually, corresponding to over 250,000 tonnes of textile waste produced every day globally, carrying 20% of global waste production. [9, 10]. The fashion sector's significant impacts on environmental pollution through textile waste from households, businesses, and the industry is well-documented in the literature. This waste has intense sustainability effects on environmental, social, and economic facets, making the industry the third most polluting globally [10]. Although ample literature on sustainable waste management approaches is prioritized, textile waste management is often neglected, generating considerable textile waste without proper disposal [11]. Despite the alarming figures, very few studies examine the use of Big Data, Artificial Intelligence, Data Analytics, the Internet of Things (IoT), and Blockchain in the management of textile waste. Thus, considering the hazards this can poses to sustainability of the planet and to hamper under-utilized fabric from ending up in landfills, all businesses, big and small, in the coming years should undergo an urgent, dramatic, and profound innovative transition that aid better economic, societal and environmental upshots through an IoT-based waste monitoring system, to promote circular end-of-life options for textile waste generated (Fig. 1).

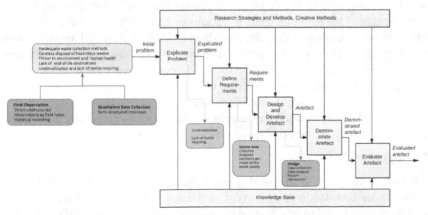

Fig. 1. Development process extended from the Design science research framework presented by Johannesson and Perjons (2014)

2 Background

The advent of Internet of Things (IoT) characterizes the technological revolution by integrating billions of sensors and actuators to build an intelligent environment. The promising sensors have demonstrated their effectiveness in several IoT applications [12], however in case of wearable textile based sensors, they have been restricted within the choice in medical applications to facilitate diseases diagnosis [13–15]. Considering the broad scope of characteristics ranging from high sensitivity, precision, range, resolution, latency, resilience, robustness, extended battery life, economical usage, and lightness, sensors have the potential for new possibilities for applications. Thus, extending the choice of detecting wear and tear, pilling and fading, stains and spots in textiles, these sensors can offer the potential to track the performance and degradation of textiles by embracing sustainability and extending the product lifespan. Through predictive analysis, they can provide early detection of damages, enabling proactive maintenance and repair, better durability, and interchangeable styles, thus hampering the amount of waste ending up in landfills or getting incinerated. Thus, the research demonstrates the valuable contribution of textile sensors in circular product design and waste reduction.

In comparison to other types of sensors, optical sensors was opted due to its significant advantages and exemption to electromagnetic waves, high sensitivity to variations in temperature, pressure, or tension, and ability to transmit signals over long distances with greater durability to withstand severe conditions of elevated temperatures, intense pressure, and chemical agents as well as their ability to be multiplexed.

2.1 The Design of Wearable Wireless-Sensor-Based Textile

The previous section of the research highlights the significant potential of utilizing optical sensors to assess the quality of textiles based on factors like yarn density and color. These sensors have the capability to detect areas of fabric that are becoming worn or weakened based on changes in texture or color, which can provide valuable information on the quality of the fabric and help to identify potential areas of concern. By utilizing optical fibers that are in direct contact with the fabric surface, these sensors can be permanently attached to the textiles and provide real-time monitoring of the fabric's quality. The results obtained from this approach can help improve the overall quality control processes in textile manufacturing and provide valuable insights for textile maintenance and repair. This section extends the discussion by proposing the framework to collect and analyze the sensor data as a means to monitor the textile quality.

Technology Stack

Sensor Data Collection. Textile quality evaluation is critical in ensuring that the products meet the desired standards in terms of yarn density and color. In this regard, optical sensors have been found to be effective in evaluating the quality of textiles. The reflective optical fibers are attached to the fabric surface to detect any changes made in the textile due to wear and tear. These sensors are permanent fixtures attached to the textiles, making them ideal for continuous monitoring of textile quality. A device, such as the Photodiode Array (PDA), is installed in a designated area where the textiles are collected for cleaning. The PDA device collects light waves reflected by the optical fiber sensors attached to the textiles and converts them into an electrical signal. This method enables continuous textile quality monitoring, which can be used to ensure that the products meet the required quality standards, leading to improved customer satisfaction and reduced product waste. The use of optical fibers and PDA devices can be a game-changer in textile manufacturing, with potential applications in the fashion and clothing industry, automotive industry, and medical textiles, among others (Fig. 2).

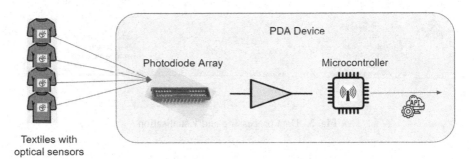

Fig. 2. Sensor data collection

After the light waves reflected by optical fiber sensors are converted into electrical signals, they are amplified and filtered before being processed by a microcontroller to detect yarn density and color changes in textiles. The resulting data is transmitted via the internet to a server using an HTTP POST API request. The transmitted data is in the form of a JSON object with unique identification numbers for each optical fiber sensor and textile batch number. This labeling system facilitates tracking of textiles with fading or reduced yarn density, thereby improving the identification of problematic textiles in the textile production process.

Data Processing and Visualization. The collected textile data described in the preceding section initiates the activation of a serverless execution environment, known as Google Cloud Platform's (GCP) Cloud Functions service. The server application is a flask application hosted on GCP, containing API endpoints for the collection of sensor data via POST requests, as well as for visualizing data intended for users responsible for monitoring textile quality and replacements (Fig. 3).

The cloud function has the python script that uses the Pandas framework to convert the JSON object received through the POST request into a dataframe, validate and process the data. The processed data, which can be directly visualized, is then stored as a CSV file in the cloud storage service by GCP. During this storage process, each data frame created as a result of an API call labeled with the textile group is mapped to the CSV file dedicated to the textile group. The data already present in the CSV file is overwritten by the new data created by the cloud function. Versioning is enabled for these files to keep track of the historical data.

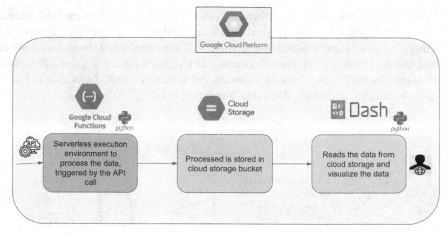

Fig. 3. Data processing and visualisation

Further in the process, the flask application with Python runtime deployed in GCP using Google Kubernetes Engine (GKE) then handles the visualization process. The flask application integrates with the Dash framework provided by Plotly. The application is accessible to customers with business contracts with sensor providers. Depending on their textile groups, related data is visualized to them on a web page. The visualization provides interactive insights about the textile quality of their textile group in comparison with the acceptable metrics that can be altered in the front-end.

Notification Distribution. Concurrent with the previous section, the flask application also uses a Machine learning model to analyze the data to determine if any of the textile data is measured below the determined threshold level of the textile quality in the metrics of color and yarn density. The ML model is trained with data collected from different types of textiles and in different quality conditions. If the python module filters the low-quality textile, a notification is sent to the user via email or SMS as per the user notification settings. The notifications are, by default, displayed on the webpage (Fig. 4).

The notification is sent through the GCP's Pub/sub service, which is a publisher and subscriber-based communication service. Pub/sub has several topics that act as publishers and are tagged with the textile group. The Pubsub also has subscriptions for each topic. The users that are related to a particular textile group are subscribed to the topic for the textile group. Once the damaged textile is identified by the flask application module, the topic is triggered, and it publishes the notification to the users who have subscribed for that topic along with the unique identifier of the damaged textile. The user can start his/her administration process to collect the damaged textile back from usage.

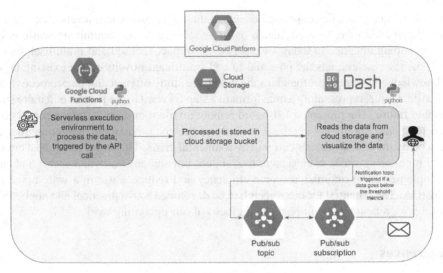

Fig. 4. Notification distribution

3 Conclusion

Optical sensing technology can be used in textiles by incorporating optical fibres into the textile materials. These sensors can send signals to the centralized IoT cloud server through wireless transmission technology and Application Programming Interface (API). The potential data collected from these sensors provide real-time monitoring, tracking, inventory control, and wear and tear analysis, making it a promising solution to waste management. The timely repairs and end-of-life alerts provided by the sensors can prolong the life of the product and facilitate easy replacement and maximize efficiency. By providing access to material reports through enterprise or manufacturer server query terminals, textile quality and transparency can be enhanced, enabling the enterprise to access pertinent product details and maintain records of any potential material damage, thus giving the advantages of Remote tracking, Condition Monitoring, Lifecycle Management and Predictive Maintenance. The implementation of encrypted cloud server backup and storage, coupled with machine learning algorithms, enables the recognition of patterns and trends in data from embedded fibre optic sensors. This facilitates predictive maintenance and informed decision-making to optimize procurement and material performance, while also allowing for improvements and recalling damaged materials to reduce waste and pollution, ultimately promoting circularity and environmental regeneration.

4 Contributions and Future Direction

Our study presents a novel framework for circularity monitoring that leverages IoT-based wearable wireless-sensor-based textiles, representing a vital area of inquiry that has yet to be explored in the literature. The resulting model holds immense promise for innovation, as well as the potential to impede socio-environmental degradation and offer both operational and strategic economic benefits at the micro and macro levels. The study's central principle of reducing reliance on finite resources and minimizing waste is of paramount significance in today's world. As an impact-focused and multidisciplinary analysis, the research has the potential to add significant novelty to the existing body of knowledge. Given its profound implications, the study offers a unique perspective on the critical issue, representing a transformative step forward in the pursuit of a more sustainable future. The presented IoT-based remote textile monitoring system contributes an ecologically intelligent approach to mitigate the socio-environmental consequence induced by the textile sector's current environmental crisis. This novel and robust circularity monitoring waste management model goes beyond any particular sector and can be implemented to optimize resource efficiency and reduce waste in a wide range of industries. The potential for our research to be developed into a practical and applicable model is significant and will be the main focus of our upcoming work.

References

1. Garcia-Muiña, F.E., González-Sánchez, R., Ferrari, A.M., Settembre-Blundo, D.: The paradigms of Industry 4.0 and circular economy as enabling drivers for the competitiveness of businesses and territories: the case of an Italian ceramic tiles manufacturing company. Soc. Sci. **7**(12), 255 (2018)
2. Dantas, T.E.T., de-Souza, E.D., Destro, I.R., Hammes, G., Rodriguez, C.M.T., Soares, S.R.: How the combination of circular economy and Industry 4.0 can contribute towards achieving the sustainable development goals. Sustain. Prod. Consum. **26**, 213–227 (2021)
3. Tarapata, Z., Nowicki, T., Antkiewicz, R., Dudzinski, J., Janik, K.: Data-driven machine learning system for optimization of processes supporting the distribution of goods and services–a case study. Proc. Manuf. **44**, 60–67 (2020)
4. Meier, H., Roy, R., Seliger, G.: Industrial product-service systems—IPS2. CIRP Ann. **59**(2), 607–627 (2010)
5. Büyüközkan, G., Karabulut, Y., Arsenyan, J.: RFID service provider selection: an integrated fuzzy MCDM approach. Measurement **112**, 88–98 (2017)
6. Esmaeilian, B., Sarkis, J., Lewis, K., Behdad, S.: Blockchain for the future of sustainable supply chain management in Industry 4.0. Resour. Conserv. Recycl. **163**, 105064 (2020)
7. de Villiers, C., Kuruppu, S., Dissanayake, D.: A (new) role for business–promoting the United Nations' Sustainable Development Goals through the internet-of-things and blockchain technology. J. Bus. Res. **131**, 598–609 (2021)
8. Torkayesh, A.E., Deveci, M., Torkayesh, S.E., Tirkolaee, E.B.: Analyzing failures in adoption of smart technologies for medical waste management systems: a type-2 neutrosophic- based approach. Environ. Sci. Pollut. Res. 1–14 (2021)
9. United Nations Environment Programme: Waste management outlook for mountain regions: Sources and solutions (2018). https://www.unep.org/resources/report/waste-management-out look-mountain-regions-sources-and-solutions. Accessed 10 Mar 2020
10. Papamichael, I., Voukkali, I., Loizia, P., Rodrıguez-Espinosa, T., Pedreño, J.N., Zorpas, A.A.: Textile waste in the concept of circularity. Sustain. Chem. Pharm. **32**, 100993 (2023)
11. Hasan, M.F., Mow, N., Alam, M.R., Hasan, S.A., Mamtaz, R.: Recycling potential of textile solid waste. Waste Manag. Environ. IX **231**, 125 (2019)
12. Sehrawat, D., Gill, N.S.: Smart sensors: analysis of different types of IoT sensors. In: 2019 3rd International Conference on Trends in Electronics and Informatics (ICOEI), pp. 523–528. IEEE, April 2019

13. Nasiri, S., Khosravani, M.R.: Progress and challenges in fabrication of wearable sensors for health monitoring. Sens. Actuators: A Phys. **312**, 112105 (2020)
14. Majumder, S., Mondal, T., Deen, M.J.: Wearable sensors for remote health monitoring. Sensors **17**(1), 130 (2017)
15. Zhang, H., et al.: Graphene-enabled wearable sensors for healthcare monitoring. Biosens. Bioelectron. **197**, 113777 (2022)

The Strength Assistant Gloves Interaction Development for Female Employment by EMG Signal Visualization Image Analysis

Fangfei Liu, Zijian Sha, and Yun Chen[✉]

Beijing Institute of Technology, Beijing, People's Republic of China
yun.chen@bit.edu.cn

Abstract. In recent years, the fertility accumulation effect has gradually disappeared, the fertility rate is low, and the number of women of childbearing age continues to decline. Therefore, it shows a social trend, that is, there is a shortage of male labor in the heavy labor industry, and more women begin to fill the gap.

By investigating the behavior characteristics of workers in heavy manual labor, the human-computer interaction needs and application scenarios of female workers in the process of labor, this paper analyzes the current situation of female workers in heavy manual labor industry, and proposes to design a hand protection product through the strength assistance structure to improve the work interaction experience on the basis of the research. On the basis of human-machine theory, the design of this product takes into account the gender difference factors and the usage habits of relevant practitioners, etc., and plays a role in helping women to improve their work preparation and strengthen safety protection. It is a practical human-computer interaction assistance product, which promotes labor liberation in the intellectual age.

Keywords: Female employment · heavy manual labor · strength assistance

1 Introduction

The traditional male industry refers to the construction, transportation, auto repair and other industries that are suitable for male physical characteristics and dominated by male practitioners in the traditional concept. Worldwide, the proportion of female practitioners in the traditional male industry is increasing year by year. In China, the labor shortage caused by the low birth rate and the aging population is prompting more Chinese women to engage in heavy manual labor. In 2020, the total number of migrant workers in China was 286 million, one third of whom were women, reflecting that Chinese women are filling the labor gap. As early as around 2010, Canadian women began to engage in traditional male industries with high physical and technical requirements, such as pipeline maintenance, metal cutting and welding [1].

Due to the small proportion of female heavy manual workers, they have not received corresponding attention in China. For example, the representative migrant women in the construction industry have poor living and working conditions, and they suffer from

C. Stephanidis et al. (Eds.): HCII 2023, CCIS 1832, pp. 264–272, 2023.
https://doi.org/10.1007/978-3-031-35989-7_34

unequal wages. As a female construction worker said, "I have never seen female workers get the same remuneration as male workers". They often work as temporary workers, lack safety protection.

In conclusion, the purpose of this article is to design a product to provide human-computer interaction assistance to female heavy manual workers by making up for their strength defects.

2 Investigation and Research

2.1 Big Data Analysis of the Current Status

All countries in the world are facing the problem of increasing female heavy manual workers, and it is a common problem to reduce the difference in treatment between men and women in this industry. The gender pay gap in the US construction industry is the smallest among all industries, and the average income of female workers is 94% of that of male workers. In China, taking the wage level of migrant workers in cities as an example, from the perspective of gender differences in wages, the wages of male migrant workers are significantly higher than those of female migrant workers. Male migrant workers with a wage level of less than 2000 yuan account for 20.37%, and female migrant workers account for 51.22% [2].

Table 1. Gender differences in wages of migrant workers in cities from the perspective of wage levels.

	Wage distribution of migrant workers					
	< 1000 ¥	1001~ 2000 ¥	2001~ 3000 ¥	3001~ 4000 ¥	4001~ 5000 ¥	> 5000 ¥
Male	2.36	18.01	38.38	19.70	11.95	9.60
Female	3.48	47.74	36.59	6.97	3.48	1.74
Cenozoic era	3.53	27.69	38.80	14.64	8.47	6.87
Older generation	1.24	27.95	35.71	17.39	10.56	7.15
local	2.86	31.43	34.05	17.38	7.86	6.42
migrant	2.56	24.52	40.94	14.07	10.45	7.46

According to the relevant survey, the primary problem faced by female heavy manual workers is the issue of safety. For example, most of the female workers recruited in the construction industry are middle-aged. Due to their low education level, their safety protection ability and self-protection consciousness are not optimistic. According to the survey, only 24% of female construction workers think that their construction site has complete protective facilities and measures. Only 48% of female construction workers received formal safety knowledge training before taking up their posts [3]. At the same time, most female workers believe that safety mainly depends on themselves. As long as they are careful and pay attention, they will be fine. From the perspective of social development trends, the problem of insufficient safety protection will continue to exist in the future. It is not an accident, so it deserves social attention.

2.2 User Research

Table 2. Comparative analysis of literature research on female workers

		Study on the living conditions of migrant women in traditional male industries	Research on the plight of migrant women workers in urban life from the perspective of gender	Construction site regime: an analysis of the formation of female construction
Crowd characteristics		– 30–50 years old – Mainly with primary and junior high school education – All married	– Born in the countryside – Unskilled and underprivileged labor – Most married and have children	– 41–50 years old – Mainly from rural areas – Low educational level – All married women
Labor content	Nature of work	They are still engaged in relatively supplementary work	High labor intensity, long overtime and high frequency	The types of work with a large number of female workers are mainly masonry, rebar and carpentry
	Specific explanation	It is not only limited to cooking and simple machines, but also involves many heavy and dangerous types of work, such as undertaking heavy manual work	Old machinery and equipment, high noise intensity in the workshop during operation, hemorrhoids caused by sitting for a long time,	There are different numbers and degrees of female workers in various types of work, and even some types of work are almost all female workers, such as elevator operators, laborers, steel bar binders, cleaners, etc.
Problems in labor	Rights and interests	Lack of awareness and ability to protect rights	Lack of access to formal network support and help from informal networks	Working income is limited, and women workers and their spouses do not have social insurance and welfare
	safety problem	Only 50% have received formal safety knowledge training before taking up their posts	Poor working environment, lack of special protection during menstruation and pregnancy	Working in the construction industry is dirty, tiring and high-risk. Compared with other industries, the salary is slightly higher

(continued)

Table 2. (*continued*)

	Study on the living conditions of migrant women in traditional male industries	Research on the plight of migrant women workers in urban life from the perspective of gender	Construction site regime: an analysis of the formation of female construction
Working scene	Most of them are construction sites, lacking gender considerations in accommodation and daily life	Gender and situational oppression exist in garment factories	The production of construction industry is mobile, open-air and diverse

By collecting existing research, combining the current situation of female workers in various representative industries for comparative analysis, the key information shown in Table 2 is summarized. Through induction and generalization, the characteristics of the surveyed group are extracted, and the work intensity of female workers is explored from the perspective of work nature and specific work content. The problems they face in the labor process are divided into three categories: employment, rights and interests, and safety. Their general needs are clarified, and the work scenes of the respondents are summarized.

User characteristics Combining with the analysis of the characteristics and behavior patterns of the analysis target users, most of the female heavy manual workers have the following characteristics:

- Low education level and less safety education.
- Hard working and increasing labor intensity, but the labor security relationship has not been gradually improved.
- Has a heavy family burden and needs to take care of the internal affairs of the family while working outside [4].
- Traditional prejudice that men are paid more by default [5].

User requirements By analyzing the characteristics and behavior patterns of target users, it is found that users need labor protection and improve labor ability. It is necessary to eliminate women's discrimination in the employment market by improving human-computer interaction in high-intensity labor.

Usage Scenario The scene is characterized by high strength requirements, high labor intensity, repetitive movements, etc. Typical scenes include construction sites, loading and unloading centers, etc.

2.3 An Overview of the Existing Products

At present, there are few safety and auxiliary products for female heavy manual workers, and there is a global market vacancy for products centered on them.

The first category of existing products is traditional protective gloves, such as labor protection gloves and rubber gloves. Their shortcomings are that the protection effect provided is poor; The second type is strength assisted gloves that apply new technologies, such as the muscle strengthening glove Robo glove developed by GM in cooperation with NASA, which is a typical case of foreign strength assisted glove development [6]. The existing products provide strong force assistance in actual labor, but less consideration is given to the social trend of increasing female workers, and the male user is the default model in terms of man-machine.

3 Relevant Theoretical Research

3.1 Research on Surface Electromyography

Surface electromyogram signal (SEMG) collects and records the bioelectrical signals generated by the corresponding nerves during muscle activity through the electrode sheet stuck on the skin surface. In recent years, they have been applied in many fields, such as motion control of external robots, biomedicine and so on [7]. Experiments show that by processing the obtained surface EMG signals, it can be found that the linear discriminant analysis (LDA), can be used to sort out the data, and the feature recognition of different hand movements can be realized [8].

3.2 Research on Female Workers

Study on the weight-bearing of female carrying workers

Because of the anatomical characteristics of their body structure, women have been engaged in heavy physical labor beyond their ability for a long time. According to the regulations of the Ministry of labor on the working conditions of loading, unloading and handling operations, it is generally recommended that the weight limit for adult women in manual handling is 10–15 kg. The total weight transported in a working day shall not exceed 7 tons [9].

Study on hand protection of female heavy physical labor

Carpal tunnel syndrome (CTS) is the most common peripheral nerve entrapment disease, mostly occurring in middle-aged and elderly women. Improper and excessive use of hands is considered to be an important pathogenic factor. Women engaged in heavy manual labor often undertake the dual tasks of domestic work and going out to work, so they have a higher risk of carpal tunnel syndrome [10].

4 Comparative Analysis and Conclusions

Referring to the literature research done by the user analysis, it is proposed to conduct user interviews in the form of semi-structured interviews. Author drew up an interview outline focusing on the research needs in the preparatory stage of the interview, and proposed some general questions related to the three focus points (Table 3).

In the actual interview, the order of questions and the form of questions were temporarily adjusted according to the situation. Moreover, as the injuries reported by the interviewees are relatively common, labor injuries are added as another focus of attention. The obtained materials are summarized according to the labor content, protection means, salary difference, labor injury and other aspects.

Table 3. Interview outline and questions

QUESTION 1 – LABOR CONTENT	What kind of heavy physical labor have you been engaged in? Why did you choose to enter the traditional male industry?
QUESTION 2 – MEANS OF PROTECTION	Is labor protection equipment allocated? What is the type, frequency and effect of the equipment allocated?
QUESTION 3 – SALARY DIFFERENCE	Are you facing difficulties in finding a job? Is there a pay difference with male workers engaged in the same or similar work? Is there a workload variance?
(ADD) QUESTION 4 – EMPLOYMENT INJURIES	What injuries (body parts) have you suffered in the process of engaging in heavy physical labor? For what reason did you finally give up the job mentioned above?

After obtaining the text materials, NVivo software is used to apply the grounded theory to carry out qualitative analysis, summarize the keywords such as protection position, work content and salary, and carry out word cloud analysis, as shown in Fig. 1. By analyzing the relevance of keywords, it is concluded that gloves, as the most frequently mentioned protective equipment by respondents, conform to user habits and it is an excellent medium for human-computer interaction in heavy physical labor. In the use scene, lifting, shoveling, pushing and other actions related to mortar and stone often occur, which provide ideas for the protection methods.

Fig. 1. Word cloud analysis of interview results

5   Design of Gloves Product

On the basis of preliminary research, the author suggests to design a product for female heavy manual workers, which will help them improve the human-computer interaction process in heavy manual labor. It is defined as a smart glove, whose function is to achieve impact cushioning through materials, and to achieve grip strength maintenance assistance through mechanical structure. During handling, grasping and other movements, the electromyography acquisition technology is used to identify the movements, and the mechanical structure is used to realize the auxiliary force maintenance during the process.

The overall structure of the product can be divided into fabric gloves, reinforcement structure, force assistance module and detection module. The operation mechanism is divided into three processes: information collection, state judgment and action feedback (Fig. 2).

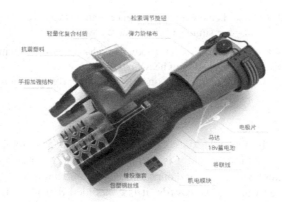

Fig. 2. Product structure diagram

The detection module includes a muscle electrical sensor and a power supply. The muscle electrical sensor uses muscle sensor V3, including an 18V electromyography module, a lead wire and three electrode pieces. After the electrode piece is pasted on the front end of the arm, the Arduino board is connected to it and powered separately to obtain the EMG signal that has been amplified, corrected and smoothed by the ADC. After the product is worn, the detection module will collect the EMG data of the user's hands during work, judge according to the data, and send an action command to the force assistance module once the user's holding and other actions are detected. In this way, the interactive mode of pre-judgment action is realized (Fig. 3).

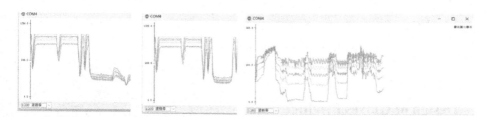

Fig. 3. EMG signal visualization image obtained by holding action in the experiment

The DC motor hidden under the glove fabric layer can change the structure of the rubber finger sleeve by pulling the plastic coated steel wire, thus providing continuous power for force maintenance. In order to ensure the stability of the structure, the plastic coated steel wire is included in a fixed nested structure to achieve the morphological stability of the fabric material when the linear material is stretched. Through physical structure traction, it makes up for the congenital weakness of women to a certain extent, reduces the burden of users' own muscles, and plays a role in preventing high-risk diseases such as carpal tunnel syndrome (Figs. 4 and 5).

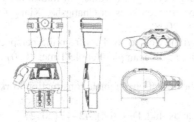
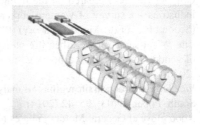

Fig. 4. Product three views   **Fig. 5.** Reinforcement structure diagram

The product hopes to provide a way of thinking focusing on product design to solve the problem of interaction inefficiency caused by insufficient strength of female practitioners in the heavy manual labor industry. After more solutions to this problem appear in the future, this product can provide service interaction contact with target users for the service system of female heavy manual workers.

6 Evaluation Plan

The product has not been put into mass production and is still in the model test stage. In the next stage, experiments will be conducted around several target users to test the high-frequency actions of more heavy manual labor, to test the adaptability of gloves to different types of labor, to evaluate the effectiveness of products, and to collect actual data in the real environment.

7 Discussion and Conclusion

Due to the small proportion of female heavy manual workers, they have not received corresponding attention in China. This topic focuses on their discomfort and insecurity in the process of work. It starts with the gender difference factors and the usage habits of relevant practitioners, using the action recognition principle of EMG technology to design glove equipment. The difference between this product and the traditional labor protection product is that it increases the auxiliary structure of strength, makes up for the lack of women's strength, and improves the human-computer interaction process in labor. At the same time, this topic hopes to guide the society to pay attention to female heavy manual workers.

Although the author believes that the use effect of this product is positive, it should be acknowledged that there are some shortcomings in the research process. The interview effect may be limited by the limited sample size, and the interviewees are concentrated in Shandong Province, and the information obtained has certain geographical limitations. In the future, this topic hopes to expand the sample research from the perspective of scale and region.

References

1. CCTV Media: The women's army took the ride of "labor shortage" to enter the traditional male industry, 12 March 2012. http://news.cntv.cn/20120312/123181.shtml
2. Yang, P., Zhang, G.: Research on gender wage difference of migrant workers in China. Manag. Obs. (12), 3 (2012)
3. Qin, A., Xie, P.: Research on the living conditions of migrant women in traditional male industries – a survey of women workers on construction sites in Changsha. Xiang Chao (Second Half of the Month) (Theory) (06), 16–18 (2008)
4. Liu, W.: A study on the urban life plight of migrant women workers from the perspective of gender – Taking Guangzhou x garment factory as an example. People Times (020), 1–2 (2020)
5. Wei, D.: Construction site regime: an analysis of the formation of female construction workers. South. Popul. **29**(03), 35–42 (2014)
6. Robo glove of General Motors imitates human hands. Ind. Des. (04), 42–43 (2012)
7. Wang, J., Jin, X.: Surface electromyography signal analysis and its application. China Sports Sci. Technol. (08), 27–29 (2000). https://doi.org/10.16470/j.csst.2000.08.009
8. Wang, H., Mao, A., Li, L.: Surface electromyography feature recognition based on linear discriminant analysis. J. Henan Univ. Technol. (Nat. Sci. Ed.) **34**(06), 831–835 (2015). https://doi.org/10.16186/j.cnki.1673-9787.2015.06.015
9. Regulations of Heilongjiang Province on labor protection of female employees. Heilongjiang Daily, 01 September 2021 (006). https://doi.org/10.28348/n.cnki.nhjrb.2021.003804
10. Zhuang, L., Tang, X.: Comparative study on manual housework of female patients with carpal tunnel syndrome. Mod. Rehabil. (03), 35 (1998)

Detection of Voluntary Eye Movement for Analysis About Eye Gaze Behaviour in Virtual Communication

Shogo Matsuno[✉]

Gunma University, Maebashi, Japan
s.matsuno@gunma-u.ac.jp

Abstract. In this study, we aim to realize smoother communication between avatars in virtual space and discuss the method of eye-gaze interaction used for avatar communication. It is necessary for this purpose, a specific gaze movement detection algorithm, which is necessary for measuring characteristic eye movements, blinks, and pupil movements. We developed those characteristic movement counting methods using an HMD built-in eye tracking system. Most input devices used in current virtual reality and augmented reality are hand gestures, head tracking, and voice input, despite the HMD attachment type. Therefore, in order to use the eye expression as a hands-free input modality, we consider an eye gaze input interface that does not depend on the measurement accuracy of the measurement device. Previous eye gaze interfaces have a difficulty called as "Midas touch" problem, which is the trade-off between the input speed and input errors. Therefore, using the method that has been developed so far, which as an input channel using characteristic eye movement and voluntary blinks, it aims to realize an input method that does not hinder the acquisition of other meta information alike gestures of eyes. Moreover, based on involuntary characteristic eye movements unconsciously expressed by the user, such as movement of the gaze, we discuss a system that enables "expression tactics" in the virtual space by providing natural feedback of the avatar's emotional expression and movement patterns. As a first step, we report the result of measured eyeball movements face-to-face through experiments in order to extract features of gaze and blinking.

Keywords: Gaze interaction · eye tracking · voluntary blink

1 Introduction

The importance of telecommunication has increased dramatically due to the voluntary curfew restrictions imposed by COVID-19. In particular, virtual reality (VR) space technology has been widely studied along with the development of various displays and interfaces. Among these technologies, a better V R space is evaluated to be one in which the user is immersed in the same way as in a real space [1]; the more similar the operation is to that in the real world when immersed in a V R space, the more the sense of discomfort is reduced and the sense of immersion is higher. However, it has been

© The Author(s), under exclusive license to Springer Nature Switzerland AG 2023
C. Stephanidis et al. (Eds.): HCII 2023, CCIS 1832, pp. 273–279, 2023.
https://doi.org/10.1007/978-3-031-35989-7_35

pointed out that while wearing a head-mounted display (H MD) for V R, interfaces such as mouse and keyboard, which are generally used for input to computers, restrict actions outside the V R space, resulting in a decrease in immersion. It has been pointed out that these conventional input methods to computers not only cause a decrease in immersion but also do not provide sufficient performance in the input operation itself [2].

In order to solve these problems, input methods with HMD for VR, including motion capture that enables intuitive operation, have been extensively studied. As a result, overall input performance has been greatly improved, and several unique input operations that differ from the conventional PC environment have been proposed. However, most of the channels used as these input interfaces are either hand-held controllers, hand gestures, or head tracking to detect and identify body movements, or input via voice information, despite the type of HMD mounting.

Therefore, the author focused on eye gaze as another input channel that can be used together without interfering with conventional input channels. Gaze input enables intuitive operation without requiring large movements. For this reason, eye gaze input has developed along with the development of computers as a communication support device for people with severe physical disabilities such as ALS, and various studies have been conducted on this subject. On the other hand, the diffusion of these devices among normal people has been very limited. The reasons for this are the harsh usage environment, such as the need for specialized equipment to use eye gaze input, and the input speed, which is more difficult to achieve than with other input interfaces. Regarding the former of these problems, the use environment is no longer a difficult constraint in a VR environment, thanks to the recent installation of line-of-sight measurement devices in VR HMD devices. Also, unlike use in real space, this disadvantage does not exist in a VR environment where HMDs are always worn. Therefore, it can be said that it is easier to demonstrate the potential specifications of gaze input in a V R space than in a real space. In addition, since eye gaze has the characteristic of strongly reflecting individual awareness and interest, it has the potential to enable the input of meta-information that is not limited to simple text or switch input.

In order to achieve true immersive VR, it is necessary to virtualize bodily sensations and enable natural two-way communication [3, 4]. Focusing on the latter, users should be able to conduct interactions in virtual worlds using facial expressions and gaze in addition to traditional means of interaction [5]. Common application scenarios include VR virtual meetings and virtual roaming. Of these, if we focus on eye gaze, ideally users should be able to see other users' expressions and make eye contact - two-way nonverbal interaction - between users in the virtual world. From these perspectives, it is expected to utilize eye gaze as nonverbal interaction [6].

In order to use such gaze expressions as an input modality, it is necessary to consider a gaze input interface that does not depend on the measurement accuracy of the measurement device. Conventional gaze input interfaces are mainly gaze-based input interfaces. Gaze-based input interfaces are compatible with the properties of HMDs and are being commercialized for actual application [7–10]. However, gaze-based input interfaces require constant gazing for a certain dwell time to strictly determine the input decision, a difficulty known as the "Midas touch" problem [11], which is a trade-off between input speed and input error. This leads to redundant input time and significantly impairs the user's experience. Thus, although there are many intuitive and accurate prior methods for traditional gaze input interfaces, there are still many limitations when utilizing them in HMD devices.

Therefore, the author aims to develop an input interface in which intuitive input is provided by voluntary eye movements and meta-information in communication, such as emotional expression, is extracted from involuntary eye movements. To solve the Midas toch problem, the author has developed an input method that uses characteristic eye movements (gestures) and voluntary blinks as input channels. In addition to this, the author has been studying the implementation of a method that acquires involuntary physiological responses such as voluntary blinks and pupil changes like mydriasis and constriction as meta-information.

In this paper, we report on a prototype system that detects eye movements that are rarely used in daily life as gestures while wearing an HMD, and at the same time identifies voluntary and spontaneous blinks separately.

2   Detection Method

In this section we use an optical method to detect eye gestures and eye blinks by measuring eye movement from periocular images captured by an infrared camera attached to an H M D through image processing. In a preliminary experiment, optical flow was measured from a periocular image captured by a normal web camera, and eye movement was vectorized using the shading of the black and white eye pixels in the image. The optical flow was measured using 900 measurement points within a fixed measurement area. The sum of the top 5% of the vector values at each measurement point was used as the evaluation value.

Next, we attempted to detect oblique eye movements, which are not usually performed. There are four possible oblique eye movements. These four types of eye movements can be discriminated by four types of vector quantities that combine the positive and negative values of the vertical and horizontal vectors in the sum of the magnitudes of the optical flow in the measurement area. Here, in the vertical direction, a positive value means upward, and in the horizontal direction, a positive value means leftward. For example, if the eye moves to the upper left, the sum of optical flow is detected to be large positive values in both horizontal and vertical directions, and if the eye moves to the lower right, it is detected to be large negative values in both horizontal and vertical directions.

In this paper, we constructed a simple discrimination algorithm based on these features. The threshold value is set empirically to a value with low misjudgment by acquiring the feature waveforms in advance through calibration for each subject. Here, since it has been pointed out that the amount of eye movement differs from left to right for some subjects, the thresholds are set separately for the left and right.

To extract oblique eye movement, the peaks of the waveform are first detected. First, we find the point where the horizontal peak and the vertical peak occur simultaneously. Next, it is determined whether a peak larger than 1/4 of the detected peak value occurs again for a while after the peak detection point. If these conditions were met, we assumed that it was a single oblique eye movement.

Next, blinks were detected in the same way, using the sum of the optical flows. A blink is a temporary response that completes a series of actions within about 1/3 s (300–400 ms). For this reason, it is difficult to distinguish between voluntary and involuntary blinks in ordinary video camera photography. On the other hand, infrared cameras often have higher resolution than ordinary video cameras, and it may be possible to discriminate voluntary blinks using methods such as those reported in previous studies even without special image processing. We adopt the algorithm for voluntary blink identification proposed in our previous study. That is, the method captures the temporal progression process of a blink as a waveform, cuts out the waveform based on abrupt changes in feature values, and further assumes that the blink is voluntary if its integral value exceeds a certain value.

3 Experiment

The hardware of the experimental system was an HP Reverb G2 Omnicept Edition head-mounted display with a built-in infrared eye tracking system. In addition, a PC was connected to the HMD for graphic output and analysis of acquired data, and the graphics were mirrored on the PC display for confirmation at the same time as the HMD.

The subjects were seated in a chair while wearing the HMD, and were asked to follow the experimental input screen and voice instructions on the display. The measured eye movement is transferred to a PC in real time via a DisplayPort connection and stored in a memory device. The recorded eye movement data were then used to detect eye movement and blinks offline.

The accuracy of the oblique eye movement detection was verified based on the algorithm described in Sect. 2 for the acquired eye movement data. First, the first set of acquired data was used as calibration data to determine the detection threshold. In this experiment, the threshold was set at 30% of the maximum and minimum values in the interval. The measured data are differenced, and the peak value exceeding the threshold is detected. The detection process was basically conducted with reference to the measurement data of both eyes, and the measurement data of the left eye was used when the measurement of eye movement failed due to a calibration failure of the HMD device.

As for the flow of the experiment, the first step was calibration to determine the discriminative thresholds for eye movement and blink. Subjects were taught in advance to blink and gaze according to the instructions displayed on the screen. They were also given the same instructions by voice at the same time as the on-screen instructions. However, subjects were also told that they did not need to hold back blinking, even when there were no clear instructions in particular. During calibration, subjects were instructed to blink three times in order to set a reference value for spontaneous blinking based on the shape features of the blink immediately after the instruction. In parallel, the reference value for spontaneous blinking was also determined based on the nonvoluntary blink waveforms detected during calibration. After the calibration was completed, the measurement experiment was conducted continuously. Subjects were instructed in advance to perform eye movements according to the directional and blink instructions for eye movement that were randomly displayed on the experimental screen. The instructional indicators were set to appear at 3-s intervals, and although the instructions set were random, each type was displayed a specified number of times (four times for each indicator in this experiment) and then terminated. The instructions for the actions are not only presented visually with the indicators on the display, but the same instructions are also read aloud at the same time. When the system detects an action performed by the subject according to the instructions, it provides feedback by changing the color and shape of the index, indicating to the subject that the input was accepted. This feedback is implemented each time an input is detected, regardless of the validity of the input. This operation was performed four times for each type of input, for a total of 20 times.

4 Results and Discussion

Table 1 shows the results of the eye movement detection. The results of the experiment show an overall discrimination accuracy of 93.75% for all six subjects. Of these, subjects B, E, and F were successful in detecting all eye movements. In addition, when we look at the failed cases of subjects A, C, and D, which have detection failures, we find that the waveform movement is often small, suggesting that there are variations in the eye movement performed by the same user depending on the state of the eye movement. In response to this, there is room to improve the detection accuracy by considering a calibration method to cope with the variations, such as by appropriately determining the number of eye movements used for calibration.

On the other hand, all errors in the table were either identification failures or missed detections, and no false detections related to oblique eye movement were observed in this experiment. From the above, it can be said that the proposed algorithm is generally successful in detecting oblique eye movement.

Table 2 shows the results of blink detection. Voluntary blinks occurred immediately after the presentation of the index, and were judged with respect to the measured blink waveform. The number of voluntary blinks was not overlooked, and it can be said that the number of blinks was accurately measured. On the other hand, since a simple counting method was used in this study, we cannot deny the possibility that voluntary blinks existed in the counts that were processed as spontaneous blinks. Therefore, we cannot evaluate the detection error. As for spontaneous blinks, we succeeded in detecting most of the spontaneous blinks that occurred during the experiment, but we believe that we missed blinks with very small movements or special movements that were slightly different from common blinks. In conclusion, we confirmed that the detection was generally sufficient when only voluntariness was used as the input channel. On the other hand, in order to use voluntary blinking as an involuntary physiological index that reflects psychological states, it is necessary to improve the detection accuracy of blinking and to successfully detect blinking in special conditions, such as when fatigue accumulates or when drowsiness is strong, and to use it to evaluate psychological states. These results suggest that it is necessary to detect blinks in a special state, such as when fatigue accumulates or when sleepiness is strong, and to use them to evaluate psychological states.

Based on these results, we confirmed that oblique eye movements and voluntary blinks can be discriminated and detected from measurements by the eye tracking sensor built into the HMD. Next, we would like to investigate an input method that combines other input channels and more precise detection of involuntary physiological indices.

Table 1. Classification results of eye movement direction of movement

Subjects	Left		Right		Total
	Up	Down	Up	Down	
A	3	3	4	4	14/16
B	4	4	4	4	16/16
C	4	4	4	3	15/16
D	4	4	2	3	13/16
E	4	4	4	4	16/16
F	4	4	4	4	16/16
Total	23/24	23/24	22/24	22/24	90/96 (84.75%)

Table 2. Detection and classification of eyeblink types

Subjects	Voluntary	Error	Spontaneous	Error	Total (Spontaneous)	
A	4	0	27	3	30	90%
B	4	0	12	4	16	75%
C	4	0	20	8	28	71%
D	4	0	6	1	7	86%
E	4	0	11	6	17	65%
F	4	0	34	11	45	76%
Total	24/24	0/24	110	33	143	77%

5 Conclusion

The purpose of this paper is to discuss the basic measurement environment for a system that enables "expressive tactics" in virtual space by providing natural feedback on the avatar's emotional expression and movement patterns based on the involuntary characteristic eye movements, such as eye movement, that users unconsciously express in the oblique direction. We proposed an automatic detection algorithm for eye movement and voluntary and spontaneous eye blinks, and evaluated its detection accuracy. From the experimental results, we confirmed that input manipulation with high accuracy is possible by using voluntary eye movements and blinks. However, it is difficult to uniformly detect very fine eye movements such as voluntary blinks and micro saccades, and to use a series of these movements as physiological indicators for estimating psychological states, it is necessary to develop a more In order to use these series of movements as physiological indicators for estimating psychological states, it is necessary to develop a detection algorithm that enables more detailed classification.

Our future plans are to improve the detection accuracy, develop algorithms to detect spontaneous blinking and micro saccades, and investigate the relationship between the psychological state and the algorithms, aiming to realize a system to evaluate the psychological state in real-time.

References

1. Zeltzer, D.: Autonomy, interaction and, presence: presence 1(1), 127–132 (1992)
2. Bowman, D.A., Rhoton, C.J., Pinho, M.S.: Text input techniques for immersive virtual environments: anempirical comparison. In: Proceedings of the Human Factors and Ergonomics Society Annual Meeting, vol. 46, no. 26, pp. 2154–2158 (2002)
3. Møllenbach, E., Hansen, J.P., Lillholm, M.: Eye movements in gaze interaction. J. Eye Movement Res. 6(2), 1–15 (2013)
4. Rosalind, W.: Picard: Affective Computing. MIT Press, Cambridge (1997)
5. Chen, S.-Y., Gao, L., Lai, Y., Rosin, P., Xia, S.: Real-time 3D face reconstruction and gaze tracking for virtual reality. In: Presented at: IEEE Conference on Virtual Reality and 3D User Interfaces, Reutlingen, Germany, 18–22 March 2018
6. Ku, P.-S., Wu, T.-Y., Chen, M.Y.: EyeExpress: expanding hands-free input vocabulary using eye expressions. In: The 31st Annual ACM Symposium on User Interface Software and Technology Adjunct Proceedings. ACM (2018)
7. Figueiredo, P., Fonseca, M.J.: EyeLinks: a gaze-only click alternative for heterogeneous clickables. In: Proceedings of the 20th ACM International Conference on Multimodal Interaction, pp. 307–314 (2018)
8. Rajanna, V., Hansen, J.P.: Gaze typing in virtual reality: impact of keyboard design, selection method, and motion. In: Proceedings of the Symposium on Eye-Tracking Research & Applications (ETRA 2018), no.15 (2018)
9. Ahuja, K., Islam, R., Parashar, V., Dey, K., Harrison, C., Goel, M.: EyeSpyVR: interactive eye sensing using off-the-shelf, smartphone-based VR headsets. In: Proceedings of ACM Interactive, Mobile, Wearable and Ubiquitous Technologies, vol. 2, no. 2, Article 57 (2018)
10. Sindhwani, S., Lutteroth, C., Weber, G.: ReType: quick text editing with keyboard and gaze. In: Proceedings of the CHI Conference on Human Factors in Computing Systems (2019, in press)
11. Jacob, R.J.K.: What you look at is what you get: eye movement-based interaction techniques. In: Proceedings of the SIGCHI Conference on Human Factors in Computing Systems (CHI 1990), pp. 11–18 (1990)

ChromicCanvas: Interactive Canvas Using Chromic Fiber

Maho Oki, Mao Wakamoto, and Koji Tsukada[✉]

Future University Hakodate, Hokkaido, Japan
{okimaho,tsuka}@acm.org

Abstract. This study aims to realize a simple and flexible method of expression by combining chromic materials and digital fabrication tools. Focusing on UV embroidery thread among chromic materials, we propose "ChromicCanvas," an interactive drawing system that allows users to draw with various colors and drawing patterns. The prototype consists of canvases created with embroidery thread and pen and stamp-type devices for switching the shape and color tone to be drawn. This paper describes the preliminary verification of UV embroidery threads, the prototype device developed, and evaluation experiments.

Keywords: Photochromism · Embroidery · Canvas · Drawing

1 Introduction

In recent years, considerable research has been conducted on wearable computers, in which the computer functions are built into clothing to support people's daily lives. In particular, research on e-textile, which incorporates sensors and electronic circuit functions into the fabric itself, is being actively pursued. Much of the previous research on e-textiles has focused on the electrical characteristics of the materials [2,6,7]. This study focuses on applying chromic materials to e-textiles. Chromic materials reversibly change their color in response to changes in the environmental conditions or other stimuli [1]. Goods and materials for manufacturing that change color with heat or ultraviolet (UV) light are sold as products, such as mugs and nails that change color with temperature, and yarn and beads that change color with UV light. These materials can be used to create fascinating works of art with interactive color changes. Nevertheless, many of these materials have limitations, such as allowing only transitions between two colors (e.g., from colorless to red), and once a pattern is determined, it cannot be changed, making it difficult to achieve flexible expression in conjunction with e-textiles. In this study, we aim to create a simple and flexible expression method by combining chromic materials and digital fabrication tools such as a CNC embroidery machine. Focusing on the UV embroidery thread among other chromic materials, we propose "ChromicCanvas," an interactive drawing system that allows users to draw with various colors and drawing patterns (Fig. 1 a).

C. Stephanidis et al. (Eds.): HCII 2023, CCIS 1832, pp. 280–287, 2023.
https://doi.org/10.1007/978-3-031-35989-7_36

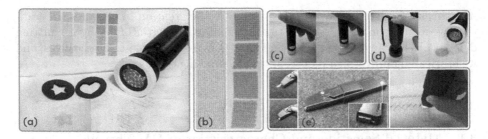

Fig. 1. (a) Overview of ChromicCanvas. (b) Trial of a new color by mixing two colors of threads in embroidery (top to bottom: blue, mix1, pink, mix2). (c) Drawing with a UV laser pointer. (d) Drawing with a UV stamp prototype. (e) Drawing with a UV pen prototype.

2   Related Work

2.1   Interaction Method Using Chromic Materials

Interactive systems have been proposed to control the color of a work using a material that changes color upon heating. Kaiho et al. [5] proposed a method for controlling the color of origami paper by applying thermochromic and conductive inks. Mosaic Textile [11] is a system that changes the color of cloth dyed with liquid crystal ink by means of heat generated by conductive threads and is proposed for use in clothing and other applications. Okazaki et al. [8] developed a method of knitting using wool dyed with an ink, whose color is fixed when a certain temperature is applied, and a special knitting rod to control the discoloration of any part of the yarn. Systems for drawing pictures on a single-color canvas coated with photochromic ink have also been proposed. Photochromic Canvas [3] allows drawing lines using a pen with a built-in projector, while Photochromic Carpet [10] permits drawing patterns as footprints by walking on it. In this study, we explored a simple method of creating canvases with color variations using a commercially available UV embroidery thread and an embroidery sewing machine. We also developed drawing devices, aiming for a system that allows users to draw pictures while easily switching color tones and patterns.

2.2   Printing Technology Using Chromic Materials

Many photochromic compounds that cause color changes due to UV rays change between specific colors and colorless, or between two specific colors. To increase the number of colors that can be represented, the following techniques have been proposed: ColorMod [9] changes the color of an object later by coloring a multicolor voxel pattern with photochromic inks during 3D printing; Photo-Chromeleon [4] improves the color tone and resolution, which can be expressed by mixing multiple colors of chromic ink into a single solution. These methods require the expertise and skill of the producer because the ink must be applied to the object, and the production procedure is complicated and difficult. Instead of dyeing with chromic ink, this study used a UV thread to facilitate the creation of canvases. In addition, we focused on the possibility that different wavelengths of UV light-emitting diodes (LEDs) can change the color of lines drawn on a single-colored canvas, and we fabricated and verified prototypes of the drawing device.

3   Materials Used in This Study

3.1   Material Selection and Characteristics of UV Threads

There are many types of chromic materials, for example, thermochromic materials, which change color depending on temperature; photochromic materials, which change color with light; and electrochromic materials, which change color with electricity [1]. We focused on photochromic materials because of their availability and ease of handling. After reviewing products with threads, fabrics, and other forms applicable to e-textiles, we obtained a "UV thread 7-color set"[1] (hereinafter referred to as UV thread). These threads are typically white and change to a unique color when exposed to UV light (Fig. 1 b), after which they gradually return to white over time. We confirmed that the UV thread could be used stably with Brother's PR655 commercial embroidery sewing machine owned by our laboratory.

The duration of coloration and effect of UV wavelength on the color tone of these UV threads were examined. We prepared embroidery samples and observed the color changes when exposed to UV light. Box-type (EKO-UV36W, 365 nm) and handheld-type (Vansky 51LED, 395 nm) UV lights were used (Fig. 2 left).

Duration of Coloration. After exposure to UV light for 30 s with the box light to activate color, the change back to white was captured on video. Under 20.9°C, the color almost disappeared after 5 min, whereas under 10.3°C, the color remained pale even after 10 min. Thus, the color duration tended to vary with temperature.

Color Tone and UV Wavelength. The results of UV irradiation of the embroidery samples using the box (365 nm) and handheld (395 nm) UV light are depicted in Fig. 2. The embroideries in blue, pink, and purple had almost the same color, but those in red, orange, yellow, and green had different color tones.

4   ChromicCanvas

We propose an interactive canvas called "ChromicCanvas," which utilizes UV threads and a sewing machine. The goals are to enable expression of a variety of colors and to achieve a flexible drawing method. To realize the former, we

---

[1] Nakamura Shoji Co. Ltd., https://angelking.co.jp/SHOP/wagon-uv-thread.html.

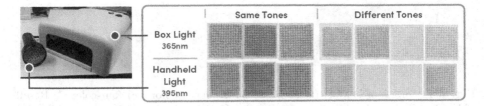

Fig. 2. UV lights used and results of UV irradiation of the embroidery.

attempted to create a variety of colored canvases by mixing multiple colors of UV threads and embroidering them. Color expression utilizing the difference in coloration according to the UV wavelength was also considered. To realize the latter, we applied devices such as laser pointers and stamped- or pen-type devices that can switch the shape and color of the drawing.

4.1 Implementation of Canvas

Single-color canvases made with a single embroidery thread and multicolor canvases made with multiple embroidery threads were created. To create a multicolored canvas, we first mixed and embroidered two colors of threads from the basic seven-color thread. We tried several stitch settings available in the sewing machine software and several patterns by sending their data to the sewing machine. As a result, it was found that the "cross stitch" and "diagonal stripe" pattern with a width of 1.5 mm blended the colors better (Fig. 1 b-mix1). Figure 3 displays 21 types of color samples mixed with two colors. Canvases with four and seven colors were also created using the same settings (Fig. 4). Although the mixed color was not as good as the two colors, it was used to validate the drawing device.

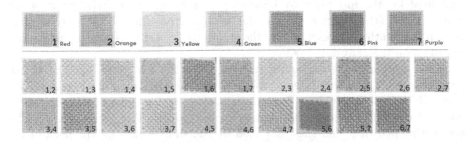

Fig. 3. Embroidery samples in seven primary colors and 21 mixed colors.

The single-color canvas was created using the "Tatami fill" stitch setting, which produces a cloth-like finish. Tatami fill can create a canvas on both sides of the fabric by using UV threads as the upper and lower threads on the sewing

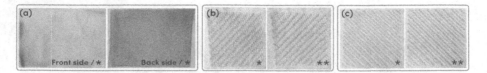

Fig. 4. Examples of canvas: (a) single-color, (b) seven-color, (c) four-color. *: Result of UV irradiation with box light. **: Result of UV irradiation with hand-held light.

machine. We used it to create a single-color double-sided canvas with different colors on the front and back sides. Figure 4 (a) shows a canvas created with the upper thread in green and the bobbin thread in pink.

4.2 Drawing on Canvas Using a Laser Pointer

Using a UV laser pointer (HTPOW Ltd., 405 nm), we confirmed that lines could be drawn freely on the canvas, similar to writing with a pen on paper (Fig. 1 c). The color density of the lines depends on the speed at which the laser pointer moves. The written lines also disappear over time.

4.3 Implementation of Stamp and Pen Type Devices

The stamp-type input device (hereinafter referred to as the UV stamp) was implemented by attaching parts created by 3D printing to a handheld UV light. When the UV stamp is pressed against the canvas, UV rays are emitted (Fig. 1 d). These are partially blocked by the attached plate, and irradiated onto the canvas in the shape of holes in the mold. This allows the user to draw stamps of various shapes on the canvas. A spring was used to fix the battery of the original handheld UV light, which was modified to emit UV rays only when the holding part is pushed all the way to be stamp-like in its usability. Flexible filaments were used for the mold cap to allow easy attachment and detachment of the stamp mold. The stamp mold was cut from a 2mm-thick black acrylic plate using a laser cutter. By exchanging the stamp mold, a stamp of any pattern can be drawn on the canvas.

A pen-type device (hereinafter referred to as the UV pen) that can switch between two UV LEDs of different wavelengths was implemented (Fig. 1 e). This allows the user to freely draw lines on the canvas. Using different UV LEDs, we aimed to control the colors that emerge on the canvas. Two types of UV LEDs were set as pen tips, and the LED used by the slide switch on the back of the pen was switched. The LED was lit only when the switch was pressed. The voltage was 4.5 V (three 1.5 V button batteries), and four types of UV LEDs with different wavelengths (375, 385, 405, and 415 nm) were used.

5   Evaluation

This section describes the usability evaluation of ChromicCanvas and the performance investigation of color drawing using the UV pen.

5.1   Usability Evaluation

We conducted a hands-on workshop using the single-color canvas, laserpointer[2], and UV stamp, and investigated the impression on the expression of the drawn pictures as well as the usability of the drawing devices through questionnaires/observations of the subjects.

Method. The experimenter verbally instructed the subjects on how to use the UV stamp, and the subjects painted on the canvas approximately 10 times without practicing, changing the stamp mold. The experimenter also instructed the subjects on how to draw using the laser pointer. The subjects practiced, and then drew a free-drawing artwork. They were then asked to complete a questionnaire. Ten subjects aged between 21 and 22 years (including four females) participated.

Result. The results of a 5-point scale for the "ease of stamping" of the UV stamp and the "ease of changing" the stamp mold showed that the average for the former was 4, while the average for the latter was 2.8. In the free description, some respondents answered that the cap was somewhat hard and difficult to remove.

Regarding free-line drawing using the laser pointer, the average scores were 4.3 for "ease of line drawing" and 4.3 for "degree of freedom in line drawing." In the free description, some users answered, "I want it to be possible to draw thin lines," and "Colors disappear faster than I expected." Fig. 5 shows examples of drawings using the laser pointer.

The question asking for "examples or places that could be used" was answered with "patch," "children's playgrounds," and "schools." In the question "How do you feel about the phenomenon of colors disappearing while drawing?" respondents answered "No problem for simple drawings" and "Can express a variety of color intensities." During the experiment, when the device colored the canvas, the subjects often exclaimed, "Oh!" and "Wow!" when the device colors the canvas. After the experiment was completed, the subjects were free to draw pictures or create complex drawings that they had not drawn during the experiment.

5.2   Performance Study of UV Pen

As discussed in Sect. 3.1, there are differences in the coloration when the wavelengths of the UV light used are different. To confirm whether this characteristic

---

[2] Since it was before the UV pen was implemented, the laser pointer was used.

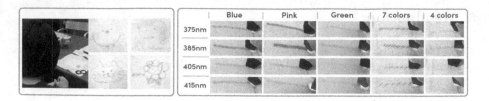

Fig. 5. Results of evaluations 5.1(left) and 5.2(right).

can be reproduced with UV pens, we compared the color outputs of LEDs with different wavelengths attached to the UV pen.

Method. The task of drawing a line on the canvas with the UV pen of approximately 5 cm for 6–7 s was performed for the single-color canvas (blue, pink, and green) and multicolor canvas (seven and four colors). LEDs with wavelengths of 375, 385, 405, and 415 nm were attached to two UV pens. The experiment was conducted in a room with a temperature of 20.5 – 21°C and fluorescent lighting, and it was filmed on video, which was used for color comparison.

Result. The color and density of the drawn lines differed depending on the UV LED wavelength. Figure 5 illustrates the lines immediately after drawing using the UV pen.

The color tone of the lines varied according to the color of the canvas. The lines drawn on the green canvas were yellow-green at 375 nm, bluish-green at 385 nm, and light blue at 405 nm and 415 nm. The lines drawn on the seven-color canvas were strong pink and blue stripes at 375 nm and 385 nm; at 405 nm and 415 nm, the pink faded, so the overall stripes appeared cold. The lines of the four-color canvas were orange/red/green at 375 nm and 385 nm but not visually visible at 405 nm and 415 nm. The blue and pink canvas did not show any differences in the color tone of the lines.

The color intensity of the lines was darker at 375 nm and 385 nm and lighter at 405 nm and 415 nm for all canvases. The yellow UV threads in the seven- and four-color canvases were difficult to confirm visually. For the aforementioned four-color canvas, the entire line was extremely thin for visual confirmation.

6 Discussion

Regarding the color duration, the positive response from 5.1 subjects suggests that the disappearance of color over time can be used for shading expression or for trial and error in expression. On the other hand, there was a comment "colors disappear faster than I expected." Because color duration is extended at low temperatures, as mentioned in Sect. 3.1, we considered adding a canvas temperature control feature to avoid interfering with the user's drawing.

For the control of the color shade/tone with the UV pen, the results in Sect. 5.2 showed that the LEDs of different wavelengths were able to switch the color tones of the green, four-color, and seven-color canvas. In all canvases, the colors were darker with 375 nm and 385 nm LEDs and lighter with 405 nm and 415 nm LEDs at the same drawing speed. In the future, we would like to improve/verify devices that can adjust the intensity of UV light and attempt to control shading and color tone.

7   Conclusion

We proposed ChromicCanvas, an interactive canvas that can express various colors and drawing patterns using a UV thread and a CNC sewing machine. New color canvases were created by combining seven colors of commercially available threads. We implemented a UV stamp that can instantaneously stamp a specific shape and a UV pen that can freely draw using UV LEDs of different wavelengths. The basic performances were verified and discussed based on the findings. In the future, we plan to pursue the improvements described in the discussion and seek applications that take advantage of the system features.

Acknowledgments. This work was partly supported by JSPS KAKENHI Grant Number 20H04231.

References

1. Bamfield, P.: Chromic phenomena: technological applications of colour chemistry. Royal Society of Chemistry (2010)
2. Enokibori, Y., Suzuki, A., Mizuno, H., Shimakami, Y., Mase, K.: E-textile pressure sensor based on conductive fiber and its structure (2013)
3. Hashida, T., Kakehi, Y., Naemura, T.: Photochromic canvas drawing with patterned light. In: ACM SIGGRAPH 2010 Posters, pp. 1–1 (2010)
4. Jin, Y., et al.: Photo-chromeleon: re-programmable multi-color textures using photochromic dyes (2019)
5. Kaihou, T., Wakita, A.: Electronic origami with the color-changing function (2013)
6. Karrer, T., Wittenhagen, M., Lichtschlag, L., Heller, F., Borchers, J.: Pinstripe: eyes-free continuous input on interactive clothing (2011)
7. Ma, H., Yamaoka, J.: Smart textile using 3d printed conductive sequins (2022)
8. Okazaki, M., Nakagaki, K., Kakehi, Y.: Metamocrochet: augmenting crocheting with bi-stable color changing inks (2014)
9. Punpongsanon, P., Wen, X., Kim, D.S., Mueller, S.: Colormod: recoloring 3d printed objects using photochromic inks (2018)
10. Saakes, D., Tsujii, T., Nishimura, K., Hashida, T., Naemura, T.: Photochromic carpet: playful floor canvas with color-changing footprints. In: Reidsma, D., Katayose, H., Nijholt, A. (eds.) Advances in Computer Entertainment (2013)
11. Wakita, A., Shibutani, M.: Mosaic textile: wearable ambient display with non-emissive color-changing modules (2006)

Analysis of Conducting Waves Using Multi-channel Surface Electromyogram Depends on Active Electrodes Supported Multiple Directions

Kohei Okura[✉], Kazuyuki Mito, Tota Mizuno, and Naoaki Itakura

The University of Electro-Communications, Chofu, Japan
xzjb2957@gmail.com

Abstract. Surface electromyogram (EMG) is recorded as interference of action potentials produced by some of the motor units of the muscle. If the composition of the interference wave can be analyzed, more detailed mechanism of muscle contraction may be elucidated. In a previous study, the triceps femoris muscle was used as the test muscle for measurement using electrodes arranged in multiple directions. Although it is possible to switch the electrode geometry and extract the obtained conducting waves, it is difficult to estimate the muscle fiber direction. To solve this problem, a new active electrode was proposed. The characteristics of the electrode shape are the same as in the previous study. The objective of this study is to analyze the conducting wave of the feather muscle by performing measurements using the m-ch method and the proposed electrode. Rom the experimental results, in total short-circuit, the electrode was observed to float from the waveform data. In all patterns, the medial head showed a higher number of conducting waves than the lateral head.

Keywords: First Keyword · Second Keyword · Third Keyword

1 Introduction

The action potentials of the muscle fibers making up skeletal muscle are generated by chemical action at the neuromuscular junction; this action conducts along the muscle fibers from the neuromuscular junction to the tendons at both ends. The con-duction velocity of the action potentials is called the muscle fiber conduction veloci-ty, and the conduction velocity is derived from the surface electromyogram (EMG) using, e.g., a cross-correlation method. The waveform obtained from the surface EMG is not the action potential in a single motor unit, but rather the interference po-tential in multiple motor units. Therefore, if we pay attention to the waveform shape as conducted over multiple channels, it is thought that a new index different from the conduction velocity can be derived.

In the previous research by Kosuga et al. [1], a multi-channel method (m-ch meth-od) was investigated, aiming to quantitatively determine the conducted wave as ob-tained

C. Stephanidis et al. (Eds.): HCII 2023, CCIS 1832, pp. 288–293, 2023.
https://doi.org/10.1007/978-3-031-35989-7_37

from the multi-channel surface EMG, its conditions, and a calculation method for the conduction velocity. According to this method, all conducting waves were extracted from the waveform of the surface EMG using array electrodes, and characteristics such as the conduction velocity, amplitude, and wavelength of each conducting wave were investigated. As a result, it became possible to consider the muscle contraction mechanisms in more detail.

In a previous study [2], we proposed an electrode with multiple directions and conducted experiments using the biceps brachii (parallelis) and triceps brachii (pectoralis) muscles as test subjects (Fig. 1). A dip switch was installed between the electrode and the amplifier, which can be turned ON (short-circuited) to change the shape of the electrode for measurement without replacing it. From the experimental results, it was found that the propagating waves could be obtained sufficiently for the parallel stripes, while almost no propagating waves could be obtained for the pinnate stripes, making measurement difficult. The reasons for the inability to acquire propagating waves include the acquisition of signals that differ from muscle potentials and the inclusion of noise due to the shaking of the electrode cable.

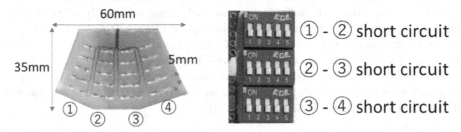

Fig. 1. Electrodes used in previous study.

To solve this problem, we propose the electrode shown in Fig. 2. This electrode features four pure silver wires of 1 mm in diameter and 9, 8, 7, 6, and 5 mm in length, each independently arranged in multiple directions. As in previous studies, a DIP switch is mounted between the electrode and the amplifier. In addition, active electrodes are used. Active electrodes are impedance conversion amplifiers mounted in the form of electrodes. It receives the input from the electrode in a high-impedance state and places the output in a low-impedance state to reduce the influence of the electrode cable. The high impedance of the active electrode is grounded to the skin surface, reducing the effect of the skin surface on the signal, as is the case with a passive electrode. The preamplifier used to activate the electrodes is mounted between the electrodes and the amplifier and is removable. The proposed electrodes are independent of each other in four rows, and the angle can be adjusted by attaching a fixed frame. In this study, a 20-degree one is used.

The objective of this study is to analyze the propagating waves obtained at the pinnacle muscle by using the m-ch method and the proposed active electrodes for measurement.

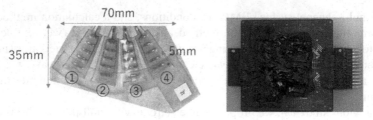

Fig. 2. "Proposed electrode" and "pre-amplifier".

2 Method

2.1 Experimental Method

The subjects were two healthy adults, and the test muscles were the triceps femoris of the dominant leg (lateral head of gastrocnemius and medial head of gastrocnemius) as self-reported by the subjects. The subjects were asked to maintain a standing position with their heel elevated 10 cm off the floor for 10 s to obtain electromyographic data. To avoid muscle fatigue, the subjects were allowed to rest sufficiently between trials, and measurements were performed multiple times in the three patterns shown in Table 1 (total short-circuit, short-circuit of ①-② and ③-④, and total open-circuit). The sampling frequency was 5 kHz, the amplifier settings were HighCut 1kHz and LowCut 5Hz, and the amplification factor was 80dB. The data obtained from the experiments were again subjected to a FIR filter with a high cutoff frequency of 500 Hz and a low cutoff frequency of 5 Hz, and the results were used for analysis (Fig. 3).

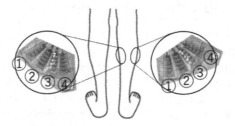

Fig. 3. Experimental system.

Table 1. Myoelectric potential data obtained in each column

Measurement channel [ch]	1–4	5–8	9–12	13–16
Fully open	①	②	③	④
Short circuit between ①-② and ③-④	①&②		③&④	
All short circuit	①&②&③&④			

2.2 Analysis Method

The m-ch method was used for the analysis. In the m-ch method, one of a pair of adjacent electrodes of the same shape is defined as a conduction source, and the other is defined as the conduction destination. The section where a zero crossing occurs twice from the source is extracted as one waveform. It is determined whether the signal has conducted over multiple channels, and then the conduction speed is calculated. When performing the conduction judgment, one waveform obtained from the conduction source is used as a conduction wave candidate. Then, the conduction wave candidate of the conduction destination existing 10 ms before and after the start point of the conduction wave candidate of the conduction source is extracted. To be able to calculate even when the waveforms have different wavelengths, the conduction wave candidates are resampled based on a sampling theorem, and the similarity ratio, amplitude ratio, and wavelength ratio are calculated.

When judging a conduction wave over multiple channels, thresholds are set for the similarity ratio, amplitude ratio, and wavelength ratio, based on the concept that if the waveform shapes between adjacent channels are similar, the action potential has conducted between the two channels. When the conduction wave candidate is equal to or larger than a threshold, it is determined as a conduction wave. The conduction speed is defined as the time difference Δt between channels, and the value is obtained by dividing the distance between channels (5 mm) by the Δt between channels. In addition, the conduction velocity variation coefficient (hereinafter referred to as CV) is used as a conduction determination condition to consider the velocity variable of the waveform for which the conduction is determined. In this study, the conduction judgment conditions were the similarity ratio, a wavelength ratio of 0.9 or more, an amplitude ratio of 0.7 or more, and a CV of 30% or less. Only conduction waves over three channels were extracted and used for analysis.

For the conducted wave(s) obtained using this analysis method, the relative frequency distribution of the amplitude and conduction velocity were compared for each electrode. The total number of conducted waves was set to 100%, and the amplitude and proportion of each conducted wave were calculated.

3 Results and Discussions

3.1 Relative Frequency Distribution and Number of Propagating Waves

The number of propagating waves obtained for the three patterns for subject A are shown in Tables 2(a) and (b).

Table 2(a) shows that there is a difference in the number of propagating waves obtained for each column in the "total short-circuit" case, and this is also true for the "total short-circuit" case shown in Table 2(b). Although it would be desirable to obtain similar data for each column because of the "total short-circuit," different results were obtained for the "total short-circuit" column. The first reason may be that the connectors of the preamplifier were not connected properly, and the myopotential data obtained in each column were not the same. The second factor could be due to noise contamination between the electrode box and the amplifier. Similar results were also shown for the "short circuit between (1)-(2) and (3)-(4)" in Table 2 (a) and (b).

Table 2. Number of conducting waves obtained in the experiment (subject A)

(a) Lateral head of gastrocnemius muscle

First column	Average value	Second column	Average value
Fully open	0.60	Fully open	2.97
Short circuit between ①-② and ③-④	1.07	Short circuit between ①-② and ③-④	1.20
All short circuit	1.47	All short circuit	1.63

Third column	Average value	Fourth column	Average value
Fully open	1.73	Fully open	0.97
Short circuit between ①-② and ③-④	1.77	Short circuit between ①-② and ③-④	2.07
All short circuit	1.53	All short circuit	1.93

[pcs/s]

(b) Medial head of gastrocnemius muscle

First column	Average value	Second column	Average value
Fully open	0.60	Fully open	33.3
Short circuit between ①-② and ③-④	2.20	Short circuit between ①-② and ③-④	20.0
All short circuit	2.97	All short circuit	26.7

Third column	Average value	Fourth column	Average value
Fully open	1.87	Fully open	1.57
Short circuit between ①-② and ③-④	2.27	Short circuit between ①-② and ③-④	3.47
All short circuit	2.00	All short circuit	2.47

[pcs/s]

3.2 EMG Data

The myopotential data obtained for subject A's "full opening" is shown in Fig. 4.

Comparing the four waveforms in Fig. 4, ups and downs of data were observed at 14ch and 15ch. This indicates that the electrodes involved in 14ch and 15ch of the proposed electrode are not properly grounded to the skin. Since accurate measurement is difficult in this condition, it is necessary to ground the electrodes not only by fixing them with tape but also with a supporter as a countermeasure.

In addition, the waveform of the blue circle in Fig. 4 is jagged. Such waveforms were not observed with conventional passive electrodes. This is thought to be because more accurate myopotential data could be obtained by measuring with active electrodes. Therefore, it can be said that the effect of noise was greater, especially for those with smaller electrode area. As a countermeasure, the amplifier settings need to be narrower than in previous studies.

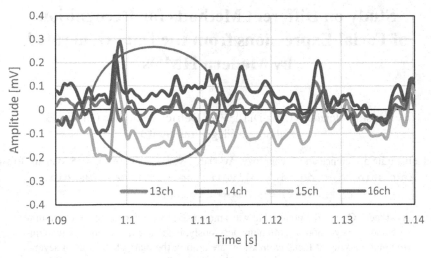

Fig. 4. Fourth row EMG data (subject A).

4   Conclusion

The purpose of this study was to analyze the propagating waves obtained in the pinnatus muscle using the m-ch method and the proposed active electrode. From the viewpoint of the number of propagating waves, similar data should be obtained in the short-circuited case, but similar myopotential data could not be obtained.

In addition, from the viewpoint of myopotential data, while active electrodes made it possible to obtain strong myoelectric signals, there was a problem that the waveforms were not smooth. From previous studies, we were able to resolve this problem to some extent by narrowing down the FIR filter.

In the future, the number of subjects, the direction of electrode attachment, and amplifier settings will be examined, and this is a guideline for detailed analysis of the seeded wave.

References

1. Kosuge, T., Itakura, N., Mito, K.: Conducting waves using multi-channel surface EMG. IEEJ Trans. **C134**(3), 390–397 (2014)
2. Okura, K., Itakura, N., Mizuno, T.: Analysis of propagating waves at electrodes in multiple directions using multichannel surface electromyography The University of Electro-Communications, Master's Research (2022)

Study on Different Methods for Recognition of Facial Expressions from the Data Generated by Modern HMDs

Agustín Alejandro Ortiz Díaz$^{(\boxtimes)}$ (ID), Delrick Nunes De Oliveira (ID), and Sergio Cleger Tamayo (ID)

Sidia Institute of Science and Technology. Av. Darcy Vargas, 654, 69055-035 Manaus, Brasil
{agustin.diaz,delrick.oliveira,sergio.tamayo}@sidia.com

Abstract. One of the non-verbal ways most used by human beings to communicate and convey emotions, often unconsciously, is facial expression. The recognition and tracking of facial expressions are among the main challenges of several companies that intend to enter virtual social environments. Virtual worlds are becoming viable due to the use of head-mounted displays (HMDs) that allow people to interact in these environments with a great deal of realism. However, recognizing and tracking facial expressions on HMDs has been challenging due to optical occlusions. The same device occludes the eyes, which are a fundamental part of facial expressions. In general, the first HMDs did not have cameras or sensors that captured what was happening behind the device. Because of this, previous research has often proposed to work by extracting partial facial features; for example, mouth, cheeks, chin, and so on). However, as of 2021, some of the latest HMDs manufactured have incorporated cameras and/or sensors for face and hand tracking. Among these modern devices, we can mention HTC-Vive-Focus-3 manufactured by HTC, HP-Reverb-G2-Omnicept-Edition manufactured by HP, Meta-Quest-Pro, manufactured by Meta, and Pico-4-Pro manufactured by Pico. This work aims to carry out a study of the main methods of recognition of facial expressions; whether they are traditional, based on deep learning, or hybrid; using as input the complete facial data provided by the new HMD devices that offer cameras and/or sensors for face tracking.

Keywords: Recognition Method · Facial Expressions

1 Introduction

Facial expressions are among the main non-verbal ways that human beings use to convey information, emotions, and feelings. This type of expression often happens even unconsciously. Currently, through facial capture technologies, it is possible to collect the different types of facial expressions that occur over time. These data can be used, for example, to replicate them within a specific virtual environment. Today, among the most widely used devices to capture these expressions are head-mounted displays (HMDs). However, until very recently, most HMDs had a lot of trouble extracting facial expressions in their entirety, due to the optical occlusions of the device itself. These occlusions occurred mainly in the eyes and eyebrows [1].

Because of this, previous research has often proposed to work by extracting partial facial features; for example, mouth, cheeks, chin, and so on). However, as of 2021, some of the latest HMDs manufactured have incorporated cameras and/or sensors for face and hand tracking. Among these modern devices, we can mention HTC-Vive-Focus-3 manufactured by HTC, HP-Reverb-G2-Omnicept-Edition manufactured by HP, Meta-Quest-Pro, manufactured by Meta, and Pico-4-Pro manufactured by Pico [2]. This work aims to carry out a study of the main methods developed for the process of recognition of facial expressions (FER). These methods can be traditional, based on deep learning, or hybrid. The complete facial data provided by the new HMD devices that offer cameras and/or sensors for facial tracking will be used as input.

For a better organization of the study, the FER process has been divided into three main scenarios: Detection and Location (Sect. 2), Extraction and Representation (Sect. 3), and Recognition and classification (Sect. 4). Then, Sect. 5 is included, where the main ideas that were extracted after analyzing each of the referenced articles are exposed. Finally, we present our general conclusions and references.

2   FER. Detection and Location

Within the FER process, the face detection stage is one of the most addressed problems in the field of computer vision. The general objective of this stage is to find human faces in digital images. Among the main challenges in solving this type of problem are occlusion, lighting, and complex backgrounds. In the scientific literature, there is a large set of methods aimed at detecting faces. Tables 1 and 2 present a summary of the relevant characteristics of the main methods of our interest. We draw directly on the work of Hasan, et al. [3], which we recommend for a detailed analysis of each method.

3   FER: Extraction and Representation

This second stage, within the FER process, is more significant for traditional proposals. In general, proposals based on deep learning merge the last two stages into one. The main objective is to find and represent features of interest within an image. In many cases, the support of human experts is required [20]. Table 3 presents a summary of the relevant characteristics of the main methods of our interest in this stage.

Table 1. Methods for detection of faces based on features. It describes the name of the method, representative reference, some strengths, and some weaknesses (*in italics*) [3].

Active shape model
Snakes [4]. It can work in real time and is easy to implement. It is little affected by noise. *It has limitations to determine contours and some convergence criteria are not the most appropriate.*
Deformable Template Matching [5]. It analyzes data in different formats, both local and global data. It can work in real-time. *It has results closely tied to the initialization point.*
Deformable Part Model [6] It is little affected by different points of view or lighting patterns. Works in real-time. *Sometimes it is sensitive to the appearance of bottlenecks.*
Point Distribution Model [7] Generate a compact structure of the face, to some extent it can treat the problem of occlusion of the face. *Control points are analyzed only linearly.*
Low-level analysis
Motion [8] It provides a robust and precise face-tracking algorithm. It can work in real-time. It is *sensitive to false positives due to facing occlusion problems.*
Color Information [9] It works very fast compared to other algorithms. *Highly affected by lighting changes, it can be inaccurate when working with side-viewed faces.*
Gray Information [10] It is computationally less complex. It is two-dimensional (2D) processing. *It can be highly affected by noise, so its efficiency is affected.*
Edge [1]. It optimizes the number of scanning. It is a robust and efficient algorithm. *It is affected by noisy images as it does not examine edges in all scales.*
Feature analysis
Feature Searching [12]. They have a high accuracy in terms of face detection. *Sensitive to lighting conditions and rotations.* A representative algorithm is ***Viola and Jones***. It is an algorithm with low computational complexity, which detects faces in real-time and with high precision, especially when working with frontal faces [3].
Constellation Analysis [13]. Handles rotation, scale, and translation problems of moderate magnitude. *Complex to implement.*

Table 2. Methods for detection of faces based on images. It describes the name of the method, representative reference, some strengths, and some weaknesses (*in italics*) [3].

Linear subspace
Eigenfaces [14]. Simple and efficient. It has a probabilistic version with excellent manipulated occlusion results. *It is affected by the variations of scales. Training the model takes a long time.*
Fisherfaces [15]. It is efficient on images with large variations in lighting and facial expression. Treat faces with glasses. *The model is greatly affected by the input data.*
Tensorfaces [16]. It deals with the influence of different factors such as lighting, and facial variation. *It has difficulty representing the nonlinearity of the subspace of the view.*
Statistical approaches
Discrete Cosine Transform (DCT) [17]. It is computationally inexpensive. It provides a simple way to deal with 3D facial distortions. *It requires quantization to ignore high-frequency components for decision-making. It is necessary to manually position the eyes in the image.*
Locality Preserving Projection (LPP) [18]. It is fast and pragmatic as it uses local pattern recognition. *It has generally low error rates. It is sensitive to noise and outliers.*
Independent Component Analysis (ICA) [19]. Its goal is to maximize the independence of the features. It is an iterative algorithm that produces an efficient probabilistic model. *It is sensitive when handling large amounts of data.*

Table 3. Methods for extraction and representation of features within the FER process. Names, some relevant characteristics, and some significant references are presented.

Active Appearance Model (AAM) is a powerful statistical model that models and records deformable objects.

[21] It evaluates various fitting methods of the AAM model. [22] It proposes the STAAM algorithm that calculates the 3D shape and rigid motion parameters using multiple calibrated perspective cameras.

Local Binary Pattern (LBP) works primarily for monochrome still images and analyses the texture of the images.

[23] It improves the traditional LBP method and proposes a surface defect detection method based on a gradient local binary pattern. [24] It uses a novel approach to extracting hybrid features from active facial patches. It also uses a variant of HOG.

Scale Invariant Feature Transform (SIFT) extracts representative and invariant features from images. Features are invariant to scaling, translation, and rotation. In addition, they are partially invariant to changes in lighting and 3D projection.

[25] The SIFT method is introduced and applied to the detection of objects. [26] The SAR-SIFT Algorithm is introduced (SAR: Synthetic Aperture Radar). It includes the detection of key points and the calculation of local descriptors.

Histograms of oriented gradients (HOG) extracts image descriptors. They are invariant to 2D rotation. Applied to problems such as facial recognition and pedestrian detection.

[27] Three main contributions: Work on the problem of facial occlusions; capture important structures for facial recognition; remove noise and treat overfitting. [28] Uses a novel framework that combines two methods; extracting inter vector angles (IVA), and HOG. It achieves promising recognition accuracy.

Gabor filter is a robust method against local distortions caused by varying lighting, expression, and pose. It has been successfully applied for facial recognition.

[29] It is applied to facial expression recognition. Combine two methods: Gabor filters and Local Gradient Code-Horizontal Diagonal. [30] Three schemes for feature extraction: Angular Radial Transform (ART), Discrete Cosine Transform (DCT), and Gabor Filter (GF). Applied to facial expression recognition.

Principal component analysis (PCA) is used for dimensionality reduction. Performs an orthogonal transformation to convert a set of values of N possibly correlated variables to a set of M uncorrelated variables. However, it is only based on linear assumptions and scale variants.

[31] It is applied to facial expression recognition. Principal Component Analysis (PCA) is used to extract the static features of facial expressions from images. [32] A hybrid PCA and local binary pattern (LBP) method is presented to resolve the environmental sensitivity of global grayscale features. It is applied to facial expression recognition.

Eigenfaces: Widely used for dimensionality reduction and recorded a great performance in facial expression recognition. The significant features are known as "eigenfaces" ("P principal components" of the set of faces).

[33] It features a functional near real-time face recognition system. This system learns to recognize new faces without supervision.

4 FER. Recognition and Classification

This last stage of the FER process aims to classify or recognize new facial expressions. The proposals based on machine learning use a traditional classifier that receives the representations of the images extracted in the previous stage as inputs. On the other hand, proposals based on deep learning merge these last two scenarios and directly extract the patterns for classification [20]. Tables 4 and 5 present a summary of the relevant characteristics of the main methods of our interest in this stage.

Table 4. Traditional Machine Learning Based Approach. Names, some relevant characteristics, and some significant references are presented.

Linear Discriminant Analysis (LDA) Its objective is to find the hyperplane of the projection that minimizes the interclass variance and maximizes the distance between the projected means of the classes.
[24] LDA is used to support the classification since the dimensionality of the extracted features is reduced. A support vector machine (SVM) is used for classification purposes.
Support vector machine (SVM) It is widely used for the classification of facial expressions. It is very effective with high-dimensional data. It minimizes the chances of overfitting. It is greatly affected by noisy image data sets. [24, 35,].
[34] Support Vector Machine (SVM) was used as a classifier. The PCA + SVM combination obtained promising results.
Random Forest (RF) is a combination of decision trees. Each tree depends on the values of an independently sampled random vector. All the trees have the same distribution.
[35] An RF algorithm is used to support the classification process. SVM is the main classifier.
Extreme Learning Machine (ELM) is a type of single hidden-layer feed-forward neural network.
[36] Three types of classifiers are evaluated: Extreme learning machine (ELM), support vector machine (SVM), and k-nearest neighbor (KNN).
Many other classification models have also been used at this stage of the FER process: **AdaBoost, Decision tree, and Naïve Bayes.**

5 Analysis and Discussion

We managed to extract the following general analyses and ideas once the investigations referenced in the previous sections were analyzed.

(1) The traditional approach usually works very well with relatively small data sets obtained under favorable conditions. In addition, they are usually quite easy-to-use proposals that train their models very quickly. They generate acceptable precisions and execution times. However, they need the "extraction and representation" stage where they usually need the support of human experts in the area.

(2) The approaches based on deep learning are better for working with data sets in real conditions. These models better cope with potential lighting and pose and resolve issues in the training data. In addition, these models can find and learn hidden facial features or patterns. However, convolutional networks consume a lot of time and memory when they have many parameters.

Table 5. Deep learning-based approach. Names, some relevant characteristics, and some significant references are presented.

Convolutional neural networks (CNN) combine functions of different levels (low/medium/high) with classifiers in an end-to-end multilayer fashion. They integrate three types of layers: convolutional layers, pooling layers, and fully connected layers [37].
[37] An architecture combining convolution layers followed by a recurrent neural network is proposed. The model extracts the relationships within the images and the temporal dependencies that exist are considered during the classification.
A deep belief network (DBN) is an evolution of the deep learning method for function learning and classification. It consists of several intermediate layers of the Restricted Boltzmann Machine and the last layer functions as a classifier. It has supervised and unsupervised learning modules.
[38] An unsupervised DBN is used for the extraction of depth-level features from fused observations of electrodermal activity sensor signals, and zygomatic electromyography.
Deep auto-encoder (DAE) is composed of two symmetrical DBNs, one for encoding and the other for decoding. Its goal is to find a reduced version of the input data without loss of information.
[39] The performance of deep auto-encoders for feature selection and dimension reduction in multi-level hidden layers is discussed. This technique achieves high performance compared to other state-of-the-art techniques.
Ensemble methods are models that combine different classifiers. They combine and group the classifiers with different techniques, such as bagging and boosting. Base classifiers can be homogeneous or heterogeneous. An efficient method must be found to combine their predictions.
[40] An ensemble face detection model that combines three state-of-the-art detectors is proposed, followed by a classification module with an ensemble of multiple deep convolutional neural networks. To combine the partial predictions, two schemes are used to learn the weights of the network: minimizing log-likelihood loss and minimizing hinge loss.
Methods that divide the human face into independent parts simplify and make the problem of facial expression detection more efficient. Each of these parts is processed independently.
[41] Divide the human face into smaller and more specific blocks based on the natural division of the muscles and organs of the face. It is proposed to divide the face in front, eyebrows, eyes, nose, mouth, and chin. Each of these parts is modeled and processed independently.

(3) Some proposals combine the two approaches. They integrate heterogeneous functions of both approaches. The goal is to take advantage of the positive features of both approaches. However, the combination of approaches could lead to the development of more complex and difficult-to-use models.

(4) Ensembles are models that combine different classifiers. Since each model works differently, their errors tend to compensate. This results in a better generalization error. However, these models tend to consume a lot of time and memory, and it is not a trivial problem to find an efficient way to combine the individual solutions of each model.

(5) Some proposal proponents divide the human face into independent parts (eyes, nose, mouth, etc.). The images or representations of each part of the face are analyzed by independent models. For our work, this idea is interesting, since our images come from a device mounted on the head. The cameras could be set to take pictures directly of a specific part of the face. However, there is the problem of unifying the solutions.

6 Conclusion

The objective of this work was to carry out a study of the main facial expression recognition methods. For a better organization, we have divided the facial expression recognition process into three main scenarios: (1) detection and location, (2) extraction and representation, and (3) recognition and classification. Furthermore, two different approaches were analyzed separately: traditional proposals based on machine learning and proposals based on deep learning.

For our project, since the data is taken from a head-mounted device, stage (1) could be simpler. We use images of human faces in stable initial conditions. A method with the characteristics of the Viola and Jones algorithm should suffice. The cameras could even be configured to divide the face into its fundamental parts (eyes, nose, mouth, etc.). Given these initial conditions, traditional models are promising if we use a suitable representation. However, due to its high accuracy values, we also decided to test deep learning models. A CNN will also be a promising model since we can increase computational resources, for example, by using many CPU and/or GPU cores.

Acknowledgment. This paper was presented as part of the results of the Project "SIDIA-M_AR_Internet_For_Bondi", carried out by the Institute of Science and Technology - SIDIA, in partnership with Samsung Eletrônica da Amazônia LTDA, in accordance with the Information Technology Law n.8387/ 91 and article at the. 39 of Decree 10,521/2020.

References

1. Suzuki, K., et al.: Recognition and mapping of facial expressions to avatar by embedded photo reflective sensors in head mounted display. In: 2017 IEEE Virtual Reality (VR), Los Angeles, CA, USA, pp. 177–185 (2017). https://doi.org/10.1109/VR.2017.7892245
2. Rory, B.: VRcompare- Largest VR & AR Headset Database (2020). https://vr-compare.com
3. Hasan, M., et al.: Human face detection techniques: a comprehensive review and future research directions. Electronics **10**, 2354 (2021). https://doi.org/10.3390/electronics10192354
4. Kass, M., Witkin, A., Terzopoulos, D.: Snakes: active contour models. Int. J. Comput. Vision **1**(4), 321–331 (1988). https://doi.org/10.1007/BF00133570
5. Yuille, A., Hallinan, P., Cohen, D.: Feature extraction from faces using deformable templates. Int. J. Comput. Vision **8**, 99–111 (1992)
6. Fischler, M., et al.: The representation and matching of pictorial structures. IEEE Trans. Comput. **C–22**(1), 67–92 (1973). https://doi.org/10.1109/T-C.1973.223602
7. Cootes, T., and Taylor, C. "Active shape models Smart snakes." In BMVC92; Springer: London, UK, 1992
8. Van Beek, P., et al.: Semantic segmentation of videophone image sequences. In: Proceedings of the Visual Communications and Image Processing'92, International Society for Optics and Photonics, Boston, MA, USA, 1992, vol. 1818, pp. 1182–1193 (1992)
9. Kovac, J., Peer, P., Solina: Human skin color clustering for face detection. In: The IEEE Region 8 EUROCON 2003, Computer as a Tool, Ljubljana, Slovenia, vol. 2, pp. 144–148 (2003)
10. Graf, H., et al.: Multi-modal system for locating heads and faces. In: The Second International Conference on Automatic Face and Gesture Recognition, Killington, USA., pp. 88–93 (1993)

11. Sakai, T.: Computer analysis and classification of photographs of human faces. In: Proceedings of the First USA—Japan Computer Conference, Tokyo, Japan, pp. 55–62 (1972)
12. De Silva, L., et al.: Detection and tracking of facial features by using edge pixel counting and deformable circular template matching. In: IEICE Transactions on Information and System, pp. 1195–1207 (1995)
13. Huang, W., Mariani, R.: Face detection and precise eyes location. In: Proceedings 15th International Conference on Pattern Recognition. ICPR-2000, Barcelona, Spain, vol.4, pp. 722–727 (2000). https://doi.org/10.1109/ICPR.2000.903019
14. Kshirsagar, V., Baviskar, M., Gaikwad, M.: Face recognition using Eigenfaces. In: 2011 3rd International Conference on Computer Research and Development, Shanghai, China, pp. 302–306 (2011). https://doi.org/10.1109/ICCRD.2011.5764137
15. Anggo, M., Arapu, L.: Face recognition using fisherface method. J. Phys. Conf. Ser. **1028**, 012119 (2018). https://doi.org/10.1088/1742-6596/1028/1/012119
16. Tian, C., Fan, G., Gao, X., Tian, Q.: Multiview face recognition: from tensorFace to V-TensorFace and K-TensorFace. IEEE Trans. Syst. Man Cybern. Part B (Cybern.) **42**(2), 320–333 (2012). https://doi.org/10.1109/TSMCB.2011.2169452
17. Chadha, A., Vaidya, P., Roja, M.: Face recognition using discrete cosine transform for global and local features. In: 2011 International Conference on Recent Advancements in Electrical, Electronics and Control Engineering, Sivakasi, India, pp. 502–505 (2011)
18. Dornaika, F., Assoum, A.: Enhanced and parameterless locality preserving projections for face recognition. Neurocomputing **99**, 448–457 (2013). https://doi.org/10.1016/j.neucom.2012.07.016
19. Lihong, Z., et al.: Face recognition based on independent component analysis. In: 2011 Chinese Control and Decision Conference (CCDC), Mianyang, China, pp. 426–429 (2011).https://doi.org/10.1109/CCDC.2011.5968217
20. Dang, V., et al.: Facial expression recognition: a survey and its applications. In: 2021 23rd International Conference on Advanced Communication Technology (ICACT), Korea (South), pp. 359–367(2021).https://doi.org/10.23919/ICACT51234.2021.9370369
21. Asthana, A., et al.: Evaluating AAM fitting methods for facial expression recognition. In: 3rd International Conference on Affective Computing and Intelligent Interaction and Workshops, Amsterdam, Netherlands, pp. 1–8, 2009, doi:https://doi.org/10.1109/ACII.2009.5349489
22. Sung, J., Kim, D.: Real-time facial expression recognition using STAAM and layered GDA classifiers. Image Vision Comput. **27**, 1313–1325 (2009)
23. Liu, X., Xue, F., Teng, L.: Surface defect detection based on gradient LBP. In: Proceedings of the 2018 IEEE 3rd International Conference on Image, Vision, and Computing (ICIVC), Chongqing, China, 27–29 June 2018; pp. 133–137 2018)
24. Happy, S., et al.: Robust facial expression classification using shape and appearance features. In: Proceedings of 8th International Conference of Advances in Pattern Recognition (2015)
25. Lowe, D.: Distinctive image features from scale-invariant keypoints. Int. J. Comput. Vis. **60**(2), 91–110 (2004)
26. Dellinger, F., et al.: SAR-SIFT: a SIFT-like algorithm for SAR images. IEEE Trans. Geosci. Remote Sens. **53**(1), 453–466 (2015)
27. Déniz, O., Bueno, G., Salido, J., De la Torre, F.: Face recognition using histograms of oriented gradients. Pattern Recogn. Lett. **32**(12), 1598–1603 (2011). https://doi.org/10.1016/j.patrec.2011.01.004
28. Islam, R., et al.: SenTion: A framework for Sensing Facial Expressions. arXiv preprint arXiv: 1608.04489 (2016)
29. Al-Sumaidaee, S., et al.: Facial expression recognition using local Gabor. Gradient code-horizontal diagonal descriptor. In: 2nd IET International Conference on Intelligent Signal Processing 2015 (ISP), London, UK (2015). https://doi.org/10.1049/cp.2015.1766

30. Tsai, H.-H., Chang, Y.-C.: Facial expression recognition using a combination of multiple facial features and support vector machine. Soft. Comput. **22**(13), 4389–4405 (2017). https://doi.org/10.1007/s00500-017-2634-3

31. Wang, X.-H., Liu, A., Zhang, S.-Q.: New facial expression recognition based on FSVM and KNN. Optik **126**(21), 3132–3134 (2015). https://doi.org/10.1016/j.ijleo.2015.07.073

32. Luo, Y., Wu, C., Zhang, Y.: Facial expression recognition based on fusion feature of PCA and LBP with SVM. Optik – Int. J. Light Elect. Opt. **124**(17), 2767–2770 (2013). https://doi.org/10.1016/j.ijleo.2012.08.040

33. Turk, M., Pentland, A.: Eigenfaces for recognition. J. Cogn. Neurosci. **3**(1), 71–86 (1991)

34. Abdulrahman, M., Eleyan, A.: Facial expression recognition using Support Vector Machines," 2015 23rd Signal Processing and Communications Applications Conference (SIU), Malatya, Turkey, 2015, pp. 276-279https://doi.org/10.1109/SIU.2015.7129813

35. Benini, S., Khan, K., Leonardi, R., Mauro, M., Migliorati, P.: Face analysis through semantic face segmentation. Signal Process. Image Commun. **74**, 21–31 (2019). https://doi.org/10.1016/j.image.2019.01.005

36. Shafira, S., et al.: Facial expression recognition using extreme learning machine. In: 3rd International Conference on Informatics and Computational Sciences (ICICoS), Semarang, Indonesia, pp. 1- 6 (2019). https://doi.org/10.1109/ICICoS48119.2019.8982443

37. Jain, N., et al.: Hybrid deep neural networks for face emotion recognition. Pattern Recogn. Lett. **115**, 101–106 (2018). https://doi.org/10.1016/j.patrec.2018.04.010

38. Mehedi, M., et al.: Human emotion recognition using deep belief network architecture. Inf. Fusion **51**, 10–18 (2019). https://doi.org/10.1016/j.inffus.2018.10.009

39. Usman, M., Latif S., Qadir, J.: Using deep autoencoders for facial expression recognition. In: 13th International Conference on Emerging Technologies (ICET), Islamabad, Pakistan, pp. 1–6 (2017).https://doi.org/10.1109/ICET.2017.8281753

40. Yu, Z., Zhang, C.: Image based static facial expression recognition with multiple deep network learning. In: ACM on International Conference on Multimodal Interaction (ICMI 2015) USA, pp. 435–442 (2015). https://doi.org/10.1145/2818346.2830595

41. Zhang, L.: Animation expression control based on facial region division. Sci. Program. **2022**, 1–13 (2022). https://doi.org/10.1155/2022/5800099

A Study on Eye-Region Expression as Naturally Expressed in a Situation of Spontaneously Evoked Emotions

Hayate Yamada[1]([✉]), Fumiya Kobayashi[1], Saizo Aoyagi[2], and Michiya Yamamoto[1]

[1] Kwansei Gakuin University, Uegahara 1, Gakuen, Sanda 669-1337, Hyogo, Japan
its51903@kwansei.ac.jp
[2] Komazawa University, Komawaza 1-23-1, Setagaya, Tokyo 154-8525, Japan

Abstract. For many years, Ekman's work on facial expressions has been the basis for research on facial expression recognition and estimation. However, there are still many unanswered questions regarding the relationship between emotions and facial expressions, such as the recent report that Japanese people do not follow Ekman's theory. In this study, we focused on the eye area, which expresses natural emotions, and analyzed the characteristics of facial feature values that are expressed in situations of internal emotional arousal. We found that the distance between the eyebrows, eye size, mouth size, mouth angle elevation, and pupil diameter were significant indicators of emotional arousal. We also found that pupil diameter is effective in estimating arousal axis by machine learning, as previous studies have shown.

Keywords: Emotion estimation · Eye features · video-watching

1 Introduction

Facial expression research has long been based on Ekman's facial expressions concerning the six basic emotions [1], but that theory does not include naturally evoked emotions. Recently, Sato et al. published a study showing that the Japanese do not follow Ekman's theory. We designed a field in which natural emotions were evoked and performed emotion estimation. We analyzed feature values using body movements, by which it is difficult to express emotions intentionally. However, we did not consider the acquisition of facial expressions in the study. In addition, the questionnaire to measure the evoked emotions in the study was insufficient as a data set for emotion estimation by machine learning. In this study, we focused on the fact that the eye region contains a great deal of information; as the saying goes, "The eye is the window of the mind." For this purpose, by focusing on the two axes of valence and arousal in Russell's core affect model, we measured and analyzed how each feature value affected the estimation by comparing it with feature values of the mouth region, which is often used in facial expression research.

C. Stephanidis et al. (Eds.): HCII 2023, CCIS 1832, pp. 303–309, 2023.
https://doi.org/10.1007/978-3-031-35989-7_39

2 Measurement Experiment

2.1 Videos for Measurement

First, we performed an experiment to select five suitable videos of about four minutes each to evoke the intended emotions (the four emotions in Russell's core affect model). The participants were 25 undergraduate and graduate students at Kwansei Gakuin University (14 males, 11 females, mean age 21.3 years, SD = 1.38). After watching five videos, the participants rated the degree of emotion the videos evoked using 7-point Likert scales. We selected the top three videos with the highest evaluation values among the five videos (Fig. 1). Figure 2 shows the set of videos used in our study [2]. Rhythm comedy, improv comedy, and Manzai (according to Wikipedia, a traditional style of comedy in Japanese culture comparable to double act comedy or stand-up comedy) were selected for fun; shark, high place, and horror were selected for fear; waiting at traffic lights, station platform, and message video were selected for bored; and hot springs, babies, and animals were selected for relaxed. None of these videos involved the performers being injured or performing life-threatening actions, and there were no ethical problems involved with the participants watching the videos.

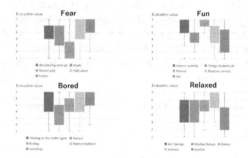

Fig. 1. The results of a questionnaire from 25 participants.

2.2 Experimental Setup

Next, we conducted video-watching experiments in which we measured facial images and eye gaze (Fig. 3 left and center) using the selected videos [3]. We placed a web camera at the top of the eye-tracking device to capture the participants' facial expressions. We placed an LED light at the bottom of the eye-tracking device to provide approximately 300 lx of illumination to the participants' faces while they watched the videos. We displayed videos on the screen of the eye-tracking device and acquired gaze and pupil diameters. We also interviewed participant about their emotions based on the eight emotions in Russell's core affect model (Fig. 3 right). The participants answered nine items: seven emotions (fun, enthusiastic, relaxed, sleepy, bored, displeased, and fear), neutral (no emotion evoked), and a free response when other emotions were evoked. We asked participants to respond to 20 scenes for each of the videos, set to coincide with the turn of the video content. The participants were 36 undergraduate and graduate students at Kwansei Gakuin University (18 males, 18 females, mean age 21.9 years, SD = 1.96).

Fig. 2. Videos for measurement experiment.

Fig. 3. The video-watching experiment (left, center) and Russell's core affect model (right).

2.3 Results

We used the data from 34 of the 36 participants in the following analyses, excluding two participants with significant missing data due to pupil measurement errors. We created a data set of 3400 s from those data. The results of the emotion arousal are shown in Table 1. The success rate is defined as the percentage of the time the intended emotion was evoked, and the expression rate is defined as the percentage of non-neutral emotions evoked. The result of emotion expression in the video-watching task showed that the highest success rate was reached with the enjoyable emotion, 86.8 percent (SD = 0.16), and the lowest was boredom, 57.1 percent (SD = 0.22). Though the participants watched the same numbers of videos, 27.5% of all the emotions evoked were fun, 16.1% were fear, 19.8% were bored, and 15.8% were relaxed, resulting in 79.3% of the four intended emotions being evoked.

Table 1. Results of the video-watching experiment.

Stimulus	Success rate [%]	Expression rate[%]
Fun	86.8	96.8
Fear	63.8	89.9
Bored	57.1	85.3
Relaxed	61.3	92.2

*Average

3   Definition of Eye and Mouth Feature Values

Next, we calculated mouth feature values as a control for the eye feature values, referring to the study by Sakagami et al. [4] (Fig. 4).

We calculated the mean in one second from facial feature points obtained by Open-Face [5]. We calculated 11 feature values for the eye region (distance between the eyes and eyebrows, eyebrow tilt, etc.), four for the mouth region (mouth size, angle of mouth corners, etc.) and eye feature value (pupil diameter).

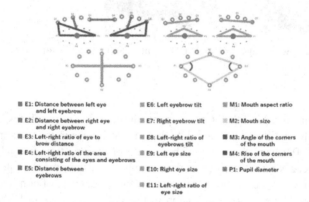

■ E1: Distance between left eye and left eyebrow

■ E2: Distance between right eye and right eyebrow

■ E3: Left-right ratio of eye to brow distance

■ E4: Left-right ratio of the area consisting of the eyes and eyebrows

■ E5: Distance between eyebrows

■ E6: Left eyebrow tilt

■ E7: Right eyebrow tilt

■ E8: Left-right ratio of eyebrows tilt

■ E9: Left eye size

■ E10: Right eye size

■ E11: Left-right ratio of eye size

■ M1: Mouth aspect ratio

■ M2: Mouth size

■ M3: Angle of the corners of the mouth

■ M4: Rise of the corners of the mouth

■ P1: Pupil diameter

Fig. 4. The feature values calculated from the feature points.

4   Expressed Feature Values

Using the data set in Sect. 3, we compared the feature values for each emotion. We normalized the feature values for each participant and calculated the mean in the evoked four emotions (fun, fear, bored, and relaxed). Via Friedman's test, we found significant differences in the distance between the eyebrows, eye size, mouth, and pupils (Fig. 5).

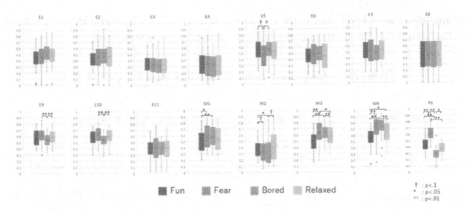

Fig. 5. Feature values averaged for each of the four emotions after normalization.

5 Analysis by Emotion Estimation Using Machine Learning

5.1 Learning Method

We used these feature values to estimate emotions with support vector machine (SVM) and decision trees. We used the hold-out method for validation. SVM was evaluated by ten-fold cross-validation using MathWorks' MATLAB numerical analysis software, and decision trees were evaluated by five-fold cross-validation using the Python package scikit-learn. The RBF kernel was used as the SVM kernel function, and for the decision tree, the best parameters were selected from max depth (one to three), the min samples leaf (six to nine), and min samples split (four or five) by a grid search. The explanatory variables were combinations of five patterns of eye-, mouth-, and pupil-feature values. The objective variables were the eight classes of emotions (seven emotions + neutral) obtained in the video-watching task, three levels of valence, and three levels of arousal. We classified the eight emotions of Russell's core affect model into three levels: pleasant (fun, enthusiastic, relaxed), neutral (sleepy, neutral), and unpleasant (bored, displeased, fear). Similarly, we classified arousal into three levels: arousing (fun, enthusiastic, fear), neutral (neutral, displeased), and sedentary (relaxed, sleepy, bored). We defined the data range used for learning as up to 5 s after the timing of the participant's emotional evocation.

5.2 Results

Next, we compared and analyzed the estimation rates. In the SVM estimation, accuracy levels for the combinations of the feature values were as follows: eye region alone (77.4%), mouth region (81.1%), and facial expressions (83.0%) (Table 2). The eye region alone was as high as other two. With decision trees, we estimated emotions using all feature values and calculated feature importance, representing the degree to which each feature values contributed to learning in the decision tree. As a result, we found that the distance between the eyebrows, eye size, mouth size, mouth angle elevation, and pupil diameter were significant (Fig. 6). The importance of the pupil was higher when estimating arousal level than when estimating valence. This result confirms the strong relationship between pupils and arousal level in the previous study [6].

Table 2. The estimation results for each individual using SVM.

Pattern	Emotion		Valence		Arousal	
	Accuracy	F value	Accuracy	F value	Accuracy	F value
Eye region feature values	77.4(8.2)	68.9(11.2)	83.3(6.1)	75.8(8.8)	83.1(7.2)	72.8(12.3)
Mouth region feature values	81.1(8.2)	73.3(11.2)	85.6(7.0)	79.0(11.2)	85.7(7.1)	77.6(13.2)
Eye region feature values · Mouth region feature values	83.0(7.0)	74.5(9.1)	87.4(5.2)	81.3(7.1)	88.1(6.1)	81.0(10.2)
Eye region feature values · Pupil feature values	80.6(7.3)	73.5(9.6)	85.6(6.9)	78.5(11.2)	85.8(6.8)	76.2(13.0)
Eye region feature values · Mouth region feature values · Pupil feature values	85.0(5.9)	77.5(8.7)	89.0(5.6)	83.9(7.1)	89.3(6.0)	82.3(10.0)

*Average(SD)

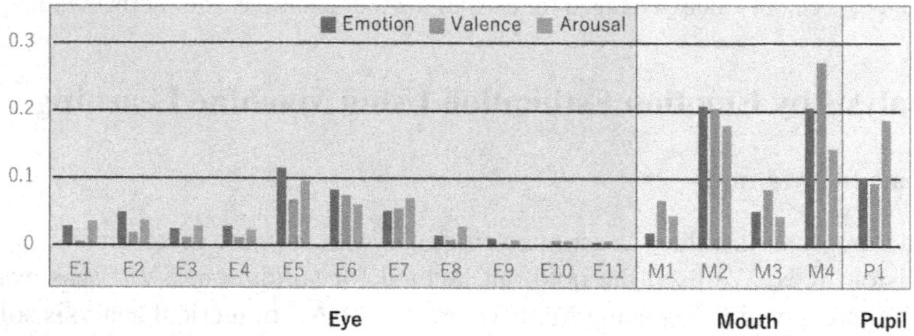

Fig. 6. The feature importance of the eye, mouth, and pupil feature values in the emotion estimation by decision tree.

6 Conclusion

In this study, we defined and analyzed eye feature values from measurement experiments in a video-watching task, and then evaluated them using machine learning. The results showed that the use of eye feature values in emotion estimation by SVM resulted in an average accuracy of 77.4% for each individual, indicating that eye feature values are useful for emotion estimation. The estimation rate was not so high and limited to each individual, but these could be higher using state of the art learning method [8]. Therefore, it is necessary to develop a method for classifying eye-expression types to perform emotion estimation using data from multiple people in the future. Expressions should be clarified during conversations, as well, because the mouth is naturally transformed while speaking. By clarifying the relationships between facial expressions and body movements, it would be possible to analyze and estimate naturally evoked emotions in various scenes.

References

1. Boucher, J.D., Ekman, P.: Facial areas and emotional information. J. Commun. **25**(2), 21–29 (1975). https://doi.org/10.1111/j.1460-2466.1975.tb00577.x

2. Kobayashi, F., Ogi, K., Aoyagi, S., Yamamoto, M.: Construction of the eye-emotion dataset and its evaluation by machine learning focusing on individual differences in emotional arousal. Corr. Human Interface **24**(3), 289–296 (2022). (in Japanese)
3. Yamada, H., Kobayashi, F., Fujiwara, S., Aoyagi, S., Yamamoto, M.: Analysis of relation-ships among body movement, eye Information, and physiological indices in emotion ex-pressions during video watching. IEICE Techn. Rep. **122**(166), 3–8 (2022). (In Japanese)
4. Sakagami, S., Nomiya, H., Hochin, T.: Estimation of facial expression intensity by using facial features based on the positions of facial feature points. In: 2016 Nendo Jouhou Shori Gakkai Kansai Shibu Shibu Taikai Kouen Rombunshuu (2016). (in Japanese)
5. Baltrusaitis, T., Zadch, A., Lim, Y.C., Morency, L.P.: OpenFace 2.0: facial behavior analysis toolkit. In 2018 13th IEEE International Conference on Automatic Face & Gesture Recognition, pp. 59–66 (2018)
6. Wang, C.-A., et al.: Arousal effects on pupil size, heart rate, and skin conductance in an emotional face task. Front. Neurol. **9**, 1029 (2018). https://doi.org/10.3389/fneur.2018.01029
7. Barros, P., Sciutti, A.: I only have eyes for you: the impact of masks on convolutional-based facial expression recognition. In: Proceedings of the IEEE/CVF Conference on Computer Vision and Pattern Recognition (CVPR) Workshops, pp. 1226–1231 (2021). https://doi.org/10.48550/arXiv.2104.08353

Perception and Cognition in Interaction

Soundscape Immersion in Virtual Reality and Living Lab: Comparison of Neuronal Activity Under Exposure to Noise and Task-Induced Mental Workload (Work in Progress)

Jan Grenzebach[✉] and Thea Radüntz

Federal Institute for Occupational Safety and Health (BAuA), Berlin, Germany
grenzebach.jan@baua.bund.de

Abstract. In occupational safety and health (OSH) research, the study of physical agents, like noise, depends on the realistic representation of workplace conditions. Both, the investigation of soundscapes in the real world and the laboratory, have each specific advantages and disadvantages. Virtual reality (VR) simulations of workplaces, including realistic soundscapes, might offer the required flexibility to probe stress-related issues imposed by noise in a rapidly changing work environment (e.g., home-based or mobile work). Like observations at the workplace, VR allows the study of a spectrum of occupational settings but under controlled conditions. In our study, we aim to measure the mental workload arising from work-related soundscapes during cognitive tasks. Eventually, we will compare neuronal activity in the real-world (i.e., living lab representation) and a VR setting.

Here, we present the planned experimental setting, the physical design of the living lab, and the implemented properties of its digital twin in VR. We introduce the electroencephalogram (EEG) as a neuro-physiological measurement for assessing the mental state, performance measurements from the cognitive tasks, and the subjective questionnaires used.

An open research question is how the specific neuronal signatures signaling mental workload in the EEG differ between living lab and VR settings. Thus, we primarily address the issue of whether the brain state differs fundamentally between the living lab and VR when observing the mental workload of a cognitive task under noise. As a second research question, we study how irrelevant sound sources increase or decrease the mental workload and identify suitable EEG markers from the time and frequency domain. The main implication of our work is to demonstrate the potential of VR for OSH research using digital twins of real-world occupational settings when considering the acoustic environment.

Keywords: soundscape · VR · EEG · living lab · occupational health · mental workload

C. Stephanidis et al. (Eds.): HCII 2023, CCIS 1832, pp. 313–320, 2023.
https://doi.org/10.1007/978-3-031-35989-7_40

1 Introduction

During the corona pandemic, many organizations decided to send their staff to their homes to fulfill work tasks remotely [1]. Especially cognitive tasks (e.g., communication, text composition, mathematical analysis, programming) that could be handled with the assistance of largely digitalized workflows and computers connected to the internet were quickly transferred to the home office [2]. Simultaneously, some employees were now able to redesign their workplace (i.e., desk layout, lighting, sound sources) while others had less freedom and had to cope with challenging domestic circumstances (i.e., using the kitchen table as a working desk). In our research, we want to focus on the sound-scapes associated with this transition. More particularly, new irrelevant sound sources emerged during that process that is specific to the home-office environment. This change in the ergonomic workplace design requires additional research for understanding and setting up a healthy and safe workplace for employees working remotely. The transition had two major implications, physical and psychological. The physical changes comprise the physical factors that changed from an occupational to a domestic environment. Since the purposes of those places are different, the physical factors alter. The psychological changes comprise, among others, the increased (perceived) controllability of some aspects of the workplace at home.

Soundscape controllability is a significant factor for well-being at work [3]. Perceived control over the distractibility evoked by specific sound sources during work is an important aspect of the ergonomics of the workplace. In better-designed work environments, the employee has control over the auditory signals that they are exposed to. Often the mere absence of predictability of certain sounds in the soundscape is identified as a leading factor for the general annoyance of sounds [4]. For that purpose, it is necessary to understand how the annoyance and subsequent effects on the mental load interact in self-controlled environments, as found in the home office workplace.

The quick transition from office workspace to home desk came abruptly and required the short-termed willingness of the employee to adopt [5]. Soundscapes during working changed drastically but it is not clear yet if the controllability of sounds at home improved (e.g., colleagues accepting long phone calls) or got worse (e.g., neighbor playing musical instruments). In the long run, this transition might influence the mental health of employees. Many employees realized the lack of dedicated extra rooms in their private homes for work-related purposes. The limited room would make it necessary to merge leisure and work duties in the private space. The dual use of the space that was originally designed to comfort recreation, eating, and entertainment (e.g., the kitchen table or the living room) could only partially be transformed into the production-centered environment required by the job.

Although the changes in the soundscape properties interact with other physical factors at the home office (e.g., lighting), in our present work, we focus only on the sound-scape and its effect on occupational health. The latter comprises the well-being, the mental workload, and the resilience of the employee [6]. To study the effects of different workspaces, occupational-health specialists were limited by recreating the observed and described properties of the field in a laboratory setting sufficiently. Thereby, they were often restricted to certain modalities (e.g., headphones). Instead of this classical approach of mimicking the workspace, a new tool is established that allows more comprehensive investigations of various types of workspaces: virtual reality (VR).

For understanding the effect of modern workplace environments on human information processing and mental workload, registration of brain activity employing the electroencephalogram (EEG) is mandatory [7]. In our study, cognitive processes can be task- or noise-related. Noise filtering asks for a secondary cognitive process that actively suppresses the irrelevant auditory information for maintaining concentration and bundles the available cognitive resources into the primary task-related process. Studying the differences between different kinds of workspaces also indicates the necessity to understand the neuronal activity that goes along with different degrees of immersion that can be induced by VR. Only then, it might be possible to identify certain markers in the neuronal response that relate to those proportions of mental workload that can be attributed to certain cognitive processes arising from the work environment itself. On this trajectory, we propose a study design for further investigation of the interrelations between EEG and VR synergy in occupational health [8, 9]. We aim to investigate if there exist relevant differences between the EEG captured in a complex VR setting and the complex naturalistic environment the VR representation stems from. In the workplace scenarios studied we focus on the transition of realistic soundscapes.

2 Methodological Approach

To be able to study in a fast and reliable manner workspaces under controlled conditions, the Federal Institute for Occupational Safety and Health creates currently a living lab to investigate certain work settings in a safe and controlled manner. We will use this platform to take a step ahead and generate a digital twin of the living lab in VR by Lidar technology. The main aim of our study is to compare the neuronal activity measured by the EEG that is going along the contrast of a living lab and the VR digital twin as its representation. This virtual representation will include visual and auditory information comparable to the real-world environment. Based on this, we can investigate the immersion level that applied soundscapes represented in VR evoke and their respective influence on the neuronal response in EEG [10].

2.1 Living Lab

The living lab is at this moment under preparation and will offer numerous opportunities to study occupational research questions in the future. The room has dimensions of ca. 7 m in length, ca. 8.5 m in width, and ca. 3.2 m in height. The room can be entered over four doors. A window can be blinded completely. The suspended ceilings will carry a minimum of 16 simple ceiling lights (fluorescent tube lamps). The floor is gray-patterned linoleum. The walls and ceiling are white and gray. The living lab offers the opportunity to control soundscapes, as they are found in regular office spaces. For example, we will place noise-emitting objects, like a printer, a telephone, and a speaker in the room. In this way, we can control the distance and the visual appearance of the environment. The sounds will be synthetically produced, presented over speakers (living lab), and presented in the VR condition over a headset speaker (digital twin).

2.2 Digital Twin of the Living Lab

We digitalized the above-described living lab with the Apple ios application "polycam" by the manufacturer Poly Inc. That automatically combines Lidar (light detection and ranging) information with photo-taking for the textures of the resulting 3-D model. We will successively increase the quality of our digital model depending on the stage of construction of the living lab. For that purpose, we will improve the quality of the used 3-D laser scanning hardware and software. A provisional 3-D model was already created and can be viewed in Fig. 2. The eye-ball validity of the resulting 3-D experience in VR was confirmed by several independent expert users.

The 3-D model has already a sufficient quality for several research questions and will improve with scanning time and the proposed improvements of the hardware and software. The noise-emitting objects in the living lab (e.g., printer, a telephone, and a speaker) will appear, as the whole environment in the digital twin. VR presentation systems (e.g., glasses and headphones) are improving in quality and affordability in recent years [11]. At this stage of development, the technology can be scientifically used for purposes desired by occupational health researchers. We have tested and selected the products "vive pro 2" and "vive pro eye" of the manufacturer HTC [10] to enable our study. The decision to choose the "vive pro 2" was mainly driven by the synchronization capabilities of the system. We want to combine the multimodal presentation of workplaces (visual) with immersive soundscapes (audio) and online registration of EEG measurements. The EEG analysis requires event triggers for the identification of relevant segments in the signal. The possibility of sending triggers of timestamps for the events presented in VR (within milliseconds) made our decision [12].

2.3 Study Design

In our research, we will then study the immersion level that the digital twin in VR can evoke compared to the living lab. For this purpose, we will expose the subject to auditory distractors in the conditions "digital twin" (VR) and "living lab" (real world). Our soundscapes will be representative of an ordinary office environment, the home office, and mobile work environments (e.g., the train, café, and co-working space). These soundscapes originate from common environments in which work-related tasks must be fulfilled.

Subjects will execute N-back and Stroop tasks that are well-established psychological tests and have been found fundamental for a myriad of occupational tasks (e.g., inhibition, updating, etc.) [10]. The mental workload and information processing during the cognitive tasks will be contrasted in the two conditions as shown in Table 1. As dependent variables, as shown in Table 2, we will register behavioral parameters (i.e., task performance), the mental workload registered by the EEG, and neuronal information processing as well as the subjectively perceived workload [13]. Furthermore, we will register the (individual) noise sensitivity [14] and the (situational) noise annoyance [15].

The physical combination of the VR headset (glasses and headphones) with the EEG cap is coming with certain challenges. The relatively heavy VR headset needs to be fixed at the head to be operated correctly. The headband of VR glasses runs from the temples,

Table 1. Cognitive tasks and the combination with the experimental setting and auditory stimulation.

		auditory stimulation			
		Silence	Noise	Noise	Silence
experimental setting	Digital twin (VR)	N-back, Stroop	no task	N-back, Stroop	no task
	Living lab (real-world)	N-back, Stroop	no task	N-back, Stroop	no task

Table 2. Recorded data during the experiment.

Type	Category	Name
Objective	Task performance	0-Back, 2-Back
Objective	Task performance	Stroop-Task
Objective	Neuronal information processing and mental workload	EEG (time/frequency)
Subjective	Self-report: Perceived mental workload	NASA task load index (TLX) [13]
Subjective	Self-report: Noise sensitivity (personal)	Weinstein's noise sensitivity scale [14]
Subjective	Self-report: Noise annoyance (situation)	Kjellberg's noise annoyance scale [15]

where it is fixated on the VR display, to the back of the head. Especially here, at the back of the head, the headband that is necessary to hold the VR glasses is touching and eventually moving the occipital electrodes of the EEG. For that purpose, a 3-D printed adapter is designed that stabilizes the support points around these electrodes (see Fig. 1). Thus, we will investigate potential differences in signal-to-noise ratio between the conditions concerning the combined use of EEG and VR [16]. Furthermore, we want to investigate the neuronal signal registered during free-movement VR experiments [11]. The advancements that have been made in measuring the mental workload using the EEG will be validated in this setting [10, 17].

Ethical research aspects of our study will be reviewed by the ethics committee of the Federal Institute of Occupational Health and Safety. All procedures will be carried out with the adequate understanding and written consent of the subjects.

Fig. 1. Combined use of mobile EEG (Brain Products) and VR headset (HTC vive pro 2) from two different angles (left / right).

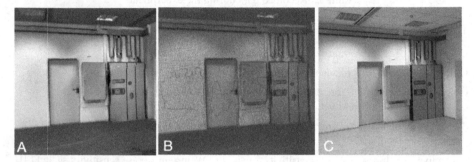

Fig. 2. The living lab: a digital twin in 3-D (A), including polygons (B), and a photo (C).

3 Expected Results

To contrast the mental workload differences between the digital twin and the living lab, we will use the well-established method of dual frequency head maps from the EEG [10, 17]. Furthermore, we will explore potential differences in the registration of the EEG regarding artifacts that might interfere with neuronal activity. Thus, our study aims in taking a first step toward the practicability of occupational-health investigations in VR.

The synthetic production of sounds and soundscapes allows for modulating psychoacoustic parameters that have been found to be annoying. Experts from within the Institute will be involved to control the physical parameters and recommend the appropriate reference values. In this process, learnings will be made about the level of immersion that different qualities of audiovisual representation can exhibit. Several qualities will be designed and tested to identify the best-fitting combination regarding the acoustic parameters and the resulting immersion level.

Nevertheless, a remaining limitation is a difference in motivation that subjects can show in contrast to their real-job performance. However, understanding the neuronal response that drives cognitive processes in controlled environments, can help initiate appropriate field studies in the future. Finally, it will be the goal of this line of research to capture employees' mental state to introduce protective mechanisms, lowering the mental burden by applying assistive technology. The health and safety of employees can be improved by the technology at hand.

4 Discussion and Conclusions

In general, the advantages of field studies come at the price of the reduced controllability of the real-working environment for research purposes. The properties of soundscapes cannot be easily parameterized and manipulated in the field. In contrast and as mentioned above, a laboratory study comes with severe limitations in terms of ecological validity but great control options. Research in VR work environments can be also better controlled than field research but might suffer from deductions in ecological validity like the lab. We suggest that the two factors controllability and validity could be optimally balanced based on the future results from our investigation regarding the differences between living lab and digital twin. The systematic investigation of the VR and living lab environments allows a better understanding of the results that are gained in VR [18].

To sum up, the investigation of physical work environment factors in VR can succeed faster, easier, and more realistic than in the regular lab and better controlled than in a field study. However, the neuronal responses of VR environments must be better understood. In case the cognitive effects of different experimentally controlled physical factors, like soundscapes, presented in VR can be determined by the EEG, a wide range of experiments could be carried out.

References

1. Von Gaudecker, H.M., Holler, R., Janys, L., Siflinger, B., Zimpelmann, C.: Labour supply in the early stages of the CoViD-19 pandemic: empirical evidence on hours, home office, and expectations (2020)
2. Valenduc, G., Vendramin, P.: Work in the Digital Economy: Sorting the Old from the New, vol. 3. European Trade Union Institute, Brussels (2016)
3. Sailer, U., Hassenzahl, M.: Assessing noise annoyance: an improvement-oriented approach. Ergonomics **43**(11), 1920–1938 (2000)
4. Lee, P.J., Jeong, J.H.: Attitudes towards outdoor and neighbour noise during the COVID-19 lockdown: a case study in London. Sustain. Cities Soc. **67**, 102768 (2021)
5. Wagner, A.J., Wang, L.M.: Effects of residential audible distractions on the performance and perception of home office workers. J. Acoust. Soc. Am. **124**(4), 2439 (2008)
6. Graeven, D.B.: Necessity, control, and predictability of noise as determinants of noise annoyance. J. Soc. Psychol. **95**(1), 85–90 (1975)
7. Grenzebach, J., Romanus, E.: Quantifying the effect of noise on cognitive processes: a review of psychophysiological correlates of workload. Noise Health **24**(115), 199 (2022)
8. Ajoudani, A., et al.: Smart collaborative systems for enabling flexible and ergonomic work practices [industry activities]. IEEE Robot. Autom. Mag. **27**(2), 169–176 (2020)
9. de Paula Ferreira, W., Armellini, F., De Santa-Eulalia, L.A.: Simulation in industry 4.0: a state-of-the-art review. Comput. Ind. Eng. **149**, 106868 (2020)
10. Radüntz, T., Fürstenau, N., Mühlhausen, T., Meffert, B.: Indexing mental workload during simulated air traffic control tasks by means of dual frequency head maps. Front. Physiol. **11**, 300 (2020)
11. Le Chénéchal, M., Chatel-Goldman, J.: HTC Vive Pro time performance benchmark for scientific research. In: Icat-Egve 2018, November 2018
12. Thompson, T., Steffert, T., Ros, T., Leach, J., Gruzelier, J.: EEG applications for sport and performance. Methods **45**(4), 279–288 (2008)

13. Hart, S.G.: NASA task load index (TLX) (1986)
14. Weinstein, N.D.: Individual differences in critical tendencies and noise annoyance. J. Sound Vib. **68**, 241–248 (1980)
15. Kjellberg, A., Landström, U.L.F., Tesarz, M., Söderberg, L., Akerlund, E.: The effects of non-physical noise characteristics, ongoing task and noise sensitivity on annoyance and distraction due to noise at work. J. Environ. Psychol. **16**(2), 123–136 (1996)
16. Radüntz, T.: Signal quality evaluation of emerging EEG devices. Front. Physiol. **9**, 98 (2018). https://doi.org/10.3389/fphys.2018.00098
17. Radüntz, T.: Dual frequency head maps: a new method for indexing mental work-load continuously during execution of cognitive tasks. Front. Physiol. **8**, 1019 (2017)
18. Tauscher, J.P., Schottky, F.W., Grogorick, S., Bittner, P.M., Mustafa, M., Magnor, M.: Immersive EEG: evaluating electroencephalography in virtual reality. In: 2019 IEEE Conference on Virtual Reality and 3D User Interfaces (VR), pp. 1794–1800. IEEE, March 2019

A Longer Viewing Distance to a Virtual Screen Could Improve Task Performance

Makio Ishihara[✉]

Fukuoka Institute of Technology, Fukuoka 811-0295, Japan
m-ishihara@fit.ac.jp
https://www.fit.ac.jp/~m-ishihara/Lab/

Abstract. This manuscript conducts a series of experiments on an impact of longer viewing distances upon mouse manipulation and calculation tasks on performance and psychological fatigue. The results show that the accuracy of tracing tends to increase while taking more time, resulting in slower speed for longer viewing distances. In addition, the speed of calculation and its accuracy tends to increase for longer viewing distances where users would relax more.

Keywords: Mouse manipulation · Kraepelin test · viewing distance · virtual display

1 Introduction

The VDT syndrome is a symptom that is caused by extensive use of eyes for long hours and pains in the neck or shoulders due to sitting at desks for long periods of time, and physiological stress that stems from monotonous and continuous work requiring no errors etc.

To deal with the VDT syndrome, the authors [2] showed that a long viewing distance to a projection screen (~3.5 m) enabled users to manipulate a computer mouse more slowly, correctly, and precisely. This outcome was however not sure to hold for longer viewing distances due to limitations on dimensions of physical rooms, so the author [1] built a virtual computer screen system. In the system, users wear an HMD to see a virtual computer screen to which the viewing distance is adjustable between 0.5 m and 128.0 m. This study aims to report the latest outcome about an influence of the longer viewing distances on task performance, psychological fatigue, and physical fatigue.

Section 2 describes a HMD-based virtual display environment and Sect. 2.1 conducts an experiment. Section 3 shows the experiment results and Sect. 4 gives the concluding remarks.

2 A HMD-Based Virtual Display Environment

Figure 1 is an immersive virtual space that a user sees in an HMD and there is a virtual computer screen just before his/her eyes. The user wears an HMD of HTC

Fig. 1. An HMD-view of an immersive virtual space and a virtual computer screen.

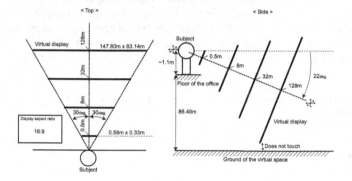

Fig. 2. Experiment design.

Vive Pro and a high-end computer of Dell Alienware is employed to compose the virtual space and run the virtual screen. Figure 2 shows the settings of the virtual computer screen. The left diagram shows the top view and the right one shows the side view. To ensure that the virtual screen is placed just in front of the user at the given viewing distance, the 3-dimensional position of the virtual screen is adjusted relatively to the position of the user's head in real time. The size of the virtual screen is enlarged or shrunk so as to hold a constant FOV of 60°. The user is located about 87 m above the virtual ground, and he/she sees the screen at the angular position of 22° below the eye level according to ergonomics of human system interaction in ISO9241.

2.1 Tasks and Subjects

There are 30 subjects. They are all students from a course of computer science and engineer in the university and all are right-handed and have experience with manipulating a computer mouse. They all have normal eyesight including corrected one. For evaluation of task performance, each subject is asked to perform three tasks in order of Tapping (mouse clicking task), Tracing (mouse dragging

Subjects	Order of vewing distance conditions			
1, 25	Near	N–Middle	F–Middle	Far
2	Near	N–Middle	Far	F–Middle
3	Near	F–Middle	N–Middle	Far
4	Near	F–Middle	Far	N–Middle
5	Near	Far	N–Middle	F–Middle
6, 29	Near	Far	F–Middle	N–Middle
7	N–Middle	Near	F–Middle	Far
8, 27	N–Middle	Near	Far	F–Middle
9	N–Middle	F–Middle	Near	Far
10, 30	N–Middle	F–Middle	Far	Near
11	N–Middle	Far	Near	F–Middle
12	N–Middle	Far	F–Middle	Near
13	F–Middle	Near	N–Middle	Far
14	F–Middle	Near	Far	N–Middle
15	F–Middle	N–Middle	Near	Far
16	F–Middle	N–Middle	Far	Near
17, 28	F–Middle	Far	Near	N–Middle
18	F–Middle	Far	N–Middle	Near
19	Far	Near	N–Middle	F–Middle
20	Far	Near	F–Middle	N–Middle
21	Far	N–Middle	Near	F–Middle
22	Far	N–Middle	F–Middle	Near
23	Far	F–Middle	Near	N–Middle
24, 26	Far	F–Middle	N–Middle	Near

Fig. 3. The order of viewing distances.

task) and Kraepelin (calculation task). For the Tapping task, two rectangles are placed on the left and right of the screen separately and the subject is asked to move the mouse cursor and click on the rectangles in an alternating manner 100 times in total as quickly and precisely as possible. For the Tracing task, a circular path is placed in the middle of the screen and the subject is asked to move the mouse cursor along the center line of the path in a clockwise direction 100 revolutions as quickly and precisely as possible. For the Kraepelin task, the subject is asked to calculate additions of a 1-digit number to a 1-digita number and answer the first digit of the obtained value for 15 min as many and correctly as possible. Each task is given with four different viewing distances of Near (0.5 m), N-Middle (8.0 m), F-Middle (32.0 m) and Far (128.0 m). To remove the order effect, each subject is assigned with each different order of viewing distances as shown in Fig. 3.

Thus the order of conditions between Near, N-Middle, F-Middle and Far is balanced among subjects to remove order effects. Each subject performs one trial at each condition for each task, resulting in

$$30 \text{ subjects} \times 3 \text{ tasks} \times 4 \text{ conditions} \times 1 \text{ trial}$$
$$= 360 \text{ trials in total.} \tag{1}$$

After each task, the subject fills out a questionnaire about his/her physical fatigue and takes a break by sitting still for 5 min then starts the next task. As regards psychological fatigue, just before and after each task, the subject performs the Flicker test.

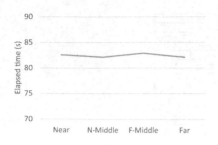

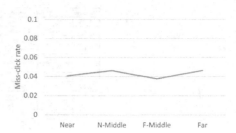

Fig. 4. Elapsed time for Tapping task.

Fig. 5. Miss clicks for Tapping task.

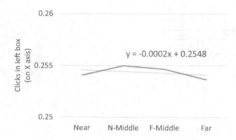

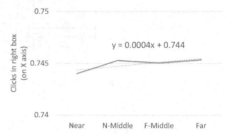

Fig. 6. Accuracy of clicking on the left target for Tapping task (0.25 is the center of the left click target).

Fig. 7. Accuracy of clicking on the right target for Tapping task (0.75 is the center of the left click target).

3 Results

Figure 4 and 5 show the elapsed time and the rate of miss clicks for the Tapping task. They indicate that the accuracy of clicking tends to become lower for longer viewing distances, spending almost the same time span. Figure 6 and 7 show the average position where clicks have happened on the left rectangle (left) and the right one (right). These graphs indicate that the average position tends to be in the center of rectangles for longer viewing distances.

Figure 8 and 9 shows the elapsed time and the accuracy of dragging for the Tracing task. They indicate that the accuracy of dragging tends to become higher for longer viewing distances, spending more time to some extent. Figure 10 shows the average track where tracing has happened (zero means that tracing happens on the center and negative values mean it happens inward the center). This graph indicates that the subject tends to move the mouse cursor on the shorter path for longer viewing distances.

Figure 11 and 12 show the speed of calculation and its accuracy. They indicate that the speed of calculation tends to become fast and the accuracy does higher for longer viewing distances. Figure 13 and 14 show that the counts of correct and wrong answers. They indicate that the impact of longer viewing distance tends to affect both the criterion.

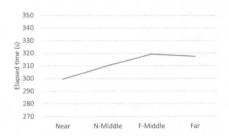

Fig. 8. Elapsed time for Tracing task.

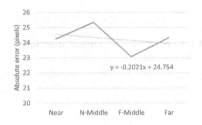

Fig. 9. Absolute error for Tracing task.

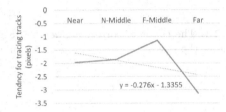

Fig. 10. Tendency for tracing tracks.

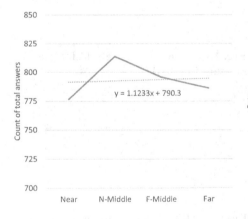

Fig. 11. The total answers.

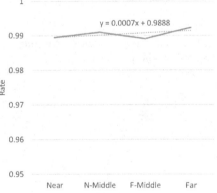

Fig. 12. The rate of correct answers.

Figure 15 and 16 show phycological fatigue by the Flicker test for all the subjects and RRIs for two subjects. These graphs indicates that the phycological stress tends to be given almost equally to them over viewing distances while the subjects would relax for longer viewing distance during the task. To see this, Fig. 17 and 18 are Lorenz plots obtained from the same two subjects. These graphs indicate that the subjects would relax for longer viewing distance during the task as well.

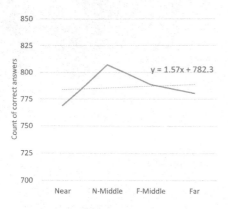

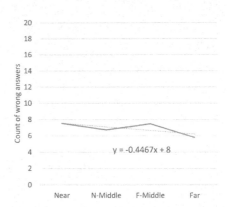

Fig. 13. The count of correct answers made in the task.

Fig. 14. The count of wrong answers made in the task.

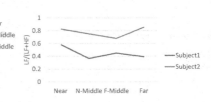

Fig. 15. The psychological fatigue measured by the Flicker test.

Fig. 16. The psychological fatigue measured by RRIs.

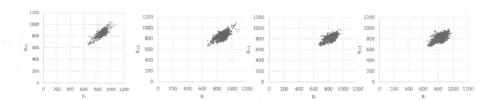

Fig. 17. Lorenz plots of RRIs from the subject 1. The left one is obtained from the Near condition and the next one is from the N-Middle one and so on.

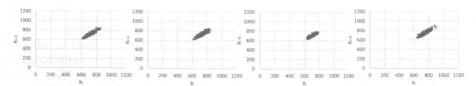

Fig. 18. Lorenz plots of RRIs from the subject 2. The order is the same with Fig. 17.

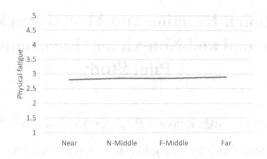

Fig. 19. The physical fatigue measured by a questionnaire of ISO9241.

Figure 19 shows physical fatigue (ISO9241) and its tends to increase to some extent at longer viewing distances.

4   Conclusions

This manuscript conducted a series of experiments on an impact of longer viewing distances upon mouse manipulation and calculation tasks on performance and psychological fatigue. The results showed that the accuracy of tracing tended to increase while taking more time, resulting in slower speed for longer viewing distances. In addition, the speed of calculation and its accuracy tended to increase for longer viewing distances where users would relax more.

In future work, the author is going to look into an impact of viewing distances on temporal changes in physiological stress during a long task.

Acknowledgement. This work was supported by JSPS KAKENHI Grant Number JP20K12522.

References

1. Ishihara, M.: Impact of longer viewing distance to virtual screen upon mouse-manipulation performance. In: Stephanidis, C., Antona, M., Ntoa, S. (eds.) HCII 2022. CCIS, vol. 1581, pp. 144–150. Springer International Publishing, Cham (2022). https://doi.org/10.1007/978-3-031-06388-6_19
2. Ishihara, M., Ishihara, Y.: Impact of viewing distance on task performance and its properties. IEICE Trans. Inf. Syst. **E101.D**(10), 2530–2533 (2018). https://doi.org/10.1587/transinf.2018EDL8117

Emotional Reaction and Mental Workload in Virtual and Non-virtual Environment: A Pilot Study

Fabiha Islam⊙, Zipporah Bright⊙, and Chao Shi[(✉)] ⊙

Binghamton University, Binghamton, NY 13902, USA
{fislam17,zbright1,cshi}@binghamton.edu

Abstract. The advanced platform of virtual reality (VR) provides fascinating experiences by offering a beyond reality, perpetual and persistent multiuser environment. However, users express dissatisfaction towards VR due to ocular problems, headache, disorientation, balance distribution, nausea, and degraded performance during exposure. Therefore, there exists a necessity to measure people's emotional responses and cognitive workload in virtual and non-virtual environment. Thus, we plan to measure 30 individuals' emotional responses and mental workload while they perform cognitively demanding tasks in virtual and non-virtual 2D environments. Until now, we hired 8 participants to play Fruit Ninja 2 at two difficulty levels: easy and hard. An iPad was used to play the game in a non-virtual 2D environment, while a head mount device was used to project the game virtually. After each game, the participants filled out the Positive and Negative Affect Schedule (PANAS) and NASA Task Load Index (TLX) questionnaires. The Friedman test result suggested that there were no significant differences between the Positive Affect (PA) scores of the game in both virtual and non-virtual environments. However, marginally significant differences were observed between the NASA TLX scores, and higher scores were associated with the hard level in the virtual environment, while lower scores were found for the easy level in the non-virtual environment. This test result indicates that people express positiveness towards the virtual environment regardless of their high mental workload. This conclusion was drawn based on the findings of a pilot study, and to obtain a better understanding, we are still recruiting participants.

Keywords: Virtual Reality · Cognitive Task Load · Emotional Response

1 Introduction

Virtual reality (VR) is an advanced computer technology that provides users with an enjoyable experience by simulating mechanisms in a real as well as imaginary world [7, 11]. In recent years, the application of VR has been predominantly found in the domain of industry and academia [7], the healthcare sector [13], clinical rehabilitation [9], gaming platforms, enhanced education learning, military training, and sports [1]. The application of VR offers people a fascinating adventure of fully immersing in a simulated environment different from traditional non-immersive environments. The main existing difference is the level of immersion the virtual world provides, as VR allows extended, three-dimensional, inclusive, and vivid computer displays covering and matching the surroundings of the projected environment [11]. Another difference is the users' engagement level in the virtual environment using their bodies. The users can interact with and manipulate the virtual content using head rotation, eye movements, and specially designed controllers, which corresponds to the user's position and movements. The interaction is achieved by using a head-mounted display (HMD) consisting of an in-build head and eye tracking system. The systems constantly coordinate the user's head and eye movements between the physical and virtual worlds and allow them to observe the virtual environment. To provide a more effective and dynamic experience, the HMDs are often coupled with hand-held controllers, which allow users to explore, reach out, and touch objects in the environment [2, 11]. Despite these numerous advantages, the application of a VR environment has some disadvantages when compared to the traditional environment. For example, VR users have reported sickness symptoms and side effects during their exposure to the VR environment, which includes motion sickness, ocular problems such as eye fatigue and blurred vision, headache, disorientation, balance disturbances, and nausea [3, 10, 12, 17]. These sickness symptoms and the user's immersive presence in VR may influence their performance, workload, and affective states [5]. Thus, it is necessary to evaluate and compare peoples' affective states as well as the mental workload in the VR and non-VR environments.

Researchers have studied affect as a psychometric tool throughout history to investigate people's emotional states in different situations. In these studies, positive and negative affect have consistently been used as dominant and independent variables. In 1988, Watson, Clark, and Tellegen developed Positive and Negative Affect Schedule (PANAS) as a psychometric scale to measure these two dimensions and demonstrate the relationship between the positive and negative affect with personality statistics and characteristics [14, 16]. In PANAS, Positive Affect (PA) is related to the plausible feeling which corresponds to well-being, satisfaction, broad social relationships, socializing, and extraversion. The ten adjectives of PANAS which represent the PA mood are interested, excited, strong, enthusiastic, proud, alert, inspired, determined, attentive, and active. On the other hand, the Negative Affect (NA) is related to distress feelings such as difficulties with overcoming difficult situations, depression, health complaints, and somatic symptoms. The ten adjectives of PANAS representing the NA mood include upset, guilty, scared, hostile, irritable, ashamed, nervous, jittery, afraid, and distressed. [14, 15]. PANAS requires the participants to respond to the 20 items using a 5-point Likert scale ranging from very slightly or not at all (1) to extremely (5). The final PA and NA scores are found by taking the sum of the ten positive and ten negative adjectives, respectively [14].

Workload is defined as the degree of processing capacity that is required to complete a task. Workload measurement indicates the relationship between the supplied resources and the demand required while performing a task. Several tools and techniques have been developed and used by several researchers to measure the mental workload while performing cognitive load-demanding tasks in many circumstances. These include subjective and objective methods such as the use of multiple questionnaires, performance outcomes, and physiological measurements. Among these methods, the National Aeronautics and Space Administration Task Load Index (NASA TLX) is the most widely known, extensively tested, and frequently used questionnaire for determining the perceived cognitive workload [4]. In 1988, Hart and Staveland developed and published the NASA TLX as a multi-dimensional survey-based instrument to collect subjective feedback and estimate mental workload [8]. The NASA LX consists of six workload components, and for measuring the workload, the respondents are asked to rate them between 0 to 100 based on their experience after completing a task. The six sub-scales include mental demand, physical demand, temporal demand, frustration, effort, and performance. The mental demand explains the attentional resources required by the task, while the physical demand accounts for the exertions or physical load demanding activities. The temporal demand measures the time pressure experienced during the completion of the task. The effort component evaluates the mental and physical effort required to accomplish a certain level of the task. Frustration correlates stress and satisfaction with task completion, and performance reflects the degree of satisfaction felt immediately after the completion of a task [18]. To evaluate each subscale's contribution, the users complete fifteen paired comparisons obtained by combining the six components. The NASA TLX global workload score is calculated as the weighted mean of the six sub-scales, which ranges between 0 and 100. The low and high NASA TLX scores mean low and high mental workload, respectively [6].

In this experiment, we focus on comparing the emotional response and mental workload of participants while they play a VR game using a head mount device and controllers and a traditional iPad game. After each trial, they were asked to rate their mental workload and emotional state subjectively using NASA TLX and PANAS questionnaires, respectively. The current paper presents a pilot study with 8 participants, while the ongoing project plans to include a total of 30 participants. The following sections of this paper represent the experimental design and procedure, data analysis, result, discussion, and conclusion.

2 Method

2.1 Participants

In this experiment, we plan to include a total of 30 participants aged between 18–35 years. So far, we have recruited eight right-hand dominant, healthy college students to participate in this study regardless of their previous VR device experience. All the 8 participants had normal or corrected to normal eye sights. The exclusion criteria were to exclude participants who had existing musculoskeletal disorders and visual impairment, which is not correctable with lenses. Table 1 demonstrates the demographic information of the 8 participants.

2.2 Apparatus

The task involves the participants playing Fruit Ninja 2 by slicing the fruits with blades as quickly and accurately as possible. Fruit Ninja 2 was adopted as it is an engaging, easy-to-play, and cross-platform game available for virtual and non-virtual devices. An Apple

Table 1. Demographic information of the participants.

Gender	No. of Participant	Mean Age (Std)
Male	6	23 (2.53)
Female	2	20 (1.42)
Total	8	22.25 (2.61)

iPad was used as a hardware device to display the game in a non-virtual environment. Fruit Ninja 2 was installed directly through the Apple App Store on the iPad. For the virtual setup, the SteamVR application was used to present the game. Varjo VR-3 (a head mount device) and two HTC Vive controllers were used to project and play the game in the virtual world. On both devices, the Fruit Ninja 2 game included two difficulty levels: Arcade (easy) and Classic (hard). The arcade mode is a timed game session that lasts approximately 1 min, offering low difficulty, while the classic mode is a more difficult game session with constraints designed to prevent the user from proceeding through the game too easily. Self-reported surveys such as NASA TLX and PANAS served as complementary tools to collect mental workload and emotional arousal data reported by the participants.

2.3 Experimental Procedure

This research was approved by the Institutional Review Board at Binghamton University. Interested participants were invited to visit the laboratory based on a previously made schedule. Upon arrival at the laboratory, the participants received a brief description of the experimental procedure. Then, their signatures were obtained on the informed consent form. Prior to the study, the demographic information of the participants, such as age, gender, etc., was collected, and training on the experimental procedure was provided to participants for approximately 10 min. During the training session, the participants were assisted in setting up and activating the Varjo VR3 Headset and placing it on their heads. They were also directed on how to adjust the headset headband so that it sits atop their face comfortably and displays a clear picture. Additional training was provided on the VR controllers and button layout. Finally, the rules and controls within the Fruit Ninja game scenarios were described to them.

Once the participants were comfortable operating the games by their own, they were asked to play the Fruit Ninja 2 game in two environments (iPad and VR) at two difficulty levels (easy and hard) with repeated measures of the factors. As a result, each participant completed a total of 8 trials (2 environments × 2 difficulty levels × 2 trials). The order of iPad and VR trials was randomly selected so that the possible effect of order was controlled. In order to collect and measure the participants' mental workload and emotional responses in each trial, they were asked to complete the self-assessment questionnaires at the end of the trials. The self-assessment questionnaires consisted of NASA-TLX and PANAS forms which included measurements of the participant's overall study experience. The participants were given a 2-min rest period after each game and self-assessment session to minimize their mental and physical fatigue. Finally, after completing a ninety-minute experiment, each participant was compensated with a $15 gift card.

2.4 Data Analysis

Participants' self-reported NASA TLX, Positive Affect (PA), and Negative Affect (NA) scores were collected and treated as dependent measures. Each participant experienced eight trials. As a result, 8 participants yielded 64 (8 × 8) trials. Table 2 lists the independent and dependent variables of the experiment.

Table 2. Independent and Dependent Variables.

Independent Variables	Dependent Variables
Environment	PANAS Scores
• VR	• PA
• iPad	• NA
Difficulty Level	NASA TLX Scores
• Easy	
• Hard	

Since we had a small sample of 8 participants, the study employed separate Friedman Nonparametric tests to observe the differences in the reported scores based on the independent variables. The independent variables were divided into four groups: iPad easy, iPad hard, VR easy, and VR hard. For an overall significant difference among the mean ranks of the groups, a Wilcoxon Signed-Rank Test was conducted with six combinations: iPad easy to iPad hard, iPad easy to VR easy, iPad easy to VR hard, iPad hard to VR easy, iPad hard to VR hard, VR hard to VR easy.

3   Result

3.1 PANAS

The Friedman Nonparametric test revealed that there were no statistically significant differences between the mean ranks of the PA scores across the two different environments and two difficulty levels ($\chi^2(3) = 4.562$, p = 0.207). However, statistically significant differences were found among the mean NA scores of the four groups ($\chi^2(3) = 20.368$, p < 0.001). The post hoc analysis demonstrated that the mean NA scores of the VR environment were significantly higher than the mean NA scores of the iPad at both difficulty levels (p = 0.012 and p = 0.011 at easy and hard level, respectively). Table 3 shows the mean with standard deviation (SD) and 95% Confidence Interval (CI) of the NA scores at both environments of the two difficulty levels.

Table 3. Mean (SD) and 95% CI of NA scores.

Difficulty level	Environment	Mean (SD)	CI
Easy	iPad	14.31 (6.99)	8.47, 20.16
	VR	20.25 (8.53)	13.12, 27.38
Hard	iPad	13.63 (4.51)	9.85, 17.40
	VR	20.50 (8.27)	13.59, 27.41

3.2 NASA TLX

The Friedman test demonstrated a marginally significant difference among the NASA TLX scores of the four groups ($\chi^2(3) = 6.3$, p $= 0.098$). The highest mean NASA TLX score (68.04) was associated with the hard level of the game played in the VR environment while the lowest score (57.61) was found in the iPad environment while playing the game at an easy level. The mean with standard deviation and 95% Confidence Interval (CI) of the NASA TLX scores at both environments of the two difficulty levels are shown in Table 4. Additionally, it was noticed that at both difficulty levels, the mean NASA TLX score was higher in the VR environment compared to the iPad environment.

Table 4. Mean (SD) and 95% CI of NASA TLX scores.

Difficulty level	Environment	Mean (SD)	CI
Easy	iPad	57.61 (16.99)	43.41, 71.81
	VR	59.67 (14.82)	47.28, 72.06
Hard	iPad	60.39 (9.90)	52.12, 68.67
	VR	68.04 (8.56)	60.89, 75.20

4 Discussion

The study investigated the effects of two different working environments and task difficulty levels on participants' perceived emotional reactions and mental workload while playing a game. Initially, 8 participants were recruited to play a fruit-cutting game in virtual and non-virtual environments at easy and hard difficulty levels with two repetitions. The perceived emotional reaction and mental workload were captured by asking the participants to fill out the PANAS and NASA TLX questionnaire at the end of each game session. The statistical analysis of the reported scores provided an understanding of the emotional response and mental workload towards the virtual and traditional non-virtual environments at two difficulty levels.

In this study participants' emotional responses to the virtual and non-virtual worlds at easy and hard levels were compared by separately analyzing the positive and negative affect scores of PANAS. The Friedman test result of the PA scores showed no statistically significant differences between the reported scores of the four groups. Therefore, it can be said that the participants demonstrated equal positiveness and possessed uniform pleasurable feelings for the game in both environments. The study also reported significant differences between the NA scores of the virtual and non-virtual environments. Higher negative affect scores were found in the virtual environment compared to the iPad at both difficulty levels. This finding may suggest that the presence of a virtual environment intensifies the distress and unpleasurable feelings of the participants regardless of task difficulty level.

The study reported that marginally significant differences exist between NASA TLX scores. This result indicates that the participants perceived a higher mental workload when they were engaged with the game in the virtual environment compared to the iPad at both difficulty levels. The observation points to the fact that the virtual environment imposes a higher mental task load compared to the traditional non-virtual environment.

5 Conclusion

This paper presented a pilot study describing peoples' perceived emotional reactions and mental workload in two different realities while being engaged in a cognitive load demanding gaming task. The study inferred that though the presence of the virtual environment develops a higher mental workload and aggravates distress feelings, the participants express equal positiveness towards the virtual world compared to the traditional environment. Nevertheless, a complete study with a larger sample size is still needed to compare the results and make a strong conclusion.

References

1. Ahir, K., Govani, K., Gajera, R., Shah, M.: Application on virtual reality for enhanced education learning, military training and sports. Augment. Hum. Res. **5**, 1–9 (2020). https://doi.org/10.1007/s41133-019-0025-2
2. Barbot, B., Kaufman, J.C.: What makes immersive virtual reality the ultimate empathy machine? Discerning the underlying mechanisms of change. Comput. Hum. Behav. **111**, 106431 (2020)
3. Chang, E., Kim, H.T., Yoo, B.: Virtual reality sickness: a review of causes and measurements. Int. J. Hum.-Comput. Interact. **36**(17), 1658–1682 (2020)
4. Devos, H., et al.: Psychometric properties of NASA-TLX and index of cognitive activity as measures of cognitive workload in older adults. Brain Sci. **10**(12), 994 (2020)
5. Faric, N., et al.: What players of virtual reality exercise games want: thematic analysis of web-based reviews. J. Med. Internet Res. **21**(9), e13833 (2019)
6. Grier, R.A.: How high is high? A meta-analysis of NASA-TLX global workload scores. In: Proceedings of the Human Factors and Ergonomics Society Annual Meeting, vol. 59, no. 1, pp. 1727–1731. SAGE Publications, Los Angeles, September 2015
7. Guo, Z., et al.: Applications of virtual reality in maintenance during the industrial product lifecycle: a systematic review. J. Manuf. Syst. **56**, 525–538 (2020)
8. Hart, S.G., Staveland, L.E.: Development of NASA-TLX (Task Load Index): results of empirical and theoretical research. In: Advances in Psychology, vol. 52, pp. 139–183. North-Holland (1988)

9. Kim, W.S., et al.: Clinical application of virtual reality for upper limb motor rehabilitation in stroke: review of technologies and clinical evidence. J. Clin. Med. **9**(10), 3369 (2020)

10. Lewis, C.H., Griffin, M.J.: Applications of virtual reality. In: Virtual Reality in Neuro-Psycho-Physiology: Cognitive, Clinical and Methodological Issues in Assessment and Rehabilitation, vol. 44, p. 35 (1997)

11. Pallavicini, F., Pepe, A., Minissi, M.E.: Gaming in virtual reality: what changes in terms of usability, emotional response and sense of presence compared to non-immersive video games? Simul. Gaming **50**(2), 136–159 (2019)

12. Saredakis, D., Szpak, A., Birckhead, B., Keage, H.A., Rizzo, A., Loetscher, T.: Factors associated with virtual reality sickness in head-mounted displays: a systematic review and meta-analysis. Front. Hum. Neurosci. **14**, 96 (2020)

13. Singh, R.P., Javaid, M., Kataria, R., Tyagi, M., Haleem, A., Suman, R.: Significant applications of virtual reality for COVID-19 pandemic. Diabetes Metab. Syndr. **14**(4), 661–664 (2020)

14. Taneja, A., Vishal, S.B., Mahesh, V., Geethanjali, B.: Virtual reality based neuro-rehabilitation for mental stress reduction. In: 2017 Fourth International Conference on Signal Processing, Communication and Networking (ICSCN), pp. 1–5. IEEE, March 2017

15. Vera-Villarroel, P., et al.: Positive and Negative Affect Schedule (PANAS): psychometric properties and discriminative capacity in several Chilean samples. Eval. Health Prof. **42**(4), 473–497 (2019)

16. Watson, D., Clark, L.A., Tellegen, A.: Development and validation of brief measures of positive and negative affect: the PANAS scales. J. Pers. Soc. Psychol. **54**(6), 1063 (1988)

17. Weech, S., Moon, J., Troje, N.F.: Influence of bone-conducted vibration on simulator sickness in virtual reality. PLoS ONE **13**(3), e0194137 (2018)

18. Young, G., Zavelina, L., Hooper, V.: Assessment of workload using NASA Task Load Index in perianesthesia nursing. J. PeriAnesthesia Nurs. **23**(2), 102–110 (2008)

Evaluation Model of Running Fatigue of Young Students Based on Characteristic Parameters of ECG Signal

Weisheng Jiang[1,2], Chao Yin[1,2], Qianxiang Zhou[1,2(✉)], and Zhongqi Liu[1,2]

[1] School of Biological Science and Medical Engineering, Beihang University, Beijing 100191, China
zqxg@buaa.edu.cn
[2] Beijing Advanced Innovation Centre for Biomedical Engineering, Beihang University, Beijing 102402, China

Abstract. Large or high-intensity running training can lead to fatigue and sports injuries; therefore, research on sports fatigue and the establishment of a fatigue analysis and evaluation model for running sports are of guiding significance for the design and training of running sports tasks. 22 subjects participated in accelerated running experiments from the slowest 8 km/h to the fastest 13 km/h, and the RPE (rating of perceived exertion) and ECG signal data were recorded. After 3 days, all subjects ran at a constant speed between 13 and 15 RPE during the acceleration run and the RPE and ECG signals were measured. To address the problem of motion artifacts in the ECG signal during exercise, a 7-layer "db8" smooth wavelet transform was used to extract ECG features. Then, five HRV (heart rate variability) indicators, NN-mean, SDNN, LF, HF, and TP, which are more sensitive to fatigue changes, were selected by applying single factor analysis of variance and single feature linear regression methods. The results showed that all five HRV indexes decelerated and decreased with the increase in exercise time, and finally reached a stable state, i.e. fatigue. Based on the subjective evaluation data and the five HRV characteristic indexes obtained, a tri-classification model for fatigue prediction was established by using a support vector machine (SVM), and its fatigue prediction accuracy was verified to be 91.06%, which can effectively evaluate running fatigue.

Keywords: ECG · heart rate · heart rate variability · exercise fatigue · SVM

1 Introduction

Running is one of the most efficient methods of physical activity of all types, yet fatigue is one of the main causes of injury for approximately 50% of runners each year [1, 2]. 60% of sports injuries are due to training errors, half of which are attributed to excessive mileage [3]. 72% of sports injuries in running are associated with sudden changes in running mileage [4]. As the frequency of running increases, the probability of injury increases, and excessive exercise can lead to localized muscle damage [2, 5].

C. Stephanidis et al. (Eds.): HCII 2023, CCIS 1832, pp. 336–342, 2023.
https://doi.org/10.1007/978-3-031-35989-7_43

Martinmki K et al. demonstrated [6] that LF, NN-mean, and SDNN showed a decreasing trend with exercise time, but only the trends of individual indicators of HRV were studied and no characteristic thresholds of exercise fatigue were summarized. The study by Malan [7] confirmed that the HRR ratio can be used as a valid evaluation index of exercise intensity for different exercising individuals, and can effectively reflect the comprehensive exercise fatigue state of individuals. However, their study evaluated exercise fatigue by a single feature without establishing an exercise fatigue detection model.

This paper proposes a method for the extraction of exercise fatigue-sensitive features of ECG signals and the classification of running exercise fatigue features. The targets, on the one hand, are the fatigue-sensitive features of running exercise and their trends, and the study of the changes in heart rate and HRV during running exercise; on the other hand, the support vector machine (SVM) classification algorithm is used to classify the time-domain, frequency-domain and non-linear features of HRV and to establish a fatigue detection model for the accurate identification of fatigue states during running exercise.

2 Method

2.1 Subjects

For the experiment, 22 male subjects aged between 20 and 28 years (mean age 23.81 years, SD = 1.59 years) and all with a BMI between 20 and 24 years were selected. They had no cardiovascular, respiratory, or musculoskeletal disease. The day before the trial, subjects were not allowed to train intensely, maintain a regular diet and good sleep, and avoid stimulants (caffeine, nicotine, etc.) or alcohol. Before the experiment, subjects should understand the purpose and procedure of the experiment, complete an informed consent form and protect the privacy of the content and data of the experiment, which has been approved by the Ethics Committee.

2.2 Experiment Equipment

This experiment uses the MP150 ECG signal acquisition system from BIOPAC, which includes an ECG signal amplifier, a 32-lead ECG signal acquisition channel, a synchronous ECG signal acquisition system, and an experimental data analysis system. And Pre-installed ECG acquisition computer with AcqKnowledge ECG signal acquisition software.

2.3 Experimental Procedures

During the experiment, ECG signals were collected from young male subjects in resting and exercise states. Exercise fatigue was induced by the subjects running on a treadmill by the experimental requirements. The MP150 device was used to collect ECG signals from the resting state before exercise and during exercise, and the RPE scale was used to experiment. The running experiment consisted of an accelerated running experiment and a constant speed running experiment, and the two experiments were separated by at least

3 days to completely relieve the fatigue caused by the accelerated running experiment. The experiments were conducted as follows:

1. Before the start of the experiment, subjects are required to be informed of the purpose, content, and procedure of the experiment, to sign an informed consent form, and to keep the data and content of the experiment confidential.
2. The subjects then rested in silence for 5 min. The experiment begins with the subject wearing the MP150 device to collect ECG signals at rest for 10 min.
3. Next, the subject wears the MP150 device to collect ECG signals during the accelerated running exercise state. Subjects ran on a treadmill at an initial speed of 8 km/h and increased their speed by 1 km/h every 5 min to a maximum speed of 14 km/h. During the run, subjects were asked about their subjective feelings of fatigue at 5-min intervals. During the run, the subjects were asked every 5 min about their subjective feelings of fatigue. The experiment continued until the subject was unable to continue running or the running time was 35 min.
4. After at least 3 days, subjects wore the MP150 device to collect ECG signals during the constant speed running exercise condition. The subject's running speed was set as the average speed at an RPE value of 13 to 15 in the accelerated running experiment. Subjects were asked about their subjective perception of fatigue every 5 min during the run. The experiment was continued until the subject was unable to continue running or the running time was 35 min.

3   Results

3.1   Subjective Fatigue Data

Data were collected from 22 subjects, of which 40 sets of data from 20 subjects were valid. The subjective exercise fatigue scores of the subjects were consistent according to the RPE scores, as shown in Fig. 1. From the data results, it can be found that running exercise can successfully induce a state of exercise fatigue and the subjective exercise fatigue perception RPE values increased with the increase of exercise time. The left graph in Fig. 1 shows the RPE data for the accelerated running and the right graph in Fig. 1 shows the RPE data for the constant speed running.

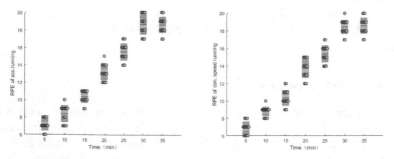

Fig. 1. RPE values in accelerated and constant speed running experiments

3.2 Screening of Fatigue Characteristics

The Shapiro-Wilk (SW) test was performed for each ECG signal characteristic and the results all had a P-value greater than 0.05, indicating that the data met a normal distribution. Therefore, in this study, the Analysis of Variance (ANOVA) method was used to examine the differences in ECG signal characteristics between fatigue states, and P values less than 0.05 were considered statistically significant. Linear regression was also applied to individual features to evaluate their ability to detect running exercise fatigue by R^2. Features with $P < 0.05$ and $R^2 > 0.7$ were defined as running exercise fatigue-sensitive features.

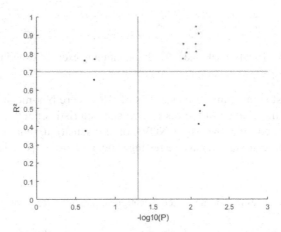

Fig. 2. Statistical distribution of running exercise fatigue characteristics (Color figure online)

In Fig. 2, the vertical coordinates are R^2 values, and the horizontal coordinates are represented by $-\log_{10}P$. When P is 0.05, $-\log_{10}P$ equals 1.3010. Therefore, the closer the ECG signal characteristic is to the upper right region of the statistical plot (red dot), the stronger the association between the characteristic and exercise fatigue, the more statistically significant it is, and the better the performance of the exercise fatigue classification model constructed with the characteristic. A total of seven ECG signals are exercise fatigue sensitive, namely HR, HRR, SDNN, NN-mean, HF, LF and TP.

3.3 Variation in Fatigue-Sensitive Characteristics of Running Exercise

The HR and HRR follow the same trend in the early stages of exercise for both accelerated and constant speed running exercise, with the heart activity increasing to adapt to the exercise state, and the HR entering a steady state after gradually adapting to the intensity of running exercise. In the later stages of running, the HR rises again significantly as the heart enters a state of exercise fatigue. The rate of increase of HR is faster than the rate of increase of constant speed. The HRR reflects that the exercise intensity of accelerated running exercise is greater than that of constant speed running exercise, as shown in Fig. 3.

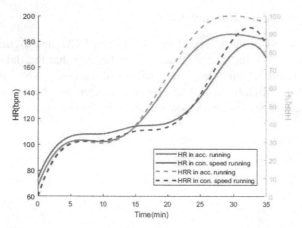

Fig. 3. Trends in HR and HRR during running exercise experiments

The top 3 most significant characteristics of HRV were NN-mean, SDNN, and HF, respectively, and the change in the distinctive characteristics per 5 min with exercise time was investigated by a one-way ANOVA on the sensitivity characteristics to HRV per 5 min in the exercise state versus the resting state, and the statistical results are shown in Table 1.

Table 1. Statistical results for the 3 exercise fatigue characteristics most sensitive to HRV

Time	NN-mean (ms)		SDNN (ms)		HF (ms²)	
	Acc.	Con.	Acc.	Con.	Acc.	Con.
0 min	974.47 ± 56.62	996.52 ± 63.23	114.05 ± 7.11	115.06 ± 6.38	609.58 ± 63.54	630.74 ± 63.10
5 min	620.21 ± 35.62	651.61 ± 35.72	68.00 ± 4.03	69.01 ± 3.78	222.59 ± 26.93	238.10 ± 27.77
10 min	572.35 ± 9.90	603.75 ± 32.92	52.71 ± 2.74	53.72 ± 2.87	120.37 ± 13.82	135.88 ± 13.14
15 min	541.1 ± 17.18	629.39 ± 39.78	45.95 ± 3.17	46.96 ± 3.65	87.47 ± 26.93	102.98 ± 10.91
20 min	536.59 ± 15.62	595.48 ± 27.46	43.46 ± 2.04	46.14 ± 3.00	40.51 ± 13.82	40.37 ± 6.27
25 min	412.65 ± 13.14	471.54 ± 21.84	37.78 ± 1.72	40.46 ± 2.37	22.33 ± 8.84	21.30 ± 5.41
30 min	350.38 ± 12.56	409.27 ± 23.00	35.09 ± 1.82	37.78 ± 2.24	13.15 ± 3.08	12.73 ± 5.21
35 min	349.49 ± 13.88	408.38 ± 24.80	114.05 ± 7.11	33.46 ± 2.30	10.52 ± 4.96	10.12 ± 5.09

Acc. in Table 1 represents the accelerated running experiment and Con. Represents the constant speed running experiment. As can be seen from the data in the table, the trend of the 5-min HRV characteristic values with exercise time for the 20 subjects was significantly different ($p < 0.01$) for all six exercise periods compared to the resting state, and there was no significant difference in the HRV characteristic values between the same exercise period of accelerated running exercise and constant speed running exercise.

3.4   Classification Models for Running Fatigue

Co-collinearity analysis was performed on the time and frequency domain feature indicators of HRV. If the correlation coefficient between two features is greater than 0.7, it indicates that there is multicollinearity between the two characteristics and one of the two characteristics needs to be eliminated. The final nine exercise fatigue-sensitive characteristics selected for SVM-MC were: HR, HRR, NN-mean, SDNN, HF, LF/HF, HF(nu), sample entropy, and approximate entropy. By arranging the kernel functions of the SVM to group and select the most appropriate classifier parameters, the results are shown in Table 2.

Table 2.   Classification results for OvO and OvR

Three classification methods	Classifier	Optimal parameters
OvO	Classifier 1	C = 3.0, kernel = 'linear'
	Classifier 2	C = 2.0, gamma = 0.038, kernel = 'rbf'
	Classifier 3	C = 1.0, gamma = 0.002, kernel = 'rbf'
OvR	Classifier 1	C = 3.0, kernel = 'linear'
	Classifier 2	C = 95, gamma = 0.003, kernel = 'rbf'
	Classifier 3	C = 2.0, gamma = 0.044, kernel = 'rbf'

Using the most appropriate multi-classifier parameters in Table 2 and the tenfold cross-validation of the running motion fatigue model, the final results are shown in Table 3.

Table 3.   Correct classification of exercise fatigue with multiple classifiers

Fatigue level	OvO		OvR	
	SVM	SVM-MC	SVM	SVM-MC
Fatigue-free	85.61%	91.21%	89.73%	92.09%
Fatigue	81.24%	89.54%	86.36%	89.68%
Heavy fatigue	85.28%	90.26%	88.43%	91.43%
Average value	84.04%	90.33%	88.17%	91.06%

The classification accuracy of OvR was significantly higher than that of OvO, and the accuracy of the classification model was higher after features with covariance were removed, indicating that feature dimensionality reduction using covariance analysis can improve the accuracy of the classifier. The model was able to achieve an accuracy of 91.06% in terms of average fatigue levels.

4 Conclusion and Discussion

This paper has successfully induced exercise fatigue in the running condition through accelerated running exercise and constant speed running exercise and has concluded the following:

1. The time-domain eigenvalues of HRV (SDNN, NN-mean) decreased as running exercise fatigue intensified, and the frequency-domain eigenvalues (TP, LF, HF) also showed a decreasing trend. This indicates that the characteristic parameters of HRV tend to decrease as running fatigue increases.
2. The change in HRV in the first half of the experiment is more dramatic during the acceleration running compared to the constant speed running. As the exercise time progressed, the trends in HRV remained more or less the same for both accelerated and constant speed running, and the eigenvalues of HRV were basically at the same level. This suggests that the acceleration running experiment causes subjects to enter a state of fatigue more rapidly. At later stages of exercise, the HRV for accelerated and constant speed running was already at a very low level.
3. This study found the relationship between HRV features and exercise fatigue, and the SVM-based exercise fatigue model can provide a feature selection basis for establishing exercise fatigue detection and provide theoretical support for subsequent wearable exercise fatigue detection equipment in real time.
4. This study was mainly based on two types of running exercise fatigue, other running patterns and sports have not been explored, and future studies should investigate the trends in HRV following multiple exercise-induced fatigues.
5. The exercise fatigue rating was based on the subjective RPE scores of the subjects, and as the subjects in this experiment were all young men, there were individual differences, and subsequent studies should increase the experimental sample of different populations.

References

1. Maselli, F., Storari, L., Barbari, V., et al.: Prevalence and incidence of low back pain among runners: a systematic review. BMC Musculoskelet. Disord. **21**(1), 343 (2020)
2. Fields, K.B., et al.: Prevention of running injuries. Curr. Sports Med. Rep. **9**(3), 176–182 (2010)
3. Jacobs, S.J., Berson, B.L.: Injuries to runners: a study of entrants to a 10,000 meter race. Am. J. Sports Med. **14**(2), 151–155 (1986)
4. Lysholm, J., Wiklander, J.: Injuries in runners. Am. J. Sports Med. **15**(2), 168–171 (1987)
5. van Gent, R.N., et al.: Incidence and determinants of lower extremity running injuries in long distance runners: a systematic review. Br. J. Sports Med. **41**(8), 469–480 (2007). Discussion 480
6. Martinmäki, K., Häkkinen, K., Mikkola, J., Rusko, H.: Effect of low-dose endurance training on heart rate variability at rest and during an incremental maximal exercise test. Eur. J. Appl. Physiol. **104**(3), 541–548 (2008). https://doi.org/10.1007/s00421-008-0804-9
7. Ma, L.: Study on the state recognition of running movement based on physiological information feedback. Zhejiang University of Technology (2018)

User-Specific Visual Axis Alignment for Reducing Eye Fatigues in HMDs

Hyosun Kim[1(✉)], RangKyun Mok[1], Young-Jun Seo[1], and Yun Taek Kim[2]

[1] Samsung Display, Yongin 17113, South Korea
cogenghyosun@gmail.com
[2] Cheonan Kim's Eye Clinic, Cheonan 31127, South Korea

Abstract. The pupillary axis and the visual axis in the eye keep a constant angle, which is called "Angle Kappa (K)" [1]. The people with exotropia (the outward deviation of one eye or both eyes) had significantly higher angle kappa than the people with normal eye [2]. Meanwhile, it is also revealed that the people with abnormal binocular vision including strabismus watched stereoscopic images (3D), they showed worse stereoacuity or felt more eye fatigue. It may be because that 3D eye fatigue may be related to kappa angles. This study is based on the hypothesis that 3D eye fatigue can result from kappa angle, the discrepancy between visual axis and the pupillary axis, even though the users do not have strabismus. The purpose of this study is to explore the possibility whether eye fatigue is reduced by matching the participants' visual axis. First, the app was developed for measuring visual axis with assist of an ophthalmologist. Second, we compared the visual fatigue of participants with and without matching user-specific visual axis alignment. As the result of the objective visual fatigue, divergence hysteresis was significant differently according to the condition of matching visual axis alignment.

Keywords: HDM · visual axis · eye fatigue

1 Introduction

When one light is presented and the person is looking at it, the light passes through the mechanics of the eye and reaches on the retina at the back of the eyeball. Due to complexity of the mechanics of the eye, there are several distinct axes by which light travels in the eye (e.g. the pupillary axis and the visual axis). The pupil axis is the imagery line through the center of cornea to the center of the pupil. The visual axis is the imagery direct line extending from the light seen, through the center of the pupil, to the fovea on which the image of the light is formed sharply. The pupillary axis is important because the center of pupil gives us the clue that we estimate viewer's attention. However, the pupillary axis is not identical to the visual axis. The pupillary axis and the visual axis keep a constant angle, which is called "Angle Kappa (K)" (Fig. 1). It is known that mean angle kappa of people with normal eyes is about $5°$ (visual angle) [1].

People with the problem in his/her eyes have the different angle kappa from that with normal eyes. Especially, people with strabismus or phoria do. When the people

C. Stephanidis et al. (Eds.): HCII 2023, CCIS 1832, pp. 343–350, 2023.
https://doi.org/10.1007/978-3-031-35989-7_44

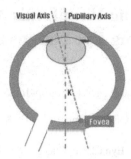

Fig. 1. The relationship between pupillary axis and visual axis

with strabismus or phoria look at an object, their eyes do not properly aligned with each other; Only one eye foveates the target and the other eye deviates nasalward or temporalward. We will see the corneal light reflex of the turned eye displaced from the pupil center. Angle kappa, the difference between the pupillary axis and the visual axis, could be higher since the one eye does not focus on an object if there is strabismus. The previous study showed that the people with exotropia (the outward deviation of one eye or both eyes) had significantly higher angle kappa than either people with normal eye or people with esotropia (the inward deviation) [2].

If the angle kappa exceeds a certain range such a exotropic strabismus, the two eyes will not be able to do their original function, especially perceiving stereopsis. The previous researches revealed that the people with abnormal binocular vision (ABV) such as strabismus showed worse stereoacuity at near and distant fixation [3–5]. Although they were able to perceive stereoscopic three-dimensional (S3D), they felt more eye fatigue [3]. This indicates that S3D symptoms are closely related to the convergence demand, which results from the difference between pupillary axis and visual axis.

Since both S3D devices and Head-Mounted Displays (HMDs) have the same operational principle in which the separate images are presented on the left- and right eye (e.g. diplopic projection), we must consider the angle kappa when a viewer is watching HMDs. Angle kappa in HMDs could be more important than in S3D devices. Because a HMD has a closed structure and a viewer see the images through the HMD lens, a viewer may feel eye fatigue or simulation sickness if the visual axis does not match the optical structure of a HMD.

In HDMs, we can adjust the distance between two lenses, which is corresponding with the pupillary distance (PD), not the distance between visual axes of two eyes. Although the pupillary axes are aligned with the center of HMD lenses, the visual axes may not match the center of HMD lenses. Adjusting the distance of two lenses will be able to solve the problem from angle kappa if following two assumptions are premised: the first assumption that all people have the identical angle kappa and the second assumption that the position of images on the HMD display is also moved as much as the distance of two lenses. If the former assumption is correct, we can get the sharp images by moving the positions of HMD lenses and the images on the display by the distance according to angle kappa (Fig. 2[b]). However, people do not have the identical angle kappa [6]. Angle kappa was measured to be as great as 9° with normal eyes. The latter assumption is also not satisfied in that there is no HMD in which the position images on the display changes according to the distance between two lenses.

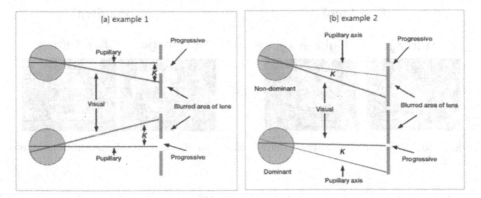

Fig. 2. The examples that the visual axes do not match the clear area in the case of fitting PALs (from Clark's article [7])

In addition, the problem from angle kappa is able to be complicated when it meets with eye dominance. Clark [7] pointed out the similar problem about the visual axes of two eyes and eye dominance in the case of fitting progressive addition lenses (PALs). In the situation where a person with binocular vision has to choose to see clearly with one eye, the dominant eye will always be chose. The direction of the visual axis on the dominant eye may not move symmetrically with that on the nondominant eye. When the dominant eye maintains the visual axis to obtain a clear image of an object, the non-dominant eye may achieve the blurry image (Fig. 2[b]). Replacing PALs with HMD lens and displays, the distance between the image on HMD displays and the visual axis of non-dominant eye may increase if we do not adjust the position of the images on the HMD display. As the result, a viewer may perceive a distorted image or (s)he hardly see S3D images. Moreover, this may cause more visual fatigue. Therefore, adjusting the position of images on the HMD display is required according to the visual axes.

The purpose of this study is to explore the possibility whether visual fatigue is reduced by matching the position of images on the HMD display with participants' visual axis. First, we measured participants' visual axis. We developed the app for measuring visual axis with assist of an ophthalmologist. Second, we compared the visual fatigue of participants with and without matching user-specific visual axis alignment. From the results, we suggest a new process for reducing visual fatigue in HMDs.

2 Experiment

2.1 Measuring Participants' Visual Axis

We developed the app for measuring participant's visual axis on HMD, assisted by the ophthalmologist, one of co-authors. This app used the diplopic projection; the left part of the display was presented to the left eye, and the right part was to the right eye. The app consisted of two steps: the first step was for macro- and the second for micro-tuning (Fig. 3).

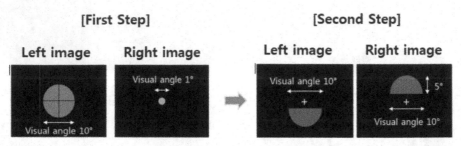

Fig. 3. Right eye and left eye images during adjustment of visual axis alignment (Color figure online)

In the first step, a red circle with visual angle 10° was presented on the left eye and a green circle with visual angle 1° was on the right eye. Complementary color (redgreen) was used for blocking the fusion of two colors. Each circle was positioned on the center of each monocular display. We asked participants to concentrate their focus to the red circle in order to maintain the angle between two visual axes of the dominant eye and the non-dominant eye. They moved the green dot until the green circle was located on the center of the red circle (Fig. 4[a]). At that time, the position of images on each eye matched the participant's visual axis. If misaligned, the green dot was located on the side of the red circle (Fig. 4[b]). Participants moved the green dot using two arrow keys ($\leftarrow$, $\rightarrow$).

Next step, an upper semicircle was showed on the left eye and a lower semicircle on the right eye. A viewer perceived that two gray semicircles were presented vertically above and below. A fixation mark, + was presented on the left and right eyes. Since two semicircles were displayed separately and a viewer did not perceived by fusing both two semicircles, we used same gray (digital value: 128). The size of a semicircle was visual angle 10°. Participants were asked to focus the + mark and then to adjust the position of the lower semicircle to match the vertical line of two semicircles. If the visual axis was aligned in the first step, two semicircles were perpendicularly located on the straight line (Fig. 4[a]). If misaligned, participants adjusted the position of the lower semicircle until two semicircles were in the vertical position (Fig. 4[b]). Although this method was referred from the test of aniseikonia, we transformed it based on the assist of the ophthalmologist.

2.2 The Effect of Matching Visual Axis on Visual Fatigue

We compared the visual fatigue of participants with and without matching user specific visual axis alignment. We measured the subjective and objective visual fatigue. The subjective visual fatigue was measured using a scale of visual fatigue [8]. Questions were rated on a 7-point Likert scale. The objective visual fatigues were fusional amplitude and vergence hysteresis. From the previous study, two variables were be utilized as an index of visual fatigue by S3D contents [9].

Binocular images

[First Step]   [Second Step]

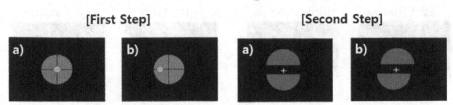

Fig. 4. Binocular images which participants see on HMD. [a] If participants' visual axis is aligned, the green dot is located on the center of the red circle or two semicircles is perpendicularly located on the straight line. [b] If misaligned, the green dot or one semicircle is not located on the center. (Color figure online)

People can see one single image when the presented images have a certain extent of binocular disparity. However, they can hardly fusion the images with binocular disparity when visual fatigue is high. We measured the break point which one single image was divided into two and the recovery point which divided images were fused with one single image. Fusional amplitude was calculated by the difference in the fusional vergence break point between convergence side and divergence side. Differences between the fusional vergence break point and recovery point was defined as the vergence hysteresis. We used two values of vergence hysteresis at convergence side and divergence side.

We developed the app for measuring fusional amplitude and vergence hysteresis on HMD (Fig. 5). Green dots with same brightness were presented on the center of the right- and left- display. Participants saw the one green dot combining the dot on the right display with that on the left display. Using two arrow keys ($\leftarrow$, $\rightarrow$), they measuring the break point and recovery point at the convergence side and at the divergence side in order. Convergence was the direction in which two green dots on the right display and the left display approached, and divergence was the direction away from each other.

Sixteen subjects were participated in this experiment for two days. They watched the same video with and without matching user-specific visual axis alignment. In the condition of matching visual axis alignment, the position of the left- and right-image was adjusted to fit the visual axis. In the condition of non-matching visual axis alignment, the image on the left was presented to a quarter point based on the x axis of the screen and the image on the right was presented at 3/4 points of the screen. Each point was the center on the left- and right display. The watching order was randomized. In order to make it unknown what condition the participants were assigned to, we measured the visual axes under all conditions.

Before watching the video, participants the score of subjective visual fatigue and then they conducted the app twice for measuring the fusional amplitude and vergence hysteresis. The first trial was the practice for learn how to operate the app, so these data were not used for analysis. Participants watched the S3D video during about 10 min. After watching video, they rated the subjective visual fatigue and performed the app for measuring objective visual fatigue (Fig. 6).

We performed the repeated ANOVA using minitab 16. As the result of the subjective visual fatigue, the main effect of the condition before and after watching the video was

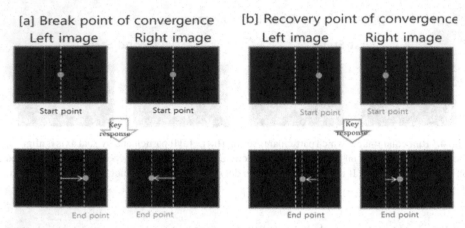

Fig. 5. Process of measuring fusional amplitude. [a] a break point is the position which one dot is divided into two. [b] a recovery point is the position which two dots are fused with one. (Color figure online)

Fig. 6. Procedure of experiment

significant (p < 0.001). The main effect of matching visual axis alignment was not significant (Fig. 7). Participants felt more fatigue after watching S3D video by HMDs, but the user-specific visual axis alignment did not affect fatigue.

As the result of the objective visual fatigue, divergence hysteresis was significant differently according to the condition of matching visual axis alignment (F(1,42) = 4.93, p = 0.032) (Fig. 8). The shorter the vergence hysteresis showed that participants merged the two dots into one dot although the positions of two dots moved slightly from the break point. This meant the muscles of eyes had less fatigue and participants were able to fuse two images easily. This result implies that when participant's visual axis and the position of images are aligned correctly, visual fatigue is able to be reduced. Fusional amplitude was marginally significant according to the condition of before and after watching (F(1,42) = 3.47, p = 0.069). However, other conditions were not significant (Table 1).

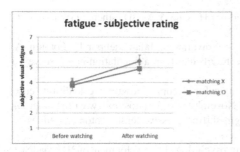
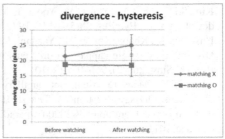

Fig. 7. (Left) The scores of subjective visual fatigue under all conditions, (Right) The vergence hysteresis at divergence side under all conditions

Table 1. Statistical values for all conditions.

Condition		Fusional Amplitude	Convergence Hysteresis	Divergence Hysteresis
Before &After	F	3.47	0.43	0.61
	p	0.069	0.53	0.44
Matching Alignment	F	2.06	0.53	4.93
	p	0.159	0.47	0.032^*

3   Conclusion

In this study, we explored the possibility whether visual fatigue is reduced by matching the position of images on the HMD display with participants' visual axis. Although the participants did not feel that visual fatigue decreased depending on matching visual axis alignment, the objective index showed that the muscles of their eyes had less fatigue.

Not everyone has the same eye shape and visual axis. If we provide images that are modified to match the characteristics of eyes of a person, people will be able to see images more comfortably. In this study, we observed the effect of matching the visual axis among several characteristics of eyes. Further researches about the effects of other characteristics are needed.

References

1. Mosquera, S.A., Verma, S., McAlinden, C.: Centration axis in refractive surgery. Eye Vis. **2**(1), 4 (2015). https://doi.org/10.1186/s40662-015-0014-6
2. Basmak, H., Sahin, A., Yildirim, N., Saricicek, T., Yurdakul, S.: The angle kappa in strabismic individuals. Strabismus **15**(4), 193–196 (2007)
3. Kim, S.-H., Suh, Y.-W., Yun, C., Yoo, E.-J., Yeom, J.-H., Cho, Y.A.: Influence of stereopsis and abnormal binocular vision on ocular and systemic discomfort while watching 3D television. Eye **27**, 1243–1248 (2013)
4. Granet, D., Rosenberg, M.A.: 3D headache may be 'avatar' of strabismus or other binocular vision condition. European Society of Cataract and Refractive Surgeons (2010)

5. Kim, S.H., Suh, Y.W., Yun, C.M., Yoo, E.J., Yeom, J.H., Cho, Y.A.: 3D asthenopia in horizontal deviation. Curr. Eye Res. **38**(5), 614–619 (2013)
6. Hashemi, H., KhabazKhoob, M., Yazdani, K., Mehravaran, S., Jafarzadehpur, E., Fotouhi, A.: Distribution of angle kappa measurements with Orbscan II in a population-based survey. J. Refract. Surg. **26**(12), 966–971 (2010)
7. Clark, T.H.: Measure visual, not pupillary, axis for accurate progressive addition lenses placement, OD says. Optometry Times, 01 November 2011. https://www.willistonoptome trist.com/wp-content/uploads/2020/09/paradigm-shiftprogressive-lenses-optometry-times-nov-dec-2011.pdf
8. Li, H.O., Kim, E.S.: The role and contribution of psychology for development of 3D broadcaste system. Korea Soc. Broadcast Eng. Mag. **6**(2), 10–21 (2001)
9. Emoto, M., Nojiri, Y., Okano, F.: Changes in fusional vergence limit and its hysteresis after viewing stereoscopic TV. Displays **25**(2), 67–76 (2004)

The Effects of Dual Display Configuration and Users' Experience on Performance and Preference in Complex Spatial-Verbal Tasks

Cheng-Jhe Lin[✉] and Yu-shao Chen

National Taiwan University of Science and Technology, Taipei 106, Taiwan
Robert_cjlin@mail.ntust.edu.tw

Abstract. Working from home has become popular during Covid-19 pandemic and it promoted the use of dual displays to handle complex information coming with multi-tasking. Previous studies have shown that the use of dual displays can produce better performance; however, the effects of different dual display configurations on users' performance in complex spatial-verbal tasks have not been systematically discussed. Furthermore, whether the user is experienced in utilizing dual displays may affect their performance and preference such as assignment of software windows. The current study investigated task completion time and user behaviors (window assignment, head turning counts and the number of window switches) in four display configurations (preferred primary-secondary screens, swapped primary-secondary screens, unified screens, and a single screen) via a realistic experimental task where participants operated 3D street view on Google Map (spatial task) to answer relevant questions in MS Word (verbal task). The results from 30 participants showed that the swapped primary-secondary screens (where the window assignment was different from the participant's preference) and the unified screen caused significant more window switching and head turning; the task completion time also increased insignificantly. The participants experienced in using dual screen performed better than the non-experienced ones in all configurations but the unified screens. The experienced participants subjectively reported that they preferred to perform longer and more complicated operations on the primary display while the non-experienced ones said the opposite. Through this study the user behaviors in spatial-verbal tasks using dual displays were understood and guidelines were provided to improve user performance.

Keywords: Dual Display · Display Configurations · Window Assignment

1 Introduction

1.1 A Subsection Sample

Since the Covid-19 pandemic many technology companies, including Facebook, Microsoft, Apple and Twitter, announced that their employees could work from home and some of them may never need to come back to offices [1]. Working from home

C. Stephanidis et al. (Eds.): HCII 2023, CCIS 1832, pp. 351–357, 2023.
https://doi.org/10.1007/978-3-031-35989-7_45

required remote conferencing and dealing with large amount of information in multiple windows. A study showed that 78.1% of time users opened more than 8 windows [2] to handle office work. Given this situation, the use of dual dis-plays has become more popular and important. Past studies also showed that using dual displays can increase work efficiency by 3.1% or more, depending on the nature of the work [3, 4]. However, various configurations of dual displays and associated window assignment were reported in the past studies, but no systematic investigation has been conducted to understand how window assignment in dual displays would affect work efficiency and effectiveness.

For example, a primary display might be placed in front of the user while a secondary display on the (left/right) side [3, 5]. This specific configuration accompanied a particular type of window assignment where important tasks (and its associated window), such as data entry and problem solving, were placed on the primary screen, while secondary tasks, such as instant messaging, referencing or entertainment, were put on the side. In contrast, two displays might be placed side-by-side so that there was no distinction between the primary and secondary screen. It was un-known, though, whether such an extended display which unified dual screens would affect users' experience and performance, especially when the task is a complex spatial-verbal task where the user needs to process spatial and verbal information simultaneously to solve a particular problem. Another factor to consider is the experience of the user in terms of using dual displays. A study has shown that users who were experienced in using dual displays would more likely benefit from switching between single and dual displays because of their familiarity to the configuration [5]. It is therefore of research interest to know whether experienced users would be influenced to a greater extent if the window assignment is not optimal/preferred when using dual displays.

2 Method

2.1 Participants

Thirty participants (24.4 ± 3.9 years old) were recruited in the experiment. Fifteen of them used one display most of the time (95 ± 9%) while the rest was accustomed to dual displays (91 ± 10% of time). The former ones was classified into single display group (SG) while the latter ones to dual display group (DG).

2.2 Experimental Task

The experimental task was a problem-solving task combing spatial and verbal parts. The participants were instructed to operate 3D street view on Google map to find a designated location so that the questions presented in MS Word files could be answered. The questions were about particular information of a building and its surrounding area. The participants needed to use the addresses provided to locate the building and manipulate the street view to obtain spatial knowledge required. After all information required by the questions was obtained, the participants should take a screenshot from a specified angle and fill all information to the table of the questions in the MS Word files.

2.3   Experimental Variables

In the experiment, participants were asked to perform the task using four kinds of display configurations:

1. Preferred: in this configuration, the participant used dual displays arranged as show in Fig. 1. The 2 software programs (windows) required for the task, i.e. Google Chrome and MS Word, were assigned according to the participant's preference. That is, the participant determined whether s/he wanted the Google Chrome for operating Google Map application to be positioned on the primary display (the one in the front) or the secondary display (the one on the right), and the MS Word would be placed on the other display. Then the separation and included angle between the two displays could be adjusted based on the participant's preference.
2. Swapped: in this configuration, the physical settings were identical to Fig. 1. However, the window assignment was the opposite to that in the preferred configuration. For example, if the participant wanted the Google Chrome to be positioned on the primary display, the Google Chrome would be placed on the secondary display instead, and vice versa.
3. Unified: in this configuration dual displays were combined as a large extended display where there was no gap between the two but the included angle (initially 160 degrees) could be adjusted (Fig. 2).
4. Single: only one display was used in this configuration.

Fig. 1. Preferred configuration

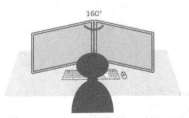

Fig. 2. Unified configuration

During the task the following response variables were measured:

1. Task completion time: the time elapsed between the onset of the task (when the experimenter said "start") and the end of the task (the participant finished the final question).

2. Head-turning count: when the participant turned her/his head from one display to another, the head-turning count would increase by one. Note that if the participant turned her/his head to the keyboard, the count remained unchanged.
3. Window-switching count: the window-switching count was calculated based on the click to the software program window. When the participant clicked one window and then another, the window-switching count would increase by one.

Besides the abovementioned quantitative and objective measures, subjective responses were also reported via questionnaire.

3 Results

3.1 Task Completion Time

The task completion time using four different display configurations were shown in Fig. 3. The results from ANalysis Of VAriance (ANOVA) demonstrated that there was neither significant main effects nor interaction among the four conditions. However, it can be found that the swapped configuration caused the task completion to increase insignificantly while the preferred one allowed the shortest completion time.

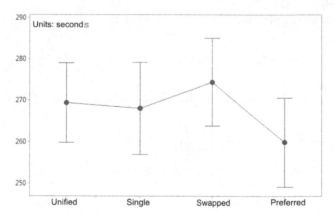

Fig. 3. Task completion time

3.2 Head-Turning Count

The head-turning counts observed from the three display configurations[1] were plotted in Fig. 4. The ANOVA revealed that there was a significant effect of display configurations (F-value = 4.73, P-value = 0.013) but not interaction. Further pair-comparison indicated that the preferred configuration caused significantly fewer head-turning count than that of the swapped one, while head-turning count from the unified configuration did not differ significantly than that from the other two.

---

[1] Head-turning count was unavailable when only one display was used.

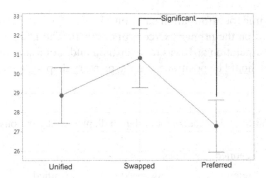

Fig. 4. Head-turning counts

3.3 Window-Switching Count

The window-switching counts observed from the four display configurations were illustrated in Fig. 5. The ANOVA revealed that there was also a significant effect of display configurations (F-value = 21.41, P-value <0.01) but not interaction. Further pair-comparison indicated that the preferred configuration caused significantly fewer window-switching count than that of the swapped one, and the count observed from single configuration was significantly lower than that from the other three.

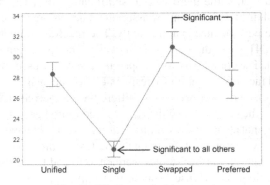

Fig. 5. Window-switching counts

3.4 Subjective Responses

In the questionnaire, the participants' preferences for the display configurations were investigated (see Table 1). It was obvious that most of the participants preferred the primary-secondary display setting with windows positioned to their preference. However, such a preference was quite different in SG and DG. For SG participants, 12/15 positioned the MS Word on the primary display, while for DG participants 13/15 positioned the Google Chrome on the primary display. Further inquiry to the participants in SG and DG revealed their different reasoning. The SG participants considered that they spent most of time for information entry on MS word, i.e. the activity intensive one should be positioned on the primary screen. In contrast, The DG participants reflected that the 3D map manipulation task was more critical and required more attention so that the Google Chrome should be positioned on the primary display, i.e. the more important one.

Table 1. The counts for preferred display configurations

User group	Reported preference			
	Preferred	Swapped	Unified	Single
SG	8/15	0/15	4/15	3/15
DG	9/15	0/15	6/15	0/15

4   Conclusion and Discussion

The current study investigated how display configurations and user experience in using dual displays would affect performance and preference in complex spatial-verbal tasks. The results showed that, while there was no significant difference in task completion time, the use of dual displays and window assignment according to the user's preference could improve time performance insignificantly. The result is compatible to that of the previous studies [3, 4] where the improvement was found to be significant but not in a great extent (3.1%). The complexity of the spatial-verbal task used in the current study could be a potential factor which might be responsible for the insignificant improvement.

The user behaviors, however, were quite different on preferred and swapped display configuration in that the swapped dual displays caused more head-turning and window-switching, implying that a higher level of physical activity might have been required, but the participant somewhat managed to complete the task at the same performance level in terms of time efficiency. Further studies were encouraged to look at this assumption by measuring physiological responses from the participants to confirm higher degree of internal resource mobilization.

Furthermore, it was quite interesting to observe participants accustomed to use dual displays preferred different window assignment than that of participants who were used to a single display. Although their preferred window assignments were contradictory to each other, they all perform better under their respective preferred conditions. User habits may explain why different display configurations served different groups of users relatively well, but from an absolute point of view, positioning the software program window associated with a critical task (not necessarily the most time consuming one) may be optimal and guarantee better performance in the long run when the task is considerably difficult and challenging. The user should therefore develop their habits carefully and choose the right configuration at the beginning so that the potential cap for the task performance can be raised at the end.

References

1. Hong Kong Economy Times, Mark Zuckerberg: half of Facebook employees are expected to work from home eternally. https://inews.hket.com/article/2650397/%E6%9C%B1%E5%85%8B%E4%BC%AF%E6%A0%BC%E6%96%99Facebook%E4%B8%80%E5%8D%8A%E5%93%A1%E5%B7%A5%E5%8F%AF%E6%B0%B8%E4%B9%85%E5%9C%A8%E5%AE%B6%E5%B7%A5%E4%BD%9C
2. Hutchings, D.R., et al.: Display space usage and window management operation comparisons between single monitor and multiple monitor users. In: Proceedings of the Working Conference on Advanced Visual Interfaces, pp. 32–39 (2004)
3. Poder, T.G., et al.: Dual vs. single computer monitor in a Canadian hospital Archiving Department: a study of efficiency and satisfaction. Health Inf. Manag. J. **40**(3), 20–25 (2011)
4. IDC. IDC Info Brief - Improving Employee Productivity with Dual Monitors (2015). http://i.dell.com/sites/doccontent/shared-content/data-sheets/en/Documents/Dual_Monitors_Boost_your_productivity.pdf
5. Kang, Y., Stasko, J.: Lightweight task/application performance using single versus multiple monitors: a comparative study. Proc. Graphics Interf. **2008**, 17–24 (2008)

The Experiment Study on Evaluation Method of Mental Fatigue in Cognitive Task Based on Physiological Signals

Zhongqi Liu[1,2], Ze Li[1,2], and Qianxiang Zhou[1,2(✉)]

[1] School of Biological Science and Medical Engineering, Beihang University, Beijing 100191, China
lzq505@163.com
[2] Beijing Advanced Innovation Centre for Biomedical Engineering, Beihang University, Beijing 102402, China

Abstract. TloadDback task experiment with personalized stimulus presentation time was designed to induce mental fatigue. The effect of mental fatigue induction was verified by analyzing the subjective score, behavioral performance data and physiological signal data (The EEG data, ECG data and eye movement data were collected in the experiment). Deep learning method was used to explore the best combination of physiological signals for mental fatigue evaluation according to different combinations of EEG, ECG and eye movement data. The results showed that the combination of EEG and eye movement signals had the highest accuracy of 92.61%.

Keywords: Mental fatigue · Evaluation · Cognition · EEG signal · ECG signal · Eye movement

1 Introduction

Mental fatigue affects the function of attentional and executive regions, leading to difficulty suppressing irrelevant information during selective attention [1], increased time required for planning, reduced task engagement [2], impaired cognitive control [3], reduced ability to process higher-level information [4], and even lead to decreased physical performance [5]. Mental fatigue affects performance in many occupations and is one of the most common causes of accidents and human error in today's world [6].

Mental fatigue is difficult to identify and quantify, and self-assessment of mental fatigue may be unreliable and cannot be monitored in real time. Therefore, it is of great theoretical significance and application value to study the evaluation method of mental fatigue based on physiological signals and provide a stable and reliable evaluation method of mental fatigue for avoiding accidents caused by mental fatigue in high-risk tasks and providing better production efficiency management in daily tasks involving manual operations.

Mental fatigue [7] is a phenomenon in which people experience subjective fatigue feeling, changes in some physiological and psychological functions of the body, and obvious decline in their ability to work during or after the cognitive activities that require continuous mental attention.

The main objective of this study is to design a reasonable cognitive task to induce mental fatigue, study the changes of physiological signal characteristics in the process of inducing mental fatigue, establish an evaluation model of mental fatigue based on physiological signals, study the best combination of physiological signals for the evaluation of mental fatigue, and provide theoretical basis for the objective evaluation of mental fatigue.

2 Method

2.1 Subjects

In this experiment, 38 subjects were selected, all male, aged 18–23 years old (mean age 20.33 years old, SD = 1.2 years old).All subjects had normal vision or corrected to normal, right-handed, no history of mental illness or neurological disorders, and no history of drug or alcohol addiction. All participants signed an informed consent form. This experiment was approved by the Ethics Committee.

2.2 Experiment Content

The research of Kate O'Keeffe [8] shows that personalized TloadDback is an effective method to induce mental fatigue, and it can maintain the physiological wake-up state in the process of inducing mental fatigue and reduce the generation of drowsiness and boredom.

TloadDback task is a dual task, consisting of a classic N-Back working memory update task and a second interference task—parity judgment task. This experiment uses a combination of 1-back task and parity judgment task. In the TloadDback task, letters and numbers appear alternately on the screen. When a letter appears on the screen, the subjects are required to judge whether it is the same as the previous letter. If it is the same, press the "s" key. If it is different, no response is required; When a number appears on the screen, the subjects are required to judge whether it is odd or even. If it is odd, press the "j" key, and if it is even, press the "k" key. The task uses 21 letters—A, C, D, E, F, G, H, J, K, L, M, N, P, R, B, T, U, V, W, X, Y and 8 numbers—1, 2, 3, 4, 6, 7, 8, 9. Visually similar letters are excluded (such as O, I, S, Z), and the number "5" is also excluded to ensure the same number of odd and even numbers. Numbers and letters are presented in pseudorandom order. Each block includes 480 stimuli, and the correct rate of each block is calculated by weighting the correct rate of letters and numbers. The correct rate of letters and numbers accounts for 65% and 35% of the total score respectively. The stimulus presentation time was personalized according to the cognitive ability of the subjects through the pre-experiment. The task diagram is shown in Fig. 1.

During the experiment, the subjects' EEG data, ECG data, eye movement (EM) data, subjective evaluation data and behavioral performance data were recorded. The subjective questionnaire was selected from the "Self-Rating Scale of Fatigue Symptoms (2002)" compiled by the Industrial Fatigue Research Institute of the Japanese Industrial

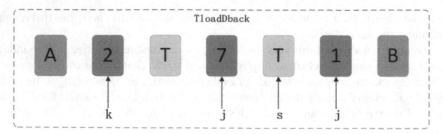

Fig. 1. TloadDback experiment task

Health Association [9]. Behavioral performance indicators include task accuracy and response time. The correct rate of tasks is calculated by weighting the correct rate of the letter task and the number task in each trial phase, with the correct rate of the letter task and the number task accounting for 65% and 35% of the total score respectively. The response time (RT) of the task refers to the time interval from the time the stimulus appears to the time when the subject presses the button to respond.

2.3 Experimental Equipment

The equipment used in the experiment is as follows:

(1) Task presentation computer

The task presentation computer is a laptop with Windows 7 system. The experimental task is written with E-prime 3.0. The task computer is equipped with E-prime 3.0, which can present the experimental task and subjective scale, and record the responses and performance data of the subjects.

(2) EEG acquisition equipment

The EEG acquisition equipment used in this experiment is a 32-channel EEG acquisition system produced by BP (Brain Products) in Germany, mainly including EEG signal amplifier, 32-channel EEG cap, and EEG signal synchronous acquisition system. The electrode arrangement of EEG cap adopts the "10–20" international standard lead placement method. Brain VisionRecorder3 software was used to record EEG signals. The sampling frequency is 1000 Hz.

(3) ECG acquisition equipment

Three-lead MP150 ECG acquisition module is selected for ECG acquisition equipment.

(4) Eye movement acquisition equipment

In this experiment, the German SMI RED eye tracker was used to record EM signals.

2.4 Experimental Procedures

This experiment is mainly divided into three stages: practice stage, pre-test stage and formal experiment stage. In the practice stage, the subjects need to be familiar with the fatigue induced task. In this stage, a block contains 60 stimuli, including 30 numbers and 30 letters. The stimulus presentation time is set to 1500 ms. The correct rate is calculated for each block practiced by the subjects, until the subjects subjectively express that they are familiar with the experimental operation and the correct rate is greater than 85%, and then stop the practice. The subjects have sufficient rest time between each block in the practice stage, to eliminate the impact of mental fatigue on task accuracy. In the pre-test stage, each block contains 60 stimuli, including 30 numbers and 30 letters, and the stimulus presentation time will decrease from 1500 ms, and the correct rate is calculated once for each block. When the correct rate is greater than 85%, the next block will be entered, and the stimulus presentation time will be reduced by 100 ms until the correct rate is lower than 85%. The subjects will repeat the experiment process with this stimulus presentation time, if the accuracy rate is still lower than 85%, then the stimulation presentation time of the above block (the shortest stimulation presentation time that the subject can maintain 85% accuracy) is used as the personalized stimulation presentation time of the subject's fatigue induction task. Before the pre-test stage, the subjects were informed that the task difficulty would increase and the reaction time would decrease. In addition, between each block, the subjects have sufficient rest time, and they can start the next block after recovering to a good state, so as to avoid the impact of mental fatigue during the pre-test on the personalized setting of the stimulus presentation time (SPT). The individualized stimulus duration set by each subject is shown in Table 1.

Table 1. Stimulus presentation time

Subject NO	S1	S2	S3	S4	S5	S6	S7	S8	S9	S10	S11	S12	S13
SPT(ms)	800	1000	600	700	600	800	500	600	800	600	700	700	900
Subject NO	S14	S15	S16	S17	S18	S19	S20	S21	S22	S23	S24	S25	S26
SPT(ms)	800	900	800	800	600	600	600	600	1000	700	1000	900	800
Subject NO	S27	S28	S29	S30	S31	S32	S33	S34	S35	S36	S37	S38	
SPT(ms)	700	800	900	1200	800	900	800	800	700	700	900	800	

3 Results

3.1 Subjective Fatigue Data

During the experiment, the subjective fatigue of the subjects showed an obvious upward trend. The average subjective score of the subjects in the first two test stages was lower than 4 points, and there was no obvious mental fatigue in the subjective sense; from the third test stage, the state of mental fatigue gradually appeared. The distribution of subjective scores in the third to fourth stages was from 4 to 6, and the subjects gradually transited to the stage of mental fatigue; From the fifth stage, the subjects showed obvious mental fatigue subjectively; In the last two experimental stages, the subjects were subjectively in a more serious mental fatigue state; After the rest and recovery stage, the subjective score of the subjects decreased significantly to less than 5 points, indicating that the mental fatigue induced by this cognitive task can be recovered through rest, belonging to acute fatigue.

3.2 Performance Data

During the task period, the correct rate of the subjects showed a significant downward trend, and the decline trend of the correct rate in the third stage was the most obvious. From the fourth test stage, the average correct rate of the subjects was lower than 85%. A repeated measure ANOVA was performed on the correct rate of the subjects during the cognitive task process, and the result was $P < 0.001$. There was significant difference in the correct rate during the cognitive task process. Mental fatigue is manifested by subjective fatigue and the decline of work ability. Therefore, the significant reduction of task accuracy can reflect that the degree of mental fatigue of the subjects gradually deepens with the extension of the test time. After the fourth stage, the correct rate could not be maintained at 85%. Combining with the subjective score, it can be seen that the subjects had obvious mental fatigue after the fourth stage.

During the task, the average reaction time of the subjects showed an upward trend. The reaction time of the subjects was prolonged, and the reaction speed became slower, which reflected the deepening of fatigue to a certain extent. After the fourth test stage, the average reaction time of the subjects was greater than the average reaction time of the pre-test stage, reflecting that the subjects entered the state of mental fatigue after the fourth stage from the perspective of reaction time.

4   EEG Signal Index

EEG Power Spectrum Feature Analysis. Selected the relative power of four waves of $\alpha, \beta, \delta, \theta$, and the relative power ratio $(\theta + \alpha)/\beta, \alpha/\beta, (\theta + \alpha)/(\alpha + \beta), \theta/\beta$, a total of eight indicators were used to evaluate the changes of EEG power spectrum characteristics during the cognitive task-induced mental fatigue.

The results showed that after cognitive task-induced mental fatigue, from the whole brain area, the relative power of δ wave and θ wave increased, the relative power ofαwave decreased significantly, and the relative power of βwave decreased slightly; The relative power of δ wave, θ wave and α wave had the same trend in the frontal region, central region, parietal region, occipital region and temporal region, showing that the relative power values of δ wave and θ wave increased, and the relative power value of α wave decreased obviously; The relative power value of β wave had different trends among different brain regions, increasing in frontal and central regions, and decreasing in parietal, occipital and temporal regions.

EEG Entropy for Assessment of Mental Fatigue. According to the change curve of the five non-linear indicators of EEG during the task—approximate entropy, sample entropy, fuzzy entropy, wavelet entropy and Hilbert yellow entropy, it can be seen that with the extension of cognitive task time, the five entropy characteristics have a downward trend on the whole. During the development of mental fatigue state, the data distribution of approximate entropy, sample entropy, fuzzy entropy and spectral entropy is similar, and the entropy value in fatigue state is lower than that in normal state. The change of EEG entropy characteristics is consistent with the subjective feelings of the subjects. Through the subjective questionnaire, when the subjects enter the fatigue state, their thinking activities will decrease, their sense of tiredness will increase, and the uncertainty of EEG signals will decrease, resulting in the decrease of EEG entropy

4.1 ECG Signal Index

It can be seen from the results that the average heart rate basically remained unchanged in the first six stages, and decreased in the seventh stage; NN-mean, SDNN, RMSSD and pNN50 showed an upward trend during the whole test, and the increase was most obvious in the last block; In the frequency domain index, total power (TP) showed an upward trend, and the rising speed gradually slowed down; Low frequency power (LF) showed an upward trend during the whole test process; High frequency power (HF) showed an overall upward trend in the seven test stages, and the upward trend was obvious in the first, second and third stages. The third, fourth, fifth and sixth stages were basically unchanged, and the last block rose significantly. There was no significant change in LF/HF as the cognitive task progressed.

4.2 Eye Movement Index

The increase of pupil diameter in the second stage of the test may be due to the increase of attention. From the third stage, the pupil diameter decreased significantly, indicating that people began to enter the fatigue state. Then, with the extension of the task time, the pupil diameter continued to decline, and the fatigue state gradually deepened. Some studies have shown that the decrease of arousal level is related to the decrease of sympathetic nervous system activity, which makes the pupil diameter smaller. The decrease of pupil diameter during fatigue induction may be related to the leading role of parasympathetic nerve, which is also similar to the mechanism of heart rate reduction under fatigue.

With the progress of mental fatigue-induced tasks, the average blink frequency first increased and then decreased, and the average blink duration showed an upward trend. Blink frequency and blink duration can well represent the changes of mental fatigue. The blink frequency increased in the second stage, and then decreased from the third stage, and from the fourth stage, the blink frequency was lower than the initial value, indicating that with the deepening of fatigue, the blink frequency decreased and the blink time extended.

5   Mental Fatigue Evaluation Model

The deep learning methods, especially the Convolutional Neural Networks (CNN) and Long Short-Term Memory (LSTM), have achieved better results in the research of mental state recognition. Both EEG and ECG signals are continuous-time signals with a lot of storage contents. LSTM has the characteristics of long-term selective memory mode, and has a good effect on feature extraction and classification of physiological signals. Because EEG signal contains channel information, two-dimensional convolution neural network is used to extract EEG signal features.

As one of the representative algorithms of deep learning, CNN can adaptively obtain useful information from the original input signal through multiple nonlinear transformations and approximate complex nonlinear functions.

In this study, a one-dimensional CNN network was used to extract fatigue-related features of heart rate variability, and a two-dimensional CNN network was used to extract fatigue-related features of EEG signals. The EM signal feature uses three EM features: pupil diameter, blink frequency, and blink duration. The extracted relevant features are fused at the full connection layer, and input into the LSTM network layer to achieve the classification and evaluation of fatigue state. The model adopts single signal of EEG and ECG for classification, evaluation of mental fatigue, as well as classification and evaluation of the fusion method of EEG and EM, ECG and EM, EEG and ECG, EEG, ECG and EM. The evaluation indexes and accuracy of classification models of different physiological signal data sets are shown in Table 2:

Table 2. Evaluation index of model

Data	Accuracy	Precision	Recall rate	F1score
EEG	87.62%	85.61%	90.40%	87.94%
ECG	63.10%	63.45%	61.84%	62.63%
ECG + EM	69.60%	68.28%	73.20%	70.65%
EEG + ECG	73.23%	73.77%	72.00%	89.37%
EEG + EM	92.61%	92.77%	92.40%	92.53^
EEG + ECG + EM	82.98%	81.94%	84.42%	83.16%

It can be seen that among the three physiological signals, EEG signal, ECG signal and EM signal, the EEG signal feature has the best effect on the evaluation of mental fatigue, while the ECG signal feature has poor effect on the evaluation of mental fatigue. The fusion analysis of EEG signal feature and EM signal feature has the best effect on the evaluation of mental fatigue, with the highest accuracy rate of 92.61%.

References

1. Faber, L.G., Maurits, N.M., Lorist, M.M.: Mental fatigue affects visual selective attention. PLoS ONE **7**(10), 1–10 (2012)
2. van der Linden, D.: The impact of mental fatigue on exploration in a complex computer task: rigidity and loss of systematic strategies. Hum. Fact. J. Hum. Fact. Ergon. Soc. **45**(3), 483–494 (2003)
3. Lorist, M.M., Boksem, M.A., Richard, K.R.: Impaired cognitive control and reduced cingulate activity during mental fatigue. Cogn. Brain Res. **24**(2), 199–205 (2005)

4. Masaaki, T., Yoshihito, S., Masami, F., et al.: Fatigue-associated alterations of cognitive function and electroencephalographic power densities. PLoS ONE 7(4), 1–5 (2012)
5. Samuele, M., Walter, S., Victoria, M.: Mental fatigue impairs physical performance in humans. J. Appl. Physiol. **106**(3), 857–864 (2009)
6. Lew, F.L., Qu, X.: Effects of mental fatigue on biomechanics of slips. Ergonomics **57**(12), 1927–1932 (2014)
7. van DLD, Eling P. Mental fatigue disturbs local processing more than global processing[J]. Psychological Research Psychologische Forschung,70(5):395–402(2006)
8. Kate, O., Simon, H., Alex, L.: A comparison of methods used for inducing mental fatigue in performance research: individualised, dual-task and short duration cognitive tests are most effective. Ergonomics **63**(1), 1–12 (2020)
9. Zhang, Z.X., Zhang, J.: About the Japanese 《Self-Rating Scale of Fatigue Symptoms.》Chin. J. Ergon. **9**(3), 60–62 (2003)

Training an EOG-Based Wordometer Without Reading – A Simple HCI Application to Quantify Reading Metrics

Matthew Mifsud[1,2(✉)], Tracey A. Camilleri[2], and Kenneth P. Camilleri[1,2]

[1] Centre for Biomedical Cybernetics, University of Malta, Msida, Malta
[2] Department of Systems and Control Engineering, University of Malta, Msida, Malta
matthew.mifsud@um.edu.mt

Abstract. Reading is the activity through which humans decipher written symbols in an effort to extract information from written text. Whether written on paper, or displayed on a screen, literacy can be considered as a valuable tool to one's social and educational development. Through the use of electrooculography (EOG), as a means of tracking one's eye movements, this work presents the development of a novel Wordometer application, capable of measuring the quantity of reading. Through the incorporation of a novel light-weight cue-based training protocol, this application obtained an average word estimation error of 8.23% when tested across five human subjects using EOG data.

Keywords: Electrooculography · Eye tracking · Wordometer

1 Introduction

The reading efficiency of an individual can be measured by calculating one's word count while reading, possibly giving an indication of any reading limitations or ophthalmological deficiencies. Furthermore, such a statistic can in turn motivate individuals to improve their reading volumes and provide clinicians with information on the reading patterns of an individual. The eye movements of an individual while reading can be tracked using EOG which is based on recording the changes in electrical potential around the eyes of the user through electrodes placed in close proximity to the user's ocular globes. The recorded potential directly reflects the nature of the eye movements performed.

Current EOG-based wordometer applications assume that the number of words read is equal to the number of detected saccades [1] or use a static average word count per line to derive a word estimate [7]. Other approaches rely on black-box Support Vector Regression (SVR)-based approaches which are training intensive [3,6]. In contrast, this work presents the development of a novel wordometer application which exploits known word skipping tendencies [10] that dictate the statistical relationship between the number of words read and the number of saccades performed by the user. These word skipping probabilities were combined with a word length distribution and used to estimate the number of words read from the detected saccades. This tool can be encapsulated within a human-computer interaction (HCI) application allowing users to read text presented on a computer screen and extract relevant metrics in a simple manner which may, for example, help motivate young readers to improve their reading skills, or provide valuable information to clinicians to help determine reading difficulties in patients.

The rest of this paper is organized as follows: Sect. 2 presents the manifestation of eye movements while reading, Sect. 3 discusses the experimental protocol together with the acquisition and processing of EOG signals while reading and Sect. 4 presents the classification measures used for the different eye movements while reading. This is followed by Sect. 5 which presents the word estimation approach and its performance when tested by a number of human subjects and Sect. 6 which concludes this paper.

2   Manifestation of Eye Movements While Reading

While reading, the human eyes tend to fixate on the majority of the words present such that they are captured into foveal vision for a detailed analysis. In turn, saccadic eye movements are performed so as to divert one's foveal vision onto a new region of text and hence proceed with the flow of the content [10]. However, whilst reading, some words, such as prepositions and pronouns, are not fixated upon. Rayner and McConkie [10] show that the probability of a fixation increases as the length of the word increases. Short two- to three-letter words are only fixated upon about 25% of the time, whilst words having eight letters or more are almost always fixated upon [10]. When reading in English, most saccades are performed from the left to the right-hand side, however, readers occasionally perform regressive saccades to previously read words [10]. Such regressions are normally attributed to the reader not understanding the text, oculomotor errors, or very long saccades which require a small corrective regression so as to proceed with the content of the text. This work aims to go beyond the state of the art by exploiting this information when extracting reading metrics, as discussed in the following sections.

3   Data Collection and Processing

3.1   Hardware Framework

Five subjects (mean age 24.0 ± 2.10 years) participated in this study which was approved by the University Research Ethics Committee (UREC) at the University of Malta. Subjects' EOG data was recorded using the conventional electrode setup which consists of six surface electrodes connected in close proximity to the user's eyes as shown in Fig. 1.

Specifically, electrodes 'A' and 'B' record data attributed to the horizontal EOG channel, 'C' and 'D' record data attributed to the vertical EOG channel, 'G' is a ground electrode and 'R' is a reference electrode. Data was recorded through the g.USBamp biosignal amplifier [4] at a sampling frequency of 256 Hz and a 50 Hz notch filter attenuated any line artefacts.

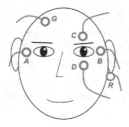

Fig. 1. Conventional six electrode EOG setup.

3.2   Pre-processing of EOG Data

Eye movement events in the electrooculogram manifest themselves with frequency components ranging from 0–100 Hz [5], however, EOG signals representing reading activities, reside at lower frequencies of around 10–11 Hz [11]. In an effort to preserve such reading signal characteristics, a filtering process was required to suppress artefacts introduced from external sources and improve the signal to noise ratio. In this regard, the first step was to determine the two bipolar channels EOG_h and EOG_v using the recorded EOG signals from the conventional setup. Subsequently, a median filter was applied to attenuate noise levels which would otherwise interfere in later stages of signal classificiation. The final step was to take the derivative of the horizontal and vertical median filtered bipolar EOG channels. This is because, saccades are represented as peaks in the derivative signal, and through proper derivative window selection, the amplitude of the saccade can be preserved. On the other hand, fixations and regions of no change in potential are diminished. An important characteristic of the difference signal is that it mitigates any wander in the baseline of the EOG signal.

3.3   Manifestation of EOG Data While Reading

Fig. 2 summarises how different eye movements manifest themselves in the electrooculogram while reading. The positive peak enclosed in a yellow rectangle corresponds to a blink and this does not appear in the horizontal EOG component. The red rectangles around the negative vertical peaks in the derivative signal represent leftward ocular movements that occur when the reader starts a new line of text, thus performing a return saccade. The blue rectangles show smaller positive peaks representing the small saccades performed by the user between successive fixations.

3.4   Cued Data Collection

The data collection process aimed at having users perform controlled eye movements similar to those carried out during reading, while also providing ground truth information on when a saccade or blink was performed and the corresponding ocular angles attributed with those eye movements. An experimental protocol

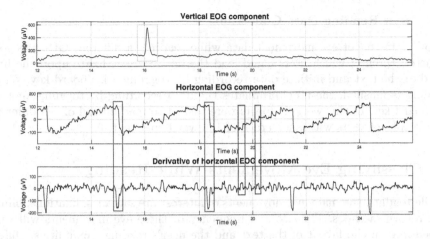

Fig. 2. Manifestation of eye movements while reading in EOG. (Color figure online)

was devised for this data collection process with a main graphical user interface (GUI) displaying cues moving in a horizontal fashion as shown in Fig. 3, mimicking human reading patterns. Cue displacements were generated randomly in order to collect a wide range of saccadic displacement sizes and to avoid having the user predict the cue's next position, hence leading to saccades being performed prematurely and interfering with the timing windows dictated by the GUI. In the cue-outputting program, an initial starting cue is displayed at the top left corner of the screen, followed by a sequence of two-second trials. Each trial consists of a yellow cue displayed for one second instructing the user to fixate upon this cue, followed by a red cue displayed for another one second instructing the user to blink. After this, another yellow cue appears in a new location, hence restarting another two-second trial whilst the previous cue is cleared.

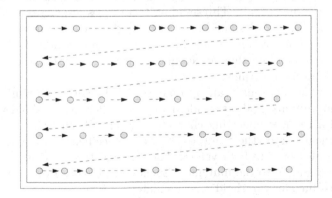

Fig. 3. Process of displayed cues mimicking reading patterns. (Color figure online)

3.5   Text Reading Data Collection

In order to collect eye movement data while reading, a different GUI was constructed through which users could load the desired text, fixate upon the first word of the text and initiate data recording by toggling a keyboard key. When reading is finished, the user terminates the data recording by toggling another keyboard key. In this work, subjects were tasked to read a total of ten different paragraphs of texts with an average of 136 words per text.

4   Classifying Eye Movements While Reading

While reading, the main eye movements of interest are saccades, fixations, blinks and return saccades. The size and frequency of these eye movements will vary depending on the layout of the text and the user's reading capabilities. Different individuals will tend to read through a section of text differently due to various psycholinguistic factors governing eye movements such as age, language proficiency and the content of the text [10]. Furthermore, the nature of the eye movements performed will vary in terms of saccade sizes, fixation durations and overall reading speed. The characteristics of these ocular activities shed light on the user's capabilities or limitations while reading such as difficulties in processing the words in the text, reflected in slow reading speeds, and possibly dyslexia, reflected through unstable fixations and erratic eye movements [9]. To this effect, the following sections will focus on the automatic detection and classification of different eye movements while reading using EOG data, which information can be presented to the user or clinician through the application.

4.1   Classifying Forward Saccades

Through proper saccade classification from the horizontal EOG channel, inferences can be carried out regarding the number of words read and other parameters such as reading speeds. Thresholding techniques are a standard approach for the detection of saccades and blinks in EOG data [6,11]. Since saccades performed while reading traverse a small distance, the amplitude of such saccades in EOG is very small and thus an adequate threshold is vital in distinguishing such events from noise within the signal.

In an effort to determine an optimal threshold which maximizes saccade detection and minimizes false saccade detection, different threshold values were iterated and a receiver operating characteristic (ROC) curve was constructed. The latter encapsulates the trade off between specificity and sensitivity of a classifier at different threshold values. The optimal threshold is taken as that value c corresponding to the minimum Euclidean distance from the (0,1) point where the distance for threshold c is calculated as follows:

$$Distance(c) = \sqrt{(1 - Sensitivity(c))^2 + (1 - Specificity(c))^2} \quad (1)$$

4.2 Classifying Blinks

Blinks manifest themselves as large peaks within the vertical EOG channel which are significantly higher than the potential on the same channel resulting from return saccades. Hence a threshold value can clearly distinguish blinks from other eye movements. To find this threshold, an average of the amplitude of ten blink related peaks from the recorded cued data was found and the threshold was set to half this value.

4.3 Classifying Return Saccades

Return saccades manifest themselves as large negative peaks in the horizontal EOG channel. The threshold for return saccades was set to three times that required for forward saccades and was operated in the negative portion of the electrooculogram.

4.4 Estimating the Number of Words Read

In this study, the word estimation procedure is based on the number of detected fixations, identified as those time windows between two successive saccades. As discussed in Sect. 2, the reader does not fixate on every word, but words are skipped. Vitu et al. [2] and Rayner et al. [10] describe various skipping probabilities associated with the length of the word considered. Based on these findings, it can be deduced that the number of fixations only represents a portion of the number of words read and excludes the number of skipped words. This implies that an estimate of the number of words read $\hat{W}$, can be found by re-compensating for the number of skipped words. Mathematically this can be done by taking the estimated number of words read $\hat{W}$, to be equal to the estimated number of fixations $\hat{F}$, multiplied by a scaling factor k where $k > 1$. In order to determine a reasonable value of k, the respective proportion of word skipping tendencies described by Rayner et al. and Vitu et al. [2,10] were taken into account together with a word length frequency distribution [8]. Determining the value of k was based on the fact that the number of words is the summation of the total number of skipped words SW and the fixated number of words $\hat{F}$. SW is the summation of the skipped words SW_i for all word lengths i, with $i = \{1,2,...,6,7+\}$, and SW_i is the product of the skipping probability P_i and the number of words N_i of that particular word length i. N_i, on the other hand, is a fraction of the total number of words $\hat{W}$ and can be calculated as $N_i = R_i\hat{W}$ where R_i is the frequency of occurrence of words with length i. Mathematically, this can be represented by:

$$SW = \sum_{i=1}^{i=7+} SW_i = \sum_{i=1}^{i=7+} P_i N_i = \sum_{i=1}^{i=7+} P_i R_i \hat{W} \qquad (2)$$

Finally, using the statistics suggested by Rayner et al. and Vitu et al. [2, 10], which describe skipping probabilities of 80% for one-letter words, 60% for three-letter words, 30% for five-letter words and 10% for seven letters or longer, together with the word length distribution [8], leads to:

$$\hat{W} = \frac{1}{0.7528}\hat{F} \tag{3}$$

Using this equation, and having derived an estimate of the number of fixations, an estimate of the number of words read could be determined.

5 Word Estimation Results

This section presents the word estimation results obtained using the proposed approach and compares them to those obtained using the SVR-based approach of Ishimaru et al. [6] and to a static word count approach assuming a static word count of 9.5 words per line as in [7]. The results of the five recruited subjects tabulated in Table 1, show that an average word estimation error of 8.23% was obtained using the proposed approach in comparison to an average of 11.83% obtained using Ishimaru et al.'s method [6] and 41.48% using the static word count approach [7]. From the obtained results it can be noted that the use of an average word count per line greatly reduces the accuracy of the Wordometer application as the performance of the system solely depends on the detection of return saccades. Furthermore, this static word count method fails to extract any information from the actual forward saccades performed by the user on each line of text. On the other hand, Ishimaru et al's approach [6] requires users to read multiple passages of text in order to train the SVR-based approach. In this regard, such a training approach is impacted by the content of the text and the user comprehending the text, which in turn impacts the fixation duration, length of the saccades and the frequency of regressions and blinks performed by the user [10].

In contrast, the proposed approach operates using subject-specific parameters which are not affected by different psycholinguistic factors governing how an individual reads through a passage of text. This is because our approach solely relies on different colored cues which instruct users to perform different ocular movements having randomly varying displacements so as to collect different saccade sizes, analogous to those performed while reading, from which an optimal threshold is determined.

Table 1. Word estimation results using the EOG data of five human subjects.

Subject	Word estimation error (%)		
	This work	SVR-based approach [6]	Static word count [7]
S1	6.45	16.62	37.92
S2	6.65	9.67	39.73
S3	10.73	11.18	61.38
S4	11.26	10.52	36.24
S5	6.04	11.19	32.14
Average	**8.23**	**11.83**	**41.48**

6   Conclusion

This work has presented the development of an EOG-based Wordometer application with a light-weight cue-based training approach, requiring users to simply gaze upon cues mimicking reading patterns. This novel training approach yields subject specific parameters used to detect multiple ocular movements, and is agnostic to psycholinguistic factors which arise when training using actual texts [6]. Furthermore, this work has exploited known word skipping tendencies [2,10] which dictate the relationship between the number of words read and the number of saccades performed by the user. The presented results show that accurate word estimates, better than the state of the art, may be obtained with relatively short training times of approximately 50 s without requiring users to read a number of texts prior to using the application.

References

1. Banerjee, A., Rakshit, A., Tibarewala, D.: Application of Electrooculography to estimate word count while reading text. In: 2016 International Conference on Systems in Medicine and Biology (ICSMB), pp. 174–177 (January, 2016)
2. Brysbaert, M., Drieghe, D., Vitu, F.: Word skipping: implications for theories of eye movement control in reading. In: Cognitive Processes in Eye Guidance, pp. 53–78. Oxford University Press (July, 2005)
3. Andreas, D., et al.: Quantifying reading habits - counting how many words you read. In: The 2015 ACM International Joint Conference on Pervasive and Ubiquitous ComputingAt: Osaka, Japan (September, 2015)
4. gtec: g.USBamp BIOSIGNAL Amplifier. https://www.gtec.at/product/g-usbamp-research/ (2019). Accessed December-2019
5. Huda, K., Hossain, M., Ahmad, M.: Recognition of reading activity from the saccadic samples of electrooculography data. In: 2015 International Conference on Electrical & Electronic Engineering (ICEEE), pp. 73–76 (November, 2015)
6. Ishimaru, S., Kunze, K., Kise, K., Dengel, A.: The wordometer 2.0: estimating the number of words you read in real life using commercial EOG glasses. In: UBICOMP/ISWC 2016 ADJUNCT, pp. 293–296 (September, 2016)
7. Kunze, K., Katsutoshi, M., Uema, Y., Inami, M.: How much do you read? counting the number of words a user reads using electrooculography. In: Proceedings of the 6th Augmented Human International Conference, pp. 125–128. AH 2015, Association for Computing Machinery, New York, NY, USA (2015)
8. Norvig, P.: English Letter Frequency Counts. https://norvig.com/mayzner.html. Accessed 20 Dec 2022
9. Prado, C., Dubois, M., Valdois, S.: The eye movements of dyslexic children during reading and visual search: impact of the visual attention span. Vis. Res. **47**, 2521–2530 (2007)
10. Rayner, K.: Eye Movements in reading and information processing: 20 Years of research. Psychol. Bull. **124**, 372–422 (1998)
11. Rui, O., Zhao, L., Pei, W., Chao, Z., GAO, X.: Design and implementation of a reading auxiliary apparatus based on electrooculography. IEEE Access PP, 1–1 (2017)

Visualization of Attention Concentration Area of P300-Speller BCI

Yusuke Minamio[1]($\boxtimes$), Hisaya Tanaka[1], Raita Fukasawa[2], Akito Tsugawa[2], and Soichiro Shimizu[2]

[1] Department of Informatics, Kogakuin University Graduate School, 2665-1, Nakano-cho, Hachioji-shi, Tokyo 192-0015, Japan
em22022@ns.kogakuin.ac.jp
[2] Department of Geriatric Medicine, Tokyo Medical University, 6-1-1, Shinjuku, Shinjuku-ku, Tokyo 160-8402, Japan

Abstract. Currently, the number of patients with dementia is increasing worldwide. The incidence of mild cognitive impairment (MCI), a pre-dementia stage, is also on the rise. It has been reported that 50% of patients with MCI will transition to dementia within 5 years. Therefore, early detection is important to prevent the progression of dementia. For the purpose, we are developing an inexpensive and simple cognitive screening method using the P300-Speller, a spelling-BCI based on event-related potential P300. It is a mechanism whereby P300 is elicited when the subject gazes at a certain letter in the matrix. Subsequently, the character is estimated using a discrimination scores (DSs) calculated based on the P300 component. As cognitive function declines, the subject's ability to pay attention concentration is impaired, thereby increasing the chance of incorrect input. By focusing on these DSs, we think that this method can be used to confirm differences and screen patients. In this study, we used the sigmoid function to represent the probability of these DSs. We created a probability distribution map. As a result, we confirmed that with each progression of dementia, the scatter of the data increased with respect to the character that was the focus of attention. In addition, statistical processing was applied to the variance values combined with SEDV. The results of Bonferroni's multiple comparisons confirmed a significant difference of 1% between all groups (i.e., normal control, MCI, and Alzheimer's disease). The differences in probability distribution maps suggest that this method is useful for screening for dementia.

Keywords: P300-Speller · Dementia · Attention

1 Introduction

The number of elderly individuals with dementia in Japan is increasing; it is expected that approximately 20% of elderly individuals aged >65 years will develop dementia [1]. As of 2012, the estimated number of individuals with mild cognitive impairment (MCI) is 4 million [2]. MCI has been linked to a high rate of transition to dementia, with 16.5% of patients developing dementia within 1 year [3]. Nevertheless, advances in medical science have led to the development of therapeutic drugs for Alzheimer's disease (AD), which can prevent disease progression [4]. In addition, in some cases (~24%), early treatment can reverse MCI to normal control (NC) [5]. Therefore, the early detection of dementia is of great importance. However, patients with dementia tend to be unwilling to seek medical attention at hospitals, thereby reducing the chance of early treatment. It has been reported that the average period from the time a family member perceives a change that triggers suspicion of dementia until the first visit to a medical institution in 7.4 months [5]. As a solution to this problem, it is expected to develop tools that can be implemented in a simple manner and can assist healthcare professionals in diagnosis. The availability of such a tool may help overcome the shortage of specialists on dementia [6].

We are currently developing an inexpensive and simple cognitive function screening tool using the P300-Speller, which uses event-related potential P300. The tool analyzes electroencephalography (EEG) when the subject gazes at a single character (target character) on a dial to estimate which character (presumed character) they view. Kurihara et al. [7] demonstrated the relationship between spelling-error distance value (SEDV), which is the distance between the target letter and the presumed letter, and cognitive decline. These findings suggested the possibility of a simple screening tool. The distance between the target letter and estimated letter of the P300-Speller is calculated. It has been found that SEDV increases as the patient's attentional focus declines. However, worsening of cognitive decline was not observed in some subjects with high SEDV despite MCI. Therefore, we evaluated the attention distribution of the surrounding characters of the estimated character by: 1) visualizing the character distribution for the discrimination score, which is the input principle of P300-Speller [8]; 2) developing a new maximum discrimination score (MDS), which is the maximum value of the discrimination score, and 3) determining the area of attention concentration (AAC), which is the number of characters for which the discrimination score takes a positive value. AAC, which is the number of letters, and the possibility of classifying NC, MCI, and AD was suggested (currently submitted to IJAE). However, MDS and AAC are calculated based on discriminant scores (DSs), which vary widely among individuals, thereby affecting the accuracy of feature classification.

The purpose of this study was to visualize the distribution of attention probability on the dial by probabilizing discriminant scores using the sigmoid function and evaluating them according to the cognitive function.

2   BCI-Based Prediction Techniques for Dementia

2.1   SEDV

SEDV is one of the parameters obtained by P300-Speller proposed by Kurihara et al. It represents the weighted average distance between the target letter and the estimated letter, and is an indicator of reduced attentional focus in patients with dementia [7]. SEDV is determined by Eq. (1).

$$SEDV = \begin{cases} 0 (i = j = 0) \\ \frac{1}{2}\sqrt{i^2 + j^2}(i = 0 \cup j = 0) \\ \sqrt{i^2 + j^2}(i = 0 \cap j = 0) \end{cases} \tag{1}$$

If i or j equals 0, then the P300-Speller principle has successfully input the row or column, and the calculation to halve the SEDV is performed. If i and j do not equal 0, both rows and columns are incorrect on the P300-Speller, and the process is continued as is.

Kurihara et al. demonstrated the association between SEDV and cognitive decline, suggesting the possibility of realizing a simple screening tool; SEDV has been found to increase with decreased attentional focus. Nonetheless, SEDV did not take a significant difference between NC-MCI, and the introduction of an index that clearly separates these two states remains a challenge.

2.2 Tsallis Entropy

Nishizawa et al. [9] evaluated cognitive function based on Tsallis entropy. The Tsallis entropy is a measure of the amount of information in data, which is lower when the time-series EEG is regular and higher when it is irregular. In particular, the Tsallis entropy decreases as cognitive function declines. Significant differences were found between NC and MCI and Cz electrodes at $p < 0.05$ in the θ- and α-wave bands. This suggested the possibility of predicting MCI by measuring the Tsallis entropy.

2.3 Classifier Cognitive Function

Fukushima et al. [10] examined the possibility of dementia classification using measures related to the type of dementia. Linear discriminant analysis, support vector machine, and K-nearest neighbor were used as classification models. The inputs were SEDV, P300 latency, P300 discrimination rate, and input letter correct response rate for each task; MCI and AD were the outputs. The results showed a high classification accuracy of 87.80% for the classification of MCI and AD. The classification accuracy by neuropsychological testing was 71.69%, suggesting that classification of cognitive function by BCI is feasible. However, the classification of three groups (i.e., AD, MCI, and dementia with Lewy bodies) exhibited low accuracy.

3 How to Visualize Attention Concentration with BCI

3.1 Letter Estimation Method by Attention Concentration

In this study, we used a system termed P300-Speller, which is a text-based BCI using event-related potentials P300. An event-related potential P300 is a positive potential that is often expressed on the parietal midline when directed at a low frequency (typically 20%) for two or more identifiable stimuli. It is named P300 because of the positive P and the latency around 300 ms. It has been found that the latency of P300 is prolonged with cognitive decline [11]. In this study, P300 was elicited using blinking letters as stimuli and target letters as low-frequency stimuli.

Figure 1 shows the P300-Speller screen used in this study. It consists of 6 rows and 10 columns according to the Japanese syllabary. The subject gazes at a predetermined target character for several tens of seconds to spell it. The system side triggers event-related potentials P300 by randomly blinking the dials on the screen in rows and columns (five times for each row and column). The computer detects the response, adds up and averages the brain waves per row and column, and estimates the estimated character that is the intersection of the row and column in which the P300 was detected.

Fig. 1. P300-Speller screen

For the detection of P300, it is necessary to obtain EEG patterns of the target letter and avoid gazing in advance. By creating a statistical discriminator, it is possible to measure the presence or absence of P300 (i.e., the degree of attentional focus on a letter) for an unknown EEG. In this study, discriminators were created using Fisher's linear discriminant. In the process, the discriminant score y(x) calculated for each matrix is determined by Eq. (2).

$$y(x) = f\left(w^T x + b\right) \tag{2}$$

Here, x is the EEG data obtained using this tool, w is the weight vector calculated by Fisher's linear discriminant, and b is the bias. The weight vector w is a linear discriminant function consisting of 120 cycles of eight electrodes × 15 cells, and the bias b consisting of 121 parameters is added. Positive and negative values for DS indicate the presence and absence of a P300 component in the EEG, respectively. The DSs are added and averaged in rows and columns to form DS(id), and the estimated character is determined from the row and column with the largest DS(id). Here, "id" indicates the number of the row/column position, and takes values from 1 to 10 for columns and from 11 to 16 for rows.

3.2 Visualization of DS by a Probabilistic Model

A probability distribution map of attentional concentration in the estimated letters was created based on the discrimination scores. The sigmoid function in Eq. (3) was used to display the probability. This function converts any input value x into a number in the range from 0 to 1.

$$sig(x) = \frac{1}{1 + e^{-x}} \tag{3}$$

The Discriminant Score Probability (DSP) is the probability representation of DS(id) obtained earlier through Eq. (4). Here, Eq. (4) is the DSP for columns. A sigmoid function was applied to each column and divided by the sum of the probabilities of all the columns, resulting in a total DSP of 1 for the column. This time col takes values from 1 to 10. For the rows, the "col" in Eq. (4) is changed to "row" and the process is repeated. The "row" can take values from 11 to 16.

$$DSP(col) = \frac{sig(DS(col))}{\sum_{k=1}^{col} sig(DS(k))} \tag{4}$$

Next, the relative probability of each character is the Spelling Attention Probability (SAP), which is calculated using Eq. (5). Since this is the relative probability in all letters in the dial, it represents the probability in the range of 6×10 for one letter of interest; the SAP is added up and visualized for the number of letters in the task. Consequently, the estimated letters are aligned.

$$SAP(row, col) = DSP(row) \times DSP(col) \tag{5}$$

4 Experiment

4.1 Subject Information

This report is based on 64 subjects aged 64–90 years who visited the Department of Geriatric Medicine at Tokyo Medical University (Tokyo, Japan) between 2018 and 2021. Table 1 shows the age, sex ratio, and mini-mental state examination (MMSE) scores of the subjects who underwent EEG measurements. MMSE is an interactive neuropsychological test that assesses cognitive function, and MMSE scores tend to be lower as cognitive function declines.

Table 1. Subject details

Variable	NC	MCI	AD
N (M/F)	8 (4/4)	33 (15/18)	23 (11/12)
Age (y) (m±SD)	71-88 (78.5 ± 3.0)	64-90 (78.9 ± 1.0)	71-89 (79.1 ± 1.1)
MMSE (m±SD)	28.8 ± 0.5	28.6 ± 1.8	23.0 ± 0.5

This study was based on the Kogakuin University's research ethics review for human subjects "New Cognitive Function Testing Method for Early Diagnosis of Dementia 2019-B-18," and the Tokyo Medical University's ethics review, "Early Diagnosis of Dementia Using Brain-Computer Interface (BCI) 2016-083."

4.2 System

The display shows a six-line, 10-column Japanese P300-Speller screen (Fig. 3); the dial flashing is operated by a laptop personal computer. Numerical analysis software MATLAB2012a (MathWorks) was used for EEG measurement, stimulus presentation, and analysis processing. In the EEG measurements, a low-pass filter of 30 Hz, a high-pass filter of 0.5 Hz, and a notch filter of 50 Hz were set. EEG was measured using active EEG electrodes (g.LADYbird; g.tec), data was collected using an electrode box (g.SAHARAbox; g.tec), and signals were amplified using a bioamplifier (g.USBamp; g.tec). A total of eight electrodes were used (Fz, Cz, P3, Pz, P4, PO7, Oz, and PO8). The back of the right earlobe and the center of the forehead were used as the reference and ground electrodes, respectively.

4.3 Task

In the measurement, the target characters were "あんこもち" (twice) and "あめのちは れ" (twice), and a total of four inputs (hereinafter referred to as the task) were performed. The subject was asked to look at the target character on the display, and to speak when the character lit up. A 1-min interval between tasks was provided to reduce subject fatigue. Of the four measured data, the first task was treated as training data for linear discriminant analysis, and the remaining three tasks ware used for analysis.

5 Results and Discussion

Figure 2 shows the relative probability diagram according to cognitive function per task. The distribution of SAP is shown with the location of the estimated letter as (0, 0, z); the z direction represents the SAP; the z direction represents the SAP.

As shown in Fig. 2, we confirmed that attention tends to be diverted to letters other than the presumed letter as cognitive function declines. The index that evaluates the degree of this distraction is the attention probability variance (APV). The SEDVmatrix is the SEDV calculated by Eq. (1) centered at (0,0) and has the same positional relationship as in Fig. 2. *mu* is the expected value, which is the sum of the product of the SEDVmatrix and the SAP corresponding to that position.

$$APV = \sum_{i=1}^{row} \sum_{j=1}^{col} (SEDVmatrix(i,j) - mu)^2 \times SAP(i,j) \tag{6}$$

Figure 3 shows the APV according to cognitive function. Analysis of variance confirmed a main effect with $p < 0.01$. In addition, Bonferroni's multiple comparisons confirmed a significant difference ($p < 0.01$) between NC and all groups, as well as between MCI and AD. This revealed a tendency for attention to be diverted beyond the estimated letters, and the APV (the variance value) tended to be significantly increased as cognitive function declined.

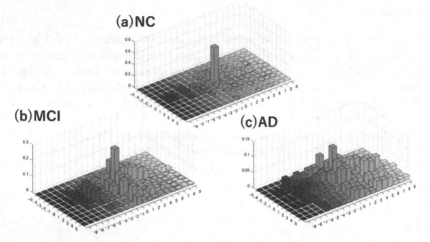

Fig. 2. The Relative probability plot according to cognitive function (a) NC patient (MMSE = 30); (b) MCI patient (MMSE = 28); (c) AD patient (MMSE = 27)

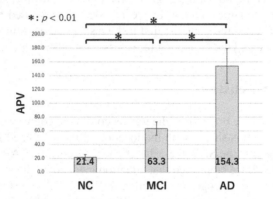

Fig. 3. APV according to cognitive function

6   Conclusion

In this study, we developed a method to visualize cognitive decline using the P300-Speller. The aim was to apply this method to the examination of MCI, a precursor stage of dementia. In previous studies, the SEDV, which represents the weighted average distance between input and estimated letters, has been effective in classifying MCI and AD. However, the classification of NC and MCI, SEDV focused on the distance between input and estimated letters. Therefore, in this study, we aimed to visualize the distribution of attentional probability on the letter board by converting DSs into probability using the sigmoid function, and evaluate the results according to cognitive function. In addition, a new index, APV, which represents the variance of the distribution of attention probability on the dial, was validated.

The results showed that the APV was significantly increased ($p < 0.01$) among all groups (i.e., NC, MCI, AD) as cognitive decline tended to divert attention beyond the estimated letters. This suggests that APV is an effective classification index for dementia. In the future, we aim to increase the number of subjects and improve the predictive accuracy of this method.

References

1. MHLW Homepage. https://www.mhlw.go.jp/file/06-Seisakujouhou-12300000-Rouken kyoku/nop1-2_3.pdf. Accessed 4 Mar 2023
2. MHLW Homepage. https://www.mhlw.go.jp/file/05-Shingikai-12601000-Seisakutoukatsu kan-Sanjikanshitsu_Shakaihoshoutantou/0000065682.pdf. Accessed Accessed 4 Mar 2023
3. Petersen, R.C., et al.: Alzheimer's Disease Neuroimaging Initiative (ADNI): clinical characterization. Neurology **74**(3), 201–209 (2010)
4. Kutoku, Y., et al.: Drug Treatments of Dementia. Jpn. J. Rehabil. Med. **55**(8), 643–647 (2018)
5. Black, C.M., et al.: The diagnostic pathway from cognitive impairment to dementia in Japan: quantification using real-world data. Alzheimer Dis. Assoc. Disord. **33**(4), 346–353 (2019)
6. MHLW Homepage. https://www.mhlw.go.jp/bunya/iryou/other/dl/01.pdf. Accessed 4 Mar 2023
7. Kurihara, R., et al.: A new assessment method for the cognitive function in dementia using the spelling-BCI. J. Hum. Interf. Soc. **21**(1), 21–30 (2019)
8. Minamio, Y., et al.: Visualization of spatial attention on the BCI cognitive test screen. In: International Symposium on Affective Science and Engineering, pp. 1–4 (2022)
9. Nishizawa, Y., et al.: Prediction of mild cognitive impairment using P300-Speller BCI - studies of the EEG with Tsallis entropy and coherence –. J. Hum. Interface Soc. **25**(1), 1–10 (2023)
10. Fukushima, A., et al.: Classification of dementia type using the brain-computer interface. Artif. Life Robot. **26**, 216–221 (2021)
11. Indoria, et al.: A study of P300 and mini mental state examination in mild cognitive impairment and Alzheimer's dementia. Sch. J. Appl. Med. Sci. **5**(8C), 3132–3140 (2017)

Two Heads Are Better Than One: A Bio-Inspired Method for Improving Classification on EEG-ET Data

Eric Modesitt[1]([✉]), Ruiqi Yang[2], and Qi Liu[3]

[1] University of Illinois Urbana-Champaign, Champaign, USA
ericjm4@illinois.edu
[2] University of California Santa Barbara, Santa Barbara, USA
ruiqiyang@ucsb.edu
[3] Palo Alto High School, Palo Alto, USA
ql39535@pausd.us

Abstract. Classifying EEG data is integral to the performance of Brain Computer Interfaces (BCI) and their applications. However, external noise often obstructs EEG data due to its biological nature and complex data collection process. Especially when dealing with classification tasks, standard EEG preprocessing approaches extract relevant events and features from the entire dataset. However, these approaches treat all relevant cognitive events equally and overlook the dynamic nature of the brain over time. In contrast, we are inspired by neuroscience studies to use a novel approach that integrates feature selection and time segmentation of EEG data. When tested on the EEGEyeNet dataset, our proposed method significantly increases the performance of Machine Learning classifiers while reducing their respective computational complexity.

Keywords: Machine Learning · SVM · KNN · Boosting · Brain-Computer Interfaces · EEG-ET Classification · Feature Selection · Bio-inspired Learning

1 Introduction

Electroencephalography (EEG) applications for classifying motor imagery tasks are significant for their medical purposes in assisting disabled civilians. However, historically Brain-Computer-Interfaces (BCI) have been limited by a lack of data, a low signal-to-noise ratio, and data's nonstationarity over time [24,25,33].

Additionally, prior neuroscience studies show that patients' neural activity tends to continually decrease as a patient learns to complete a new task (Fig. 1). Based on these results, we expect that different time-segmented partitions of EEG data produce vastly different feature representations. After all, according to previous neuroscience studies, well-learned tasks produce completely different neural signals than tasks that haven't been learned [14], so it follows that distinct time-segmented data partitions should be treated as different. In this work, we were motivated by such findings to create the Two Heads method, where we split the EEG-ET (EEG-Eye Tracking) data by individual

---

E. Modesitt, R. Yang and Q. Liu—These three authors contributed equally.

C. Stephanidis et al. (Eds.): HCII 2023, CCIS 1832, pp. 382–390, 2023.
https://doi.org/10.1007/978-3-031-35989-7_49

subject, concatenated the results, and applied feature selection. Our method was tested on EEGEyeNet's Left Right (LR) task dataset (publicly available) to classify saccade direction using EEG-ET data [17].

2   Related Work

Classification models are typically designed in such a way that assumes every input corresponds with a fundamentally similar set of features to other inputs, thus allowing the models to learn these essential features [12, 16, 31, 38, 48]. Most popular feature selection methods for EEG take into account this typical design [10, 34, 35]. Such approaches include simple statistical transformations such as Principal Component Analysis (PCA) and Independent Component Analysis (ICA) [2, 13, 43], the selection of filter banks [19, 44], and other algorithms that transform high dimensional feature spaces based on individual model performance [5, 22, 23, 37].

However, given the adaptive nature of the brain when learning a new task, it is unclear whether the features learned in one segment of our data would share underlying features with data in another time segment. Current approaches that work towards a solution to the non-stationarity of EEG include adding adaptiveness to the model in either feature extraction process [21, 29, 41] or the classification process [1, 4, 20]. However, relevant solutions in the process of feature selection for EEG datasets are relatively lacking. Hence, we introduce the Two Heads method to address the dynamic nature of EEG data through a novel approach to selecting the best feature of subsets of data.

3   Methods

3.1   Two Heads Data Segmentation

Previous work introduces this segmentation of learning as a three-stage process, where the learner progresses from Novice to Intermediate, and finally to Skilled (Fig. 1). However, in this work, we decided to split the data into two parts. We made this deviation to reflect the difference in data collected per individual. Notably, the three fMRI shown in Fig. 1 images were taken over a 60-min interval per subject [14], whereas the EEGEyeNet dataset only records over a 15-min period per subject [17]. Therefore, to make up for the differences in length, we reduced the number of segmented stages of learning from three to two.

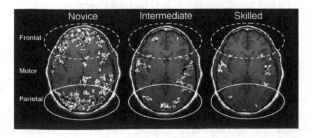

Fig. 1. Neural activity after 0 min (Novice), 30 min (Intermediate), and 60 min (Skilled) in a motor imagery task [14]

Starting from EEGEyeNet's baseline, we took EEG-ET data for each participant in the Left-Right task and modified the data. Accordingly, we split each individual subject's data into two disjoint time intervals of equal length. After splitting the first and second halves of individuals' data into groups 1H (1st Half) and 2H (2nd Half) respectively, we applied feature selection algorithms to these two separate data arrays.

3.2   Two Heads Feature Selection

After our data segmentation process, we extracted features by following the existing pipeline suggested by EEGEyeNet benchmark. The feature extraction process includes band-pass filtering at the alpha band (8–13 Hz), and applying a Hilbert transform on the filtered data. Finally, the phase and amplitude for each of the 129 channels were extracted as features [17]. Then we applied feature selection to our two distinct groups of features, each representing different time intervals (1H and 2H), separately. There are three common ways to select features, filter-based feature selection, wrapper-based feature selection, and embedded methods [18]. However, in this work, we only applied a filter-based feature selector due to concerns about the increased computational complexity that other feature selection methods could add. In particular, our results demonstrate our usage of Univariate Feature Selection from the implementation in the sklearn package, using the ANOVA F-value as our scoring mechanism. In the context of EEG, integrating these techniques could contribute to enhancing feature selection and classifier performance (Fig. 2) shows our entire pipeline.

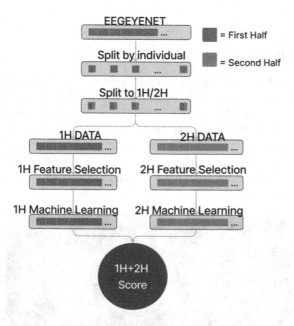

Fig. 2. Model flowchart, from EEGEyeNet to splitting by individual, to taking 1H/2H, to separate feature engineering and classification

3.3   Two Heads Training

As Fig. 2 shows, 1H and 2H feature sets were processed into separate training pipelines. The training pipeline split each segmented dataset into train, validation and test sets based on a proportion of 0.7:0.15:0.15. For our work, each of the eight ML classifiers shown in Table 1 was trained on five iterations of the same data, and we present the mean scores. Our results show little to no significant deviation in accuracy across iterations, resulting in us not reporting the standard deviation. The final score for each classifier is a weighted average of 1H and 2H classification accuracies.

4   Results

Table 1 shows the mean scores from the SOTA benchmark in EEGEyeNet and the mean scores of ML classifiers coupled with feature selection models without segmenting the EEG data into different time series. As portrayed in the table, this traditional method of implementing feature selection has improved the performance of all ML classifiers from the original SOTA benchmark.

The results demonstrated in Table 1 suggest that a traditional feature selection approach significantly improved all ML classifiers overall. However, the results of our Two Heads method in Table 1 suggest that our novel approach also improves the performance of ML classifiers on a grander scale.

Table 1. Results (classification accuracies in %) for state-of-the-art (SOTA) benchmark from EEGEyeNet, traditional feature selection (FS) and our 1H+2H approach of implementing feature selection. Mean scores of 5 runs of each considered classifier.

ML Classifier	SOTA	FS	1H (1st Half)	2H (2nd Half)	1H+2H
Gaussian NB	87.7	90.8	**94.6**	91.4	93.0
LinearSVC	92.0	92.1	**96.8**	88.7	92.7
KNN	90.7	96.1	**96.9**	95.7	96.3
RBF SVC/SVR	89.4	96.5	**97.5**	95.9	96.7
AdaBoost	96.3	96.5	**97.7**	95.2	96.4
Random Forest	96.5	96.9	**97.9**	96.4	97.1
Gradient Boost	97.4	97.5	**98.2**	96.9	97.5
XGBoost	97.9	98.1	**98.6**	97.6	98.1

In addition to our novel approach's contribution to expanding the marginal increase of ML classifiers' performance in comparison to both the SOTA benchmark and traditional feature selection, our procedure also manages to achieve a lower or equal runtime on all ML classifiers tested except random forest and gradient boost, as shown in Fig. 3. It suggests that our approach is promising not only in achieving higher accuracy but also in reducing computation complexity – which optimizes the performance-to-computation ratio for ML classifiers in comparison with current procedures.

Moreover, the result for 1H based on XGBoost even exceeds some deep learning classifiers. As tested in the EEGEyeNet benchmark, CNN achieves a mean accuracy of 98.3 [17] which is lower than the 98.6 mean score by our 1H approach using XGBoost.

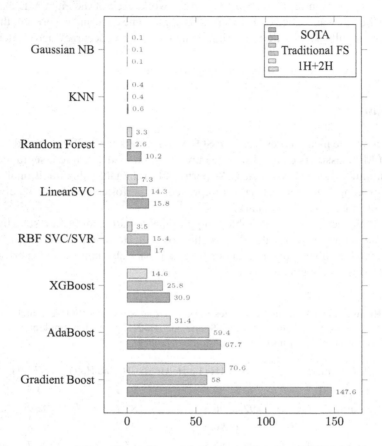

Fig. 3. Comparison of Run Time (Seconds) for state-of-the-art (SOTA) benchmark from EEGEyeNet, traditional feature selection (FS) method, and our 1H+2H approach of implementing feature selection. The mean of 5 trials for each method is measured.

5   Discussion

The comparison of our results to those from EEGEyeNet's SOTA benchmark and the traditional feature selection method suggests that our approach increases the performance of ML classifiers by a significant margin. In addition, although general feature selection also decreases the runtime for ML models to finish training, our novel method achieves an even lower runtime involved in training most of the ML models. Generalizing these accurate results suggests a new method for researchers to maximize the accuracy of ML classifiers while minimizing their computation complexity (namely, feature selection and splitting data into different time intervals). This could potentially lower the barrier to entry for EEG classification tasks, as successful future implementations of this method should guarantee that people would need fewer data samples and thus less computational power to achieve cutting-edge results.

Our work has two main directions for future work. Currently, our work has been tested only on the EEGEyeNet dataset. We would need more evidence to claim with certainty that this result generalizes to other EEG datasets such as GigaDB [9] and BCI Competition IV dataset [39]. Second, we tested our results on several machine learning models. We can not generalize that all types of predictive models (especially deep learning models) will follow the same trend of increased performance given our Two Heads method. Future work will focus on testing our method in SOTA deep learning architectures, including CNN, AutoEncoders [2], and so on. Other machine learning analysis for biomedical data [2,6,7,11,30,32,36,42] or other time series data [8,26–28,40,45–47] could be worth trying to compare with our approach on the same dataset. We would also like to examine the robustness of the models we have investigated, given the widespread attention to the vulnerability of machine learning models [15].

Finally, we urge future research to take into account the dynamic nature of the brain in their experiments. For example, researchers might create an ML model which helps steer a cursor on a screen for paralyzed patients. In this case, researchers could strategically focus their models on the segment of data where patients have learned how to complete the task, as this subset of data would produce a distinct result from the data collected while the patient is still learning. To tackle this issue, transfer learning can be employed to design a task-specific model with minimum effort of fine-tuning [3]. Regardless, this result motivates us to treat EEG data collected on novel tasks differently from EEG data collected on more well-learned tasks.

6 Conclusion

This paper proposes and tests a novel bio-inspired method to implement feature selection with ML classifiers. Through this approach, we found that the Two Heads method optimizes ML classifiers' performance-to-computation ratio and outperforms both the SOTA benchmark on EEGEyeNet and the traditional feature selection approach. Our findings suggest that time segmentation has a notable impact on EEG signals and prompts future research to consider the time component of EEG data during the data collection process and the training of ML classifiers.

References

1. Abu-Rmileh, A., Zakkay, E., Shmuelof, L., Shriki, O.: Co-adaptive training improves efficacy of a multi-day EEG-based motor imagery BCI training. Front. Hum. Neurosci. **13** (2019). https://doi.org/10.3389/fnhum.2019.00362, https://www.frontiersin.org/articles/10.3389/fnhum.2019.00362

2. Al-Saegh, A., Dawwd, S.A., Abdul-Jabbar, J.M.: Deep learning for motor imagery EEG-based classification: a review. Biomed. Signal Process. Control **63**, 102172 (2021)

3. An, S., Bhat, G., Gumussoy, S., Ogras, U.: Transfer learning for human activity recognition using representational analysis of neural networks. arXiv preprint arXiv:2012.04479 (2020)

4. Antony, M.J., et al.: Classification of EEG using adaptive SVM classifier with CSP and online recursive independent component analysis. Sensors **22**(19), 7596 (2022)

5. Baig, M.Z., Aslam, N., Shum, H.P., Zhang, L.: Differential evolution algorithm as a tool for optimal feature subset selection in motor imagery EEG. Exp. Syst. Appl. **90**, 184–195 (2017). https://doi.org/10.1016/j.eswa.2017.07.033, https://www.sciencedirect.com/science/article/pii/S0957417417305109

6. Bashivan, P., Rish, I., Yeasin, M., Codella, N.: Learning representations from EEG with deep recurrent-convolutional neural networks. arXiv preprint arXiv:1511.06448 (2015)

7. ChedID, N., Tabbal, J., Kabbara, A., Allouch, S., Hassan, M.: The development of an automated machine learning pipeline for the detection of Alzheimer's disease. Sci. Rep. **12**(1), 18137 (2022)

8. Chen, L., et al.: Data-driven detection of subtype-specific differentially expressed genes. Sci. Rep. **11**(1), 332 (2021)

9. Cho, H., Ahn, M., Ahn, S., Kwon, M., Jun, S.C.: EEG datasets for motor imagery brain-computer interface. GigaScience **6**(7), gix034 (2017)

10. Craik, A., He, Y., Contreras-Vidal, J.L.: Deep learning for electroencephalogram (EEG) classification tasks: a review. J. Neural Eng. **16**(3), 031001 (2019)

11. Deb, R., An, S., Bhat, G., Shill, H., Ogras, U.Y.: A systematic survey of research trends in technology usage for Parkinson's disease. Sensors **22**(15), 5491 (2022). https://doi.org/10.3390/s22155491

12. Deb, R., Bhat, G., An, S., Shill, H., Ogras, U.Y.: Trends in technology usage for Parkinson's disease assessment: a systematic review. MedRxiv. pp. 2021–02 (2021)

13. Guo, X., Wu, X., Gong, X., Zhang, L.: Envelope detection based on online ICA algorithm and its application to motor imagery classification. In: 2013 6th International IEEE/EMBS Conference on Neural Engineering (NER), pp. 1058–1061 (2013). https://doi.org/10.1109/NER.2013.6696119

14. Hill, N.M., Schneider, W.: Brain changes in the development of expertise: neuroanatomical and neurophysiological evidence about skill-based adaptations. In: Ericsson, K.A., Charness, N., Feltovich, P.J., Hoffman, R.R. (eds.) The Cambridge Handbook of Expertise and Expert Performance, pp. 653–682. Cambridge University Press (2006). https://doi.org/10.1017/CBO9780511816796.037

15. Jiang, C., He, Y., Chapman, R., Wu, H.: Camouflaged poisoning attack on graph neural networks. In: Proceedings of the 2022 International Conference on Multimedia Retrieval, pp. 451–461 (2022)

16. Jiang, C., Ngo, V., Chapman, R., Yu, Y., Liu, H., Jiang, G., Zong, N.: Deep denoising of raw biomedical knowledge graph from Covid-19 literature, Litcovid, and Pubtator: framework development and validation. J. Med. Internet Res. **24**(7), e38584 (2022)

17. Kastrati, A., et al.: Eegeyenet: a simultaneous electroencephalography and eye-tracking dataset and benchmark for eye movement prediction. arXiv preprint arXiv:2111.05100 (2021)

18. Khaire, U.M., Dhanalakshmi, R.: Stability of feature selection algorithm: a review. J. King Saud Univ. Comput. Inf. Sci. **34**(4), 1060–1073 (2022)

19. Kumar, S., Sharma, A., Tsunoda, T.: An improved discriminative filter bank selection approach for motor imagery EEG signal classification using mutual information. BMC Bioinform. **18**(S16),(2017). https://doi.org/10.1186/s12859-017-1964-6

20. Lahane, P., Jagtap, J., Inamdar, A., Karne, N., Dev, R.: A review of recent trends in eeg based brain-computer interface. In: 2019 International Conference on Computational Intelligence in Data Science (ICCIDS). pp. 1–6 (2019). https://doi.org/10.1109/ICCIDS.2019.8862054

21. Li, M.a., Zhu, W., Liu, H.n., Yang, J.f.: Adaptive feature extraction of motor imagery eeg with optimal wavelet packets and se-isomap. Applied Sciences 7(4), 390 (2017)

22. Liang, N., Bougrain, L.: Decoding finger flexion from band-specific ECOG signals in humans. Front. Neurosci. **6** (2012). https://doi.org/10.3389/fnins.2012.00091, https://www.frontiersin.org/articles/10.3389/fnins.2012.00091

23. Liu, A., Chen, K., Liu, Q., Ai, Q., Xie, Y., Chen, A.: Feature selection for motor imagery EEG classification based on firefly algorithm and learning automata. Sensors **17**(11) (2017). https://doi.org/10.3390/s17112576, https://www.mdpi.com/1424-8220/17/11/2576

24. Lotte, F., et al.: A review of classification algorithms for EEG-based brain-computer interfaces: a 10 year update. J. Neural Eng. **15**(3), 031005 (2018)

25. Lotte, F., Congedo, M., Lécuyer, A., Lamarche, F., Arnaldi, B.: A review of classification algorithms for EEG-based brain-computer interfaces. J. Neural Eng. **4**(2), R1 (2007)

26. Lu, Y., et al.: COT: an efficient and accurate method for detecting marker genes among many subtypes. Bioinformatics Advances **2**(1), vbac037 (2022)

27. Luo, X., Ma, X., Munden, M., Wu, Y.J., Jiang, Y.: A multisource data approach for estimating vehicle queue length at metered on-ramps. J. Transp. Eng. Part A Syst. **148**(2), 04021117 (2022)

28. Ma, X., Karimpour, A., Wu, Y.J.: Statistical evaluation of data requirement for ramp metering performance assessment. Transp. Res. Part A Policy Pract. **141**, 248–261 (2020)

29. Mousavi, M., Lybrand, E., Feng, S., Tang, S., Saab, R., de Sa, V.: Spectrally adaptive common spatial patterns. arXiv preprint arXiv:2202.04542 (2022)

30. Qian, P., Zhao, Z., Chen, C., Zeng, Z., Li, X.: Two eyes are better than one: exploiting binocular correlation for diabetic retinopathy severity grading. In: 2021 43rd Annual International Conference of the IEEE Engineering in Medicine & Biology Society (EMBC), pp. 2115–2118. IEEE (2021)

31. Qu, X., Liu, P., Li, Z., Hickey, T.: Multi-class time continuity voting for EEG classification. In: Frasson, C., Bamidis, P., Vlamos, P. (eds.) BFAL 2020. LNCS (LNAI), vol. 12462, pp. 24–33. Springer, Cham (2020). https://doi.org/10.1007/978-3-030-60735-7_3

32. Qu, X., Liukasemsarn, S., Tu, J., Higgins, A., Hickey, T.J., Hall, M.H.: Identifying clinically and functionally distinct groups among healthy controls and first episode psychosis patients by clustering on EEG patterns. Front. Psych. **11**, 541659 (2020)

33. Qu, X., Mei, Q., Liu, P., Hickey, T.: Using EEG to distinguish between writing and typing for the same cognitive task. In: Frasson, C., Bamidis, P., Vlamos, P. (eds.) BFAL 2020. LNCS (LNAI), vol. 12462, pp. 66–74. Springer, Cham (2020). https://doi.org/10.1007/978-3-030-60735-7_7

34. Qu, X., Sun, Y., Sekuler, R., Hickey, T.: EEG markers of stem learning. In: 2018 IEEE Frontiers in Education Conference (FIE), pp. 1–9. IEEE (2018)

35. Roy, Y., Banville, H., Albuquerque, I., Gramfort, A., Falk, T.H., Faubert, J.: Deep learning-based electroencephalography analysis: a systematic review. J. Neural Eng. **16**(5), 051001 (2019)

36. Saeidi, M., et al.: Neural decoding of EEG signals with machine learning: a systematic review. Brain Sci. **11**(11), 1525 (2021)

37. Tan, P., Wang, X., Wang, Y.: Dimensionality reduction in evolutionary algorithms-based feature selection for motor imagery brain-computer interface. Swarm and Evol. Comput. **52**, 100597 (2020). https://doi.org/10.1016/j.swevo.2019.100597, https://www.sciencedirect.com/science/article/pii/S221065021930286X

38. Tang, J., Alelyani, S., Liu, H.: Data classification: algorithms and applications. In: Data Mining and Knowledge Discovery Series, vol. 56, pp. 37–64. CRC Press (2014)

39. Tangermann, M., et al.: Review of the BCI competition IV. Front. Neurosci. **6**, 55(2012)

40. Vaswani, A., et al.: Attention is all you need. In: 30th Proceedings of Advances in Neural Information Processing Systems (2017)

41. Woehrle, H., Krell, M.M., Straube, S., Kim, S.K., Kirchner, E.A., Kirchner, F.: An adaptive spatial filter for user-independent single trial detection of event-related potentials. IEEE Trans. Biomed. Eng. **62**(7), 1696–1705 (2015). https://doi.org/10.1109/TBME.2015. 2402252

42. Yi, L., Qu, X.: Attention-based CNN capturing EEG recording's average voltage and local change. In: Artificial Intelligence in HCI: 3rd International Conference, AI-HCI 2022, Held as Part of the 24th HCI International Conference, HCII 2022, Virtual Event, June 26–July 1, 2022, Proceedings. pp. 448–459. Springer (2022). https://doi.org/10.1007/978-3-031-05643-7_29

43. Yu, X., Chum, P., Sim, K.B.: Analysis the effect of PCA for feature reduction in non-stationary EEG based motor imagery of BCI system. Optik **125**(3), 1498–1502 (2014). https://doi.org/10.1016/j.ijleo.2013.09.013, https://www.sciencedirect.com/science/article/pii/S0030402613012473

44. Zhang, Y., Zhou, G., Jin, J., Wang, X., Cichocki, A.: Optimizing spatial patterns with sparse filter bands for motor-imagery based brain-computer interface. J. Neurosci. Methods **255**, 85–91 (2015). https://doi.org/10.1016/j.jneumeth.2015.08.004, https://www.sciencedirect.com/science/article/pii/S016502701500285X

45. Zhang, Z., Duffy, V.G., Tian, R.: Trust and automation: a systematic review and bibliometric analysis. In: Stephanidi, C., et al. (eds.) HCII 2021. LNCS, vol. 13094, pp. 451–464. Springer, Cham (2021). https://doi.org/10.1007/978-3-030-90238-4_32

46. Zhang, Z., Tian, R., Ding, Z.: TrEP: transformer-based evidential prediction for pedestrian intention with uncertainty (2023)

47. Zhang, Z., Tian, R., Sherony, R., Domeyer, J., Ding, Z.: Attention-based interrelation modeling for explainable automated driving. IEEE Trans. Intell. Veh. **8**, 1564–1573 (2022)

48. Zhao, Z., Zeng, Z., Xu, K., Chen, C., Guan, C.: DSAL: deeply supervised active learning from strong and weak labelers for biomedical image segmentation. IEEE J. Biomed. Health Inform. **25**(10), 3744–3751 (2021)

Reflected Light vs. Transmitted Light: Do They Give Different Impressions to Users?

Ryohei Nakatsu[1]([✉]), Manae Miyata[2], Hirotaka Kawata[2], Naoko Tosa[1], and Takashi Kusumi[3]

[1] Disaster Prevention Research Institute, Kyoto University, Kyoto 606-8501, Japan
nakatsu.ryohei@gmail.com
[2] Seiko Epson Corporation, Nagano 392-8502, Japan
[3] Graduate School of Education, Kyoto University, Kyoto 606-8501, Japan

Abstract. The difference in information display between a projector (reflected light) and a display (transmitted light) is an essential issue. Marshal McLuhan proposed in his book "Laws of Media" the well-known hypothesis that "reflected light makes people analytical and transmitted light makes them emotional." In this study, we matched the display conditions of the projector and display as much as possible. Then we presented the subjects with emotional content (landscape video) and analytical content (three-digit multiplication) and asked them to evaluate their experiences. As a result, we found no statistical difference between the projector and the display evaluations.

Keywords: Reflected light · Transmitted light · Psychological experiment · Marshall McLuhan

1 Introduction

Information display and viewing include two methods. One is displaying information on a screen with a projector (PJ), by which we receive information through the reflected light. Another is displaying information using an LED or liquid crystal display (DP), by which we get information by transmitted light. DP has the characteristic of clearly showing even in the daytime because of its high brightness. On the other hand, PJ can project images not only on a flat surface but also on a curved surface.

Due to these differences in characteristics, PJ and DP are appropriately used depending on each scene. However, as to what kind of effect information displayed by these different methods would give human psychology, there still needs to be more accumulation of essential data.

This psychological experiment aimed to clarify the difference in appearance between PJ and DP through psychological experiments after adjusting various conditions of DP and PJ devices as much as possible.

C. Stephanidis et al. (Eds.): HCII 2023, CCIS 1832, pp. 391–399, 2023.
https://doi.org/10.1007/978-3-031-35989-7_50

2 Related Research

Regarding reflected and transmitted light, Marshall McLuhan made a well-known statement in his book "Laws of Media" that "reflected light makes people logical and transmitted light makes them emotional [1]" based on the experiment by Herbert E. Krugman [2]. However, investigations have yet to be undertaken to examine the difference in appearance between PJ (reflected light) and DP (transmitted light) after strictly controlling the conditions. Based on this, in this study, we conducted psychological experiments after matching the display conditions of PJ and DP as much as possible.

3 Environmental Conditions

3.1 Display Device

In this research, we investigated how the difference in devices, such as whether to use reflected light or transmitted light, affects the appearance when conditions, such as brightness, contrast, etc., of these devices are adjusted as much as possible. We adopted the device size of 55 inches (screen size: 139.7 cm diagonal x 121.7 cm horizontal x 68.5 cm vertical). We used the following display devices in the experiment.

Fig. 1. A display and a projector used for the experiment.

Display device 1: SONY KD-55X8500B (55-inch liquid crystal display) (Fig. 1: left).

Display device 2: Epson EF-11 (Brightness: 1000 lumens, resolution: Full HD, laser light source) (Fig. 1: right).

3.2 Setting the Experimental Environment.

Figure 2 shows the settings for the entire experimental environment. The DP was set on the front side of the room. Also, the projector and the screen were placed on the side of the room. When changing the display device, the subjects changed their sitting position to always sit in front of the displayed content.

Fig. 2. Setting of the experiment

3.3 Display Device Condition Settings

We have set the conditions for the DP and PJ as similar as possible as follows.

- Screen size: 55 inch
- Brightness: 163cd / m2
- Resolution: Full HD
- SRGB (Cover rate is 94% for both PJ and DP, the area ratio is PJ / 107%, DP / 96%)
- White color temperature: PJ/7231K, DP/6792K
- Contrast PJ/580, DP/1148

3.4 Lighting Conditions

Initially, we planned to secure about 200 lx on the desk to maintain the minimum illuminance required for work. However, in the projection by a PJ, the illumination is reflected on the projection surface, reducing the actual brightness and contrast and not making an equal comparison with the DP. Therefore, the experiment was carried out without lighting.

4 Experimental Conditions

4.1 Scene

The following two scenes were targeted.

Scene 1: Passively watch the displayed video (landscape video).
Scene 2: Actively watch the displayed image while doing some work (mathematical task).

4.2 Subject

In this psychological experiment, we used 34 students of Kyoto University as subjects (Male: 21 and female: 13).

4.3   Content

We prepared multiple contents and provided them to the subjects in a well-balanced manner for each condition and subject according to the design of the experiments. Specifically, we used the following contents.

Content 1: 4 Types of Landscape Videos (Resolution: Full HD)

https://www.youtube.com/watch?v=Q98ACV6SVe8
https://www.youtube.com/watch?v=mee3u5jJTts
https://www.youtube.com/watch?v=4ijYpgSkxPo
https://www.youtube.com/watch?v=E5hZKq_broQ

Figure 3 shows the situation in which a subject is watching the landscape video.

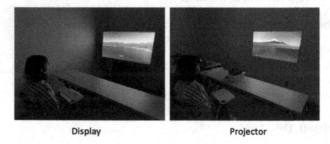

Display   Projector

Fig. 3. A subject watching a landscape video

Content 2: 3 Digits x 3 Digits Multiplication

Initially, we thought about displaying only the problem on the screen and having the subjects carry out multiplication on the work desk. However, since it was necessary to have them pay close attention to the display screen, we decided for them to perform the multiplication using the keyboard while watching the display screen.

Several multiplication practices were conducted before achieving the actual experiment. Almost all subjects could get used to multiplication using the keyboard and screen by practicing only one problem.

4.4   Measurement Method

The seven-scale SD method was adopted as the subjective evaluation method.

Experimental procedure.

Based on the preliminary experiment, the viewing duration of the landscape image was set to 5 min, and multiplication was set to 7 min.

4.5   Evaluation Items

The following items selected from the evaluation items used in the literature [3, 4] were used as evaluation items. Also, we have added several evaluation items depending on our experiment [5]. In addition, for scene 2, the number of multiplications the subjects could answer, and the correct answer rate of the task are also evaluated.

1) **What did you feel? (Impression)**

Comfortable – Uncomfortable, Familiar – Unfamiliar, Beautiful - Not beautiful, Calm – Restless, Interesting – Boring, Warm – Cold, Changeable - Not changeable, Flashy – Plain, Unique – Ordinary, Like – Dislike

2) **What kind of effect does it have? (Effect)**

Work goes well - Work does not go well, Can relax - Cannot relax, Can be creative – Cannot be creative, Motivated - Not motivated, Can face difficulties - Cannot face difficulties, Can get rid of tiredness - Cannot get rid of tiredness.

5   Experimental Result

5.1   Comparison of Average Values

Figure 4 compares the DP and PJ when targeting landscape images,

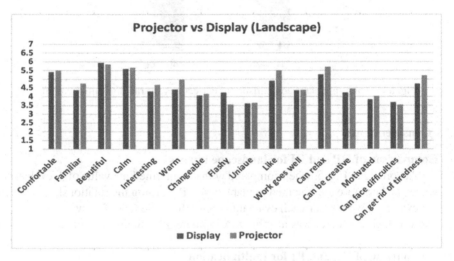

Fig. 4. Comparison of display and projector for landscape video

In addition, Fig. 5 compares the DP and PJ regarding the number of answers in multiplication (the average number of multiplications performed in time). Figure 6 shows the comparison between the DP and PJ regarding the correct answer rate (the average percentage of correct answers among the obtained answers).

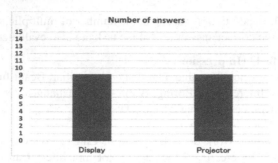

Fig. 5. Display-projector comparison for the number of obtained answers in multiplication.

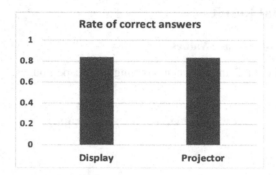

Fig. 6. Display-projector comparison for correct answer rate in multiplication.

5.2 Consideration1

(1) **Comparison of DP and PJ for landscape images**

According to Fig. 5, when compared with the intermediate value of 4, evaluation values of 4 or more are obtained in many cases. Regarding the relationship between the evaluation values for each evaluation item, the same tendency was observed: if one was high, the other was also high. A more detailed analysis is given in 5.3 and 5.4.

(2) **Comparison of DP and PJ for multiplication**

Regarding the number of answers and the rate of correct answers, the results showed almost no difference between the display and the projector.

From these results, when multiplication is targeted, in other words, when logical processing is performed, there is almost no difference between DP and PJ. This indicates that transmitted and reflected light has almost no effect on humans when performing logical processing.

Therefore, in the following, the difference between DP and PJ will be analyzed in more detail regarding the impact on human non-logical processing.

5.3   Factor Analysis

A similar tendency is obtained for the averaged evaluation values in Fig. 14. But it is unclear whether there is a difference due to many evaluation items. Therefore, we conducted a factor analysis on ten evaluation items related to "How did you feel (impression)?".

First, an exploratory factor analysis (Maximum Likelihood method, Promax Rotation) was performed on the ten evaluation items. Based on the results, three factors were considered based on the attenuation pattern of the eigenvalues (3.806, 2.084, 1.124,…). Next, factor analysis (Maximum Likelihood method, Promax Rotation) was performed with three factors. The results are shown in Table 1.

Factor 1 includes four items: "interesting," "unique," "changeable," and "flashy." As these are considered to mean a sense of dynamism, they are grouped into a variable called a "dynamism factor." Factor 2 includes four items, "beautiful," "comfortable," "calm," and "liking," which can be summarized as a composite variable named "serenity factor." Factor 3 consists of two items, "warm" and "familiar," which can be combined into a composite variable called "familiarity factor.".

Table 1. Results of factor analysis of 3 factors on "impression."

Item	Factor1	Factor2	Factor3	Synthesized factor
Interesting	.830	−.031	.076	Dynamism factor
Unique	.794	.043	−.065	
Changeable	.769	−.137	.183	
Flashy	.592	.092	−.308	
Beautiful	.087	.933	−.246	Serenity factor
Comfortable	−.009	.716	.097	
Calm	−.258	.680	.282	
Liking	.339	.432	.325	
Warm	.023	−.040	.808	Familiarity factor
Familiar	−.025	.045	.403	
α coefficient	.822	.825	.490	

Next, we conducted a factor analysis on the six items in "What kind of effect does it have (effect)." First, an exploratory factor analysis (Principal Factor method, Promax Rotation) was performed on the six evaluation items. Based on the results, two factors were considered based on the attenuation pattern of the eigenvalues (3.079, 1.234,…). Next, factor analysis (Principal Factor method, Promax Rotation) was performed with two factors. The results are shown in Table 2.

Factor 1 includes four items: "motivated," "can face difficulties," "can be creative," and "work goes well." These are summarized as a composite variable named the "motivation factor." Factor 2 includes two items, "I can relax" and "I can get rid of tiredness", which are combined into a composite variable named "relaxation factor.".

Table 2. Results of factor analysis of two factors on "effect."

Item	Factor1	Factor2	Synthesized factor
Motivated	.946	-.050	Motivation factor
Can face difficulties	.727	-.083	
Can be creative	.652	.093	
Work goes well	.599	.130	
Can relax	-.073	.934	Relaxation factor
Can geti rid of tiredness	.118	.873	
α coefficient	.826	.776	

5.4 Anova

Regarding "impression," the ten evaluation items were combined into three composite variables. A two-way ANOVA was performed on these three synthetic variables. The constituent elements are two factors: two levels of display methods (DP, PJ) and three levels of impressions (dynamism, serenity, and familiarity) using synthetic variables. The result shows no difference since the main effect for the display method is not significant $(F(1, 33) = 2.16, p = .151)$. This result indicates no significant difference between PJ and DP.

Next, regarding "effects," the six evaluation items were combined into two synthetic variables, and a two-way ANOVA was performed on these two synthetic variables. The constituent elements are two factors: two levels of display methods (display, projector) and two levels of effects (motivation, relaxation) using synthetic variables. The result shows that the main effect of the display method is not significant $(F(1, 33) = 1.89, p = .178)$, indicating that there is no significant difference between the two display methods of PJ and DP.

5.5 Consideration2

The results of the ANOVA, when viewing a landscape image, showed no significant main effect between DP and PJ for the evaluation items regarding "impression" and "effect." This indicates no significant difference between DP and PJ while performing activities that appeal to the senses and emotions, such as viewing a landscape image.

In addition, in performing multiplication, which involves performing logical processing while looking at the screen, it was found that there was no significant difference between DP and PJ in terms of the number of multiplications and the accuracy. This indicates no significant difference between DP and PJ when performing the logical multiplication activity.

6 Conclusion

It is well known that Marshall McLuhan proposed a hypothesis in his book "Laws of Media" that "reflected light makes people logical and transmitted light makes people emotional." However, our experiments did not support the hypothesis proposed by him.

However, regarding the validity of this hypothesis, it is necessary to examine its validity further using more highly valid experimental tasks, which is our future.

References

1. McLuhan, M., McLuhan, E.: Laws of Media: The New Science, University of Toronto Press (1992)
2. Krugman, H.E.: Brain wave measures of media involvement. J. Advert. Res. **11**(2), 3–9 (1971)
3. Ni, T., et al.: Increased display size and resolution improve task performance in information-rich virtual environments. Graph. Interface **2006**, 139–146 (2006)
4. Narita, N., Kanazawa, M.: Psychological factors of 2D/3D HDTV sequences and evaluation method of their overall impressions. J. Inst. Image Inf. TV Eng. **57**(4), 501–506 (2003)
5. Nakatsu, R., Tosa, N., Takada, H., Kusumi, T.: Comparison of viewing contents using large LED display and projector by psychological evaluation. In: Baalsrud Hauge, J., C. S. Cardoso, J., Roque, L., Gonzalez-Calero, P.A. (eds.) ICEC 2021. LNCS, vol. 13056, pp. 3–14. Springer, Cham (2021). https://doi.org/10.1007/978-3-030-89394-1_1

Preliminary Experiments in Hybrid Moving Images

Hidetaka Okumura[1], Peeraya Sripian[2]([⊠])[id], and Hiroki Nishino[1]

[1] School of Informatics, Kochi University of Technology, A417, 185, Miyano-kuchi,
Tosayamada-cho, Kami-shi, Kochi, Japan
230310p@ugs.kochi-tech.ac.jp, hiroki.nishino@acm.org
[2] College of Engineering, IGP, Shibaura Institute of Technology, Main building
Room 11I10-2, 3-7-5, Koto-ku, Tokyo, Japan
peeraya@shibaura-it.ac.jp

Abstract. We describe our preliminary experiments in hybrid moving images. A hybrid image is generated by synthesizing two different still images into one in such a way that the interpretation can change depending on the viewing distance of either of these two images. However, existing works on hybrid images only apply this technique to still images, and the application to moving images is still largely unexplored. Thus, investigating hybrid moving images has the potential to contribute to both research and artistic practices. We have developed software to create video clips of hybrid images and have performed a preliminary investigation into hybrid moving images. The results suggest that hybrid moving images still retain the characteristics of hybrid images, but the synthesis of a moving image and a still image may likely extend the range over which the synthesized moving image can still be perceived. On the other hand, the synthesis of two moving images seems to narrow the possible viewing distances for both synthesized images. Faster movement may also improve visibility.

Keywords: hybrid image · moving image · visual arts · digital arts · optical illusion

1 Introduction

A hybrid image is a picture that combines the low spatial frequencies of one picture with the high spatial frequencies of another picture, producing an image with an interpretation that changes with viewing distance [5].

In this article, we describe our preliminary experiments on the application of hybrid image generation techniques to moving images. As we are not aware of any previous research that investigates hybrid moving images to date, we begin with a simple experiment applying the original hybrid image generation technique described by Olivia et al. [5]. We then extend our study to an advanced technique developed by Sripian and Yamaguchi [11], which allows for greater flexibility in shape similarity between source images. Our preliminary investigation suggests that the synthesis of a moving image and a still image may extend the distance over which the synthesized moving image can be perceived. However, the synthesis of two moving images may narrow the viewing distances for both synthesized images. Faster movement may also improve the visibility of synthesized moving images. Such characteristics of hybrid moving images are worthy of further investigation.

2   Related Work

2.1   Oliva's Hybrid Image Generation Technique

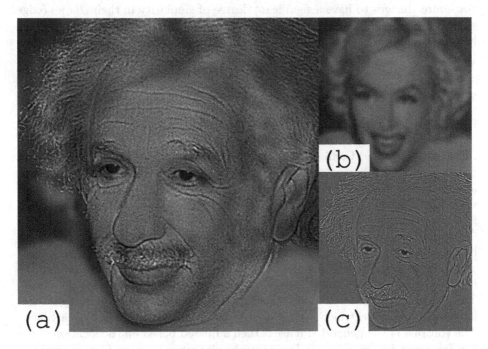

Fig. 1. A hybrid-image example generated with Oliva's technique. (a) The generated hybrid image, (b) the low-frequency component perceived at far distance (Monroe), and (c) the high-frequency component perceived at near distance (Einstein).

Oliva et al. described their original technique for generating hybrid images in their paper [5]. In this technique, one image to be viewed from a far distance (I_1) is filtered with a low-pass filter (G_1), while the other to be viewed up close (I_2) is filtered with a high-pass filter $(1 - G_2)$. Here, G_1 and G_2 are Gaussian filters associated with specific parameters, such as the expected viewing distance for I_2. The resulting hybrid image (H) is synthesized by adding these two filtered images: $H = I_1 \cdot G_1 + I_2 \cdot (1 - G_2)$ [5]. Figure 1^1 (a) shows a well-known

---

[1] Image: A hybrid image constructed from the low-frequency components of a photograph of Marilyn Monroe (left inset) and the high-frequency components of a photograph of Albert Einstein (right inset), https://en.wikipedia.org/wiki/Hybrid_image#/media/File:Hybrid_image_decomposition.jpg (public domain).

example of a hybrid image composed of two portraits: Marilyn Monroe in the low spatial frequencies (Fig. 1 (b)), which can be seen from a far distance, and Albert Einstein in the high spatial frequencies (Fig. 1 (c)), which can be seen from a close distance. The concept of a hybrid image presents a novel paradigm wherein a single image can be perceived as two distinct types of information with the modulation of viewing distance, creating an ambiguous image. This type of image, also known as a double image, is not only utilized for artistic purposes but also serves as a common experimental stimulus in the field of psychology [2,3,8] and enables the study of scene perception in the brain [4,7]

While this hybrid image generation technique is widely used, it requires the two source images to have a significant degree of similarity in their shapes (edge alignment) to be effectively presented. Otherwise, as shown in Fig. 2[2] (a), the high-frequency (HF) image may appear as if it is embossed on the low-frequency (LF) image, regardless of viewing distance.

2.2   Sripian's Hybrid Image Generation Technique

Creating a hybrid image that does not rely on overlapping the source images requires maintaining the separation of two spatial frequency images with respect to viewing distance. Unaligned parts of hybrid images can cause an ambiguous perception of both images, especially when viewed closely, so to achieve an edge-alignment-free hybrid image, it is necessary to cover the low-frequency image with high-frequency noises that do not deteriorate the perception of the high-frequency image.

Sripian et al. proposed a hybrid image generation technique called "the noise insertion method" that can effectively synthesize images without requiring much similarity in shape (edge-alignment-free hybrid image) [11]. In their method, the high-frequency image is preprocessed to enhance small noises within the image. This is done by first extracting the high-frequency information using a two-level high-pass filter, which is then used to intentionally create ringing artifacts. The contrast of the generated noise is then adjusted based on the location of the low-frequency image. Figure 2 illustrates the difference between Oliva's and Sripian's noise insertion techniques. Furthermore, they proposed an extended version of the method, which involves creating a hybrid image from three different sources [12].

Fig. 2. Hybrid-image examples with limited edge alignment between source images. (a) With Oliva's technique, the high-frequency image (lioness) appears as if it were embossed on the low-frequency image (puppy), and (b) Sripian's noise insertion technique allows for the generation of a hybrid image even from source images with limited edge alignment.

3   Research Objective

In addition to the primary application of hybrid images in vision psychology experiments, they have been utilized for security [6] and vision testing [9,10].

Furthermore, efforts have been made to integrate hybrid images into large displays as an emerging visualization technique [1].

The objective of this study is to investigate the application of hybrid images in a video format, which has not been explored previously. By examining the potential utility of hybrid images in a dynamic image configuration, this study contributes to the expanding range of applications for hybrid images in visual media.

4   Preliminary Investigation

We conducted a preliminary user study to build hypotheses about the characteristics of hybrid moving images. In the study, we conducted qualitative interviews to gather information about participants' viewing experiences. We also recorded the appropriate viewing distances that participants claimed for high-frequency (HF) and low-frequency (LF) images. We developed software to generate hybrid image video clips and created three video clips as listed in Table 1 (above). To investigate how differences in movements and shapes may influence viewing experiences, we divided each hybrid moving image into four sections as described in Table 1 (below).

Table 1. Hybrid moving images for our initial study.

Clip No	HF image (move)	LF image (move)	shape
#1	elephant (slow)	rhinoceros (slow)	similar
#2	duck (slow)	dog (slow)	different
#3	lion (slow)	puppy (fast)	different
Section No	HF image	LF image	duration
#1	still image	still image	10 s
#2	still image	moving image	10 s
#3	moving image	still image	10 s
#4	moving image	moving image	10 s

We recruited five undergraduate students (four male and one female) for our preliminary user study. We repeatedly presented three video clips to one participant in each session on a 40-inch LCD monitor. We asked the participant to move freely forward or backward to find the best viewing positions for HF and LF images while also asking them to explain their viewing experience.

In general, the hybrid moving images maintained the characteristics of hybrid still images but with some noteworthy changes in viewing distances, according to the participants. They also noted that the visibility of the moving images was improved when combined with a still image (Sections #2 and #3) in comparison with the still images section of the same video clip. This applied to all three video clips. They especially noticed the effectiveness when the shapes of the source images were quite different, as in video clips #2 and #3, where the details of the HF image were presented. This was reflected in the appropriate viewing distance range they claimed. In Section #2, the nearest distance to the LCD monitor at which the LF moving image could still be perceived became closer than in Section #1 (hybrid still image). In Section #3, the furthest distance at which the HF moving image could still be perceived became more distant than in Section #1.

Interestingly, our findings reveal that when synthesizing two moving images (as detailed in Section #4), the perceptual ranges for both high-frequency (HF) and low-frequency (LF) images were reduced. Participants had to approach closer to perceive the HF moving image and retreat further away to perceive the LF image. Additionally, participants reported that the increased movement speed in the video made perceiving both HF and LF images easier. Furthermore, the participants noted that the details of the HF moving images enhanced their perceptibility when synthesized using Sripian's method, rendering the HF moving images more discernible than their still counterparts.

5   Conclusion

We described our preliminary investigation into hybrid moving images, and this is possibly the first known investigation of the topic. While user study participants could precept both HF and LF moving images similarly as in hybrid still images, we also observed a noteworthy difference between hybrid still images and hybrid moving images that influence viewing experiences. We are currently designing formal user studies with controlled experiments based on findings obtained from our preliminary study.

References

1. Isenberg, P., Dragicevic, P., Willett, W., Bezerianos, A., Fekete, J.D.: Hybrid-image visualization for large viewing environments. IEEE Trans. Vis. Comput. Graph. 19(12), 2346–2355 (2013)
2. Long, G.M., Toppino, T.C.: Enduring interest in perceptual ambiguity: alternating views of reversible figures. Psychological bulletin 130(5), 748 (2004)
3. Oliva, A., Torralba, A.: Modeling the shape of the scene: A holistic representation of the spatial envelope. International journal of computer vision 42, 145–175 (2001)
4. Oliva, A., Torralba, A.: Building the gist of a scene: The role of global image features in recognition. Progress in brain research 155, 23–36 (2006)
5. Oliva, A., Torralba, A., Schyns, P.G.: Hybrid images. ACM Transactions on Graphics (TOG) 25(3), 527–532 (2006)
6. Papadopoulos, A., Nguyen, T., Durmus, E., Memon, N.: Illusionpin: Shoulder-surfing resistant authentication using hybrid images. IEEE Transactions on Information Forensics and Security 12(12), 2875–2889 (2017)
7. Parkkonen, L., Andersson, J., Hämäläinen, M., Hari, R.: Early visual brain areas reflect the percept of an ambiguous scene. Proceedings of the National Academy of Sciences 105(51), 20500–20504 (2008)

8. Schyns, P.G., Oliva, A.: Dr. angry and mr. smile: When categorization flexibly modifies the perception of faces in rapid visual presentations. Cognition 69(3), 243–265 (1999)
9. Sripian, P.: Toward using hybrid image as a visual acuity assessment tool. In: 2016 Nicograph International (NicoInt). pp. 171–177. IEEE (2016)
10. Sripian, P.: Computational visual illusion and its application. In: ICGG 2018-Proceedings of the 18th International Conference on Geometry and Graphics: 40th Anniversary-Milan, Italy, August 3–7, 2018 18. pp. 106–113. Springer (2019)
11. Sripian, P., Yamaguchi, Y.: Shape-free hybrid image. In: Proceedings of the Symposium on Non-Photorealistic Animation and Rendering. pp. 11–19 (2012)
12. Sripian, P., Yamaguchi, Y.: Hybrid image of three contents. Visual Computing for Industry, Biomedicine, and Art 3(1), 1–8 (2020). https://doi.org/10.1186/s42492-019-0036-3

Where Does the Attribute Framing Effect Arise If a Pie Chart is Given Along With a Verbal Description?

Kaede Takamune(✉), Kazushi Nishimoto, and Kentaro Takashima

Japan Advanced Institute of Science and Technology, 1-1 Asahidai, Ishikawa 923-1292, Nomi, Japan
s2220023@jaist.ac.jp

Abstract. The framing effect is a phenomenon in which differences in positive or negative verbal expressions change a person's decision. A recent study revealed that people made biased decisions, even when given a supplementary pie chart, thus demonstrating that the attribute framing effect is maintained. However, the stage of the process wherein the attribute framing effect arises remains an open question. In this paper, we conducted two investigations to determine whether differences in verbal expressions affect how people read and create pie charts. In Experiment 1, we investigated whether differences in verbal expressions positively or negatively affect reading a pie chart. In Experiment 2, we investigated whether differences in verbal expressions positively or negatively affect drawing a pie chart. As a result of the two experiments, subjects answered the pie chart values correctly. In other words, it was suggested that the framing effect occurs during the final decision-making step, not during the rate-drawing or rate-reading step.

Keywords: The framing effect · Pie charts · Reading · Drawing

1 Introduction

The framing effect is a phenomenon in which differences in descriptive expressions affect the evaluation or decision-making of a subject, despite being logically equivalent [1]. This phenomenon is classified into three different types: the risky-choice framing effect, the attribute framing effect, and the goal-framing effect. The attribute framing effect focuses on one of the attributes of an object, with the difference in descriptive expressions [2]. For example, about the identical beef, there are two different descriptions with a positive description such as "75% lean" or a negative description such as "25% fat". These different descriptions affect the evaluation of the beef, with the positive explanations rated higher than the negative ones [3].

Most studies on attribute framing effects focused on the verbal descriptions of objects. More recently, the effects of attributes by non-verbal means, such as graphs and sounds, have been investigated [4]. However, to the best of our knowledge, there are no studies on the effects of drawing or reading pie charts. In this paper, we investigate the attribute framing effect of a pie chart as supplementary non-verbal information in addition to the verbal description of attributes.

C. Stephanidis et al. (Eds.): HCII 2023, CCIS 1832, pp. 407–413, 2023.
https://doi.org/10.1007/978-3-031-35989-7_52

2 Related Works

There have been several research attempts that investigated how nonverbal information, such as voice and facial expressions [5] and supplementarily added pie chart [6–8], influenced the framing effect.

Garelik et al. [5] investigated the effects of emotional information by speech and facial expressions that are supplemented to task sentences in positive and negative descriptions. The results showed that the evaluation of the object changed in a positive or negative direction depending on the change of emotion in the voice and the facial expression. Furthermore, several recent studies have investigated the framing effect with a supplementary presentation of pie charts [6–8]. Gamliel and Kreiner showed that the risky-choice framing effect occurs even when the pie chart is supplementary added to the verbal descriptions [8].

However, there is still an open question remaining. The question is whether the difference in verbal description changes the way of reading the pie chart (e.g., more values are read in the positive description) which results in biased decision-making, or does not particularly influence the way of reading the pie chart and only the difference of the verbal description influence the bias of the decision-making. In other words, when different verbal descriptions are given, at which stage does the bias arise: in reading the pie chart or in making the final decision? This point is not yet revealed. Hence, in this study, by conducting two experiments described in Sect. 3 and 4, we attempt to identify at which stage of the decision-making process the attribute framing effect occurs when the pie chart is supplementarily provided to the verbal descriptions.

3 Experiment 1: Effect of Different Descriptions When Reading Values from Pie Charts

In the first experiment, we examined whether the attribute framing effect affects reading values from a pie chart.

3.1 Task and Procedure

In Experiment 1, we employed 38 experimental participants who were graduate students at our institute and their related people (18–39 years old). We showed them a task set that contains a sentence with a pie chart and asked them to read the sentence and pie chart and to answer the rate that the pie chart indicated.

We presented 12 task sets in total that consisted of tasks with positive descriptions, those with negative descriptions, and some dummy tasks for preventing the participants from inferring that this experiment is related to the attribute framing effect. For example, in a positive description task, the given sentence was such as "This pie chart illustrates the result of the effectiveness of a specific medication. The part of the graph filled in black shows the rate of people whose disease has been made recovery by this medicine. Please estimate and answer the rate." The black part of the pie chart showed a rate of 70%, but no numerical values were shown in the pie chart (see Fig. 1). The participants were required to answer the rate of the pie chart in the range of 0–100%. In the case of the negative description task, a part of the presented sentence, "the rate of people whose disease has been made recovery by this medicine," was replaced with the sentence, "the rate of people whose disease has not been made recovery by this medicine."

Additionally, we also investigated cases where the participants had relations with the presented task set. For example, we showed a sentence, "Now you are suffering from a serious disease. You are told that a new medicine has recently been developed to treat it. This pie chart shows the results of a medication administration. The rate of people who benefited from the medication was shown in the black part of the pie chart. Please answer the rates of this pie chart numerically." Like this, the task description used "you" to make the things his/her own problem. We hypothesized that the participants would answer with higher value in case the participants were related to the presented descriptions than in the cases not related to them.

This pie chart illustrates the result of the effectiveness of a specific medication. The part of the graph filled in black shows the rate of people whose disease has been made recovery by this medicine. Please estimate and answer the rate.

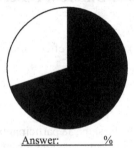

Answer:＿＿＿＿＿＿％

Fig. 1. An example of a task set in Experiment 1

3.2 Results

Table 1 shows the results of Experiment 1 in which the maximum, minimum and average values of the participants' answers are shown. For all conditions in Experiment 1, the average values were almost 70%: the estimated values were accurate. An analysis of variance was conducted for two factors i.e., description type and relationship with the participants; the main effect was not significant for either factor. Neither the difference in the description type presented nor the difference in the relationship with the participants affected the reading of the pie chart. Therefore, we can conclude that the attribute framing effect did not occur at the stage of reading the pie chart.

Table 1. Results of Experiment 1

Description type	Relationship with the participants	Maximum value	Minimum value	Average	STDV
Positive description	**Total**	**78**	**60**	**70.0**	**2.2**
	Related to the participants	75	60	69.7	2.4
	Not related to the participants	78	68	70.4	1.9
Negative description	**Total**	**78**	**63**	**70.2**	**2.2**
	Related to the participants	78	65	70.3	2.4
	Not related to the participants	75	63	70.3	1.9

4 Experiment 2: Effects of Different Descriptions When Drawing Pie Charts

In the second experiment, we examined the effect of different descriptions on drawing pie chart proportions.

4.1 Tasks and Procedure

Experiment 2 was conducted with the same 38 participants as Experiment 1. We provided them with a task set that contains a sentence and a blank pie chart and asked them to read the sentence and draw a line in the blank pie chart to express the rate described in the sentence.

We presented 12 task sets in total that consisted of tasks with positive descriptions, those with negative descriptions, and some dummy tasks for preventing the participants from inferring that this experiment is related to the attribute framing effect. Each task set is printed on a paper sheet. For example, in a positive description task, the given sentence was such as "A certain medicine is effective for 70% of people. Please draw a line in the pie chart below to express the rate." After reading this sentence, the participants drew a straight line in a blank pie chart on the paper sheet by hand (see Fig. 2). In the case of the negative description task, a part of the presented sentence, "The medicine is effective" was replaced with the sentence, "The medicine is not effective."

Additionally, we also investigated cases where the participants had relations with the presented task set. For example, we showed a sentence in the case of a task with a positive description, "You are suffering from a severe disease. You are told that a new medicine has recently been developed. The medication is effective for 70% of people. Please draw this rate on the pie chart below." Like this, the task description used "you" to make the things his/her own problem. We hypothesized that the participants would answer with higher value in case the participants were related to the presented descriptions than in the cases not related to them in case of the positive descriptions. The value of the rate drawn in the graphs was calculated from the angle between the line drawn by the participants and the line initially drawn at the 0% position.

A certain medicine is effective for 70% of people. Please draw a line in the pie chart below to express the rate.

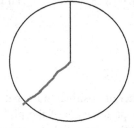

Fig. 2. An example of a task set in Experiment 2 and an answer

4.2 Results

Table 2 shows the results of Experiment 2 in which the maximum, minimum and average values of the participants' answers calculated from the drawn lines are shown. For all conditions in Experiment 2, the average values were almost 70%. This result indicates that the graphs are generally drawn accurately. An analysis of variance was conducted on two factors i.e., description type and relationship with the participants; the main effect was not significant for either factor. Neither the difference in the description type presented nor the difference in the relationship with the participants affected the drawing of the pie chart. Therefore, we can conclude that the attribute framing effect did not occur at the stage of drawing the pie chart.

Table 2. Response values for pie chart drawing in each descriptive phrase

Description type	Relationship with the participants	Maximum value	Minimum value	Average	STDV
Positive description	**Total**	**91**	**62**	**70.3**	**5.8**
	Related to the participants	89.5	64.5	70.2	5.8
	Not related to the participants	91	62	70.3	5.9
Negative description	**Total**	**91**	**60**	**70.1**	**6.2**
	Related to the participants	91	61	70.2	6.5
	Not related to the participants	87.5	60	70.2	5.9

5 Discussions

This paper investigated the impact of positive and negative descriptions on the reading (Experiment 1) and drawing (Experiment 2) of the pie charts. Those results indicated that neither description significantly impacted the accuracy of reading as well as drawing the pie charts. Additionally, we hypothesized that relating the tasks to the participants themselves may lead to egocentric judgments. However, even in this condition, no significant effects have been found and the hypothesis was not supported. These findings demonstrated that the attribute framing effect does not occur at the stage of estimating the rate in the pie chart; it occurs in the final decision-making step after the accurate estimation of the pie chart.

In a pie chart, even if you are only interested in one part of the information, other information is always presented at the same time. For example, in case of our experiments described in Section 3 and 4, the presented pie chart always shows both the positive description (e.g., the medicine is effective for 70% of the people) and the negative description (e.g., the medicine is ineffective for 30% of the people) at the same time. The pie chart shown in Fig. 1 highlighted the 70% area in black and presented it to the participants, while the remaining white area clearly shows the existence of the 30% counterpart. The attribute framing effect is a phenomenon that the evaluation of the object (the effectiveness of the medicine in this case) is affected when a one-sided description is presented (positive or negative). However, if the rate is presented by using a pie chart, not only the focused part but also the counterparts are presented and probably recognized simultaneously, even if only the focused part is described in the verbal descriptions. Therefore, the attribute framing effect may not occur or is weakened when a pie chart is presented alongside a biased verbal description. This point should be studied in the future.

6 Concluding Remarks

In this paper, to identify at which stage of the decision-making process the attribute framing effect occurs when the pie chart is supplementarily provided to the biased verbal descriptions, we conducted two experiments to examine how people estimate the pie charts alongside a biased verbal description. The results are as follows:

- The attribute framing effect does not occur in the stage of reading the rate from the pie chart (Experiment 1),
- The attribute framing effect does not occur in the stage of drawing the pie chart based on the given rate in the verbal description (Experiment 2), and
- The results of Experiments 1 and 2 suggest that the attribute framing effect occurs in the final decision-making stage after the stage of reading or drawing the pie chart.

The pie charts always show the entire information regardless of whether each part is focused on or not, which may weaken the attribute framing effect. In contrast, there are some types of graphs such as a bar graph that can indicate only the focused part without explicitly showing the other parts. Such graphs may strengthen the attribute framing effect. Further experiments should be conducted on the other types of graphs on attribute framing effects.

References

1. Tversky, A., Kahneman, D.: The framing of decisions and the psychology of choice. Science **211**(4481), 453–458 (1981)
2. Levin, I.P., Schneider, S.L., Geath, G.J.: All frames are not created equal: a typology and critical analysis of framing effects. Organ. Behav. Hum. Decis. Process. **76**, 149–188 (1998)
3. Kühberger: The influence of framing on risky decisions: a meta-analysis. Organ. Behav. Hum. Decis. Process. **75**(1), 23–55 (1998)
4. Kreiner, H., Gamliel, E.: Looking at both sides of the coin: mixed representation moderates attribute-framing bias in written and auditory messages. Appl. Cognit. Psychol. **30**, 332–340 (2016)
5. Schneider, T.R., Salovey, P., Pallonen, U., Mundorf, N., Smith, N.F., Steward, W.T.: Visual and auditory message framing effects on tobacco smoking. J. Appl. Soc. Psychol. **31**(4), 667–682 (2001). https://doi.org/10.1111/j.1559-1816.2001.tb01407.x
6. Gamliel, E., Kreiner, H.: Is a picture worth a thousand words? The interaction of visual display and attribute representation in attenuating framing bias. Judgm. Decis. Mak. **8**(4), 482–491 (2013)
7. Kreiner, H., Gamliel, E.: Are highly numerate individuals invulnerable to attribute framing bias? Comparing numerically and graphically represented attribute framing. Eur. J. Soc. Psychol. **47**(6), 775–782 (2017)
8. Gamliel, E., Kreiner, H.: Applying fuzzy-trace theory to attribute-framing bias: gist and verbatim representations of quantitative information. J. Exp. Psychol. Learn. Mem. Cogn. **46**(3), 497–506 (2020)

Cloud Illusion: A New Optical Illusion Induced by Objects Rotating Around a Blank Area

Kazuhisa Yanaka[✉] and Kazuki Watanabe

Kanagawa Institute of Technology, Atsugi-Shi, Kanagawa-Ken, Japan
yanaka@ic.kanagawa-it.ac.jp

Abstract. A new motion illusion has been discovered in this study. Three filled-in circles were placed on a PC screen to form an equilateral triangle whose centers were connected, and they rotated at approximately one revolution per second. Subsequently, a non-existent cloud-like object appeared in an empty area in the center. This illusion is named the "cloud illusion". The hue of the cloud-like object is very close to that of the circle. For example, when the circle was black, the cloud was gray. When the number of circles was increased to 4 or more or when the size of the circles was increased, the clouds were darkened. When a circle was colored, the hue of the cloud was almost the same as its color. This illusion resembles the Hermann grid illusion in that something like a cloud appears, but it is the opposite of the Hermann grid illusion in that it appears when rotated.

Keywords: Motion Illusion · Kanizsa Triangle · Cloud Illusion

1 Introduction

A new motion illusion was observed in this study. This research first estimated the latency of the "Kanizsa Triangle" [1, 2], an illusion known as "subjective contour". An experiment was conducted to rotate the Kanizsa triangle, and the extent to which the number of rotations should be increased was determined to determine if the processing in the brain could not keep up and the optical illusion would disappear. Then, an unexpected optical illusion appeared. When the stimulus was rotated at approximately one revolution per second around the center, a cloud-like object appeared in the blank area inside the triangle, as shown in Fig. 1. [3]. The direction of rotation can be either clockwise or counterclockwise. This illusion was named the "cloud illusion".

At that time, the illusion was thought to be related to subjective contours. However, it was not correct, because further experiments revealed that this illusion occurs even when subjective contours are unrelated, as shown in Fig. 2. In this case, no subjective contours are perceived, because black circles were used instead of Pacman-like shapes. Nevertheless, the cloud illusion occurred.

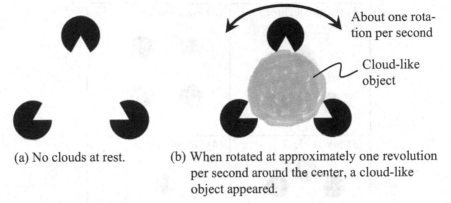

(a) No clouds at rest.

(b) When rotated at approximately one revolution per second around the center, a cloud-like object appeared.

Fig. 1. Cloud illusion caused by the rotation of the Kanizsa Triangle.

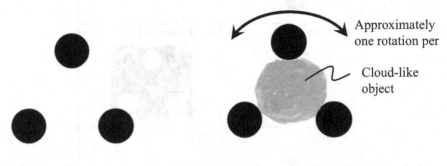

(a) No clouds at rest

(b) When rotated at approximately one revolution per second around the center, a cloud-like object appeared.

Fig. 2. Cloud illusion caused by the rotation of three circles.

2 Variants

The optimum rotation speed is approximately one rotation per second, which produces the densest clouds. When the number of circles in the original image in Fig. 3 (1) was increased, as shown in Fig. 3 (2)(3), the illusion was reduced. As shown in Fig. 3 (4), denser circles increased the illusion. As shown in Fig. 3 (5), sparse circles reduced the illusion. When the entire figure was inverted in brightness as shown in Fig. 3 (6), the cloud color was also inverted. When the color of the circles was changed to gray, as shown in Fig. 3 (7), the illusion was reduced. When the color of the circles was changed to one of the primary colors (red, green, or blue) as shown in Fig. 3 (8) (9) (10), the color of the cloud will have similar hue.

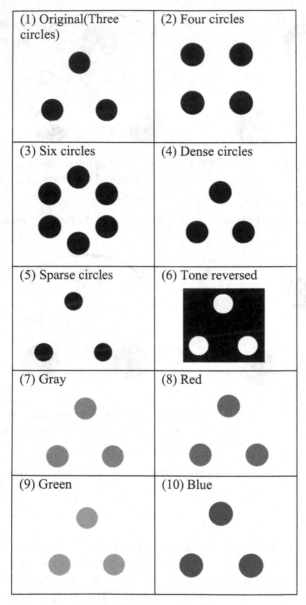

Fig. 3. Various stimuli.

3 Stimulus Rotated by a Motor

The illusion is possibly affected by the limited number of pixels on the screen and the frame rate of the PC. To eliminate this possibility, the PC screen was not used, and a geared motor was used to rotate the stimuli printed on paper mechanically, as shown in Fig. 4. Even in this case, clouds were observed in the white area at the center of the disk.

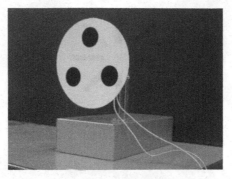

Fig. 4. Device that uses a motor to rotate a circular piece of paper with a figure printed on it.

4 Comparison with Other Optical Illusions

The cloud illusion resembles the Hermann grid illusion [4] shown in Fig. 5, in which a cloud appears in or around each intersection. However, it is the opposite of the Hermann grid illusion, in which the cloud appears when rotated. In Hermann grid, illusory black clouds appear when the image is stationary, but disappear when the whole image is rotated. This phenomenon occurred possibly because the Hermann grid illusion has a long latency from when the stimulus enters the eye to when the cloud-like object is perceived. Consequently, the illusion does not occur when the stimulus changes in a short period of time.

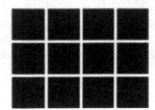

Fig. 5. Hermann grid.

The Ehrenstein illusion [5] shown in Fig. 6, along with the Kanizsa triangle already mentioned, is related to a phenomenon called subjective contours. In Kanizsa's triangle, a non-existent triangle is perceived, whereas in the Ehrenstein illusion, a non-existent circle is perceived. In both illusions, when the stimulus is stationary, the interior of a triangle or circle appears brighter than its surroundings, but no clouds are present. When the stimulus is rotated, a cloud-like object appears in both cases.

Fig. 6. Ehrenstein illusion.

5   Conclusion

A new motion illusion was discovered, in which a cloud-like object appears near the center when three circles are placed so that their centers form an equilateral triangle, and the circles are rotated approximately once a second on the PC screen. Although the mechanism of the illusion has not been determined, investigating other similar illusions such as the Hermann grid and the Ehrenstein illusion may lead to a unified understanding of illusions.

References

1. Kanizsa, G.: Margini quasi-percettivi in campi con stimolazione omogenea. Riv. Psicol. **49**(1), 7–30 (1955)
2. Wikipedia, Kanizsa triangle. https://en.wikipedia.org/w/index.php?title=Kanizsa_triangle&direction=next&oldid=156014567. Accessed 16 Mar 2023
3. Yanaka, K., Watanabe, K.: Cloud illusion - illusion caused by rotation of subjective contours. In: 16th Illusion Workshop Abstract, one page, 2 Mar 2022 (in Japanese)
4. Michael Bach, Hermann Grid. https://michaelbach.de/ot/lum-herGrid/. Accessed 16 Mar 2023
5. Michael Bach, Ehrenstein Illusion. https://michaelbach.de/ot/lum-Ehrenstein/. Accessed 16 Mar 2023

The Effects of Expertise on Airline PILOT'S Eye Activities in Flight Tasks with Different Complexity

Yiyuan Zheng[1]([✉]), Yuwen Jie[1], and Shan Fu[2]

[1] Shanghai Aircraft Airworthiness Certification Center of CAAC, Shanghai, China
zhengyiyuan@saacc.org.cn
[2] Shanghai Jiao Tong University, Shanghai, China

Abstract. Information processing remains one of the key elements of aviation safety, and eye is the most essential sensory organ as it almost processed 80% of flight information. In order to improve the operating efficiency and safety level of airlines, the impacts of expertise on the qualified civilian airmen's eyes activities is still needed to be studied, especially under multiple flight scenarios with different complexity. Three types of eye movement parameters, including eye blinks rate, pupil size and dwell time were compared in three different flight tasks. Besides, fourteen pilots with airlines background were classified into two groups depending on their flight hours. This experiment was carried out in a CRJ-200 full flight simulator. The factor of task complexity indicated significant effects on eye blinks rate ($F(2, 12) = 17.833$, $p < 0.001$), and dwell time ($F(2, 12) = 17.317$, $p < 0.001$), and expertise showed a significant influence on dwell time ($F(1, 18) = 8.532$, $p = 0.006$). Furthermore, neither of the factor had effect on pupil size. Although expertise seemed no effect on commercial airline pilots in routine tasks, the phenomenon of difference existed when encountering unusual surroundings or situations of aircraft. Unlike the irregular fluctuation of pupil size, and eye blinks rate that only presented difference in most sophisticated tasks, dwell time could be an ideal indicator to distinguish less expert and more expert in whatever the complexity of the tasks.

Keywords: Expertise · Eye activity · Commercial airline pilots

1 Introduction

Information processing remains one of the key elements of aviation safety and effectiveness, which provides comprehensive understanding of what was happened and what is going on in the ambient environment. If information could not be acquired and maintained validly, disasters might occur. For instance, the flight accident of VD8387 resulting in 44 people died at Yichun Airport in August 2010, China, was primarily because the flight crew was in a poor visual perception condition. They insisted landing even did not intercept the runway, and failed to establish the required visual reference. In addition, the accidents of Lion Air Flight 610 and Ethiopian Airlines flight 302 in 2018 and 2019 both revealed that the flight crews were unable to effectively recognize and respond to undesired stabilizer movement and the effects of potential Angle of Attack (AOA) sensor failure, i.e. the information provided gave rise to pilots' confusion and perceptual illusion potentially.

Eye is the most essential sensory organ as it almost processed 80% of flight information. Eye movements can be considered as indicators of cognition behavior and situation awareness definitely, regardless of being regulated by bottom–up processes, i.e., spontaneous orientation towards an oncoming stimulus, or by top–down processes, i.e., intentionally and driven by knowledge, expectation and goals [1]. The two most important and highly correlated parameters in eye activities are fixations and saccades. A fixation is a set of look-points or a series of eye gaze vector data points that is focused on a stationary target in the individual's visual field. More prosaically, it is the duration for individuals visually acquiring and interpreting the information within the field of vision. A saccade is a small rapid jerky movement of the eye especially as it jumps from fixation on one point to another. Due to visual acuity is highest at the point of gaze, we have to move our eyes in a sequence of saccades with intermittent fixations on areas of interest [2]. As saccadic movements trace the area of desired information, fixations could collect all the information essential for the brain to interpret the overall image. As long as the processing of information on each fixation is efficient, humans achieve nearly optimal search performance [3].

Besides, eye blinks rate and pupil size are also two effective indexes to characterize cognitive activities. Blinks rate has been observed to correlate with memory and respond demands. In general, the increased requirements of the amount of time for individuals acquiring information results in a decreased blinks rate, however, it has been pointed out to increase with increased memory task load [4]. Moreover, pupil dilation has been found with the increased demand of information processing [5]. In flight deck, either obtaining information from displays or recalling information from quick reference handbook (QRH) might lead to pupil change.

On the other wise, it is widely accepted that individual expertise has an obvious influence on comprehending current situation and predicting future status [6]. Expertise plays a significant role in developing and maintaining situation awareness in the face of high volumes of information transfer and system complexity. The characteristics that allow people to cultivate high levels of situation awareness are often developed silently alongside more observable features like skilled performance. With increased experience and practice, most people could cognitively organize the more available information in their working, and they could also observe and handle problems at a deeper level than novices in their domain. In aviation, generally, the more expert pilots made better decisions in terms of flight attitude and speed [7]. Taylor and Kennedy found more expert pilots had better flight summary scores at baseline and showed less decline over time [8]. Moreover, expert ability to organize information into meaningful units appears to facilitate future flight state projections [9]. Most eye tracking experiments studying the expertise effects of pilots are focused on one specific task. For instance, Kasarskis et al. found that experts had significantly shorter dwells, more total fixations, more aim point and airspeed fixations and fewer altimeter fixations than novices during VFR flight [10]. Yu and Wang indicated experienced and novice helicopter pilots differ in scanning pattern among different areas of interest (AOIs) during the pursuit of a dynamic target [11]. Kim and Palmisano revealed that experienced pilots established unique eye-scanning strategies in a glideslope control [12]. During landing operations, experts could be able to attend to relevant display elements for required information more quickly compare with novices. However, the novices selected in most studies were flight cadets or students with aviation background, who might not be the properly representative population of civilian airmen, as they could not satisfy the minimum requirements of the commercial airlines.

Although some general conclusions were achieved, in order to improve the operating efficiency and safety level of airlines, the impacts of expertise on pilots' eyes movement is still needed to be studied, especially under multiple flight scenarios with different complexity. Therefore, three tasks possessing significant complexity differences according to the Task Complexity in Flight method (TCIF) were selected. To be more representative and practical, all the fourteen subjects with various flight hours experience in this experiment were from commercial airlines. Furthermore, three different kinds of eyes movement parameters were chosen in this research, including eye blinks rate, pupil size and dwell time. The experiment was carried out in a CRJ-200 level D flight simulator.

2 Methods

2.1 Subjects

Fourteen Chinese male pilots, ranging in age from 33 to 52 (Mean = 38.19, SD = 7.09), were participated in this study. These pilots consisted of two test pilots recruited from Civil Aviation Administration of China (they also worked for airlines as part-time pilots), two flight instructors from China Eastern Airline, and ten commercial airline pilots (Six from China Eastern Airline, two from China Southern Airline, and the rest two from Chengdu Airline). Their mean flight hours were 6622 ± 4911 (range from 1200 to 16,000), and the average flight hours in the last half month before this study were 12.36 ± 8.57 (range from 4 to 23). Each pilot has been either captain or first officer of CRJ-200 for more than 1 year (Mean = 3.89 ± 3.22). Concurrently, they have all been recruited as captains or co-pilots for other types of aircrafts. These subjects were classified into two groups, more expert (ME), and less expert (LE), based on a 4000 h threshold to ensure equal cohorts. Thus, half of the pilots belonged to the more expert group (10659 ± 4235.6 h), and the other half pertained to the less expert group (2317.4 ± 1026.8 h). All subjects had normal vision and showed no signs of visual or vestibular pathology. The institutional review board of the School of Aeronautics and Astronautics, Shanghai Jiao Tong University had approved the study in advance, and each participant have signed the informed consent before the commencement of their experiment.

2.2 Equipment

The experiment was carried out on a CRJ-200 level D full flight simulator, which was belonged to China Eastern Airline. The flight simulator was conforming to the guidance presented in Federal Aviation Administration Advisory Circular AC 120-40B (Airplane

Simulator Qualification) [13]. Expect for this study, the flight simulator has also been used as pilot training for the airline.

In addition, one head-mounted eye tracker (Tobbi Glass II, Sweden), was used in this experiment to capture the required data of the subjects' dominant eyes. The eye tracker was calibrated by instructing participants to gaze at one fixed point. Horizontal and vertical eye movement trajectories were interpolated to determine fixation point with a resolution of approximately less than 0.2 cm. The sample of the eye tracker was 50 Hz.

2.3 Procedure

For the sake of investigating the expertise effects in various flight conditions with different complexity, three scenarios were established, consisting of one normal task, standard instrument approach (SIA), one specific environment task, flying in icing condition (IC), and one emergency task, one engine failure after V1 (EF). According to the results of TCIF, EF is most complicated task in these three scenarios, the complexity of IC is medium, and SIA is least. Before the experiment, each subject was trained in the same flight simulator for one hour to be familiar with the simulator configurations and the procedures. Simultaneously, one flight instructor stayed with the flight crew in the same simulator, who was responsible for task configuring or acted as ATC if necessary. Only the data of pilots flying were recorded in this study. The relevant tasks configurations and the procedures of the crew operating are as following.

Standard Instrument Approach. This flight task was performed at Chengdu Shuangliu International Airport. The task was started in 40 nautical miles away from descending point. After slowing down the speed to 145 knots, and descending the altitude to 1500 feet, the aircraft was in the landing pattern. The pilots flying then were required to execute a CAT I standard instrument approach procedure and landed the aircraft on the runway.

Flying in Icing Condition. This flight task was carried out at Shanghai Hongqiao Airport. Firstly, pilot flying was required to perform a standard instrument departure according to the corresponding procedure, and when reaching the cruise altitude (10000ft), a moderate freezing on wings was configured by the flight instructor. As the icing condition was noticed, the order of 'turn on the anti-icing of wing and fairing' was given by the pilot flying. Subsequently, a new route was set to avoid cumulus as needed in light of the terrain and weather conditions. After getting rid of the frozen area, the task was finished.

One Engine Failure after V1. This flight task was conducted in Kunming Wujiaba Airport. The task was initiated when the TOGA (Takeoff/Go-around) button was pressed. Then, the pilot flying pushed the throttle and kept accelerating until the aircraft reaching V1 (takeoff decision speed). When the speed being increased to V1 + 3 kn, the left engine failure was settled by the flight instructor. The flight crew had to make sure the throttle was on maximum position, and manipulate rudders to keep the aircraft running along the runway central line. When the aircraft reaching VR (rotation speed), they needed to rotate and maintain a pitch angle of 12 degree climbing, and retract the landing gear when the climbing rate was positive. At the height of 400 feet, the flight crew had to select and confirm the roll mode of autopilot, and executed the engine failure procedure when possible. After that, they were required to follow one engine approach procedure, and landed the aircraft on the same runway. The process of this flight task was shown in Fig. 1.

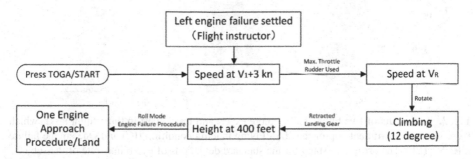

Fig. 1. The flow chart of One Engine Failure after V1

2.4 Statistical Analysis

SPSS 17.0 for Windows was used to process the experiment data. ANOVA analysis and t-test were implemented in this study. When $P < 0.05$, the results were considered statistically significant.

3 Results

3.1 Eye Blinks Rate

In this study, the averages of eye blinks rate of less expert were all slightly lower than the more expert. Meanwhile, with the increase of complexity, the value of eye blinks rate kept a download trend as shown in Fig. 2. Nevertheless, only in One Engine Failure after V1 task, the difference of more expert and less expert was significant ($t = 3.08$, $p = 0.01$). Furthermore, the factor of task complexity ($F_{(2, 12)} = 17.833$, $p < 0.001$) indicated a significant impact on the blinks rate, but the expertise effect ($F_{(1, 18)} = 3.551$, $p = 0.068$) was insignificant. Simultaneously, the interaction of complexity and expertise was insignificant ($F_{(2, 12)} = 1.308$, $p = 0.283$).

3.2 Pupil Size

The results of pupil size in this experiment was depicted as in **Fig. 3**. The pupil diameter of more expert expanded slightly as the complexity of flight scenarios increased. The less expert group, however, presented an irregular fluctuation, and the smallest average size was in most complicated task, One Engine Failure after V_1. Neither expertise ($F_{(1, 18)} = 0.013$, $p = 0.911$) nor task complexity ($F_{(2, 12)} = 0.001$, $p = 0.999$) had significant influence on pupil size, and the interaction of these two factor ($F_{(2, 12)} = 0.006$, $p = 0.994$) was insignificant either.

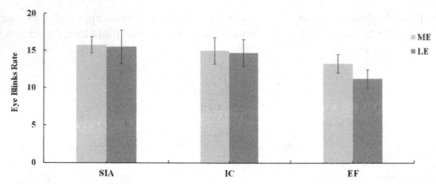

Fig. 2. The results of Eye blinks rate of more expert and less expert in three flight tasks, which were standard instrument approach (SIA), Flying in icing condition (IC) and One engine failure after V1 (EF). The error bars stand for the standard deviations of eye blinks rate of the subjects either for more expert or for less expert.

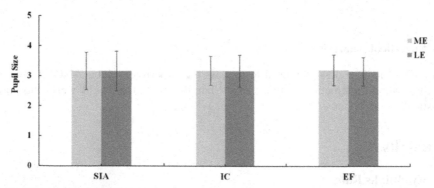

Fig. 3. The results of Pupil size of more expert and less expert in three flight tasks, which were standard instrument approach (SIA), Flying in icing condition (IC) and One engine failure after V1 (EF). The error bars stand for the standard deviations of pupil size of the subjects either for more expert or for less expert.

3.3   Dwell Time

The influences of expertise ($F (1, 18) = 8.532$, $p = 0.006$) and task ($F (2, 12) = 17.317$, $p < 0.001$) on dwell time were both significant, and the interaction of these two factors was insignificant ($F (2, 12) = 1.619$, $p = 0.212$). Dwell time uniformly became longer as the flight tasks complexity increased, both for more expert and less expert, as shown in Fig. 4. Specifically, expect for Standard Instrument Approach, the differences of ME and LE were significant in both tasks of Flying in icing condition ($t = 2.24$, $p = 0.045$) and One engine failure after V_1 ($t = 2.20$, $p = 0.048$). The results of dwell time in the experiment was shown in Fig. 4.

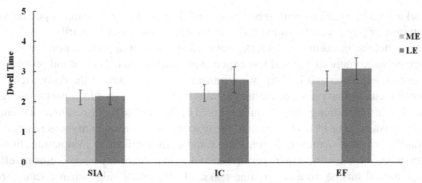

Fig. 4. The results of Dwell time of more expert and less expert in three flight tasks, which were standard instrument approach (SIA), Flying in icing condition (IC) and One engine failure after V1 (EF). The error bars stand for the standard deviations of dwell time of the subjects either for more expert or for less expert.

4 Discussion

Poor situation awareness was found to be the main cause in one review of over 200 flight accidents [14], and in another study, more than 85% of major aircraft accidents, which involving human error could be attributed to situation awareness deterioration [15]. Acquiring and maintaining the acceptable and appropriate situation awareness depends on capability of information processing and individual expertise level. Eye activity is the critical element of information processing, which could be regarded as the indicator of cognition behavior and fundamental source of situation awareness. Furthermore, it is generally acknowledged that with the increase of expertise, individuals could comprehend current situation and predict future status better. In this research, we selected three representative parameters including eye blinks rate, pupil size and dwell time in three flight tasks with different complexity to study the expertise influence on eye movements of commercial airlines pilots.

The phenomenon of difference between more expert and less expert existed in this experiment, especially in two more sophisticated scenarios. This was reasonable. More expert pilots adapted their visiting strategy more flexibly in response to variable changes of the task demands [16]. Expert superiority involved "chunking" in perception and cognition. With more experience, experts obtain a relatively greater memory store, of board patterns involving groups of pieces, or what could be called as chunks. A chunk is a perceptual or memory mechanism that organizes a large quantity of more elementary units into an integrated component. The influence of this chunking capability is amplified in complicated situations, which require much more information storage and advanced skill. In contrary, novices would be severely hampered in their efforts because of both limited attention and working memory [17]. A person who is fresh to the systems or situations in a particular domain will be considerably overloaded in seeking to gather information, understand what it means, and formulate correct responses. Lacking such structure, the scan patterns of novices would be sporadic and non-optimal, therefore, they would have to confront each piece of data discretely and be obliged to process it in working memory along with other pieces of data, and might neglect specific vital information or pay excessive attention on other information unnecessarily.

Nevertheless, in normal flight task, standard instrument approach, none of the difference between more expert and less expert was conspicuous. The normal procedures, like takeoff, approach and landing, were routine operations during the daily flight. All the commercial airline pilots, no matter captain or first officer, should master those basic skills. With initial training and compulsory fixed cycle repetition, the resource demanded to accomplish such tasks decreased until the resource-free automaticity was reached for the qualified civilian airmen. Differing from some studies indicating in situations that are not necessarily routine the expert performance would reduce, expertise seems no effect on commercial airline pilots in routine tasks. On the other side, when encountering unusual surroundings or situations of aircraft, more expert could be able to rapidly recognize such familiar patterns. They could then associate these patterns with operations stored in memory that had proven to be effective in the past. They could even reconstruct familiar fragmented information to manage unexpected situations. For instance, under the circumstances that the front windshield of the right seat of the cockpit broke and fell off, most of the instruments failed, and the first officer was once sucked out of the aircraft, the captain of 3U8633, a former air force pilot with nearly twenty years flight experience, made safe preparations for landing at Chengdu Shuangliu International Airport in May, 2018. However, less expert might not have enough exposure to those configurations to have developed many of these kinds of patterns. Hence they deal with the emergencies in a piece-by-piece manner.

Considering the detailed results, firstly, although eye blinks rate manifested a negative relationship of the complexity, only in most sophisticated flight task, the difference between more expert and less expert was significant. It conformed to the evidence that blinks rate decreased slightly with task load, however the correlation between workload and blinks rate was fairly weak [18]. Several studies also indicated that blinks rate might be more efficacious in fatigue measurement, for example, it could be served to distinguish pilots-flying and co-pilots in military aircraft [18]. Secondly, neither expertise nor task complexity had significant impact on pupil size. It seemed inconsistent with Chen SY and J. Epps conclusion, as they found pupil diameter variation was larger during the high perceptual load task than the low, supported by the significant effect on the task type [19]. The discrepancy of the results might probably because pupil diameter is more sensitive to ambient environment than other parameters, such as display polarity or illumination conditions [20]. Besides, Wilson noted that when overload occurs, pupil diameter could become unresponsive to changes or even reverse its response [21]. This could explain the irregular fluctuation of less expert. Moreover, dwell time, directly related to saccadic and fixation behaviors, was an ideal indicator to express the significant effects of expertise and task complexity. Generally, that saccades presented the focus attention on important information, and fixations are necessary for information processing [22]. Longer dwell time is often connected with the difficulty of information extraction [23]. The monitoring strategy of experts afforded greater control and precision of the aircraft. In some extent, the short dwell time reflected their skill level; they simply needed less time to extract relevant information. In some other domains, similar conclusions were found, for instance, in a given writing system, experience had a large impact on fixation durations and saccade lengths [24].

However, it is worth noting that expertise sometimes does not guarantee the better performance. A particularly improper and problematic misunderstanding about the nature of skilled human performance is that, if experts can easily carry out some tasks, they then could always be able to execute those tasks correctly [25]. Yet in fact, experts from time to time make inadvertent errors at tasks they normally perform without difficulty in all fields. This might be the consequence of the combination of subtle changes in task demands, inadequate information available to complete the task, or the inherent characteristics of the cognitive processes that influence skilled performance [26].

Currently, although plenty of novel techniques and approaches have been implemented in aviation industry, for example, prognostics health management and safety management system, pilots themselves are still the predominate element of flight safety. In sum, we studied the effects of expertise on commercial airline pilots' eyes activities, including eye blinks rate, pupil size and dwell time, in three flight scenarios with different complexity. The further attentions would be paid on the following three aspects. Firstly, more flight tasks will be considered, especially, including the abnormal and emergency procedures. Secondly, the distinction of the more expertise and the less expertise is still under controversy, some other measurements that can reflect real flight skills except for the flight hours need more concern. Last but not least, more samples will be selected to represent a wider range of qualified pilots who meet airline's operational requirements.

References

1. Hahn, B., Ross, T.J., Stein, E.A.: Neuroanatomical dissociation between bottom–up and top–down processes of visuospatial selective attention. Neuroimage **32**(2), 842–853 (2006)
2. Cajar, A., et al.: Coupling of attention and saccades when viewing scenes with central and peripheral degradation. J. Vis. **16**(2), 8 (2016)
3. Najemnik, J., Geisler, W.S.: Optimal eye movement strategies in visual search. Nature **434**(7031), 387–391 (2005)
4. Van Orden, K.F., et al.: Eye activity correlates of workload during a visuospatial memory task. Hum. Factors **43**(1), 111–121 (2001)
5. Ellis, K.K.E.: Eye tracking metrics for workload estimation in flight deck operations. Dissertations & Theses - Gradworks (2009)
6. Charness, N., Feltovich, P.J., Hoffman, R.R.: The Cambridge Handbook of Expertise and Expert Performance. vol. 20, no. 7, p. 560–560 (2006)
7. Schriver, A.T., et al.: Expertise differences in attentional strategies related to pilot decision making. Hum. Fact. J. Hum. Fact. Ergon. Soci. **50**(6), 864–878 (2008)
8. Taylor, J.L., et al.: Pilot age and expertise predict flight simulator performance. A 3-year Longitudinal Study **68**(9), 648–654 (2007)
9. Doane, S.M., Sohn, Y.W., Jodlowski, M.T.: Pilot ability to anticipate the consequences of flight actions as a function of expertise **46**(1), 92–103 (2004)
10. Kasarskis, P., et al.: Comparison of expert and novice scan behaviors during VFR flight. In: Proceedings of the 11th International Symposium on Aviation Psychology (2001)
11. Yu, C.S., et al.: Pilots' visual scan patterns and attention distribution during the pursuit of a dynamic target. Aerospace Med. Hum. Perform. **87**(1), 40–47 (2016)
12. Kim, J., et al.: Pilot gaze and glideslope control. Acm Trans. Appl. Percept. **7**(3), 1–18 (2013)

13. FAA, A.C.: Airplane Simulator Qualification (AC 120–40B), F.A. Adminstration, Editor. Washington, DC (1991)
14. Stanton, N.A., Chambers, P.R.G., Piggott, J.: Situational awareness and safety. Saf. Sci. **39**(3), 189–204 (2001)
15. Gawron, V.J., Human Performance, Workload, and Situational Awareness Measures Handbook. CRC Press, Boca Raton (2008)
16. Schriver, A.T., et al.: Expertise differences in attentional strategies related to pilot decision making. **50**(6), 864-878 (2008)
17. Dukas, R.: Causes and consequences of limited attention. Brain Behav. Evol. **63**(4), 197–210 (2002)
18. Marquart, G., Cabrall, C., De Winter, J.: Review of eye-related measures of drivers' mental workload. Procedia Manuf. **3**, 2854–2861 (2015)
19. Stern, J.A., Boyer, D., Schroeder, D.: Blink rate: a possible measure of fatigue. **36**(2), 285–297 (1994)
20. Chen, S., Epps, J.: Using task-induced pupil diameter and blink rate to infer cognitive load. Hum.-Comput. Interact. **29**(4), 390–413 (2014)
21. Taptagaporn, S., Saito, S.: How display polarity and lighting conditions affect the pupil size of VDT operators. Ergonomics **33**(2), 201–208 (1990)
22. Wilson, G.F.: An analysis of mental workload in pilots during flight using multiple psychophysiological measures. Int. J. Aviat. Psychol. **12**(1), 3–18 (2002)
23. Unema, P.J.A., et al.: Time course of information processing during scene perception: the relationship between saccade amplitude and fixation duration. Vis. Cogn. **12**(3), 473–494 (2005)
24. Boucheix, J.-M., et al.: Cueing animations: dynamic signaling aids information extraction and comprehension. Learn. Instr. **25**, 71–84 (2013)
25. Rayner, K., et al.: Eye movements during information processing tasks: individual differences and cultural effects. Vision. Res. **47**(21), 2714–2726 (2007)
26. Ericsson, K.A.: Deliberate practice and acquisition of expert performance: a general overview. Acad. Emerg. Med. **15**(11), 988–994 (2008)
27. Dror, I.E., Charlton, D.: Why experts make errors. JFI **56**(4), 600–616 (2006)

Study on EEG Characteristics of Different Personality Risk Decision Making Under Time Pressure

Qianxiang Zhou[1,2], Bangnan Ye[1,2], and Zhongqi Liu[1,2(✉)]

[1] School of Biological Science and Medical Engineering, Beihang University, Beijing 100191, China
lzq505@163.com
[2] Beijing Advanced Innovation Centre for Biomedical Engineering, Beihang University, Beijing 102402, China

Abstract. Two experimental conditions (Experiment 1: No time pressure, Experiment 2: Time pressure) were designed and 50 volunteers participated in the experiment. Subjective scale data (Big Five Personality Scale and Time Pressure Self-Rating Scale), decision-making behavior performance data (decision time, risk preference, etc.) and EEG data under two experimental conditions were collected respectively. According to the Big Five personality scale scores (neuroticism, openness, pleasantness, extraversion, conscientiousness), volunteers were divided into two personality types (ie flexible personality and troubled personality), and the analysis was conducted under two experimental conditions Differences in risk decision-making behavior characteristics and EEG characteristics of people with different personalities.

Keywords: Time pressure · Risk decision-making · Big Five personality · EEG characteristics

1 Introduction

Time pressure is one of the problems that everyone needs to face, and Svenson and Edland [1] argued that time pressure arises as a feeling of anxiety that individuals experience when the remaining available time for a task is less than the remaining time necessary for the task. Zakay [2] concluded from previous studies that individuals' perception of the existence of time pressure is due to certain specific mental activities with negative emotional experiences are stimulated. When people are faced with emergencies, they often do not have enough time to make decisions due to time pressure caused by external time constraints, which can lead to poor decisions. Different populations have significant behavioral and psychological differences when facing stress, which means different populations have different abilities to deal with time pressure [1]. Screening for populations that can still perform effectively in the face of emergencies in critical tasks is important to ensure the successful performance of critical tasks.

C. Stephanidis et al. (Eds.): HCII 2023, CCIS 1832, pp. 429–436, 2023.
https://doi.org/10.1007/978-3-031-35989-7_55

Currently, a large number of studies have focused on the effects of time pressure on decision making [3, 4], and research on factors specific to different personality traits is not yet mature. There is a growing body of research showing that physiological signals, such as the characteristics of EEG, can respond well to the brain's stress state and risk decision-making behavior [2]. Because the origin of stress is the brain, examining and analyzing a person's stress through electroencephalography (EEG) is also a reliable means of assessing stress levels [5, 6].

In this study, through subjective scale data, decision-making behavior performance data, and EEG data, we tried to find the differences in decision-making characteristics of volunteers under temporal stress and the patterns of changes in EEG characteristics, and to explore the differences in decision-making characteristics of different personalities under temporal stress EEG characteristics differences for subsequent personnel selection and training.

2   Method

2.1   Subject

The volunteers were 50 undergraduate students, who were 18 to 24 years old. All had visual acuity or corrected visual acuity of 1.0 or above; no record of smoking, drinking, or drug use within one week, and no history of psychiatric disorders. All volunteered to participate in the experiment and filled out a written consent form to receive some remuneration upon completion of the experiment. All participants signed an informed consent form.This experiment was approved by the Ethics Committee.

2.2   Experimental Tasks

The experiment consisted of two parts, Experiment 1 and Experiment 2. Experiment 1 was a no time pressure situation, in which a time limit of 60s was imposed to allow the volunteers to focus on their attention; Experiment 2 was set at 80% of the average response time of the volunteers in Experiment 1. Each experiment consisted of 48 trails, and two pie charts (Fig. 1) appeared on the screen when each trial was conducted, representing two different "lotteries", A and B, respectively. Lottery A had a 67% chance of getting $48 and a 33% chance of losing $12. Lottery B had a 68% chance of getting $15 and a 32% chance of getting $37.50. The expectation for Lottery A was $28.2 and Lottery B was $22.2. Volunteers who tend to be risk seeking chose Lottery A because Lottery B had a 67% chance of getting $48, which is more than Lottery A's maximum payout of $37.50. Volunteers who tended to be risk averse were more likely to choose Lottery A because Lottery B had a 33% chance of a losing situation. This allowed the subjects' risk attitudes to be explored. Each pie chart was colored with two different area ratios to represent the probability of gain or loss after selecting that "lottery".

During the experiment, a red cross was first presented on the screen for 0.5 s, then two "lottery tickets" were presented on the screen, and when the stimulus was presented, the volunteer had to think about the "lottery ticket" that he/she thought was more profitable by pressing "F" to select the "lottery ticket" on the left side of the screen and "J" to

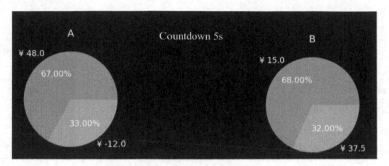

Fig. 1. Task screen

select the "lottery ticket" on the right side of the screen. Each experiment had 48 trails, and the time pressure was set at 80% of the average time for all responses without time pressure for each individual.

2.3 Experimental Equipment

(1) EEG acquisition system

A complete set of Brain Products EEG equipment, including EEG signal amplifier (Brain Products, antiCHamp), 64-lead EEG signal acquisition cap (Brain Products, actiCAP), EEG signal synchronization acquisition system, and EEG stimulation system, manufactured by BP, was used in this experiment.

(2) Task presentation and data collection computer

The task presentation computer was preloaded with E-Prime2 tasks to present the experimental tasks, and performance data related to the experimental tasks were recorded in the background while the experiment is in progress. An additional EEG acquisition computer with Brain Vision Recoder 3.0 EEG signal acquisition software was pre-installed.

3 Results

3.1 Data from Subjective Scales

Big Five Inventory Data. Volunteers' scores on five personality traits were measured using the Big Five Inventory (BFI), which divide personality into five dimensions: neuroticism, extraversion, openness, agreeableness, and responsibility. It contained a total of 60 questions, each with five options corresponding to a score of 1 to 5. Each personality dimension had a maximum score of 60 and a minimum score of 0. Table 1 showed the scores of the subjects.

Using the K-Means algorithm to cluster personalities, it was possible to classify personality types into two categories: One was the resilient (neuroticism score below normal, extraversion, openness, and responsibility scores above normal, and agreeableness score within the normal range (-0.5 to 0.5)), with a total of 20 (40%); the other was disturbed (neuroticism score above normal, responsibility score below normal), a total

Table 1. Subjects' Big Five personality score statistics

Idex	Average	Standard deviation	Minimum	Maxmam
Neuroticism	35.72	7.99	23	51
Extraversion	37.76	6.69	22	50
Openness	43.22	7.56	29	60
Agreeableness	35	3.01	30	43
Responsibility	41.48	4.56	30	57

of 30 volunteers (60% of the total). Individuals with the disturbed personality type were prone to more negative emotions, while the resilient personality type was able to face different scenarios in life, such as stress and conflict, more easily.

Time Stress Data. The time stress scale was used to measure the level of time stress perception, and the test paper consisted of 6 questions, each with a score range from 0 to 5 out of 30. The mean values and standard deviations of the time stress scale scores of the volunteers with different personalities were shown in Table 2.

Table 2. Time stress scale scores of volunteers with different personalities

	No time pressure			Time pressure		
	Resilient	Disturbed	All subjects	Resilient	Disturbed	All subjects
Average	15.79	16.76	16.38	21.89	21.36	21.57
Standard deviation	1.47	2.09	1.9	2.05	2.48	2.29

Using Pearson correlation analysis, correlations were made between the volunteers' Big Five personality scores and their scores on the Time Stress Scale, and the results of the analysis showed that under the condition of Experiment 1 without time stress, none of the volunteers' scores on the Big Five personalitiAes were significantly correlated with their scores on the Time Stress Scale. In the condition of Experiment 2, the volunteers' scores on the agreeableness scale showed a significant positive correlation with their scores on the time stress scale ($r = 0.369$, $p = 0.035$), that is, the higher the scores on the agreeableness scale, the higher the volunteers' scores on the time stress scale. Under time stress, the correlation between the neuroticism score and the time stress scale approached a significant positive correlation ($r = 0.237$, $p = 0.054$).

3.2 Performance Data

Decision-Making Time. The means and standard deviations of the decision times of volunteers with different personalities in Experiment 1 and Experiment 2 were shown in Table 3.

Table 3. Decision-making time of volunteers with different personalities

	No time pressure			Time pressure		
	Resilient	Disturbed	All subjects	Resilient	Disturbed	All subjects
Average (s)	21.55	19.98	20.66	10.58	9.83	10.15
Standard deviation (s)	3.99	3.45	3.69	2.14	1.85	1.97

Resilient volunteers had longer decision times than distressed volunteers in both experimental conditions due to the fact that resilient personalities have higher responsibility scores, and volunteers' responsibility scores showed significant positive correlations with decision times in both experiments, so resilient personalities with higher responsibility scores had longer decision times.

Quality of Decision Making. Decision quality was defined as the number of volunteers choosing the "lottery" with higher expectation in the decision task, and the statistics of all volunteers choosing the "lottery" with higher expectation in the two different experimental conditions were shown in Table 4.

Table 4. Decision quality of volunteers with different personalities

	No time pressure			Time pressure		
	Resilient	Disturbed	All subjects	Resilient	Disturbed	All subjects
Average	26.35	25.36	25.8	19.6	19.03	19.2
Standard deviation	3.32	3.51	3.4	2.81	3.07	2.93

The quality of volunteers' decision making in Experiment 1 was higher than that in Experiment 2. In Experiment 1, resilient personalities had higher decision quality than disturbed personalities. Similarly, in Experiment 2, resilient personality volunteers had higher decision quality than disturbed personality, but the main effect of personality was not significant.

Risk Attitudes. Risk attitude was measured by the number of times volunteers chose the risk-taking option in the decision-making task, and the statistics of the number of volunteers who chose the risk-seeking "lottery" were shown in Table 5.

Correlational analysis showed that in Experiment 1, the Neuroticism score ($r = -0.323$, $p = 0.022$) was significantly and negatively correlated with volunteers' risk preferences, and the Extraversion score ($r = 0.348$, $p = 0.013$) was significantly and positively correlated with risk preferences; the same results were found in Experiment 2, where the Neuroticism score ($r = -0.403$, $p = 0.004$) was significantly negatively correlated with volunteers' risk preferences, and the extraversion score ($r = 0.385$, $p = 0.006$) was significantly positively correlated with risk preferences; in both experimental conditions, volunteers with higher neuroticism scores tended to be more risk averse,

Table 5. Risk preferences of volunteers with different personalities

	No time pressure			Time pressure		
	Resilient	Disturbed	All subjects	Resilient	Disturbed	All subjects
Average	26.45	24.03	25	22.45	18.73	20.22
Standard deviation	3.39	4.75	4.39	3.92	5.11	4.97

and those with higher extraversion scores tended to be more risk seeking. Resilient personality volunteers both preferred the risk-seeking option and showed higher risk-seeking preferences than troubled personality volunteers.

3.3 EEG Data

Power Spectrum Characteristics. In Experiment 2, the relative power of theta waves in the central (p = 0.025) and occipital (p = 0.027) regions of the resilient personality increased compared to Experiment 1. In contrast, for the disturbed personality, the relative power of theta waves in the prefrontal and central regions decreased under temporal stress.

In the Experiment 2 condition, the relative power of theta waves in the central region (r = 0.235, p = 0.039) was significantly and positively correlated with the open personality score, and the relative power of theta waves in the central region (r = 0.275, p = 0.017), parietal region (r = 0.306, p = 0.008) and occipital region (r = 0.245, p = 0.034) was significantly and positively correlated with the agreeableness score The relative power of β waves in the central (r = 0.244, p = 0.04), parietal (r = 0.228, p = 0.045) and occipital (r = 0.219, p = 0.037) regions had a significant negative correlation with the livability score. Relative power in other frequency bands was not significantly correlated with Big Five personality.

Wavelet Packet Energy Characteristics. In Experiment 2 with time pressure, the δ-wave relative wavelet packet energy in the prefrontal and central regions was significantly lower than in Experiment 1, and the δ-wavelet energy in the occipital region decreased under time pressure, but the results did not reach the significance level; the relative wavelet energy of α-wave was significantly lower on all four brain regions; the relative wavelet energy of β-wave was significantly higher in the prefrontal and central regions, and in the parietal and occipital regions, the wavelet energy of β-wave was likewise The relative wavelet energy of β-wave was significantly higher in the prefrontal and central regions, and in the parietal and occipital regions, the wavelet energy of β-wave was also higher, but the results did not reach the significance level.

The results of the correlation analysis showed that the scores of the five dimensions of the Big Five personality and the relative wavelet packet energy of the EEG did not correlate in Experiment 1 without time stress. In the conditions of Experiment 2, the volunteers' theta wave relative wavelet packet energies in the prefrontal (r = 0.258, p = 0.025), central (r = 0.232, p = 0.042), parietal (r = 0.241, p = 0.04), and occipital (r =

0.257, p = 0.024) regions all showed significant positive correlations with the scores of agreeableness.

Sample Entropy Characteristics. A two-factor ANOVA was conducted on the sample entropy of the EEG signals in the four brain regions, and the time-stress and personality main effects of the sample entropy data were not significant on any of the four brain regions, and the interaction term was likewise not significant.

Using Pearson correlation analysis, the correlations between the sample entropy values of the four brain regions of the volunteers in the two experiments and the Big Five personality scores were calculated separately, and the results showed that the sample entropy of the EEG signals of the volunteers was insensitive to the personality characteristics of the volunteers under both experimental conditions, and there was no significant correlation.

Wavelet Entropy. Wavelet entropy can visually reflect the distribution of energy in different rhythmic signals, the larger the wavelet entropy, the more dispersed the energy distribution of different rhythmic signals. In the study of relative wavelet energy, the relative energy of fast waves (δ, α), which originally accounted for more in the prefrontal and central regions of volunteers under time pressure, decreased, and the relative energy of slower waves (β, γ), which accounted for less, increased, making the energy of EEG waves dispersed to a relatively wide frequency band range, the disorderly set of EEG signals was enhanced, the complexity was increased, and therefore the wavelet entropy value was increased. This fully illustrated that the disorder and complexity of the brain were elevated and the brain activity was more active under time stress.

Micro-State Analysis. Microstates of EEG are a method of using spontaneous neuronal activity to parse brain function. Brain topographies do not change randomly over time; instead, a certain EEG topography can remain stable for a certain period of time, and then quickly switch to another topography afterwards, each of which can remain stable for a period of time. It has been found that these relatively stable EEG topographies and topological transition processes can reflect the brain's processing of information and were called microstates of EEG signals [7].

By means of clustering, the microstates of EEG could be classified into microstates alike A, microstate B, microstate C, and microstate D. The average duration of microstates was about 80 to 120 ms, after which they are transformed into another microstate.

Correlation analyses of the microstate parameters with the Big Five personality showed that the neuroticism personality score was significantly and positively correlated with the duration of microstate B (r = 0.327, p = 0.02) and borderline significantly and negatively correlated with the responsibility score (r = -0.268, p = 0.06). The percentage of microstates C had a significant positive correlation with neuroticism scores (r = 0.289, p = 0.042). The number of occurrences of microstate B had a borderline significant positive correlation with the neuroticism score (r = -0.261, p = 0.067). In contrast, disturbed personality volunteers had higher neuroticism scores and lower responsibility scores, which may have led to a higher duration of microstate B than resilient personality, as well as a higher percentage of occurrences of microstate C than resilient personality.

4 Conclusion

Individual temporal stress was successfully induced using a personalized stress elicitation method, and the temporal stress condition resulted in a significant increase in the individual's sense of temporal stress; the individual's decision making performance decreased; and the EEG characteristics showed stress state-related features.

References

1. Svenson, O., Edland, A.: Change of preference under time pressure: choices and judgements. Scand. J. Psychol. **28**(4), 322–330 (1987)
2. Zakay, Dan: The impact of time perception processes on decision making under time stress. In: Ola Svenson, A., Maule, John (eds.) Time Pressure and Stress in Human Judgment and Decision Making, pp. 59–72. Springer US, Boston (1993). https://doi.org/10.1007/978-1-4757-6846-6_4
3. Bernoulli, D.: Exposition of a new theory on the measurement of risk. Econometrica **22**(1), 23–36 (1954)
4. Dahl, R.A., Simon, H.A.: Administrative behavior: a study of decision-making proceses in administrative organization. Adm. Sci. Q. **2**(2), 244 (1957)
5. Seo, S.H., Lee, J.T.: Stress and EEG. In: Crisan, M. (ed.) Convergence and Hybrid Information Technologies INTECH, Croatia, pp. 413–426 (2010)
6. Slobounov, S.M., Fukada, K., Simon, R., et al.: Neurophysiological and behavioral indices of time pressure effects on visuomotor task performance. Cogn. Brain Res. **9**(3), 287–298 (2000)
7. Lehmann, D., Ozaki, H., Pal, I.: EEG alpha map series: brain micro-states by space-oriented adaptive segmentation. Electroencephalogr. Clin. Neurophysiol. **67**(3), 271–288 (1987)

Ethics, Transparency and Trust in HCI

A Transparency Framework for App Store Descriptions

Adel Alhejaili[1,2][✉] and James Blustein[1]

[1] Dalhousie University, Halifax, NS, Canada
adel.alhejaili@dal.ca, jamie@ACM.org
[2] Taibah University, Medina, Saudi Arabia

Abstract. Apps that address health issues, including mental health, are emerging as essential categories. People worldwide are increasingly using smartphone apps for mental health support, especially in the wake of the COVID-19 pandemic.

Prior research has indicated that finding the right app is challenging. Part of the problem is the absence of or lack of the necessary information people need to know before downloading such a vital app.

In this work, we created a transparency framework that compounded several challenges and barriers and presented possible design guidelines that bridge this gap and mitigate users' burden when searching for health apps by communicating health information effectively.

Keywords: Transparency · Apps · Research-based evidence content · Claims · Effectiveness · Hidden costs · Privacy

1 Introduction

As we move through these uncertain times, people worldwide increasingly use smartphone apps for mental health support [35]. There is a worldwide increase in the use of smartphone apps for mental health support [35]. Mental health apps can help people manage their mental health and well-being for less money and time than traditional options, and increase access to care, which has become increasingly important, especially in the wake of the COVID-19 pandemic [28].

According to the Organization for the Review of Care and Health Apps (ORCHA), there was a 200% increase in the use of mental health apps [21]. This pandemic has "exposed crucial gaps in mental health care systems, which significantly impact the well-being of many people globally" [28, p.2].

Considering the number of mental health apps available, it is a challenge for consumers to find the right ones [29, 30]. They often rely on app reviews and in-store ratings, or they might follow given advice through social media or personal recommendations [30].

© The Author(s), under exclusive license to Springer Nature Switzerland AG 2023
C. Stephanidis et al. (Eds.): HCII 2023, CCIS 1832, pp. 439–446, 2023.
https://doi.org/10.1007/978-3-031-35989-7_56

The app stores offer little information when it comes to the app description since all the necessary information people need to know before downloading such a vital app might be buried in the app description, not visible at first sight, or might be absent or inadequate [4,12,14,18,23,29,31,32]. Despite the efforts that have been made to address this issue, there is still an urgent need to change the app store design [17,34].

This research aims to showcase a transparency framework of the app descriptions in the app stores that compounded several challenges and barriers. More importantly, it also offers possible design guidelines that can be used to bridge the gap in communicating health information to users effectively.

2   Background and Related Work

This section provides a brief and holistic overview of our theoretical transparency framework of the app description based on a comprehensive literature review of prior work[1]. Also, we shed some light on temporary solutions.

2.1   Transparency in the App Description

"App descriptions are a crucial channel for developers to communicate apps' information to users" [5, p. 3]. A critical challenge in the app stores is that important information about the app may be absent [23]. App descriptions may not be readable by target users, which can negatively impact app adoption and usage [32].

Research-Based Evidence Information. Due to the "lack of scientific evidence, the absence of scientific requirements for mental health apps on the Apple App Store or Google Play Stores, and limitations in existing app evaluation methods, relatively little is known about the effectiveness of popular mental health apps or even the extent to which mental health apps include content consistent with empirically supported interventions" [37, p.1]. The literature on the "efficacy of mobile health apps is still evolving" [15, p.106]. The supporting evidence base of even using the best available apps is scant, and most of these apps "do not deliver value, especially for those who are sick or have chronic conditions" [6, p.1].

Claims and Effectiveness. Marshall et al. reported that only 3% of mental health apps were backed by research (e.g., claims of effectiveness) [22, p. 5]. In another study, Marshall et al. [23] stated that only 6.2% of the 162 apps had published evidence of their effectiveness. More importantly, users were found to be skeptical of the effectiveness of the treatments [34,36].

---

[1] The complete list of references associated with this work is available upon request from the corresponding author.

Credentials and Credibility. Users face challenges, especially when they try to judge that an app is credible and of good quality, which may not be since the provided information in the app stores is insufficient [14]. Organizations such as the UK NHS's app library "can lend credibility to and have the potential to promote the uptake of selected health apps by providing a list of safe, evidence-informed, tested, and, where possible, clinically effective health apps for the general public to choose from" [34, p.2].

Hidden Costs. Many users stated they want to know the hidden costs of free apps. Users were looking specifically for that information, especially the difference between the free and paid version. Furthermore, they want to know beforehand whether they would be required to pay overtime and pay for an upgrade (e.g., extra functionally) [9].

Hudson et al. stated that "apps should be transparent about their costs, rather than hiding features behind a paywall, where it is not possible to evaluate the usefulness of those features before making a payment" [11, p.8]. More importantly, in-app purchases are not sufficiently disclosed in all the apps and can only be seen when using the app.

Privacy Concerns. Previous findings suggested that the regulations related to the data privacy of apps remain inadequate, and one of the reasons is the poor regulations in the app stores [26, 38]. A great deal of research showed that users are concerned about their privacy [12, 13, 20, 25, 34, 38].

Many available apps rely on selling the collected data to fulfil "their business plan, jeopardizing personal privacy" [38, p.3]. Also, evidence of poor privacy practices has been found, resulting in fines because of selling users' sensitive information [38].

To ensure the data privacy and security of health apps, a great deal of research has presented guidelines and recommendations that can be followed by app stores and incorporated into the app development practices [12, 25, 38]. The app's description needs better transparency of data protection to help users make an informed choice upfront by providing them with the risks associated with sharing their sensitive information with third parties for commercial purposes and how their data are handled [25, 34, 38].

Clinical and Professional Reviews. Prior research has found that when users search for apps, the most influential cue they consider is the app reviews [1]. Unfortunately, app developers often lack clinical expertise [14]. Because of that, they are asked to integrate the information from professionals (e.g., academic researchers and clinicians) [24, 27, 29, 38] since the importance of app reviews is aligned with the app description [1].

Problems with the Current App Stores Delivery Models. Prior work suggested that some participants found that the information in the app stores is disorganized and causes confusion, representing a barrier to using health apps [33,34]. They are "inherently designed poorly and limit the effectiveness of patients and clinicians to actively identify and utilize such apps without using outside resources" [2, p.5]. Helf and Hlavacs suggested "new app store formats need to be explored and evaluated" [8, p.20].

2.2   Curated Health Tools and Portals as Temporary Solutions

Several tools have emerged over the past few years to assist consumers and clinicians navigate crowded app stores [16,24,27,36]. Szinay et al. [34] study explored if the general public is willing to use curated health app portals. They found that half of their participants preferred to use Google when searching for a health app as their first choice, whereas the other half decided to use the app store [34]. Surprisingly, even with the health app portals, users were unaware of their existence [34]. Despite the appealing factor of health portals to users, only 3 out of 18 have searched for a health app from the health portal, whereas the rest decided to search using the app stores. [34]. Still, any "potential consumer would have to search in two places for the information they need to make a choice" [38, p.2].

3   Research Objective

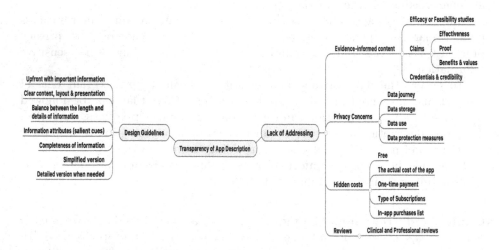

Fig. 1. Transparency framework of app description and design guidelines.

The information people need to know before downloading a critical app is buried in the description (e.g., evidence-informed content and hidden costs). When users have adequate information about the app they are evaluating, they can choose the right app that matches their needs.

As seen in Fig. 1, this research intends to showcase our transparency framework of the app descriptions in the app stores that compounded several challenges and barriers. More importantly, following discussed earlier work, it also offers possible design guidelines that can effectively bridge the gap in communicating health information to users and can be applied to other health app categories (e.g., eating disorders).

Earlier studies showed that the depth of the available information influences people's decisions. It is essential to consider the information attributes and the completeness of the provided information [7].

Overall, the app description should be designed not to overwhelm the users. Instead, the presented information should be complete, so users can avoid looking or searching in multiple resources [38] or trying to infer what is missing [7]. We aim to maximize the impact and benefits of specific information cues to support people's decisions when searching for health apps [30].

4 Discussion

The implications of our transparency framework are tremendous and pervade many levels. Numerous parties (e.g., "stakeholders in public health, policymakers, government bodies, health organizations," researchers, providers and developers) are involved in bridging the gap and mitigating users' burden when searching for health apps [34, p.11]. The needed changes are enormous since the lack of information found in the app description could impact users' expectations.

It is essential and crucial to providing users with all the necessary information about health apps upfront at the point of download without burdening them with finding them on their own. Finding information about the evidence-informed content and whether the app does what it claims to do is challenging. In the current app stores, the app description is lengthy. The direct mention of that information is absent, even for popular health apps. Furthermore, finding the hidden costs of the app features beforehand does not exist. More importantly, users want to know who has access to their data, whether the collected data is shared with healthcare professionals or others, where the information is stored in the app, where it will go, and if they can delete it [13,38]. The majority of those apps did not clearly disclose this type of information to their respective users [10].

Regarding the curated health portals such as One Mind PsyberGuide [27] and MIND database [16], users are unaware of their existence, and they cannot be expected to look or search in multiple resources [38]. Also, navigating curated health tools was difficult and characterized as "cumbersome" [34].

Overall, this work is the first step and the starting point towards finding a suitable solution that addresses all the issues surrounding how we assist users when searching for health apps.

5   Conclusion and Future Work

In this work, we reviewed prior research and provided an important opportunity to advance and contribute to the understanding of the lack of transparency in the app description of app stores. Our transparency framework compounded several challenges and barriers and presented possible design guidelines for the discussed issues.

The app store design should serve as "a gateway — ... [not a] barrier — for effective communication of health information" [19, p. 136]. Consumers must be able to easily access and view the complete information about the apps they are curious about [3]. The app stores should provide a mechanism for developers to add all the addressed issues in the app description.

In the follow-up phase of our work, using a mix-method approach, we plan to conduct an evaluation study with users to test a proposed prototype's design.

In conclusion, given the lack of mental health app resources for clinicians, researchers, developers and users, this research will serve as an essential resource to bridge the gap and provide valuable information.

Acknowledgments. The first author gratefully acknowledges a scholarship from Taibah University, Saudi Arabia.

References

1. Alhejaili, A., Blustein, J.: A study on how users choose apps. In: Human-Computer Interaction: User Experience and Behavior. Springer, Heidelberg (2022). https://doi.org/10.1007/978-3-031-05412-9_1
2. Aungst, T., Seed, S., Gobin, N., Jung, R.: The good, the bad, and the poorly designed: The mobile app stores are not a user-friendly experience for health and medical purposes. Dig. Health (2022). https://doi.org/10.1177/20552076221090038
3. Chakraborty, D., Kayal, G., Mehta, P., Nunkoo, R., Rana, N.P.: Consumers' usage of food delivery app: a theory of consumption values. J. Hosp. Mark. Manag. (2022). https://doi.org/10.1080/19368623.2022.2024476
4. Eis, S., et al.: Mobile applications in mood disorders and mental health: systematic search in apple app store and google play store and review of the literature. Int. J. Environ. Res. Public Health (2022). https://doi.org/10.3390/ijerph19042186
5. Feng, Y., Chen, L., Zheng, A., Gao, C., Zheng, Z.: Ac-net: assessing the consistency of description and permission in android apps. IEEE Access (2019). https://doi.org/10.1109/ACCESS.2019.2912210
6. Gordon, W.J., Landman, A., Zhang, H., Bates, D.W.: Beyond validation: getting health apps into clinical practice. NPJ Dig. Med. (2020). https://doi.org/10.1038/s41746-019-0212-z
7. Haugtvedt, C.P., Herr, P.M., Kardes, F.R.: Handbook of Consumer Psychology. Psychology Press, New York (2008). https://doi.org/10.4324/9780203809570
8. Helf, C., Hlavacs, H.: Apps for life change: critical review and solution directions. Entertain. Comput. (2016). https://doi.org/10.1016/j.entcom.2015.07.001
9. Hendriks, Y., Peek, S., Kaptein, M., Bongers, I., et al.: Process and information needs when searching for and selecting apps for smoking cessation: qualitative study using contextual inquiry. JMIR Hum. Fact. (2022). https://doi.org/10.2196/32628

10. Huckvale, K., Torous, J., Larsen, M.E.: Assessment of the data sharing and privacy practices of smartphone apps for depression and smoking cessation. JAMA Netw. Open (2019). https://doi.org/10.1001/jamanetworkopen.2019.2542

11. Hudson, G., et al.: Comparing professional and consumer ratings of mental health apps: mixed methods study. JMIR Form. Res. (2022). https://doi.org/10.2196/39813

12. Jilka, S., et al.: Terms and conditions apply: critical issues for readability and jargon in mental health depression apps. Internet Intervent. (2021). https://doi.org/10.1016/j.invent.2021.100433

13. Kabacińska, K., et al.: What criteria are young people using to select mobile mental health applications? a nominal group study. Dig. Health (2022). https://doi.org/10.1177/20552076221102775

14. Kanthawala, S., Joo, E., Kononova, A., Peng, W., Cotten, S.: Folk theorizing the quality and credibility of health apps. Mob. Media Commun. (2019). https://doi.org/10.1177/2050157918796859

15. Kao, C.K., Liebovitz, D.M.: Consumer mobile health apps: current state, barriers, and future directions. PM&R (2017). https://doi.org/10.1016/j.pmrj.2017.02.018

16. Lagan, S., D'Mello, R., Vaidyam, A., Bilden, R., Torous, J.: Assessing mental health apps marketplaces with objective metrics from 29,190 data points from 278 apps. Acta Psychiatrica Scandinavica (2021). https://doi.org/10.1111/acps.13306

17. Larsen, M.E., et al.: Using science to sell apps: evaluation of mental health app store quality claims. NPJ Dig. Med. (2019). https://doi.org/10.1038/s41746-019-0093-1

18. Larsen, M.E., Nicholas, J., Christensen, H.: Quantifying app store dynamics: longitudinal tracking of mental health apps. JMIR mHealth uHealth (2016). https://doi.org/10.2196/mhealth.6020

19. Lazard, A.J., Brennen, J.S., Adams, E.T., Love, B.: Cues for increasing social presence for mobile health app adoption. J. Health Commun. (2020). https://doi.org/10.1080/10810730.2020.1719241

20. Lipschitz, J., et al.: Adoption of mobile apps for depression and anxiety: cross-sectional survey study on patient interest and barriers to engagement. JMIR Mental Health (2019). https://doi.org/10.2196/11334

21. Ashall-Payne, L.: On World Mental Health Day, ORCHA reports that the use of mental health apps is still on the rise (2021). https://orchahealth.com/on-world-mental-health-day-orcha-reports-that-the-use-of-mental-health-apps-is-still-on-the-rise/

22. Marshall, J.M., Dunstan, D.A., Bartik, W.: The digital psychiatrist: in search of evidence-based apps for anxiety and depression. Front. Psychiatry (2019). https://doi.org/10.3389/fpsyt.2019.00831

23. Marshall, J.M., Dunstan, D.A., Bartik, W.: Apps with maps-anxiety and depression mobile apps with evidence-based frameworks: systematic search of major app stores. JMIR Mental Health (2020). https://doi.org/10.2196/16525

24. New Zealand Ministry of Health: Health Navigator app library (2022). https://healthify.nz/apps/

25. Nurgalieva, L., O'Callaghan, D., Doherty, G.: Security and privacy of mhealth applications: a scoping review. IEEE Access (2020). https://doi.org/10.1109/ACCESS.2020.2999934

26. O'Loughlin, K., Neary, M., Adkins, E.C., Schueller, S.M.: Reviewing the data security and privacy policies of mobile apps for depression. Internet Intervent. (2019). https://doi.org/10.1016/j.invent.2018.12.001

27. One Mind PsyberGuide: About One Mind PsyberGuide (2022). https:// onemindpsyberguide.org/about-psyberguide/

28. Philippe, T.J., et al.: Digital health interventions for delivery of mental health care: systematic and comprehensive meta-review. JMIR Mental Health (2022). https:// doi.org/10.2196/35159

29. Porras-Segovia, A., Díaz-Oliván, I., Gutiérrez-Rojas, L., Dunne, H., Moreno, M., Baca-García, E.: Apps for depression: are they ready to work? Curr. Psychiat. Rep. **22**(3), 1–9 (2020). https://doi.org/10.1007/s11920-020-1134-9

30. Schueller, S.M., Neary, M., O'Loughlin, K., Adkins, E.C.: Discovery of and interest in health apps among those with mental health needs: survey and focus group study. J. Med. Internet Res. (2018). https://doi.org/10.2196/10141

31. Stafford, E., Brister, T., Duckworth, K., Rauseo-Ricupero, N., Lagan, S., et al.: Needs and experiences of users of digital navigation tools for mental health treatment and supportive services: survey study. JMIR Mental Health (2021). https:// doi.org/10.2196/27022

32. Su, W.C., Mehta, K.Y., Gill, K., Yeh, P., Chih, M.Y., Wu, D.T.: Assessing the readability of app descriptions and investigating its role in the choice of mhealth apps: retrospective and prospective analyses. In: AMIA Annual Symposium Proceedings. American Medical Informatics Association (2021). https://pubmed.ncbi. nlm.nih.gov/35308941

33. Szinay, D., Jones, A., Chadborn, T., Brown, J., Naughton, F., et al.: Influences on the uptake of and engagement with health and well-being smartphone apps: systematic review. J. Med. Internet Res. (2020). https://doi.org/10.2196/17572

34. Szinay, D., Perski, O., Jones, A., Chadborn, T., Brown, J., Naughton, F., et al.: Influences on the uptake of health and well-being apps and curated app portals: think-aloud and interview study. JMIR mHealth uHealth (2021). https://doi.org/ 10.2196/27173

35. Torous, J.: Matching Mental Health Apps with Trust and Transparency (2020). https://www.psychologytoday.com/us/blog/digital-mental-health/202004/ matching-mental-health-apps-trust-and-transparency

36. Wasil, A.R., Palermo, E.H., Lorenzo-Luaces, L., DeRubeis, R.J.: Is there an app for that? a review of popular apps for depression, anxiety, and well-being. Cogn. Behav. Pract. (2021). https://doi.org/10.1016/j.cbpra.2021.07.001

37. Wasil, A.R., Venturo-Conerly, K.E., Shingleton, R.M., Weisz, J.R.: A review of popular smartphone apps for depression and anxiety: assessing the inclusion of evidence-based content. Behav. Res. Therapy (2019). https://doi.org/10.1016/j. brat.2019.103498

38. Wykes, T., Schueller, S., et al.: Why reviewing apps is not enough: transparency for trust (t4t) principles of responsible health app marketplaces. J. Med. Internet Res. (2019). https://doi.org/10.2196/12390

Offensive Play Recognition of Basketball Video Footage Using ActionFormer

Tafadzwa Blessing Chiura and Dustin van der Haar[✉]

Academy of Computer Science and Software Engineering, University of Johannesburg, Corner of Kingsway Avenue and University Road, Auckland Park, Johannesburg, Gauteng, South Africa
bless.mukuru@gmail.com, dvanderhaar@uj.ac.za

Abstract. This paper will aim to conduct 3 experiments to determine the best-performing action recognition approach on the SpaceJam dataset. The 3 experiments are Temporal Segment Network (TSN), Inflated 3D-CNN (I3D) and Pose-estimation (Pose-C3D). TSN and I3D yielded similar results with TSN scoring 54.88% for the mean accuracy, 94.33% for top-5 accuracy and 54.88 top-1 accuracy. And I3D scored 53.07% mean accuracy, 91.65% for top-5 accuracy and 53.07 mean accuracy. When Pose-C3d is run for 240 epochs it achieves better results with a top 1 accuracy and mean-class accuracy of 63.15% and a top-5 accuracy of 95.51. These results indicate that the models can distinguish between similar actions such as running and walking in basketball with relative success.

Keywords: Basketball · Action Recognition · Offensive Play Recognition

1 Introduction

The application of technology in sports ranges from statistical analysis, and score prediction to performance tracking using wearable technology [1]. Another significant factor that influences match outcomes is coaching, as evidenced by the better-coached teams usually outperforming their opponent [2]. With the influence of coaching ever-increasing, it is imperative to develop a better understanding of the sport.

This study will carry out a comparison of action recognition methods applied to the SpaceJam dataset and discuss the outcome as well as benchmark the results against past experiments. The discussion will start with a background overview, along with other action recognition datasets, and then the methods and similar works section. The experiment details are outlined, along with their results and a discussion. The article is then concluded.

2 Background

Plays in basketball are comprised of mainly two phases, offence, and defence. Offence is when one team has the ball and is trying to score. While defence is when the opposing team is trying to get the ball back and stop the opposition from scoring. Within either

C. Stephanidis et al. (Eds.): HCII 2023, CCIS 1832, pp. 447–454, 2023.
https://doi.org/10.1007/978-3-031-35989-7_57

phase lies a multitude of set plays. Set plays can be viewed as a coordinated sequence of movements that take place leading up to an attempt to score. DiFiori, et al. describe a play as an interactive drill that is dynamic and requires a certain level of skill from the players [3].

Action recognition is the process of labelling visual data with action labels. Factors such as motion differences in the manner each subject performs each action in question can influence and add complexities in this area [4]. Regarding action recognition, the goal is generally well understood and predominately revolves around the correct identification and classification of action(s) that are being carried out in said footage or video stream. Traditionally action recognition falls into one of two categories, namely human-human and human-object interactions [5]. Based on the length of the video and the activity in the video both human-human and human-object may be present and may even overlap. The tasks in this domain involve locating the subject or region of interest. Once the subject is found in a frame, the next step will be to try to find the same subject in the following frames, essentially tracking its movement throughout the video.

2.1 Justification

Computer vision has shown that computers can identify complex human movement patterns given adequate training data. Getting similar performance to the sport of basketball would save coaches countless hours preparing video snippets for their players eliminating the element of human error resulting in mislabelling for example. It furthermore shows the need and advantage of content-based video indexing. To add to this, most sports video consumers (fans, players, coaches, media) are rarely ever interested in the entire game footage but rather in certain key action points.

The complexities and intricacies of basketball are multi-faceted as highlighted above. Being able to break down the game is invaluable to all stakeholders, from new players to old fans to broadcasters and so forth. Giving visual breakdowns improves the understanding of game strategy, and improves training and execution, thus reducing chances of injury and resulting in an overall better sports experience. The intervention of computers in video analysis allows for the simplification of labour-intense processes. Further benefits will arise from the ability of the models to distinguish fine-grained motions such as the ones found in basketball. Given the fast-paced nature of basketball, positive outcomes could inherently mean better localization and tracking, ultimately providing better insight into how to deal with fast-paced action videos.

Successful offensive play recognition enables computers to obtain a deeper level of understanding that is context-driven in basketball. Past research has looked at the classification of actions in isolation or detecting stoppages during gameplay of broadcasts [6]. This research aims to move from successful action recognition to chaining those actions to determine if the sequence of events falls within the offensive phase of the team.

2.2 Datasets

This section will look at some popular data sets used to tackle action recognition problems. Publicly accessible datasets are important as creating a new data set can be time-consuming and may prove to be financially expensive (equipment, labour etc.). It is also easier for the community to determine the best-performing approaches if similar datasets are used.

UFC-101 is a dataset from the University of Florida Central which has 101 common action classes (such as applying lipstick, cliff diving and dunking a basketball) distributed across roughly 13000 videos and spanning 27 h [7]. The video clips are all standardised to 25 fps (frames per second) with a resolution of 320 × 240 pixels. The average clip length is 7.21 s, the shortest being just over 1 s and the longest being 71 s.

Sports-1M is a dataset made up of 1 million videos that span over 480 different sports activities. The activities or actions are specific in nature and do not follow the convention of general "actions" as seen in the above datasets. To elaborate the data set has basketball, 3-on-3 basketball, and wheelchair basketball, and swimming has both medley and synchronized swimming [8]. The videos are on average longer than 5 min. The dataset is not standardised, requiring its users to have a pre-processing step before using it as done by [8]. They cropped the frames to the size of 200 × 200 pixels.

ActivityNet is a dataset aimed at tackling human activity understanding. The objective of the dataset was to compare approaches aimed at untrimmed video classification, trimmed activity classification and activity detection. The dataset covers a wide range of daily human activities ranging from "mowing the lawn" to "paying delivered pizza". ActivityNet is made up of videos of varying lengths up to 20 min and are largely 30 fps. The dataset is comprised of 203 classes, spanning 849 h and on average each video depicts on average 1.41 activities. The classes can be grouped into broad categories namely, "personal care", "eating and drinking", "household", caring and helping", "working", "socialising and leisure" and "sports and exercises" [9].

SpaceJam is a dataset that is focused on specific basketball movements [10, 11]. SpaceJam looks at some actions that take place during a basketball game (e.g. passing and running). The other datasets listed above are geared towards large-scale audiences and span over multiple general action categories or classes. SpaceJam is made up of 32000 short video clips that span 10 classes (e.g., walk, pass, shoot). It is the most suited, publicly available dataset to date for the goals set out for this study. Each video is made up of 15 frames, with a frame rate of 10fps and a resolution of 128 × 176 pixels.

3 Similar Work

Action recognition has garnered much attention and inspired various innovative approaches. This section will look at works that are similar to the study that is carried out in this paper. It will discuss some of the recent developments and implementations in action recognition such as 2 stream approaches and transformers.

3.1 Learning Spatio-Temporal Features with 3D-CNN

Tran et al. (2015) looked at applying deep 3D-CNNs that could model temporal information using 3D convolutions and 3D-pooling operations [12]. This was to overcome the shortfalls of 2D-CNNs which do not utilise temporal information. In 3D-CNNs, convolution and pooling operations are performed spatio-temporally as opposed to 2D-CNNs where the operations are done only spatially. Learning spatio-temporal features showed promising results as it outperformed some of the best-performing models on several datasets, showing the ability to generalise well. Some of the notable datasets they performed well on include UMD, UFC101 and Action Similarity Labeling (ASLAN). For action recognition on UFC-101 C3D archived an accuracy rate of 85.2%.

3.2 Long-Term Recurrent Convolutional Network (LRCN)

Donahue et al. (2016) proposed a deep hierarchical visual feature extractor such as a CNN and a model that can learn to recognise and process temporal data for tasks having sequential data [13]. The approach was to pass each input (RGB frame or flow) into a CNN to get a fixed-length vector representation which is then passed into a recurrent sequence learning module. This recurrent model uses set parameters to map the input to output, taking previous step outputs into account and using them to update the parameters. This process is carried out in sequence and ensures that the model's weights are reused and/or updated at every time step and that each pass-through is built on top of the previous one. The model was trained end-to-end and to guard against the model overfitting the authors applied a vigorous dropout of 0.9. When compared to a single-frame baseline model the LRCN slightly outperformed it on both RGB and flow inputs. LRCN obtained an accuracy of 68% on RGB input and 77% on the flow input type.

3.3 Video Transformer Network

Neimark et al. (2021) looked at video transformer networks (VTNs) to improve CNN performance by reducing training times with less computational demands [14]. VTN operates on a single stream of data (video) from frame level to action recognition. Their architecture is composed of 3 key parts, 2D-spatial feature extraction, temporal attention-based encoder and a classification multilayer-perceptron head (MLP). The faster training times are attributed to the architecture having fewer pass-throughs of data and aiding the capability of consuming long video streams or token sequences. This approach yielded some positive results including shorter training time, reaching inferences faster and achieving higher accuracies compared to I3D and SlowFast models.

3.4 Action Former

Zhang et al. (2022) set out to identify actions in time and recognise their categories in a single shot without using action proposals. They came up with ActionFormer, which combines multiscale feature representation with local self-attention and uses a lightweight decoder to classify every moment in time and estimate the corresponding action boundaries [15]. ActionFormer uses local self-attention to model temporal context in untrimmed videos, classifies every moment in the video and reduces their corresponding action boundaries. The end model is trained using standard classification and regression loss and can localise the movements of actions in a single shot. The model integrates local self-attention to extract a feature pyramid from the input video and is treated as an action candidate. A convolutional decoder is also used with a feature pyramid to classify the candidates into foreground and background actions. The key idea is to classify each movement as either one of the action categories or the background and further regress the distance between the current time step and the action's start time and end time, referred to as onset and offset respectively. One of the experiments that Zhang et al. ran was to apply ActionFormer on the ActivityNet dataset, they achieved an average mAP of 35%. At the time it was only outperformed by TCA-Net [15].

3.5 UniFormer

Li et al. (2022) designed a unified transformer that would be able to handle spatiotemporal data well. They called it UniFormer, it is built on a vanilla transformer architecture with a unifier block at the end to complement the transformer [16]. The unifier block consists of 3 modules namely dynamic position embedding (DPE), multi-head relation aggregator (MHRA) and feed-forward network (FFN).

DPE is responsible for integrating position information into the tokens effectively introducing the spatiotemporal aspect. MHRA is used to handle video redundancies and highlight dependencies. MHRA achieves this by unifying 3D convolution and spatiotemporal self-attention in a transformer layout. MHRA solves for both shallow and deep layers. FFN applies a point pointwise enhancement to each token passed through the transformer. UniFormer performed better on the Something-Something dataset compared to other approaches, achieving an accuracy rate of 60% on V1 and 70% on v2.

The above discussion shows a various number of approaches that have been applied in the field of activity recognition. A significant amount of the studies and datasets are however focused on general human movements executed in day-to-day tasks. This study aims to learn and model general movements and then identify movements in a specific context of basketball. This will show how these approaches and models fare in the narrow and specialized context of offence in basketball.

4 Experiment Setup

The SpaceJam dataset (as discussed in Sect. 2.2) has an uneven distribution of classes. For example, more than half the dataset is either walk, run or no action. To ensure that every class has fair weighting on the model(s) training, part of the pre-processing step involves extracting an equal number of videos per class. The data will follow the conventional 70:30 split between training and validation respectively. The shooting class has a total of 426 videos, thus the training set is made up of 298 videos for each action class and 127 for the evaluation. All models will be trained for a reasonable number of epochs until a significant landmark is observed be it an increase in loss, no increase in accuracy, overfitting and so forth. The final dataset resulted in 2980 training videos and 1270 validation videos.

4.1 Temporal Segment Network (TSN – MMAction2)

Temporal Segment Networks (TSN) aim to expand on the concept of 2-stream CNNs which set out to separate the learning into spatial and temporal streams [17]. As opposed to using RGB images for the spatial stream and stacked optical flows for the temporal stream, TSN uses RGB-difference for the spatial and warped optical flow fields for the temporal stream [18]. The approach used in this study uses a pre-trained model from MMAction2 trained on the Kinetics-400 dataset and uses a Resnet50 backbone as opposed to ImageNet as used by [17]. A Stochastic Gradient Descent (SGD) optimizer is applied, the dropout ratio is set to 0.4, momentum is set to 0.9 and input frames are resized to 224 × 224.

4.2 Inflated-3D (I3D – MMAction2)

Before training can begin further pre-processing is required to extract frames from videos. I3D takes in videos in the form of frames with each video being represented by a directory containing frames. This I3D implementation is also pre-trained on Kinetics-400 and uses a ResNet50 backbone. Uses an SGD optimizer as well with momentum set to 0.9, batch normalization is applied at each layer and ReLU is used as the activation function. For this implementation, the pipeline will scale each frame to 256 pixels then proceed to randomly crop a 224 × 224 patch and each video is flipped from left to right for training.

4.3 Pose Estimated Convolutional 3D (PoseC3D – MMAction2)

PoseC3D aims to make use of skeleton points of human subjects in a video by locating and tracking them. Before implementing PoseC3D, further pre-processing is required on the dataset to obtain 2D-pose data to use in this pipeline. The pose data is extracted using a Faster-RCNN detector and RGB-inputs. The pose3D implementation used is instantiated with SlowOnly backbone which is inflated from Resnet50 and pre-trained on kinetics-400, and uses an SGD optimizer, momentum 0.9, learning rate 0.2.

5   Results

This section will discuss the results obtained from the pipelines described above (Sect. 4). All three pipelines made use of the MMAction2 platform, running a backbone of Resnet 50 and pre-trained on Kinetics-400. TSN scored 54.88% for the mean accuracy and top-1 accuracy, and 94.33% for top-5 accuracy. I3D scored 53.07% for mean accuracy and top-1 accuracy, and 91.65% for top-5 accuracy. Pose-C3D scored a mean accuracy and top-1 accuracy of 36.69%, and top-5 accuracy of 90.55%. This can be attributed to the complex modalities that this architecture uses, 2D skeletons and 3D-heatmap volumes which require longer learning time [18]. When Pose-C3d is run for 240 epochs it achieves better results with a top-1 accuracy and mean-class accuracy of 63.15% and a top-5 accuracy of 95.51. These results show promising signs mainly as models seem to be able to distinguish between actions carried out in a basketball game with relative success, with some actions being similar to each other such as running and walking.

6 Conclusion

This paper aimed to compare 3 different approaches to tackling action recognition in basketball. These 3 approaches namely TSN, I3D and PoseC3D have largely been applied in areas of general human activity recognition on datasets such as Kinetic-400 and UFC-101 which have a wide array of actions with hundreds of classes. Basketball actions are relatively few in comparison to the broader human action spectrum and even fewer when it comes to SpaceJam with 10 action classes. SpaceJam encompasses some movements that are similar such as running and walking but all models seemed to fare well enough handling such similarities. PoseC3D required the most training to get comparable results with the other models, as when trained at just 20 epochs it was outperformed by both TSN and I3D by around 20 percentage points. For PoseC3D it then achieved a top-1-accuracy of 63% breaking the 60% mark, furthermore, the model scored 95% for top-5-accuracy. This shows the models' ability to be pre-trained on a large action dataset such as Kinetics-400 and then fine-tuned domain such as basketball with a largely reduced dataset size (SpaceJam).

References

1. Adesida, Y., Papi, E., McGregor, A.: Exploring the role of wearable technology in sport kinematics and kinetics: a systematic review. Sensors **19**, 1597 (2019)
2. Mallett, C.J., Lara-Bercial, S.: Serial winning coaches. In: People, Vision, and Environment. Sport and Exercise Psychology Research, pp. 289–322 (2016)
3. DiFiori, J.P., et al.: The NBA and youth basketball: recommendations for promoting a healthy and positive experience. Sports Med. **48**(9), 2053–2065 (2018). https://doi.org/10.1007/s40 279-018-0950-0
4. Poppe, R.: A survey on vision-based human action recognition. Image Vis. Comput. **28**, 976–990 (2010)
5. Zhang, S., Wei, Z., Nie, J., Huang, L., Wang, S., Li, Z.: A review on human activity recognition using vision-based method. J. Healthc. Eng. **2017**, 1–31 (2017)
6. Carbonneau, M., Raymond, A., Granger, É., Gagnon, G.: Real-time visual play-break detection in sport events using a context descriptor. In: IEEE International Symposium on Circuits and Systems (ISCAS), pp. 2808–2811 (2015)
7. Soomro, K., Zamir, A.R., Shah, M.: UCF101: a dataset of 101 human actions classes from videos in the wild. arXiv.org arXiv:1212.0402 (2012)
8. Karpathy, A., Toderici, G., Shetty, S., Leung, T., Sukthankar, R., Fei-Fei, L.: Large-scale video classification with convolutional neural networks. In: IEEE Conference on Computer Vision and Pattern Recognition 2014, pp. 1725–1732 (2014)
9. Caba Heilbron, F., Escorcia, V., Ghanem, B., Carlos Niebles, J.: ActivityNet: a large-scale video benchmark for human activity understanding. In: Proceedings of the IEEE Conference on Computer Vision and Pattern Recognition, pp. 961–970 (2015)
10. Francia, S.: Classification of Basketball Actions through Deep Learning Techniques (2018). https://github.com/simonefrancia/SpaceJam. Accessed 05 Mar 2022
11. Zakharchenko, I.: Deep learning in basketball action recognition (2020). https://s3.eu-central-1.amazonaws.com/ucu.edu.ua/wp-content/uploads/sites/8/2020/11/Zakharchenko-Iryna_188601_assignsubmission_file_Iryna-Zakharchenko.pdf. Accessed 10 Mar 2022
12. Tran, D., Bourdev, L., Fergus, R., Torresani, L., Paluri, M.: Learning spatiotemporal features with 3D convolutional networks. In: IEEE International Conference on Computer Vision 2015 (ICCV), pp. 4489–4497 (2015)

13. Donahue, J., et al.: Long-term recurrent convolutional networks for visual recognition and description. In: Proceedings of the IEEE Conference on Computer Vision and Pattern Recognition, pp. 2625–2634 (2015)
14. Neimark, D., Bar, O., Zohar, M., Asselmann, D.: Video transformer network. In: Proceedings of the IEEE/CVF International Conference on Computer Vision, pp. 3163–3172 (2021)
15. Zhang, C., Wu, J., Li, Y.: ActionFormer: Localizing Moments of Actions with Trans-formers. arXiv.org, arXiv:2202.07925 (2022)
16. Li, K., et al.: Uniformer: Unified Transformer for Efficient Spatiotemporal Representation Learning. arXiv.org, arXiv:2201.04676 (2020)
17. Simonyan, K., Zisserman, A.: Two-stream convolutional networks for action recognition. In: Advances in Neural Information Processing Systems (NIPS), vol. 27 (2014)
18. Duan, H., Zhao, Y., Chen, K., Lin, D., Dai, B.: Revisiting skeleton-based action recognition. In: Proceedings of the IEEE/CVF Conference on Computer Vision and Pattern Recognition, pp. 2969–2978 (2022)

MedAIcine: A Pilot Project on the Social and Ethical Aspects of AI in Medical Imaging

Sophie Jörg[1]([✉]) [iD], Paula Ziethmann[2] [iD], and Svenja Breuer[3] [iD]

[1] Munich School of Philosophy, Kaulbachstraße 31/33, 80539 Munich, Germany
sophie.joerg@hfph.de
[2] University of Augsburg, Universitätsstraße 2, 86159 Augsburg, Germany
[3] Technical University of Munich, Augustenstraße 46, 80333 Munich, Germany

Abstract. As artificial intelligence continues to advance and permeate various aspects of our lives, it is crucial that we consider the ethical and social implications of these developments. With its pilot project 'MedAIcine' the newly founded Center for Responsible AI Technologies ('CReAITe') strives for critically reflecting vital concepts and conflicts regarding the responsible design and use of AI in medical imaging, using an interdisciplinary approach called 'embedded ethics and social science'. Drawing on perspectives of developers, physicians, and patients across three different use cases (radiology, endoscopy, and dermatology), we identify key social, political, and ethical challenges associated with medical AI, such as issues of trust, privacy, explainability, bias, equity, and responsibility in relation to AI technologies.

Keywords: Embedded Ethics · Artificial Intelligence · Medical Imaging · Human-Computer-Interaction

1 Introduction

1.1 AI in Medicine

We have long known about the potential of so-called *artificial intelligence* (AI), but with the release of *ChatGPT*, a chatbot or text-based dialog system from the U.S. company *OpenAI*, in November 2022, the world has once again witnessed the capabilities these modern technologies hold. Thanks to advances in *machine learning* (ML) and *deep learning* (DL), AI can now process, analyze, and interpret data in very short time and thereby preparing and enhancing human decision-making.

Especially in the medical context, AI is seen as a *key technology*: Computer programs, for example, learn to predict the individual course of illness and therapy by means of AI-supported analysis of an infinite number of medical records. Intelligent assistance systems and care robots assist people with limited mobility. Medical wearables measure, record and interpret the patient's vital signs contributing to the continuous monitoring of chronic diseases. Hence, AI-based prognostics and methods not only help with *diagnosis* and *therapy*, but also with the reliable and yet cost-efficient *care* of patients (Siontis et al. 2021).

C. Stephanidis et al. (Eds.): HCII 2023, CCIS 1832, pp. 455–462, 2023.
https://doi.org/10.1007/978-3-031-35989-7_58

AI is ubiquitous. It is making its way into our everyday practices. By doing so, it is not only changing the way we *perceive* and *interact* with our environment but is *transforming* it at the same time. This becomes particularly evident in the medical context (cf. Rajpurkar et al. 2022): AI in medicine is not only changing the way of patient examination, perception of that examination and the interaction with physicians, it is also reshaping the very context in which we live. By using AI-based remote diagnostic tools or optimizing the processes of existing medical infrastructure, medical care can be improved in large parts of the world and the overall human right to health can be protected more consistently (Raso et al. 2018).

Although the use of AI in medicine may sound promising at first, ethical considerations point to certain risks of the current use and design of AI in medicine: Lack of transparency, explanation, and fairness, but also insufficient protection of patients' privacy and their sensitive health data are just a few examples of the specific challenges in dealing with medical AI.

1.2 Objective: Interdisciplinary Research on the Social and Ethical Aspects of Medical AI

As AI continues to advance and permeate various aspects of our lives, it is crucial that we consider the ethical and social implications of these developments. From issues of bias and discrimination, privacy and autonomy, transparency, and accountability, to questions of human-machine-interaction, the ethical and social issues surrounding AI are complex and multifaceted and need to be addressed carefully and responsibly.

Due to the interdisciplinary character of AI itself and its application contexts (cf. Zhuang et al. 2020), we assume that AI and its impact can only be comprehensively researched on an *interdisciplinary* basis. Accordingly, AI must be problematized and analyzed in light of various disciplines—such as *computer science, science and technology studies, medicine,* and *philosophy.* By exploring the ethical and social aspects of AI in such cross-disciplinary frameworks, it is possible to draw on the different expertise and findings without disregarding the respective focus, approaches, and methods of each discipline.

The overall objective of this project can be classified on three levels:

(*Descriptive level*) Identifying conflicts of interest between stakeholders within health-care AI innovation (e.g., physicians, patients, health insurers, caregivers).

(*Theoretical level*) Uncovering and deconstructing key terms and philosophical concepts—such as autonomy, vulnerability, explainabililty or responsibility—as well as their mutual relation within sociotechnically transformed practices.

(*Normative level*) Developing concrete proposals for the responsible and trustworthy use and design of AI in the medical context based on *empirical* and *hermeneutic research.*

2 'CReAITe' and Its Pilot Project 'MedAIcine'

2.1 'CReAITe': Center for Responsible AI Technologies

The Center for Responsible AI Technologies (*CReAITe*), founded by the Technical University of Munich (TUM), the Munich School of Philosophy and the University of Augsburg in February 2022, pursues the goal of incorporating philosophical, ethical, and social science inquires throughout the process of developing, implementing, and critically reflecting on AI technologies. *CReAITe* has set itself the task of rethinking human-machine interaction and contributing to a better understanding of the transformative power of technologies, such as ML and DL.

CReAITe intends on expanding this integrated view on interdisciplinary AI research and its (techno)philosophical, ethical as well as societal and political dimensions to four different—albeit crucial—fields of application: (i) Medicine/Care/Health; (ii) Future of work; (iii) Mobility; (iv) Climate/Environment.

By involving politics, ethics, law, computer science, science and technology studies as well as cultural studies, *CReAITe* aims to facilitate the emergence of technical innovations that can perform the tasks assigned to them *reliably*, but also in a *socially responsive* and *responsible* manner.

2.2 'MedAIcine': Pilot Project

With the research on the social and ethical aspects of AI in medicine, *CReAITe* started its pilot project: *MedAIcine*. In this particular project the main focus is on the use of AI in medical imaging, such as X-ray, MRI or CT.

Especially in the field of imaging diagnostics, AI systems are already widely used and researched. According to preliminary results, integrating AI and *computed-aided detection* (CAD) with screening methods, in fact, has shown reliable and accurate screening results (Goyal et al. 2020, 18). However, *MedAIcine* also highlights the aforementioned conflicts and challenges of embedding AI technologies into our practices: For example, if AI systems are trained with data sets that do not represent all skin colours and ethnicities, patterns such as tumour thickness or the size of a suspected melanoma cannot be recognised and determined equally well for all skin colours and ethnicities either. As a result, patients are being discriminated, putting some people at a disadvantage when it comes to medical care.

3 Use Cases and Methods

3.1 Embedded Ethics

In *MedAIcine*, we apply an innovative interdisciplinary approach known as embedded ethics and social science (Breuer et al. 2023). 'Embedded ethics' denotes a research practice that involves an ongoing integration of ethical and social analyses into the entire development process (McLennan et al. 2020). As a research team comprising scholars from science and technology studies (STS), philosophy, and ethics, we share a common interest in investigating the complex social and ethical issues arising in the development of machine learning systems in medical imaging. We study these issues empirically, leveraging long-term integrated collaboration with engineering researchers and medical practitioners.

We use a qualitative, inductive, and interpretivist approach, following grounded theory methodology (Charmaz 2006) with an iterative process of data collection and analysis. For data collection, we conduct ethnographic field studies where we write field notes as embedded, overt, participant observers at AI research labs and in hospitals; we obtain pseudonymized qualitative semi-structured interviews with AI researchers, medical experts, and patients, as well as scenario-based focus groups with patients. Throughout the process, we adapt our sampling strategy based on insights from ongoing analysis of our incoming data. In our analysis, we apply analytical lenses from STS, philosophy, and ethics to come to a rich understanding of the practices at hand in the development and clinical implementation of medical AI.

Ultimately, we aim for interdisciplinary co-design of medical AI applications, where ethical and social analyses constitute integral parts of design processes and workplace integration. This empirically based approach thus constitutes an alternative to the prevalent more abstract, planning- and, principle-oriented efforts in technology ethics and innovation that have often fallen short of expectations to ensure responsible conduct in research and development (Winfield and Jirotka 2018).

In its empirical orientation, our approach draws on and complements traditions of parallel and collaborative interdisciplinary research. It resonates with approaches of value-sensitive design (Friedman et al. 2012) and relational empirical ethics of care technologies (Pols 2015). It shares with ethics parallel research (van der Burg 2009) the interest in investigating social and ethical aspects alongside and in concert with research in science and engineering. Yet, embedded ethics and social science goes beyond this goal in its aim to achieve long-term *integration* of social, ethics, science, and technology research. Our approach is thus squarely rooted in a tradition of sociotechnical integration research (Fisher and Schuurbiers 2013; Fisher et al. 2015). It draws from the field of STS viewing emerging technologies as complex, sociotechnical compounds that mediate interactions between researchers, developers, users, and other affected or involved stakeholders and machines-interactions we aim to better understand by looking at concrete case studies.

3.2 Use Cases: Radiology, Endoscopy, and Dermatology

Radiology: AIM Lab. The first use case we focus on is ML in radiology. We investigate this field by way of a case study of a university research laboratory, the Lab for Artificial Intelligence in Medicine (*AIMLab*) at TUM. Into the *AIMLab*, embedded STS researchers are integrated, conducting a social science laboratory field study. They undertake regular lab visits, attend lab meetings, shadow AI researchers in their everyday work and conduct peer-to-peer interviews with them. The combination of computer science research tradition and an university hospital radiology department allows us valuable insights into the synergies and tensions that emerge between disciplinary research and an application domain. Focus of this case study is to gain an in-depth understanding of the particularities of the *practices* in AI research for radiology, as well as the specific social and ethical issues that arise in relation to this domain.

Endoscopy: Achalasia. The second use case being researched in *MedAIcine* addresses the diagnosis and treatment of achalasia—a rare dysfunction of the esophageal muscles and the lower sphincter. In the gastroenterology department of Augsburg University Hospital, physicians are leading a study concerning the 3D-reconstruction of the esophagus with a multimodal data system. Their goal is to program a model of the esophagus using specially developed algorithms, to specify its stretching ability, inclination, and muscle thickness. In accordance with the embedded ethics approach described above, the researchers involved in *MedAIcine* are already engaged in the early phase of the development of such a prototype for the digital, AI-supported augmentation of human organs. Thus, ethical research on possible standards of fair training data or a sufficient degree of explainability of technology is involved even before the AI-systems are programmed.

Dermatology: OCTOLAB. Further, we are embedded into the OCTOLAB project of the University Hospital Augsburg, where optical coherence tomography for the diagnosis of basal cell carcinomas is to be integrated into a long-pulsed infrared laser for the therapy of basal cell carcinomas. The associated diagnostics and therapy will be based on AI. The aim of the project is that the combined device will contribute to automated diagnostics and therapy in the early detection and individualized minimally invasive therapy of basal cell carcinomas. Our focus of this case study is to gain a deeper understanding of the use of the AI system in (changing) medical practice, exploring in particular ethical implications of using a *closed-loop system* for automated diagnostics and therapy. To achieve this, we participate in consultations with patients and meetings of medical and scientific stakeholders involved in OCTOLAB. Additionally, we conduct *scenario-based focus group discussions* with physicians and patients.

4 Preliminary Findings and Emerging Topics

As a reaction to socio-technical changes in medical contexts and practices, the preliminary findings of the interview study (*peer-to-peer researcher interviews*) at *AIMLab* already show that people often demand the respective technology to be explainable. Especially in critical areas of application, such as military defense or medicine, transparency regarding the reasoning of the AI-based decision-making process are seen as essential. The output of an AI-system should therefore be visible as well as comprehensible to other external agents. For instance, the final decision, such as a recommendation for emergency surgery or a patient's cancer diagnosis, should remain comprehensible and understandable to medical staff. *Explainablility* is therefore stressed as a key aspect for developing transparent and trustworthy AI, leading to a thriving stream of research: the so-called 'eXplainable Artificial Intelligence' (XAI). It is assumed that sufficient explainability may overcome the black box issues of opaque AI systems. But when is something considered sufficiently justified or comprehensible? Which criteria constitute explainability, as it is often emphasized in the context of AI? The interviews conducted so far indicate that, even among experts, no shared understanding of (sufficiently) explainable AI prevails yet. Gaining insights into a variety of explainability and interpretability techniques employed in the *AIMLab*, will help us investigate the concrete research and technical practices related to making ML-machine learning models interpretable and explainable. Complementing our empirical research, philosophical reflections on *explanation*—as raised in the history of ideas or the philosophy of science—here can contribute to provide a conceptual basis for the discussion on medical XAI. In philosophy different schemes of explanation are distinguished (e.g., *statistical relevance*-model or *causal mechanical*-model). In a generic sense, however, all philosophical concepts think of explanations as a *linguistic and logical construct*, which reveals the central causes of a certain phenomenon and thereby demonstrates its *causality* (Hocutt 1974, 385). By means of formal logical reconstructions, a kind of *regularity* (if *p*, then *q*) is to be made explicit, which establishes a logical (causal) relation between cause *p* (*explanans*) and effect *q* (*explanandum*) (Ruben 2004, 110).

In the further course, *MedAIcine* will explore the limitations of these explanatory models—hitherto known in philosophy—in the context of modern technologies, such as AI, and strives for refining a new understanding of explanatory power in contrast to correlated yet distinct concepts, such as reliability, transparency or understanding (cf. Abel 1948).

Moreover, issues concerning the altering relationship between humans and machines in general and the human-computer-interaction in particular emerged in the course of the interviews. For instance, how is medical AI affecting established—in the medical context, mostly asymmetrical—power and trust relationships? Against this backdrop, *MedAIcine* is currently exploring these possible transformations along considerations of *power* and ethics on *vulnerability*. Being and becoming vulnerable by technology can generally be understood on three levels: Due to its very essence all humans are vulnerable (*ontological* vulnerability)—some moreover by situation (*situational* vulnerability) or by structure (*structural* vulnerability). Since all people are to be understood as vulnerable, the focus of thinking is less on risk and more on the positive direction of understanding people as vulnerable beings (cf. Haker 2021). By recognising the ontological vulnerability of all individuals—in the sense of a *conditio humana*—and the situational and structural factors that can exacerbate vulnerability, we can approach the use of AI systems in medicine with empathy and a commitment to protecting the welfare of all involved (i.e., patients, medical staff, companies producing medical technologies etc.).

In addition to making people vulnerable via technology, *MedAIcine* examines power structures in the context of medical human-machine interactions. Drawing on emerging theories such as data colonialism (cf. Ricaurte 2019) and data feminism (D'Ignazio and Klein 2020), *MedAIcine* explores power structures underlaying the development, use and design of medical AI. Here, scholars in these fields emphasize to reflect on the initial mechanisms and the extent to which these power structures are altered and (re)produced through algorithmic biases.

5   Concluding Thoughts

In our project, *MedAIcine,* we investigate various aspects that pertain to Human-Computer-Interaction (HCI). In exploring human-centered AI design, our focus lies on studiying philosophical and ethical implications of the HCI regarding specialized AI systems in imaging diagnostics. Grounded on our 'embedded ethics and social science' research, we offer an interdisciplinary, empirically, and philosophically informed sensitivity to issues of explantion, trust, and power relations arising in various dimensions of HCI. We are convinced that reflections of the philosophy of AI and STS analyses on behavioral change in context of AI contribute to advance our understanding of HCI. We are eager for an exchange on these matters with the community at HCI International 2023.

References

Abel, T.: The operation called 'Verstehen.' Am. J. Sociol. **54**(3), 211–218 (1948)

Breuer, S., Braun, M., Tigard, D., Buyx, A., Müller, R.: How engineers' imaginaries of healthcare shape design and user engagement: a case study of a robotics initiative for geriatric healthcare AI applications. Trans. Hum.-Comput. Interact. (TOCHI) **30**(2), 1–33 (2023). https://doi.org/10.1145/3577010

Charmaz, K.: Constructing Grounded Theory: A Practical Guide Through Qualitative Analysis. SAGE Publication, London, Thoursand Oaks, New Deli, Singapore (2006)

D'Ignazio, C., Klein, L.F.: Data Feminism. Strong Ideas Series. The MIT Press, Cambridge (2020)

Fisher, E., O'Rourke, M., Evans, R., Kennedy, E.B., Gorman, M.E., Seager, T.P.: Mapping the integrative field: taking stock of socio-technical collaborations. J. Responsible Innov. **2**(1), 39–61 (2015). https://doi.org/10.1080/23299460.2014.1001671

Fisher, E., Schuurbiers, D.: Socio-technical integration research: collaborative inquiry at the midstream of research and development. In: Doorn, N., Schuurbiers, D., van de Poel, I., Gorman, M.E. (eds.) Early Engagement and New Technologies: Opening up the Laboratory. PET, vol. 16, pp. 97–110. Springer, Dordrecht (2013). https://doi.org/10.1007/978-94-007-7844-3_5

Friedman, B., Kahn, P., Borning, A.: Value sensitive design: theory and methods. University of Washington Technical report, 02-12 (2002)

Goyal, H., et al.: Scope of artificial intelligence in screening and diagnosis of colorectal cancer. J. Clin. Med. **9**(10), 3313 (2020)

Haker, H.: Verletzliche Freiheit. Zu einem neuen Prinzip der Bioethik. In: Keul, H. (eds.) Theologische Vulnerabilitätsforschung. Gesellschaftsrelevant und interdisziplinär, pp. 99–118. Kohlhammer, Stuttgart (2021)

Hocutt, M.: Aristotle's four becauses. Philosophy **49**(190), 385–399 (1974)

McLennan, S., et al.: An embedded ethics approach for AI development. Nat Mach Intell **2**(9), 488–490 (2020). https://doi.org/10.1038/s42256-020-0214-1

Pols, J.: Towards an empirical ethics in care: Relations with technologies in health care. Med. Health Care Philos. **18**(1), 81–90 (2015)

Raso, F.A., Hilligoss, H., Krishnamurthy, V., Bavitz, C., Kim, L.: Artificial intelligence & human rights: opportunities & risks. Berkman Klein Center Research Publication (2018)

Rajpurkar, P., Chen, E., Banerjee, O., et al.: AI in health and medicine. Nat. Med. **28**, 31–38 (2022). https://doi.org/10.1038/s41591-021-01614-0

Ricaurte, P.: Data epistemologies, the coloniality of power, and resistance. Telev. New Media **20**(4), 350–365 (2019). https://doi.org/10.1177/1527476419831640

Ruben, D.: ExplRaining Explanation. Routledge, London/New York (2004)

Siontis, K.C., Noseworthy, P.A., Attia, Z.I., et al.: Artificial intelligence-enhanced electrocardiography in cardiovascular disease management. Nat. Rev. Cardiol. **18**, 465–478 (2021). https://doi.org/10.1038/s41569-020-00503-2

Winfield, A.F.T., Jirotka, M.: Ethical governance is essential to building trust in robotics and artificial intelligence systems. Philos. Trans. Ser. A Math. Phys. Eng. Sci. **376**(2133) (2018). https://doi.org/10.1098/rsta.2018.0085

van der Burg, S.: Imagining the future of photoacoustic mammography. Sci. Eng. Ethics **15**(1), 97–110 (2009). https://doi.org/10.1007/s11948-008-9079-0

Zhuang, Y., Cai, M., Li, X., Luo, X., Yang, Q., Wu, F.: The next breakthroughs of artificial intelligence: the interdisciplinary nature of AI. Engineering **6**(3), 245–247 (2020)

Exploring Gender Nonbinary Experiences Through the Lens of the 7th HCI Grand Challenge

Reactions to the Categorization of Nonbinary Users in AI-Generated Online Advertising Profiles

Sam Leif[1]([envelope]) [iD], Nina Exner[2] [iD], and Ari Gofman Fishman[3] [iD]

[1] University of Nevada, Las Vegas, Las Vegas, NV 89154, USA
sam.leif@unlv.edu
[2] Virginia Commonwealth University, Richmond, VA 23284, USA
[3] Analog Devices Inc., Wilmington, MA 02155, USA

Abstract. Gender-based societal bias can lead to digital inequality and digital exclusion. An under-addressed marginalized group is the non-binary community, comprised of those who do not fully identify their gender as male or female. The assumption of a gender binary can become ingrained in the systems and algorithms undergirding technology. AI provides companies the ability to leverage tracked online behaviors to create targeted advertising profiles based on systematic, algorithmic-assigned personal characteristics. Given the potential for digital exclusion, digital inequality, and data violence, these online advertising profiles may be inaccurate and even harmful to non-binary people. This poster presents preliminary findings from a survey of nonbinary participants on perspectives on the representation of their identities in AI-generated online advertising profiles.

Keywords: Gender Nonbinary · HCI Grand Challenges · Digital Inequality

1 Introduction

In investigating the Grand Challenges facing HCI as a discipline, Stephanidis [1], along with 32 experts in HCI, identified the seventh challenge as "Social and Organizational Democracy," specifically highlighting gender as a factor affecting digital inequality and digital exclusion. When considering gender-based inequalities, an un-der-addressed gender group is non-binary people: people who do not fully identify their gender as male or female. Analyses estimate upwards of 2.6 million people in the United States alone identify as gender nonbinary. It is likely that this number is higher due to under-reporting for fear of social repercussions. The gender non-binary population faces both digital exclusion and digital inequality [2]. As such, research into this community also addresses the third HCI Grand Challenge: "Ethics, Privacy, & Security".

People often assume binary genders, reflecting an ingrained social assumption that everyone's gender identity is exclusively either male or female based on their assigned sex

C. Stephanidis et al. (Eds.): HCII 2023, CCIS 1832, pp. 463–470, 2023.
https://doi.org/10.1007/978-3-031-35989-7_59

at birth. When these exclusionary binary values are structured into systems, nonbinary people are erased in a form of data violence. Data violence refers to the potential harm inflicted on gender nonconforming people by systems that serve as the foundation for the ubiquitous presence of technology encountered every day.

Once seen as neutral and free of bias, society is becoming more aware of the potential for harm when AI algorithms are developed by those with conscious or unconscious bias [3–5]. One area permeated by AI is online behavioral advertising. AI provides companies the ability to leverage tracked online behaviors to create targeted advertising profiles based on systematic, algorithmic-assigned personal characteristics [6]. Personal profiles include the categories used by large-scale marketing systems to determine and record a per-son's advertising interests in order to match people with advertisements. In assigning people to categories, AI-generated profiles attempt to represent or proxy individuals' characteristics as a way to represent their potential interests. This utilizes and reinforces algorithmic associations between gender and the resulting advertisements, and encodes individuals incorrectly. For nonbinary people, this means that multiple layers of assumption create the risk of marginalization.

Given the potential for digital exclusion, digital inequality, and data violence, these online advertising profiles may be inaccurate and even harmful to nonbinary people. This poster presents preliminary findings from a survey of nonbinary and gender non-conforming participants who shared their perspectives on the representation of nonbinary identities in AI-generated online advertising profiles.

2   Methods

2.1   Materials

This multimethod study used a survey to collect quantitative and open-entry responses from participants. The survey structure included two sections. The survey's first section, the "short survey," asked for the participant's country and gender identity. It explained the concept of AI-driven assignment of categories for the purpose of creating a computer profile describing the person. The short survey asked what category/ies they wanted representing them in a computer-generated profile, and whether they had concerns about automated gender profiles.

The participant then could choose to exit the survey or navigate to the second section, the "long survey". The long survey presented the concept of online advertising profiles used by platforms to tailor advertisements to a person. It first asked about the assignment of categories in an imaginary profile, and then gave directions on how the participant could find their own Google user profile. Participants were then asked about their reactions and thoughts about their personal profile and the general idea of profiles after seeing the real-world example. While this does not represent the "in the wild" study of ethics recommended in the HCI Grand Challenges discussion of ethics and trust [1], it approaches that target more than an abstract example can.

Many questions included an open-text field prompting elaboration. All answers were optional; thus, the n of responses varies.

2.2 Participants

This study used purposive sampling to collect 152 responses. Links to the survey were shared online in spaces dedicated to the gender non-binary community (i.e., Reddit, Twitter, and Facebook groups specifically for people who identified as non-binary). Participation was voluntary and anonymous. Consent was obtained by click-through without signature. No identifiers were collected, and review for indirect identifiers was performed and indirect identifiers were redacted permanently, and no inducement or reward was proffered as part of participation.

The study was conducted under the supervision of the Tufts and Virginia Commonwealth University Institutional Review Boards. It was determined to be Exempt from active monitoring, Exemption Category 2i.

2.3 Analysis

The quantitative answers lend themselves to descriptive statistics. To our knowledge, this is the first exploration of larger-scale categorization of the nonbinary community, as opposed to manual in surveys and forms, or descriptive metadata.

Qualitative text responses were condensed and coded via iterative rounds of inductive coding. The team did not attempt exhaustive and exclusive coding; instead, the researchers coded all texts and attempted to reflect the naturalistic phrasing of the participants. We prioritized investigator triangulation with frequent check-ins to compare code structures and wording to best represent concepts. Trustworthiness of the analysis is improved through this investigator triangulation.

3 Results

3.1 Quantitative Results

Participants described their gender identity and were allowed to select all relevant gender identities. The resulting list of participant gender identities had 152 respondents who checked a total of 521 categories, representing a mean 3.4 identities per participant summarized in Table 1.

In the short survey, participants were prompted to answer in an open-text box, "What gender categories would you want computerized data systems to have available to assign to people generally?" 140 participants typed in responses. Out of those entries, the researchers harmonized any category labels as best possible (such as combining "gender fluid" and "genderfluid"). Many of the entries were explanations or perspective statements rather than specific categories, but for those that specified categories, Table 2 lists the category labels that were named at least 5 times. Over 30 different labels were listed by participants less than 5 times each.

The short survey also asked, "Do you have any concerns about automated gender profiles?" 115 out of 152 participants, or 76%, responded yes. 18 indicated Maybe, and a further 16 indicated the "Not sure or undecided" option. Only three replied No.

In the longer survey, participants were asked whether advertising profiles could potentially meet the needs of the nonbinary community. 104 participants elected to respond to this question (Fig. 1).

Table 1. Participant identities - 152 respondents were able to select all that applied

Selected	Count
Nonbinary	137
Transgender	79
Genderqueer	63
Transmasculine	45
Agender	42
Genderfluid	36
Androgynous	20
Transfeminine	19
This list does not represent my gender identity fully. The researchers should add (open response)	17
Questioning gender identity	16
Woman/female	16
Demigender	10
Man/male	7
Bigender	4
Neutrois	4
Pangender	2
Two Spirit	1
Grand Total	521

Table 2. What gender categories would you want computerized data systems to have available to assign to people generally?

String	Count	String	Count
Non-binary	59	Man	18
None/no answer/undesignated	59	Woman	18
Female	33	Transgender	6
Male	33	Genderfluid	6
Agender	21	"By open text entry"	5
Other	19	Feminine	5
		Genderqueer	5

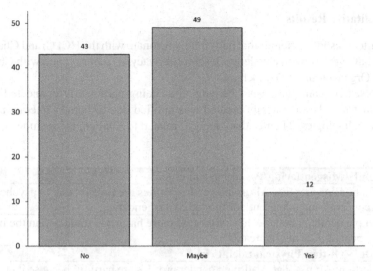

Fig. 1. "Can advertising profiles meet needs specific to the nonbinary community?"

The longer survey also directed participants that had Google accounts in how to find and look at their Google Ad profile. They were then asked to rate a Likert-type scale response of how well the profile described them. 62 participants elected to respond to this question (Fig. 2).

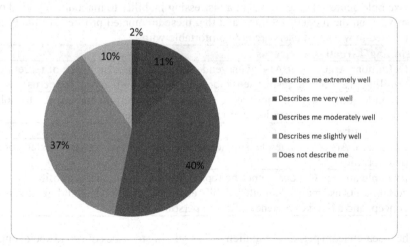

Fig. 2. "How well are you represented by the data categories in your ad personalization profile?"

3.2 Qualitative Results

The open-text response themes that particularly resonate with the HCI Grand Challenges are those having to do with Challenge 3: Ethics, Privacy, & Security; and with Challenge 7: Social Organization & Democracy.

The research team perceives Challenge 3 as being particularly connected to risks of harm that may be unethically created or amplified due to human interactions with computer technologies. Themes that emerged related to Challenge 3 include:

Harmful - Misgendering/Psychological risks
Definition: Argues that AI-driven gender profiles are harmful due to psychological concerns, including but not limited to misgendering.
Example quote: "I believe they will cause more harm and trauma than the monetary benefit they might create."
Harmful - Outing/Physical/Social risks
Definition: Argues that AI-driven gender profiles are harmful because it creates social risks, which may or may not be implied to lead to physical risks. This category includes "outing" nonbinary and gender-non-conforming users.
Example quote: "If the data is leaked, people could be subject to targeted harassment."
Privacy concern
Definition: Argues that AI-driven gender profiles represent a privacy concern, either specific to the nonbinary population or in general.
Example quote: "These represent a distressing inability to maintain any kind of privacy on the modern Internet, and that these automated profiles are likely to be used in ways that users are not comfortable with."
Profiling/Targeting Concerns
Definition: Argues that AI-driven gender profiles represent a risk of targeting, profiling in a criminal justice sense, or other hypervisibilization concerns.
Example quote: "Will a transphobic employer or governmental agency be able to see and use the information that I am trans and queer?"
Remove entirely
Definition: Argues that gender should be removed entirely from automated computer profiles.
Example quote: "Gender cannot be represented in an automated profile. To list certain traits as "male", "female", "nbi", etc. is to fail to understand gender as a concept and a lived experience of every person."

The research team perceives Challenge 7 as relating to issues of broad social engagement, including but not limited to avoiding the exclusion of social minorities from technology-mediated practices. As we understand it, Challenge 7 is not about absolute exclusion through in/accessibility, which is covered in Challenge 5. Rather, it is about social improvement, including ensuring that technology decreases inequity rather than exacerbating existing inequities. Themes that emerged related to Challenge 7 include:

Active management options
Definition: Argues that AI gender categorization requires options to actively manage and change categories on an ongoing basis
Example quote: "Without the ability to self-describe and make updates to that self-description, I'm not sure that it would even be possible to create profiles describing nonbinary people."
Capitalism/advertising is bad
Definition: Argues that AI-driven profiles are de facto problematic due to heavy use in advertising or as part of the capitalist economy.
Example quote: "Advertisements are garbage and automated profiles are also garbage. They're all about commodifying actual human beings and turning them into data slurry with the goal of profiting off humans more "efficient." No thank you."
Interests
Definition: Argues that interests should define categories instead of gender being assigned as a proxy variable.
Example quote: "Where would they derive the automated gender assignment? If it's by search history or implied stuff, boo assumptions are lame. If its by the user's chosen label, I could get behind it."
Opt-out / Opt-in / visible categories
Definition: Argues that categories should be opt-in, should allow opting out, should be visible and togglable on and off by personal preference, or otherwise allow periodic management including deactivation or reassignment.
Example quote: "All gender should be opt in or based on explicit self-identification"
Stereotypes/biases
Definition: Argues that AI-driven gender categorization inherently is based on or replicates stereotypes and biases about the nonbinary community or gender concepts.
Example quote: "This is super annoying and bad and just serves to reinforce gender binaries and gender stereotypes within the dominant gender narratives."
Useful/accurate
Definition: Argues that AI-automated gender profiles are or can be useful and accurate.
Example quote: "I don't see if it matters to much? AI tends to correct itself over time."
Useless/inaccurate
Definition: Argues that AI-automated gender profiles are useless or inaccurate.
Example quote: "Probably no really useful, most people are more complex, than those profiles could ever understand."

4 Discussion and Conclusion

Digital exclusion, through non-representation or misrepresentation, is the most obvious concern given classification systems' default to the male/female binary. When data collection instruments first identify the need for additional gender representation, a common choice is to add the gender category of "other." Unfortunately, this quite literally relegates nonbinary people as 'the other', identifying them as inherently alien, strange, or not normal. Better options exist to fully and respectfully represent participants whose gender is not fully captured as male or female; this data would also be more accurate.

Digital inequality issues also emerged as participants described concerns about embedding biases and stigmas into representations through the AI-driven connections harvested from large-scale data sources and reflected into profiles. Further research can explore how widely these concerns are shared by other populations. Algorithm developers can and should incorporate these issues into development pipelines and algorithm audits.

Still, over 50% of respondents believed that AI-generated personal profiles could potentially meet needs specific to the nonbinary community. The preliminary review of the data suggests modifications could improve the engagement, inclusion, and representation of nonbinary computer users. Examples of identified modifications include building greater nuance into the categories, personal management of profile categories, and tight scoping on interests as defining categories instead of gender being assigned as a proxy variable. There is still much data to be analyzed in this survey, and we anticipate additional findings which can support a more just, accurate, and inclusive digital world.

References

1. Stephanidis, C., et al.: Seven HCI grand challenges. Int. J. Hum.-Comput. Interact. **35**(14), 1229–1269 (2019). https://doi.org/10.1080/10447318.2019.1619259
2. Robinson, L., et al.: Digital inequalities and why they matter. Inf. Commun. Soc. **18**(5), 569–582 (2015). https://doi.org/10.1080/1369118X.2015.1012532
3. Green, B., Viljoen, S.: Algorithmic realism: expanding the boundaries of algorithmic thought. In: Proceedings of the 2020 Conference on Fairness, Accountability, and Transparency, pp. 19–31 (2020). https://doi.org/10.1145/3351095.3372840
4. Mehrabi, N., Morstatter, F., Saxena, N., Lerman, K., Galstyan, A.: A survey on bias and fairness in machine learning. ACM Comput. Surv. **54**(6), 1–35 (2022). https://doi.org/10.1145/3457607
5. Noble, S.U.: Algorithms of Oppression: How Search Engines Reinforce Racism. NYU Press (2018)
6. Varnali, K.: Online behavioral advertising: an integrative review. J. Mark. Commun. **27**(1), 93–114 (2021). https://doi.org/10.1080/13527266.2019.1630664

Pseudo Happiness in Artificial Intelligence

Anniez Rachmawati Musslifah and Akif Khilmiyah[✉]

Department of Islamic Educational Psychology, Universitas Muhammadiyah Yogyakarta, Kasihan, Indonesia
akif.khilmiyah@umy.ac.id

Abstract. Happiness is one of the main goals of human life. Various ways are taken in order to achieve a certain level of happiness that involves experiences and emotions. *Artificial Intelligence* (AI) is present as one of the human efforts to achieve happiness. Through Artificial intelligence, humans are facilitated in supporting various activities. This paper aims to find out the impact of *Artificial Intelligence* on human happiness. This research uses qualitative research methods with a literature study approach. Data collection through literature review is related to the research focus, in the form of literature review, theory and government regulation documents. The source of primary material in this study is various literature that directly discusses *Artificial Intelligence* and the Psychology of Happiness through the Theory of Literature. Other sources are research findings, discussion results, seminars, etc. Library materials are then discussed and analyzed critically and in depth to support existing propositions and ideas from various references. The results showed that as an innovation, Artificial Intelligence clearly affects various aspects of human life, one of which is the mobility aspect. With the convenience obtained with Artificial Intelligence allows the occurrence of negative impacts that have the potential to appear in line with the negative impacts of the use of technology itself but, in the view of happiness psychology, as expressed by Seligmen, *Artificial Intelligence* is not fully capable of guaranteeing one's happiness. The sense of comfort and security offered by *Artificial intelligence* is pseudo-happiness in the perspective of happiness theory.

Keywords: Happiness · Artificial Intelligence · Technology

1 Introduction

Throughout human civilization is always looking for ways to be able to live in this world in various ways to achieve certain goals. One of the goals of human beings to live is to achieve a condition that is comfortable, happy, and to gain affection and a sense of security. Human happiness is measured through various indicators that cannot be generalized or applied in general. There are main indicators that human beings achieve a state of happiness when they feel a positive emotional feeling, and are able to be felt by birth and mind. Happiness is basically a level of achievement in a person that creates a sense of satisfaction both physically and mentally, and is able to describe oneself positively [1]. Through this positive outlook, individuals are able to show their existence

C. Stephanidis et al. (Eds.): HCII 2023, CCIS 1832, pp. 471–478, 2023.
https://doi.org/10.1007/978-3-031-35989-7_60

in society, and are able to show patterns of behavior that are in line with prevailing moral values. Thus, human happiness can be achieved by each individual, even if it goes a different way or path.

Some of the things that affect happiness are factors of religiosity, emotional intelligence, income, work and social relations [2]. The religiosity factor is the initial foundation in its relationship with God. The conviction and determination that things come and come back because God is the basic principle of a person achieving a satisfactory condition, as well as answering the questions in his brain. The second factor is related to emotional intelligence that is able to encourage humans to always master themselves internally in direct contact with other individuals within a group. The third and fourth factors related to income and employment have almost the same correlation, where both are a process and an outcome in an action. The fifth factor is social relations which is a factor of happiness that directly intersects with a choice and the ability of the human mindset to adapt to the environment. It is these various ways and techniques of relating that then have an impact on the happiness of an individual.

Happiness is a variable that correlates positively with well-being, security, and meeting needs [3]. These three things encourage individuals to achieve a certain level of happiness that in some conditions cannot be described in just words. By returning these three things in the concept of Maslow's Theory of Motivation, happiness correlates indirectly with the 5 (five) main elements of human needs, namely: breathing, moving; a sense of security; Compassion; appreciation; and self-actualization. Happiness is one of the main discussions in psychology, where many scientists incorporate the element of happiness into scientific development.

Happiness according to Seligman is the overflow of positive feelings in the past, present, and future that form a positive emotion. The overflow of positive feelings or positive emotions in the past consists of: satisfaction, peace, and a feeling of relief. While positive emotions in the future consist of confidence, hope, optimism, and certainty. Positive emotions in the present consist of sensoryly acquired pleasure and gratification obtained from activities involving the individual himself [4].

Research shows that individuals who are able to adapt to new environments or habits have the potential to become happy individuals. Happiness becomes the ultimate goal in the attainment of human life [5]. One of the human adaptations in this Century is a change in attitudes and mindsets towards technology. In a sense, humans today are required to achieve certain competencies in mastering technology. Science and knowledge are the main requirements in this competence, where individuals must be able to show existence in the midst of the pace of change and development of the times. Technology is present as a solution to various human problems, including in techniques for solving human problems.

One of the technologies that is present as one to help solve human problems is Artificial intelligence or commonly abbreviated as AI. Artificial intelligence (AI) is a breakthrough in technology, where technology through engineering is directed at a certain level of intelligence as can be done by humans. Like humans, Artificial intelligence is able to analyze, make decisions, and even make predictions [6]. Artificial intelligence is defined as Artificial Intelligence, where in that intelligence, technology is able to replace humans in certain things. With AI, humans are able to limit mobility, and at the same time are able to solve various problems they find.

The concept of Artificial Intelligence is basically a concept that directly intersects with the Smart City Concept, the Smart Government Concept, the Internet of Things Concept, and the Big Data Concept. The whole concept in the perspective of a government is directed at smart government, where there is a smart system platform integration that integrates all data in a platform. That's why in many countries, AI is an important part of cyber-security policy as well as mapping cyber-security development prospects [7]. Various potential developments of Artificial Intelligence have shown that Artificial intelligence in the present and in the future is able to maintain itself as one of the main problem solvers in human life. Artificial intelligence which is in line with the concept of Industry 4.0 and Society 5.0 has now changed many aspects of human life, even to the private realm.

Data in 2022 shows that 24.6% of organizations in Indonesia have adopted Artificial intelligence. Meanwhile, Thailand is in second place (17.1%), followed by Singapore (9.9%) and Malaysia (8.1%). A study conducted by PricewaterhouseCoopers (PwC) revealed that 52% of companies in the world accelerated the adoption of Artificial intelligence due to the emergence of COVID-19 in late 2019 or early 2020. While 86% of CEOs stated that Artificial intelligence became a mainstream technology in their companies in 2021. This is evidenced that in 2021, the increased use of Artificial intelligence in various business sectors creates business value of US$ 2.9 trillion and 6.2 billion hours of worker productivity. The contribution of Artificial intelligence to the global economy is expected to reach US$15.7 trillion by 2030. Indonesia itself is the 3rd most internet user country in Asia after China and India. Based on 2021 data, as many as 212.35 million people in Indonesia use the Internet. Indonesia is also expected to become the largest digital economy in Southeast Asia. In 2025, the value of digital economy transactions is projected to reach US$ 124 billion or around Rp 1.775 trillion.

Research shows that Artificial intelligence also penetrates the security side of a country, which has the potential to have an impact on a person's security or privacy [8]. Artificial intelligence is not only developed for the benefit of the business world, but also for education, health, and the military. Artificial intelligence in the field of business or start-ups shows the potential for negative impacts in line with the Industry 4.0 revolution, namely: risks to human comfort and safety. That's why artificial intelligence "certification" is needed in line with the regulations set out [9]. This certification is useful for ensuring that humans remain in control of their every act. In the view of legal science, every human act is a legal act that has implications for the law as well. Artificial intelligence certification creates a certain trust in individuals and communities in engaging themselves in the world of technology. The development of Artificial intelligence technology is expected to be able to support the ease of work from humans. This ability to support or alleviate man's work ultimately boils down to man's ultimate goal of achieving happiness. The achievement of happiness with Artificial intelligence technology is because human work becomes lighter, the workload is also reduced. If this can be achieved, then human productivity in work will increase.

But a frightening fact comes from the military world, that the use of Artificial intelligence has penetrated into weapons that do not need to be controlled by humans. Technology in this case is simply a time bomb for human existence [10]. This has led to much speculation by military observers who predict that an individual's security will be vulnerable, given the large number of artificial intelligence-based tools that can threaten at any time. One vivid example in this regard is the presence of drones or unmanned aircraft capable of being equipped with various weapons, and capable of moving automatically.

The overall negative impact of using artificial intelligence can obviously affect a person's happiness level, considering that in many studies, happiness is influenced by one of the main factors, namely safety. It is undeniable that Artificial intelligence has answered various questions and is able to solve various human problems. But on the other hand, there is the potential for insecurity that at any time can arise due to the absence of strict supervision of technological developments. The phenomenon of using AI deserves attention even to the point of making regulations so as not to cause a wider negative impact on the lives of individuals and society [11]. The impact of a technology is like a snowball that can turn big and uncontrollable. Failure of Artificial intelligence in one place will give rise to potential failures elsewhere. This can be the result of hacking or non-optimal surveillance. Based on this description, this paper seeks to explain the impact of artificial intelligence on a person's happiness from a psychological perspective.

2 Research Methods

This research uses a type of literature research. Data collection through literature review is related to the research focus, in the form of literature review, theory and government regulation documents. The source of primary material in this study is various literature that directly discusses Artificial Intelligence and the Psychology of Happiness through the Theory of Literature. Other sources are research findings, discussion results, seminars, etc. Library materials are then discussed and analyzed critically and in depth to support existing propositions and ideas from various references. Data collection in this study uses documentation techniques, data search or theories that are relevant to the research question, namely: how artificial intelligence impacts a person's happiness in the perspective of psychology in the form of notes, books, reports, research findings, scientific articles, etc. After the data is collected, it is analyzed. The analysis methods used are content analysis and descriptive analysis.

3 Result and Discussion

Happiness is an emotionally pleasurable experience, as well as achieving a certain level of satisfaction in life [12]. With happiness, a person is able to push himself to perform positive actions. In addition, a happy individual is able to show quality works in life as traces of his life. Happiness in some theories is mentioned as having an inherent perspective, as explained as follows (Table 1):

One of the quality works born of productive individuals is Artificial intelligence. Artificial intelligence was originally developed in America through the companies IBM and Microsoft, which were started 25 years ago [13]. This tech giant company devotes

Table 1. Happiness Theory Expert Perspective

Perspective	Carr	Fromm	Diener	Seligman
Definition	Positive psychological state	Productively oriented	Cognitive and affective evaluation	The results of self-assessment
Factor	1. Satisfaction with the past 2. High level of positive emotions 3. Low level of negative emotions	1. Gratitude 2. Forgiving and Forgetting	1. Positive relationship 2. Discovery of meaning in life 3. Resilience Ability	1. Past satisfaction 2. Future optimism 3. Happiness in the present

itself to fundamental changes in the facet of human life supported by the use of technology followed by other companies, various developments and innovations emerged from Artificial intelligence technology that can be applied in various fields, including education, economics, and in the military field. Its use that began to lead to military purposes lured other countries to do the same. China and the European Union allocated some funds as an investment in the development of Artificial intelligence. This is not only for military purposes, but also for business and health purposes. It is proven by the emergence of Digital Market Systems as well as various medical devices that are able to diagnose in a relatively shorter time. Various businesses that prioritize the convenience and comfort of technology-based humans are one of the primary needs today, ranging from gadgets to modes of transportation.

In terms of Artificial intelligence surveillance, the European Union is a pioneer. Not only that, the European Union is even at the forefront of the development of Artificial intelligence in the private and public sectors. The European Union even issued regulations that have several main points, namely: first, the ethics of using Artificial intelligence; second, identification of risks in the use of Artificial intelligence; third, Artificial intelligence does not threaten human rights and democracies; fourth, there are prevention mechanisms, for example, system hacking can be anticipated immediately; fifth, Artificial intelligence is the responsibility of the state that develops it; and sixth, Artificial intelligence does not represent humans, where humans must obtain information if they communicate with Artificial intelligence [14].

The use of Artificial intelligence, whatever its purpose cannot be done to replace the elements inherent in humans. Artificial intelligence must be developed while maintaining humans as the center, considering that human characteristics are as beings who have intentions, emotions, aesthetics, values, and morals. The emphasis of Artificial intelligence that is not a substitute for humans in this point is clearly to maintain human existence with its various fitrahs, including in terms of mobility. In addition, the various affections shown by humans are also imitable and replaced by Artificial intelligence. Without inherent values and morals, Artificial intelligence has the potential to run out of control. Man remains the holder of control over the Artificial intelligence he created, and is not enslaved by it.

The transparency of the use of Artificial intelligence in the field of security is also questionable, considering the impact that is often not identified by the people in a country. One example is the use of Artificial intelligence in the military field which has the potential to become a killer robot [15]. In addition, various algorithmic systems in Artificial intelligence have the potential to lock humans to the side of momentary happiness and distance themselves from more essential happiness. Happiness is obtained through various processes directed towards the achievement of a more optimistic and positive experience in seeing each side of life [16]. Artificial intelligence must be directed to the positive side of humans with various regulations and strict supervision of it. Thus, Artificial intelligence does not get out of control, further distancing humans from reality.

Seligman is an American psychologist. He was born August 12, 1942. He is an educator, and author of self-help books. Since the late 1990s, Seligman has been an avid promoter in the scientific community for the field of positive psychology. His theory of learned helplessness is very popular among psychological scientists and clinical psychologists. A Review of General Psychology survey, published in 2002, ranks Seligman as the 31st most referenced psychologist of the 20th century. Seligman views that human beings have two potentials, namely good potential and bad or negative potential, which he means that humans can be good and can also be bad. According to him, by developing the positive potential of human beings, the sense of suffering will be reduced to bring him happiness. So that his studies so far he has focused on seeing and developing human potential. In addition, he also thinks that every human being has the potential to be happy and live a good life [17].

Seligman divides happiness into 3 (three) positive emotions, namely: first, past satisfaction. It is influenced entirely by the thoughts of individuals in the past [18]. Artificial intelligence is able to show itself as an admirable "figure", able to solve problems that have not been solved before. Artificial intelligence in this case is a euphoria in itself for some people, where emotions can become one in experiences involving technology. Based on Seligman's Theory of Happiness, Artificial intelligence meets the criteria of positive emotions in past satisfaction. With the technology that exists now, humans are able to express themselves as desired, and can even achieve a picture of past and future experiences.

Second, optimism for the future. Positive emotions about the future include: faith, trust, confidence, and hope [19]. Artificial intelligence in many studies has the potential to be able to distance human beings from individual beliefs and beliefs with their God. The farther an individual enters Artificial intelligence, the farther the potential for closeness to God becomes. The certainty of Artificial intelligence in science and knowledge can be maintained, but individually the existence of Artificial intelligence is a threat that can interfere with human survival. The certainty of the existence of artificial intelligence can be influenced by its surveillance system. This is true for both the developer and the user. Great hope is pinned on Artificial intelligence which is considered capable of solving various human problems in the modern world today. But the existence of Artificial intelligence is also a scary scourge of the risk of physical human relationships. In some cases, learning has been replaced by artificial intelligence "figures" who are scientifically able to explain each material, but forget the value and moral side that should also be conveyed.

Third, happiness in the present. This emotion has a strong sensory and emotional component, is temporary in nature and involves little thought. That's why it is also called basic feelings or emotions, considering that there is the involvement of the five senses there [29]. Artificial intelligence can achieve this emotional state. For example, the development of social media with various algorithms in it is able to make individuals "trapped" in their world. Thus it can be concluded that in measuring the indicators of the emotion of happiness in the present, artificial intelligence is able to achieve it. However, when viewed from the impact indicators, individuals have the potential to move away from the world of reality. And this will have a bad impact on AI users.

Every technology, like a currency coin, has 2 (two) sides, both positive and negative. Based on the description above, it can be seen that AI has the potential to have a negative impact on a person's happiness. Artificial intelligence puts itself in a middle position, where in the indicator of positive emotions of happiness, AI is not fully achieved. For this reason, attention is needed, especially to the education of AI actors, researchers, users, and observers [20]. This is in line with one of the studies that recommends the need for AI development by paying attention to 5 (five) aspects, namely: legal certainty; user education; technical and procedural acts; organizational structure, capacity building; and international cooperation.

Seligman explains that to know a person's level of happiness can be measured or known by looking at the level of satisfaction of himself. According to him, happiness can be influenced by several things, the main ones are overall satisfaction, the environment beyond self-control (circumstances beyond our control) and voluntary action [21]. In terms of past satisfaction emotions, Artificial intelligence is able to meet human expectations. Artificial intelligence is able to position itself as a form of life satisfaction; environment beyond self-control; and voluntary action. But on the other hand, Artificial intelligence has not been able to answer happiness in the perspective of future optimism emotions. This is the main point based on Seligman's theory of happiness, that artificial intelligence is pseudo-and momentary happiness which is not the ultimate happiness.

4   Conclusion

Artificial Intelligence is one of the boredom in the field of technology that allows users to do various activities without having to spend a lot of energy. As an innovation, Artificial Intelligence clearly affects various aspects of human life, one of which is the mobility aspect. With the convenience obtained with Artificial Intelligence, it is possible to have negative impacts that have the potential to arise in line with the negative impacts of utilizing the technology itself. In the view of Seligmen's Theory of Happiness, Artificial Intelligence is not fully capable of guaranteeing one's happiness. The sense of comfort and security offered by Artificial intelligence is pseudo-happiness in the perspective of happiness theory. An in-depth study is needed on the development of Artificial intelligence accompanied by strict regulation and supervision, before Artificial intelligence creates itself as a substitute for humans in many aspects of life.

References

1. San Martín, J., Perles, F., Canto, J.M.: Life satisfaction and perception of happiness among university students. Span. J. Psychol. **13**(2), 617–628 (2010)
2. Permana, Y.: The relations between gratitude and happiness among students of divorce victims at SMA PGRI Purwoharjo. In: 3rd Asean Conference on Psychology, Counseling, & Humanities, pp. 92–96 (2017)
3. Romadhani, R.K.: Meaning of happiness in children: an exploratory study. Psychol. Res. Interv. **3**(1), 42–46 (2020)
4. Lu, L., Bin Shih, J.: Sources of happiness: a qualitative approach. J. Soc. Psychol. **137**(2), 181–187 (1997)
5. Koc, K., Pepe, O.: The investigation of the relationship between happiness levels of the faculty of sports sciences and the levels of life satisfaction and optimism. World J. Educ. **8**(6), 74–81 (2018)
6. Cioffi, R., Travaglioni, M., Piscitelli, G., Petrillo, A., De Felice, F.: Artificial intelligence and machine learning applications in smart production: progress, trends, and directions. Sustainability **12**(2), 492 (2020)
7. Dignum, V.: Responsible artificial intelligence: designing AI for human values. ICT Discov. (1), 1–8 (2017)
8. Shukla Shubhendu, S., Vijay, J.: Applicability of artificial intelligence in different fields of life. Int. J. Sci. Eng. Res. **1**(1), 28–35 (2013)
9. Jha, K., Doshi, A., Patel, P., Shah, M.: A comprehensive review on automation in agriculture using artificial intelligence. Artif. Intell. Agric. **2**, 1–12 (2019)
10. Li, J., Herdem, M.S., Nathwani, J., Wen, J.Z.: Methods and applications for artificial intelligence, big data, internet-of-things, and blockchain in smart energy management. Energy AI 100208 (2022)
11. Agbai, C.M.: Application of artificial intelligence (AI) in the food industry. GSC Biol. Pharm. Sci. **13**, 171–178 (2020)
12. Phillips, J., De Freitas, J., Mott, C., Gruber, J., Knobe, J.: True happiness: the role of morality in the folk concept of happiness. J. Exp. Psychol. Gen. **146**(2), 165 (2017)
13. Makridakis, S.: The forthcoming Artificial Intelligence (AI) revolution: Its impact on society and firms. Futures **90**, 46–60 (2017)
14. Nilsson, N.J.: The Quest for Artificial Intelligence. Cambridge University Press, Cambridge (2009)
15. Stahl, B.C.: Artificial Intelligence for a Better Future: An Ecosystem Perspective on the Ethics of AI and Emerging Digital Technologies. Springer, Cham (2021). https://doi.org/10.1007/978-3-030-69978-9
16. Tamir, M., Schwartz, S.H., Oishi, S., Kim, M.Y.: The secret to happiness: feeling good or feeling right? J. Exp. Psychol. Gen. **146**(10), 1448 (2017)
17. Diener, E., Seligman, M.E.P.: Very happy people. Psychol. Sci. **13**(1), 81–84 (2002)
18. Triantoro, S.: Forgiveness, gratitude, and happiness among college students. Int. J. public Heal. Sci. **3**(4), 241–245 (2014)
19. Veenhoven, R.: Happiness: also known as 'life satisfaction' and 'subjective well-being. In: Land, K., Michalos, A., Sirgy, M. (eds.) Handbook of Social Indicators and Quality of Life Research, pp. 63–77. Springer, Dordrecht (2011). https://doi.org/10.1007/978-94-007-242 1-1_3
20. Moyano-Diaz, E., Mendoza-Llanos, R., Paez-Rovira, D.: Psychological well-being and their relationship with different referents and sources of happiness in Chile. Rev. Psicol. **39**(1), 162–182 (2021)
21. Seligman, M.: PERMA and the building blocks of well-being. J. Posit. Psychol. **13**(4), 333–335 (2018)

A Novel Human-Centered Trust Framework: Applications for Assured AI and Autonomy

Sarah Rigsbee[✉] [iD], Alexis Basantis[iD], Matthew Gubanich, and Cara LaPointe[iD]

Johns Hopkins University Applied Physics Laboratory, Laurel, MD 20723, USA
{Sarah.Rigsbee,Alexis.Basantis,Matthew.Gubanich,
Cara.LaPointe}@jhuapl.edu

Abstract. Highly advanced technologies, such as AI-enabled systems, are becoming more integrated into the daily lives of humans. These systems have the potential to provide incredible utility and benefit to end users. However, in order to maximize their benefit, these systems must be designed and integrated in ways that are thoughtful, intentional, and ethical, while accounting for the diverse perspectives that exist in these technical ecosystems. In order to understand system assurance in a meaningful and impactful way, it is important to look across all system stakeholders, including individuals representing diverse perspectives such as engineers, legislators, end users, and community leaders. Therefore, our research aimed to better understand: what does assurance of autonomous and AI-enabled systems look like from a human-centered perspective?

This paper presents the human-centered approach taken to begin to answer this research question and outlines culminating insights and a framework that can be leveraged to ensure core perspectives are being considered when designing and building advanced technologies, such as automated and AI-enabled systems.

Keywords: Trust · Human-Centered Design · Assurance · AI · Autonomy

1 Introduction

With the emergence of artificial intelligence (AI) and AI-enabled autonomous systems, the technological landscape is becoming more complex. In addition to advancing technological complexity, these systems are also becoming increasingly more integrated into the daily life of humans. From the emergence of highly automated vehicles onto our roadways to automated digital assistants that are a button push away, technologies are continually evolving and becoming more indispensable. While useful, permitting technical systems unrestricted access to ourselves, data, and homes come with inherent risks. Systems can be easily hacked, misused, or designed with bias, potentially causing harm to both humans using the system and bystanders [1–3].

If our goal is for these systems to be beneficial contributors to society, it is important to understand how to ensure they are safe, reliable, secure, and ethical [4]. Because technologies are inherently linked to people, with humans designing, building, integrating, and using these systems, it is only logical to also approach understanding system assurance from a human-centered perspective.

C. Stephanidis et al. (Eds.): HCII 2023, CCIS 1832, pp. 479–485, 2023.
https://doi.org/10.1007/978-3-031-35989-7_61

Human-centered design (HCD) and design thinking (DT) are creative problem-solving processes which aim to develop usable systems by focusing on integrating the human perspective throughout the entire design process [5, 6]. These methods can be applied to a variety of applications including engineering, organizational design, and strategic visioning, with user feedback providing the basis for design and prototyping. Previous work has applied DT and HCD principles to develop ethical and human-centered systems [7], to better understand bias and explainability of AI-enabled systems [8, 9], and prototype autonomous systems, like intelligent robotics used in healthcare and emergency response applications [10, 11]. However, although studies have been conducted to dive deep into understanding isolated components of assurance, limited work has been done that leverages human-centered methods to holistically examine autonomous systems and AI assurance. Therefore, our research sought to use HCD and DT methods to understand the question: *what does assurance of autonomous and AI-enabled systems look like from a human-centered perspective?*

2 Approach

To gain insight into the different challenges and opportunities that exist and to better understand the current technology landscape, qualitative data was collected through an ethnographic interview approach. Ethnography is "the hallmark of qualitative inquiry" [12], and ethnographic interviewing focuses on building a comfortable, productive relationship through the use of friendly, structured, interviewee-driven conversation [13]. When developing the interview structure, it is crucial to understand that an individual's perspectives will be shaped by their personal bias, including the knowledge they have gained over time and through their own lived experiences [14]. With this understanding in mind, the team developed a set of descriptive and structural interview questions. Descriptive questions are general and broad and are designed to better understand how the interviewee sees their world around a given topic [13]. An example descriptive question used during the team's interviews was "What does assurance mean to you? How do you know when something is assured?" Structural questions help explore the responses to descriptive questions and provide additional insight into how interviewees organize their knowledge [13]. An example structural question used during interviews was "What does it mean for a system to be [safe and reliable], [secure and resilient], [predictable and seamless], and [beneficial impact on society]?".

To capture a wide range of perspectives, twenty-five ethnographic interviews were held with a diverse set of individuals across nine entities, representing the leadership team of the Johns Hopkins Institute for Assured Autonomy (IAA), private industry, academia, and government. The interviews focused on perceptions and viewpoints of technical assurance, trust, ethical system development, and the impact of autonomous systems on individuals and communities. Anonymized interview notes were captured in-situ, and the team synthesized the information to identify common and unique themes across the data. Synthesis is an abductive sensemaking process that manages, organizes, and filters data in an effort to produce relevant information and knowledge [15]. Therefore, the output of the synthesis process highlighted core insights and findings, driving the creation of the framework outlined below.

3   Results

3.1   Core Research Insights

From the synthesis process and our observations during the ethnographic research phase, a large number of broad and deep insights were generated and derived from the interview data. For simplification and clarity, below is a subset of the core research findings that were the main drivers of the framework development.

Assurance is a Relationship. Assurance arises as the result of a social relationship built between the stewards of technology and the recipients of technology. The recipients of technology are the people who use or are impacted by systems. Technology recipients put their trust into the stewards that the system will perform in the way that is expected and do no harm. The stewards of technology are the individuals and organizations in charge of building, managing, and integrating technical systems. Stewards are responsible for considering the ways in which their systems will affect the technology recipients, both within and outside its original design scope.

Trust is a Complicated Word. The concept of trust often describes the way people relate to technology. Technology could likely serve as a proxy for the trust more appropriately applied to people, not machines. Technologies are not moral or ethical agents, but depending on people's past experiences they may interact with technology as if it was.

All Humans Influence Technology. Users of technologies are not the only people who are impacted by them. People exist throughout the entire lifecycle of technological systems – from design and engineering, building, marketing, selling, maintenance, legislating, and disposal. These people have different perspectives, incentives, and values, and therefore might engage with technology in different ways. For example, experts in a specific technology may interact with it in a different way, compared to a "normal" end user, due to their experience with and education on the system. Different cultures and communities may also interact with technology in different ways, due to their priorities and historical experiences.

3.2   The Johns Hopkins Human-Centered Trust (JHHT) Framework

The culminating result of the approach and insights described above is the Johns Hopkins Human-Centered Trust Framework (JHHT, pronounced "jet"). This framework (Fig. 1) was developed to visualize and communicate the core components and perspectives of technical assurance that were derived from the HCD approach. The sections below outline framework components and discoveries in greater detail.

Trust of Recipients. The recipients of technology are impacted by systems, either wittingly or unwittingly. These witting populations, or active recipients, explicitly choose to engage with technology. The unwitting populations, or passive recipients, are affected by technology and must engage with it, even if they did not directly choose to do so. All technology recipients must trust that the technology will perform in the way that is expected and will do them no harm. The technology recipients are both people and

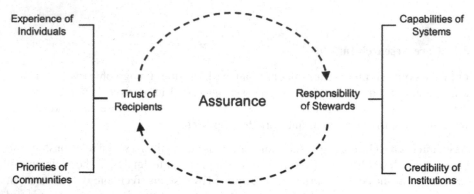

Fig. 1. The Johns Hopkins Human-Centered Trust (JHHT) Framework outlining the assurance relationship and perspectives important to automated system assurance.

communities, and it is important to note that how they approach, think about, and engage with technology will vary.

Experience of Individuals. Individuals bring their own values and experiences to bear on every interaction they have with technology. These experiences and values influence how individuals perceive and interact with autonomous systems. Humans may choose to trust technology until proven wrong. Similarly, if a person has a negative experience with a technology, that might bias their willingness to trust a future technology.

Priorities of Communities. Humans are generally social creatures, often resulting in individuals assembling themselves into multiple value-based communities. For example, these communities may be affinity-based, governmental, and/or institutional. Communities often serve to codify, protect, and enforce the values of the members that comprise them through rules, ethical standards, laws, policing, and social repair programs. The communities need to decide what is desired from technology, if it is beneficial, and what is most important to the community.

Responsibility of Stewards. The stewards of technology are the individuals and institutions in charge of building, managing, and integrating technical systems. Stewards are responsible for considering the ways in which their systems will affect the technology recipients, both within and outside its original design scope. The trust that individuals and communities have in technical systems is not only based on their performance capabilities, but also directly related to the credibility of the steward's institution.

Capability of Systems. Core and enabling autonomous technologies comprise the systems in the assurance trust relationship. These systems must be highly capable and perform in their operating environment as designed. In addition, for assurance, these systems must appropriately communicate their intentions – especially when they are capable of autonomous and self-learned behavior – and be safe, reliable, resilient, and secure against attack. Furthermore, when resilient systems fail, recovery actions must be clearly outlined and understood by the technology recipients.

Credibility of Institutions. Stewards must act in ethical, fair, and just ways to maintain their credibility. Many different types of institutions are stewards, and it is often believed that the institutions most central to assurance are the actual organizations that build the technology. However, there are other institutions that validate, educate, analyze, oversee, or regulate these technology-building institutions. The credibility of those who represent technology building institutions and the institutions themselves can enhance, displace, degrade, or destroy the trustworthiness of the technology.

4 Applications for Assured AI and Autonomy

The JHHT framework can be used to understand all of the complex components that should be considered when designing and developing a wide range of assured AI and automated systems. Below outlines some potential use cases, developed by our team, where the JHHT Framework could be leveraged to foster human-machine trust.

4.1 Voice Assistants

The availability and use of AI-enabled voice assistants has proliferated with the introduction of these technologies by large technology firms such as Apple's Siri, Amazon's Alexa and Google's voice assistant. Previous research has shown the disparities in effectiveness and cultural competence of these systems across the world [16, 17]. Leveraging the JHHT Framework could help technology developers understand that working with underrepresented communities and individuals to develop voice assistants is important and will assist in meeting the various needs of those diverse populations.

4.2 Social Robotics

As countries around the world face aging populations [18], social robotics are a potential solution to the resulting challenges such as shortages in healthcare, increasing loneliness, and the need for assistance with life tasks [19, 20]. The JHHT Framework can aid designers through the development process by highlighting the need for these social robotic technologies to be culturally competent and tailored to meet the needs of the users AND communities, thus fostering appropriate levels of human trust in those systems.

4.3 Emergency Response Technologies

Autonomous technologies are being explored and leveraged for emergency response situations, including mobile robots to guide human evacuees to safety. In emergency evacuation situations, timely evacuation is often critical and human emotions are heightened. Accounting for cultural human dynamics is important in the design of mobile evacuation robots in order to lead to positive outcomes [21].

5 Conclusion

The JHHT Framework can enable developers and providers of technology to understand how the capability of the system and the credibility of institutions both affect recipient perception and emotions. The framework can also highlight how the needs of both individuals and communities should be considered when designing and developing technology. An additional intent of the JHHT Framework is to foster a strategic feedback loop between the recipients and the stewards, resulting in the co-development of more trustworthy and trusted technology. Although many HCD tools for human-centric technology development exist, the JHHT Framework makes a novel contribution to the current research landscape by providing a more holistic framework which facilitates the understanding of the complex ecosystem of components and trust relationships that contribute to technical assurance.

References

1. Al-Sabaawi, A., Al-Dulaimi, K., Foo, E., Alazab, M.: Addressing malware attacks on connected and autonomous vehicles: recent techniques and challenges. In: Stamp, M., Alazab, M., Shalaginov, A. (eds.) Malware Analysis Using Artificial Intelligence and Deep Learning, pp. 97–119. Springer, Cham (2021). https://doi.org/10.1007/978-3-030-62582-5_4
2. Asaro, P.M.: The Liability Problem for Autonomous Artificial Agents. Association for the Advancement of Artificial Intelligence (2015). https://peterasaro.org/writing/Asaro,%20E thics%20Auto%20Agents,%20AAAI.pdf
3. Cowgill, B., Dell'Acqua, F., Deng, S., Hsu, D., Verma, N., Chaintreau, A.: Biased programmers? Or biased data? A field experiment in operationalizing AI ethics. In: Proceedings of the 21st ACM Conference on Economics and Computation, pp. 679–681 (2020). https://pap ers.ssrn.com/sol3/papers.cfm?abstract_id=3615404
4. National Defense Industrial Association System Assurance Committee (2008). Engineering for System Assurance. https://www.ndia.org/-/media/sites/ndia/meetings-and-events/div isions/systems-engineering/sse-committee/systems-assurance-guidebook.ashx?la=en
5. Meinel, C., Leifer, L.: Design thinking research. In: Design Thinking Research, Understanding Innovation (2012). https://doi.org/10.1007/978-3-642-21643-5_1
6. Razzouk, R., Shute, V.: What is design thinking and why is it important? Rev. Educ. Res. **82**(3), 330–348 (2012). https://doi.org/10.3102/0034654312457429
7. Xu, W.: Toward human-centered AI: a perspective from human-computer interaction. Interactions (2019). https://dl.acm.org/doi/pdf/10.1145/3328485
8. Kronqvist, A., Rousi, R.A.: A quick review of ethics, design thinking, gender, and AI development. Int. J. Des. Creativity Innov. **11**(1), 62–79 (2022). https://www.tandfonline.com/doi/full/10.1080/21650349.2022.2136762
9. Yang, L., Wang, H., Deleris, L.A.: What does it mean to explain? A user-centered study on AI explainability. In: Degen, H., Ntoa, S. (eds.) HCII 2021. LNCS (LNAI), vol. 12797, pp. 107–121. Springer, Cham (2021). https://doi.org/10.1007/978-3-030-77772-2_8
10. Green, A., Huttenrauch, H., Norman, M., Oestreicher, L., Eklundh, K.S.: User centered design for intelligent service robots. In: Proceedings 9th IEEE International Workshop on Robot and Human Interactive Communication, pp. 161–166 (2002). https://ieeexplore.ieee.org/abstract/document/892488
11. Doroftei, D., et al.: User centered design. In: Search and Rescue Robotics - From Theory to Practice (2017). https://www.researchgate.net/publication/319388805_User-Cen tered_Design

12. Marshall, C., Rossman, G.B., Blanco, G.L.: Designing qualitative research. SAGE Publishing, Inc. (2014)
13. Westby, C., Burda, A., Mehta, Z.: Asking the right questions in the right ways: strategies for ethnographic interviewing. ASHA Leader **8**(8), 4–17 (2003). https://doi.org/10.1044/leader. FTR3.08082003.4
14. Riquelme, L.F.: Ethics and diversity: doing the right thing? Perspect. ASHA Special Interest Groups **7**(1), 27–34 (2022). https://doi.org/10.1044/2021_PERSP-21-00261
15. Kolko, J.: Abductive thinking and sensemaking: the drivers of design synthesis. Des. Issues **26**(1), 15–28 (2010). https://doi.org/10.1162/desi.2010.26.1.15
16. Ma, Y., et al.: Enthusiasts, pragmatists, and skeptics: investigating users' attitudes towards emotion- and personality-aware voice assistants across cultures. In: MuC 2022: Proceedings of Mensch und Computer 2022, pp. 308–322 (2022). https://dl.acm.org/doi/10.1145/3543758. 3543776
17. Linxen, S., Strum, C., Bruhlmann, F., Cassau, V., Opwis, K., Reinecke, K.: How WEIRD is CHI? In: CHI 2021: Proceedings of the 2021 CHI Conference on Human Factors in Computing Systems, vol. 143, pp. 1–14 (2021). https://dl.acm.org/doi/10.1145/3411764.3445488
18. World Health Organization: Ageing and health: Key facts (2022). https://www.who.int/news-room/fact-sheets/detail/ageing-and-health
19. Pedersen, I., Reid, S., Aspevi, K.: Developing social robots for aging populations: a literature review of recent academic sources. Sociol. Compass **12**(6) (2018). https://doi.org/10.1111/ soc4.12585
20. Broekens, J., Heerink, M., Rosendal, H.: Assistive social robots in elderly care: a review. Gerontechnology **8**(2), 94–103 (2009). https://ii.tudelft.nl/~joostb/files/Broekens%20et% 20al%202009.pdf
21. Wagner, A.R.: Robot-guided evacuation as a paradigm for human-robot interaction research. Front. Robot. AI Hum.-Robot Interact. **8** (2021). https://www.frontiersin.org/articles/10.3389/ frobt.2021.701938/full

An Exploratory Study of Programmer Bias Transfer: Investigating Colorblind Racial Attitudes Among Hispanic Students and Their Influence on Algorithmic Systems

Ana Cecilia Sánchez Ramos(⊠)

The University of Texas Rio Grande Valley, Edinburg, TX 78539, USA
acecysanchezr@gmail.com

Abstract. Algorithm-driven systems are increasingly ubiquitous, but concerns about their potential biases against racially marginalized groups persist. Although previous research has identified sources of algorithmic bias, such as biased datasets, little is known about the influence of personal biases of programmers on the algorithms they create. This study draws from Sociological theories on racialized organizations and color blind ideology to investigate this issue. To this end, a mixed-methods survey was conducted on Computer Science and Computer Engineering undergraduate students at a Hispanic-serving institution, examining the effects of demographics, cultural background, and color blind beliefs on a series of hypothetical programming tasks. As data analyses are still in progress, this paper reviews relevant Sociological literature and provides an overview of the survey methodology, as well as preliminary findings.

Keywords: First keyword · Second keyword · Another keyword

1 Introduction

Computer systems are increasingly being used across a variety of settings for the automation of a wide range of tasks: companies employ hiring tools that perform the screening of job applications [11] k-12 education institutions used monitoring systems to enforce social distancing guidelines during the COVID-19 pandemic [17], and robots are deployed in industrial and social settings [14]. Although these tools have facilitated the execution of many processes, scholars have found racial biases embedded in computer programs that resulted in discriminatory outcomes, disproportionately impacting Black individuals and other people of color [3,7,11]. Examples of this include smartwatch sensors and facial recognition systems that perform poorly on dark skin tones [7,9], surveillance systems where Black people are more likely to be flagged as a threat [2], and chatbots that reproduce racist speech [6,15,16].

While in some cases an algorithm - the sets of instructions given to a computer to perform a given task - is expected to favor a particular group over another to produce more equitable outcomes [4], biased programs may produce negative consequences through the systematic and unfair discrimination of already marginalized groups. For example, in 2015 a photo-tagging algorithm developed by Google was reported to have mislabeled pictures of Black people. The problem likely arose from an "unbalanced dataset", wherein the data used by the program to identify a human face lacked a representative number of images depicting Black individuals [7,9]. This case illustrates the overrepresentation of elements in a data-driven algorithm, a well-known source of bias in computer systems, albeit not the only one. Programs can be racially biased due to different reasons, such as a system being deployed in a context for which it was not designed to be used, or through the deliberate non-use of data that leads to unintended outcomes [4,5].

One particular source of bias that has been acknowledged in algorithmic bias literature but that remains understudied is the transfer of personal prejudices, often originating from society at large - organizations, institutions, and the overall culture surrounding an individual - onto a system [4,5].

A system's execution and limitations reflect the values and priorities of its creators [3,11], and it has been argued that if those behind the development of algorithmic systems hold racial prejudices, then they are likely to perpetuate oppressive dynamics through said artifacts [4], but there is no research that systematically evaluates the transfer of personal racial prejudices onto algorithms. Ensuring that software development teams are more racially diverse, as scholars have proposed [3,7,9], would improve the performance of computer systems by incorporating different perspectives, thus increasing awareness on limitations that might have gone unnoticed otherwise. However, this measure does not consider the underlying structures that in the first place enable racial prejudices to enter technologies. In order for racial biases to enter technologies, there must be a system in place that allows for this transfer to occur. One such system is present in modern mainstream organizations.

2   Racialized Organizations and Colorblind Programs

According to racialized organizational theories, organizations in industrial countries are social institutions that uphold Whiteness as a standard. Through policies and everyday work procedures, these institutions reproduce racial and gender hierarchies [1,12,18] The result can be seen in most of the executive positions held in organizations in the United States and Europe, which are occupied by White men [1,13]. This is particularly true for large, influential institutions, as are prominent technology companies [6,8].

In the past, organizational procedures were explicitly racialized, but due to the growing stigmatization of overt discrimination following the Civil Rights movement, companies began to adopt apparently race-neutral policies and practices. This new, subtle form of racism is termed "colorblind" because it claims to not "see" race, and is the prevalent racial ideology of the post Civil Rights era [13,19]. Colorblind racism is characterized by subsuming its racist intent under apparently non-racial discourse and practices, making it difficult to identify and address.

In the case of technology, in addition to mainstream tech companies being overwhelmingly white and male, whiteness is also present in the emerging technologies developed by said organizations. As Benjamin (2019) shows, the design process of algorithms is inherently racialized and white-centered. Still, there is a widespread belief that emerging technologies are racially neutral [2,6,11] even though there are several examples that prove otherwise. This notion of race-neutrality in technological tools likely arose from the fact that algorithms that discriminate against racially underrepresented groups often do so through proxies (e.g., zip code) rather than through criteria that explicitly targets individuals [7,11]. Colorblindness is, then, present in biased algorithms.

I argue that this is due to the culture surrounding technology organizations. Individual racial attitudes are guided by organizational routines, meaning that people can reproduce racial inequalities even in the absence of malicious intent by conforming to organizational norms. This is true for people of color who, while they may be able to challenge racial hierarchies, they can also reproduce structures of inequality by conforming to racialized organizational scripts [12]. In addition to reproducing racial hierarchies inadvertently, members of racially underrepresented groups may navigate a racialized environment through White cultural assimilation to avoid being ostracized [13]. In racialized organizations whiteness is embedded in norms, values, ideologies, and policies in a way that is often unremarkable and taken for granted, and any threats to their established hierarchy are seen as illegitimate intrusions into their meritocratic, "normal" functioning [12]. Further, the incorporation of previously excluded groups into mainstream organizations has been central to their whitening [12], so integrating into mainstream organizational culture could also be a way for a person to increase their chances of attaining White status in the U.S. racial/ethnic hierarchy, even if this means reinforcing the legitimacy of racialized procedures. Additionally, organizations tend to select people of color that are highly integrated into mainstream culture because they are less likely to challenge entrenched racial hierarchies [13]. This could be yet another reason why people of color conform to the White standard.

In describing how developers in tech companies may perpetuate inequalities through the design of algorithm-driven systems, Benjamin (2019) writes: "we could expect a Black programmer, immersed as she is in the same systems of racial meaning and economic expediency as the rest of her co-workers, to code software in a way that perpetuates racist stereotypes" (p. 61).

Focusing solely on the diversification of software development teams fails to address the structural aspect of the issue of programmer bias transfer, as diversity policies do little to change the racial distribution of organizational power [12] Moreover, approaching programmer bias transfer as only a matter of diversity in development teams ignores the fact that people of color can also internalize biased racial beliefs and reproduce them [2], especially as they are in an environment that enables them to do so.

3   Present Work

Drawing from prior research, I propose technological companies are racialized institutions that perpetuate racial hierarchies through colorblind practices. Further, because organizational practices guide individual attitudes, leading members of an organization to conform to racialized scripts - whether consciously or not -, I argue that developers that conform to the values upheld in technology companies internalize colorblind ideas and reproduce them through algorithmic systems. This is true as well for individuals of color, who may partake in the creation of a racially biased system due to the unconscious adoption of racist beliefs. They may also conform to racialized scripts to become more integrated into U.S. culture. As previous research shows, the practice of becoming integrated into the mainstream has become central in attaining a White status in the U.S. racial/ethnic hierarchy. Thus, individuals of color that are more incorporated into U.S. culture may be more likely than non-incorporated ones to endorse the racial ideology prevalent in the United states (i.e., color blindness). Another reason why people of color may conform to organizational racial practices is to avoid being ostracized [13]. In the present work I investigate the issue of programmer bias transfer from a Sociological perspective. Drawing from theories of racialized organizations and on color blind ideology, I explore the transfer of personal racial prejudices from individuals pertaining to an underrepresented group, onto algorithmic systems. In particular, I seek to answer the following research questions:

- RQ 1. Do developers at a Hispanic-serving institution hold colorblind racial beliefs?
- RQ 2. Do such colorblind racial beliefs transfer to algorithmic systems?
- RQ 3. Are individuals more integrated into mainstream culture more likely to transfer their racial prejudices than less incorporated ones?

I address the above inquiries through an exploratory, quasi-experimental study consisting of a mixed-methods survey. In the survey I gather demographic information and data on the cultural background, personal experiences, and colorblind racial beliefs of Computer Science (CSCI) and Computer Engineering (CMPE) students at a Hispanic-serving institution, and investigate the correlation of these characteristics with students' responses to a series of hypothetical programming scenarios. I evaluate participants' beliefs in color blind ideas using the Color-blind Racial Attitudes Scale (CoBRAS) developed by [10], and conduct a content analysis to identify themes reflecting a colorblind ideology in the responses provided to the experimental tasks. To examine the relationship between these two, I conduct a series of statistical analyses.

My research centers on Hispanic students and their involvement in the development of racially biased programs. By examining their experiences I aim to shed light on the ways in which marginalized individuals can be complicit in perpetuating discriminatory systems. Additionally, I explore whether students who aspire to join the tech industry are inclined to adopt its organizational culture, including colorblind beliefs that may contribute to the development of biased technologies. I focus on students because I believe it is during this formative stage that the incorporation of measures to mitigate the development of biased programs, for example through specialized courses, would be more efficient. The objective of this research is to further our current knowledge on how racial prejudices are transferred from developers to algorithms, and to inform potential strategies for creating more equitable and inclusive systems. In doing so, this work contributes to the growing field of algorithmic bias, and the literature on color blind racism and organizational theories, and also aims to create an impact at the educational level by providing insights that can potentially aid in the design process of coursework for CSCI/CMPE majors.

4   Method

I developed an exploratory, mixed-methods study to understand the extent to which individual experiences and racial prejudices of Computer Science and Computer Engineering students at a Hispanic-serving institution impact the design process of computer systems.

4.1   Participant Recruitment and Sample

Undergraduate and graduate students were recruited at a Hispanic-serving university located on the South Texas border. Eligibility criteria included being 18 years or older, full-time enrollment, and pursuing a major in Computer Science (CSCI) and/or Computer Engineering (CMPE). Students were recruited through CSCI/CMPE courses and through a student organization's Discord server. Some courses that promoted the study offered extra credit to participating students. Students that did not wish to participate in the survey had the alternative option of writing an essay to qualify for extra credit. Participation was completely voluntary, and students who abandoned the survey received no penalty. Students taking the survey for extra credit were still eligible for it even if they abandoned the survey. I received a total of 77 responses, with a remaining sample of 40 surveys. Selection criteria of the surveys included having completed demographic questions, as well as the CoBRAS scale and the experimental tasks used to evaluate transfer of colorblind ideas to algorithm design.

4.2   Survey

I designed a mixed-methods survey on Qualtrics consisting of a series of demographic and cultural background questions, scales, and three experimental tasks. These described hypothetical scenarios, for which participants were then prompted to design algorithmic solutions.

Consent Form and Extra Credit Information. At the beginning of the survey participants were shown a consent form disclosing the purpose of the survey and a description of its content. To avoid priming, the consent form used deception in describing the study's purpose, stating that the goal was to evaluate CSCI/CMPE students' experiences at the university. The consent form also provided an estimate of the survey's completion time, benefits and risks associated with it, and requirements for receiving extra credit for eligible courses. Additionally, it stated that participation was completely voluntary and that the information gathered was confidential. Lastly, it provided resources and contact information so students could learn more about the research being conducted and their rights as a participant. Upon reading the disclosure form, participants were given the eligibility criteria to participate in the study, and then chose either to consent or not. If consent was provided, they could move onto the next section. All participants were given a randomly-generated code. Students from eligible courses could submit their code to the Primary Investigator to receive extra credit.

Demographics and Cultural Background. The survey explored participants' background through a series of demographic questions, as well as participants' level of cultural assimilation into mainstream Western culture, reflections on school experiences (e.g., whether they are comfortable with their degree program and the classes they have taken; involvement in student activities, etc.), and perceptions towards the field of CSCI and/or CMPE, such as what they value from these careers and why they chose to pursue a degree in them.

Beliefs in Tech Neutrality and Colorblindness. To identify beliefs in the racial neutrality of computer systems -particularly those driven by Artificial Intelligence-, and the tech industry, participants were asked to select their level of agreement to a series of statements regarding algorithmic fairness. To assess participants' beliefs in color blind ideas, I utilized the Color-Blind Racial Attitudes Scale, or CoBRAS, developed by Neville and colleagues.

All questions and scales were distributed to mitigate priming.

Experimental Tasks. I developed three experimental tasks to evaluate the extent to which personal background and colorblind beliefs transfer to computer systems. Each question presented students with hypothetical system development scenarios, asking them to propose a solution. The scenarios presented allowed for discrimination proxies to be incorporated into their implementation and thus, into participants' responses.

Post-Completion Survey and Debriefing. To assess suspicion, at the end of the survey participants were asked to give a description of what they thought the survey evaluated. Participants could also ask any questions they had about the study and add comments. These last questions serve as feedback for the Primary Investigator. Students were then debriefed and disclosed the real intent of the survey. A link to a website with resources on colorblind racism and algorithmic bias was provided. The website was created with Glitch.

4.3 Data Analyses

Data is being analyzed using statistical software STATA, version 17. I conducted descriptive statistics of the resulting sample (n=40), and coded the CoBRAS scale to get the scores for each participant. I also performed a content analysis on the responses provided in the experimental tasks to identify recurrent themes that correlated with the central themes of colorblind racial ideology: abstract liberalism, naturalization of racial phenomena, cultural racism, and minimization of racism. I first developed a preliminary coding device that included said themes. This coding artifact was modified in subsequent iterations as I analyzed participants' responses to include any additional themes that I had not foreseen.

5 Preliminary Results and Future Work

The sample of respondents in this study consisted of 36 male CSCI/CMPE majors and 4 female CSCI/CMPE majors, with an average age of 23 years old and an annual average income of 54.2. The vast majority (90%) of participants identified as Hispanic, with half of the sample identifying as Democrat and leaning more Liberal (45%) and Moderate (30%) than Conservative (7.5%) and Other (17.5%). Currently, the answers provided to the experimental tasks are undergoing content analysis, and as such, no significant results can be reported at this time. Upon completion of this project, future work could investigate potential differences between the responses of students at a Hispanic-serving institution and those at institutions with primarily White populations, which will provide a more nuanced understanding of the role of personal biases in algorithmic systems.

References

1. Acker, J.: Inequality regimes: gender, class, and race in organizations. Gender Soc. **20**(4), 441–464 (2006)
2. Benjamin, R.: Race after technology: Abolitionist tools for the new JIM code (2020)
3. Crawford, K.: Artificial intelligence's white guy problem. The New York Times **25**(06), 5 (2016)
4. David Danks and Alex John London: Algorithmic bias in autonomous systems. IJCAI **17**, 4691–4697 (2017)
5. Friedman, B., Nissenbaum, H.: Bias in computer systems. ACM Trans. Inf. Syst. (TOIS) **14**(3), 330–347 (1996)
6. Garcia, M.: Racist in the machine. World Policy J. **33**(4), 111–117 (2016)
7. Hankerson, D., et al.: Does technology have race? In: Proceedings of the 2016 CHI Conference Extended Abstracts on Human Factors in Computing Systems, pp. 473–486 (2016)
8. Huisache, S.: 2020 People of Color in Tech Report, September 2020
9. Lee, W.: How tech's lack of diversity leads to racist software, July 2015
10. Neville, H.A., Lilly, R.L., Duran, G., Lee, R.M., Browne, L.: Construction and initial validation of the color-blind racial attitudes scale (cobras). J. Counsel. Psychol. **47**(1), 59 (2000)

11. O'neil, C.: Weapons of math destruction: How big data increases inequality and threatens democracy. Crown (2017)
12. Ray, V.: A theory of racialized organizations. Am. Sociol. Rev. **84**(1), 26–53 (2019)
13. Ray, V., Purifoy, D.: The colorblind organization. In: Race, Organizations, and the Organizing Process. Emerald Publishing Limited (2019)
14. Sauppé, A., Mutlu, B.: The social impact of a robot co-worker in industrial settings. In: Proceedings of the 33rd Annual ACM Conference on Human Factors in Computing Systems, pp. 3613–3622 (2015)
15. Schlesinger, A., O'Hara, K.P., Taylor, A.S.: Let's talk about race: identity, chatbots, and AI. In: Proceedings of the 2018 CHI Conference on Human Factors in Computing Systems, pp. 1–14 (2018)
16. Stuart-Ulin, C.R.: Microsoft's politically correct chatbot is even worse than its racist one, July 2018
17. Ramos, C.: Emerging safety technologies in schools: addressing privacy and equity concerns to ensure a safe in-person school, September 2021
18. Wooten, M.E.: Soapbox: Editorial essays: Race and strategic organization (2006)
19. Zamudio, M.M., Rios, F.: From traditional to liberal racism: living racism in the everyday. Sociol. Perspect. **49**(4), 483–501 (2006)

Highly Automated and Master of the Situation?! Approach for a Human-Centered Evaluation of AI Systems for More Sociodigital Sovereignty

Ulrike Schmuntzsch[✉] [iD] and Ernst A. Hartmann [iD]

Institute for Innovation and Technology within the VDI/VDE Innovation + Technik GmbH, Steinplatz 1, 10623 Berlin, Germany
{schmuntzsch,hartmann}@iit-berlin.de

Abstract. In this paper, the framework of sociodigital sovereignty and an according classification matrix will be presented. Both have been developed on the basis of action regulation and sociotechnical theories in order to analyze and design different aspects of sociodigital sovereignty within sociotechnical systems. By using this matrix, it is possible to identify and address biases and potential conflicts in terms of transparency, reliability, trust, and fairness. The sociotechnical approach presented here addresses the three aspects - human, technology and organization – and will be complemented by an action-theoretical perspective that includes the three aspects of "transparency/explainability", "confidence of action/efficiency" and "freedom of action/divergence". This results in a matrix of nine fields in which different facets of sociodigital sovereignity are systematically adressed (e. g. Hartmann & Shajek, 2023). Furthermore, the resulting implications from a use case will be presented in this paper. There, the classification matrix was used in a workshop to analyze a highly automated technical system. Finally, future developments of the framework and the according classification matrix are outlined.

Keywords: sociodigital sovereignty · explainable AI · sociotechnical systems · action regulation theories

1 Introduction

1.1 Project Background and Preliminary Work

Increasing competition as well as new technologies, e.g. Artificial Intelligence (AI) especially in the field of industrial production, are leading to an equally increasing specialization of products and services. This digitalization and automation have a significant impact on the interaction between human and machine. In order for this complexity to remain manageable by humans and for them to remain capable and ready for action that cannot be automated, and in the event of sudden incidents, the development of secure and user-friendly concepts and technologies is essential.

But what does 'capable of action' mean, especially in terms of AI? The capability to act is closely related to the concept of sociodigital sovereignty of individuals and organizations in sociotechnical systems.

C. Stephanidis et al. (Eds.): HCII 2023, CCIS 1832, pp. 494–501, 2023.
https://doi.org/10.1007/978-3-031-35989-7_63

For the exploration of this concept in an industrial context, the project "Digital Sovereignty in the Economy" has been launched at the Institute for Innovation and Technology (iit) in 2019. Purpose of this project is to investigate the working conditions in industrial workplaces with highly automated systems for skilled workers in terms of transparency, comprehensibility, and controllability.

In this context, since 2019, several research studies were conducted in order to gain a more comprehensive understanding of trends and innovations as well as challenges of highly automatized industrial workplaces (Pentenrieder et al., 2021). The first interviews took place in 2019 with experts from industry and academia. These expert interviews were complemented with workplace studies in 2020 at several medium-sized companies in the German machine tool industry (Pentenrieder et al. 2021, 2022). Here, workers were accompanied in their working environment and interviewed directly about their everyday practice and their concerns and wishes in terms of digitalization in future. Results showed that, due to increasingly complex automation, restrictions and dependencies on actions are one part of the expressed worries. Another problematic aspect is the intransparency of complex machine logics, especially of AI components. Due to the lack of explainability and controllability, skilled workers have problems to stay informed about what is going on and why. Being not master of the situation makes it hard for the workers to maintain their high level of skills and then to intervene correctly and in time in situations when it is needed. This dilemma was already defined and discussed as Ironies of Automation by (Bainbridge, 1983) and is still relevant.

Having these wishes and concerns of practitioners regarding explainability and controllability in mind, a participatory online workshop, also named as co-creation workshop, was designed and held in December 2021. Using three uses cases from different industrial fields, AI-based technologies and their impact on the practical work were discussed closely application-oriented with experts from business, politics, and science. Based on these three use cases from brewery, machine building, and automotive industry, workplaces were analyzed as sociotechnical systems. The different ideas were structured using a classification matrix based on the concept of sociodigital sovereignty (Pentenrieder et al., 2023; Hartmann, 2022).

All this preliminary work clarified that even the highest automated technical system, even when using AI, can still be seen as a sociotechnical system. This perspective underlines the importance to design and analyze them by having the human users and their concerns and needs in mind, as well as issues related to the organization. To sum up research so far, especially the aspects explainability and controllability as well as certain degrees of freedom to act in highly automated and regulated technical systems are extremely essential for skilled workers in order to fulfill their task as best as possible nowadays and in future (Oesterreich, 1981; Hacker, 2005; Mumford, 2006; Gunning et al., 2019). For designing and analyzing those human-centered sociotechnical systems, the concept of digital sovereignty and the developed classification matrix can be useful.

In the following chapter, the concept of digital sovereignty, the classification matrix, and the corresponding theoretical background will be presented.

2 Theoretical Background of the Concept of Digital Sovereignty and the According Classification Matrix

Following concepts from work psychology, a conceptual approach for analyzing and designing work systems regarding digital sovereignty was developed. Relevant theories include action regulation theory (Hacker, 2005), control theory – in the sense of psychological control, control of humans over their environments – as applied to action regulation (Oesterreich, 1981), and sociotechnical systems theory (e.g. Mumford, 2006).

Combining core aspects of these theories, a matrix can be constructed, consisting of three columns and three rows (Hartmann, 2022; the following description is very close to Hartmann & Shajek, 2023).

The three columns describe three aspects of digital sovereignty at the workplace:

- Transparency and Explainability: Transparency of the technological system is necessary for humans being able to exercise control. Complex algorithmic and AI-based systems are inherently complex and intransparent. Thus, transparency must be provided with extra effort. There is a rapidly growing field of research addressing these aspects of explainable AI (XAI, Gunning et al., 2019).
- Confidence of action means that humans, when acting in sociotechnical systems, can be confident that the effects of their action are those which they expected when deciding to implement these actions (*Efficiency*, Oesterreich, 1981).
- Finally, freedom of action describes situations offering humans a range of different courses of action from which they may choose autonomously (*Divergence*, Oesterreich, 1981).

The three rows of the matrix in Fig. 1 relate to the three sub-systems of sociotechnical systems – technology, people, and organization. Combining the three columns and three rows, nine facets of sociodigital sovereignty in sociotechnical systems are constructed.

In Fig. 1, leading questions are provided for these nine facets, to make the meaning of each facet more easily understood.

Starting with these nine questions, more specific questions were developed to cover more detailed aspects of each facet. In this way, a (preliminary) set of 40 questions was designed, which served as an input to the workshop described in the following section.

3 Workshop on the Evaluation of the Classification Matrix

3.1 Preparation and Implementation of the Workshop

Having developed the classification matrix and a first set of questions covering the nine aspects of digital sovereignty, both have been applied in a first industrial use case. There, the launch of a new planning software was assessed with the help of the matrix and the questionnaire. At the time of the workshop, a test run of the new software had already taken place, but it was not yet implemented for everyday operation. This launch as well as the technical system itself were critically and emotionally discussed among employees because not only a new system should be introduced, but because also some working routines would have to be changed. In order to structure the variety of arguments

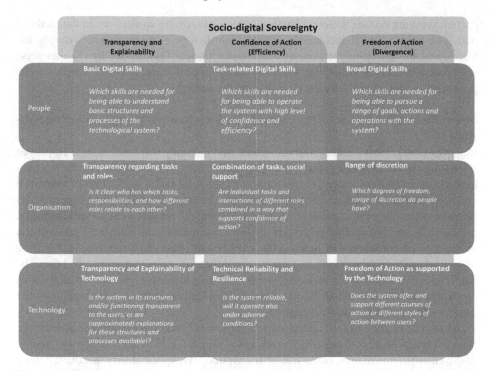

Fig. 1. Dimensions and facets of digital sovereignty at the workplace (Hartmann, 2022; Hartmann & Shajek, 2023)

from opponents and supporters as well as to consider all aspects of the sociotechnical system and working routines, the developed classification matrix was used for a stepwise consideration of both sides.

After introducing the matrix to the three participants of the company, in the first part, the current working routine without new planning software was considered. Employees were asked to write down positive and negative ideas on cards, which were then sorted into the matrix. In the subsequent evaluation, these answers represent the strengths (positive) and weaknesses (negative) of the current working routine without using the new planning software. In the second part, another assessment took place with the help of the matrix and its questionnaire. This time, employees were asked to predict positive and negative aspects connected with the usage of the planning software and the new working routine as well as to express their experiences during a test run. Again, ideas were written on cards and sorted into the matrix. In the subsequent evaluation, experienced or predicted positive aspects represent opportunities and negative ones are seen as threats.

3.2   Results – SWOT Analysis

For further evaluation, a SWOT analysis was conducted. It contains a summary of the results of the first part (without planning software) and second part (with planning software). The fields S and W represent the strengths (S) and weaknesses (W) of the current working routine without planning software that were worked out in the analysis part. The fields O and T include the aspects identified from the experiences during the test run of the planning software and the opportunities (O) and threats (T) that arise with future use. In the following, since the mapping of the matrix is too complex to be presented in this article, only the main results are described.

Strengths and Weaknesses of the Current Working Routine Without Planning Software

Regarding the current working routine without new planning software, a single employee is in charge of the complete process from start to finish. Looking at the strengths, in a positive sense, employees appreciate the variety of different tasks, the feeling of relevance and responsibility as well as the general overview because of having all information get together. Regarding the classification matrix in terms of **transparency/explainability,** the current working routine is perceived to be transparent and holistic. Furthermore, in the area of **confidence of action/efficiency**, established processes enable a feeling of competence and process control among employees in a positive sense. Additionally, employees also appreciate a varied spectrum of tasks and that each worker or each group can apply individual methods and processes. This leads to positive assessments in the category **freedom of action/divergence**.

However, because of staff shortage and a huge set of tasks each employee is in charge for, the current process shows many weaknesses. These can also structured with the help of the classification matrix. In the area of **transparency/explainability** this overcharged process often leads to a lack of project overview and untraceable information, especially in case of sickness leave cover and training new staff. The current working conditions with high workload lead to enormous stress among the employees and also create a feeling of loss of control. The individual procedures of each worker also lead to inefficiencies. The fact that, due to the specialized knowledge required, different employees can only replace and support each other very poorly and that the training phase is very long results in a poor adherence to delivery dates which is an enormous problem for the company. To sum up, in a negative sense, both employees and company face weaknesses according to **confidence of action/efficiency.** Additionally, the lack of structured documentation of implicit knowledge proves to be problematic, e.g. for the onboarding of new employees, resource planning for a more constant workload and avoidance of load peaks, the improvement of on-time delivery and the continuous training of employees. These aspects lead to less flexibility and limit the **freedom of action/divergence** of employees and company as a whole.

Opportunities (O) and Threats (T) of the Test Run and Future Working Routines with the New Planning Software

Regarding the test run and future working routines with new planning software positive (opportunities) as well as negative (threats) aspects were expressed by the participants and structured by using the classification matrix.

Looking at the predicted opportunities, the new planning software should lead to more transparency on available equipment and competences of the employees. Overall, knowledge and systems are to be merged and expert knowledge (e.g. help texts, interpretations, best practice examples), but also practical procedures, should be made transparent and explainable to everyone. In the end, this should lead to more **transparency/explainability** for the company and employees. In the area of **confidence of action/efficiency**, the planning software should lead to a relief of workload by providing an individual project overview of the weekly schedule. In addition, a specialization of roles should reduce the range of tasks and with that the disadvantages of multitasking. Ultimately, this can also lead to an optimization of on-time delivery and efficiency. Regarding the area of **freedom of action/divergence**, the planning software and the new working routines should lead to more flexibility in the company's resource planning, but can also be used for the personal development of each employee by identifying and offering systematic training needs. In addition, employees are given the opportunity to actively help shape new processes and systems.

Beside the predicted opportunities, participants also expressed their concerns about the new planning software and procedure. Regarding the area of **transparency /explainability**, a certain mistrust in the reliability of the technical system was stated. Due to the reduced range of tasks, employees fear a loss of transparency over the complete process. Having all the implicit knowledge in the system, in the area of **confidence of action/efficiency**, employees feared being replaced by less qualified staff. Furthermore, a loss of competence is also worried about. In addition, there are concerns about usability, e.g. that the input in weekly planning leads to additional work and inefficiency. Looking at the area of **freedom of action/divergence**, there are concerns about a reduced scope of action because of rigid software specifications. Due to a reduced set of tasks, there exists also the fear that working routines will become more monotonous and less varied.

3.3 Summary Assessment

In summary, it can be stated that on the one hand there are various positive aspects associated with the current working routine without a planning software. On the other hand, there are various risks and fears associated with the introduction of the planning module. For a successful introduction, these two views need to be addressed directly. The goal should be to incorporate the positive aspects into the new system and to invalidate or dissolve any concerns. The many weaknesses of the current working routine without the planning software should be openly stated, and the opportunities opened up by the introduction of the planning module, on the other hand, should also be proactively worked out and disseminated at the personal level of the staff.

Concretely, the workshop showed very clearly that employees are longing for a working environment, tasks and technology which are transparent and comprehensible to them (**transpareny/explainablility**). Furthermore, employees prefer working routines where they feel confident that their actions will lead to the desired outcomes efficiently (**confidence of action/efficiency**). They expressed fear of losing control because of not knowing what the machine is doing and why, but still being responsible for the result. Other expressed concerns deal with the category **freedom of action/divergence**. Here, it was stated by the participants that they appreciate a work which is seen as holistic and diverse. This includes accompanying a product from start to finish as well as being in charge of information and able to employ personal routines for different tasks.

4 Discussion and Conclusion

In conclusion, the workshop showed that the concept of sociodigital sovereignty and the classification matrix as well as the questionnaire based on it are useful tools to structure a debate about implementing new technologies and working routines. Nearly all the expressed concerns and fears as well as wishes and hopes of the participants of the workshop are reflected in the nine facets of the matrix. Generally, it turns out that focusing at first on the current working routine without new planning software and after that analyzing the predicted situation with new planning software was suitable. Consequently, positive and negative arguments for both working routines could be captured and structured holistically with the help of the matrix. This resulted in two comprehensive and comparable pictures. As already stated in the summary assessment, the whole process showed very clearly that both working routines have their strengths/opportunities and weaknesses/threats and it is now necessary to regard both sides to make the best out of it. Therefore, again, the concept of sociodigital sovereignty and the classification matrix provide on the one hand as an evaluation tool well-structured results from the participants. On the other hand, it can also serve as a guideline to design new technologies and working routines in a holistic and human-centered way. In the future, it is therefore planned to further develop and validate the framework as well as the questionnaire. Based on the experiences of this workshop – and more workshops as planned for the future – an assessment grid will be developed which might be used for formal assessment, evaluation, and auditing of applications of algorithmic systems in industry, with respect to sociodigital sovereignty of the individuals and the organization.

To end this article, it should be stated that even the highest automated system can still be seen as a sociotechnical system and it should be designed in a way that possibly all the negative effects Bainbridge (1983) postulated as ironies of automation should be prevented or mitigated. The human has to be in the loop and in charge of the situation and therefore the aspects of explainability and controllability are of enormous importance. The demand is even more urgent in AI-based systems. Finally, in order to positively answer the initial question – Highly automated and Master of the Situation?! – a human-centered design of technology and working routines covering the nine facets of sociodigital sovereignty can therefore make a relevant contribution.

References

Bainbridge, L.: Ironies of automation. Automatica 19(6), 775–779 (1983)

Gunning, D., Stefik, M., Choi, J., Miller, T., Stumpf, S., Yang, G. Z.: XAI—explainable artificial intelligence. Sci. Robot. 4(37), eaay7120 (2019)

Hacker, W.: Allgemeine Arbeitspsychologie. 2., vollständig überarbeitete und ergänzte Auflage. Huber, Bern (2005)

Hartmann, E.A.: Digitale Souveränität: Soziotechnische Bewertung und Gestaltung von Anwendungen algorithmischer Systeme. In: Hartmann, E.A. (ed.) Digitalisierung souverän gestalten II, pp. 1–13. Springer, Heidelberg (2022). https://doi.org/10.1007/978-3-662-64408-9_1

Hartmann, E.A., Shajek, A.: New digital work and digital sovereignty at the workplace – an introduction. In: Shajek, A., Hartmann, E.A. (eds.) New Digital Work – Digital Sovereignty at the Workplace, pp. 1–15. Springer, Heidelberg (2023). https://doi.org/10.1007/978-3-031-26490-0_1

Mumford, E.: The story of socio-technical design: reflections on its successes, failures and potential. Inf. Syst. J. **16**(4), 317–342 (2006)

Oesterreich, R.: Handlungsregulation und Kontrolle. Urban & Schwarzenberg, München (1981)

Pentenrieder, A., Bertini, A., Künzel, M: Digitale Souveränität als Trend? – Der Werkzeugmaschinenbau als wegweisendes Modell für die deutsche Wirtschaft. In: Hartmann, E.A. (ed.) Digitalisierung souverän gestalten: Innovative Impulse im Maschinenbau, pp. 17–30. Springer, Heidelberg (2021). https://doi.org/10.1007/978-3-662-62377-0_2

Pentenrieder, A., Hartmann, E.A., Künzel, M.: Nachweislich eine gute Entscheidung: Qualitätssicherung für künstlich-intelligente Verfahren in der Industrie. In: Hartmann, E.A. (ed.) Digitalisierung souverän gestalten II, pp. 51–63. Springer, Heidelberg (2022). https://doi.org/10.1007/978-3-662-64408-9_5

Pentenrieder, A., et al.: Designing explainable and controllable artificial intelligence systems together: inclusive participation formats for software-based working routines in the industry. In: Shajek, A., Hartmann, E.A. (eds.) New Digital Work – Digital Sovereignty at the Workplace, pp. 135–148. Springer, Heidelberg (2023). https://doi.org/10.1007/978-3-031-26490-0_8

Ethical Concerns of COVID-19 Contact Tracing: A Narrative Review

Zhiyin Shi[1(✉)], Zhixuan Zhou[2(✉)], Abhinav Choudhry[2], Mengyi Wei[3], Xiang Chen[1], and Bohui Shen[5]

[1] Macau University of Science and Technology, Macau, China
1809853gpa11003@student.must.edu.mo
[2] University of Illinois at Urbana-Champaign, Champaign, USA
{zz78,ac62}@illinois.edu
[3] Technical University of Munich, Munich, Germany
mengyi.wei@tum.de
[4] King Abdullah University of Science and Technology, Thuwal, Saudi Arabia
xiang.chen@kaust.edu.sa
[5] Champaign, USA
r130233082@mail.uic.edu.cn

Abstract. Contact tracing has been widely adopted during COVID-19 to curb the spread of infection. Despite its effectiveness, ethical issues abound and many people are not willing to use it. Toward understanding the ethical issues arising from contact tracing and informing future epidemic intervention, we conducted a narrative review of 26 papers addressing ethical concerns of COVID contact tracing (N = 26). The issues identified by researchers included data leakage, surveillance, lack of accessibility, etc., and proposed solutions included data minimization, transparency, voluntary and temporary use, adhering to data protection standards, designing affordable wearable devices, etc. Based on the findings, we propose research and design implications to make future epidemic contact tracing effective and ethical at the same time.

Keywords: COVID contact tracing · Privacy · Accessibility

1 Introduction

The COVID-19 pandemic has greatly bothered people's lives since its outbreak. Different strategies were adopted to suppress the virus transmission. Medical measures, such as cascaded therapy systems, anti-COVID drugs, and vaccines, have been developed. Public health strategies, such as mask wearing, social distancing, frequent sanitization, and digital contact tracing techniques, were also implemented to curb the epidemic. Among them, contact tracing is the most technology-centric approach, relying heavily on digital technologies such

---

Z.Shi and Z.Zhou—The first two authors contributed equally to this paper.
B.Shen—Independent Researcher

© The Author(s), under exclusive license to Springer Nature Switzerland AG 2023
C. Stephanidis et al. (Eds.): HCII 2023, CCIS 1832, pp. 502–511, 2023.
https://doi.org/10.1007/978-3-031-35989-7_64

as smartphones and people's mobility data. Simply put, contact tracing curbs the spread of infection by identifying people who might have been infected or exposed to contagious individuals. Digital contact tracing has been extensively utilized during the COVID-19 pandemic, sometimes used in combination with manual contact tracing [7].

With the end of the pandemic in sight, the efficacy and public engagement of contact tracing have been retrospectively evaluated by researchers. Several countries and regions, where collectivism is valued, including China, Singapore, and Hong Kong, achieved remarkable epidemiological success through contact tracing techniques. One major reason behind their success was the mandatory use of contact tracing apps, resulting in a higher level of technology uptake and adherence, which was key to the efficacy of contact tracing [14]. In other countries which did not force people to use contact tracing apps, the uptake rate could hardly reach 60% [24], which was a threshold to make contact tracing effective [17]. The prevalent ethical issues of contact tracing, such as privacy concerns, have limited people's willingness to use it [2,14], though people were sometimes ready to sacrifice their individual privacy for the wider goal of public health [19,21,29,38].

Toward understanding main ethical concerns surrounding COVID contact tracing and identifying potential solutions, we conducted a narrative review of 26 relevant papers. We aimed to answer the following two research questions (RQs):

- **RQ1:** What are the major ethical issues raised by COVID contact tracing?
- **RQ2:** What are potential solutions to these ethical issues?

Our analysis concluded two main ethical issues that could radically lower the level of contact tracing uptake: privacy concerns and a lack of accessibility. Privacy concerns may strongly affect people's willingness to use contact tracing apps and manifest itself in two ways, namely, data leakage and government surveillance. The lack of accessibility of digital contact tracing, which required the use of smartphones, effectively marginalized financially vulnerable populations, as well as certain demographics, such as older adults and children. Limited participation from these populations not only hindered the success of contact tracing, but also put them at higher health risks. Technological and administrative solutions have been proposed to increase the uptake and thus efficacy of contact tracing. We further synthesized research and design implications for future epidemic intervention based on the evidence.

Our contribution is two-fold. First, we summarized ethical issues arising from COVID contact tracing, including the sporadically expressed ones, to present a high-level understanding of its ethical aspect. Second, we outlook effective and ethical data solutions for future epidemic intervention based on the lessons learnt from the COVID-19 case.

2   Background: AI and ICT for COVID-19

During the COVID-19 pandemic, Artificial Intelligence (AI) and Information and Communications Technology (ICT) played crucial roles in various fields, including diagnosis, public health, clinical decision-making, therapeutics, resource prioritization, virus tracking, etc. [12,34]. Although the applications of AI and ICT have produced positive outcomes, ethical principles were often compromised during their deployment, such as autonomy, privacy, and fairness [36]. Veinot et al. warned that unethical utilization of AI could adversely affect already vulnerable populations [35]. Contact tracing has attracted wide attention in epidemic control but the numerous ethical concerns raised may arise again in a future pandemic [27]. Thus, it is of timely interest to comprehensively understand the outcomes of contact tracing and come up with a more ethical approach to contact tracing and epidemic intervention in general.

3   Method

We conducted a narrative review by analyzing 26 papers related to contact tracing during COVID-19 with ethical relevance. We searched Google Scholar for articles published between January 1, 2020 and February 28th, 2023. Search terms included ("SARS-CoV-2" OR "COVID-19") AND "contact tracing" AND "ethical issues". A final set of 26 papers was used for later qualitative synthesis.

We started by summarizing main research findings of the papers, especially regarding ethical issues and corresponding solutions. Two authors independently conducted the thematic coding [9] and used mind-mapping to organize the findings into a hierarchy of themes. Discussions were held regularly to reach a consensus and arrive at the current results.

4   COVID Contact Tracing and Privacy Concerns

Privacy concerns are expressed in two ways. On the one hand, people are fearful that their mobility data and personal information collected by contact tracing apps may be acquired by unauthorized individuals, leading to privacy breaches. On the other hand, people are not comfortable with the government collecting citizens' data and intruding their private realm. Distrust toward governments was commonly expressed.

4.1   Data Leakage

De-anonymized information is likely to put contact tracing app users at risk, especially vulnerable groups, leading to stigmatization [38]. For instance, gay people in Morocco were outed through proximal location tracking [5]. Even anonymous information sharing could lead to data leakage [4,18,22,31]. By contributing data anonymously, one also revealed information about other people [6]. Individuals' behavior and choices could be easily inferred based on "group" data [5,10]. In the case of contact tracing apps, one may receive a notification telling them to "stay inside" or "get tested" based on anonymized geo-location and biometric data of the people in their neighborhood — similar information inference attacks apply to this scenario. Ali Alkhatib showed how even the well-intentioned, privacy-preserving digital contact tracing apps risked trampling upon delicate balances in social and natural ecologies [5].

One interesting phenomenon is that the context of COVID-19 prevention appeared to increase people's willingness to share personal information [29]. A similar finding was that of Jahari et al. who found that reciprocal benefits and reputation enhancement mediated the relationship between privacy concerns and intention to use contact tracing applications; people were more willing to forsake privacy if they gained societal benefits or reputation [19]. In some contrast, a study found that participants concerned about the disease were more concerned about privacy and more unwilling to use contact tracing apps [11].

4.2 Surveillance

Surveillance often came in the form of manipulation or coercion. Governments may practice societal exclusion, i.e., limiting people's social participation, to force them to use contact tracing apps [3, 22]. For example, in China's excessive measures of zero-COVID policy, the government only granted people access to public venues if they could prove that they were not infected with or exposed to COVID-19 with a contact tracing app [40]. The Indian government's Aarogya Setu app was made mandatory for use in several public contexts [8] despite collecting highly intrusive location and biometric data [31].

In authoritarian regimes such as China, the implementation of contact tracing has expanded the central government's power over people's political and data rights [32]. The removal of local power in pandemic administration has led to the production of a unified national subject. Such concerns also existed in relatively democratic countries. For instance, Israel passed a legislation that allowed the government to track the mobile phone data of individuals suspected to be infected [33]. The South Korean government has also maintained a public database of known patients which contained information about their occupation, age, gender, and travel routes [20]. A major concern arising from the expansion of governments' power is that increased surveillance and harsher law enforcement tend to "stick" after they are justified by crisis events, evidenced by such cases as the persistence of Homeland Security activities against terrorism in the United States following the 9/11 tragedy [23]. This is a serious concern which was also highlighted in a systematic review on the topic: habituation to security policies may lead to discrimination and cause distrust, imperilling long-term health [3].

The adoption of contact tracing apps in China, Hong Kong, Singapore, Israel, South Korea, and India has caused the governments to experience varying levels of distrust from their citizens [8, 18, 23]. Public distrust in centralized data governance and data privacy risks have long existed, but were exacerbated by COVID-19. Further, people thought governments were unable to tame the *dataveillance* practices routinely carried out by corporate actors, showing the major limitations of the current data governance models [25]. The inclusion of large corporate technology companies in health, which is monopolistic in nature, has also been questioned, being termed the "googlization" of health crisis management [22]. Doubts have been cast over whether it is wise to risk access to such data by technology companies with their business models focusing on harnessing data for profit, because they might affect public policy for financial gains [3].

5 COVID Contact Tracing and Accessibility

Accessibility of contact tracing apps may further hinder its wide adoption and thus efficacy. Several papers pointed out that the efficacy of contact tracing apps heavily relied on the number of users [3, 16, 17]. For example, Hinch et al. suggested that the epidemic could only be stopped if up to 60% of the whole population used the contact tracing app and adhered to its public health recommendations [17].

Contact tracing apps often required the use of smartphones and mobile Internet access. However, smartphones were not financially accessible to a large portion of the global population, and even older smartphones were not always able to run digital contact tracing apps [5]. Children and older adults needed extra protection since they were physically vulnerable, but most of them were not able to use a smartphone device, which put them at higher risks [5, 39]. Advocation of adoption of contact tracing technology might aggravate inequalities in society due to existing unequal access to technology [18]. This reduces the accuracy of any models based on the contact tracing data, and policy makers should thus integrate factors of inclusion and accessibility into data solutions beforehand [5].

6 Solutions

Trust is essential to the general effectiveness of contact tracing [28]. To mitigate the aforementioned ethical issues of contact tracing and raise people's trust and willingness in using the technology, technological and administrative solutions have been proposed.

6.1 Data Minimization

Some researchers argued that where people got in contact with an infected individual was not important; what mattered was proximity to a contagious person. They suggested that it was neither necessary nor useful to collect sensitive location data, such as GPS or radio cell data [1, 18]. The principle of data minimisation is that "a data controller should limit the collection of personal information to what is directly relevant and necessary to accomplish a specified purpose." In the case of contact tracing which has raised major concerns about privacy breaches, it is of vital importance to implement the data minimization principle in its deployment.

6.2 Transparency

Informed consent and transparency about data sharing and usage can mitigate some privacy concerns [30]. Making contact tracing apps open-sourced may help keep them transparent, avoid the misuse of the technology for surveillance, and raise people's trust [15]. A trade-off between transparency and voluntariness was expressed by Afroogh et al.: they felt that compulsory use of tracking apps was more transparent [3]. False expectations should be prevented. The government should make an effort to clearly communicate the goals and functions as well as possible benefits, risks, and limitations of the contact tracing apps to the public in advance [28]. Only in this manner, can a trusting relationship between the government and the public likely be built.

6.3   Voluntary and Temporary Use

Lanzing argued that the use of contact tracing apps should be voluntary, and pre-conditional social participation should be prohibited [22]. This view is also echoed by others [3,18,31]. The coercive use of contact tracing in China, the restriction of people's mobility, and the sanction of online discussions on such issues [13] have been a major human rights disaster [40].

It is also a common belief that contact tracing apps should only be used during the pandemic and the data should be destroyed after the pandemic is over. Thus, a review and exit strategy must be in place to establish when and how fast this should happen by an independent body [26].

6.4   Adhering to Data Protection Standards

Adhering to data protection standards can help ensure accountability of contact tracing practices. Sowmiya et al. suggested building contact tracing apps upon the Advanced Encryption Standards (AES) encryption standard and random cloud storage for protecting the collected data [31]. Idrees et al. listed the rights conferred under the General Data Protection Regulation (GDPR), and argued that they needed to be enhanced in the context of healthcare data [18]. More auditing efforts are needed to assess the adherence of contact tracing apps to data privacy and security standards, and thus ensure accountability and people's data rights.

6.5   Decentralized Vs Centralized Contact Tracing

Idrees et al. proposed a blockchain-based digital contact tracing technique which could effectively provide contact tracing functionalities without compromising users' privacy or confidentiality [18]. According to them, a blockchain provided users with total control over their data throughout the data life cycle and allowed for withdrawal at any time. Moreover, the data stored were encrypted, time stamped, and immutable, making access by unauthorized individuals impossible, which promoted transparency and eliminated discrepancy. Surveys of contact tracing apps revealed a mix of centralized and decentralized architectures with proximity-based methods largely being decentralized while location-based ones being centralized [4,18,31].

Grekousis & Liu argued that while a decentralized architecture offered more privacy, it was not as efficient as its centralized counterpart [16]. Ahmed et al.

further stated that none of the centralized, decentralized, or hybrid architectures were impervious to attacks, and even privacy-preserving mechanisms could be subverted [4]. Since decentralized systems were not inherently safe, White & van Basshuysen proposed that if the likelihood of a system being effective was higher, a higher level of risk for privacy should be regarded as acceptable [37]. It has been posited that even centralized systems with enough privacy safeguards are justified as public health interventions in a pandemic [8].

6.6   Affordable Wearable Devices to Improve Accessibility

Making contact tracing more accessible to all demographics both helps improve its efficacy and benefits a wider population. However, smartphones which contact tracing apps rely on are not accessible to financially vulnerable groups, children, and older adults [3,5]. Grekousis et al. suggested that efforts should be devoted to creating stand-alone, smaller, and cheaper wearable devices with low energy consumption so that they could be distributed freely among economically or physically vulnerable people in future pandemics [16].

7   Discussion

7.1   Research Implications: Epidemic, Data Governance, and Surveillance

Despite the proven effectiveness of contact tracing apps in curbing the pandemic [23], spontaneous and wide adoption of contact tracing is not very likely. Relatively democratic governments like the US seldom forced their citizens to use contact tracing apps. As a result, fewer than 60% of the people in these countries used them, making them less effective [17]. On the contrary, some countries like China enforced the use of contact tracing apps more strictly, experiencing varying levels of distrust from their citizens [23].

People widely express their concerns over data privacy. In times of crisis, they experience additional concerns of governmental surveillance, which might stick after the crisis [23]. People showed a low level of trust toward the centralized data governance model, and did not believe the governments could effectively manage the collected data [25]. While researchers have suggested making contact tracing apps adhere to security and privacy standards [31], centralized data governance by governments is intrinsically harder to regulate since it is less subject to auditing compared to their corporate counterparts, especially in authoritarian regimes. Future research could explore the public attitudes toward contact tracing in countries with different levels of democracy and collectivism.

7.2   Design Implications: Toward Effective and Ethical Contact Tracing

To address people's privacy concerns of contact tracing apps, various solutions have been proposed in prior literature, such as minimizing data collection [1], transparently communicating benefits and risks of contact tracing [28], making the use of contact tracing apps voluntary [22] and temporary [26], and adhering to data protection standards [31]. Neither decentralized nor centralized architectures could fully address the privacy concerns [4], and researchers generally accepted the trade-off between privacy and efficacy [37]. Research efforts are urgently needed to develop more privacy-preserving contact tracing technologies without degrading their efficacy.

While accessibility issues of contact tracing apps may prevent them from achieving their efficacy and wider social benefits [5], researchers have suggested the creation and distribution of affordable wearable devices to replace smartphones [16]. Such designs and controlled experiments would be valuable.

8   Conclusion

In this paper, we conducted a narrative review to understand ethical issues of COVID contact tracing apps and potential solutions. Privacy concerns center around data leakage and surveillance, accompanied by people's long-standing distrust toward the government. Accessibility issues prevent contact tracing from fulfilling its potential in curbing the pandemic and benefiting the wider population. Unfortunately, no solutions so far could achieve a satisfactory level of privacy, leading to insufficient community uptake except when enforced strictly. Based on existing evidence and solutions, we proposed design and research suggestions for effective and ethical contact tracing.

References

1. Abeler, J., Bäcker, M., Buermeyer, U., Zillessen, H.: COVID-19 contact tracing and data protection can go together. JMIR mHealth uHealth. 8(4), e19359 (2020)
2. Abuhammad, S., Khabour, O. F., Alzoubi, K.H.: COVID-19 contact-tracing technology: acceptability and ethical issues of use. In: Patient Preference and Adherence, vol. 14, 1639–1647 (2020)
3. Afroogh, S., et al.: Tracing app technology: an ethical review in the COVID-19 era and directions for post-COVID-19. Ethics Inf. Technol. 24(3), 30 (2022)
4. Ahmed, N., Michelin, R. A., Xue, W., et al.: A survey of COVID-19 contact tracing apps. IEEE Access. 8, 134577–134601 (2020)
5. Alkhatib, A.: We need to talk about digital contact tracing. Interactions 27(4), 84–89 (2020)
6. Barocas, S., Levy, K.: Privacy dependencies. Wash. L. Rev. 95, 555 (2020)
7. Barrat, A., Cattuto, C., Kivelä, M., Lehmann, S., Saramäki, J.: Effect of manual and digital contact tracing on COVID-19 outbreaks: a study on empirical contact data. In: J. R. Soc. Interface, 182020100020201000 (2021)
8. Basu, S.: Effective contact tracing for COVID-19 using mobile phones: an ethical analysis of the mandatory use of the Aarogya Setu application in India. Cambridge Q. Healthcare Ethics. 262, 1–10 (2020)
9. Braun, V., Clarke, V.: Using thematic analysis in psychology. Qual. Res. Psychol. 3(2), 77–101 (2006)

10. Breebaart, L.: Filosofen over de corona-app: begrijpt de overheid privacy wel? https://www.trouw.nl/gs-be38a475. Accessed 1 June 2020
11. Chan, E.Y., Saqib, N.U.: Privacy concerns can explain unwillingness to download and use contact tracing apps when COVID-19 concerns are high. Comput. Human Behav. **119**, 106718 (2021)
12. Chen, J., See, K.C.: Artificial intelligence for COVID-19: rapid review. J. Med. Internet Res. **22**(10), e21476 (2020)
13. Chen, X., Xie, J., Wang, Z., Shen, B., Zhou, Z.: How we express ourselves freely: censorship, self-censorship, and anti-censorship on a Chinese social media. In: iConference, Part II, pp. 93–108 (2023)
14. Colizza, V., Grill, E., Mikolajczyk, R., et al.: Time to evaluate COVID-19 contact-tracing apps. Nat. Med. **27**(3), 361–362 (2021)
15. Dar, A.B., Lone, A.H., Zahoor, S., Khan, A.A., Naaz, R.: Applicability of mobile contact tracing in fighting pandemic (COVID-19): issues, challenges and solutions. Comput. Sci. Rev. **38**, 100307 (2020)
16. Grekousis, G., Liu, Y.: Digital contact tracing, community uptake, and proximity awareness technology to fight COVID-19: a systematic review. Sustain. Cities Soc. **71**, 102995 (2021)
17. Hinch, R., Probert, W., Nurtay, A., et al.: Effective configurations of a digital contact tracing app: a report to NHSX (2020)
18. Idrees, S.M., Nowostawski, M., Jameel, R.: Blockchain-based digital contact tracing apps for COVID-19 pandemic management: issues, challenges, solutions, and future directions. JMIR Med. Inform. **9**(2), e25245 (2021)
19. Jahari, S.A., Hass, A., Hass, D., Joseph, M.: Navigating privacy concerns through societal benefits: a case of digital contact tracing applications. J. Consum. Behav. **21**(3), 625–638 (2022)
20. Kim, M.J., Denyer, S.: A 'travel log' of the times in South Korea: Mapping the movements of coronavirus carriers. The Washington Post. **13** (2020)
21. Kostka, G., Habich-Sobiegalla, S.: In times of crisis: public perceptions toward COVID-19 contact tracing apps in China, Germany, and the United States. New Med. Soc. 14614448221083285 (2022)
22. Lanzing, M.: Contact tracing apps: an ethical roadmap. Ethics Inf. Technol. **23**(1), 87–90 (2021)
23. Li, V.Q., Ma, L., Wu, X.: COVID-19, policy change, and post-pandemic data governance: a case analysis of contact tracing applications in East Asia. Policy Soc. **41**(1), 129–142 (2022)
24. LibertiesEU: COVID-19 Contact Tracing Apps in the EU. https://www.liberties.eu/en/stories/trackerhub1-mainpage/43437. Accessed 2 June 2021
25. Lucivero, F., Marelli, L., Hangel, N., et al.: Normative positions towards COVID-19 contact-tracing apps: findings from a large-scale qualitative study in nine European countries. Crit. Public Health **32**(1), 5–18 (2022)
26. Morley, J., Cowls, J., Taddeo, M., Floridi, L.: Ethical guidelines for COVID-19 tracing apps. Nature **582**(7810), 29–31 (2020)
27. Parker, M.J., Fraser, C., Abeler-Dörner, L., Bonsall, D.: Ethics of instantaneous contact tracing using mobile phone apps in the control of the COVID-19 pandemic. J. Med. Ethics **46**(7), 427–431 (2020)
28. Ranisch, R., Nijsingh, N., Ballantyne, A., et al.: Digital contact tracing and exposure notification: ethical guidance for trustworthy pandemic management. Ethics Inf. Technol. **23**, 285–294 (2021)

29. Romero, R.A., Young, S.D.: Ethical perspectives in sharing digital data for public health surveillance before and shortly after the onset of the COVID-19 pandemic. Ethics Behav. **32**(1), 22–31 (2022)

30. Simko, L., Chang, J., Jiang, M., Calo, R., Roesner, F., Kohno, T.: COVID-19 contact tracing and privacy: a longitudinal study of public opinion. Digital Threats Res. Pract. (DTRAP) **3**(3), 1–36 (2022)

31. Sowmiya, B., Abhijith, V. S., Sudersan, S., Sakthi Jaya Sundar, R., Thangavel, M., Varalakshmi, P.: A survey on security and privacy issues in contact tracing application of COVID-19. SN Comput. Sci. **2**, 1–11 (2021)

32. Sun, Y., Wang, W.Y.: Governing with health code: Standardising China's data network systems during COVID-19. Policy Internet **14**(3), 673–689 (2022)

33. Tidy, J.: Coronavirus: Israel enables emergency spy powers. In: BBC News, vol. 17 (2020)

34. Van der Schaar, M., Alaa, A. M., Floto, A., et al.: How artificial intelligence and machine learning can help healthcare systems respond to COVID-19. In: Machine Learning, 110, 1–14 (2021)

35. Veinot, T.C., Mitchell, H., Ancker, J.S.: Good intentions are not enough: how informatics interventions can worsen inequality. J. Am. Med. Inform. Assoc. **25**(8), 1080–1088 (2018)

36. Wei, M., Zhou, Z.: AI ethics issues in real world: Evidence from AI incident database. In: 56th Hawaii International Conference on System Sciences (2022)

37. White, L., van Basshuysen, P.: Privacy versus public health? A reassessment of centralised and decentralised digital contact tracing. Sci. Eng. Ethics **27**(2), 23 (2021)

38. Williams, S.N., Armitage, C.J., Tampe, T., Dienes, K.: Public attitudes towards COVID-19 contact tracing apps: a UK-based focus group study. Health Expect. **24**(2), 377–385 (2021)

39. Zastrow, M.: Coronavirus contact-tracing apps: can they slow the spread of COVID-19? In: Nature (2020)

40. Zhan, Z., Li, J., Cheng, Z. J.: Zero-covid strategy: what's next? Int. J. Health Policy Manage. **12**(Continuous), 1–7 (2023)

Understanding the Acceptance of Artificial Intelligence in Primary Care

Teresa Sides(✉) , Tracie Farrell , and Dhouha Kbaier

The Open University, Milton Keynes, Buckinghamshire, UK
Teresa.Sides@open.ac.uk

Abstract. AI has made significant advancements in healthcare, yet its applications are limited to secondary care, with little evidence of its use in primary care. Trust has been identified as a significant factor affecting AI usage, but it does not entirely explain why AI is deployed in some NHS sectors and not others. Organizational infrastructure may also contribute to the lack of AI use in primary care.

Macro level stakeholders such as government bodies and health trusts have expressed interest in integrating AI, allocating resources, and providing training for employees to encourage trust and acceptance of AI. Conversely, at the micro-level stakeholders such as general practitioners and patients, have identified factors such as fairness, accountability, transparency, and ethics as having an impact on trust in AI.

Despite their potential influence, meso-level stakeholders such as managers and IT experts have been largely overlooked in AI research. Investigating their perspectives on trust and relationships across organizational levels is crucial for successful implementation of AI in primary care.

We propose a mixed-methods study design based on a conceptual framework that combines the Technology Acceptance Model-3, Unified Theory of Acceptance and Use of Technology-2, and trust attributes. By combining these models, we aim to gain a better understanding of how stakeholders perceive AI both individually and across organisational levels. Using the proposed model, we present our early findings on the enablers and barriers to AI acceptance in UK primary care. Finally, we discuss future directions on how to overcome the identified barriers.

Keywords: Artificial Intelligence · primary care · AI acceptance · trust

1 Introduction and Background

In recent years the integration of artificial intelligence (AI) has grown rapidly in many sectors of society. In the UK, the healthcare sector has introduced AI into some departments of secondary care, while primary care has been largely disregarded. This lack of acceptance of AI technology contradicts the National Health Service (NHS) long term plan that puts the digitalisation of primary care as a top priority [1]. Therefore, it is crucial to understand the factors that may influence the acceptance of AI technology, given the structural and organisational differences between secondary and primary care.

© The Author(s), under exclusive license to Springer Nature Switzerland AG 2023
C. Stephanidis et al. (Eds.): HCII 2023, CCIS 1832, pp. 512–518, 2023.
https://doi.org/10.1007/978-3-031-35989-7_65

While prior research has identified trust as a significant factor affecting the acceptance of AI in primary care, it remains unclear how other organisational factors or stakeholder perspectives may impact AI adoption. The structure of primary care as a sector of private businesses operating under one main contract with the NHS [3] may negatively impact the acceptance of AI. According to NHS Digital, there were 6,514 primary care practices in England in 2022 [2], all operating independently. The organisational levels within the NHS are described by Asthana, Jones and Sheaff [4] as macro, meso and micro levels. The macro level includes the government, and the entire NHS network, who seek to leverage technology to improve efficiency [5]. Primary care management, technology providers, and secondary care health boards constitute the meso level, which has largely focused on the perspectives of technology providers. The micro level is comprised of individual stakeholders, so the perspectives may be more variable, having differing requirements and views on AI. Thus, the complexity of the NHS and its multiple organisational levels, as noted by Asthana, Jones and Sheaff, represents a significant barrier to the integration of technology. In particular, a study by Ferreira, Ruivo and Reis concluded that perspectives from meso level stakeholders are particularly important to understand, but their views are often not present [6]. For example, although meso level practice managers have been identified as gatekeepers to GP practices, their perspectives have not been fully explored in the literature. Next, we explore the organisational levels in more detail to identify what we already understand about the perspectives of AI at each level.

Macro. Morrison [7] conducted interviews with macro level stakeholders to identify facilitators and barriers to the adoption of AI. Findings from the study indicate that barriers to AI adoption include regulatory constraints, cost implications, inadequate training, and suboptimal IT infrastructure. These findings are in line with the UK's national AI strategy, which seeks to address the identified barriers and promote AI development across all sectors of society [5]. Macro level stakeholders are not just talking about how AI can deliver, they are actively advocating for changes to facilitate the smooth delivery of new and emerging technologies. This stands in contrast to meso level stakeholders who have not had the opportunity to express their perspectives on this subject, as discussed in the subsequent section.

Meso. Organisational levels within primary care are complex as GP practices are run as individual private businesses with NHS contracts [2]. In a global study, 84% of meso level managers believed AI would increase efficiency, while 36% expressed concerns about job security [8]. Further, Leyer and Schneider [9] reported that 50% of managers identified opportunities for AI implementation in their businesses. These findings suggest that meso level managers in the business world have expressed concerns regarding AI adoption, which are similar to those recognised by macro level stakeholders. In contrast, the perspectives of meso level stakeholders within primary care have yet to be investigated. However, if their perspectives are consistent with those of business managers, macro level stakeholders are already addressing some of the identified concerns.

Micro. Lebcir et al. [10] have documented a body of literature that examines the perspectives of micro level stakeholders regarding AI. The authors concluded that in order for healthcare to fully leverage the potential of AI, a holistic approach should be considered. Such an approach would take into account not only technological infrastructure but also organisational management factors. Among the existing studies, Blease et al. [11] conducted a qualitative investigation into the views of doctors on the potential of AI in primary care. This study was particularly interesting because while previous studies have indicated that doctors do believe that AI could augment medical diagnoses [12], doctors in this study were skeptical. Instead, the study found that doctors viewed AI as most beneficial for administrative tasks. As previously discussed in this study, trust-building in AI has been a focal point for researchers to facilitate the integration of AI into all sectors of society. Characteristics such as fairness, accountability, transparency, and ethics have been identified as pivotal in establishing trust. Previous research has shown that barriers to the adoption of new technologies differ among stakeholders, and opinions differ on the most effective strategies for fostering trust among them.

Research Aims. This research aims to advance the understanding of the different levels of stakeholders and their requirements in the context of promoting acceptance and trust of AI within primary care. The existing literature indicates that there is a lack of trust and acceptance towards AI in primary care. Possibilities to improve acceptance or help researchers to understand the priorities of primary care, may lie in gathering more stakeholder perspectives. Our study intends to explore whether there are differing requirements across the various organisational levels that could influence acceptance and trust of AI. The research objectives being addressed within this initial study to advance the understanding of stakeholder levels and requirements are:

1. What are the current levels of acceptance for AI within primary care?
2. What level of influence does each stakeholder level have over the introduction of AI within primary care?
3. What are the barriers to trust and acceptance of AI within primary care at each stakeholder level?

To answer these research objectives, each question will be broken down into specific hypotheses questions developed using a conceptual framework.

2 Conceptual Framework

Several frameworks have been developed to understand the characteristics that influence the acceptance of novel technologies. For this study, the most relevant frameworks are TAM3 [13], developed to assist managers in understanding the factors influencing technology acceptance with characteristics such as 'perceptions of external control' and 'computer anxiety'. Additionally, UTAUT2 [14], which provides insight into technology acceptance from an individualistic perspective and introduces characteristics such as 'social influence' and 'facilitating conditions'. The characteristics of trust are also key factors identified within the literature as a barrier to AI acceptance, which are fairness, accountability, transparency, and ethical considerations [15]. To address the research questions in this study, our conceptual model combined TAM3, UTAUT2 and trust models. This enabled a thorough investigation of stakeholders' perspectives on AI and the determinants that influence the use of AI and its adoption. The combined frameworks (Fig. 1) guided the development of hypotheses, which determined the online survey questions. Seven key question areas have been identified through the hypothesis questions. These include who the stakeholders are, what levels of acceptance or influence they have, the barriers, benefits, and stakeholders' views towards explanations and AI. The mixed methods between-subjects study will help us to understand how different factors influence AI acceptance for different stakeholders across organisational levels. By understanding the influence of stakeholders, it will be easier to identify potential barriers that need to be addressed to increase the acceptance of AI within primary care.

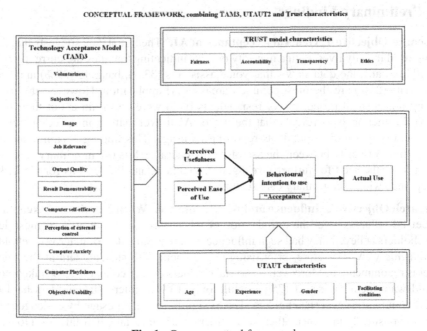

CONCEPTUAL FRAMEWORK, combining TAM3, UTAUT2 and Trust characteristics

Fig. 1. Our conceptual framework

3 Methods

A series of hypotheses were defined to enable the required data to be collected. The online survey questions were designed with hypotheses in mind, using constructs and questions from previously validated surveys. An online survey targeting stakeholders from primary care was conducted with HREC approval to gather research data. The survey was piloted and tested prior to its release with 6 primary care employees and colleagues. The survey was hosted on JISC, and a link was posted on Prolific to recruit participants. The survey attracted 60 responses from primary care employees across the UK, with additional responses obtained through snowball sampling. There are currently 64 responses in total, with 10 at the macro level, 4 at the meso level and 50 at the micro level. The survey is still open and remains active until 31st March 2023. Therefore, this initial statistical analysis is based on the data currently available. The data was then examined and cleaned with one response being excluded due to plagiaristic responses within the open-ended questions. Descriptive analysis revealed that 75% of the population was female, and 22% were male respondents which is representative of the workforce of the NHS [16], (31%) fell within the age range of 26–35 years. Both quantitative and qualitative data were analysed using statistical and thematic analysis techniques [17]. Key words or phrases were identified from the open-ended questions. The preliminary findings of the analysis are discussed in the next section.

4   Preliminary Findings

Research Objective 1: General Acceptance of AI. The initial data suggests that AI is being used in daily lives, with a majority of 59% indicating that they are currently using it. Additionally, the data shows that voice assistants (33%), banking (22%) and travel directions (25%) are the most common areas of AI application. However, it is worth noting that a small proportion of respondents (9%) were uncertain about their usage of AI. Further analysis reveals that the use of AI in work situations is comparatively low, with only 3% of respondents reporting its usage. This finding is significant as it highlights a disparity between the use of AI in general and its use in primary care. This emphasises the need for further investigation to understand the reasons for the lack of acceptance within the primary care sector.

Research Objective 2: Influence and AI Acceptance. When examining stakeholders' perceived influence over the introduction of AI, it was found that 50% of meso level stakeholders believed they had such influence, whereas only 10% of macro stakeholders shared this view. Therefore, prioritising engagement with stakeholders at the micro-level is recommended. Moreover, meso stakeholders perceived that macro stakeholders would want them to use AI (75%), while only 40% of micro stakeholders held this belief about meso-level stakeholders. This is significant, as AI usage by colleagues was found to positively influence other stakeholders' trust in AI and their intention to use it. However, initial findings suggest that the influence of colleagues was dependent on the transparency and appropriateness of the data being examined. These findings suggest that stakeholder perceptions of influence, as well as trust and intention to use AI, are influenced by stakeholder level, and that engaging with meso-level stakeholders is crucial for the successful implementation of AI. Further research is needed to validate these results and to explore in more depth the factors that influence stakeholder perceptions of influence and trust in AI.

Research Objective 3: Barriers to Acceptance. The perceived barriers to AI being introduced in primary care were deskilling of the workforce, the need for training and concerns about data accuracy or the decisions made by AI. Participant P35 expressed that "it may deskill the workforce and put jobs at risk", while participant P58 discussed "resistance from management or current interested parties who would lose work/contracts". Specifically, 75% of meso level stakeholders identified deskilling as a barrier to acceptance, while only 50% of micro and macro-level stakeholders shared similar concerns. Additionally, stakeholders at all levels identified training as a significant barrier. Participant P55 expressed fear "that it further diminishes role of clinical training or human interactions". Most stakeholders also believed that AI would need to demonstrate cost savings, while also worrying about the high risk of misuse. Participant P26 declared that "it would need to be proven to be efficient and cost effective before being rolled out". These findings highlight the need for careful consideration of the potential implications of AI implementation. This includes the impact on the workforce, the necessity for training, and the need for clear cost savings and efficacy data. Further research is needed to explore these barriers in more depth and to identify potential strategies for overcoming them. The initial analysis shows that several factors affected the level of trust for AI among stakeholders, including deskilling of the workforce, data security, accountability, fairness, and understanding. Macro and micro stakeholders ranked the most significant characteristic for trust in AI as ethics. In contrast, meso stakeholders emphasised the importance of accountability to enable trust in AI. When looking at all stakeholder views, ethical and moral standards were highlighted as the most important characteristics, followed by compliance with primary care policies and regulations. For example, participant P36 described how "a lot of our work depends on humans to make decisions that may not be replicated fairly by an AI." Some respondents declared that they would not trust AI at all. Participant P41 declared "I am pro human service only", and participant P42 stated "I don't believe in using it full stop". However, others expected AI to make decisions that aligned with their own choices, as in participant P47 who expressed a need for "proof that it was making the decisions I would make". These findings suggest the need for AI to be developed and implemented with strong ethical considerations, accountability, and transparency to foster trust among stakeholders in primary care. Future research could explore ways to address stakeholders' concerns about the ethical implications of AI use and the potential impact on human decision-making in primary care settings.

5 Conclusion and Next Steps

This research has taken the first step to identify the views of all stakeholders within primary care. The findings suggest that AI is being used in daily life, with voice assistants, banking and travel directions being the most common areas of use. However, the use of AI in work situations needs further investigation to understand the reasons for the lack of acceptance in the primary care sector. The initial findings also revealed that stakeholder perceptions of influence, trust and intention to implement AI are influenced by stakeholders' levels. Meso level stakeholders were found to have the highest perceived influence, therefore, prioritising engagement with them is recommended. Moreover, stakeholder trust and intention to use AI were positively influenced by colleagues using AI. While transparency and the appropriateness of the data being examined were also highlighted as influential characteristics. The perceived barriers to the introduction of AI in primary care were identified as deskilling of the workforce, the need for training, concerns about data accuracy, and the decisions made by AI. The findings highlight the importance of careful consideration of potential implications. This includes the impact on the workforce, the necessity for training and the need for clear cost savings and efficacy within the data. Finally, the initial findings found that stakeholders' trust in AI was influenced by several factors including ethics, accountability, fairness and understanding.

This suggests the need for AI to be developed and implemented with strong ethical considerations, accountability, and transparency to foster trust among stakeholders in primary care. These initial findings are based on preliminary data from our ongoing survey. To continue with this research, the next step will be to further analyse in detail the full data set, across organisational levels. The findings from the survey will then guide the next stage of this research.

References

1. NHS. https://www.longtermplan.nhs.uk. Accessed 22 May 2022
2. Davidson, S.: https://lowdownnhs.info/explainers/how-do-gps-fit-into-the-nhs/, https://lowdownnhs.info/explainers/how-do-gps-fit-into-the-nhs/. Accessed 14 Jan 2023
3. NHS Digital. https://www.statista.com/statistics/891854/number-of-general-practices-in-the-united-kingdom/. Accessed 14 Jan 2023
4. Asthana, S., Jones, R., Sheaff, R.: Why does the NHS struggle to adopt eHealth innovations? A review of macro, meso and micro factors. BMC Health Serv. Res. 19(1), 984 (2019). https://doi.org/10.1186/s12913-019-4790-x
5. UK Government. https://www.gov.uk/government/publications/national-ai-strategy-ai-action-plan/national-ai-strategy-ai-action-plan. Accessed 16 Dec 2022
6. Ferreira, H., Ruivo, P., Reis, C.: How do data scientists and managers influence machine learning value creation? Procedia Comput. Sci. 181, 757–764 (2021)
7. Morrison, K.: Artificial intelligence and the NHS: a qualitative exploration of the factors influencing adoption. Future Healthc. J. 8(3), e648–e654 (2021). https://doi.org/10.7861/fhj.2020-0258
8. Kolbjørnsrud, V., Amico, R., Thomas, R.J.: Partnering with AI: how organizations can win over skeptical managers. Strategy Leadersh. 45(1), 37–43 (2017)
9. Leyer, M., Schneider, S.: Decision augmentation and automation with artificial intelligence: threat or opportunity for managers? Bus. Horiz 64(5), 711–724 (2021)
10. Lebcir, R., et al.: Stakeholders' views on the organisational factors affecting application of artificial intelligence in healthcare: a scoping review protocol. BMJ Open 11(3), e044074 (2021). https://doi.org/10.1136/bmjopen-2020-044074
11. Blease, C., et al.: Artificial intelligence and the future of primary care: exploratory qualitative study of UK general practitioners' view. Med. Internet Res. 21(3), e12802 (2019). https://doi.org/10.2196/12802
12. Summerton, N., Cansdale, M.: Artificial intelligence and diagnosis in general practice. Br. J. Gen. Pract. 69(684), 324–325 (2019). https://doi.org/10.3399/bjgp19X704165
13. Venkatesh, V., Bala, H.: Technology acceptance model 3 and a research agenda on interventions. Decis. Sci. 39(2), 273–315 (2008)
14. Venkatesh, V., Thong, Y.J.L., Xu, X.: Consumer acceptance and use of information technology: extending the unified theory of acceptance and use of technology. Mis. Q. 36(1), 157 (2012). https://doi.org/10.2307/41410412
15. UK Government. https://www.gov.uk/government/publications/data-ethics-framework. Accessed 26 Feb 2023
16. NHS Employers. https://www.nhsemployers.org/articles/gender-nhs-infographic. Accessed 17 Mar 2023
17. Braun, V., Clarke, V.: What can "thematic analysis" offer health and wellbeing researchers? Int. J. Qual. Stud. Health Well-Being 9, 10.3402 (2014)

Heightened Cyber Vulnerability to Patients with Cardiac Implantable Electronic Devices

Leanne N. S. Torgersen[1]([✉]) [iD], Rupert E. D. Whitaker[1] [iD], Ricardo G. Lugo[2] [iD],
Stefan Sütterlin[2,3] [iD], and Stefan M. Schulz[4] [iD]

[1] Tuke Institute, London, UK
l.torgersen@tukeinstitute.org
[2] Centre for Digital Forensics and Cybersecurity, Tallinn University of Technology, Tallinn,
Estonia
[3] Faculty of Computer Science, Albstadt-Sigmaringen University, Sigmaringen, Germany
[4] Department of Behavioural Medicine and Principles of Human Biology for the Health
Sciences, Trier University, Trier, Germany

Abstract. Cardiac implantable electronic devices (CIEDs) have shown to
improve autonomy, quality of life, morbidity and mortality (relative reduction
of mortality by 30% at 3 years follow-up) [1]. However, CIEDs possess a cyber
vulnerability. With these exemplary safety concerns, we theorise: 1) Cybersecurity risks are difficult for medical institutions to plan (ambiguous nature of threat),
which results in ineffective cyber defense measures, 2) Cyber threats can impair
trust in the device, treatment plan and patient-provider relationship; and 3) As
CIEDs "go" with the patient and the cyber risk can not be quantified, patients'
stress levels are higher from the perceived cyber threats than from a technical
malfunction.

From a literature review and subsequent position paper submission, the rationale for the research project was formulated. The methodology consists of two
qualitative studies assessing both providers' and patients' perspectives of cybersecurity risks with CIEDs and a risk assessment of CIED manufacturer manuals.
For designing the two qualitative studies, we postulated: 1) providers lack understanding about cybersecurity risks with CIEDs and thus do not include these risks
in the informed consent due to either "not wanting to raise patients' anxiety levels
except for known serious adverse events", or not wanting to "extend time with
consenting patients for low-probability issues" [13] and 2) patients are not aware
of the cyber risks with CIEDs. From the results of these studies, we plan to develop
white papers to promote standards and guidelines for cybersecurity related risks
with CIEDs to the inform consent-processes as well as manufacturers' manuals.

Keywords: Cybersecurity Vulnerability · Cardiac Implantable Electronic
Devices · Perceived Cyber Risks and Threats

1 Introduction

With the advancements in digitalisation for cardiac implantable electronic devices
(CIEDs), patients are provided greater opportunities for improved autonomy, quality
of life and a potential increase in life expectancy. In addition, a CIED can help reduce

© The Author(s), under exclusive license to Springer Nature Switzerland AG 2023
C. Stephanidis et al. (Eds.): HCII 2023, CCIS 1832, pp. 519–528, 2023.
https://doi.org/10.1007/978-3-031-35989-7_66

unnecessary provider visits [14], which in turn results in more cost-effective services. Specifically, CIEDs allow for: 1) monitoring in real-time by acquiring physiological data automatically on a frequent basis (e.g., daily), 2) alerting a provider of the resultant information including warnings related to device integrity; and 3) allowing for remote surveillance of the patient's physical condition without any tangible interventions from providers [2, 3]. For patients with significant cardiac disease and/or arrhythmias, implantable electronic devices such as permanent pacemakers, defibrillators and cardiac resynchronization therapy devices can assist with maintaining baseline cardiac function for the patient and incidences of life-threatening events [4]. Despite the digital and functional practicalities of CIEDs, cyber safety issues when transferring wireless information exists. While proprietary communication and data safety protocols support the secure transfer of data between patients and providers, this does not safeguard the device in its entirety. As CIEDs do not connect directly to the internet, they tend to connect via a secondary device, be that a bedside or home monitor that can be stationary or mobile, which in turn transmits patient data to the manufacturer service centers and thereafter to the provider [1, 5, 6]. Despite most data transfers being encrypted, messages can still be intercepted or blocked. In the case of data transmissions between medical devices and providers, manufacturers are aware of the risk of communication tampering within medical institutions and thus expect medical institutions and their clinical network administrations to have cyber defense practices in place in order to "identify, analyze, evaluate and control these risks" [7]. If adequate measures are not in place, then the primary burden of legal accountability shifts to medical institutions. It is known that hospitals lag behind other institutions of comparable size in terms of their cybersecurity standards, and despite this understanding that cyber attacks can threaten an institution's entire IT-infrastructure primarily due to its interconnectedness, some hospitals continue to direct suboptimal resources towards their IT-infrastructure [8]. Furthermore, the attribution problem associated with cyber attacks, makes it also difficult to establish standard guidelines for protecting an institutional database when leadership is unsure to whom and what they are protecting against or from what direction [8]. For this reason, negligence towards cybersecurity measures could be found at the institutional level, where financial resources that could have been directed to a known and increasing risk were instead utilised in other areas. Unfortunately, suboptimal cyber defense measures at medical institutions is not the only cyber vulnerability patients with CIEDs can experience. Other vulnerabilities to CIEDs include close proximity to radio frequencies similar to the pulse generator frequency or electromagnetic interferences, which can provide opportunities for device compromise [7]. With the many variations of cyber vulnerabilities, CIED patients could possibly experience either or both the loss sensitive data and the loss of device control. For those patients with CIEDs, should a physician choose to withhold information after determining or downplaying the risk level of injury from a cybersecurity compromise, and a cyber attack subsequently occurs and results in: 1) a serious adverse event and injury, be that physical or mental, and/or 2) a lethal outcome, this could be considered negligence, and could result in both legal and reputational consequences to the provider. Thus, the emergence of cybersecurity risks, such as "being hacked" by anonymous individuals with malicious intent, can shape and alter how we view and practice patient-centred care, how services are experienced by the patient, what risks are communicated in the informed consent and how to support the patient's ability to make an informed decision.

Research on human factors in cybersecurity acknowledges that technology does not exist in isolation, but rather the interpretations, conclusions and decisions made by individuals or groups of humans provide an "inbuilt guarantee" that a whole range of human failures, if given the opportunity, will occur [8]. Human factors, resulting in cyber attacks targeting the healthcare sector, have been associated with a specific type of lack of security awareness, training, and security-related attitudes [9]. A likely consequence of human factors, that result in a cybersecurity breach, is a mistrust in the system's integrity and provision of those care services. If mistrust were to develop in the system, this could impact: 1) the political incentives to support digitalisation's advancement, 2) the financial and organizational costs of enhancing cyber resilient IT-systems within the institution; and 3) the patients' confidence in these healthcare IT-systems to protect their information. Patients are expected to place complete trust in their healthcare services and the data transferred to their CIEDs or device data sent and shared to the providers, are available in real time. As patient data must remain confidential in accordance with legal mandates, these requirements of maintaining a confidential data system are dependent upon having a stable information and communication technology platform. In the healthcare field, human factors and errors unfortunately play a strong role in the occurrence of cyber attacks and such breaches place patients at an increased risk. Should a digital system become compromised, such a breach could negatively affect the trust in the healthcare institution, the patient-provider relationship and could eventually result in the patient's decision not to pursue or obtain needed treatments due to the fear of a cyber attack overweighing the benefit of the treatment. Also, by not informing a patient during the informed consent process that these cyber vulnerabilities exist, this could result in legal implications to the provider and medical institution as well. Furthermore, if such an attack were to become public, impaired trust in the healthcare system and legal consequences could further result. Therefore, a cyber attack not only directly threatens both the patient's health and the confidentiality, integrity and availability of the CIED but also the integrity of the medical institution and patient provider relationship.

2 Rationale for Current Project

When considering the impact of IT-security vulnerabilities with CIEDs and the implications to medical practice and patient safety, we postulated the following premises for which we created the rationale for the research project: 1) **Low level of institutional readiness:** Low-probability-high-impact scenarios are difficult to imagine or plan for [10] and constitute an ambiguous threat. Ambiguous threats are associated with delayed planning as well as ineffective and inconsistent implementation of protective measures and in most cases, these threats are often downplayed or ignored., 2) **Trust:** These cyber threats can impair trust in the device, the treatment plan and in the patient – provider/-medical institution relationship(s); and 3) **Subjective Threat Potential:** Compared to cyber threats in the healthcare sector, where medical devices are temporarily out of order as a result of a cyber attack, the perceived threat to integrity of the system (as depicted under point 2) is increased in smart CIEDs due to: a) being unlike other medical devices, the CIED is not stationary but travels with the patient, rendering the perceived threat a consistent "patient-centred threat", b) the threat can not be quantified in a conceivable way as it is not statistical, c) being subjected to a crime, including the malicious intent by a third person, can cause more anxiety and stress than a purely technical failure with the device itself. From the above points, those medical institutions and providers that are not preparing or informing their patients of the possible risks when choosing CIED treatment in the presence of this highly individualized, unescapable and unquantifiable vulnerability, have the potential to involuntarily shift patients' risk perceptions and thus treatment preferences and choices. Furthermore, providers are responsible for adhering to the ethical principles of autonomy, beneficence, non-maleficence and justice during the consenting process [15]. At present, there are no standardised guidelines for listing cybersecurity risks within the informed consent and thus the decision to include cybersecurity risks is mainly left to the provider's discretion, who may also have limited cyber risk information. Without effective and in-depth communication about all possible cybersecurity risks during the consent process, CIED patients can be left unaware of the privacy and physical risks they possess by wearing such a device. Therefore, cyber risk factors should be covered within the patients' informed consent and reviewed on an ongoing basis as new risk information becomes available. By including cyber risk information in the informed consent process, patients are given the autonomy to make the best-informed decision.

For the development of the research project, an initial literature review and assessment were performed and a position paper was written based on these continually emerging safety challenges with cybersecurity and the ever-growing "patient-centred threat" to CIED patients. In addition, both legal and ethical implications as well as proposed solutions for the continued adherence to patient-centred care practices and authentication of the informed consent were presented. From this position paper the subsequent design of the research project was mapped. While the research project focuses primarily on the providers' and patients' understanding and perceptions of cybersecurity risks with CIEDs with the main aim of developing standardized cyber risk information that can be placed in informed consents and discussed with patients during the informed consent process, a secondary set of studies could subsequently evolve that target medical institutions with the intent of assisting in the design and development of interdepartmental cyber risk management teams, the creation and implementation of effective cyber resilient training programs for employees, which would provide detailed education on human factors and how, for example, slips and mistakes can affect cyber resilient practices. These training modules could be standardized and utilised across all medical institutions as well and be promoted in the form of white papers to the health care sector.

3 Methodology

The methodology for the studies within the research project consists of two qualitative studies assessing both providers' and patients' perspectives of cybersecurity risks with CIEDs as well as a risk assessment of the CIED and secondary device manuals from the main manufacturers who sell these devices. From the two studies, we postulated: 1) providers lack understanding about the increased cybersecurity risks with CIEDs and presently do not include these risks in the informed consent either due to not wanting to "unnecessarily" raise patients' anxiety and stress levels or extend time with lengthier discussions about cyber risks with patients [13]; and 2) patients are not sufficiently aware of their cyber risks with having a CIED, state that this ambiguous threat would produce higher levels of anxiety due to not feeling prepared and informed, and thus would impact the patient-provider relationship. In addition, we assumed there may exist cultural differences among patients residing from different countries as to whether they would prefer to be informed or not. From the results of these qualitative questionnaire and interview studies, we plan to develop standardized cybersecurity risk guidelines for CIED informed consents.

3.1 Research Question and Objectives of the Provider Perception Study

The primary research questions proposed for the provider study were: What do providers know about the cybersecurity risks with CIEDs and do they convey these risks to their patients within the informed consent and during the consenting process or is this risk information downplayed and determined to not be necessary to communicate to patients with CIEDs either due to cultural practices in medicine, professional opinions or concerns that the patient may chose/refuse the proposed treatment plan?

The objectives of the study were to understand the providers' perspectives regarding: 1) level of knowledge they have about cybersecurity risks with CIEDs, 2) how much information they have about CIED cybersecurity risks from the manufacturer or other sources of information, 3) how much do they communicate to their patients about these risks during the informed consent process and when new information comes available, 4) do they feel prepared to discuss cybersecurity risks with patients, 5) are they concerned about cyber attacks, 6) what are their opinions with the current informed consent process as to whether is it lacking or satisfactory, 7) if providers choose to avoid discussions regarding cybersecurity vulnerabilities with their patients, what is their rationale for doing so; and 8) understanding what providers would like to see done most or perceive as most important in presenting cybersecurity information effectively to their patients. We hypothesized that providers did not perceive the risk level with cybersecurity as high enough to deem necessary to include cybersecurity risk information within the informed consent or be discussed during the consent process, and possessed also alternative reasons that prevented them from fully disclosing cybersecurity risks to patients (e. g. lack of understanding, avoidance of overburdening the patient with information that was determined as not helpful, and avoiding extended conversations that were perceived as not necessary).

3.2 Design of Provider Study

This study was a multi-center, qualitative study in which an online questionnaire as well as semi-structured interviews were conducted. As this is a hermeneutics approach in study design, we desired to understand the rationale, for not informing patients about cybersecurity vulnerabilities, if this were indeed occurring. The study questions were subsequently designed with this in mind, reviewed and assessed by the research team to ensure the objectives of the study were effectively being addressed. All study documentation, questionnaire and interview questions were submitted to and approved by the ethical review board prior to the commencement of the study. The online study questionnaire was created utilising the SoSci Survey platform, which was hosted exclusively by the University of Würzburg for study purposes; and not through publicly available servers [11]. The SoSci Survey platform adheres to German data privacy laws [11]. All study practices, consenting process, data collection and integrity followed GDPR guidelines for participant privacy assurance and data privacy authenticity and the Declaration of Helsinki for maintaining ethical principles in clinical research study design. Data collection and entry practices followed GDPR regulations for pseudonymisation and anonymisation.

We anticipated to enrol and interview 2–3 providers per institution and country from at least 3 different countries (approximately 6–7 providers per country) but continued to actively enrol participants until saturation of responses was achieved. Providers represented either cardiologists or surgeons who consented patients and surgically implanted cardiac implantable electronic devices (CIEDs). These providers were invited to enrol in the study, complete an online questionnaire including uploading their current informed consent that was anonymised (not linked to the medical institution where they work) as well as be interviewed and recorded in a private Zoom meeting. All providers were consented first via the online questionnaire and then asked again via verbal consent prior to all interviews beginning. During the provider interviews, open-ended questions were also posed to allow for free commentary and the gathering of additional information about the providers' perspectives. Question areas whether from the online survey or interview included: demographics, types of CIEDs used on patients, sources of information about devices and cybersecurity information, perceived cybersecurity risks to patients and institution, the current consenting process and whether these processes were satisfactory or lacking, and if providers were not informing patients of the cybersecurity vulnerabilities with CIEDs, what was their rationale for not informing them.

Participants created their own study subject codes and the participants' names, email addresses and phone numbers, along with their study subject codes, were linked on a separate identification spreadsheet. This spreadsheet key remained on one of the investigator's cyber and password protected institutional computers and the personal data remained pseudonymised while the interviews were being conducted in case follow up questions developed from either the interviewers or the participants. Thus, only those investigators who were involved in the direct consenting and interviewing process had access to the spreadsheet and study subject codes for each of the study participants. The other investigators did not have access to the pseudonymised data and thus only had access to the deidentified data. Upon completion of the interviews and after all data was entered, the identification spreadsheet key was deleted and the data became deidentified/anonymous. While the personal data was deidentified and anonymised on the data spreadsheet, the demographic data collection included gender, age, years of practice and country location. Practices of pseudonymisation and anonymisation followed GDPR regulations. Data were analyzed using JASP statistical program. Descriptive statistics as well as multivariate statistical analyses was performed to assess for associations between variables or within-subject factors. Data could be stratified based on country and for example, Chi-square tests performed especially if there were observed cultural differences between responses (in particular in the aspects of liability concerns). Results will be published and disseminated.

3.3 Objectives of Patients' Perceptions Study

The main research questions proposed for the patient study are: How aware are patients of their increased physical and privacy risks because of possessing a CIED, how concerned or anxious are they of learning about these cybersecurity risks and would they want to be informed of these risks?

The objectives of this study will be to understand the patients' perspectives specifically to the following points: 1) their levels of knowledge regarding cybersecurity risks with having a CIED and how these types of risks can: a) affect them physically and/or personally with the stealing of privacy data; and b) the cyber attack can occur either at the medical institutional or patient levels, 2) how much information have their providers communicated to them about CIED cybersecurity risks whether during the informed consent process or anytime thereafter (i.e. updated patch required), 3) how concerned or anxious do they feel about cyber attacks compared to other risks (i.e. infection, device malfunction, risk from leads burning), 4) what are their opinions with the current informed consent process as to whether is it lacking or satisfactory; and 5) to what level of detail, if any, do patients wish to be informed regarding cybersecurity risks and how should this information be presented to patients.

3.4 Design of Patient Study

This qualitative questionnaire study will be conducted primarily online. Similar to the provider study, we will continue to actively enrol until saturation of responses is achieved. These potential study subjects will be recruited in countries similar to where providers practice medicine. We will recruit both through providers, through postings at medical institutions as well as through online advertising of the study such as via support groups, other CIED information organisations and LinkedIn. However, we do recognize some selection bias maybe unavoidable if those who enrol in the study tend to be a category of patients who are more active with responding. The inclusion criteria for enrolling in the study will include those patients who have consented to receive a CIED and are able to read and write in English. General categories of data collected include: 1) demographics, 2) knowledge level about types of cyber attacks and understanding about possible targeted locations for such attacks, 3) state and trait anxiety measurements (current levels as well as assessment of anxiety levels based on hypothetical cyber attacks and possible consequences), 4) current depression measurement scale such as Beck Depression Inventory (BDI-II), 5) current consent process understanding, 6) how comfortable are the patients able to communicate with the provider, 7) perceived anxiety levels towards cyber attacks compared to infections, lead burns and device malfunctions; and 8) measurement of self-efficacy in their perceived capacity to maintain reduced levels of anxiety and rumination during communications with providers regarding the receipt of possible new cyber risk information whether during the informed process or thereafter. The study questions will be designed, reviewed and assessed by the research team to ensure the objectives of the study are being effectively addressed. All study documentation, questionnaire and interview questions will be submitted and approved by the ethical review board prior to the commencement of the study. The online study questionnaire will be created utilising the SoSci Survey platform, which is hosted exclusively by the University of Würzburg for study purposes; and not through publicly available servers [11]. The SoSci Survey platform adheres to German data privacy laws [11]. All study practices, consenting process, data collection and integrity will follow GDPR guidelines for participant privacy assurance and data privacy authenticity and the Declaration of Helsinki for maintaining ethical principles in clinical research study design. Data collection and entry practices will follow GDPR regulations for pseudonymisation and anonymisation.

As this study is an online questionnaire study only, participant data will be anonymised such that the data can not be traced back to an individual subject. Descriptive statistics as well as multivariate statistical analyses will be performed to assess for associations between variables or within-subject factors. Data could be stratified based on country and Chi-square tests performed especially if there are observed cultural differences between responses (in particular wanting to be informed or not of cybersecurity risks). Results will be published and disseminated.

3.5 Risk Assessment of CIED and Secondary Device Manufacturer Manuals

The final component of the research project will be a risk assessment of the manufacturer manuals that are specific for both CIEDs (pacemakers, defibrillators and cardiac resynchronization devices) and secondary device support systems. From a preliminary assessment of the patient counseling manual from one manufacturer there was no reference of suggesting or providing suggestions for cybersecurity risk discussions for providers [7]. We theorize that hospitals, who primarily purchase the CIEDs from manufacturers, receive limited information on device details and performance, which in turn is needed for providers to convey pertinent information to patients who are considering obtaining a CIED or possess one [12]. From the manufacturer manuals, we plan to search for information on and assess: 1) what information, if any, about cybersecurity risk with CIEDs and secondary devices is mentioned, 2) are there manufacturer propriety protocols identified with the transfer of private patient data, 3) is that transfer of data one-way or two-way, 4) does the data transfer occur only in the patient's home or can the data transfer occur while the patient is in the community (mobile secondary device), 5) does the data transfer occur one time per day or more frequently, 6) does the patient need to be a specific distance from the secondary device for the data to transfer; and 7) are there references or directly stated comments in which manufacturers are subtlety shifting the risk and accountability to medical institutions and/providers. A list of known device manufacturers has been created and all CIED and secondary device manuals will be retrieved from online websites. A spreadsheet identifying the key objectives of the manual reviews will be created and points of interest will be highlighted. Data will be reviewed with fellow investigators and determined from group discussions if the information in the manuals is sufficient, lacking or if manufacturers are shifting potential cybersecurity risks to medical institutions and/or patients. Results from the risk assessment will be included in the two study publications.

4 Next Generation of Studies

Results obtained from this research project will shape future research directions and the next generation of studies. For example, a long-term plan is to conduct a randomised control study to assess the effectiveness of standardised cyber risk information in the informed consent and consenting process compared to a control group (standard informed consent without cyber risk information included). This standardised cyber risk information that would be developed from the results found from the two qualitative studies and risk assessment. In addition, results from this research project will allow us to understand current cultural and operating practices by providers and medical institutions. A secondary set of studies could subsequently evolve to target medical institutions to understand: 1) their current cybersecurity standards, 2) what trainings, if any, are available and how frequently are they conducted, 3) how often are employees updated by IT departments of possible cybersecurity risks and practices that can promote an attack; and 4) the medical institutions' and employees' levels of understanding of human factors and common errors performed. The purpose of this proposed operational procedure assessment, as well as results from the initial research project, will assist in the creation and implementation of effective cyber resilient training programs for employees and leadership, which would include detailed education on human factors such as how, for example, slips and mistakes can affect cyber resilient practices. Furthermore, cyber resilient practices could also include the design and development of interdepartmental cyber risk management teams, which could be piloted and tested for effectiveness in improved cyber resilient practices with the goal of creating standard operating procedures within a medical institution. If standardized, these training modules and interdepartmental cyber risk management teams could be made available and utilised across all medical institutions and be promoted in the form of white papers to the health care sector.

References

1. Hussein, A.A., Wilkoff, B.L.: Cardiac implantable electronic device therapy in heart failure. Circ. Res. **124**, 1584–1597 (2019)
2. Kwarteng, E., Cebe, M.: A survey on security issues in modern implantable devices: solutions and future issues. Smart Health **25**, 100295 (2022)
3. Zeitler, E.P., Piccini, J.P.: Remote monitoring of cardiac implantable electronic devices (CIED). Trends Cardiovasc. Med. **26**(6), 568–577 (2016)
4. Epstein, A.E., DiMarco, J.P., Ellenbogen, K.A., Mark Estes, N.A., Freedman, R.A., Gettes, L.S., et al.: ACC/AHA/HRS 2008 guidelines for device-based therapy of cardiac rhythm abnormalities: a report of the American college of cardiology/American heart association task force on practice guidelines and developed in collaboration with the American association for thoracic surgery and society of thoracic surgeons. J. Am. Coll. Cardiol. **51**(21), e1–e62 (2008)
5. Leavitt, N.: Researchers fight to keep implanted medical devices safe from hackers. Computer **43**(8), 11–14 (2010)
6. CardioMessenger Smart Technical Manual. Biotronik. CardioMessenger Smart (biotronik. com), Berlin, Germany (2023)

7. Physician's Technical Manual, Pacemakers and Operator's Manual Latitude Programming System, Boston Scientific. 359248-002_multi_PTM_en-US_S.pdf (bostonscientific.com), 359487-008_LATITUDE Prog System 3300_OM_en_S.pdf (bostonscientific.com), St. Paul, Minnesota (2023)

8. Sütterlin, S., Knox, B.J., Maennel, K., Canham, M., Lugo, R.G.: Contribution title: On the relationship between health sectors' digitalization and sustainable health goals: a cybersecurity perspective. In: Flahault, A. (ed.) Transitioning to Good Health and Well-Being, 1st edn, pp. 133–155. MDPI Books, Basel (2022)

9. Kim, L.: Cybersecurity awareness: protecting data and patients. Nurs. Manage. **48**(4), 16–19 (2017)

10. Das, S., Siroky, G.P., Lee, S., Mehta, D., Suri, R.: Cybersecurity: the need for data and patient safety with cardiac implantable electronic devices. Heart Rhythm **18**(3), 473–481 (2021)

11. SoSci Survey GmbH. Questionnaire title: Providers' perspectives of how prepared they are and how much they communicate to their cardiac implantable electronic device (CIED) patients about cybersecurity risks during the informed consent process. Login SoSci Survery (uni-wuerzburg.de), Munich, Germany (2023)

12. Lind, K.D.: Understanding the Market for Implantable Medical Devices. Issue Brief Public Policy Institute (American Association of Retired Persons) (2017)

13. Braddock, C.H., Fihn, S.D., Levinson, W., Jonsen, A.R., Pearlman, R.A.: How doctors and patients discuss routine clinical decisions. J. Gen. Int. Med. **12**(6), 339–345 (1997)

14. Hassija, V., Chamola, V., Bajpai, B.C., Naren, Zeadally, S.: Security issues in implantable medical devices: fact or fiction? Sustain. Cities Soc. **66**, 102552 (2021).

15. Varkey, B.: Principles of clinical ethics and their application to practice. Med. Princ. Pract. **30**, 17–28 (2020)

Exploring Emotional and Physiological Reactions to Linguistic Racism: A Case Study in Higher Education

Linghan Zhang[1]([✉]), Jung Yeon Park[2], and Elizabeth T. Kwari[2]

[1] Eindhoven University of Technology, Eindhoven, Netherlands
zhang1@tue.nl
[2] George Mason University, Fairfax, USA
{jpark233,ekwari}@gmu.edu

Abstract. Linguistic racism can cause complex negative emotions and mental health issues in individuals. This study investigates how linguistic racism affects Non-Native English Speakers (NNES) and Native English Speakers (NES) in higher education (students and faculties) with physiological signal-based methods and survey responses. Participants ($N = 13$) watched a video showing a new immigrant experiencing linguistic racism while their physiological signals were measured. Moreover, the participants self-reported their emotions before and after they watched the video. Results indicate that the video especially makes NNES participants scared and nervous, which is not observed in NES. The study also found acute physiological reactions in NNES during experiments. The findings encourage further research on the relationship between linguistic racism and NNES's mental health, especially providing insights into how to support NNES in higher education.

Keywords: Linguistic Racism · Physiological Signals · Affective Computing · Higher Education

1 Introduction

Linguistic racism (LR), the ideologies and practices that conform to an uneven power structure between language users in a group, has been prevalent all over academia [1, 2]. For example, racialized students with English accents dissimilar to white native English speakers (NES) are not treated as respectfully because their accents are associated with negative stereotypes. Moreover, they are often stigmatized by various microaggressions (e.g., exclusions, lack of respect) that may impact emotions such as non-belonging, low self-esteem, and anxiety [3]. While the literature review presents research on LR experiences based on (semi-structured) interviews and questionnaires, to our knowledge, few studies have utilized quantitative approaches to present a unified understanding of LR-triggered emotions. Hence, the study aims to facilitate the measurement of participants' emotional states with two approaches, i.e., self-report surveys [4, 5] and physiological signals [6–12]. We use the E4 wristband [13] to collect physiological signals triggered

C. Stephanidis et al. (Eds.): HCII 2023, CCIS 1832, pp. 529–535, 2023.
https://doi.org/10.1007/978-3-031-35989-7_67

by the LR experience. The contribution of this work is threefold. First, we examine the LR experience and emotions among students and faculty in higher education. Secondly, we compare NES's and NNES's emotional changes when experiencing LR. Third, we explore the association between self-reported emotional intensity triggered by LR and individuals' physiological reactions.

		E4 Starts Recording 1st Event Marker	2nd Event Marker	3rd Event Marker	E4 Finishes Recording 4th Event Marker	
LSAS-SR	**PANAS**	**Pre-task**	**LR Experience (task)**		**Post-task**	**PANAS**
exclude participants with extreme high level of anxiety	identify participants' emotion types and intensities before task	enable the participants to relax while collect baseline signals	Measure the participants' physiological responses to LR video	Help the participants to calm down and recover from the LR video while tracking physiological signal		Identify participants' emotion types and intensities caused by the LR video

Fig. 1. Experimental Procedures and Purposes

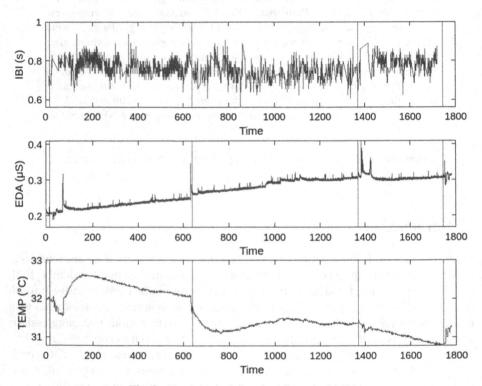

Fig. 2. Physiological signals collected with E4

2 Methods

We invited 13 participants at George Mason University to join controlled lab-based experiments with IRB approval. As illustrated in Fig. 1, the participants conducted three phases of experiments, i.e., 10-min relaxing music listening as a baseline study, 20-min LR video watching, and 5-min music listening for recovery. We used Liebowitz Social Anxiety Scale (LSAS-SR) to screen highly anxious participants [14] before the experiment and the Positive and Negative Affect Schedule (PANAS) to assess emotion types and intensities before and after watching the video.

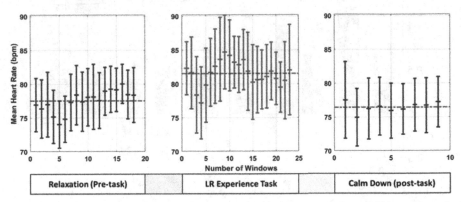

Fig. 3. Mean HR interval over one experiment. Markers denote mean value, whiskers are standard deviation, and the black dash lines show the participant's average heart rate in a given stage

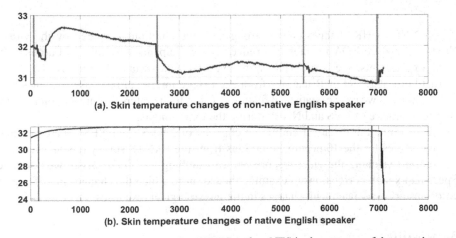

Fig. 4. Skin temperature changes of an NNES and an NES in three stages of the experiment

The LR video clip [15] includes a few episodes of an NNES immigrant in the US who was exposed to verbal harassment and ridicule in daily life because of her thick accent. During the experiment, we collected the physiological signals and the event marks [38–41], as shown in Fig. 2, where we could observe that the NNES' physiological signals changed drastically during the experiments. Then we analyze the recorded Electrodermal Activity (EDA), Blood Volume Pulse (BVP), body temperature, and exact features from these signals in each experiment stage. Specifically, we extract BVP features, including mean, minimum, maximum, standard deviation, range of Heart Rate (HR), SDNN, RMSSD, pNN50, pNN20, LF ratio, HF ratio, and LF/HF. Figure 3 shows.

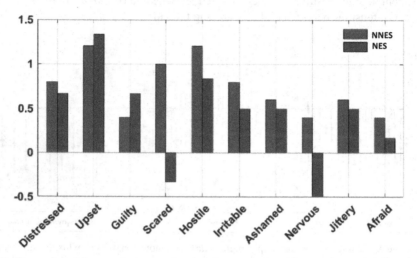

Fig. 5. Examples of change scores: a comparison between non-native speakers (NNES) and native speakers (NES)

an NNES's HR changes due to strong negative emotions triggered by the video. Next, we analyze EDA features that reflect the participants' physiological arousal. In these experiments, the participants were exposed to a sustained stimulus. Thus, we extract both SCL and SCR features from each stage instead of response windows [16, 17]. Moreover, we extract statistical features of skin temperature. Figure 4 compares the skin temperature of NES and NNES during the experiments.

To examine the extent of emotional changes of NNESs and NESs, we computed change scores for the 10 negative emotions from the PANAS survey (change score = score after watching the video - score before watching the video). Also, we compute Spearman's rank correlations to examine the extent to which the changes in self-report emotions are associated with changes in the physiological responses.

3   Results

Figure 5 demonstrates the change scores in the PANAS survey. In general, after watching the video, both NES and NNES participants reported intensified negative emotions, such as distress, upset, and hostility. Moreover, NNES participants reported increased levels of scaredness and nervousness, whereas NES did not.

Figure 6 presents directions and magnitudes of the relationships between the change in self-report emotion and physiological responses. For EDA, we found that about 27% of all pairs of the changes (in self-report emotions and physiological responses) have Spearman's r greater than or equal to 0.3. For example, we found changes in the figure of F2 (Number of Significant SCRs) are related to changes in *scared* and *distressed* ($r = 0.55, 0.46$), relatively stronger than other emotion types. For HRV, we found that about 22% of all pairs have Spearman's r greater than or equal to 0.3. Among them, the figure of F1 (Mean HR) was strongly correlated with the emotion type, *scared* ($r = 0.73$); F7 (RMSSD) with *nervous* ($r = 0.70$); F2 (Std HR) with *ashamed* ($r = 0.50$). For skin temperature, the correlation between F1 (Mean Temp) and *ashamed* was the highest ($r = -0.41$).

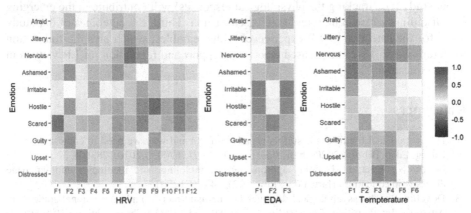

Fig. 6. Correlations between self-report emotion change and change in physiological data

4   Discussion and Conclusion

Our study based upon quantitative approaches suggests that Linguistic Racism (LR) experiences are generally associated with triggering negative emotions as measured by physiological signals as well as survey responses. Our lab-based experiment found noticeable and characteristic physiological reactions while NNES participants watch the LR video. The intermedium results of physiological signals show strong connections between the emotion sets triggered by LR and individuals' physiological signal changes. Moreover, we believe the experimental video could impact most participants and cause physiological changes, especially the NNES, as observed by the noticeable increments in some HR and EDA features.

From their survey responses before and after the video, the NNES participants tend to have elevated levels of scaredness and nervousness in response to the LR-related stimulus, whereas the NES participants show similar negative emotions, nevertheless, at lower overall intensities. Moreover, statistical analysis shows correlations in many pairs of LR-triggered emotions and physiological reactions. We believe that this work provides insightful information to advance interdisciplinary research in the areas of anti-racism, critical race theory, and emotion computing.

In future work, we plan to expand the experiment by using multiple videos with LR-related episodes closely tied to students and faculty members in higher education and recruiting more student and faculty participants to improve statistical power in data analysis. In addition, we will invite a few of our participants from the experiment to a semi-structured interview to obtain in-depth information about their emotional changes in relation to the LR-related experience, which would, in turn, help enhance the validity of our research design and measurement tools.

We strongly believe our study contributes to the literature in various ways. First, this study provides a comprehensive understanding of LR-triggered emotions to NNESs in the context of higher education. Second, the novel quantitative techniques presented in our study (i.e., tracking the physiological responses) will contribute to the emerging interdisciplinary research around race-based trauma. Third, the outcomes of our study allow for the detection of LR experiences with wearables, which lays the foundation for future work of wearable-based emotional support and regulation for LR victims in higher education.

References

1. De Costa, P.I.: Linguistic racism: its negative effects and why we need to contest it. Int. J. Biling. Educ. Biling. (2020). https://doi.org/10.1080/13670050.2020.1783638
2. Flores, N., Rosa, J.: Undoing appropriateness: raciolinguistic ideologies and language diversity in education. Harv. Educ. Rev. **85**(2), 149–171 (2015)
3. Dovchin, S.: The psychological damages of linguistic racism and international students in Australia. Int. J. Biling. Educ. Biling. **23**(7), 804–818 (2020). https://doi.org/10.1080/136 70050.2020.1759504
4. Watson, D., Clark, L.A., Tellegen, A.: Development and validation of brief measures of positive and negative affect: the PANAS scales. J. Pers. Soc. Psychol. **54**(6), 1063 (1988)
5. DePaoli, L.C., Sweeney, D.C.: Further validation of the positive and negative affect schedule. J. Soc. Behav. Pers. **15**(4), 561–568 (2000)
6. Subhani, A.R., Xia, L., Malik, A.S.: Evaluation of mental stress using physiological signals. In: 2011 National Postgraduate Conference, pp. 1–4. IEEE (2011)
7. Shi, H., et al.: Differences of heart rate variability between happiness and sadness emotion states: a pilot study. J. Med. Biol. Eng. **37**(4), 527–539 (2017)
8. Chung, J.W.Y., So, H.C.F., Choi, M.M.T., Yan, V.C.M., Wong, T.K.S.: Artificial Intelligence in education: using heart rate variability (HRV) as a biomarker to assess emotions objectively. Comput. Educ.: Artif. Intell. **2**, 100011 (2021)
9. Choi, K.H., Kim, J., Kwon, O.S., Kim, M.J., Ryu, Y.H., Park, J.E.: Is heart rate variability (HRV) an adequate tool for evaluating human emotions?–A focus on the use of the international affective picture system (IAPS). Psychiatry Res. **251**, 192–196 (2017)
10. Guo, H.W., Huang, Y.S., Lin, C.H., Chien, J.C., Haraikawa, K., Shieh, J.S.: Heart rate variability signal features for emotion recognition by using principal component analysis and support vectors machine. In: 2016 IEEE 16th International Conference on Bioinformatics and Bioengineering (BIBE), pp. 274–277. IEEE (2016)
11. Wu, G., Liu, G., Hao, M.: The analysis of emotion recognition from GSR based on PSO. In: 2010 International Symposium on Intelligence Information Processing and Trusted Computing, pp. 360–363. IEEE (2010)

12. Egger, M., Ley, M., Hanke, S.: Emotion recognition from physiological signal analysis: a review. Electr. Notes Theor. Comput. Sci. **343**, 35–55 (2019)
13. E4 wristband. https://www.empatica.com/en-int/research/e4/. Access 2022
14. Liebowitz, M.R., et al.: Efficacy of sertraline in severe generalized social anxiety disorder. J. Clin. Psychiatry **64**(7), 785–792 (2003). https://doi.org/10.4088/jcp.v64n0708
15. YouTube.: Immigrant Shamed For Her English. YouTube (2021). https://www.youtube.com/watch?v=LACUT5PKEeg Retrieved October 19, 2022
16. Lutin, E., Hashimoto, R., De Raedt, W., Van Hoof, C.: Feature extraction for stress detection in electrodermal activity. In: BIOSIGNALS, pp. 177–185 (2021)
17. Benedek, M., Kaernbach, C.: A continuous measure of phasic electrodermal activity. J. Neurosci. Methods **190**(1), 80–91 (2010)

User Experience and Technology Acceptance Studies

Are Scrutiny and Mistrust Related?
An Eye-Tracking Study

Danushka Bandara[1]([✉]) [iD] and Sambhab Sau[2]

[1] Fairfield University, Fairfield, CT 06824, USA
dbandara@fairfield.edu
[2] Georgia Institute of Technology, Atlanta, GA 30332, USA

Abstract. Eyes are an important organ in both information processing and communicating. Eye gaze contains rich information about our attention and internal state. It has previously been studied as a measure of trust in various contexts such as air traffic control, driving, and online shopping. The study uses fixation and saccadic measurements to obtain a viable measure of human trust. The experiment involved nine participants and their trust level was indicated by whether they accepted or rejected a decision made by an Artificial Intelligence (AI). A Tobii pro nano eye-tracker and psychopy software were used to track the participants' eye gaze and responses. Results indicate that saccade count shows a statistically significant variation between trust and mistrust conditions with $p < 0.05$, while the fixation count showed a variation at $p < 0.2$. Through this study, we show that the count of saccades is a viable measure of a human's mistrust in an AI system.

Keywords: Eye tracking · Trust · Human-AI interaction

1 Introduction

Eye gaze tracking is a data-rich behavioral measure for Human Computer Interaction (HCI) researchers. It is used as a usability metric and a control mechanism [4]. In this study, we are interested in delineating the connection between eye gaze and perceived level of trust in a human-AI interaction scenario. Several research areas have used eye gaze as a measure of trust. It has been used in air traffic controller scenarios where it was used to measure stress-related task overload [1] because stress is connected to low levels of trust; eye tracking can be an indicator of trust levels. Researchers have shown in driving scenarios that there is a connection between the frequency and duration of eye glances and trust in the system [2, 3]. In a study examining the effect of human brands on consumers' trust levels in online shopping, it was ascertained that longer fixation durations on brand images, calculated from eye tracking data, indicated greater trust in specific products [12]. Moreover, in an unmanned aerial vehicle control study, participants were shown to trust high-reliability automation more than low-reliability automation with several key eye tracking metrics (total fixation duration, backtrack rate, scanpath length per second, etc.) being closely correlated with trust levels [14, 15].

© The Author(s), under exclusive license to Springer Nature Switzerland AG 2023
C. Stephanidis et al. (Eds.): HCII 2023, CCIS 1832, pp. 539–545, 2023.
https://doi.org/10.1007/978-3-031-35989-7_68

Analysis of eye movements is typically conducted in terms of fixations (pauses over informative regions of interest) and saccades (rapid movements between fixations). Given the strong link between fixations and overt visual attention, fixations have been widely studied in experimental psychology to evaluate reading comprehension, facial processing, and online learning [18]. Typically, subjects exhibiting mistrust will pay greater attention to evaluating the system in question. Saccadic measurement has become prominent in many research fields as deficient saccadic function is helping in examining neurological activity and diagnosing various disorders [19]. Eye tracking metrics, such as fixations and saccades, extracted from raw eye movement data have been proven to work well as input to various modeling methods [16]. The parameters for identifying fixations and saccades are commonly either velocity-based or dispersion-based. For example, identifying a fixation might mean specifying the allowed dispersion from a single point in a subject's field of vision for a minimum time threshold. On the other hand, a saccade may be specified by defining a minimum velocity threshold for the pupil to be moving from one fixation to the next. A fixation and saccade can never occur at the same time. The exact parameters for identification are a matter of debate among researchers and are generally chosen based on what serves the model in question best [17]. This study explores the connection between eye tracking features and the trust level of a human. The trust and mistrust are measured by the humans' acceptance or rejection of decisions made by an Artificial Intelligence (AI) agent.

Research Hypothesis: Eye tracking features (fixations and saccades) can be used to distinguish trust and mistrust conditions.

2 Method

2.1 Experiment Design

We conducted a human subject study where nine subjects participated in a 'Human-AI Interaction' experiment. Participants completed a pre-experiment questionnaire to gauge their base level of trust in computers. We adopted the disposition to trust inventory [7] and adjusted the questions to reflect human-computer trust. When participants arrived for the experiment, they were seated in front of the computer and presented various images consecutively with 10 s of rest between each trial. Their job was to judge whether the images were authentic or 'doctored' (manipulated in any way). We used the CASIA [7] dataset as the source for the images. In addition to the images, participants were shown the AI decision of whether the image was authentic or not authentic. We used a 'wizard of oz' methodology for this study (i.e., we simulated the AI response) to show the participants a variety of AI responses. We also administered a trust measurement survey during the experiment to gauge how trust varies subjectively [9]. During the experiment, a Tobii pro nano eye-tracker was used to track their eye gaze continuously. The Tobii eye-tracker was calibrated to track the eye gaze location on the computer screen at 20 Hz. The user responses were tracked by the psychopy [10] software, which was also utilized to present the experiment materials; it tracked the time of presentation of each question as well. As indicated above, we combined eye tracking with the user responses to evaluate eye tracking data as trust indicators (Fig. 1).

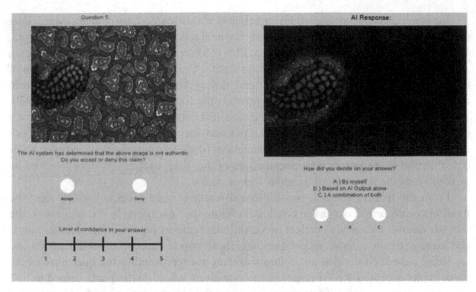

Fig. 1. An example screen that was shown to participants.

2.2 Data Collection

The participants completed the consent form and pre-experiment questionnaire before attending the experiment. When they arrived for the experiment, they were asked to sit in front of the computer comfortably. Then, the Tobii pro nano eyetracker was calibrated for their eye gaze. The eyetracking data was collected in a csv file along with timestamps. The psychopy experiment was run and collected the user response for each question along with the time stamps. The starting and ending timestamps for each question was used to extract the eye tracking data for each question. Then the eyetracking data was further processed to obtain features such as fixations and saccades.

2.3 Data Processing and Modeling

A fixation is defined here as a state in which the eye is focused on a point of interest with some maximum limit in variation and minimum time limit. For this study, the maximum allowed variation from the point of interest was 25 pixels and the minimum duration was 200 ms. A saccade is defined as a state in which the eye moves rapidly from one point of interest to another for some minimum time period, minimum velocity threshold, and minimum acceleration threshold. After doing a grid search over the parameters, these three parameters were chosen to be 5 ms, 60 pixels/second, and 150 pixels/seconds^2, respectively. Fixations and saccades were calculated for each question asked to participants. Each fixation was documented using the start time, end time, total duration (calculated as start time subtracted from end time), and x and y coordinates of the fixation. Each saccade was documented using the start time, end time, total duration, and two pairs of x and y coordinates representing the start and end of the saccade [11].

Incomplete data from one of the participants was discarded, leaving the eyetracking data and levels of trust of 8 participants for analysis. For the raw eyetracking data, (0,0) represents the top left of the screen, (0.5, 0.5) represents the center of the screen, and (1,1) represents the bottom right of the screen. Using the resolution information of the computer screen used (1920 x 1080), the raw eyetracking data was converted from these ratios to pixels where (0,0) still represents the top left of the screen, while (1920, 1080) represents the bottom right of the screen. Further, we only used the left eye's coordinates for feature extraction of fixations and saccades in this paper as using both eyes' coordinates was assumed to be redundant. Moreover, any rows of the eyetracker data that had 0s, assumed to be output errors of the Tobii eyetracker, were removed so as not to bias the detection of fixations and saccades.

From the fixation dataset, two additional features were collected which were the fixation counts and the average fixation durations per question. In the same way, the saccade dataset was used to collect two additional features representing saccade counts and average fixation durations per question. These two features from both fixations and saccades were then divided again into two datasets representing the questions where participants accepted the AI response and questions where participants denied the AI response. Overall, a total of 685 questions were asked to participants with 416 questions being accepted by participants and 269 of them being denied.

3   Results

Here we show the results of our analysis for the trust vs mistrust conditions. The mistrust group is defined as the set of questions where participants denied the AI's recommendation, and the trust group is defined as the set of questions where participants accepted the AI's recommendation. We have left out the fixation duration and saccade duration results because they did not show any variation between trust and mistrust conditions.

The top left boxplot in Fig. 2 represents the fixation counts for all subjects divided between mistrust and trust. The mean for the mistrust group was 29 fixations, while the mean for the trust group was 27. The interquartile range (IQR) for the mistrust group was 14, while the IQR for the trust group was 15. Upon conducting a one-way ANOVA test to compare the means of the trust and mistrust group for all subjects, the p-value was found to be approximately 0.155512.

The top left boxplot of Fig. 3 represents the saccade counts for all subjects divided between mistrust and trust. The mean for the mistrust group was 43 saccades, while the mean for the trust group was 38. The interquartile range (IQR) for the mistrust group was 26, while the IQR for the trust group was 24. Upon conducting a one-way ANOVA test to compare the means of the trust and mistrust group for all subjects, the p-value was found to be approximately 0.001995. Assuming an alpha value of 0.05, a statistically significant difference was observed between the two groups for saccadic counts (0.001995 < 0.05).

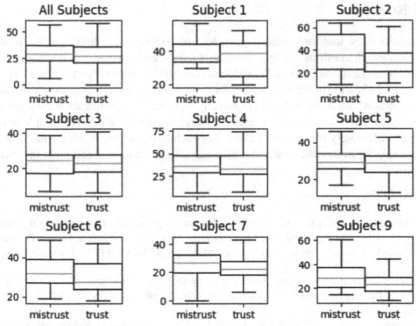

Fig. 2. (Top left) Per question average fixation counts for all subjects in the dataset. Fixation counts are higher for the mistrust condition across all subjects. (the rest of the plots) Per question average fixation counts for each individual subject.

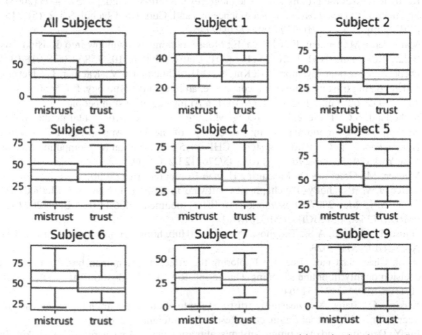

Fig. 3. (Top left) Per question average saccade counts for all subjects in the dataset. Saccade counts are higher for the mistrust condition across all subjects. (the rest of the plots) Per question average saccade counts for each individual subject.

4 Discussion

The results show that the count of saccades and fixations was higher in the mistrust condition which confirms our hypothesis that a trust and mistrust can be distinguished by saccade and fixation features. We did see a variation between subjects of how large this effect was. Indicating that there is inter subject variation on the effect of trust level on eye gaze. Saccadic counts provided a statistically significant discrimination between trust and mistrust conditions than fixations and, therefore, could be a novel complementary feature to accurately predict trust levels. In conclusion, our study shows the utility of eye tracking for evaluating trust and mistrust conditions in human computer interaction.

References

1. Prinet, J.C., Sarter, N.B.: The effects of high stress on attention: a first step toward triggering attentional narrowing in controlled environments. In: Proceedings of the Human Factors and Ergonomics Society Annual Meeting, vol. 59(1), pp. 1530–1534 (2015). https://doi.org/10.1177/1541931215591331
2. Geitner, C., et al.: A link between trust in technology and glance allocation in on-road driving. In: Driving Assessment Conference, vol. 9 (2017). https://doi.org/10.17077/drivingassesment.1645
3. Hergeth, S., Lorenz, L., Vilimek, R., Krems, J.F.: Keep your scanners peeled: gaze behavior as a measure of automation trust during highly automated driving. Hum Factors. 58(3), 509–519 (2016). https://doi.org/10.1177/0018720815625744. Epub 2016 Feb 3 PMID: 26843570
4. Jacob, R.J., Karn, K.S.: Eye tracking in human-computer interaction and usability research: Ready to deliver the promises. In: The mind's eye, North-Holland, pp. 573–605 (2003)
5. Freeman, J.B.: Doing psychological science by hand. Curr. Dir. Psychol. Sci. 27(5), 315–323 (2018). https://doi.org/10.1177/0963721417746793
6. Maldonado, M., Dunbar, E., Chemla, E.: Mouse tracking as a window into decision making. Behav. Res. Methods 51(3), 1085–1101 (2019). https://doi.org/10.3758/s13428-018-01194-x
7. Disposition to trust inventory [McKnight, D.H., Choudhury, V., Kacmar, C.: Developing and validating trust measures for e-commerce: an integrative typology. Inf. Syst. Res. 13(3), 334–359 (2002).] modified to cater to trust in AI instead of trust in people
8. Sutherland, S.C., Harteveld, C., Young, M.E.: the role of environmental predictability and costs in relying on automation. In: Proceedings of the 33rd Annual ACM Conference on Human Factors in Computing Systems (CHI' 2015). Association for Computing Machinery, New York (2015). https://doi.org/10.1145/2702123.2702609
9. Madsen, M., Gregor, S.D.: Measuring Human-Computer Trust (2000)
10. Peirce, J.W.: PsychoPy--Psychophysics software in Python. J. Neurosci. Methods 162(1–2), 8–13, 15 May 2007. https://doi.org/10.1016/j.jneumeth.2006.11.017. Epub 2007 Jan 23. PMID: 17254636; PMCID: PMC2018741
11. Ghose, U., Arvind, A.S.: Titoghose/Pytrack. GitHub. https://github.com/titoghose/PyTrack. Accessed 15 Mar 2023
12. Wook Chae, S., Chang Lee, K.: Exploring the effect of the human brand on consumers' decision quality in online shopping. Online Inf. Rev. 37(1), 83–100 (2013). https://doi.org/10.1108/14684521311311649
13. Jenkins, Q., Jiang, X.: Measuring trust and application of eye tracking in human robotic interaction. In: Industrial Engineering Research Conference (2010)
14. Lu, Y.: Detecting and overcoming trust miscalibration in real time using an eye-tracking based technique (dissertation) (2020)

15. Lu, Y., Sarter, N.: Eye tracking: a process-oriented method for inferring trust in automation as a function of priming and system reliability. IEEE Trans. Hum.-Mach. Syst. **49**(6), 560–568 (2019). https://doi.org/10.1109/thms.2019.2930980
16. Lu, Y., Sarter, N.: Modeling and inferring human trust in automation based on real- time eye tracking data. In: Proceedings of the Human Factors and Ergonomics Society Annual Meeting, vol. 64(1), pp. 344–348 (2020). https://doi.org/10.1177/1071181320641078
17. Salvucci, D.D., Goldberg, J.H.: Identifying fixations and saccades in eye-tracking protocols. In: Proceedings of the Symposium on Eye Tracking Research & Applications - ETRA 2000 (2000). https://doi.org/10.1145/355017.355028
18. Steil, J., Huang, M.X., Bulling, A.: Fixation detection for head-mounted eye tracking based on visual similarity of gaze targets. In: Proceedings of the 2018 ACM Symposium on Eye Tracking Research & Applications (2018). https://doi.org/10.1145/3204493.3204538
19. Stuart, S., et al.: Eye-tracker algorithms to detect saccades during static and dynamic tasks: a structured review. Physiol. Meas. **40**(2) (2019). https://doi.org/10.1088/1361-6579/ab02ab

Exploring the Intersection of Storytelling, Localisation, and Immersion in Video Games – A Case Study of *the Witcher III: Wild Hunt*

Vanessa Cesário[1](✉) ⓘ, Mariana Ribeiro[2], and António Coelho[2,3] ⓘ

[1] Interactive Technologies Institute (ITI/LARSyS), IST University of Lisbon, Lisbon, Portugal
vanessa.cesario@tecnico.ulisboa.pt
[2] Faculty of Engineering of the University of Porto, Porto, Portugal
[3] Institute for Systems and Computer Engineering, Technology and Science (INESC/TEC), Porto, Portugal

Abstract. Video games have become an increasingly popular and influential form of entertainment in recent years, with a growing market and diverse range of players. As a result, there is a need to better understand and improve various aspects of the video game industry, including storytelling, localisation, and immersion. Storytelling in video games refers to the use of narrative elements, such as character development, plot, and dialogue, to create a compelling and engaging experience. Localisation involves adapting a game for different cultural and linguistic audiences, which can be a complex process that requires careful consideration of the original content and the target audience. This can include translation, voice acting, and other modifications to ensure a seamless and enjoyable experience for players. Immersion refers to the extent to which the player feels fully absorbed and engaged in the game world and its gameplay. By understanding and addressing these three areas, game developers can create more engaging and successful games for players around the world. This study focuses on the interrelated areas of storytelling, localisation, and immersion within the context of role-playing games, using *The Witcher III: Wild Hunt* as a case study. The study used 41 participants who played the game in both English and Brazilian-Portuguese localised versions and completed questionnaires and interviews about their perceptions of these three areas. The results of the study offer recommendations for improving graphic design in video games and suggest the need to explore whether the impact of localisation on story and immersion is dependent only on language or influenced by other factors.

Keywords: Video games · Entertainment · Storytelling · Localisation · Immersion · Role-playing games (RPGs) · The Witcher III: Wild Hunt

1 Introduction

Video games have gained significant importance and dimensions within our culture in recent years [1–6]. The entertainment market has witnessed a growing demand for immersive gameplay and alternative reality experiences [7–9]. As the market expands,

C. Stephanidis et al. (Eds.): HCII 2023, CCIS 1832, pp. 546–552, 2023.
https://doi.org/10.1007/978-3-031-35989-7_69

the pool of consumers and players increases, leading to a need to enhance and explore the localisation process of video games and the features and stages it entails. Technological advancements now enable greater interactivity and agency between players and their gameplay experiences.

Interactive storytelling involves the player's actions within the story, shaping the rest of its development according to their needs and interests, creating more emotional involvement [10]. This field is ripe for expansion, and game localisation requires new translation approaches. While sharing some similarities with screen translation and software localisation, game localisation distinguishes itself by aiming to create an immersive experience for players, allowing localisers to modify, omit, or add elements as necessary to bring the game closer to the player and convey the original feel of gameplay [11]. Regarding localisation, several possibilities, alternatives, and techniques are critical for the distribution, reach, and success of any video game [12]. These include market research, localisation implementation, facial animation modelled on real-life acting through motion-capture techniques, similarities in voice acting between versions, familiarity between the video game and players, and content adaptation to fit the target language's background and history. Video games encompass all of these components as "a medium of entertainment and present a variety of different forms of storytelling and information. The stories within games come in the form of text, speech, activities, and cinematic narratives – cutscenes" [13].

Research on narrative, immersion, and localisation, individually or together, has been extensively conducted [14–24]. However, this article distinguishes itself by focusing on all three elements within the field of video games, specifically the Role-Playing Game (RPG) genre, with a study involving *The Witcher III: Wild Hunt*.

2 Methodology

The study recruited a total of 41 participants (9 females and 32 males) aged between 17 and 35 years, with the majority being of European-Portuguese background. The participants were required to play *The Witcher III* for approximately two hours, one hour each in English and Brazilian-Portuguese, and were asked to complete the Game Experience Questionnaire (GEQ) [25] after each playthrough. The localised versions of the game provided the players with an opportunity to experience the cinematic introduction, tutorial, and various early quests, allowing for a deeper interaction with different elements of the game within a limited time frame. After the gameplay, the participants were interviewed to provide their views on how the three areas of storytelling, localisation, and immersion would impact the transmission of the same story and overall video game in different cultural languages.

2.1   A the RPG in Study: *The Witcher III: Wild Hunt*

RPGs are known for their intricate and interactive storylines, making them a perfect example of translation and localisation challenges. As with writers creating a story from scratch, translators working on RPGs must be creative [11, 27]. *The Witcher III: Wild Hunt*, a 2015 action RPG developed and published by CD Projekt, is the third game in the series, featuring an open world with a third-person perspective. According to Maziarz and Onik [24], *The Witcher III: Wild Hunt* boasts a rich, captivating narrative, replete with jokes, puns, songs, customs, and other cultural references. The game was released in various languages, including English, German, French, Brazilian-Portuguese, Russian, Japanese (dubbed), Spanish, Italian, Korean, Chinese, Czech, Hungarian, Arabic, and Turkish. In an interview, Szwed [28] opined that "there is no original language" for *The Witcher III*, as all languages were developed simultaneously, and "Polish and English are probably the richest in Easter eggs".

The storytelling in video games is a crucial element that can make the gameplay immersive and enjoyable for players. These games' narratives usually involve a combination of humour and folklore, which can be challenging to translate into other languages or cultural contexts. Vickery [26] examined how players interacted with the English narrative in this video game and identified three types of interactions: passive, active, and dialogue choices. The authors also identified two narrative structures within the game: linear and branching. The study found that players interacted with the story even when performing tasks outside the main quest. The semantic layer of a game, which includes idiomatic expressions, sayings, slang, and jokes, can be difficult to translate effectively, as the desired comic effect or meaning may be lost in the target language. In such cases, the source expression must be adapted to the target context, which may potentially impact the player's comprehension or enjoyment of the game [24].

3   Results of the Game Experience Questionnaire

For each played version, a questionnaire was filled in individually and was composed by the core module of the GEQ [25] which assesses game experience as scores on 7 components with a total of 33 questions: 1) *competence*, 2) *sensory and imaginative immersion*, 3) *flow*, 4) *tension/annoyance*, 5) *challenge*, 6) *negative affect*, 7) *positive affect*. By applying the GEQ, we were able to understand how players perceived each played version. This quantitative measure was helpful in complementing the qualitative data collected through post-game interviews.

We checked the normality of the data. All dependent variables (all of 7 components reported above) were not normally distributed ($p < 0.005$), hence we applied non-parametric tests – *Wilcoxon signed rank test*. This test showed us that: (i) Values of *sensory and imaginative immersion* are significantly lower on the Brazilian-Portuguese version (mean 2.84; mdn 3.00) than on the English version (mean 3.54; mdn 3.67) – this difference is significant, $Z = -3.801$, $p < 0.001$, $r = -0.59$; (ii) Values of *flow* are significantly lower on the Brazilian-Portuguese version (mean 2.02; mdn 2.20) than on the English version (mean 2.77; mdn 2.80) – this difference is significant, $Z = -3.560$, $p < 0.001$, $r = -0.56$; (iii) Values of *positive affect* are significantly lower on the Brazilian-Portuguese version (mean 2.85; mdn 3.00) than on the English version (mean 3.60; mdn 3.80) – this difference is significant, $Z = -4.067$, $p < 0.001$, $r = -0.64$; (iv) Values of *tension/annoyance* are significantly higher on the Brazilian-Portuguese version (mean 0.80; mdn 0.33) than on the English version (mean 0.37; mdn 0.00) – this difference is significant, $Z = -2.255$, $p = 0.024$, $r = -0.35$; (v) Values of *negative affect* are significantly higher on the Brazilian-Portuguese version (mean 1.32; mdn 1.25) than on the English version (mean 0.74; mdn 0.75) – this difference is significant, $Z = -2.975$, $p = 0.003$, $r = -0.46$; (vi) Values of *competence* and *challenge* between both versions are non-significant ($p > 0.05$).

In other words, our findings show that when playing the Brazilian-Portuguese version of the game, participants were unable to fully immerse themselves in the game, feeling a lack of enjoyment and positive emotions such as joy and interest. Instead, they experienced negative emotions like irritation, frustration, anxiety, stress, sadness, and worry. However, there was no difference in the perceived level of challenge or in the characteristics and skills that enhance the performance of the game between the Brazilian-Portuguese and English versions.

4 Results of the Interviews

During the interview, participants were asked about the effects of storytelling, localisation, and immersion on the transmission of the same story and overall video game in different cultural languages. We noted that the curiosity factor increases when people discover that there are versions that differ greatly from those they know, leading to an increased interest in understanding the changes that the game may undergo in these adaptations. The discussion touched on the differences between the Polish, Japanese, and Arabic language versions.

Overall, it was considered that these versions would pose evident differences and affect the connection and relation developed with the game, particularly with Polish being the one where language-wise differences would be felt since it is the original country of development and inspiration for the game, which some considered to be closer to an "original" or more faithful version. Although the interviewees agreed that "if the different adaptations can still transmit the same feeling and message in different cultures and languages, then they are good," there was some concern regarding the changes the Japanese and Arabic versions encompassed, such as censorship or core modifications (graphic or linguistic).

While the participants understood why these changes were made, their opinions were divided between those who condoned such measures in adaptation and those who criticized them. Regarding the Japanese and Arabic versions, changing, adding, or removing elements that censor any content from the originally developed and intended video game and story was considered to definitely affect the connection made with the story and the video game. Despite cultural differences, the participants agreed that a video game is a work of art, originally conceived in a certain way to be experienced in that way, and censorship is still gravely frowned upon, no matter how understandable the changes may be to make the game accessible to everyone.

In conclusion, participants debated that since players from countries that only have access to certain versions, such as the Arabic, Japanese, or Chinese versions, are actively losing content and information that make the game what it is, even if they are not aware of it. These changes could result in missed opportunities for the players to experience lore, contextualization, references, or visual content. Such changes affected by the localisation component, in turn, creates a linked effect on the storytelling and therefore the immersion that the player will feel when playing the video game.

5 Recommendations for Improving Graphic Design in Video Games

Regarding graphical content, it is important to consider feedback received from players when making adaptations to video games. Active removal, censorship, or modification of content or materials in a video game is generally viewed negatively. While these changes may be necessary for global distribution, they should not significantly alter the game's original lore, concept, or intended features. Otherwise, players may perceive and interpret the story differently, impacting their immersion during gameplay.

To minimize the need for essential adaptations or modifications to a game's lore when released worldwide, communication and compromise should be established within the video game industry regarding localisation. Standardization or acceptance of the original content, regardless of country or culture, would allow players more freedom of choice regarding the version of the game they are playing. This would ensure that players can fully interpret and appreciate the game according to their own preferences.

However, it can be challenging to achieve this objective. Ideally, players should be given the option to choose the level of censorship, visible change, or obliteration of content in the version of the game they are playing. This is especially important when only one version of the game is available in their country. Providing players with control over the content they are exposed to might enable them to fully immerse themselves in the game and enhance their overall experience.

6 Guidelines for Future Research

The research of the intersection of storytelling, localisation, and immersion in video games has opened up a vast spectrum of research opportunities. As evidenced by the present study, there is still much to be explored and analyzed in this area, particularly in relation to the RPG genre and beyond. The research has demonstrated considerable potential for further design developments and considerations, and one key guideline for future research is to explore the possibility of recreating and expanding upon this study with the use of other available languages in *The Witcher III: Wild Hunt* video game, as well as in other RPGs that have different structural components, and other genres that may differ significantly from those explored in this study.

The comparison of the impact of localisation on storytelling and immersion in different genres of video games is a crucial area for future research. It is worth contemplating the differences between the use of English and Portuguese in the RPG genre, and in other types of games such as tabletop games, MOBAs, and horror games. Exploring the differences in the impact of localisation on immersion and storytelling in these genres could provide valuable insights into the language-specific impact of localisation on video games, as well as the unique intricacies and specificities inherent to each game genre.

Furthermore, it would be interesting to consider how well-known titles from different genres, such as *Bioshock* (2007), *Uncharted: Drake's Fortune* (2007), *Horizon Zero Dawn* (2017), and *Deponia* (2012), would respond to the same study when exploring how localisation affects immersion and storytelling in their respective contexts. For example, *Deponia*, a text-heavy point-and-click game, would be a suitable candidate for exploring how localisation affects immersion and storytelling in puzzle games.

In conclusion, the present study has highlighted the need for further investigation into the intersection of storytelling, localisation, and immersion in video games. This research has demonstrated considerable potential for further design developments and considerations, and future research in this area could provide valuable insights into the language-specific impact of localisation on video games, as well as the unique intricacies and specificities inherent to each game genre.

Acknowledgements. This project has received funding from the ARDITI's postdoctoral scholarship M1420–09-5369-FSE-000002.

References

1. deHaan, J., Diamond, J.: The experience of telepresence with a foreign language video game and video. In: Proceedings of the 2007 ACM SIGGRAPH symposium on Video games, pp. 39–46. Association for Computing Machinery, New York (2007). https://doi.org/10.1145/1274940.1274951
2. Gómez-Maureira, M.A., van Duijn, M., Rieffe, C., Plaat, A.: Academic games - mapping the use of video games in research contexts. In: Proceedings of the 17th International Conference on the Foundations of Digital Games, pp. 1–10. Association for Computing Machinery, New York (2022). https://doi.org/10.1145/3555858.3555926
3. Klarkowski, M., Johnson, D., Wyeth, P., Smith, S., Phillips, C.: Operationalising and measuring flow in video games. In: Proceedings of the Annual Meeting of the Australian Special Interest Group for Computer Human Interaction, pp. 114–118. Association for Computing Machinery, New York (2015). https://doi.org/10.1145/2838739.2838826
4. Kultima, A.: Game design research. In: Proceedings of the 19th International Academic Mindtrek Conference, pp. 18–25. Association for Computing Machinery, New York (2015). https://doi.org/10.1145/2818187.2818300
5. Nóbrega, F., et al.: Designing multi-gateway interactions in: a multi-player strategy game. In: Proceedings of the 2017 CHI Conference Extended Abstracts on Human Factors in Computing Systems, pp. 226–229. ACM, New York (2017). https://doi.org/10.1145/3027063.3048411
6. Wardrip-Fruin, N.: Games, hypertext, and meaning. In: Proceedings of the 31st ACM Conference on Hypertext and Social Media, p. 3. Association for Computing Machinery, New York (2020). https://doi.org/10.1145/3372923.3404477
7. Cesário, V., Radeta, M., Matos, S., Nisi, V.: The ocean game: assessing children's engagement and learning in a museum setting using a treasure-hunt game. In: Extended Abstracts Publication of the Annual Symposium on Computer-Human Interaction in Play, pp. 99–109. ACM, New York (2017). https://doi.org/10.1145/3130859.3131435
8. Cesário, V., Trindade, R., Olim, S., Nisi, V.: Memories of Carvalhal's palace: haunted encounters, a museum experience to engage teenagers. In: Lamas, D., Loizides, F., Nacke, L., Petrie, H., Winckler, M., Zaphiris, P. (eds.) INTERACT 2019. LNCS, vol. 11749, pp. 554–557. Springer, Cham (2019). https://doi.org/10.1007/978-3-030-29390-1_36
9. Cesário, V., Olim, S., Nisi, V.: A natural history museum experience: memories of Carvalhal's palace – turning point. In: Bosser, A.-G., Millard, D.E., Hargood, C. (eds.) ICIDS 2020. LNCS, vol. 12497, pp. 339–343. Springer, Cham (2020). https://doi.org/10.1007/978-3-030-62516-0_31

10. Crawford, C.C.: Chris Crawford on Interactive Storytelling. New Riders, Berkeley (2012)
11. Mangiron, C., O'Hagan, M.: Game localisation: unleashing imagination with 'restricted'translation. J. Specialised Transl. **6**, 10–21 (2006)
12. Domsch, S.: Storyplaying: Agency and Narrative in Video Games. De Gruyter, Berlin (2013). https://doi.org/10.1515/9783110272451
13. Somerdin, M.: The game debate: video games as innovative storytelling (2016)
14. Aarseth, E.: A narrative theory of games. In: Proceedings of the International Conference on the Foundations of Digital Games, pp. 129–133. ACM, New York (2012). https://doi.org/10.1145/2282338.2282365
15. Agrawal, S., Simon, A., Bech, S., Bæntsen, K., Forchhammer, S.: Defining immersion: literature review and implications for research on audiovisual experiences. JAES **68**, 404–417 (2020)
16. Bernal-Merino, M.A.: The Localisation of Video Games (2013). https://doi.org/10.25560/39333
17. Cesário, V., Coelho, A., Nisi, V.: Enhancing museums' experiences through games and stories for young audiences. In: Nunes, N., Oakley, I., Nisi, V. (eds.) ICIDS 2017. LNCS, vol. 10690, pp. 351–354. Springer, Cham (2017). https://doi.org/10.1007/978-3-319-71027-3_41
18. Cesário, V., Coelho, A., Nisi, V.: Design patterns to enhance teens' museum experiences. In: 32nd British Human Computer Interaction Conference, pp. 1–5 (2018). https://doi.org/10.14236/ewic/HCI2018.160
19. Cesário, V., Nisi, V.: Designing mobile museum experiences for teenagers. Museum Manage. Curatorship (2022)
20. Cesário, V., Nisi, V.: Designing with teenagers: a teenage perspective on enhancing mobile museum experiences. Int. J. Child-Comput. Inter. **33**, 100454 (2022). https://doi.org/10.1016/j.ijcci.2022.100454
21. Green, A.M.: Storytelling in Video Games: The Art of the Digital Narrative. McFarland & Company, Jefferson (2017)
22. Hevia, C.M.: Video games localisation: posing new challenges to the translator. Perspectives **14**, 306–323 (2007). https://doi.org/10.1080/09076760708669046
23. Jennett, C., et al.: Measuring and defining the experience of immersion in games. Int. J. Hum Comput Stud. **66**, 641–661 (2008). https://doi.org/10.1016/j.ijhcs.2008.04.004
24. Maziarz, P., Onik, D.: cultural barriers in equivalence - the English localization of the video game Wiedźmin 3: Dziki Gon. Explorations **7**, 45–57 (2019). https://doi.org/10.25167/EXP13.19.7.6
25. IJsselsteijn, W.A., de Kort, Y.A.W., Poels, K.: The Game Experience Questionnaire. Technische Universiteit Eindhoven, Eindhoven (2013)
26. Vickery, N., Tancred, N., Wyeth, P., Johnson, D.: Directing narrative in gameplay: player interaction in shaping narrative in the witcher 3. In: Proceedings of the 30th Australian Conference on Computer-Human Interaction, pp. 495–500. Association for Computing Machinery, New York (2018). https://doi.org/10.1145/3292147.3292201
27. Mangiron, C.: Localizing Final Fantasy–bringing fantasy to reality. LISA Newsl. Glob. Insider **13**, 5 (2004)
28. Noclip - Video Game Documentaries: Translating & Adapting The Witcher 3 (2017). https://www.youtube.com/watch?v=Gxg5INjNopo

Utilizing Different Voice Value to Understand Voice Assistant Users' Enjoyment

Ai-Ni Cheng[✉]

Syracuse University, 900 South Crouse Ave., Syracuse, NY 13244, USA
aicheng@syr.edu

Abstract. This study aims to understand if various voice assistants' (VAs') voice parameters (i.e. pitch range and speech rate.) that may have effect on users' enjoyment and preference. VAs follows various voices as Siri has five kinds of recordings in the English (American) channel. For the reason that Siri has diversified voices, this research aims to use a non-binary voice (i.e. ios 15.4, recording 5) as a sample and use AUTO-TUNE software to modify their pitch ranges and speech rates. Through a web-based survey conducted on Qualtrics, participants—recruited from Amazon Mechanical Turk (MTurk)—were asked their feelings after listening to 4 patterns, which included higher pitch range, lower pitch range, higher speech rate, and lower speech rate. I ask about their enjoyment of listening to those patterns across five different categories: motivation, goal, proof, evaluation, and potential. In a sample size of 114, this study discusses how the responses differ between the different categories and how they link to various VA voice parameters. In this study, I demonstrate that various VA voice parameters have no significant effect on users' motivation, goals, proof, and evaluation. Users' potential is slightly affected by the changeable voice parameters of this human-computer interaction however it is still not significant. With this study, I indicate that the pitch range and speech rate of the voice assistant, Siri iOS 15.4 recording 5, has no effect on the enjoyment of their user's experience.

Keywords: Human-Computer Interactions · Voice Assistant · User Experience · Nonverbal Perception · Enjoyment · Voice Parameter · Siri

1 Introduction

1.1 Voice Assistants (VAs) and VA's Voice

Voice Assistants (VAs) are often used as a form of personal assistant for many people. VAs are voice-controlled mobile or personal devices which allow users to communicate with, to make some queries and have emotional connection VAs, such as Google Assistant, Microsoft Cortana, Amazon Alexa, Apple Siri and Yandex Alice [1–3].

During VA's interaction, users prefer more personalize voice assistants [4–6]. VA has personalized relation during interaction are more effective than impersonalized such as changed pitch value [4]. Social robots, included VAs, during the interaction between users are seeking to develop in a socially enriching way [5]. By personalized users'

© The Author(s), under exclusive license to Springer Nature Switzerland AG 2023
C. Stephanidis et al. (Eds.): HCII 2023, CCIS 1832, pp. 553–560, 2023.
https://doi.org/10.1007/978-3-031-35989-7_70

engagement during the interaction, this fact will raise the relationship between users and social robots [6].

On the other hand, VAs' voice might be a way to increase VAs' personalization because voice is a way to transport information [7, 8]. Pitch range and speech rate are the fundamental characteristics of the voice that indicate personality [7]. People who have loud, rapid, and broad-pitched voices are most likely extroverts [8]. Moreover, voice is important for people's enjoyment. Niculescu et al. (2011) state that using different pitches can increase overall enjoyment and interaction quality [9]. That is to say different voices' value in voice assistants might influence user experiences.

1.2   Users' Experience (UX) and VA's Voice

Enjoyment is defined as a good experience [10]. Enjoyment is the effect produced by functional and nonfunctional interactions and reflects the users' feelings during the experiment. It includes enjoying the interaction while using the voice assistant such as feeling nervous, satisfied, anxious, etc. [11].

The frequency use of VA can influence emotional aspects of this voice-controlled device's user experience [1]. Players who have positive enjoyment, such as fun, pleasure, and enjoyment, with the target device often tends to affect their motivation to interact with the device continually [12].

In short, this study aims to use enjoyment as a standard to value the users' satisfaction with various voice parameters of VA. By understanding the relationship between user's enjoyment and VA's multiple pitch range and speech rate, this research hypothesizes that VA's various voice parameters can influence users' experience and enhance their enjoyment of the interaction.

2   Methodology

This author has completed the Collaborative Institutional Training Initiative (CITI) Training and taken the Social/Behavioral Research Course (Appendix 1). This research is approved by Syracuse University Human Research Protections Program and the Institutional Review Board (IRB) authorization has been given (Appendix 2). After receiving IRB approval for the study protocol, changed voice parameters were created using AUTO software, and a web-based survey was conducted using Qualtrics.

2.1   Voice Parameters Created

Study voice parameters were created through AUTO software, Voice Recorder Pro, an audio editor platform widely used for signer, musicians, and creators. This software supports sharable files in iTunes and iCloud Drive, and has an affordable interface for users to record audio, audio mixing, modify voice value, etc. [13]. To select a more neutral voice for this study, I used IOS 15.4 Siri recording 5 in English (American) as a sample. Recording 5, according to Apple, was recorded by a non-binary person and as the reason to provide more diversified-choice voices for users [14]. As a second step, I studied the frequency pattern consumers used and chose a pattern with questions be-cause the question pattern is classified in high-arousal target audiences emotion [15]. I recorded the pattern by asking how's the weather and recorded Siri's response "The forecast is calling for a mix of rain, partly cloudy skies, and clear skies this week. Daytime temperatures will fluctuate between 43°F and 66°F, with overnight lows between 28°F and 52°F." Moreover, the speakers' voice affects personal attributions due to being raised or lowered by 20% of pitch or expanded or compressed by 30% of speech rate [7]. Therefore, I utilized the AUTO software to modify this record into four different pieces of audio: raised 20% of pitch, lowered 20% of pitch, expanded 30% of speech rate and, expanded 30% of speech rate.

2.2 Participants Recruitment

Study participants were recruited through Amazon's Mechanical Turk (Mturk), a data collection platform widely used for survey or experimental studies. Despite some constraints, many studies have found that the MTurk sample and the benchmark survey have no statistically significant difference [16]. To select the most appropriate survey participants for our study, only MTurk panelists with a previous Human Intelligence Tasks (HIT) approval rating 95% or higher were allowed to participate in the survey. As a second requirement, since our survey is conducted in English and audio pattern recorded in the United States, participation was restricted to MTurkers located in the United States. Each participant who successfully finished the survey to the end received a $0.5 reward.

2.3 Survey and Data Cleaning Process

Participants will be asked to answer survey questions about their enjoyment of voice assistant voice recordings. The survey will be based on Urakami et al research [11], the effect of naturalness of voice and empathic responses on enjoyment, attitudes and motivation for interacting with a voice user interface ,and Kono & Araake's research [12], Is it Fun?: Understanding Enjoyment in Non-Game HCI Research, to build questionnaires to measure participants' enjoyment. The questionnaire will measure how much participants enjoyed the interaction answering on 5-point Likert scales ranging from 1 (Strongly disagree) to 5 (Strongly agree) regarding enjoying the interaction; the questionnaire will measure subjective enjoyment, the questionnaire statements are in forms such as: "I enjoyed ~," "~was fun," "How enjoyable ~," and "~was enjoyable."

The questionnaire used five classifications to understand the enjoyment: background and motivation, objective and goal, support and proof, results and evaluation, and application and potential [12]. Background and motivation refer to the reason why fun is required or important in VA' voice pitch or speed rate; objective and goal refer to VA's voice pitch or speed rate aims to make users feel fun; support and proof refer to VA's voice pitch or speed rate is a supportive element to strength the pleasure of HCI; results and evaluation refer to VA's voice pitch or speed rate in HCI is enjoyable; application and potential refer to propose or mentions applicable use case or describes potentials of methods such as if I can modified VA's voice pitch or speed rate, I will feel more pleasure. These questionnaires in the survey will be recruited using Amazon's MTurk to seek respondents.

One-hundred-forty-six participants were initially recruited through MTurk. Because this study investigated the enjoyment of HCI after listening to four modified audios, this survey asked participants to listen to an original recording and a changed pitch and speed-rate audio in order to make sure interviewees feel comfortable to listen to several modified voice audio recordings. The sample was reduced to one-hundred-fourteen participants who successfully completed the survey.

3 Result

This study recruited survey participants by posting a message on the MTurk site with a title of "Utilizing different voice values to understand the enjoyment of voice assistants users". MTurk panels were then able to access an encrypted link that leads panels to the web-hosted survey. In the task description, participants were informed that they will be asked to answer about their enjoyment after listening to a recording.

Based on the enjoyment of VA's interaction [11, 12], this article captures five items to capture five dimensions of enjoyment for listening to VA's modified pitch and speed rate recording. The five categories, follow as background and motivation, objective and goal, support and proof, results and evaluation, and application and potential, are documented below.

3.1 Background and Motivation

In the background and motivation category, among one-hundred-fourteen participants, disagreements (which included strongly disagree and disagree) were 52.6% and agreements (which included strongly agree and agree) were 22.0%. Neither agree nor disagree stated 25.4%.

3.2 Objective and Goal

In the objective and goal category, among one-hundred-fourteen participants, disagreements (which included strongly disagree and disagree) were 45.8% and agreements (which included strongly agree and agree) were 29.4%. Neither agree nor disagree stated 24.8%.

3.3 Support and Proof

In the support and proof category, among one-hundred-fourteen participants, disagreements (which included strongly disagree and disagree) were 52.9% and agreements (which included strongly agree and agree) were 26.1%. Neither agree nor disagree stated 21.0%.

3.4 Results and Evaluation

In the evaluation category, among one-hundred-fourteen participants, disagreements (which included strongly disagree and disagree) were 49.2% and agreements (which included strongly agree and agree) were 24.1%. Neither agree nor disagree stated 26.6%.

3.5 Application and Potential

In the application and potential category, among one-hundred-fourteen participants, disagreements (which included strongly disagree and disagree) were 27.7% and agreements (which included strongly agree and agree) were 48.4%. Neither agree nor disagree stated 24.0%.

4 Conclusion

The findings of this study do not lend support to the hypothesis that VA's various voice parameters have significant effects on influencing UX of their enjoyment.

52.6% participants disagree that voice's higher or lower pitch and expanded or compressed speed rate are important factors that can entertain them. 45.8% participants disagree that they feel that a voice's higher or lower pitch and expanded or compressed speed rate is fun as a personal assistant. 52.9% participants disagree that after hearing the recording, they feel it gives participants pleasure. 49.2% participants disagree that those are a fun experience after listening to the recordings. On the other hand, 48.4% participants agree that if one can modify the voice, the voice assistant will amuse the user more.

Regarding the overall enjoyment of VA's voice parameters, it yielded no statistical difference between the voice pitch and speed rate. Even though 48.4% of interviewees agree that the potential category – modify the voice, the voice assistant will amuse the user more – this sample is still not a significant result. That is to say, this study is unable to make an assertion in favor of a significant difference.

5 Limitation and Challenge

Throughout the study, a number of limitations impeded achieving the kind of results sought. One limitation that we faced was users' nonverbal perception. Response length (syllables) and response time in communicate interaction are affect one's perception [7], making it a challenge with a limit to pitch and speed rate. In addition, because participants can't modify the pitch and speed rate during the survey, this fact might lead to impersonalization and decrease their enjoyment. Another limitation that we faced was the absence of different voices, such as Siri record 1 to record 4. This limited the diversity of these results in terms of recording 5 individuals. Since no respondents identified significant enjoyment with those changed voice pitch and speed rate, it was there-fore impossible to make a connection between other VA's voices. Had this study been able to get a greater pattern of nonverbal perceptions and diversity vocal recording, these results would've held more significance.

6 Future Works

The goal of this study is aim to gain knowledge that can be used in the further research, design a foreign language (FL) learning support with the potential aspect.

This author is a graduate student that grew up in Taiwan and then moved to upstate New York. For foreign students, it's possible to learn English before entering the US, however, the English proficiency we built up for the TOEFL exam is still deficient for the real world. Given that a large percentage of conversational English is only understood at a deeper level. Therefore, based on the challenge and research, I worked with SU English Language Institute (ELI) to understand if a changeable speed rate of VA can support users' learning FL experience.

In short, this author want to design a VA that can enhance target users' UX and support FL learners. This further research uses the changeable speed rate in VA to do a further design, and conducts target users' experience to create a language learning support VA.

Appendices

Appendix 1. Collaborative Institutional Training Initiative (CITI) Training

Completion Date 17-Sep-2021
Expiration Date 16-Sep-2024
Record ID   45139862

This is to certify that:

Ai-Ni Cheng

Has completed the following CITI Program course:

Not valid for renewal of certification through CME.

Basic/Refresher Course - Human Subjects Research
(Curriculum Group)
Social/Behavioral Research Course
(Course Learner Group)
2 - Refresher Course
(Stage)

Under requirements set by:

Syracuse University

Collaborative Institutional Training Initiative

Verify at www.citiprogram.org/verify/?w5cb96a31-6fe2-451c-9136-8eb813f64abf-45139862

Appendix 2. Institutional Review Board (IRB) Authorization

 Syracuse University

INSTITUTIONAL REVIEW BOARD
MEMORANDUM

TO: James Fathers
DATE: November 4, 2022
SUBJECT: Determination of Exemption from Regulations
IRB #:   22-334
TITLE: *Design a Personalize Voice Assistant by Utilizing Different Voice Value to Understand the Enjoyment of Voice Assistant Users*

The above referenced application, submitted for consideration as exempt from federal regulations as defined in 45 C.F.R. 46, has been evaluated by the Institutional Review Board (IRB) for the following:

1. determination that it falls within one or more of the eight exempt categories allowed by the organization;
2. determination that the research meets the organization's ethical standards.

It has been determined by the IRB this protocol qualifies for exemption and has been assigned to category 2. This authorization will remain active for a period of five years from **November 4, 2022** until **November 3, 2027**.

CHANGES TO PROTOCOL: Proposed changes to this protocol during the period for which IRB authorization has already been given, cannot be initiated without additional IRB review. If there is a change in your research, you should notify the IRB immediately to determine whether your research protocol continues to qualify for exemption or if submission of an expedited or full board IRB protocol is required. Information about the University's human participants protection program can be found at: http://researchintegrity.syr.edu/human-research/. Protocol changes are requested on an amendment application available on the IRB web site; please reference your IRB number and attach any documents that are being amended.

STUDY COMPLETION: Study completion is when all research activities are complete or when a study is closed to enrollment and only data analysis remains on data that have been de-identified. A Study Closure Form should be completed and submitted to the IRB for review (**Study Closure Form**).

Thank you for your cooperation in our shared efforts to assure that the rights and welfare of people participating in research are protected.

Tracy J Cromp

Tracy Cromp, M.S.W.
Director

DEPT: VPA School of Design, 100 Crouse Dr, Syracuse, NY 13244   STUDENT: A-Ni Chang

Office of Research Integrity and Protections   T: 315.443.3013
214 Lyman Hall, 100 College Place   orip@syr.edu
Syracuse, NY 13244

References

1. Arlinghaus, C.S, Ollermann, F.: Hey, Siri®! ok, Google®! does talking to voice assistants enhance emotional aspects of mobile phone user experience? In: Mensch und Computer 2022, pp 382–388. ACM, Darmstadt Germany (2022)

2. Al-Kaisi, A.N., Arkhangelskaya, A.L., Rudenko-Morgun, O.I.: The didactic potential of the voice assistant "Alice" for students of a foreign language at a university. Educ. Inf. Technol. **26**(1), 715–732 (2020). https://doi.org/10.1007/s10639-020-10277-2

3. Le Pailleur, F., Huang, B., Léger, P.-M., Sénécal, S.: A new approach to measure user experience with voice-controlled intelligent assistants: a pilot study. In: Kurosu, M. (ed.) HCII 2020. LNCS, vol. 12182, pp. 197–208. Springer, Cham (2020). https://doi.org/10.1007/978-3-030-49062-1_13

4. Machado, S., Duarte, E., Teles, J., Reis, L., Rebelo, F.: Selection of a voice for a speech signal for personalized warnings: the effect of speaker's gender and voice pitch. Work **41**, 3592–3598 (2012). https://doi.org/10.3233/WOR-2012-0670-3592

5. van Doorn, J., et al.: Domo arigato Mr. Roboto: emergence of automated social presence in organizational frontlines and customers' service experiences. J. Serv. Res. **20**, 43–58. https://doi.org/10.1177/1094670516679272 (2017)

6. Khan, S., Iqbal, M.: AI-powered customer service: does it optimize customer experience? In: 2020 8th International Conference on Reliability, Infocom Technologies and Optimization (Trends and Future Directions) (ICRITO), pp 590–594. IEEE, Noida (2020)

7. Apple, W., Streeter, L.A.: Effects of pitch and speech rate on personal attributions, J. Pers. Soc. Psychol. (1979)

8. Eden, B.L: Clifford Nass and Scott brave's wired for speech: how voice activates and advances the human-computer relationship. J. Assoc. Hist. Comput. (2006)

9. Niculescu, A., Dijk, B., Nijholt, A., See, S: The influence of voice pitch on the evaluation of a social robot receptionist (2011)

10. Brandtzæg, P.B., Følstad, A., Heim, J.: Enjoyment: lessons from Karasek. In: Blythe, M., Monk, A. (eds.) Funology 2. HIS, pp. 331–341. Springer, Cham (2018). https://doi.org/10.1007/978-3-319-68213-6_21

11. Urakami, J., Sutthithatip, S., Moore, B.A.: The Effect of naturalness of voice and empathic responses on enjoyment, attitudes and motivation for interacting with a voice user interface. In: Kurosu, M. (ed.) HCII 2020. LNCS, vol. 12182, pp. 244–259. Springer, Cham (2020). https://doi.org/10.1007/978-3-030-49062-1_17

12. Kono, M., Araake, K.: Is it fun?: Understanding enjoyment in non-game HCI research (2022)

13. Linfei Ltd. Voice Recorder Pro, App Store (2022)

14. Axon, S.: HEY SIRI - Apple will add fifth US English Siri voice in iOS 15.4. In: ars TECHNICA (2022). https://arstechnica.com/gadgets/2022/02/apple-will-add-fifth-us-english-siri-voice-in-ios-15-4/

15. El Ayadi, M., Kamel, M.S., Karray, F.: Survey on speech emotion recognition: features, classification schemes, and databases. Pattern Recogn. **44**, 572–587 (2011). https://doi.org/10.1016/j.patcog.2010.09.020

16. Buhrmester, M.D., Talaifar, S., Gosling, S.D.: An evaluation of amazon's mechanical Turk, its rapid rise, and its effective Use. Perspect. Psychol. Sci. **13**, 149–154 (2018). https://doi.org/10.1177/1745691617706516

User Experience of Croatian National & Nature Parks' Website – A Comparison

Mihaela Franjić[1]([⊠]) [iD], Tihana Galinac Grbac[2], and Boštjan Brumen[3]

[1] Faculty of Tourism, University of Maribor, Cesta Prvih Borcev 36, 8250 Brežice, Slovenia
mihaela.franjic1@um.si

[2] Department of Engineering, Juraj Dobrila University of Pula, Zagrebačka 30, 52100 Pula, Croatia
tgalinac@unipu.hr

[3] Faculty of Electrical Engineering and Computer Science, University of Maribor, Koroška Cesta 46, 2000 Maribo, r, Slovenia
bostjan.brumen@um.si

Abstract. Tourism is a dynamic area, as the COVID–19 pandemic has shown. Many external factors influence tourism, including the development of digital technologies, which must be monitored in parallel to other developments in the field. In this paper, we research the user experience of websites of Croatian National and Natural parks, which are a national treasure of exceptional importance for Croatian tourism, and which annually attract around 3.5 million tourists. For the first time, in 2017, the parks of Croatia integrated all the parks on one website through the PARCS project to better inform users and promote the parks as a brand in the tourist market. Precisely for this reason, we are interested in how users interact with the website www.parkovihrvatske.hr, since the site's appearance has not been renewed since 2017. It is crucial to know the opinion of potential users because, more than half of the time, they plan and book their trip via the Internet, which is an example of Human-Computer Interaction. The research enabled us to compare respondents, connect expectations and evaluations, and ultimately provide an additional opinion about the website. Based on the analysis, we present guidelines for upgrading the website.

Keywords: Human-Computer Interaction · User Experience · Croatian National and Natural Park(s)

1 Introduction

Croatia is a popular tourist destination with up to 20% tourism share in GDP through the past [1, 2], together with nature as one of the essential factors for tourism success [3] and European trip motivators [4]. Before the COVID-19 pandemic, Croatia had a record number of tourist overnight stays, especially foreign (87%), while domestic had a lower share of 13% [3]. It is important to mention that 10% of Croatia's surface is protected by Nature Protection Act, and that includes eight National parks (hereinafter NP) and twelve Nature parks (hereinafter PP) as the basis of natural diversity along the geographic

C. Stephanidis et al. (Eds.): HCII 2023, CCIS 1832, pp. 561–570, 2023.
https://doi.org/10.1007/978-3-031-35989-7_71

park Vis archipelago and Papuk and one biosphere reserve Mura–Drava–Danube [3]. To raise the quality of service and remove barriers to effective management of protected areas and connectivity of the park, in 2017, the PARCS project was completed, based on which the website www.parkovihrvatske.hr was created [5]. Through the project, a marketing and communication strategy was developed, a web portal with a web shop for online ticket purchases was launched, and a mobile application was created (which no longer exists today). The brand's digital pages also appeared on social networks such as Facebook and Instagram [6] for the 19 parks. Additionally, PP Dinara, which was declared a PP after the completion of the PARCS project, was added to the website.

For a long, researchers have been aware that it is essential to understand how users perceive a website and that getting feedback is a very expensive and time–consuming task. Therefore, they linked good survey results with quality implementations, i.e., the quality of the website was measured by how users saw it–User Experience (UX) and Interface (UI). Also, the Internet has enabled the development of new ways of selling the distribution of tourist services and products with specific opportunities and challenges in the market [7]. Websites have evolved mainly because they help small and medium–sized (SMEs) organizations reduce costs, time and help them market and present themselves to users [8]. For the above reasons, we decided to investigate user satisfaction with the website www.parkovihrvatske.hr.

2   Literature Review

The latest International Telecommunication Union (ITU) data showed the difference between 2019 and 2021 was in 782 million Internet users, an increase of 10% at the time of the COVID-19 pandemic [9]. We can say that a "mini-revolution" occurred during the current 4th Industrial Revolution overwhelmed by digital technologies [10, 11], which brought changes in the way people do certain things and how society behaves [12, 13].

The use of digital enables cross–border interactions with suppliers, competitors, and, most importantly, customers [14, 15]. User expectations and habits have changed, which required the modernization and introduction of digital, which also represented additional pressure on organizations [16, 17].

2.1   Digital Platforms in Tourism

Digital tourism development is focused on learning, sharing experiences and creativity, reaching a broad audience and they are, before everything, interdependent for further development and realization of opportunities [18]. According to the OECD, 77% of business services (food, beverage and accommodation) in 2020 had a website and use social networks, what shaped tourism ecosystem. This means that tourism has accepted e-commerce, internet platforms and payment systems [19]. For success, there are specific rules that a digital product must meet, i.e., it should be: easy to use, provide a rich UX, be visually pleasing, have a positive contribution to society and a specific value, and its performance conclusively influences user behaviour, which means that should be adaptable and usable [20].

Foreign users rely heavily on digital platforms when planning their trips, comparing specific destinations and gathering information which helps users in decision-making process for purchase. Research has shown a positive connection between tourist arrivals and the size of the tourism industry at a destination that has adopted digital tools [21].

A more straightforward online way, a comparison with other providers, "new" consumer habits and a broader marketing approach are just some of the main reasons for the growing development of digital platforms and online travel reservations [22]. The implementation of modern technologies is essential because it makes the difference between being chosen or not being chosen. It is the first and most important step, which affects the satisfaction of the tourist, who, if she encounters obstacles, cannot plan on her own and be autonomous [23]. According to the 2018 data, 82.2% of users booked a service or product without human interaction [24]. Just this fact is highlighting the importance of optimized Human-Computer Interaction (HCI) on websites.

2.2 Satisfaction as a Key Factor

HCI is considered as a multidisciplinary field focused on humans, i.e., the design pays attention to the usability [25] and how a person will approach a particular product from a different point of view [26, 27]. Users have certain expectations before the interaction, which is necessary to meet and find out what they do and do not prefer to adapt the website as much as possible [28]. In some studies, authors noted that HCI, together with UX and UI as key for designing services [29] are also culture–dependent. Different cultures have different attitudes towards things and people, lifestyles, personalities, emotions, aspects, thinking, and categorization, and this is also the basis of user behaviour and at the end of their experience [30]. It was demonstrated that different cultures react differently and have experience with the product based on: colour, material, visual display, speed, scenario, communication, style and the like [31]. From the point of view of website owners and practitioners, it is necessary to adapt the content for different ethnic groups if the goal is promotion outside their own country. They also mentioned the need for additional research related to cultural dimensions to create a web page with as many languages, content and customised structures as possible. If websites want satisfied users worldwide, they should design a "culturally sensitive website" to be competitive in the marketplace [32]. That is why we need a clearer picture of services to provide users with an adequate and interesting digital platform [33]. Likewise, we must consider that if technology advances, it is not proportionate and necessary for users to change. Also to pay attention on their emotional state, culture, nationality and other.

As a rule, official digital sites should have a "good" plan [34], i.e., with their simple, clear and consistent design [26] and approach to facilitate interaction, shorten "steps", and thus reduce errors by users [35].

Iitsuka and Matsuo found that the requirement to sign up slows down online purchases and increases the likelihood that customers will abandon the purchase. As many as 45% of researchers in this study said they left the site after forgetting their login information [35]. Company PwC researched how to give users a great UX, i.e., how to be loyal, buy more, or share their experiences with others. The survey showed that 32% of all customers are willing to terminate any cooperation and interaction with an organisation or brand after only one bad experience [36]. Also, some previous research noted that

Internet users can easily and quickly assess whether the things presented to the user are worthy of attention and that the site user or visitor can make a positive or negative decision within 8 s. This is evidenced by a study conducted by Microsoft, which found that the average range of human attention decreased from 12 s in 2000 to only 8 s in 2013 [37].

3 Problem Statement, Objectives and Aim

Tourism websites are constantly changing over the years – from performance, style, advertising, online shopping and others. Since, according to the data, 87% of the guests are foreigners, and Croatia turns out to be nature as its tourist trump card together with parks, our aim was to find out more about the opinion of users who visited the website www.parkovihrvatske.hr. It is important because, according to our literature, about half and more of them plan or book travel over the Internet, so this is another reason to test UX and UI on the chosen website. We were interested in how different users (not only from Croatia) perceive the mentioned website from UX and UI and whether their experiences are different or the same. For the same reason, we will examine whether a correlation exists between the expectations of the park representatives and the users whose opinions we are interested in, but we will focus on the experience and mostly on satisfaction.

We believe that users and designers want the products to be easy to use, have a purpose, contribute to society and be attractive. So, our objective was to find out if the expectations of owners and UI together with UI are matched.

So far, no research has been known to us that includes respondents from several different countries for the UX related to www.parkovihrvatske.hr or any other Croatian tourism website. We believe the data collected would provide a clear picture of how users experience the website and guide the administrators in planning further steps in design, marketing and other fields through which end users are reached. Also, this research aims to check the current state of connection with users and what needs to be done in their opinion to maintain contact and to define the direction of improvement [34].

4 Methods

We used both qualitative and quantitative research methods. For getting the expectations of site owners, we used the interview as a starting point and general information about the project and data about users. We received the UX and UI through a survey for which we had 3 groups: Foreign, Domestic and Representatives respondents.

4.1 An Interview as a Starting Point

In May 2022, we interviewed the responsible person from the Directorate for Nature Protection, Ministry of Economy and Sustainable Development (MINGOR), under whose administration the website belongs.

We found out that the site has not been updated since its inception, that they have never checked user satisfaction, and that foreign users can only use email for contact, but that there have been no major problems so far. The errors that occur most often are related to double registration of the user, a long sales route, and a lack of foreign languages. Through interviews, we found out that their user data management is poorly developed and that the website is managed by an outsourced company and they don't track site statistics. Most important was that they believe in importance of newer technologies.

4.2 Survey and Data Analysis

Guided by the literature [38–41], we divided answers in eight variables/elements: Design and layout, Technical Factors, Accessibility, User-friendliness, Adequacy of content, Quality of content, Functionality of webshop and Overall Satisfaction. We used and adapted the questionnaire from different sources [42–44, 45]. We had a questionnaire for our users in two different languages; Croatian for domestic and English for foreign respondents. Another questionnaire was a bit different and was intended for representatives of the parks. They had the task of predicting how the respondents would evaluate certain elements. The respondents had the condition that they had to visit the website and complete one task on it, and if they did not do it, then the survey was over for them. The method we used was snowball sampling [sedgwick] and our respondents had special traits (to visit the website). The survey was open online at www.1ka.si from the end of May until July 2022. We processed certain data and tests using the IBM SPSS Statistics 27 tool, using alpha value of 0.05. We followed GDPR limitations and our surveys were anonymous.

4.3 Results

We had 636 people clicking on the invitation link to participate at the survey. Overall, a total of 168 people answered the surveys correctly (valid answers), and the percentage of complete surveys is about 26%. Domestic respondents (N = 60) were are coming from Croatia as representatives (n = 43). Our foreign respondents (N = 65) were mostly from the following countries: Serbia, United Kingdom, Bosnia and Herzegovina, Netherlands, Slovenia, Austria, France, Italy, Finland and others. We cannot say that certain respondents represent their home country based on a low number of respondents from a given country. Respondents were mostly female with completed higher education and were about 27 years old, while representatives were on average 42 years old.

We wanted to get a broader picture from the data, so we analyzed data with Costumer satisfaction evaluation (CSAT), Net promoter score (NPS) and test with SPSS tool; Pearson Correlation Coefficient – r and ANOVA test in the example of evaluation.

From Table 1 is obvious that foreign and representatives are close with the CSAT evaluation with almost 69% and that domestic users have the lowest average and satisfaction of 63%. They are most satisfied with the Quality of the content and unhappy with the functionality of webshop. Looking at 8 variables, the highest ratings were given by foreign respondents, who rated 5 variables the best, followed by park representatives. The strictest were domestic respondents, who rated 7 variables with the lowest of all three mentioned groups. We can conclude that in CSAT there is the biggest difference between foreign and domestic respondents (11%).

Table 1. Average CSAT evaluations of each element by groups

Element/variable	Average of foreign	Average of domestic	Average of representatives
Design and layout attractivness	75%	69%	72%
Technical factors	71%	67%	73%
Accessibility	65%	59%	62%
User-friendliness	69%	66%	68%
Adequacy of content	71%	66%	58%
Quality of content	75%	68%	75%
Functionality of webshop	53%	42%	67%
Satisfaction	72%	66%	72%
Average	**69%**	**63%**	**68%**

As for the NPS score, all groups are classified as detractors bordering with passive users, which means they are critical of the website and would not recommend to others.

Also, Pearson's correlation test showed that says there is a strong and high correlation between the expectations of park representatives and user experience ($r = 0,79$, $r2 = 0,6241$, $p < 0,000$).

ANOVA showed that the difference exists ($F = 26,560$, $P < 000$, $df = 2$). Using the Post Hoc tests, we can say that the most common difference between foreign and domestic respondents is in each variable, but there is not only in difference in User–Friendliness. This means that in the end, based on the tests, we can say that there are differences between satisfaction of domestic and foreign users and park representatives in all variables except User–Friendliness.

The hypotheses that between the groups were no significant difference were rejected, which means that each group evaluated differently, while park representatives and foreigners shared a somehow similar opinion, and that there is a connection between the expectations of the representatives and the user experience.

5 Discussion and Conclusion

Finally, regarding user opinion, we can say that it is divided, although it is more critical. Respondents like the design, colours and maps the most. On the other side, there is a room for improvement. The devastating fact is that they would not recommend the website to others, which greatly affects the brand as such. We can assume that domestic respondents are more critical because they know the offer "better", expect to learn something new on the website and be able to buy tickets for all the parks. This kind of (dis)satisfaction greatly affects their autonomy when planning their trip, and we believe that the renewal of the website will attract more potential visitors. They lack tickets for all parks in one place, they expect higher security with https protocol. One of the problems is that the site lacks FAQ, a contact phone number and a chatbot that most modern sales sites use. Some of the respondents stated that it is necessary to add other additional options, such as accommodation, weather forecast, packages and promotional discounts and other. In their opinion, the prices, working hours of the parks, instructions on transport and available transport, directory and list of parks should be specially emphasized, to highlight for whom the services and products are suitable, and to emphasize whether it is allowed to take animals.

At the end of the research, we can say that there is a high correlation between the representatives' expectations user's actual evaluation. This means that representatives are probably aware that they are unhappy with the current state of the website, engagement and that the site's out-of-datedness greatly affect UX and UI. Representatives believe that the UX and UI can be improved with the benefits of newer technologies (Artificial Intelligence, Cloud computing and other), implementation of App, the progress of social media and with translation into several languages. They see this way of promotion as an opportunity for "less-known" parks, but when we asked them about the future of further development, they did not have any form of strategic planning.

In case all the pieces of information are in one place would shorten the steps for the user, user would choose the most similar package and, in this way, without "heavy" research, get to know what she can expect in a particular park and its surroundings. Such platforms already exist on the European and World markets, they achieve the competitiveness and sustainability of tourism at the local, regional and national level.

5.1 Limitations

The key limitations are that we could not access all information classified as internal within NP and PP organisations. Also, we lack access to the site as an administrator so that we could assign tasks to our respondents, and measure time and performance. For this reason, we will not be able to measure two of the three UX indicators according to ISO standards (effectiveness, efficiency). Due to the chosen methodology, we could not monitor how people respond and how much time they need to complete a given task.

5.2 Concluding Remarks

Finally, the National Parks are facing numerous challenges, in attracting funding for their maintenance but also in meeting user experience criteria while facing tourist cultural diversity. Furthermore, new ideas are needed to deal with parks operational efficiency and effectiveness while addressing global sustainability goals. In that avenue, the wider adoption of ICT technologies can bring numerous benefits.

Acknowledgement. We acknowledge the support of the Croatian Science Foundation research project no. HRZZ-IP-2019-04-4216.

References

1. Statista. https://www.statista.com/topics/7340/travel-and-tourism-in-croatia/#topicHeader__wrapper. Accessed 17 Aug 2022
2. HGK. https://hgk.hr/documents/hrvatsko-gospodarstvo-2020-web6107a81e2f243.pdf. Accessed 2022/5/7
3. CNTB. https://croatia.hr/hr-HR/dozivljaji/priroda?term_node_tid_custom%5B0%5D=1097#view-id-personalize_your_trip. Accessed 3 Apr 2022
4. Flash Eurobarometer, https://mtu.gov.hu/documents/prod/fl_392_sum_en.pdf, last accessed 28. 8. 2022
5. MZOE, Project PARCS: Brochure. Tiskara Grafing, Zagreb (2017)
6. GEF. https://www.thegef.org/search?search=PARCS&btnSearch=Search. Accessed 19 Jun 2022
7. Buhalis, D.: eTourism: Information technology for strategic tourism management. Harlow. Pearson/Prentice Hall, UK (2003)
8. Corigliano, M.A, Baggio, R.: On the significance of tourism website evaluations. In: Hitz, M., Sigala, M., Murphy, J. (eds) Information and Communication Technologies in Tourism 2006, pp 320–321, Springer, Vienna (2006)
9. ITU. https://www.itu.int/itu-d/reports/statistics/2021/11/15/internet-use/. Accessed 19 Jun 2022
10. Fernández–Macías, E.: Automation, digitalisation and platforms: Implications for work and employment. Publications Office of the European Union Luxembourg (2018)
11. Smith, C., Crespo–Dubie, D.: What is the Digital Age and the Internet of Things. Carefree, Arizona: Smith & Associates (2018)
12. Merritt, B.: The digital revolution. Synthesis. Lectures on Emerging Engineering Technologies, vol. 2, no. 4, pp 1–109 (2016). https://doi.org/10.1007/978-3-031-02029-2_4
13. Nankervis, A., Connell, J., Montague, A., Burgess, J. (eds.): The fourth industrial revolution. Springer, Singapore (2021). https://doi.org/10.1007/978-981-16-1614-3
14. Verhoef, P.C., et al.: Digital transformation: a multidisciplinary reflection and research agenda. J. Bus. Res. **122**, 889–901 (2021)
15. Yokogawa. https://www.yokogawa.com/library/resources/white-papers/the-differences-between-digitization-digitalization-and-digital-transformation-in-manufacturing/, 12 Jun 2022
16. Sht, K.: Impact of covid–19 on tourism industry: A review. Department of Operations Management, Faculty of Management, University of Peradeniya (2020)
17. OECD, How's Life in the Digital Age? Opportunities and Risks of the Digital Transformation for People's Well–being. OECD Publishing, Paris (2019)
18. Dredge, D., Phi, G.T.L., Mahadevan, R., Meehan, E., Popescu, E.: Digitalisation in Tourism: In–depth analysis of challenges and opportunities. Executive Agency for Small and Medium–sized Enterprises (EASME), European Commission (2019)
19. OECD, Tourism Trends and Policies 2020. OECD Publishing, Paris (2020)
20. Nylén, D., Holmström, J.: Digital innovation strategy: a framework for diagnosing and improving digital product and service innovation. Bus. Horiz. **58**(1), 57–67 (2015)
21. Lopez Cordova, J. E.: Digital platforms and the demand for international tourism services. World Bank Policy Research Working Paper, vol. 9147, pp. 1–34 (2020)
22. Dominique–Ferreira, S., Viana, M., Prentice, C.: Developing a digital platform based on a design and marketing approach. In: 2021 16th Iberian Conference on Information Systems and Technologies (CISTI). Chaves: IEEE (2021)
23. Fernández-Herrero, M., Hernández-Maestro, R.M., González-Benito, Ó.: Effects on the "self-organization- satisfaction" relationship of changes in the economic context. Asia Pacific J. Tourism Res. **24**(7), 658–668 (2019)

24. Papadakis, S., Tsakirakis K.: The digital transformation of the tourism industry. (Magister thesis). International Hellenic University, Hospitality and Tourism Management, Thessaloniki (2020)

25. Janzen, S.: Advancing the advanced search: improving the web of science user experience with a spreadsheet search query tool. In: Stephanidis, C., Antona, M., Ntoa, S. (eds) HCI International 2022 Posters. HCII 2022. Communications in Computer and Information Science, vol. 1580, pp. 292–299, Springer, Cham (2022). https://doi.org/10.1007/978-3-031-06417-3_40

26. Marcus, A.: HCI and user–experience design. Human–Computer Interaction Series, pp. 265–269, Springer, London (2015). https://doi.org/10.1007/978-1-4471-6744-0

27. Kim, G.J.: Human–Computer Interaction: Fundamentals and Practice. CRC Press, Boca Raton (2015)

28. Michalco, J., Simonsen, J.G., Hornbæk, K.: An exploration of the relation between expectations and user experience. Int. J. Hum.-Comput. Interact. **31**(9), 603–617 (2015)

29. Baird, C.: Useful, usable, desirable: applying user experience design to your library: Aaron Schmidt and Amanda etches. J. Electron. Resour. Librariansh. **27**(2), 142–143 (2015)

30. De Mooij, M., Hofstede, G.: Cross–cultural consumer behaviour: a review of research findings. J. Int. Consum. Mark. **23**(3–4), 181–192 (2011)

31. Liu, P., Keung, C.: Defining cross-culture theoretical framework of user interface. In: Rau, P.L.P. (eds.) Cross-Cultural Design. Methods, Practice, and Case Studies. CCD 2013. Lecture Notes in Computer Science, vol. 8023, pp. 235-242. Springer, Berlin (2013). https://doi.org/10.1007/978-3-642-39143-9_26

32. Fletcher, R.: The impact of culture on web site content, design, and structure: an international and a multicultural perspective. J. Commun. Manag. **10**(3), 259–273 (2006)

33. Albert, B., Tullis, T.: Measuring the user Experience: Collecting, Analyzing, and Presenting Usability Metrics, 2. Newnes, Elsevier (2013)

34. Sabukunze, I.D., Arakaza, A.: User experience analysis on mobile application design using user experience questionnaire. Indonesian J. Inf. Syst. **4**(1), 15–26 (2021)

35. Iitsuka, S., Matsuo, Y.: Website optimization problem and its solutions. In: Proceedings of the 21st ACM SIGKDD International Conference on Knowledge Discovery and Data Mining, pp 447–456 (2015)

36. PwC. https://www.pwc.com/us/en/advisory-services/publications/consumer-intelligence-series/pwc-consumer-intelligence-series-customer-experience.pdf. Accessed 29 Jul 2022

37. MatAllenProductions. https://mattallenproductions.com/the-power-video-infographics/. Accessed 30 May 2022

38. Morville, P.: Ambient Findability: What we find Changes who we become. O'Reilly Media, Inc, Sebastopol (2005)

39. Lewis, J.R., Sauro, J.: Item benchmarks for the system usability scale. J. Usability Stud. **13**(3), 158–167 (2018)

40. Knight, W.: What is user experience? In: UX for Developers. 1–12. Apress, Berkeley, CA (2019)

41. Arthana, I., Pradnyana, I., Dantes, G.: Usability testing on website wadaya based on ISO 9241–11. J. Phys: Conf. Ser. **1165**(1), 1–8 (2019)

42. UEQ. https://www.ueq-online.org/. Accessed 31 May 2022

43. QuestionPro survey software. https://www.questionpro.com/survey-templates/user-interface-survey-questions/. Accessed 31 Apr 2022
44. McLellan, S., Muddimer, A., Peres, S.C.: The effect of experience on system usability scale ratings. J. Usability Stud. **7**(2), 56–67 (2012)
45. Ibadi, T., Yolanda, A., Raihan, M., Wirawan, A.: Analisa Website Coursera menggunakan metode system usability ScalE (SUS). Prosiding Seminar Hasil Penelitian Vokasi (Semhavok) **3**(2), 193–197 (2022)

Time Loss Aversion

Ziwei Gao[✉]

University College London, London, UK
annannika.biu@gmail.com

Abstract. The present paper introduces "Time Loss Aversion" - people's tendency to fear previous misallocations of time, which then motivates people to change their future behaviour. Loss aversion has previously been achieved through framing outcomes as losses. Previous research has induced loss aversion by framing monetary outcomes as losses rather than gains.. It presents a case study where time loss aversion was used to decrease people's social media use. Social media use was framed in a manner of time spent in one week, a month or a year, rather than in terms of daily averages (the usual approach in screen time apps). This framing significantly motivated people to reduce their future social media use. Time loss aversion has implications for "time-based addictions" - addictions where the misallocation of time results in negative outcomes to people's health, productivity and well-being. Finally, the paper discusses how time loss aversion can be implemented in the UX and UI of mobile devices and wearables to promote better outcomes for users.

Keywords: Time Loss Aversion · Social Media · Behaviour Change

1   Introduction

The present paper introduces and describes "Time Loss Aversion" - a tendency for people to fear previous uses of their time, usually due to over engaging with a certain activity. As people see this as a misallocation of time, they are then motivated to change their future behaviour by engaging with that activity less and engaging in other activities more. For example, people often feel regret after binge watching multiple episodes of a television program (Pittman and Steiner 2019). Time loss aversion does not only motivate people to change their behaviour, but it also helps people realise how they spent their time. Thus, time loss aversion can promote better time organisation.

This paper will start with a review of the loss aversion literature. It will then discuss time as an important factor to human decision making and its relation to loss aversion. Then it will introduce and define Time Loss Aversion, and outline a case study of how it influenced people's willingness to use social media in the future. Finally, the findings and implication of using time loss aversion for HCI, UX and UI will be discussed.

2 Loss Aversion

Older theories in economics positing that people are rational actors that maximise their utility (Von Neumann and Morgenstern 1947) has since been challenged and disproved by work done within the tradition of bounded rationality. Bounded rationality is a concept proposed by Herbert Simon which suggests that people's ability to be rational is bounded by factors, including limited information, limited time, limited attention, as well as social, emotional and practical factors (Simon 1990). People don't fully analyse all the available information, options and consequences before making a decision but rather rely on heuristics and assumptions to make decisions more efficiently.

Loss aversion is a behavioural economics concept that describes the tendency of people to prefer avoiding losses over acquiring gains of equal or greater value (Kahneman and Tversky 1984). Individuals are more likely to feel the pain of a loss more acutely than they feel the pleasure of an equivalent gain, and will often take greater risks to avoid losses than to achieve gains. The tendency was discovered by Kahneman and Tversky who modelled and explained it through prospect theory. Prospect theory suggests people make decisions based on perceived gains and losses rather than on absolute outcomes (Kahneman and Tversky 1979). It proposes that people evaluate potential losses and gains relative to a reference point, and the perceived value of the outcomes is influenced by the way they are presented or framed. Framing refers to the way that a decision or problem is presented can influence an individual's perception and subsequent choices (Novemsky and Kahneman 2005).

For instance, people might give a scenario where they are given the choice between 100% chance of losing $50 or a 50% chance of losing $100. In this "loss" frame, people are more likely to choose the 50% chance of losing $100, exhibiting risk-seeking behaviour. Conversely, if presented with the choice between a 100% chance of gaining $50 or a 50% chance of gaining $100, people are more likely to choose the 100% chance of gaining $50, exhibiting risk-averse behaviour.

Studies have shown that loss aversion can also be induced for outcomes that are not monetary. In the earliest example of non-monetary loss aversion, when a public health policy outcome is presented as the number of lives lost instead of saved, it can lead to an increased risk-taking behaviour due to the fear of loss (Kahneman and Tversky 1984). People on average thus are more likely to pick a policy where there is a 50% chance of saving 100 people from getting an illness, versus a 100% chance of saving 50 people from getting an illness.

Loss aversion is also present in productivity. When grades are framed in terms of losses, it motivates students to work harder to achieve higher grades (McEvoy 2016). Students who received feedback in "points lost" and started with 100 percent earned statistically higher grades than students who received feedback in "points earned" and started at 0, while controlling the other factors that may have affected student performance e.g. previous GPA, attendance.

2.1 Decision-Making on Time Allocation

Research has now shown that participants show similar decision patterns when making trade-offs about time. In one study, participants were given a total amount of participation time in a study (Paese 1995). They had a chance to make a decision involving risk that would either increase or decrease their participation time. The way people made decisions about allocated time replicated the way they made decisions in other domains. These patterns replicate when people are making real time allocation decisions outside of laboratory settings. People perceive time they spend waiting as a loss, which results in a greater amount of risk-seeking behaviour (Kroll and Vogt 2008). Another study found that children at school have a time loss aversion during their lunch break which influences their choices for school lunch (Sharma et al. 2018).

Loss aversion can also drive people's behaviour. Recent research has shown that Fear of Missing Out (FOMO) can be explained in terms of loss aversion - people dislike missing out a part of an experience and as a result will engage with it more (Gupta and Shrivastava 2021). Indeed, a recent systematic literature review found that for some social media users, avoiding FOMO is a strong motivating factor driving their social media use (Tandon et al. 2021).

From reviewing the previous literature, it becomes clear that there is a novel opportunity to frame people's previous behaviour and to see which types of behaviour induce a sense of loss aversion. With the help of data from wearables and mobile devices, researchers can now explore this area of research. By showing people their past behaviour and inducing a sense of loss, researchers can investigate how people react to their own previous behaviour that is subjectively perceived as misallocated time.

3 Time Loss Aversion

Time loss aversion is a type of loss aversion (and thus cognitive bias) where the object of attention is the allocation of time rather than money or another resource. "Time Loss Aversion" is people's tendency to fear previous misallocations of time, which then motivates people to change their future behaviour. People will perceive time to be as misallocated if they over engage in activities that they themselves perceive to be unnecessary or excessive, and under engage in activities that are important to or beneficial for them. It thus differs from other types of loss aversions temporally as it makes people focus on previous allocations of time and how this should influence the way they allocate their time in the present and in the future. Further it can be directed towards a fear of not engaging enough in certain activities in the past, which motivates an increased engagement with that activity in the future, or over-engaging in certain activities in the past, which in turn motivates a decreased engagement with that activity in the future.

The reason why people misallocate their time in the first place is because time allocation decisions are the result of a series of psychological factors including: emotional drives, personal goals, resources restraints and preferences (Coleman and Iso-Ahola 1993). To give an example, O'Lea (2011) reviewed the many factors that drive people's allocation of time towards social media. On one hand, *gratification theory* posits that people use the media to satisfy four primary needs: diversion, personal relationships, personal identity, and surveillance needs (Bumgarner 2007). Another explanation is that *social networking* is deeply ingrained in the human psyche, and virtual communities such as different social media platforms have become increasingly popular for participants seeking to keep in touch with friends (Coyle and Vaughn 2008).

Time loss aversion is experienced as fear of wasting time (rather than money), which can manifest in different ways depending on an individual's perception of how they have allocated their time in the past. Time loss aversion has significant implications for decision-making in various domains, such as work, leisure, and education. Individuals who feel they have not spent enough time with their loved ones may prioritise spending time with them in the future, even if it means sacrificing other activities. On the other hand, individuals who feel they have spent too much time on social media in the past may be motivated to decrease their social media use in the future.

Monitoring apps, such as Apple's Screen Time allow people to review how they have allocated their time on average, per day towards using different apps on a smartphone. Research shows that screen time can successfully reduce Facebook use (Doğan et al. 2019). Another study found that half of its participants using monitoring apps reduced their overall social media time (Tiller et al. 2021). However, most participants did not stick to their goal, thus these apps did not achieve time loss aversion. The negative aspects of screen time apps could be the way in which it presents its information to users, specifically it shows people averages. It may be the case that with loss aversion focused on monetary outcomes, people are more likely to react to total money lost or gained, rather than averages.

Another potential problem is that of magnitude. People looking at their daily average use of different apps might perceive this time as relatively insignificant. It may be that to achieve time loss aversion, larger magnitudes of time that go beyond that amount achievable in a day is required; for instance, giving people data on time spent on an activity in a week, month or year. This is now possible due to the mobile and wearable revolution, giving people more granular data on how they are spending their time both on-screen and off-screen (Hernandez et al. 2020).

3.1 Case Study

Inspired by the concept of time loss aversion, a study conducted by the author has tested two novel interventions aimed at reducing people's daily social media use and increasing their engagement in non-digital activities (Gao 2023a). The time loss aversion intervention told participants what their daily social media (self-reported from their Screen Time app) use equated to on the level of a week, month, and year. This intervention aimed to induce a sense of loss in participants by showing them the amount of time they had wasted on social media. The tailored loss aversion intervention was similar to the time loss intervention but additionally gave people examples of how they could have spent their time differently on non-digital activities. This intervention aimed to show participants the alternative activities they could engage in instead of social media to induce a sense of loss. Thus it aimed to induce a similar effect to the previously conducted FOMO studies (Tandon et al. 2021).

Results suggested that both interventions were significant in reducing intentional social media use as well as increasing willingness to engage in non-digital activities. However, there was no significant difference between the two interventions. The exception to this were participants who were considered to be heavy social media users as they used 4 or more social media platforms on a regular basis. This group additionally benefited from the tailored loss aversion's use of examples of other activities.

The study was the first to frame people's real past behaviour as a way of inducing a sense of time loss aversion that in turn motivated people's future behaviour; specifically, a decrease in a behaviour that appears as excessive, and an increase in alternative behaviours that take time away from the excessive behaviour. This finding has specific implications for apps such as screen time, revealing that screen time, with its use of daily averages, will not be effective until it switches to an interface that displays weekly, monthly, and even yearly averages that are time loss aversion inducing.

3.2 Difference Between Lost Money and Lost Time

Time and money are both important resources that people use to achieve their goals, but they are fundamentally different. This is because time is a finite resource that cannot be regained once it is spent, while money is a flexible resource that people can earn and save. This raises the question of how money loss aversion and time loss aversion are similar and how they are different.

The way in which money is framed in terms of losses and gains is more reliable with a more clear reference point (i.e., the amount of money someone has now). Time loss aversion relies on more modern measurement approaches and has a less clear reference point. Spending 5 h on social media may be seen as lost time by most but for people that are social media influencers it will be seen as time well spent. However, certain techniques such as the use of persuasive language can frame spent time as lost time, for most people.

In the aforementioned case study, time loss aversion was achieved through the use of visual data and persuasive language that allowed people to view time as a resource. This opens up opportunities for future research to explore how people view time when framed in different ways and how this influences their behaviour. Time is a more dynamic concept than money as it is spent in every moment of one's life. Further research could explore the differences, similarities, and dynamics of how people view and use time and money by allowing them to allocate the resources in parallel.

4 Implications for HCI

Wearable and mobile technologies have resulted in data that allow us to have a more detailed understanding of how and where we spend our time (Hernandez et al. 2020). HCI paradigms could incorporate time loss aversion in a way that is more reliable than ever before. Modern tech ecosystem combining mobile (e.g., smartphone), wearable (e.g., watch) and smart home data can tell us how we spend our time on-screen and off-screen (Oliveira and Lóscio 2018).

Loss aversion can be used to combat the addictive design present in UX, UI and algorithms behind social media, streaming and games. Such addictive design results in "time-based addictions" - addictions where the regularly repeating misallocation of time results in negative outcomes to people's health, productivity and well-being (Gao 2023b). Such addictive design is usually referred to as "dark patterns" - deceptive or manipulative design elements intentionally used to keep users engaged (Gray et al. 2018). For example, auto-play in most video streaming sites keeps users watching. Social media platforms like TikTok, Instagram and SnapChat, often use algorithms that show users notifications when they haven't logged in for a while. This creates a sense of FOMO that encourages the users to keep spending time on these sites to not miss out on anything (Gupta and Shrivastava 2021). Such design might be good for user retention, but not for user wellbeing. It would be more beneficial if users could gain access to how much time they were spending on the sites.

For example, time loss aversion can help users in designing features that control excessive social media use (Gao 2023a). By implementing the concept of loss aversion, interventions can be used to encourage users to reduce social media use and increase the engagement of non-digital activities. Smartphone software designers can create features to show their users how their social media use equates to timelines beyond a day. By inducing a sense of loss, providing alternative activities, and rewarding users for their efforts, Apple Screen Time can create a more effective and user-friendly interface that encourages healthy usage of social media.

5 Conclusion

In conclusion, this paper defines time loss aversion. The case study presented in this article provides evidence for the existence of time loss aversion, which can have significant implications for the design of screen time and social media apps. The differences between time and money loss aversion have been discussed, emphasising the need for a more nuanced approach to design. Better design can motivate people to devote more time to meaningful activities, rather than losing the balance between time well-spent and time lost. Overall, this article contributes to a better understanding of human behaviour and how it can be leveraged to create better technological solutions that enhance our lives.

References

Beam, E.A., Masatlioglu, Y., Watson, T., Yang, D.: Loss aversion or lack of trust: why does loss framing work to encourage preventative health behaviors? (No. w29828). National Bureau of Economic Research (2022)

Bumgarner, B.A.: You have been poked: exploring the uses and gratifications of Facebook among emerging adults. First Monday (2007)

Coleman, D., Iso-Ahola, S.E.: Leisure and health: the role of social support and self-determination. J. Leis. Res. 25(2), 111–128 (1993)

Coyle, C.L., Vaughn, H.: Social networking: communication revolution or evolution? Bell Labs Tech. J. 13(2), 13–17 (2008)

Doğan, U.: Effects of social network use on happiness, psychological well-being, and life satisfaction of high school students: case of Facebook and Twitter. Egitim ve Bilim 41(183), 217–231 (2016)

Gao, Z.: Personalizing time loss aversion to reduce social media use. Pending Review (2023a)

Gao, Z.: Time-Based Addiction. In the CHI Conference on Human Factors in Computing Systems (CHI'23) Workshop on Behavioural Design in Video Games: Ethical, Legal, and Health Impact on Players (2023b)

Gray, C.M., Kou, Y., Battles, B., Hoggatt, J., Toombs, A.L.: The dark (patterns) side of UX design. In: Proceedings of the 2018 CHI Conference on Human Factors in Computing Systems, pp. 1–14. April 2018

Gupta, S., Shrivastava, M.: Herding and loss aversion in stock markets: mediating role of fear of missing out (FOMO) in retail investors. Int. J. Emerg. Mark. 17(7), 1720–1737 (2021)

Hernandez, N., Lundström, J., Favela, J., McChesney, I., Arnrich, B.: Literature review on transfer learning for human activity recognition using mobile and wearable devices with environmental technology. SN Comput. Sci. 1, 1–16 (2020)

Kahneman, D., Tversky, A.: Prospect theory: an analysis of decision under risk. Econometrica 47(2), 263–291 (1979)

Kahneman, D., Tversky, A.: Choices, values, and frames. Am. Psychol. 39(4), 341 (1984)

Kőszegi, B., Rabin, M.: A model of reference-dependent preferences. Q. J. Econ. 121(4), 1133–1165 (2006)

Kroll, E.B., Vogt, B.: Loss aversion for time: an experimental investigation of time preferences. In: Working Paper Series (2008)

McEvoy, D.M.: Loss aversion and student achievement. Econ. Bull. 36(3), 1762–1770 (2016)

Novemsky, N., Kahneman, D.: The boundaries of loss aversion. J. Mark. Res. 42(2), 119–128 (2005)

Paese, P.W.: Effects of framing on actual time allocation decisions. Organ. Behav. Hum. Decis. Process. 61(1), 67–76 (1995)

O'Lea, K.A.: An examination of social media technology and its impact on the pursuit and allocation of personal leisure time (2011)

Oliveira, M.I.S., Lóscio, B.F.: What is a data ecosystem?. In: Proceedings of the 19th Annual International Conference on Digital Government Research: Governance in the Data Age, pp. 1–9, May 2018

Pittman, M., Steiner, E.: Transportation or narrative completion? Attentiveness during binge-watching moderates regret. Soc. Sci. 8(3), 99 (2019)

Sharma, A., Moon, J., Bailey-Davis, L.: Loss aversion of time: serving school lunches faster without impacting meal experience. Ecol. Food Nutr. 57(6), 456–472 (2018)

Simon, H.A.: Bounded rationality. Utility and probability, pp. 15–18 (1990)

Tandon, A., Dhir, A., Almugren, I., AlNemer, G.N., Mäntymäki, M.: Fear of missing out (FoMO) among social media users: a systematic literature review, synthesis and framework for future research. Internet Research (2021b)

Tiller, H.: Analysis of the function time limits within the IPhone feature screen time. In: Conference in interaction technology and design, p. 141

Von Neumann, J., Morgenstern, O.: Theory of games and economic behavior, 2nd rev (1947)

Multimodal Interaction in Virtual Reality: Assessing User Experience of Gesture- and Gaze-Based Interaction

Lisa Graichen$^{(\boxtimes)}$ and Matthias Graichen

TU Berlin, Berlin, Germany
lisa.graichen@web.de

Abstract. Virtual reality (VR) applications are entering people's everyday lives and being used in professional applications, research, and science. The question arises as to whether there may be interaction modes that are more suitable than the standard controllers with which these devices are typically equipped. To address this question, it is necessary to conduct human-centered studies, which is typically done in the field of human factors research. We present a forthcoming study in which we integrate mid-air gesture-based interaction and gaze-based interaction into a VR setup so that users can interact with the system without touching a button, surface, or device. We then compare these two approaches to the controllers that are provided with the VR device. For gesture recognition, we use a Leap Motion device, which is mounted on the front of the VR device. For gaze-based interaction, we use the eye-tracking system that is integrated into the HCT Vive. We use a basic application, in which users can rotate and move virtual 3D blocks. In the study described, we will focus on user experiences and ask the participants to rate the prototypes according to their subjective impressions. Additionally, we will document errors caused by the system or participants' incorrect actions to investigate whether perceived errors affect user experiences. Lastly, we will ask for reports of pain or discomfort in the body parts involved and measure the size of the participants' fingers and hands.

Keywords: Gesture-Based Interaction · Virtual Reality · Gaze-Based Interaction

1 Introduction

Over the last decade, extended reality applications have emerged rapidly, entering people's everyday lives as well as research and science. The term "extended reality" (XR) involves different levels of immersion, including virtual reality (VR), augmented reality (AR), and mixed reality (MR). Although XR systems have existed for decades, recent technological progress has accelerated the development of numerous applications and research questions. Additionally, affordable systems such as the HTC Vive and Oculus Rift have entered the market, making the VR experience available to researchers and private users.

© The Author(s), under exclusive license to Springer Nature Switzerland AG 2023
C. Stephanidis et al. (Eds.): HCII 2023, CCIS 1832, pp. 578–585, 2023.
https://doi.org/10.1007/978-3-031-35989-7_73

In the domain of human–computer interaction, there is a wide range of movements that are referred to as "gestures." These include clicking, pointing, and moving a traditional computer mouse; touching a screen with one's fingers; using different tools (e.g., a controller) or the entire body as an input mode; and using other parts of the body such as the eyes (gaze) or the head (head movements). In this paper, we use the term "gesture-based interaction" to denote mid-air gestures that are performed in the air and do not involve physical contact with a surface [15]. According to [13], these gestures are defined by the absence of 1) proximity to a surface, 2) pressure on a surface, 3) transfer of matter, 4) momentum, 5) constraint of movement (i.e., freedom of movement is high), 6) attrition or wear, and 7) haptic feedback. Although several studies have shown that gestures are attractive to users (see e.g., [2, 4, 9]), gestures in VR applications are only beginning to be studied (see e.g., [1, 11, 14]). The same holds for gaze-based interaction (see e.g., [10, 16]).

In this forthcoming study, we investigate how different interaction modes – namely gestures and gaze as input methods – affect user trust, users' assessments of attractivity, and acceptance. We will use a VR environment in which participants will be asked to perform basic tasks using mid-air gestures and gaze (i.e., head movements). A Leap Motion device will be employed for gesture recognition. We will address the following research questions:

1) How do different interaction modes affect user trust?
2) How do different interaction modes affect perceived system attractivity?
3) How do different interaction modes affect user acceptance?
4) How do different interaction modes affect user workload?

2 Methods

2.1 Design

We selected a one-way repeated measures design with interaction mode (controller vs. mid-air gestures vs. gazes) as the factor. The controller interaction mode was employed as a comparison mode because it is the device that comes standard with the VR device. Use of the standard controller would also be considered as use of gestures, but users perceive the performance of mid-air gestures as more natural because, as in human communication, they do not need to touch a tool. Therefore, we refer to this interaction mode as "gesture-based interaction." Gaze-based interaction would also be considered a specific form of gesture-based interaction. To distinguish between interaction modes, we refer to this mode as "gaze-based interaction." The order of interaction types during the study will be counterbalanced using the standard Latin Square to avoid sequence or learning effects.

2.2 Participants

An opportunity sample of approximately 35 persons, composed primarily of students, will be selected using the TU Berlin mailing lists. This study will comply with the tenets of the Declaration of Helsinki, and informed consent will be obtained from each participant.

2.3 Facilities and Apparatus

We will use a VR headset equipped with standard controllers. To implement gesture-based interaction, we will use a Leap Motion controller (https://www.ultraleap.com) that is connected to the VR device and mounted on the front of the VR device (see Fig. 1a-b).

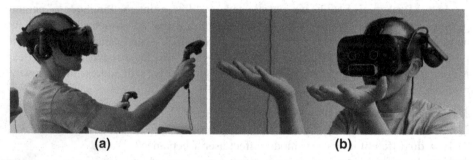

(a)   **(b)**

Fig. 1. a-b. Setup for gestures and controller with Leap Motion mounted on the front of the VR device.

We will use three basic applications that allow users to perform basic tasks such as creating 3D blocks, resizing them, and picking up and moving the created objects (see Fig. 2a-c). The applications using the controller and gestures, respectively, are existing example applications called "Blocks" [3, 18], while the application using gazes has been developed in-house using Unity and the software and plug-ins of the Tobii eyetracker integrated into the HTC Vive [17]. The experimenter will be able to follow all the participants' actions on a connected laptop. We will use a video camera to record the gestures performed and the laptop screen to enable analysis of the participants' gesturing behavior and the system's reactions.

The VR device is available with an integrated eye tracker, which we have tested comprehensively. Eye-tracking, despite the technical improvements that have occurred in recent years, can be difficult for various known and unknown reasons. Based on the tests we conducted and our extensive experience using eye-tracking in prior studies, we decided to not use the integrated eye tracker but rather to use head movement as a detection method for participants' gazes. Extensive testing of this approach demonstrated acceptable detection accuracy. Participants will be asked to look at one of the interactive fields (see Fig. 2a) to trigger a specific task.

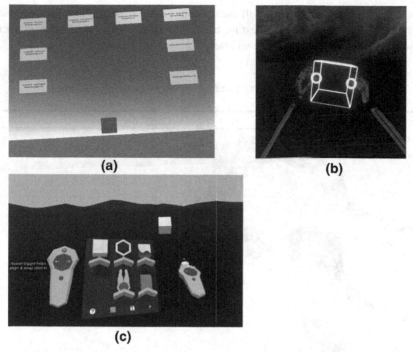

Fig. 2. a-c. Virtual environment displayed to participants for gestures (left), gazes (right), and controller (bottom)

2.4   Interaction Tasks

Six tasks were designed for controller and gesture-based interaction. These tasks were derived from basic tasks that can be used to cover a wide range of possible activities. To ensure that the respective gesture was suitable for the interaction tasks selected, a pre-test was conducted with 17 participants using an online questionnaire. Participants were presented with images of different gestures and asked to rate the appropriateness of each gesture for each related task. For the forthcoming study, we selected six gestures that were rated as highly appropriate for the interaction tasks selected. Table 1 presents the task descriptions and the corresponding gestures/controller actions (the controller figure can be retrieved from [12]).

2.5   Procedure

Upon arrival, participants will be introduced to the VR device, the general use of the system and the Leap Motion, and the tasks that they will be asked to perform during the study. Each participant will be given as much time as necessary to learn and practice all the interaction tasks and will be repeatedly tested on their interaction performance to reduce training effects during the experiment and the likelihood of them making an incorrect gesture during a task. In the first phase, participants will use a small application to familiarize themselves with the VR device. In the second phase, participants will perform tasks in three trials. They will use the controllers for controller-based interaction and the Leap Motion device for gesture-based interaction and gaze-based interaction. The sequence of interaction modes will vary for each participant.

Table 1. Tasks with corresponding mid-air and controller gestures.

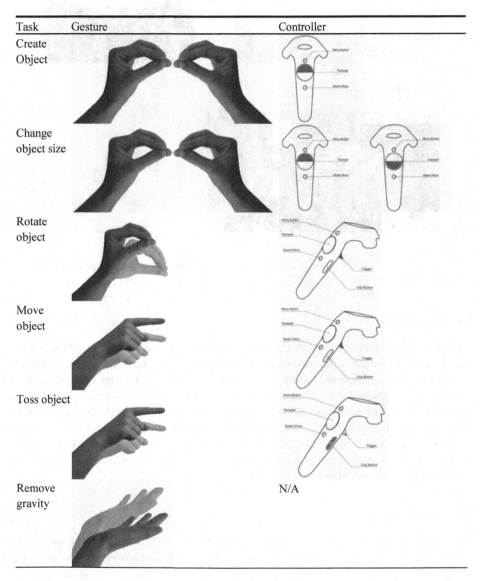

Task	Gesture	Controller
Create Object		
Change object size		
Rotate object		
Move object		
Toss object		
Remove gravity		N/A

After completing the task in each interaction mode, participants will complete a questionnaire focused on their subjective impressions, including impressions related to trust, acceptance, and hand comfort. At the end of the experiment, participants will complete additional demographic questionnaires, in which we will obtain their hand measurements and ask them about their sense of immersion and simulator sickness. In total, the experiment will take approximately 1.5 h per participant.

2.6 Dependent Variables

Participants will assess their trust in the system using a 12-item unidimensional scale from a questionnaire that measures trust [7]. Acceptance will be measured using a 9-item questionnaire developed by [19] that consists of two subscales: "usefulness" (five items) and "satisfying" (four items). Participants will also be asked to rate the level of attractivity using a questionnaire created by [5]. Additionally, we will use a self-developed questionnaire to ask them about their feelings of presence and immersion [8] and simulator sickness [6] as well as their comfort or discomfort when performing the movement for each interaction mode.

Error rates will be documented by the examiner during the study. A video recording will be made to enable the analysis of gesturing behavior.

3 Implications

In the presented study, we aim to investigate whether gestures and gaze are suitable and attractive interaction modes for VR applications. VR devices such as the HTC Vive usually come with a standard controller. However, the need to hold a controller might be disruptive in some situations and applications. Some applications might require the user to have their hands free. It might be uncomfortable for the user to hold the controller if it does not suit their hand size or is too heavy. If several persons are supposed to use the application and hardware, it can also be unhygienic to use controllers. Therefore, other interaction modes might have advantages. As previous studies have shown, gestures are difficult to implement. Therefore, their detection rate tends to be relatively low, which may lead to errors or system malfunction. However, in previous studies, we have found that gestures are attractive, stimulating, well accepted, and trusted by users [4]. As gaze is also an innovative and intuitive way of interaction, which should even offer more robust detection rates than gestures due to its lower level of movement complexity, we additionally aim to investigate whether this mode of interaction could also be acceptable. However, it is possible that users may feel insecure when using gaze-based interaction, as they may be concerned about accidentally triggering actions simply by moving their eyes as they are used to doing.

There are many open questions regarding gesture-based interaction. Currently, there is no established set of gestures that is widely known and accepted. Developers need to implement gestures carefully. Having a high number of gestures makes it more difficult for users to learn and remember them but also allows for the selection of gestures that are well adapted to the particular task, which makes the interaction more natural and intuitive. In addition, developers need to consider which gestures meet the technical preconditions of the chosen detection tool. In our forthcoming study, we aim to contribute to the field by addressing all these open questions.

References

1. Rahul, A., Rubaiat, H.K., Danny, M.K., Wilmot, L., Karan, S.: MagicalHands: mid-air hand gestures for animating in VR. In: Proceedings of the 32nd Annual ACM Symposium on User Interface Software and Technology, ACM, New York, NY, USA, pp. 463–477 (2019). https://doi.org/10.1145/3332165.3347942
2. Fariman, H.J., Alyamani, H.J., Kavakli, M., Hamey, L.: Designing a user-defined gesture vocabulary for an in-vehicle climate control system. In: Proceedings of the 28th Australian Computer-Human Interaction Conference (OzCHI 2016). 29 November - 2 December 2016, University of Tasmania, ACM, New York, NY, USA, pp. 391–395 (2016). https://doi.org/10.1145/3010915.3010955
3. Google. Blocks. Accessed 16 Mar 2023. https://store.steampowered.com/app/533970/Blocks_by_Google/
4. Graichen, L., Graichen, M., Krems, J.F.: Evaluation of gesture-based in-vehicle interaction. User experience and the potential to reduce driver distraction. 1–19 (2019). https://doi.org/10.1177/0018720818824253
5. Hassenzahl, M., Burmester, M., Koller, F.: AttrakDiff: ein fragebogen zur messung wahrgenommener hedonischer und pragmatischer Qualität. In: Mensch & Computer 2003. Interaktion in Bewegung, Gerd Szwillus and Jürgen Ziegler, Eds. Berichte des German Chapter of the ACM, 57. B.G. Teubner, Stuttgart, Leipzig, 187–196 (2003)
6. Kennedy, R.S., Lane, N.E., Berbaum, K.S., Lilienthal, M.G.: simulator sickness questionnaire. An enhanced method for quantifying simulator sickness. Int. J. Aviation Psychol. 3(3), 203–220 (1993). https://doi.org/10.1207/s15327108ijap0303
7. Körber, M.: Theoretical considerations and development of a questionnaire to measure trust in automation. In: Bagnara, S., Tartaglia, R., Albolino, S., Alexander, T., Fujita, Y. (eds.) Proceedings of the 20th Congress of the International Ergonomics Association (IEA 2018). IEA 2018. Advances in Intelligent Systems and Computing, vol. 823, pp. 13–30. Springer, Cham (2019). https://doi.org/10.1007/978-3-319-96074-6_2
8. Lessiter, J., Freeman, J., Keogh, E. and Davidoff, J.: A cross-media presence questionnaire: the ITC-sense of presence inventory. Presence: Teleoperators Virt. Environ. 10(3), 282–297 (2001). https://doi.org/10.1162/105474601300343612
9. Loehmann, S., Knobel, M., Lamara, M., Butz, A.: Culturally independent gestures for in-car interactions. In: Kotzé, P., Marsden, G., Lindgaard, G., Wesson, J., Winckler, M. (eds.) INTERACT 2013. LNCS, vol. 8119, pp. 538–545. Springer, Heidelberg (2013). https://doi.org/10.1007/978-3-642-40477-1_34
10. Mutasim, A.K., Batmaz, A.U., Stuerzlinger, W.: Pinch, click, or dwell: comparing different selection techniques for eye-gaze-based pointing in virtual reality. In: ACM Symposium on Eye Tracking Research and Applications, ACM, New York, NY, USA, pp. 1–7 (2021). https://doi.org/10.1145/3448018.3457998
11. Narayana, P., et al.: Cooperating with avatars through gesture, language and action. In: Arai, K., Kapoor, S., Bhatia, R. (eds.) IntelliSys 2018. AISC, vol. 868, pp. 272–293. Springer, Cham (2019). https://doi.org/10.1007/978-3-030-01054-6_20
12. NicePNG. Free PNG Image Library. Accessed 9 Mar 2023. https://www.nicepng.com/ourpic/u2w7a9e6t4o0o0q8_htc-vive-controls-htc-vive-controller-guide/
13. O'hara, K., Harper, R., Mentis, H., Sellen, A., Taylor, A.: On the naturalness of touchless: putting the interaction back into NUI. ACM Trans. Comput.-Hum. Interact. 20(1), 1–25 (2013). https://doi.org/10.1145/2442106.2442111

14. Pustejovksy, J., et al.: Interpreting and generating gestures with embodied human computer interactions (2020). https://doi.org/10.5281/zenodo.4088625
15. Saffer, D.: Designing Gestural Interfaces. O'Reilly Media Inc, Sebastopol (2008)
16. Salam, H., Seguier, R., Stoiber, N.: Integrating head pose to a 3D multitexture approach for gaze detection. IJMA 5(4), 1–22 (2013). https://doi.org/10.5121/ijma.2013.5401
17. Tobii. HTC Vive Pro Eye. Accessed 16 Mar 2023. https://www.tobii.com/products/integration/xr-headsets/device-integrations/htc-vive-pro-eye
18. Ultraleap. Blocks. Accessed 16 Mar 2023. https://gallery.leapmotion.com/blocks/
19. Van der Laan, J.D., Heino, A., de Waard, D.: A simple procedure for the assessment of acceptance of advanced transport telematics. Transp. Res. Part C: Emerg. Technol. 5(1), 1 (1997). https://doi.org/10.1016/S0968-090X(96)00025-3

Research on Evaluation of Cabin Design Based on Virtual Reality

Wei Guo[✉], Xiaoli Wang, Yanbo Li, and Liyao Wang

Beijing Aircraft Technology Research Institute COMAC, Beijing, China
guowei0224@foxmail.com

Abstract. With the development and maturity of virtual reality technology, it has been rapidly developed in various fields, and it is also gradually promoted in the aviation field. The paper established an evaluation environment for the overall design of the cabin in the initial stage of civil aircraft based on the virtual reality technology, which supported designers to design and determine the overall parameters of the cabin in the virtual reality environment quickly, such as cabin division, seat arrangement, service facility layout, emergency exit layout, crew seats and rest area layout et al. At the same time, it provided designers with a virtual evaluation environment and method for the cabin general layout parameters design from the perspective of human factors, which was used to provide cabin designers and human factors experts with a rapidly changing virtual cabin at the initial stage of design, and supported them to complete cabin design and evaluation. And the paper chose cabin designers, human factors experts and passengers with rich design or flight experience, built an evaluation experiment of cabin virtual reality environment. The paper conducted human factors evaluation on the overall cabin design in the virtual reality environment, formed a cabin usability evaluation index system of human factors in the virtual reality environment, which was used to guide the application of virtual reality technology in cabin design and human factors design.

Keywords: Cabin Design · Virtual Reality · Index System

1 Introduction

The cabin is the only space for passengers to move and rest during flight. From boarding to disembarking, passengers are in the space and environment of the cabin. In order to attract passengers, from cabin designers to airlines, they hope to provide passengers with a more comfortable cabin space. With the development and maturity of virtual reality technology, it has been rapidly developed in various fields, and it is also gradually promoted in the aviation field.

The design analysis and evaluation of traditional civil aircraft cabin design is usually carried out based on the desktop simulation and demonstration prototype, but the former is not a human in loop interactive environment, which is not good to the completion of human performance evaluation at the initial stage of design, the latter cannot form a fast iteration in the design process [1]. Some researchers believe that, traditional design methods cannot always bring out the best in all aspects of a designed product when trying to communicating it to all different levels of stakeholders. So in the fields of interior design, automobile design and aircraft cabin design, more and more researchers have introduced virtual reality technology into the display and design process in order to achieve product success.

In the early stage, the VR applications used in aircraft cabin design were concentrated in the detailed design stage in the later stage of design. In 2007, Airbus showed its new cabin design to customers based on virtual reality technology in the Cabin Definition Center in Hamburg (CDC). Through this technology, the customer and the designer completed the final inspection before acceptance, mainly including the color and pattern design of the cabin interior, seats and other parts. However, this technology has not been used in the cabin design process [2].

In 2019, De Crescenzio et al. have conducted a study within Horizon 2020 project CASTLE (Cabin Systems Design Toward Passengers Well-being). In their findings, published in the International Journal on Interactive Design and Manufacturing, they state that VR has been recognized as a powerful tool to get the intended user closer to the product even before it has been manufactured [3].

Based on virtual reality technology, this paper establishes a system integrating the overall design and evaluation of civil aircraft cabin. It can support designers to provide rapid design and evaluation in virtual reality environment. At the same time, this paper also established the evaluation index of virtual reality cabin to guide the cabin design.

2 System Design

This paper constructs a virtual reality civil aircraft cabin design environment and evaluation environment in the Unreal Engine 5. For the overall design of the cabin at the conceptual stage, it can quickly provide a realistic virtual reality environment for cabin designers and various stakeholders to conduct design evaluation.

2.1 Import Aircraft Shape Surface

For the work related to the general arrangement of the cabin, the fuselage shape surface is its basic constraint condition (see Fig. 1). The fuselage shape surface is constructed in industrial 3D design software by a complex surface generated by multiple arcs. It is more complex to build this kind of model directly in the virtual reality environment. Therefore, the system uses the method of model import to simplify the model generated by CATIA and other software while preserving the constraints as much as possible, to obtain a complete and usable fuselage shape in the virtual environment.

2.2 Interior Matching

In order to obtain a more realistic display effect in the cabin, this paper builds a model library of interior panels with different curvature in blocks to adapt to different body

Fig. 1. Aircraft shape surface

shapes. The designer can select the interior model as close as possible under the condition of ensuring constraints to obtain a complete interior model of the cabin. The built interior model library includes ceilings, side wall panels, partitions, partition boards, interior doors and carpets. At the same time, the model library also provides editing and customization functions for model maps and materials.

2.3 Seat Arrangement

As an important facility for passengers in the cabin, the seat can focus on the comfort design of democratic manufacturers and airlines in the cabin. This system establishes a common seat model library in service. These include four types of first-class seats, business class seats, super economy class seats and economy class seats. This article uses the parameterized modeling of the seat to realize the designer's design of different seats. The seat parameters that can be adjusted by designers include: seat height, width of the seat surface, depth of the left side, handrail width, handrail height, back height, back angle, cabin entertainment system type, and entertainment system display size. In addition, this system also establishes a customized seat color, pattern, and material model material library, which can provide a richer customized option for the seat.

For the ranking of cabin seats, the system provides designers to adjust the interactive interface of the discharge and seat configuration. At the same time, it also supports designers to arrange data drivers through existing seats to complete the seat layout in the cabin.

In order to present the interaction of more realistic personnel in the virtual environment and seats, we also provide model elements such as bookbags, small table boards, power sockets and other model elements in the design of the seat design for the user's interactive experience (Fig. 2).

2.4 Boarding Doors, Service Doors and Emergency Doors

This article also designs the design interface of the aircraft cabin door, which is used to select the type of the cabin door and determine the position of the cabin door. In the model library, the boarding door, service doors and emergency doors of type I-IV and

Fig. 2. Business class seats

type A-C, includes the upper pull type, side pull type, downward type, external opening type, open type, external opening type 4 categories (Fig. 3).

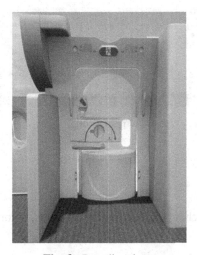

Fig. 3. Boarding doors

2.5 Service Facilities

This article builds the basic model library of the service facilities in the cabin, mainly including bathrooms, kitchens, cloakrooms, units lounges and luggage racks. The models of the bathroom, kitchen and cloakroom can be adjusted according to the size and location of the spatial size and location; The luggage rack can adjust its height, volume, opening and closing method, and interval size. In addition, the meal cars and unit lounges can be adjusted according to the expected number (Fig. 4).

Fig. 4. Kitchens

2.6 Portal

The system provides an interactive interface that regulates the height, size, spacing and type of porthole (Fig. 5).

Fig. 5. Portal

2.7 Light

The system can support changing the number of lights, colors, and types in the cabin (Fig. 6).

Fig. 6. Lights

2.8 Identifier

The system provides a typical cabin internal sign. At the same time, it can also support changes in the colors, fonts, patterns, and layout positions of signs and marks. Due to the differences in different airlines and even different models, the system provides more self-determination functions of model materials.

3 Index System

8 subjects are involved in the test aging from 25 to 55 years old, of which 5 males and 3 females. All participating personnel have a variety of modeling experience and have a cabin design experience in a certain aspect. This includes two human factors experts.

We used HTC's Vive Pro Eye and integrated a Leap Motion Controller on the headset. In this setup, the position and orientation of the headset in the virtual scene are controlled through the SteamVR Tracking system.

The participants completed the design and evaluation of the cabin in the virtual reality environment. They referred to the existing cabin evaluation indicators [4], and determined the virtual reality cabin evaluation indicator system (see Table 1) through questionnaire survey and centralized meeting discussion.

Table 1. Virtual reality environment cabin assessment index system

Primary Factor	Secondary Factor	Third Factor	Detailed Index Description
Cabin Space Comfort	Cabin Layout Design	Cabin Length	Cabin Length Value
		Cabin Width	Cabin Width Value
		Cabin volume	Cabin Volume Value
		Aisle Height	Aisle height Value
		Entrance Height	Center Overhead Entrance Height
			Lateral Overhead Entrance Height
		Pitch	Economy Class Minimum Pitch
			Business Class Minimum Pitch
		Aisle Width	Main Aisle Width of Different Class
		Seat Number in a Row	Seat Number in a Row of Different Class
		Cabin Window	The Height Value of the Lower Edge of the Cabin Window from the Floor
			Cabin Window Width

(continued)

Table 1. (*continued*)

Primary Factor	Secondary Factor	Third Factor	Detailed Index Description
	Passenger Seat Design	Back Space	Seat Back Width
		Activity Space	Upper Seat Back Thickness
			Distance Between Seat Backs
			Folding Table Width and Inclination Angle
		Seat Width	Seat Width, Armrest Width
		Seat Fixed Angle and Reclining Adjustment Angle	Initial Fixed Angle for seat Installation and the Angle Adjustment Range
		Seat Design	Seat Material, Seat Color, Seat Style
	Luggage Rack Space	Luggage Rack Height	Height from the Lower Edge of the Luggage Rack to the Cabin Floor
		Luggage Rack Volume	The Total Volume of the Luggage Rack, the Size of a Single Suitcase that Can be Accommodated
Cabin Environment Comfort	Thermal Comfort	Temperature Range	Temperature Adjustable Range in Cabin Area
	Lighting	Brightness level	Cabin Overall/Partial Lighting Brightness Level, Individual Lighting Brightness
		Uniformity of Brightness Distribution	Cabin Lighting Contrast
		Color Temperature	Cabin Overall/Partial Lighting Color Temperature Value
Interaction Comfort	Cabin Amenities	Interaction of IFE Facilities	Operation Convenience, Interface Design
		Virtual Porthole Design	Virtual Portholes Dimension, Passenger Vision Fidelity, Interface Design, Operation Convenience, etc
		Interior Design	Interior Design Shape, Color, and Material
		Virtual Interaction Design	Interactive Facilities Type, Interface Design, and Operation Convenience

4 Conclusion

This paper mainly aims at the requirements of civil aircraft cabin design, decomposes the cabin elements, and constructs the cabin design system and evaluation system in the virtual environment using virtual reality technology. And organize cabin designers to use the system to complete the task of cabin layout. At the same time, based on the system, a series of indicators supporting cabin assessment in the virtual reality environment have been determined. In subsequent work, we will continuously improve the system and index system to design and evaluate the factors of the people's cabin as the factors.

References

1. Guo, W., Wang, X., Deng, Z., Li, H.: A civil aircraft cockpit control device design using mixed reality device. In: Chen, J.Y.C., Fragomeni, G. (eds.) Virtual, Augmented and Mixed Reality: Applications in Education, Aviation and Industry, HCII 2022. LNCS, vol. 13318, pp. 196–207. Springer, Cham (2022). https://doi.org/10.1007/978-3-031-06015-1_14
2. Moerland-Masic, I., Reimer, F., Bock, T.M., Meller, F., Nagel, B.: Application of VR technology in the aircraft cabin design process. CEAS Aeronaut. J. 1–10 (2021)
3. Rydström, A., Broström, R., Bengtsson, P.: A comparison of two contemporary types of in-car multifunctional interfaces. Appl. Ergon. **43**, 507–514 (2012)
4. Wang, X., Guo, W., Deng, Z., Yang, C.: Research on the cabin evaluation index system for future passenger flight experience. In: Stephanidis, C., Antona, M., Ntoa, S. (eds.) HCI International 2022 Posters, HCII 2022. CCIS, vol. 1583, pp. 317–327. Springer, Cham (2022). https://doi.org/10.1007/978-3-031-06394-7_41

Gender Effects on Creativity When Pair Programming with a Human vs. an Agent

Jacob C. Hart[1]([✉])(iD), Marcus Ensley[1](iD), and Sandeep Kaur Kuttal[1,2](iD)

[1] University of Tulsa, Tulsa, OK 74104, USA
jch389@utulsa.edu
[2] North Carolina State University, Raleigh, NC 27695, USA

Abstract. This paper explores the effect of introducing a pair programming agent on creativity and gender. To understand this, we conducted
two studies on pair programming: Study 1: between two humans, and
Study 2: between a human and an agent using a Wizard-of-Oz simulation method. We labeled the conversations using the Osborn-Parnes
creative problem-solving process that contains four phases: clarify, idea,
develop, and implementation, to analyze the data. We found that when
working with an agent both genders discussed more ideas rather than
develop, but overall favored to clarify and implement; whereas, when
working with a human, participants tended to favor developing their
ideas. Further, men participants clarify more in the presence of an agent
than with a human while women spent more time on implementation
with a human. Based on our findings, we present design guidelines for
future pair-programming agents.

Keywords: Creativity · Conversational Agents · Pair Programming ·
Gender Effects

1 Introduction

Advancements in agents such as ChatGPT, Dall-E-2, and Copilot have changed
the way humans approach problems. These agents directly provide solutions to
the human that may affect their creative thinking. Programming is a creative
task that requires developers to clarify a problem space and implement developed
ideas. Developers may work together using pair programming – an agile method
where programmers switch roles between driver (actively coding) and navigator
(reviewing work, asking clarifying questions, and proposing suggestions) [1,2].
In this article, we are interested in exploring the effect of introducing a pair
programming agent on creativity from a gender perspective.

Prior work introduced PairBuddy, a pair programming agent that helps
address current limitations such as pair incompatibility [10], geo-temporal limitations associated with remote multi-national teams, and the need for a second
developer [12,22,23]. These prior studies have found the performance of Pair-
Buddy to be on par with a human [13]. However, researchers also found that

© The Author(s), under exclusive license to Springer Nature Switzerland AG 2023
C. Stephanidis et al. (Eds.): HCII 2023, CCIS 1832, pp. 594–602, 2023.
https://doi.org/10.1007/978-3-031-35989-7_75

creativity is affected by the introduction of an agent, especially for idea generation, as humans depended more on PairBuddy for code suggestions instead of exploring alternative solutions to the programming tasks [11].

To understand how an agent may effect a developers creative thinking process, we conducted two gender-balanced studies on pair programming: one between two developers (9 pairs) and the second between a developer and an agent (14 pairs) using a Wizard-of-Oz method. This method allows researchers to simulate the behavior of an agent prior to its development [14,27]. To analyze the data, we labeled the conversations using phases in the Osborn-Parnes creative problem-solving process: **clarify, idea, develop, and implementation** [19,20]. Furthermore, clarify breaks down into three sub-phases: exploring the vision, gathering data, and formulating challenges.

We investigated:

- *RQ1: How were creative phases affected in same and mixed-gender pairs?*
- *RQ2: How were creative phases affected when interacting with a developer vs. an agent?*

This article is organized as follows: Sect. 2 discusses Related Work, and our methodology is outlined in Sect. 3. Section 4 then highlights key findings with Sect. 5 concluding.

2   Related Works

2.1   Developer Creativity

One benefit of pair programming is increased creativity [3] and it has been suggested that programs created by pairs would be better due to combined experience and creativity [4]. In the classroom, researchers have found pair programming to be an effective teaching strategy [25,26] as students are more creative and experience more enjoyment [8]. To investigate the creative phases used by developers, we utilized the Osborn-Parnes Creative Problem Solving process (CPS) [9,18,19]. CPS uses 4 distinct phases, clarify, idea, develop, and implement, to model the creative process and is further elaborated in Sect. 3.3. Finally, CPS has been used in educational setting to help teach future developers programming [16,21].

2.2   Understanding Pair Programming Conversations

Prior work by Kuttal et al. investigated the effects of gender in remote pair-programming finding gender differences in role preference, same-gender pairs were more democratic, and in mixed-gender pairs women's self-efficacy was not improved [10,12,15,24]. Additionally, Kuttal et al. explored the effects of substituting a developer with a pair programming agent finding that such an agent could support active learning, motivation, and address compatibility issues, but developers trusted the agent too much as the agent could not explain itself or the concept being used to solve the problem [11,13,22,23]. Finally, prior work has explored the ability of BERT to classify the intent and slots of pair programming conversations finding gender bias in their performance [7,17].

3   Methodology

A lab study between a Developer-Developer (DD) was conducted with 9 gender-balanced (3 man-man, 3 man-woman, 3 woman-woman) participant pairs followed by a Developer-Agent (DA) study using Wizard of Oz Method. The DA lab data was collected virtually during the Covid-19 pandemic allowing us to collect data outside of the local area. The dataset contained 23 conversations, representing 8,324 utterances of both Developer-Agent (DA) and Developer-Developer (DD) dialogue.

3.1   Wizard of Oz Method and Agent Design

To conduct the Developer-Agent study, we used a Wizard of Oz (WoZ) method, a type of simulation where part or all of a systems functions are secretly controlled by a researcher known as the wizard [14,27]. WoZ methods allow researchers to collect dialogue that is unique to the interaction with agents. This dialogue is separate from the broader human discourse and lays the groundwork for future ML Algorithms [6]. In our study, one graduate and undergraduate student followed a script of templated responses with select options and simulated all other aspects of the agent [11,12,23]. Preliminary studies were conducted to train the wizards prior to those included here.

3.2   Task Design

Prior to starting the study, participants completed a background questionnaire and tutorials on the think-aloud method, test-driven development, pair programming, and, in DA studies, the capabilities of the agent. Alternatively, DD participants performed pair jelling tasks with their partner as prior research has shown that even small amounts of pair jelling can increase performance [5].

During the study, participants were given forty minutes to complete an implementation of Tic-Tac-Toe in Java using test-driven development and the think-aloud method. The time limit was chosen to avoid developer's fatigue. Further, test-driven development encourages developers to go through all stages of the software development lifecycle while the think-aloud method allows researchers to better model the participants cognitive process. Participants utilized the Eclipse IDE and JUnit testing framework as well as user stories and acceptance criteria to help solve their task.

3.3   Labeling

All lab studies were recorded and transcribed. The transcripts were labeled using the Osborn-Parnes Creativity Problem Solving (CPS) which consists of four phases: **clarify, idea, develop, and implement** [18,20]. The first phase, **clarify**, is used to gain a better understanding of the problem and consists of three sub-phases: **exploring the vision, gathering data, and formulating challenges**. Developers start in the **clarify** phase with **explore the vision** by identifying broad challenges or goals. Once a target is set, developers may **gather data** by turning to user stories, documentation, errors, or the code itself. Finally, participants **formulate challenges** by asking questions or focusing the goal in such a way that it invites solutions.

After **clarify** and **formulate challenges**, developers need to generate **ideas** to solve the current problem. Ideally, **idea** results in several possible solutions which can further be developed. Next, **develop** involves enumerating ideas, strengthening possible candidate solutions and eliminating nonviable alternatives. Finally, the developed idea needs to actually be **implemented** which includes the process of identifying the resources or actions necessary to do so.

Two researchers labeled the data, each labeled the first study settling disagreement through discussion. One researcher labeled six studies and the other researcher labeled seven. To measure inner-rater reliability, 20% of the data was labeled by each researcher achieving a Cohen's Kappa of 81.1%, which is considered substantial agreement.

4   Results

In this section we use either DD or DA to describe the partner type (developer or agent), S followed by a number to signify the study number, and either WW, MW, or MM to refer to woman-only, mixed, or man-only pairings respectively.

Table 1. Creativity stage usage by gender pairing

	WW		MW		MM	
Phase	#	%	#	%	#	%
Clarify	242	20.93	301	27.44	298	27.54
-Explore the Vision	17	12.5	23	12.85	9	3.10
-Gather Data	80	58.82	131	73.18	170	58.62
-Formulate Challenge	39	28.68	25	13.97	111	38.28
Idea	175	15.14	158	14.40	209	19.32
Develop	308	26.64	307	27.99	290	26.80
Implement	431	37.28	331	30.17	285	26.34

4.1   How Were Creative Phases Affected in the Same and Mixed Gender Pairs?

Table 1 shows the usage of each creativity phase and sub-phase grouped by the DD gender pairing.

Women-Only Pairings Clarified While Implementing

Overall, women-only pairings spent more time **implementing** (37.28%) at the expense of **clarifying** (20.93%) compared to other pairings (MW: 30.17%, 27.44% and MM: 26.34%, 27.54%). For example, in DD S4, a WW pairing, P2 clarified to her partner *"so this i equals to zero and if...zero one and two [und] three are all marked as the [same]...we consider it to be a winner"*, while writing an if statement for the horizontal win condition inside of a nested for loop. Then, her partner asked a quick **clarify** question about syntax before the pair continued to **implement**. In contrast, MM pairing preferred to run test cases to **clarify** functionality in order to **formulate challenges**. Such as in DD S1, a MM pairing, P1 was working on a similar loop when he said, *"It's ugly, but it should work...let's test what we have though"* after finishing the implementation of the pair's idea. Then, the pair received one failed test case which led them to formulate challenges about one of their methods.

Mixed-Gender Pairings Tended to Clarify by Gathering Data

Mixed pairings (73.18%) spent significantly longer on **gather data** compared to similar-gender pairings (MM 58.62% and WW 58.82%). This can best be seen in DD S3, where the MW pairing was attempting to use print statements to verify functionality when they realized nothing printed and decided to *"...just go from top bottom, [and] just check what each thing does."* The pair went back and forth clarifying each line of code *"..it calls tic tac toe game game...it'll start a new game g..."* before deciding to *"...focus on getting it to like actually say that we win"* and moving forward with the problem. However, in DD S2, the MM pair realized *"...the false [test case] is not right so let's check out [the] method"* and were quickly able to realize that they had not properly accounted for empty cells, resolving the test case, without the need for so much **gather data**.

Men-Only Pairings Favored Formulating Challenges to Explore their Vision

While all groups tended to start **clarify** after **implement** with **gather data**, MM groups would transition from **gather data** to **formulate challenges** rapidly without further use of **explore the vision**. This can be seen in DD S1 when the pair received *"...one failure, checkIsWinner"* while testing their implementation of a for-loop to check all the win condition the pair **formulated the challenge** that *"...if one of those diagonals or one of the columns is um all empties, then this would return true."* Instead of asking open ended questions and using **explore the vision**, MM pairing tended to focus on the challenge directly in front of them. As a result, men-only pairings (38.28%) spent the longest time formulating challenges when compared to women-only (28.68%) and mixed (13.97%) pairings.

All Pairings Developed Ideas

A common pattern observed for all DD interactions was that problem clarification persisted until a challenge was identified. **Ideas** could be generated and then evaluated, selected and/or strengthened through the **develop** phase, and finally **implemented**. For example in DD S7, P1 had the **idea** to *"...identify who* *has three columns first...* ", which P2 **developed** by suggesting they *"...could create another function..."* before P1 ultimately **implemented** the *"...function...winner check.".* Regardless of pairing, we found that developers spent a similar amount of time on **idea** (WW: 15.14%, MW: 14.40%, and MM:19.32%) and **develop** (WW:26.64%, MW:27.99%, and MM: 26.80%).

4.2 How Were Creative Phases Affected when Interacting with a Developer vs. an Agent?

Table 4.2 shows the usage of each creativity phase and sub-phase grouped by the gender and partner-type.

	Women				Men			
	DD		DA		DD		DA	
Phases	#	%	#	%	#	%	#	%
Clarify (Total)	366	22.76	759	44.78	475	27.50	725	51.49
-Explore the Vision	27	12.74	118	15.55	22	5.60	137	18.90
-Gather Data	137	64.62	292	38.47	244	62.08	268	36.97
-Formulate Challenges	48	22.64	349	45.98	127	32.32	320	44.14
Idea	253	15.73	142	8.38	289	16.73	104	7.39
Develop	444	27.61	112	6.61	461	26.69	86	6.11
Implement	545	33.89	682	40.24	502	29.07	493	35.01

All Participants Clarified more with an Agent by Exploring the Vision and Formulating Challenges, but Gathering Less Data
We found that men and women participants working with an agent **explore the vision** (M:18.90% and W:15.55%) and **formulate challenges** (M:44.14% and W:45.98%) more than participants working with another developer (M:5.60% and W:12.74%, M:32.32% and W:22.64%). This increase is most notable in men participants as when working with another developer only 27.50% of utterances were dedicated to **clarify**, with only 5.60% going towards **explore the vision**, but when working with an agent this increases to 51.49%, of which 18.90% is **explore the vision**. When working with an agent, developers would quickly **gather data** (M: 36.97% and W: 38.47%) by checking the current error message, reading a user story, or reviewing code and then start asking **clarify** questions to the agent. This can seen in DA S4 when the participant verifies that the user story *"...says that [if] you can't play it anywhere, then it should be a tie."* and then immediately asks *"so, we need some way to check and make sure that there are no spaces left right?"* By attempting to ask the agent for solutions, developers depended on **clarify** over **develop** or **idea**. However, when working with another developer participants would often go back and forth discussing **gathered data** (M: 62.08% and W: 64.62%). For example, in DD S9 the pair went *"..back to the tic tac toe game, [thinking] it was supposed to return true, after the first move anyways"* which led them to realize the test was *"...calling game.checkWinner"* and the pair continued to gather data by tracing through

the code. Without a human partner there was no interjecting or need to verify that the other human was following along.

DD Pairs Developed Ideas Together more While in DA Pair Developers Asked the Agent for the Ideas
When developers worked with other developers they tended to spend a proportionate amount of time on each of the creative problem solving phases including **idea** (W:15.73% and M:16.73%) and develop (W:27.61% and M:26.69%). However, when developers worked with an agent they tended to spend less time on **idea** (W:8.38% and M:7.39%) and **develop** (W:6.61% and M:6.11%). Further, DD pairs would explore 2–3 **ideas** whereas DA pairs only focused on 1–2 **ideas**, for instance, P2 in DD S8, presented several **ideas** such as using *"a zero or an o uhh Mark test here"* for marking the board. Additionally, those working with an agent tended to focus on evaluating and selecting ideas without strengthening them. For example, in DA S5 the participant had the idea to *"...check every column and then check the two diagonals"* which the agent replied *"how would that look like?"*, selecting the idea for implementation. Often, the agent would develop an idea by asking the developer to clarify the code after implementation without strengthening the idea. Occasionally, the agent would express doubt after an implementation by saying, *"I'm not sure if this is right."* To which the developer would either try again or allow the agent to write the code.

5   Conclusion

This work explored the gendered effects of pair programming with a developer and an agent. We found that when DD pairs spent roughly proportionate utterances in each of the Osborn-Parnes creativity problem solving phases. However, when working with an agent, developer's spent little time on the **idea** or **develop** phase. Additionally, women-only pairings would combine **clarify** with **implement** to facilitate understanding; whereas, men-only pairing tended to **clarify** by **gathering data** from test cases. Further, mixed gendered pairs tended to **gather data** going through the code line by line to **formulate a challenge**. Regardless of gender, participants working with an agent tended to **gather data** quickly so that they could formulate a new challenge for the agent.

References

1. Arisholm, E., Gallis, H., Dybå, T., Sjøberg, D.: Evaluating pair programming with respect to system complexity and programmer expertise. In: TSE, pp. 65–86 (2007)
2. Baheti, P., Gehringer, D., Stotts, P.: Exploring the efficacy of distributed pair programming (2002)
3. Begel, A., Nagappan, N.: Pair programming: what's in it for me? In: ESEM 2008: Proceedings of the Second ACM-IEEE International Symposium on Empirical Software Engineering and Measurement, pp. 120–128. ACM, October 2008
4. Bipp, T., Lepper, A., Schmedding, D.: Pair programming in software development teams - an empirical study of its benefits. Inf. Softw. Technol. **50**(3), 231–240 (2008). https://doi.org/10.1016/j.infsof.2007.05.006

5. Cockburn, A., Williams, L.: Extreme programming examined. chap. The Costs and Benefits of Pair Programming, pp. 223–243 (2001)
6. Dahlbäck, N., Jönsson, A., Ahrenberg, L.: Wizard of OZ studies: why and how. In: International Conference on Intelligent user Interfaces, pp. 193–200 (1993)
7. Hart, J. Aubuchon, J., Kuttal, S.K.: Feasibility of using youtube conversations for pair programming intent classification. In: VL/HCC (2022)
8. Howard, E., Evans, D., Courte, J., Bishop-Clark, C.: A qualitative look at alice and pair-programming. In: Number, vol. 7, August 2009
9. Isaksen, S., Treffinger, D.: Celebrating 50 years of reflective practice: versions of creative problem solving. J. Creative Behav. **38**(2), 75–101 (2004)
10. Kaur Kuttal, S., Gerstner, K., Bejarano, A.: Remote pair programming in online CS education: investigating through a gender lens. In: VL/HCC, pp. 75–85 (2019)
11. Kuttal, S.K., Myers, J., Gurka, S., Magar, D., Piorkowski, D., Bellamy, R.: Towards designing conversational agents for pair programming: accounting for creativity strategies and conversational styles. In: VL/HCC, pp. 1–11 (2020)
12. Kuttal, S.K., Sedhain, A., AuBuchon, J.: Designing a gender-inclusive conversational agent for pair programming: an empirical investigation. In: Degen, H., Ntoa, S. (eds.) HCII 2021. LNCS (LNAI), vol. 12797, pp. 59–75. Springer, Cham (2021). https://doi.org/10.1007/978-3-030-77772-2_4
13. Kuttal, S.K., Ong, B., Kwasny, K., Robe, P.: Trade-offs for substituting a human with an agent in a pair programming context: the good, the bad, and the ugly. In: CHI (2021)
14. Landauer, T.K.: Psychology as a mother of invention. In: ACM SIGCHI Bulletin, pp. 333–335 (1987)
15. Lott, C., McAuliffe, A., Kuttal, S.K.: Remote pair collaborations of CS students: Leaving women behind? In: VL/HCC (2021)
16. Mayer, R.E.: The psychology of how novices learn computer programming. ACM Comput. Surv. **13**(1), 121–141 (1981)
17. McAuliffe, A. Hart, J., Kuttal, S.K.: Evaluating gender effects in pair programming conversations. In: VL/HCC (2022)
18. Osborn, A.F.: Applied Imagination : Principles and Procedures of Creative Thinking. C. Scribner New York (1953)
19. Page-Jones, M.: The Practical Guide to Structured Systems Design. Prentice Hall, Prentice-Hall International Editions (1988)
20. Parnes, S.: Creative Behavior Workbook. Scribner, New York (1967)
21. Perkins, D.N., Martin, F.: Fragile knowledge and neglected strategies in novice programmers. In: Papers Presented at the First Workshop on Empirical Studies of Programmers on Empirical Studies of Programmers, pp. 213–229. Ablex Publishing Corp. (1986)
22. Robe, P., Kaur Kuttal, S., Zhang, Y., Bellamy, R.: Can machine learning facilitate remote pair programming? challenges, insights & implications. In: VL/HCC, pp. 1–11 (2020)
23. Robe, P., Kuttal, S.K.: Designing PairBuddy - conversational agent for pair programming **29**, 1–13 (2021)
24. Robe, P. Kuttal, S.K.A.J., Hart, J.: Pair programming conversations with agents vs. developers: challenges & opportunities for se community. In: The ACM Joint European Software Engineering Conference, and Symposium on the Foundations of Software Engineering (2022)
25. Ruvalcaba, O., Werner, L., Denner, J.: Observations of pair programming: variations in collaboration across demographic groups. In: Proceedings of the 47th ACM Technical Symposium on Computing Science Education, pp. 90–95. ACM (2016)

26. Seo, Y.H., Kim, J.H.: Analyzing the effects of coding education through pair programming for the computational thinking and creativity of elementary school students. Indian J. Sci. Technol. **9** (2016). https://doi.org/10.17485/ijst/2016/v9i46/107837

27. Yang, Q., Steinfeld, A., Rosé, C., Zimmerman, J.: Re-examining whether, why, and how human-AI interaction is uniquely difficult to design, pp. 1–13. ACM (2020)

Angular Foot Movement Time Variability in Foot-Based Interaction

Seung-Kweon Hong$^{(\boxtimes)}$ and Sangwon Kim

Korea National University of Transportation, Chungbuk 27469, South Korea
skhong@ut.ac.kr, sangwon7904@naver.com

Abstract. In the foot-based interaction studies, the typical pattern of foot movement is to lift the foot, move horizontally or vertically to approach an input button, and then click the button. This study is a research on angular foot movement in which the heel is fixed in one place and the foot/leg is rotated to approach the input button. The participants' posture (sitting/standing) did not affect the foot movement time. According to the previous studies, the time required in the other types of foot movement was shorter in the standing position than in the sitting position. It took less time to move the feet in the space on the front right side of the body than in the front center of the body. This indicates that it is effective to place the input device on the front right side of the worker's body rather than the front center of the body in the input task requiring angular foot movement. On the other hand, the input task requiring angular foot movement can be explained and predicted by Fitts' law, similarly to the input task requiring the other types of foot movement.

Keywords: Foot Movement Time · Angular Movement · Fitts' Law

1 Introduction

Typically, input devices are operated using human hands, but relying too much on the hands can decrease efficiency in input work [1]. To address this issue, the foot has been explored as an alternative or complementary input device, leading to increased research on foot-controlled input devices [2]. Our study focuses on the speed and accuracy of foot movements used for button clicking. Previous studies on foot movement speed and accuracy have mainly focused on buttons placed in the sagittal and frontal planes [3, 4], with foot movement involving lifting the foot and moving horizontally or vertically to approach the button before clicking it.

However, in our study, we consider a different pattern of foot movement, specifically angular foot movement. Angular foot movement involves moving the foot in a circular or angular direction, including rotational movements with the toes while keeping the heel in place. This type of movement is commonly used when moving the foot between the brake and accelerator pedals in a car and may be more efficient than lifting the foot from the floor in terms of speed and accuracy.

Despite the importance of angular foot movements in input work, there have been insufficient studies on the topic. Hong and Chae [5] measured foot movement time in

© The Author(s), under exclusive license to Springer Nature Switzerland AG 2023
C. Stephanidis et al. (Eds.): HCII 2023, CCIS 1832, pp. 603–608, 2023.
https://doi.org/10.1007/978-3-031-35989-7_76

various button arrangement situations and found that arrangements requiring angular foot movement resulted in shorter movement times and higher accuracy. Park and Myung [6] showed that angular foot movement time could be explained by a modified Fitts' law, although their study was limited to angular foot movement in a sitting posture. In our study, we conducted an experimental study on angular foot movements in both sitting and standing postures and compared our results to those of Park and Myung's study in terms of Fitts' law.

2   Methods

2.1   Participants and Tasks

This experiment involved ten college students between the ages of 22 and 27, consisting of 7 males and 3 females, who had no physical limitations in moving their feet and legs. The participants were instructed to fix their right foot's heel and use their toes to rotate their foot and leg to click an input button. As shown in Fig. 1, the input buttons were placed at angles of $-20°$, $0°$, $20°$, $40°$, and $60°$, with the participant's exact front set at $0°$. The distance between the heel position and the input button was determined by the participants based on the size of their foot.

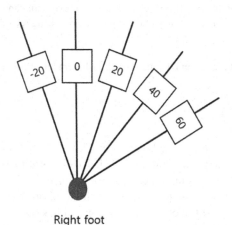

Right foot

Fig. 1. Positions where the input buttons can be installed and right heel position.

The buttons were square in shape with a width and height of 5 cm and were placed such that the foot's rotational direction and the vertical line of the button intersected at right angles, allowing participants to use the full width of the button. Only two buttons for the experiment were placed in front of the participants. Space between two buttons was set according to the experimental conditions. The participants were instructed to click two buttons reciprocally. The click times of two buttons were measured and the interval time between the two clicks was also recorded.

2.2 Experimental Design

The experimental design for this study is within-subjects design, where each participant is exposed to all experimental conditions. This design helps to control for individual differences between participants and increases the statistical power of the analysis. The two independent variables are posture (sitting and standing) and position of input buttons (front right side and front center of the body), and the dependent variable is angular movement time. Each participant is asked to perform the task 20 times under each experimental condition, and the conditions are randomized to prevent fatigue and learning effects.

To measure the time for angular foot movement based on the input button's position, two types of button arrangements were considered. The first type of arrangement consisted of setting one button on the −20-degree reference line and the other button on the reference line of 0, 20, 40, or 60° to change the foot rotation angle. This type of button arrangement induces input work on the front center of the body. The second type of arrangement consisted of setting one button on the 60-degree reference line and the other button on the reference line of −20, 0, 20, or 40° to change the foot rotation angle. This type of button arrangement induces input work on the front right side of the body.

3   Results

3.1   Variance Analysis of Foot Movement Time

Figure 2 displays the average angular foot movement times according to the foot rotation angle, working posture, and button position. A series of two-way analysis of variance for angular foot movement time was conducted. Table 1 presents the effect of working posture and button position on angular foot movement time at each foot rotation angle and also shows the interaction effect of the two variables.

In all rotation angles, there was no statistical difference in average angular foot movement time between standing and sitting postures. This result differs from those of experiments on the other types of foot movement pattern. For instance, in case of moving the foot vertically or horizontally, the foot movement time in the standing position was significantly shorter than that in the sitting position [3].

On the other hand, the time required for buttons on the front right side of the participants' body was significantly less than the time for buttons on the front center of the participants' body. This suggests that the participants felt more comfortable to rotate their foot in the front right side of the body. However, the interaction effect between posture and button position did not appear to be significant.

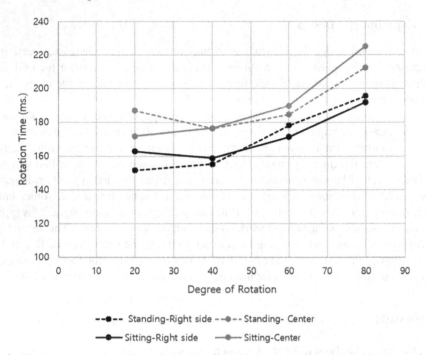

Fig. 2. Foot movement times depended on the foot rotation degree, posture and button position.

Table 1. Effects of working posture and button position on angular foot movement time at each foot rotation angle and the interaction effects.

Turning Angle	Variables	F	P
20°	Posture	F(1, 36) = 0.04	0.844
	Button position	F(1, 36) = 4.79	0.035*
	Interaction	F(1, 36) = 1.67	0.204
40°	Posture	F(1, 36) = 0.05	0.831
	Button position	F(1, 36) = 4.85	0.034*
	Interaction	F(1, 36) = 0.04	0.843
60°	Posture	F(1, 36) = 0.01	0.933
	Button position	F(1, 36) = 1.78	0.190
	Interaction	F(1, 36) = 0.40	0.530
80°	Posture	F(1, 36) = 0.26	0.617
	Button position	F(1, 36) = 8.18	0.007*
	Interaction	F(1, 36) = 0.86	0.359

3.2 Fitts' Model for Angular Foot Movements

According to traditional Fitts' law, the movement time can be described by the width of the target and the distance from the starting point to the target. However, in the angular movements, the width of the target has little influence on the time taken to complete the movement [6]. A modified Fitts' law has been proposed to account for movement time in these cases [7]. In this study, this model was applied to the collected data, except for the case where the rotation angle was 20-degrees. There was little difference in the time required for 20-degree turn and 40-degree turn. This can be said to be the result of an experimental error in which the foot rotation time was not accurately measured when at a small angle. The measured foot rotation time included not only the pure foot rotation time but also the time to click the start button and the target button. This result may appear when the button click time is longer than the pure foot rotation time and the variance of the button click time is large.

Equation 1 to 4 represent the modified Fitts' model for each posture and each button position. The models had a high explanatory power for the all cases. Park and Myung's experiment was limited to a button position in the front center of the body while seated. The coefficient of determination of their linear regression model was very high at 0.99. Our findings also showed high coefficients of determination under the same conditions, as well as under different conditions.

$$MT = 15.42 + 57.99\sqrt{A}, \quad R^2 = 0.999, \quad \text{Right} - \text{side } \textit{in standing posture} \tag{1}$$

$$MT = 13.55 + 87.21\sqrt{A}, \quad R^2 = 0.880, \quad \text{Center } \textit{in standing posture} \tag{2}$$

$$MT = 12.46 + 78.39\sqrt{A}, \quad R^2 = 0.965, \quad \textit{Right} - \textit{side in sitting posture} \tag{3}$$

$$MT = 18.27 + 56.94\sqrt{A}, \quad R^2 = 0.909, \quad \textit{Center} - \textit{side in sitting posture} \tag{4}$$

4 Discussion and Conclusion

Input work by foot is not superior to input work by hand in terms of the speed and accuracy [8]. In order for the foot to substitute for or assist the hand, foot-based interaction must be more efficient. Compared to foot movement lifting the foot from the floor and moving horizontally and vertically, the angular foot movement can be said to have higher speed and accuracy. Therefore, it would be desirable to utilize more angular foot movement when manipulating the input device.

In this study, angular foot movement times according to the working posture and the space in which the foot moves were investigated. Working posture did not affect foot movement time. The angular foot movement time was shorter when the foot moved to the font right side of the body rather than the front center of the body. This suggests input button should be located at the front right side of the body. On the other hand, input tasks requiring angular foot movement can be explained and predicted by Fits' law, just like input tasks requiring the other types of foot movement pattern.

Overall, this experiment provides important insights into the efficiency and accuracy of foot-controlled input devices, particularly when using angular foot movements. It should be noted, however, that there were some limitations to the study. The experiment only considered two types of button arrangements and did not investigate other variables such as button size or spacing. In addition, the experiment did not measure the muscle activation patterns during foot movement, which could provide insights into the biomechanical mechanisms of foot movement. Despite these limitations, the study provides valuable insights into the use of foot movement as an input method and may inform the design of input devices that utilize foot movement.

Acknowledgment. This research was supported by Basic Science Research Program through the National Research Foundation of Korea (NRF) funded by the Ministry of Education (Grant number #NRF-2022R1F1A1076475).

References

1. Hong, S.K.: A pilot study on the control performance of foot-controlled mouse devices for the nondisabled people. J. Ergon. Soc. Korea **35**(3), 175–184 (2016)
2. Velloso, E., Schmidt, D., Alexander, J., Gellersen, H., Bulling, A.: The feet in human–computer interaction: a survey of foot-based interaction. ACM Comput. Surv. (CSUR) **48**(2), 1–35 (2015)
3. Chan, A.H., Hoffmann, E.R.: Effect of movement direction and sitting/standing on leg movement time. Int. J. Ind. Ergon. **47**, 30–36 (2015)
4. Chan, A.H., Hoffmann, E.R., Wong, K.P.: Seated leg/foot ballistic and visually-controlled movements. Int. J. Ind. Ergon. **56**, 25–31 (2016)
5. Hong, S.K., Chae, J.S.: Work efficiency and layout of foot push buttons. J. Korean Inst. Plant Eng. **18**(1), 73–79 (2013)
6. Park, J.-E., Myung, R.-H.: Fitts' law for angular foot movement in the foot tapping task. J. Ergon. Soc. Korea **31**(5), 647–655 (2012)
7. Gan, K.-C., Hoffman, E.R.: Geometrical conditions for ballistic and visually-controlled movements. Ergonomics **31**(5), 829–839 (1988)
8. Hoffmann, E.R.: A comparison of hand and foot movement times. Ergonomics **34**(4), 397–406 (1991)

Into the Dark World of User Experience: A Cognitive Walkthrough Study

Rohit Jaiswal(✉) 🆔 and Harishankar Moosath

CHRIST (Deemed to Be University), Bengaluru, India
`rohit.jaiswal@psy.christuniversity.in`

Abstract. In this age of AI, the unison of man and machine is going to be more prominent than ever, thus creating a need to understand the underlying framework that is adopted by app designers and developers from a psychological point of view. Research on the various benefits and harmful effects of user experience design and furthermore developing interventions and regulations to moderate the use of dark strategies in digital tools is the need of the hour. This paper calls for an ethical consideration of designing the experience of users by looking at the unethical practices that exist currently. The purpose of the study was to understand the cognitive, behavioural and affective experience of dark patterns in end users. There is a scarcity in the scientific literature with regard to dark patterns. This paper adopts the methodology of user cognitive walkthrough with 6 participants whose transcripts were analysed using thematic network analyses. The results are presented in the form of a thematic network. A few examples of the themes found are the experience of manipulation in users, rebellious attitudes, and automatic or habitual responses. These findings provide a basis for an in-depth understanding of dark patterns in user experience and provide themes that will help future researchers and designers develop ethical and more enriching user experiences for users.

Keywords: User Experience · Dark Patterns · Cognitive Walkthrough

1 Introduction

In this age of AI, the unison of man and machine is going to be more prominent than ever, hence it is necessary to understand the underlying framework that is being used and developed by app designers and developers from a psychological point of view to necessitate research on the various benefits and harmful effects that they have to offer and furthermore create an analytic strategy to design interventions and regulations to moderate the use of addictive strategies and manipulative strategies in digital applications.

Dark patterns are misleading features that are purposefully designed to lead people to do activities that they otherwise wouldn't. The user is not benefited from these patterns but the benefit lies in those who are responsible for the product [4]. Dark patterns may be seen in many web products that are utilised all over the world, including social networking sites, different applications, and web services [4]. Organisations can direct users toward a desired conclusion from their point of view by developing interfaces deliberately and manipulatively [9]. Harry Brignull used the term "dark pattern" to describe this user exploitation phenomenon, which he characterised as "a user interface intentionally built to fool people into doing things they may not otherwise do" [2, 8]. Researchers have written several papers regarding dark patterns [3, 6], yet there is little research on the issue, indicating that it is understudied. The study by Mathur and colleagues [9] is an exception since they utilised an automated method—a web crawler created for experts—to find occurrences of dark patterns on over 11,000 shopping websites. The crawler found 1,818 examples of dark patterns inside these sites, even though it just looked at textual data and so ignored patterns enabled by colour, design, and other non-textual factors. Recent studies on the topic have been conducted at Purdue University, mainly by emphasising ethical aspects [5, 6]. In order to characterise numerous deceptive tactics, Brignull [2] created 12 different forms of dark patterns. Gray et al. [6] added to this by categorising them into five different groups: nagging, obstruction, sneaking, interface interference, and compelled action which is given below.

Fig. 1. Summary of dark pattern strategies [6].

2 Methods

2.1 Aim

To understand the user's experience of dark patterns in user experience design.

2.2 Research Question

- What are the cognitive aspects of the experience of dark patterns in user experience design?
- What is the user's emotional experience of dark patterns in user experience design?
- What is the user's behavioural response to dark patterns in the experience design?

2.3 Research Design

The study will follow a qualitative design. The qualitative phase will entail a cognitive walkthrough, where a set of stimuli will be presented to participants and their responses to the open-ended questions about each stimulus will be recorded.

2.4 Participants

The participants for the study were anyone who had a more than 3-h engagement on their mobile phone or pc/laptop. They must be users of services such as e-commerce and social media. The sampling technique followed is that of purposive sampling. The age group for the study is emerging adults (18–25). The total number of participants was n = 6.

2.5 Tools

The interview guide used for the purpose of the interview was validated by 4 expert validators and necessary changes were made by taking their feedback into account. Furthermore, the tools for the study include screenshots of the dark patterns that exist on the internet.

3 Results

The procedure for the formulation of the results displayed above was inspired and guided by Thematic network analysis [1]. The resultant themes were namely, Negative Experience Of Dark Patterns in users (affective), Avoidance and Withdrawal as Behavioural Responses in users (behavioural) and Interference with the Decision-Making Process in Users (cognitive).

A visual network map is given below.

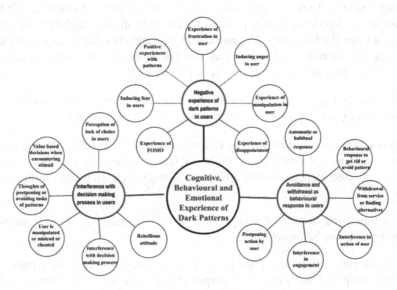

Fig. 2. Network Representation of analysis.

3.1 Theme 1: Negative Experience of Dark Patterns in Users

Experience of Frustration in Users. The theme comprises various experiences of users who experience frustration when they come in contact with dark patterns such as nagging, obstruction etc. They highlight that such experiences persist because dark patterns interrupt the engagement process of a user such as reading or browsing. This interrupted experience leads to feelings of frustration in users.

> "I feel frustrated that I was doing something that I was enjoying. Yeah. And then I have to pause in the middle and deal with this."

This experience then further leads to a sustained mark in the user during the use of the app which stings of discomfort and unpleasant emotions which the user seems to remember when a screenshot of dark patterns such as "nagging", "sneaking", "forced action" and "obstruction" was displayed to the user.

> "So what I have experienced so far is honestly that these pop-ups are kind of irrelevant, right? Yeah. So I would feel very annoyed at having wasted my time and I'm anticipating reading like finding out what the article's about, I read some genetic stuff leading into the article, then this thing pops up and then I feel annoyed at having wasted my time"

Most of the users reported feeling on a similar note, which led them to have thoughts about not wanting to continue to use the service, especially if such patterns are too frequent during the course of the users' use of the service.

Inducing Anger in Users. Anger and annoyance were common emotions felt by the users due to the experience of dark patterns, for instance, the user highlights that in their experience when the frequency of a pattern such as obstruction becomes too much, they experience the emotion of anger and feel annoyed at the fact that they are repeatedly disturbed from their experience of a particular service.

> "At first it does anger me because it's like, I mean, it says you can create a free account, but if it was free, it just might as well have, let me read it."

Experience of Manipulation in Users. Users also feel manipulated in the majority, as many experiences provoke them to think or feel a certain way they don't intend to or they are cheated by pre-selecting a bunch of items which are hidden from the user's obvious eye.

> "I think that it's to sort of manipulate you into spending more, without even realising that you're spending more."

It is with great bemusement that the users find these patterns to have manipulated them in the first place. Many users were surprised and when asked about their experience, their reflection on what they felt or thought about when the stimulus was shown was answered with an ecstatic response of them saying "I feel cheated".

"It's not a good feeling to be deceived by anyone, especially when you, uh, when you are using a laptop and using your PC, you're doing any work"

"It would make me feel cheated. So there's a clear sense of deception and also I might feel suspicious because, uh, I mean, this information is something that a lot of service providers do and you also openly accept and agree to the terms and conditions"

This was commonly seen in the patterns of "sneaking", "bait and switch" and "forced action".

Experience of Disappointment. Users are also disappointed at large as they end up losing trust in the service or they are made to feel sad for unsubscribing or quitting the use of a service they are engaging in and have an overall "sad" user experience.

"I don't like it at all. So if I think something is free, but I have to give my details, I will be disappointed"

Users generally have a certain expectations especially when they are doing a task at hand such as scrolling or reading. Upon an encounter with a dark pattern, their expectations of the service with regards to doing their task do not seem to meet and they feel disappointed. It is imperative to note that this experience turns into sheer disappointment when the frequency of the pattern is very high as some users noted that if it's only once in a while it may not bother them too much.

"I don't mind it because I like ads or games that may be fun but of course, I think after a point of time when it becomes too much it'll get very disappointing to use the app"

The user responds with the above statement when asked how they felt about an instance of "interface interference" whose stimulus was displayed on the screen. They mention that ads sometimes can be interesting and that it's okay to have them once in a while, it can be a good break from what they are engaged in. But, again, if the frequency of such patterns increases this will lead to a negative user experience of the app.

Inducing Fear in Users. A few patterns such as sneaking have been found to induce fear in users as they feel scared to use such services where pre-selected items are hidden from the user's knowledge and when they come to realise it which is very rare, they are fearful about using the product itself which then definitely urges them to terminate their service with the application. It is also mostly associated with scenarios where privacy of date and sharing is commonly pre-selected as shown by the stimuli during the interview. It is also important to note that, a few participants weren't aware of such a scenario and only became aware after displaying the stimulus.

"it sort of scares me to think about how many instances I would've missed out like this"

Experience of FOMO. Users are also made to feel fear in terms of missing out on exciting updates and influencing the users to retract their original decision. They end up feeling like they are going to miss out on something which in reality may not be really necessary such as air ticket insurance.

"make you feel like if you don't do it, you're actually losing out on something, something bad will happen to you. So they're sort of backing on that fact to make you engage with it more."

A few users also mention that patterns that induce "FOMO" don't really disrupt the user experience, instead, it is a smart way of getting users out of autopilot mode and actually may encourage them to think about making a decision without the element of manipulation.

Positive Experience. A few users don't mind experiencing a dark pattern such as FOMO and some even find it fascinating because the choices are clear and there is transparency involved in comparison to the rest of the patterns.

"You have options. It just opens up different possibilities. And I have a choice. I feel like I have a choice as a user, This definitely makes me feel much better as a user"

When compared to different stimuluses displayed, users realise that transparency and availability of choice is most important in their outlook towards user experience when using web applications.

3.2   Theme 2: Avoidance and Withdrawal as Behavioural Response in Users

Behavioural Response to Get Rid or Avoid Patterns. Getting rid of a dark pattern that seems to interfere with the user's engagement process is common among users. It is found that users are quite engrossed in what they do and such dark patterns are like house flies buzzing about your head when one is trying to concentrate.

"my first instinct would be to still remove it anyway because I didn't choose to add it."

Withdrawal From Service or Finding Alternatives. Users are found to withdraw and look for other alternatives when they encounter a dark pattern. It is interesting to note that some users indicate that if the content of the application is necessary for them it is only, in that case, they choose to continue the service.

"If I have no intentions of making an account, I will probably never use this website again, because I know I will not get the complete information that I need."

Interference in Action of User and Interference in Engagement. Users also encounter interference in the action they wish to perform. Users indicate that when a dark pattern is interfering with their screen, there is a lot of delays to find the close button because of which they are forced to view the ad for a while which again definitely frustrates the user in the experience of a service.

"It's not like I have the choice immediately. There is a choice to close it, to continue with my game, but usually, the choice comes a little later. So that waiting period ends up becoming very, very frustrating"

Postponing Action by Users. Users are found to postpone the task displayed by the stimulus most of the time by either clicking not now or remind me later. They say this process is a very unconscious response.

"Even if I'm actually not doing anything, I would, my first instinct would be just to not want to update it because yeah. It's just an added step to whatever I'm doing. postpone it as much as I could"

Automatic or Habitual Response. Most users claim that when they encounter a pattern that might ask them to rate the app or switch on a notification or any ad that interferes with the interface, most users click on the "not now", "maybe later" or "click on x button", without thinking. They claim that it has become a habitual experience and does not involve much thought process.

"It also happens that I press not now because it's such an autopilot response, That's not like a new stimulus for me. So again, the autopilot response is still there and that's not helping me deal with it all"

Many apps have such patterns that are quite recurring, this has helped the users learn their response and without reading what the interface has to say they click on a response that they are used to clicking.

3.3   Theme 3: Interference with Decision-Making Process in Users

Users are found to face difficulties and disturbances in their thought processes when trying to make a decision when they encounter a dark pattern. Their thoughts revolve around wanting a transparent choice but are loaded with triggers that confuse them or make them make a decision they never intended to make.

Perception of Lack of Choice in Users. An illusion of choice is what is encountered by users. With regards to patterns such as forced action, bait and switch etc. users are seen to perform an action they never intend to make and mostly go ahead with performing the action because they need the book or the update at some point. But the entire user experience of deceiving the users into thinking they have a choice does create a negative impression on the product.

"but here, even if I don't want to make an account, I have to in order to continue reading it, reading it. So I feel more restricted"

Worth or Value-Based Decision Making When Encountering with Stimuli. As described in the theme above, a decision such as rating or creating an account is taken ahead only if it matters to the user. In most users it is found that rating a famous app does not necessarily matter to the user and hence they don't engage in the process of rating instead they really need the content or really like they decide to create an account when they encounter the dark pattern.

"I was just, if it was a random use article that I'd open, you know, just for time pass and I was reading it, then it doesn't matter too much to me if I didn't finish reading the article because I was just reading it to pass the time"

Thoughts of Postponing or Avoiding Tasks of Patterns
It is found that users think about postponing the alert notifications or rating notifications or thinking about avoiding a particular service when they encounter a dark pattern.

"Maybe I'll think about it later. I'm not deciding in my head a clear no, either."

The User is Manipulated Misled or Cheated. Users are found to be misled as there is a mismatch between the user's intention and the intention of the service, this is commonly seen in bait and switch and sneaking patterns.

"I would feel manipulated because that's not the action that I was intending."

Interference with Decision-Making Process. Users also are found to suddenly get into a state of confusion or take unexpected time to perform an action. It is found that certain triggers like wording or colours interfere with the user's original decision.

"I think when they add that extra step of asking, are you sure? And yeah. And like, even if I'm still very sure about it, just because they've again said that I might miss things. It's very confusing."

Rebellious Attitude. It is interesting to note that some users have developed a rebellious attitude towards the service because of their encounter with the dark pattern. This is commonly seen in sneaking or nagging where pre-selected items are hidden even if the user wants to select those items they do not select them.

"Second, *like the fact that I didn't choose it anyway, so I don't want it, you know, that would drive me to remove it immediately."*

4 Discussion and Conclusion

"I wish I could cut off from the phone and internet world and just be like a hermit or something"

The development of technology so far has been for the people. Every advancement in the world of tech necessitates a fluid and satisfactory user experience. Without the effort in understanding human-computer interaction, technology would be a book lying on the shelf gathering dust. Research on user interface and user experience has enabled technology and humans to come closer together and work as one. This study is aimed at the same. Dark patterns are deceiving components that are purposefully designed to lead people to take activities that they otherwise wouldn't. The user is not the intended audience for these patterns [4]. The study has been in line with the understanding of dark patterns. It is interesting to know that the participants who spoke about their experience with a particular pattern pointed out a business angle towards why such a pattern is used. None of the participants was a designer working for technology companies. There is a general air of knowledge which possesses an understanding of why dark patterns are the way they are and users do not shy away from talking about it.

"They're like kind of gotten into your head and they they're getting you to like, say the words I'll do this later, perhaps priming you to do it in the future"

Negative feelings experienced when browsing might have an adverse effect on customer loyalty or buying intention [7]. The result of this study does take on similar lines, where users are interestingly seen to develop a "rebellious attitude" as mentioned in the result section, which is unique to this study, where it is found that negative experiences with patterns such as "sneaking", "bait and switch" etc. lead to termination of use of the service or closing the application and finding other alternatives.

An interesting finding during the course of the analyses was the theme of "positive experiences", where a few patterns helped the user. A suggestive pop-up to download a pdf, or even patterns that induce FOMO was seen to help the user get out of their autopilot mindset and actually think at that instance. Thinking enabled them to really consider insurance or subscribing to a certain service. This brings us to another important finding which is the "illusion of choice". Users reiterate that freedom of choice should never be taken away from the users when they encounter such patterns when patterns are presented with two or more courses of action such as "switch on alert" or "not now" even though it's obstructing their interface, they feel valued as a customer as the autonomy of choice rests with them and those who do not want alerts can simply click on not now allowing them to think about their decision at a later time.

Advertisements, sign-ups, checking out on e-commerce websites or apps etc., are designed in a way so that the experience of the user using their service is smooth and intuitive. But, this paper highlights important design strategies that are leading to poor user experience in users. A summary of this is given in Fig. 1. This article focuses on 3 target areas namely, cognitive, behavioural and affective experience in users. Hence, it has tried to gauge a wholesome picture of how the experiences are shaped using cognitive walkthrough as the primary methodology in the study. The results (Fig. 2) show that there is a negative impact on users and research in human-computer interaction must be directed towards mitigating such patterns that exist in the majority of applications we use every day. The implications concerning Human-computer Interaction open up an important dialogue and scientific research on creating ethical designs. Furthermore, the article provides an understanding of the cognitive, behavioural and affective experiences or dark patterns, that can act as a base to conduct future research.

References

1. Attride-Stirling, J.: Thematic networks: an analytic tool for qualitative research. Qual. Res. 1(3), 385–405 (2001)

2. Brignull, H.: Dark patterns: Inside the interfaces designed to trick you (2013). Accessed 19 Mar 2019
3. Brownlee, J.: Why dark patterns won't go away (2016). Accessed 21 Feb 2019
4. Cara, C.: Dark patterns in the media: a systematic review. Netw. Intell. Stud. 7(14), 105–113 (2019)
5. Chivukula, S.S., Brier, J., Gray, C.M.: Dark intentions or persuasion? UX designers' activation of stakeholder and user values. In: Proceedings of the 2018 ACM Conference Companion Publication on Designing Interactive Systems, pp. 87–91 (2018)
6. Gray, C.M., Kou, Y., Battles, B., Hoggatt, J., Toombs, A.L.: The dark (patterns) side of UX design. In: Proceedings of the 2018 CHI Conference on Human Factors in Computing Systems, pp. 1–14 (2018)
7. Hibbeln, M., Jenkins, J.L., Schneider, C., Valacich, J.S., Weinmann, M.: How is your user feeling? Inferring emotion through human–computer interaction devices. MIS Q. 41(1), 1–22 (2017)
8. Kim, W.G., Pillai, S.G., Haldorai, K., Ahmad, W.: Dark patterns used by online travel agency websites. Ann. Tour. Res. 88, 1–6 (2021)
9. Maier, M., Harr, R.: Dark design patterns: an end-user perspective. Hum. Technol. 16(2), 170 (2020)
10. Mathur, A., et al.: Dark patterns at scale: findings from a crawl of 11K shopping websites. Proc. ACM Hum.-Comput. Interact. 3(CSCW), 1–32 (2019)

User Reaction to AI Interview: Focusing on Emotion and Intentions Expressed in an Online Community

Hye Min Lee and Young June Sah[✉]

Graduate School of Metaverse, Sogang University, Seoul, Republic of Korea
ysah@sogang.ac.kr

Abstract. AI interviews are widely expanding as the need for transparent processes in hiring employees increases and in-person interviews shrink due to the Covid-19 pandemic. The current study examined how people respond to AI interviews and whether their responses change over time, using data from Blind, a Korean online community for workers, where users share information and opinions related to the company they work for. We collected a total of 263 posts and 1,832 comments on the subject of 'AI interview' and classified them into the emotional expressions and intentions of posts. The results revealed that the majority of the posts expressed negative emotions rather than positive ones. The negative emotions were expressed mostly toward self or the AI interviewer, the hiring company, or the AI interview solution company. Furthermore, posts and comments not revealing emotions were requesting or sharing information. It is also found that posts expressing negative emotions were likely to receive supportive comments whereas informative posts were likely to garner sneering comments. To sum up, users appreciate fully the online social platform to reduce uncertainty and mitigate any negative feelings from the unexperienced technological challenge.

Keywords: AI Interview · Online Community · Sentiment Analysis

1 Introduction

AI interviews are a brand-new technology in real life. AI interview is progressed by asking questions to the interviewee in real time and recording the process of answering, while analyzing non-verbal factors such as the interviewee's expression, eye movement, and voice pitch. It consists of self-introduction, personality trait tests, or role plays in an office situation, and a structured in-depth interview [1]. In South Korea, it was first introduced by public enterprises in 2018 and has been gradually expanded, and currently more than 600 companies have used AI interviews as part of their recruitment process [2]. This expansion had been based on the need for a fair recruitment process, and the demand for online interviews during the COVID-19 pandemic. It means that AI interviews have become a kind of rite of passage not only for students who have just graduated from college but also for office workers preparing for better companies. To this end, this study investigated people's perceptions of AI interviews using data from

© The Author(s), under exclusive license to Springer Nature Switzerland AG 2023
C. Stephanidis et al. (Eds.): HCII 2023, CCIS 1832, pp. 619–625, 2023.
https://doi.org/10.1007/978-3-031-35989-7_78

'Blind', a Korean online community where users share various information including personal or social issues.

In online communities, users can share information and state their opinion. In social media, knowledge and opinion are widely diffused when it comes to negative or positive rather than neutral [4]. Knowledge diffusion refers to the spread and dissemination of knowledge, information, or innovation from one individual, organization, or community to another. It can occur through various channels, including social networks, publications, conferences, workshops, training programs, collaborations, and partnerships. The goal of knowledge diffusion is to facilitate learning, innovation, and problem-solving, and to enhance the adoption and implementation of new knowledge or practices.

Blind is an anonymous online community for workers and a venue for knowledge diffusion among company workers. For joining Blind, it is required to certify the users' company emails. After identifying the company emails, a user can freely read and write posts and comments. When users write a post or comment, their nicknames and their current companies are displayed with their messages. It means that users' current company is the only information available to other users. As of 2023, more than eight million workers participate in the community regardless of sectors, job positions, and scales of companies [3], rendering Blind an appropriate venue for collecting data for the purpose of the current study. In Blind, we can collect posts not only generated by job seekers who are preparing for an AI interview but also by stakeholders such as HR staff from hiring companies or programmers from AI solution companies. We expect users to reveal their emotions about AI interview in posts and comments.

Previous studies reported that posts in online communities can be classified into two categories, one requesting information and the other sharing information or opinion [4]. In line with this finding, we expect that Blind posts related to AI interview and comments on the posts are either requesting information or expressing opinion. In addition, we predict that posts also include emotional expressions toward AI interview. Users may request or share information in comments as well as reveal their attitude towards the author of a post. The attitude toward posters expressed in the comments can be supportive or sneering.

About the comment, we expect most comments are supportive of the poster, because the comments are dependent on the content of the posts. Earlier research on emotional contagion suggests that when people express positive or negative emotions in their posts, it can influence the emotions expressed in the comments. In written communication, emotional expression can grab the attention of others, which can increase their cognitive engagement and likelihood of responding to emotional stimuli by sharing information. Additionally, attention plays a role in emotional contagion, which is the spread of mood and affect through populations simply by exposure. [5]. In line with this literature, we assume that the purpose and sentiment in the comments are correlated with the posts' purpose and sentiment. For example, when the post is negative then the mainstream of comment would be supportive by mentioning negative aspects of AI Interview.

Based on the argument stated above, we propose our research questions as follows.

RQ 1: What are the contents of the post regarding the AI interview?

RQ2: What is the overall content of the comments? Are they supportive or critical of the post author? If they are supportive, how are they showing support? And what types of critical comments are there?

RQ3: How are comments different across the post types? In a post requesting information or sharing information, are there supportive comments for the author of the post, or are there sneering at comments? On the other hand, in posts that express emotions, will there be comments requesting or sharing information? Or will there be comments that express agreement or sarcasm?

2 Method

This study collected 263 posts and 1,832 comments on the subject of 'AI interview' in the blind for 4 years from May 18, 2018, when AI interview was introduced, to December 31, 2022. We used content analysis methodology to examine the intent of posts and comments (whether they were requesting information or sharing information), emotional states, and the recipient of negative emotions. This involved manually processing the data and performing semantic analysis.

2.1 Data Analysis

Intention. According to the intention of writing posts and comments, they were classified as 'requesting information' or 'sharing information.' 'Request for information' was coded when a post is asking questions about an AI interview, and 'sharing' was coded when the intention was to share know-how and tips on AI interview or to present opinions on the subject.

Emotional State. We coded posts whether the user's emotional expression toward the 'AI interview' was positive or negative.

Targets of Negative Emotions. In the case of posts expressing negative emotions, the types of subjects were subdivided. There are four main categories: self (e.g., "I screwed up the AI interview because I couldn't concentrate on the interview."), AI interviewer (e.g., "A machine dares to evaluate a human being."), hiring company (e.g., "The company did delegate everything to AI interviewers. AI interviews were introduced to reduce labor costs without considering the recruitment of talented individuals"), and AI interview solution company ("The company which developed AI interview should be cursed.").

Attitudes in Comments. Comments reveal users' reactions and show their attitudes to posts. It is reasonable to assume that they are affected by the content and emotion of the post, and by other comments left early to the post. We coded comments as 'supporting' when they sympathized with or defended the post author, and as 'sneering' if they criticize or refute the post author.

3 Result

Results showed that the posts are divided into three categories. One is a negative emotion toward an AI interview. We further analyzed these and classified into four categories depending on the targets of the emotion. They include 'self,' 'AI interviewer,' 'hiring company' and 'AI-solution company.' Posts not revealing emotions were coded as either requesting information or sharing information. The percentage of posts requesting information was more than twice the percentage of posts sharing the information (see Table 1). However, the number of posts sharing information about AI interviews has gradually increased. There are three categories for requesting information: (1) asking for compatible devices, appropriate dress code such as casual or formal, (2) expected time for the result to be announced, and (3) strategies to do well on an AI interview. In contrast, two types emerged in posts sharing information: (1) know-hows or tips for AI interview and (2) personal opinions about AI interviews (see Table 1).

All emotional expressions in the posts accounted for negative emotion. In the online community postings, 69% of the negative expressions were toward 'self.' Furthermore, the target for negative expression also suggested that users tend to feel humiliated how robots (AI interviewers) can evaluate human beings when they failed AI interview. However, it is interestingly shown that the percentage of posts expressing negative emotion to hiring companies and AI-solution companies are about the same. This means users do not blame companies but speak ill of themselves or AI-interviewer (see Table 1).

Table 1. Distribution of post ($N = 263$)

Definition	Example	n (%)
Requesting Information	*"Can you give me some tips for an AI interview?"*	83 (32%)
Sharing Information	*"It would be helpful to search through YouTube."*	36 (14%)
Negative		144 (54%)
Self	*"I screwed up AI interview because of my incapability"*	100 (69%)
AI interviewer	*"A machine dares to evaluate a human being"*	20 (14%)
Hiring company	*"AI interviews were introduced to reduce labor costs without thinking about recruiting talented people"*	12 (8%)
AI-Solution Company	*"company which developed AI interview should be cursed"*	12 (8%)
Positive		0 (0%)

In the comments, users are more willing to share information (31%) rather than simply providing information (20%). Generally, it shows that users are willing to answer the questions in the posts instead of ignoring the posts. Furthermore, a large portion of the comments are about supporting original post writers (35%). Supporting original post writers are divided into three parts: (1) to sympathize with the author (35%), (2) to advocate the posters' opinions (25%), and (3) to trust tips for original posters (40%).

Secondly, the act of sneering at the poster (11%) is also classified into three categories: (1) to make fun of the original poster's situation, such as mocking their failure in an AI interview (45%), (2) to oppose the poster's opinion (37%), and (3) to doubt the original posters' know-hows (17%) (see Table 2).

Table 2. Distribution of comments (N = 1,832)

Definition	Example	N (%)
Requesting information	*"Can you share your experience with AI interview?"*	383(20%)
Sharing information	*"AI interview result will be announced within a week"*	573(31%)
Supporting comments		649(35%)
advocate poster's opinion	*"I agree with the idea that an AI interview is just reducing cost for recruiting."*	260(40%)
sympathize with poster	*"I feel sorry that author failed the AI interview."*	227(35%)
trust poster's know-hows	*"Your tips are helpful. Thanks."*	162(25%)
Sneering comments		195(11%)
make fun of poster	*"You lost the robot. Shame on you, human."*	88(45%)
oppose poster's opinion	*"I don't think AI interviews matter during the recruitment process."*	72(37%)
doubt poster's know-hows	*"Your tips are out of date."*	35(18%)
Off-Topic		35(0.02%)

We further analyzed how comments and posts are associated. It is shown that informative comments such as requesting or sharing information are mainly attached to the posts requesting information. In contrast, emotional comments (e.g., supportive or sneering) are shown in negative posts.

Regarding posts that request information, the comment that elicits the highest number of replies is the one that provides information, which makes up 43% of all comments. The second most common comment, comprising 26% of all comments, is the one that seeks more information. These comments can either be supportive (22%) or sarcastic (7%) in nature. Supportive comments tend to mirror the questions that the post author has, while sneering comments often ridicule the author's "stupid" question.

As for posts that share information, the majority of comments (37%) are supportive, with users expressing trust in the poster's tips on AI interviews. Another significant portion of comments (26%) provide related tips, while some (22%) ask for more information or express doubt in the poster's tips (13%).

Negative posts attract the most comments, accounting for 55% of all comments (1,008 out of 1,832). Of these, supportive comments account for the largest percentage (45%), with users questioning the AI interviewer's ability to evaluate human beings and sharing their own experiences or knowledge on how to handle non-human interviewers.

Additionally, users ask for tips on how to overcome interview-related stress (17%) and share humor at the poster's expense (14%). Posts requesting information make up the next largest percentage of comments, comprising 41% of all comments. It's interesting to note that posts sharing information only account for less than 5% of comments. Therefore, most comments are concentrated in negative posts or posts requesting information (See Table 3).

Table 3. The distribution of comments by the post type ($N = 1,832$)

Comment (N = 1,832)	Post (N = 263)			
	Requesting information	Sharing information	Negative	Total
Requesting information	198(26%)	16(22%)	169(17%)	383
Sharing information	327(43%)	19(26%)	227(23%)	573
Supporting comments	167(22%)	27(37%)	455(45%)	649
Sneering comments	49(7%)	9(13%)	137(14%)	195
NA	11(2%)	1(1%)	20(2%)	32
Total	752	72	1,008	1,832

4 Discussion

The current study found that Blind users show their perception toward AI interview in posts or comments. In the posts, users tend to ask for how to do well on AI interview. Furthermore, they blame themselves or AI-interviewers when they did not pass the AI interview rather than attributing the failure to hiring companies or AI-Solution companies. In contrast with the post, the authors in the comments are willing to share information. Regarding the portion of comment, informative comments are mainly attached to posts requesting information, while emotional comments are predominantly found in negative posts. For posts that request information, the comment that elicits the most replies is the one that provides information, while for posts sharing information, the majority of comments are supportive. Negative posts attract the most comments, with supportive comments being the largest percentage. It's also interesting to note that posts sharing information account for less than 5% of comments, with the majority of comments being concentrated in negative posts or posts requesting information. These findings suggest that emotional content and requests for information are significant factors in driving engagement and interaction on online platforms.

The current study has several limitations that should be acknowledged. First, it only represents Korean companies and does not account for other domains, such as education, where AI interviews may be applied, such as university entrance exams. In the educational field, AI-interviewers may be used to assess an applicant's ability to work well with others. Future studies in different fields may yield different findings. Additionally, analyzing changes between posts and comments over time could provide meaningful insights. Through an examination of the temporal differences between posts and comments, it is possible not only to determine the thresholds for positive and negative comments directed at the poster, but also to ascertain when users abstain from writing comments.

As AI interviews are becoming more common in Korea, lots of people will have to interact with AI. We anticipate that users may be able to reduce their negative feelings towards AI interviewers and overcome challenges in the interview process by proactively seeking advice and expressing their emotions through online communities. Moving forward, we plan to collect samples over a long period of time through continuous monitoring and use factor analysis to explore additional factors that influence posts and comments.

Acknowledgement. This research was supported by the MSIT (Ministry of Science and ICT), Korea, under the Graduate School of Metaverse Convergence support program (IITP-2023-RS-2022-00156318) supervised by the IITP (Institute for Information & Communications Technology Planning & Evaluation).

References

1. MidasIT. https://www.midashri.com/intro/ai. Accessed 12 Mar 2023
2. Donga news. https://www.donga.com/news/Economy/article/all/20220502/113177779/1. Accessed 12 Mar 2023
3. MT news. https://news.mt.co.kr/mtview.php?no=2023022810185565400. Accessed 13 Mar 2023
4. Savolainen, R.: Asking and sharing information in the blogosphere: the case of slimming blogs. Libr. Inf. Sci. Res. **33**(1), 73–79 (2011)
5. Stieglitz, S., Dang-Xuan, L.: Emotions and information diffusion in social media—sentiment of microblogs and sharing behavior. J. Manag. Inf. Syst. **29**, 217–248 (2013)
6. Wagg, A.J., Callanan, M.M., Hassett, A.: Online social support group use by breastfeeding mothers: a content analysis. Heliyon **5**(3), e01245 (2019)
7. Bălău, N., Utz, S.: Information sharing as strategic behaviour: the role of information display, social motivation and time pressure. Behav. Inf. Technol. **36**, 589–605 (2017)

Study on the Consumption Difference of Children's Smartwatches Under SOR Theory

Tianhao Li, Xinyi Xu, and Cong Cao[✉] [iD]

Zhejiang University of Technology, Hangzhou 310023, China
congcao@zjut.edu.cn

Abstract. Smart wearable devices are being introduced as the next generation of ubiquitous technologies after smartphones. With the booming development of the smart wearable devices market, children's smart wearable devices represented by children's smartwatches have become a new force. However, the response of the Chinese and western countries markets to children's smartwatches is quite different. This paper builds a model based on the SOR theory. This model summarizes the influencing factors of consumers' purchase intention from three aspects: functional characteristics, situational characteristics and flow experience. This model has both theoretical and practical value. The results can enrich the research of related theories, and play a certain guiding role in the market development of manufacturers.

Keywords: Children · Smartwatches · Demand Boosting Effect · Problem Suppression Effect · Regional Differences

1 Introduction

Smart wearable devices are being introduced as the next generation of ubiquitous technologies after smartphones [1]. In China, according to data from Zhongyan.com, the number of children aged 5–12 in China is about 170 million in 2021, and the market penetration rate of children's smartwatches is about 30%. However, the most western consumers of children's smartwatches enthusiasm are not high. What's more, the German federal network agency announced a ban on children's smartwatches in 2017 and encouraged parents to destroy the children's smartwatches they already have. It is worth pondering why there is such a big difference between Chinese and western countries' responses to children's smartwatches.

The academia has conducted in-depth research on the related issues of smart wearable devices, which are mainly divided into two aspects: user willingness and privacy protection. In terms of users' willingness to use smart wearable devices, users intentions to use smart wearable devices are determined by five influential factors: satisfaction, enjoyment, usefulness, flow state, and cost [2]. Privacy issues have become important for consumers who, for the most part, expect some control over their privacy when using wearable devices [3]. In terms of privacy protection involved in smart wearable devices, smart wearables are revolutionizing how users communicate and acquire information

[4]. Yet, the user benefits of smart wearables largely depend on the devices ability to collect and analyze a large amount of user data, shaping the smart wearables-privacy paradox. Wearable devices can also collect user data regardless of time and place, uploading data to the cloud can easily make the wearable device's system vulnerable to attacks and data leakage [5].

In general, flow experience partially mediates the effects of interaction on repurchase intention. Therefore, this paper chooses flow experience as the intermediary and SOR theory as the research basis. By establishing a model, the influences of functional diversity, functional practicality, privacy disclosure and comparison of flow experience are discussed.

2 Literature Review

Mehrabian and Russell (1974) first proposed the stimulus-organic-response (SOR) theory, confirming that when an individual is stimulated by external stimuli (S), some emotion (O) will be generated in his heart, which will then trigger the individual response (R). The SOR theory has been empirically tested in many fields and is a typical theoretical model for the study of individual behaviour.

Csikszentmihalyi focuses on consumer experience and first proposed the concept of "flow experience". He focuses on the psychological satisfaction of online consumers in the process of online shopping. When individuals are in a state of flow experience, they are completely absorbed in what they are doing. The mood was very happy and it felt like time passed very quickly. Flow experience is often used as an important mediator when the academic community uses SOR theory to build models.

The current studies covered different research themes which are related to the smart wearables area, particularly user behaviour, technology-focused, security and privacy, design, and social acceptability [6]. However, academic researchers have some limitations. On one hand, the geographical region has an impact on buying behaviour [7]. However, most studies are based on the actual situation of their own countries or regions. When customers journey from a need to a purchase decision and beyond, they rarely do so alone [8]. We need to recognize regional differences in consumption behaviour. In addition, there are few studies on children's smart wearable devices represented by children's smartwatches. The current studies stop at the category of smart wearable devices, without corresponding mining and analysis of the problems involved in the market expansion of segmented products.

To sum up, the current problems are as follows:

- Research on purchasing behaviour of smart wearable devices is limited to the country or the region, with few cross-regional studies.
- There is insufficient research on the market segment of intelligent wearable devices.
- Studies on privacy paradox or user intention ignore the mediating role of flow experience, so the conclusions are often limited

Therefore, the SOR model using flow experience as a mediator is appropriate. By studying the influence of various factors on flow experience, the model can finally determine the source of differences in purchase intention.

3 Theoretical Development

This paper aims to establish a model of influencing factors of consumers' purchase intention. The internal mechanism of sales differences in children's smartwatches is explored through influencing factors of consumers' purchase intention. The SOR model has been evolving and developing for a long time and has an authoritative position in the academic circle. Therefore, the SOR model is widely used in research on consumers' purchase intentions.

For example, upon the SOR framework, a multi-mediation model is proposed to address this relatively new research avenue. It was discovered that the environmental stimuli (i.e., perceived mobility, social presence, and system and service quality) directly and indirectly influence tourists' MST shopping intention through their inner organism changes (i.e., perceived usefulness and perceived enjoyment) [9]. To address the research gap, researchers conducted a systematic review of studies on online impulse buying and used the SOR framework to identify and classify the factors that affect online impulse buying [10]. The results showed that: information and service quality are key antecedents of perceived value, whereas rewards and recognition, and customization are non-significant [11].

Therefore, this paper intends to refer to relevant literature studies and combine the features of smart wearable devices such as children's smartwatches, and comprehensively utilize SOR to establish the influencing factor model of consumers' purchase intention.

4 The Proposed Model

This paper builds a model based on the SOR theory. This model summarizes the influencing factors of consumers' purchase intention from three aspects: functional characteristics, situational characteristics and flow experience. This model has both theoretical and practical value. The results can enrich the research of related theories, and play a certain guiding role in the market development of manufacturers.

4.1 Functional Diversity

As for individual consumers, they are more willing to try and use products with a higher degree of diversity [12]. This means that the variety of product features can affect the flow experience of consumers.

Product function diversity can stimulate consumers' curiosity and desire to explore. When consumers buy a product, they will be interested in and curious about the various functions and features of the product. This curiosity and exploratory desire can help consumers have a deeper understanding of the features and use methods of the product, to improve the user experience.

Product function diversity can meet the needs of different consumers. Consumers have different needs. Some consumers focus on the appearance and design of products, while others focus on the practicality and function of products. If the product has a variety of functions and features, it can meet the needs of different consumers, thus improving the market competitiveness of the product (Fig. 1).

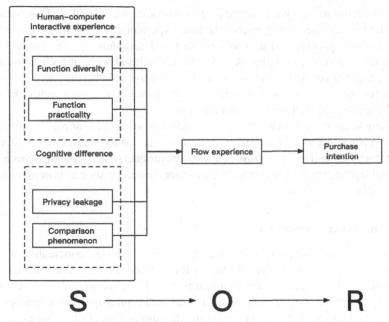

Fig. 1. Influence factor model of consumption difference based on the SOR

4.2 Functional Practicality

Finneran and Zhang [13] proposed in the PAT (Person-Artifact Task) model that the tool should be aligned with the task, that is, the user believes that only the use of a tool is appropriate to accomplish a task or function, and flow experiences are more likely to occur in this situation. Ghani and Deshpande [14] summarized two important manifestations of flow experience: total commitment to activity and pleasure from the activity. The results of the flow experience make participants focus on the body experience of the process, thus losing the sense of time. That means that the usability of the product affects the flow experience of the consumer.

Product functionality utility can increase consumers' confidence in using the product. When a product's functions and features are useful and practical, consumers are more likely to feel confident in using the product. This confidence can help consumers enter a state of flow, where they are fully immersed in the product and its functions, leading to a more satisfying user experience.

Product functionality utility can increase the overall satisfaction of consumers. When consumers use a product with practical and useful functions and features, they are more likely to feel satisfied with their purchase. This satisfaction can further enhance the flow experience, leading to a heightened sense of enjoyment and pleasure.

4.3 Privacy Leakage

Studies have shown that the importance of users' perception of privacy has a significant impact on their attitudes [15]. In the development of customer relationship planning, privacy concerns will play a negative role in customer feelings [16]. That means that privacy leakage can negatively impact the flow experience of consumers.

Privacy leakage can lead to a loss of trust and confidence in the product. When consumers' personal information is accessed or disclosed without their consent, they may feel that the product is not secure or trustworthy. This loss of trust can make it difficult for consumers to enter a state of flow, as they may be distracted or worried about the security of their personal information.

Privacy leakage can lead to negative emotional states, such as anger, frustration, and anxiety. When consumers' personal information is accessed or disclosed without their consent, they may feel angry or frustrated with the product or the company. This negative emotional state can make it difficult for consumers to enter a state of flow and enjoy the product fully.

4.4 Comparison Phenomenon

Bertrand and Morse have found that non-rich families will have the mentality of keeping up with the Joneses when they are at a higher level of Top Income and consumption, and thus consume a larger share of their current income [17]. For some commodities, their ownership or value is likely to be correlated with the "keeping up with the Joneses effect" of promoting household consumption through the motivation of highlighting their own status [18]. Therefore, for parents, they do not want their children to use smartwatches as the capital to show off and reduce their purchase intention. However, some parents are buying their children expensive smartwatches to show off their status. Therefore, the influence of comparison phenomenon on flow experience is two-sided. This is reflected in the following aspects.

Comparison phenomenon can influence consumers' values. People tend to measure their self-worth and compare themselves with others based on their material possessions and social status. This value system can affect consumers' purchasing behaviour, leading them to pursue more expensive and luxurious products, thereby increasing their pressure and financial burden. Comparison phenomenon can affect consumers' emotional states. People in this atmosphere often feel anxious, insecure, and dissatisfied, which can undermine their flow experiences and diminish their purchasing satisfaction.

4.5 Flow Experience

Trevino and Webster [19] believe that flow experience is an important factor in human-computer interaction design. Many studies have confirmed that flow experience is positively correlated with purchase intention [20]. Therefore, the change in flow experience will directly affect the change in consumers' purchase intention.

Flow experience can improve consumers' sense of self-efficacy and self-affirmation. In a state of flow, consumers feel focused and confident that they can overcome challenges and difficulties. This sense of self-efficacy and self-affirmation will enhance consumers' confidence and determination, thus improving their purchase intention.

Flow experiences can satisfy consumers' needs and desires. In shopping activities, consumers often have a variety of needs and desires, such as getting recognition, satisfying curiosity, improving self-confidence, and so on. When consumers experience a state of flow during shopping activities, these needs and desires will be satisfied, thus increasing their purchase intention.

Flow experiences can stimulate consumers' desire to buy. In the state of flow, consumers will feel very happy and excited, thus increasing their desire to buy. Flow can also give consumers a sense of detachment from reality, making them more likely to make impulsive purchases.

5 Comprehensive and Multi-level Support

In the process of research and analysis, different factors have different impacts on flow experience. We summarize functional diversity and functional utility as a human-computer interactive experience. Good human-computer interaction experience has a positive effect on consumers' flow experience. We summarize the privacy leakage and compare climate as cognitive differences. People in different countries and regions have different levels of acceptance of privacy leaks. People in different countries and regions have different definitions of keeping up with the Joneses. Children have very limited purchasing power. For smart wearable devices aimed at children, such as children's smartwatches, parents' opinions on the products often decide whether to buy or not. Children often have the will but not the right to decide in this process.

Since parents have certain rights to operate children's smartwatches, the feelings of parents and children should be considered at the same time when studying the human-computer interaction experience. In addition, children's cognition is limited, and it is difficult to play a decisive role in purchasing decisions. Therefore, in the study of cognitive differences, we should focus on the cognitive differences of parents.

Manufacturers want to consider as many factors as possible when researching the market. Some factors do not directly affect buying intentions. This can lead to a less comprehensive analysis of the market. Selecting a certain medium can integrate various influencing factors. This paper considers the influence of various factors on flow experience. The model integrates various influencing factors through the mediation of flow experience.

In conclusion, the model proposed in this paper provides multi-faceted and multi-level guidance for manufacturers to investigate the market.

6 Conclusion

This paper is based on the existing research about the smart wearable device, adopting literature analysis and secondary data analysis to analyze various influencing factors. This model is based on SOR theory and has theoretical authority. We classify functional diversity and functional availability as human-computer interactive experiences. We classify privacy leakage and the climate of comparison as cognitive differences.

The current academic research on consumer behavior has limitations. The foregoing summarizes three points. (1) The research has regional limitations. (2) Research on market segments is insufficient. (3) Most studies only study the factors that influence purchasing behavior. Due to the neglect of mediating factors, it is easy to consider the influencing factors incomprehensively.

The model established in this paper summarizes the superficial factors into two modules and four aspects. By summarizing, we can take into account the factors that affect consumers' purchase intention more comprehensively. This is because many superficial factors are essentially the same. For example, parents buying smartwatches for the convenience of monitoring their children can also be analyzed. The need for parents to supervise their children is the demand for human-computer interaction experience. Children's smartwatches can meet this demand, making parents' flow experience a positive change. After a comprehensive analysis of a large number of surface and secondary factors, we summarized the influencing factor model of children smartwatch consumers' purchase intention based on SOR theory.

Due to the lack of data support for the qualitative hypothesis, we need to quantify the impact of the hypothesis and assign certain impact factors in the follow-up work. In future studies, we will collect relevant literature and secondary data based on this model. At the same time, we will design relevant questionnaires based on the two modules of human-computer interaction experience and cognitive differences. Quantitative analysis of qualitative assumptions by collecting and analyzing large amounts of data. The above work can enrich the content of the model, enhance the practicality of the model, and provide better decision support for manufacturers in future production decision.

Acknowledgments. The work described in this paper was supported by grants from the Humanities and Social Sciences Research Project of Zhejiang Provincial Department of Education, grant number Y202248811; the Zhejiang Provincial Federation of Social Sciences, grant number 2023N009; and China's National Undergraduate Innovation and Entrepreneurship Training Program, grant number 202210337052.

References

1. Park, E., Kim, K.J., Kwon, S.J.: Understanding the emergence of wearable devices as next-generation tools for health communication. Inf. Technol. People **29**(4), 717–732 (2016)
2. Park, E.: User acceptance of smart wearable devices: an expectation-confirmation model approach. Telemat. Inform. **47** (2020)
3. Perez, A.J., Zeadally, S.: Privacy issues and solutions for consumer wearables. IT Prof. **20**(4), 46–56 (2018)
4. Kang, H., Jung, E.H.: The smart wearables-privacy paradox: a cluster analysis of smartwatch users. Behav. Inf. Technol. **40**(16), 1755–1768 (2020)
5. Jiang, D., Shi, G., Gao, Y.: Research on data security and privacy protection of wearable equipment in healthcare. J. Healthc. Eng. **2021**, 1–7 (2021)
6. Niknejad, N., Ismail, W.B., Mardani, A., Liao, H., Ghani, I.: A comprehensive overview of smart wearables: the state of the art literature, recent advances, and future challenges. Eng. Appl. Artif. Intell. **90** (2020)
7. Gajdoš Kljusuric, J., Čačić, J., Misir, A., Čačić, D.: Geographical region as a factor influencing consumers' perception of functional food – case of Croatia. Br. Food J. **117**(3), 1017–1031 (2015)
8. Hamilton, R., Ferraro, R., Haws, K.L., Mukhopadhyay, A.: Traveling with companions: the social customer journey. J. Mark. **85**(1), 68–92 (2020)
9. Hew, J.-J., Leong, L.-Y., Tan, G.W.-H., Lee, V.-H., Ooi, K.-B.: Mobile social tourism shopping: a dual-stage analysis of a multi-mediation model. Tour. Manag. **66**, 121–139 (2018)

10. Chan, T.K.H., Cheung, C.M.K., Lee, Z.W.Y.: The state of online impulse-buying research: a literature analysis. Inf. Manag. **54**(2), 204–217 (2017)
11. Molinillo, S., Aguilar-Illescas, R., Anaya-Sánchez, R., Liébana-Cabanillas, F.: Social commerce website design, perceived value and loyalty behavior intentions: the moderating roles of gender, age and frequency of use. J. Retail. Consum. Serv. **63** (2021)
12. Iyengar, S.S., Lepper, M.R.: When choice is demotivating: can one desire too much of a good thing? J. Pers. Soc. Psychol. **79**(6), 995–1006 (2000)
13. Finneran, C.M., Zhang, P.: A person–artefact–task (PAT) model of flow antecedents in computer-mediated environments. Int. J. Hum. Comput. Stud. **59**(4), 475–496 (2003)
14. Ghani, J.A., Deshpande, S.P.: Task characteristics and the experience of optimal flow in human—computer interaction. J. Psychol. **128**(4), 381–391 (1994)
15. Cases, A.-S., Fournier, C., Dubois, P.-L., Tanner, J.F.: Web Site spill over to email campaigns: the role of privacy, trust and shoppers' attitudes. J. Bus. Res. **63**(9–10), 993–999 (2010)
16. Ashley, C., Noble, S.M., Donthu, N., Lemon, K.N.: Why customers won't relate: obstacles to relationship marketing engagement. J. Bus. Res. **64**(7), 749–756 (2011)
17. Bertrand, M., Morse, A.: Trickle-Down Consumption, vol. 98, no. 1, pp. 863–879. Social Science Electronic Publishing (2013)
18. Brown, P.H., Bulte, E., Zhang, X.: Positional spending and status seeking in rural China. J. Dev. Econ. **96**(1), 139–149 (2011)
19. Trevino, L.K., Webster, J.: Flow in computer-mediated communication. Commun. Res. **19**(5) (1992)
20. Hausman, A.V., Siekpe, J.S.: The effect of web interface features on consumer online purchase intentions. J. Bus. Res. **62**(1), 5–13 (2009)

The Evaluation of Heart Rate and Presence in Virtual Reality Games

Po-Hung Lin$^{(\boxtimes)}$, Ting-Jui Yang, and You-Fang Luo

National Kaohsiung University of Science and Technology, Kaohsiung 807618, Taiwan
franklin@nkust.edu.tw

Abstract. This study explores the effects of gender, viewing time, and game category on heart rate and presence. A total of 20 participants were enrolled in a three way mixed factorial design to investigate the effects of gender (male, female), viewing time (5, 10, 15 min) and game category (horror, action) on change of heart rate and iGroup presence questionnaire (IPQ). The ANOVA results indicated that game category was significant on change of heart rate, where action games have a higher change of heart rate than horror games. However, the results indicated that no significant variable was found on IPQ.

Keywords: Heart rate · Presence · Virtual reality

1 Introduction

Past research has shown that gender was affected by hormones no matter in psychological differences, personality traits, behavioral patterns, or interests, where men may have better spatial abilities than women in a virtual reality environment [1]. In facts, people of various genders react differently when playing games. Lin and Ku [2] found that females feel more visual fatigue when playing 3D games. Lin and Chen [3] also showed that males did better than females in 3D interfaces.

Moreover, Obrist et al. [4] tested four types of movies on 3D displays, including skiing, space leaping, breakdance, and body painting. According to previous research, different video types were also investigated [5, 6]. Lin [5] examined the sports and travel videos in the evaluation of visual fatigue. Lin and Chen [6] investigated the three video types (horror, action, and comedy) and showed that horror videos showed the greatest effects on iGroup presence questionnaire (IPQ). Actually, game categories with different video types may bring the impacts on participants' visual and physiological performance it's also worthy to be investigated in this study.

Finally, viewing time is also a critical consideration when play games. Obrist et al. [4] established a time limit of 3 min for individuals to watch the four types of 3D videos. Lin [5] further investigated the viewing time of 3D TVs and set 5, 10, and 15 min to investigate the visual performance. Based on above studies, this study also considered viewing time as an independent variable investigated in this study.

© The Author(s), under exclusive license to Springer Nature Switzerland AG 2023
C. Stephanidis et al. (Eds.): HCII 2023, CCIS 1832, pp. 634–636, 2023.
https://doi.org/10.1007/978-3-031-35989-7_80

2 Method

Twenty college students took part in this experiment. All had corrected visual acuity better than 0.8. A three way mixed factorial design was used to investigate the effects of gender (male, female), viewing time (5, 10, 15 min), and game category (horror, action) on change of heart rate and IPQ. Viewing time and game category were within-subject factors and gender was a between-subject factor. Six experimental combinations were completed by each participant in a random order. Analysis of variance (ANOVA) was conducted with repeated measures on change of heart rate and IPQ. The Least Significant Difference (LSD) test was used to find the significance among the levels of independent variables.

3 Results and Discussion

As shown in Table 1, the ANOVA results for change of heart rate indicated that game category ($F = 85.082$, $p < 0.05$) was significant, and action games ($M = 22.883$) have a higher change of heart rate than horror games ($M = 3.017$) (see Fig. 1). The reason may be that participants need to punch left and right and move back and forth from time to time when playing action (boxing) games, resulting in a high change of heart rate. On the contrary, the tempo of horror games (escape room) was too slow and static, resulting in a low change of heart rate.

The ANOVA results for IPQ indicated that no significant factor was found. Since all participants wore HTC VIVE Focus 3, they also reported that spatial presence, involvement, and realness were observed in virtual reality games. That may be a reason for the insignificance on IPQ.

Table 1. ANOVA results for change of heart rate

Source of variance	Sum of square	Degree of freedom	Mean square	F value	Significance
Gender (G)	45.633	1	45.633	0.196	0.663
Viewing time (B)	1058.850	2	529.425	2.247	0.120
Game category (GC)	11840.533	1	11840.533	85.082	0.000**
G * B	222.217	2	111.108	0.472	0.628
G * GC	111.000	1	90.133	0.648	0.431
B * GC	662.317	2	331.158	2.133	0.133
G * B * GC	101.617	2	50.808	0.327	0.723

* $p < 0.05$; ** $p < 0.01$

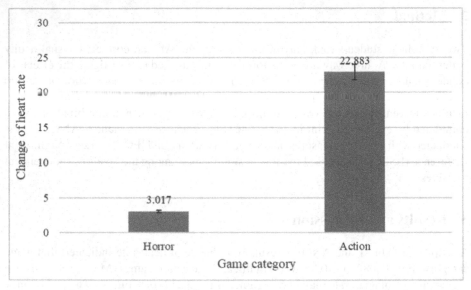

Fig. 1. The main factor effect of game category for change of heart rate

4 Conclusions

This study explores the effect of gender, viewing time, and game category on change of heart rate and IPQ. The results indicated that game category was significant on change of heart rate, where action games have a higher change of heart rate than horror games. However, the results indicated that no significant variable on IPQ. The main contribution of this study is to provide ideas for game players to pick suitable games when playing virtual reality games.

References

1. Cutmore, T.R.H., Hine, T.J., Maberly, K.J., Langford, N.M., Hawgood, G.: Cognitive and gender factors influencing navigation in a virtual environment. Int. J. Hum. Comput. Stud. **53**(2), 223–249 (2000)
2. Lin, P.H., Ku, W.C.: Visual fatigue evaluation of a glasses-free 3D handheld console, august. In: 19th Triennial Congress of the IEA, Melbourne, Australia, pp. 9–14 (2015)
3. Lin, P.C., Chen, S.I.: The effects of gender differences on the usability of automotive on-board navigation systems-a comparison of 2D and 3D display. Transp. Res. F Traffic Psychol. Behav. **19**, 40–51 (2013)
4. Obrist, M., Wurhofer, D., Meneweger, T., Grill, T., Tscheligi, M.: Viewing experience of 3DTV: an exploration of the feeling of sickness and presence in a shopping mall. Entertain. Comput. **4**, 71–81 (2013)
5. Lin, P.-H.: The evaluation of visual fatigue in 3D televisions. In: Stephanidis, C. (ed.) HCI 2016. CCIS, vol. 617, pp. 216–219. Springer, Cham (2016). https://doi.org/10.1007/978-3-319-40548-3_36
6. Lin, P.H., Chen, J.H.: Effects of video type, display technique, and ambient illumination on visual and psychological performance. J. Ambient Intell. Hum. Comput. (2020)

What Linguistic Considerations Should Smart Speakers Adopt in Error Notification?

Tomoki Miyamoto(✉) [ID]

Graduate School of Informatics and Engineering, The University of
Electro-Communications, Chofu 182-8585, Japan
miyamoto@uec.ac.jp

Abstract. This study proposes three experimental frameworks to systematize linguistic considerations (politeness) when smart speakers notify users of errors: (1) Measuring the effects of apologies and asking expressions, (2) The relationship between the number of errors and the effect of politeness and (3) The relationship between the appearance of the smart speaker and the politeness effect. The smart speaker's utterances in these experiments are designed based on the politeness theory, which systematizes politeness between humans in pragmatics. This poster presents the details of these three experimental frameworks and the preliminary results of (1).

Keywords: smart speakers · politeness · trust

1 Introduction

Speech recognition errors are a semi-permanent problem for smart speakers. The politeness and phrasing (linguistic considerations) of the speech used by the smart speaker in the event of a speech recognition error may affect the user's psychology, lowering (or raising) reliability and willingness to continue using the speaker. Previous studies of linguistic considerations in HCI [1–6] have reported several significant effects of linguistic considerations in conversation assuming a first meeting and in driver assistance. However, the effect of linguistic considerations on error notification by smart speakers is not clear.

This paper proposes three experimental frameworks to systematize linguistic considerations when a smart speaker notifies a user of an error.

- (1) Measuring the effects of apologies and asking expressions.
- (2) The relationship between the number of errors and the effect of politeness.
- (3) The relationship between the appearance of the smart speaker and the politeness effect.

The smart speaker utterances in these experiments are designed based on the politeness theory [7], which systematizes linguistic considerations between humans in sociolinguistics and pragmatics. This paper discusses the details of these three experimental frameworks and the preliminary experimental results of (1).

2   Experimental Frameworks

This section presents the three experimental frameworks to systematize linguistic considerations (politeness) when smart speakers notify users of errors.

2.1   (1) Measuring the Effects of Apologies and Asking Expressions

Apologies and asking expressions are part of Negative Politeness Strategies (NPS) [7] NPS is a speech strategy for communicating to the interaction partner that there is no intention to violate the freedom of action. For example, when a smart speaker asks a user to correct their speech input, NPS conveys an intention of consideration to the user and is expected to improve trust. An apology is a strategy commonly used by conventional smart speakers in error notifications. Asking expressions are useful in studies of driver assistance tasks [4]. However, the interaction between these strategies is not clear.

This experiment was conducted in a 2 × 2 mixed design. Factor A (within-participants design) was an asking expression to the user (Direct vs. Asking). The specific utterances were as follows. In these experimental conditions, we counterbalanced order effects. In addition, Amazon echo (Alexa) (Amazon) was employed as the smart speaker in this experiment, and the appearance of Alexa is shown in Fig. 1. This experiment has passed ethical review at the research ethics committee of The University of Electro-Communications.

- Direct: So, please instruct me again.
- Asking expressions: So, could you please instruct me again?

Factor B (between-subjects design) is the apology expression (No apology vs. Apology). Specifically, in the Apology level, "Sorry" is added at the beginning of the utterance.

This experiment is video-based. The video scenarios show Alexa's behavior when a user purchases Alexa and then makes a voice input to play music. These scenarios were explained to the participants via text.

The dependent variable in this experiment is the degree of improvement in the smart speaker's trust. Participants in the experiment evaluated their trust in the smart speaker twice: in the first evaluation (pre-evaluation), participants evaluated a video in which the smart speaker behaved differently than the user expected. The video used the same utterances in all experimental conditions. In the video subject to the second evaluation (post-evaluation), the smart-speaker asks the user to modify his or her speech input. The smart speaker's speech in this video was designed based on experimental factors A and B. Based on the results of the two evaluations, the difference between the post-evaluation value and the pre-evaluation value is the dependent variable.

2.2   (2) The Relationship Between the Number of Errors and the Effect of Politeness

Experiment (1) cannot discuss the medium- to long-term effects of error notification. In this experiment, based on the design of experiment (1), I examine

Fig. 1. The smart speaker adopt on this experiment.

the effect of the number of smart speaker errors on trust. Specifically, I set the number of errors (1, 2, or 3) as the experimental factor C. The number of errors is set to a maximum of three as an exploratory study. It may be necessary to include a larger number of errors in the study, but this point will be discussed based on the experimental results.

2.3 (3) The Relationship Between the Appearance of the Smart Speaker and the Politeness Effect

It is also important to discuss the influence of the appearance of the Smart speaker. This experiment set up Amazon echo (Amazon), Google home (Google), Sota (Vstone), and RoBoHoN (SHARP) as experimental conditions and compares the evaluation results. Of these, Sota and RoBoHoN in particular have anthropomorphic appearances, and I expect that their evaluations will differ significantly from those of general smart speakers such as Amazon echo and Google home.

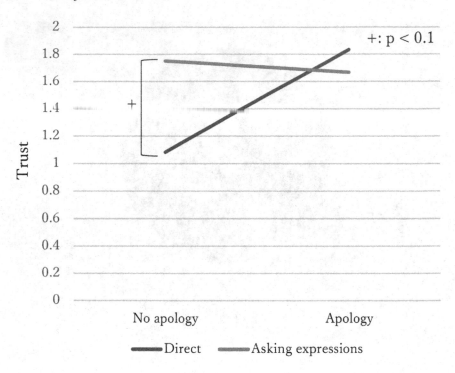

Fig. 2. Trust of this experiment means the value of improvement about trust in pre and post-evaluations.

3   Results

This section reports the preliminary results of the experimental framework (1). Participants in this experiment were recruited by a crowdsourcing service (Crowd Works) (n = 24). Twelve participants were assigned to each level of Factor B.

Two-way ANOVA was applied to examine the effects of experimental factors A and B. Fig. 2 shows the evaluation results. The results suggest that the influence of politeness is larger for utterances without an apology, and smaller for utterances with an apology. Although previous studies [3,4] have reported results suggesting the usefulness of the NPS, it was not clear whether the effect of an apology changed trust.

4   Conclusion

This paper discussed the effectiveness of linguistic consideration strategies used by smart speakers in error notification. The experimental framework and results proposed in this paper are an important contribution to establishing an improvement method that can be utilized by anyone without the need to develop an engineering level to deal with the negative effects of speech recognition errors, which is a problem that speech interfaces are always faced with.

References

1. Miyamoto, T., Katagami, D., Shigemitsu, Y.: Improving relationships based on positive politeness between humans and life-like agents. In: Proceedings of the 2017 HAI Conference on Human-Agent Interaction, pp. 451–455. ACM Digital Library, New York (2017)
2. Miyamoto, T., et al.: Proposal of driving support agent which speak based on politeness theory. In: HCI in Mobility, Transport, and Automotive Systems: First International Conference, MobiTAS 2019, Held as Part of the 21st HCI International Conference, HCII 2019, pp. 235–244 (2019)
3. Miyamoto, T., et al.: Influence of social distance expressed by driving support agent's utterance on psychological acceptability. Front. Psychol. **12**, 526942 (2021). https://doi.org/10.3389/fpsyg.2021.526942
4. Miyamoto, T., Katagami, D., Tanaka, T., Kanamori, H., Yoshihara, Y., Fujikake, K.: Should a driving support agent provide explicit instructions to the user? Video-based study focused on politeness strategies. In: Proceedings of the 9th International Conference on Human-Agent Interaction, pp. 157–164 (2021)
5. Miyamoto, T., Katagami, D., and Usami, M.: A politeness control method for conversational agents considering social relationships with users. In: Advances in Artificial Intelligence: Selected Papers from the Annual Conference of Japanese Society of Artificial Intelligence (JSAI 2020), pp. 224–231 (2021)
6. Lee, J., Lee, K.M.: Polite speech strategies and their impact on driver's trust in autonomous vehicles. Comput. Hum. Behav. **127**, 107015 (2022)
7. Brown, P., Levinson, S.C.: Politeness: Some Universals in Language Usage. Cambridge University Press, Cambridge (1987)

Comparison of Psychological Evaluation of KANSEI Lighting Using Large and Small Numbers of Subjects

Ryohei Nakatsu[1]([✉]), Naoko Tosa[1], Satoru Okagaki[2], Muneharu Kuwata[2], and Takashi Kusumi[1]

[1] Kyoto University, Sakyo, Kyoto 606-8501, Japan
`nakatsu.ryohei@gmail.com`, `{tosa.naoko.5c,`
`kusumi.takashi.7u}@kyoto-u.ac.jp`
[2] Mitsubishi Electric Corporation, Advanced Technology R&D Center, Amagasaki, Hyogo 661-8661, Japan
`Okagaki.Satoru@aj.MitsubishiElectric.co.jp,`
`Kuwata.Muneharu@cs.MitsubishiElectric.co.jp`

Abstract. It is an important issue whether the results of psychological experiments targeting a small number of people can be extended to a large number of people. We are conducting joint research between the university and the company on KANSEI lighting that combines glass art and lighting. About 1,800 visitors were asked to evaluate the developed KANSEI lighting at an exhibition intended for the general public. We used the evaluation items that had already been conducted on a small number of people. Therefore, the results of both experiments could be compared. In this paper, we report the results of comparing an evaluation experiment with a large number of people and that with a small number of subjects.

Keywords: Kansei lighting · Large number of subjects · Psychological experiment

1 Introduction

KANSEI evaluation is often conducted using psychological experiments. Psychological experiments conducted in university laboratories usually focus on exacting conditions, and the number of subjects is often limited to a few dozen. In addition, since the target is mainly students, the age distribution is also biased. For this reason, when we report the results of psychological experiments using university students at academic conferences, etc., we are often asked questions about the generality of the results when the subjects are extended to a large number of ordinary people. For such questions, a typical answer is, "we will consider this as a future issue". However, it is rarely considered because it is challenging to conduct psychological experiments on a large number of ordinary people in the same conditions as those on a small number of people.

C. Stephanidis et al. (Eds.): HCII 2023, CCIS 1832, pp. 642–649, 2023.
https://doi.org/10.1007/978-3-031-35989-7_82

In this research, we compared the results of a small-scale psychological experiment conducted in our laboratory, mainly using students, with the results of a psychological experiment conducted on the same problem on a large number of ordinary people. Thus, we will present an answer to the above question.

Kyoto University and Mitsubishi Electric have conducted joint research to develop new KAKNSEI lighting that appeals to people's sensibility by applying art created by one of the authors, Naoko Tosa. As a result, we developed a prototype of KANSEI lighting named "Light Table". First, we evaluated this Light Table in a small-scale psychological experiment targeting dozens of Kyoto University students [1]. Then we had the opportunity to exhibit it at Mitsubishi Electric's showroom. We conducted a questionnaire survey targeting visitors and asked about 1,800 to evaluate it.

In this paper, we will report the results of comparing psychological experiments with a large number of people and those with a small number of people.

2 Light Table

One of the authors, Naoko Tosa, has been creating video artwork called "Sound of Ikebana" by giving sound vibrations to viscous liquids, such as paint, and shooting the jumping-up paints with a high-speed camera at 2000 frames per second [2].

The "Sound of Ikebana," obtained as a two-dimensional video image, has an organic and beautiful shape. When exhibiting this video art, there have been many requests to make it a three-dimensional shape. One of the attempts to make the Sound of Ikebana three-dimensional is to use multiple high-speed cameras to film the creation of the Sound of Ikebana and to create the 3D Sound of Ikebana from the images captured by the multiple cameras [3].

As another attempt to create a three-dimensional version of the Sound of Ikebana using a different material, we tried to create a similar shape using glass. As the actual Ikebana is made up of multiple types of flowers and plants, combining the created glass art pieces, we tried to create a three-dimensional object similar to the Sound of Ikebana.

As a glass art production method, we used "hot work," where glass is melted by heat and then molded. We created various shapes by twisting and dropping the soft glass. In the process, we also tried coloring the created glass art by adding various pigments. Figure 1 shows examples of the glass art pieces created.

Using these glass art pieces as parts, creating a shape that combines multiple parts, placing them on a table, and illuminating them from the side, we found that a beautiful table that appeals to human sensitivity can be created. It was named the "Light Table" [1, 4].

In addition, we found that by using the light source which emits parallel light, an even more beautiful light shape called caustic was created. Parallel light produces cleaner caustic than ordinary diverging light. Parallel rays can reach a long distance, so they are suitable for car lights, etc.

Also, by hitting parallel rays of light on glass or water, a collection of reflected or refracted light is generated to create a unique and beautiful shape. This is called "caustic [5]". Sunlight, far enough away from the light source, is a parallel ray, so when it hits the

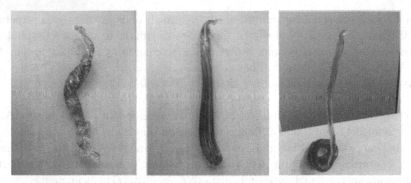

Fig. 1. Examples of produced glass art pieces.

surface of the water, it forms a beautiful glow through the waves on the water's surface, which is an example of caustic.

Glass art is suitable for creating caustic, and in fact, using Mitsubishi Electric's light source creates beautiful caustic, as shown in Fig. 2. Rotating this table changes the caustic produced over time, creating more effective light shapes.

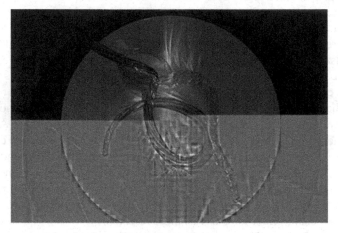

Fig. 2. Light Table

3   Psychological Evaluation Experiment of "Light Table"

3.1   Basic Concept

There are many emotional evaluations based on psychological experiments, and they can be divided into KANSEI evaluations as research at universities and those aimed at commercialization at companies. The former attempts to analyze the characteristics of human sensibility by setting strict conditions and finely analyzing the difference in evaluation between different conditions. Subjects are mainly university students, and the number of people is often limited to a few dozen. Therefore, a problem is whether or not the KANSEI evaluation conducted on a small number of students at a university has generality when extended to a large number of ordinary people.

On the other hand, KANSEI evaluation by companies aims at commercialization, so generality is emphasized rather than strictness. In order to emphasize generality, the number of subjects is often significant. However, there are several limitations. One is that the results often belong to trade secrets and are often not disclosed. Another is that evaluation is often conducted using a questionnaire format at product exhibitions, etc. However, as the aim is to have people purchase the product as a product, the evaluation items usually differ from the KANSEI evaluation at universities. Therefore, only some studies have compared these two different assessments.

As one answer to such a problem, we decided to compare the evaluation of a small number of people at the university and the evaluation of a large number of people targeting the general public. We have already conducted and published an evaluation experiment with a small number of people at a university [1]. Since the evaluation experiment was conducted with a large number of people this time, we decided to compare the results of the evaluation experiment with a small number of people.

3.2   Evaluation by a Small Number of People

A total of 24 Kyoto University students and staff (13 males, 11 females, ages 20 to 40) were used as subjects for the evaluation of the Light Table [1, 4].

3.3   Evaluation by a Large Number of People

In contrast to the evaluation of a small number of people at a university, we evaluated the Light Table for a large number of ordinary people. We had the opportunity to exhibit the Light Table at the exhibition space "METoA Ginza" owned by Mitsubishi Electric in Ginza. Many people visited the venue during the event, and about 1,800 evaluated the Light Table.

3.4   Evaluation Items

A questionnaire was prepared to evaluate the Light Table, and we asked the subjects to answer the questionnaire on a 5-point scale. The questions consist of three groups: "What do you feel about the lighting?" (impression), "What kind of effect does the lighting have?" (effect), and "What kind of scene is lighting suitable for?" (scene). They consist of a total of 19 items belonging to these three groups. Table 1 shows the content of specific questions. Regarding the item "What do you feel about the lighting?" we decided on the evaluation items based on previous research [6–8]. In addition, we formed questions about "What kind of effect does the lighting have?" and "What kind of scene is lighting suitable for?" through discussion among the participants of this joint research.

Table 1. Contents of the questionnaire

1. What do you feel about the lighting? (Impression)	2. What kind of effect does the lighting have? (Effect)
Comfortable – Uncomfortable	I can relax – I cannot relax
Friendly – Unfriendly	I can be creative – I cannot be creative.
Beautiful – Not beautiful	I feel energetic – I do not feel energetic
Calm – Restless	I can face difficulty – I cannot face difficulty
Interesting – Boring	I feel refreshed – I do not feel refreshed
Warm – Cold	**3. What kind of scene is the lighting suitable for? (Scene)**
Changeable – Not changeable	Appropriate for sleeping – Inappropriate
Luxury - Sober	Appropriate for eating – Inappropriate
Unique - Mediocre	Appropriate for relaxing – Inappropriate
	Appropriate for working – Inappropriate
	Appropriate for chatting – Inappropriate

4   Comparative Analysis of Evaluation Results for Large and Small Groups

4.1   Experiment Results

For each of the three major question groups: "What do you feel the about lighting?", "What kind of effect does the lighting have?" and "What kind of scene is the lighting suitable for?" Figs. 3, 4, and 5 show graphs obtained by averaging the evaluation values. (Each figure also shows the variance analysis results, which will be described later.)

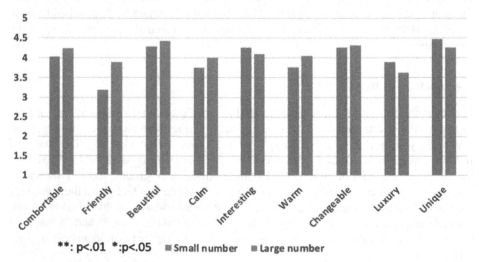

Fig. 3. Mean value of evaluation results for "What do you feel about the lighting?"

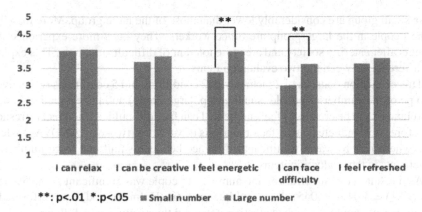

Fig. 4. Mean value of evaluation results for "What kind of effect does the lighting have?"

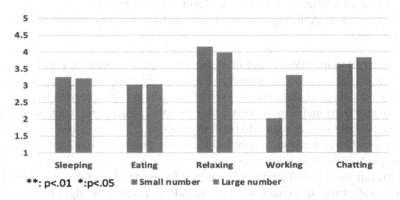

Fig. 5. Mean value of evaluation results for "What kind of scene is the lighting suitable for?"

4.2 Considerations

(1) Consideration on "What do you feel about the lighting?"

The trends for both small and large groups are very similar. This evaluation is based on the type of target audience (small group, large group) and evaluation items (comfortable, friendly, beautiful, calm, interesting, warm, changeable, luxury, and unique). Therefore, we conducted a two-factor analysis of variance (two-way ANOVA) to determine whether there was a significant difference between small and large numbers of participants in the evaluation items.

As a result, the main effect was insignificant for the two groups ($F(1897, 1) = 0.824$, $p = .364$). This result shows no significant difference between the small and large groups.

(2) Consideration on "What kind of effect does the lighting have?"

The trends for each evaluation item for small and large groups are very similar. However, regarding the evaluation items of "I feel energetic" and "I can face difficulties," the results of the small group are considerably lower than those of the large group. More than 70% of the people in the large group are office workers. They have more experience than students after entering society and are more tolerant of difficult situations. This explains the difference between the two evaluation items.

This evaluation consists of 2 factors with 2 conditions and 5 conditions respectively: the type of the number of people (small group, large group) and the evaluation items (I feel relaxed, I can be creative, I feel energetic, I can face difficulties, and I feel refreshed). Therefore, we conducted a two-factor analysis of variance (two-way ANOVA) to determine whether there was a significant difference between small and large numbers of participants in the evaluation items.

As a result, the main effect on the number of people was significant at the 5% level $(F(1897,1) = 4.04 \ p = .045)$. Then multiple analysis (Holm method) was performed on the number of people for each evaluation item, and the results are as follows.

I can relax: $p = $ n.s., I can be creative: $p = $ n.s., I feel energetic: $p = .004(**)$, I can face difficulties: $p = .003 \ (**)$, I feel refreshed: $p = $ n.s.

This shows that ANOVA confirmed the results intuitively obtained from Fig. 4 mentioned above.

(3) Consideration on "What kind of scene is the lighting suitable for?"

The trends for each evaluation item for small and large groups are very similar. This evaluation consists of 2 conditions: the type of the number of people to be targeted (small group, large group) and 5 evaluation items (sleeping, eating, relaxing, working, and chatting). Therefore, we conducted a two-factor analysis of variance (two-way ANOVA) to determine whether there was a significant difference between small and large numbers of participants in the evaluation items.

As a result, the main effect was insignificant for the number of people $(F(1897, 1) = 2.47, p = .116)$. From this result, we can conclude that there is no significant difference between a small number of people and a large number of people regarding "What kind of scene is the lighting suitable for?".

However, from Fig. 5. For the evaluation item of "working," the evaluation for the small group is considerably lower than that for the large group. As a precaution, multiple analysis (Holm method) was performed on the number of people for each evaluation item, and the results were as follows.

Sleeping: $p = $ n.s., Eating: $p = $ n.s., Relaxing: $p = $ n.s., Working: $p < .01(**)$, Chatting: $p = $ n.s.

This confirms that the result for the small group is significantly lower than that of the large group. The reason is probably the same as in the case of Fig. 4. At the same time, office workers evaluate KANEI lighting as effective in an office environment.

5   Conclusion

It is an exciting question in psychological experiments whether the results of psychological experiments conducted in university laboratories on a small number of students can be extended to a large number of ordinary people. In this research, we conducted a psychological evaluation experiment with a large number of subjects and that with a small number of subjects, targeting KANSEI lighting that combines glass art and lighting.

As an evaluation experiment with a small number of people, we have already conducted an experiment targeting 24 people, including university students. Regarding the psychological evaluation of a large number of people, we conducted a questionnaire survey asking the visitors when the KANSEI lighting was exhibited for the general public. About 1,800 visitors responded to the questionnaire, double-digit compared to the psychological experiments conducted on dozens of university people.

We compared the results of two psychological evaluation experiments; the results with a small number of subjects with those with a large number of people. When we analyzed the results based on ANOVA, we found that there is mostly no significant difference regarding the number of people. This is an exciting result because it shows that the results of psychological experiments conducted on a small number of people at universities are essentially the same as the results of psychological experiments conducted on a large number of ordinary people.

As this experiment was limited to KANSEI lighting, however, in the future, it will be necessary to verify the generality of the results by expanding the experiment to other subjects.

References

1. Nakatsu, R., Tosa, N., Okazaki, S., Yamazaki, H., Kuwata, M., Hirai, T.: Evaluation of art lighting combining LED lighting and glass art by psychological experiment. In: 18th International Conference of Asia Digital Art and Design (ADADA2020), December 2020
2. Tosa, N., Pang, Y., Yang, Q., Nakatsu, R.: Pursuit and expression of Japanese beauty using technology. In: Special Issue "The Machine as Artist (for the 21st Century)," Arts journal, MDPI, vol. 8, no.1, p. 38, March 2019. https://doi.org/10.3390/arts8010038
3. Tosa, N., Yunian, P., Nakatsu, R., Yamada, A., Suzuki, T., Yamamoto, K.: 3D modeling and 3D materialization of fluid art that occurs in very short time. In: Nunes, N.J., Ma, L., Wang, M., Correia, N., Pan, Z. (eds.) ICEC 2020. LNCS, vol. 12523, pp. 409–421. Springer, Cham (2020). https://doi.org/10.1007/978-3-030-65736-9_37
4. Nakatsu, R., et al.: Evaluation of artistic lighting combining LED light and glass art by psychological experiment. Int. J. Humanit. Soc. Sci. Educ. 8(5), 76–88 (2021)
5. https://en.wikipedia.org/wiki/Caustic_(optics)
6. Oi, N.: The difference among generations in evaluating interior lighting environment. J. Physiol. Anthropol. Appl. Hum. Sci. 24(1), 87–91 (2005)
7. Noguchi, H., Sakaguchi, T.: Effect of illuminance and color temperature on lowering of physiological activity. Appl. Human Sci. 18(4), 117–123 (1999)
8. Kobayashi, H., Sato, M.: Psychological responses to illuminance and color temperature of lighting. J. Physiol. Anthropol. 11(1), 45–49 (1992)

An Analysis of the Impact of Bench Placement Angle on Comfortableness and Interaction

Wataru Oomoto and Saerom Lee[✉]

Faculty of Engineering and Design, Kagawa University, Takamatsu, Japan
lee.saerom@kagawa-u.ac.jp

Abstract. There is a worldwide movement to transform streets into pedestrian-centered spaces currently. It is desirable that the new street spaces be used by many people to use for various activities and interact with each other. However, the possibility of interaction is one of the factors that make people feel uncomfortable in the streets. To solve this complex problem, it is necessary to rethink the quality of stay on the streets. In this study, we focused on benches, the basic facility for stay in street spaces, and investigated the effect of bench placement angles on the "comfortableness". In the experiment, we used 3D street model to perform virtual evaluations. As a result of analysis, it was found that the bench placement angle may have direct effects on the evaluation of "other users" and indirect effects as the "calmness" and "size" factors. The results should contribute to improved comfortableness in bustling street spaces.

Keywords: Street Bench · Placement Angle · Comfortableness · Space Design

1 Introduction

In the past, streets have played an important role in society as the key to traffic and functioned as automobile-centered spaces. However, there is now a growing trend worldwide to reconfigure street space as a space for pedestrians. In Japan, for example, some communities are gradually expanding the percentage of sidewalks on their main streets and considering various ways to utilize this space [1]. Behind this reworking of the streets is the aim to make there function not only for passage, but also for various activities [2]. In particular, the ideal would be for users to interact with each other, but several issues must be considered to realize this vision. For example, it is important in communication to be aware of the presence of others. On the other hand, for people who want to take a break alone, it becomes a factor that makes them feel uncomfortable. In addition, some people nowadays avoid approaching others under the effects of COVID-19 [3]. Therefore, it is important to consider the balance between "comfortableness" and "interaction", and to design more appropriate relationships among users.

In related previous studies, researchers analyzed relationships between the staying behavior and human factors or investigated the effect of activities on the impression of the landscape [4, 5]. The characteristic of these studies is that the perspective of the analysis is outside of the space. Therefore, it is considered that analyzing from the

C. Stephanidis et al. (Eds.): HCII 2023, CCIS 1832, pp. 650–657, 2023.
https://doi.org/10.1007/978-3-031-35989-7_83

viewpoint inside will lead to some novelty. In this study, we focused on bench as a perspective inside the street space [6, 7]. Specifically, through evaluating and comparing 4 layouts with different bench placement angles, it was investigated how angles affect the "comfortableness" when people using. Results of this study is expected to contribute the realization of a lively street space that satisfies both "comfortableness" and "possibility of interaction".

2 Methods

In this study, we defined "possibility of interaction" as the condition that bench users can see each other and "comfortableness" as the degree of psychological burden caused by the presence of others. Methods of this study are executed based on these definitions. The outline of the methods is shown as follows. First, the preliminary research to examine the conditions of this experiment is executed and a street model is created using the results of preliminary research. Then, an evaluation experiment is conducted using the created street model in the form of a questionnaire. Finally, we investigate the effect of installation angle using an analysis of variance and multiple comparisons.

2.1 SD Method

For the evaluation of comfortableness, three items using a 5-point scale are prepared. In addition, we used the SD (Semantic Differential) method to evaluate impressions. Since the same scale can be used to evaluate different objects, we adopted this method to compare the impressions among the placements.

2.2 Factor Analysis

In the evaluation of impressions, the factor analysis is performed to estimate factors shared by the entire placement. Then, we investigate the relationship between the factor scores of each placement and the evaluation of comfortableness. Based on this result, we analyze the indirect effects of the placement angle on the evaluation of comfortableness. In this step, we used the maximum likelihood method as the extraction method and Promax rotation as the rotation method.

3 Preliminary Research

3.1 Outline

To examine the conditions of experiment, the questionnaire was conducted targeting 40 Japanese university students. The questionnaire consisted of four sections, "Basic Characteristics," "Bench Use Experience," "Unique Landscape Elements," and "Other Users". We performed this survey by Google Forms.

3.2   Results

This section presents some results particularly related to conditions of the experiment. Regarding the frequency of bench use, 19 of the total respondents answered "frequently" or "occasionally," so we asked them when and for what purpose they use benches. The result showed that they tended to use benches in the afternoon, especially in 12:00 to 15:00. In addition, it was the most common for purpose of bench use that "Eating and drinking" and "Resting (choose "Other" and answer by additional comments)", followed by "Chatting". Also, some people used bench for "looking at the scenery" and "operating a smartphone". This mean that some people using benches for lunch and other breaks.

Furthermore, the effect of the other people's characteristics on comfortableness was surveyed for 40 respondents with multiple-choice. Regarding other's age, the most common answer was "not influenced for comfortableness". Also, it was shown that a certain number of respondents who felt uncomfortable with "10 s" and "20 s," which are the same age groups as theirs. In addition, the most common response for gender was "not affected the comfortableness".

3.3   Creation of Street Model

In this study, a virtual survey is conducted using a 3D street model not real street. Figure 1 shows the model created based on the results in Sect. 3.2. For the production, the 3D modeling software "SketchUp" and the rendering tool "Twinmotion" were used. In detail, the overall landscape was designed without any sense of local characteristics, referencing some actual streetscapes. The surrounding facilities were set up with stores along the street, as a space for shopping and other activities. In addition, the time of day in the model was set around 14:00.

Fig. 1. 3D street model used in the experiment

4 Experiments

4.1 Outline

Experiment was conducted assuming a situation where two benches were set up on the street and the respondent and another person were sitting on each bench. Figure 2 shows the arrangement that was the subject of this survey. In the street, a female model was placed as an example of the other user, and the respondent's position was presented as a gray silhouette. In addition, 4 patterns with different angles of bench placement were defined on the experiment. The angles were considered 0, 20, 40, and 90°.

The experiment was performed following the below steps. First, the scenario was created for "eating and drinking" and "resting," which were the most common activities in the preliminary survey results, and this scenario was presented with the images of benches. Then, 3 images with different viewing directions shown in Fig. 3 were presented as the scenery when people were seated. Finally, the respondents were asked some questions about their evaluation of comfortableness and impression.

Fig. 2. 4 patterns with different angles of bench placement

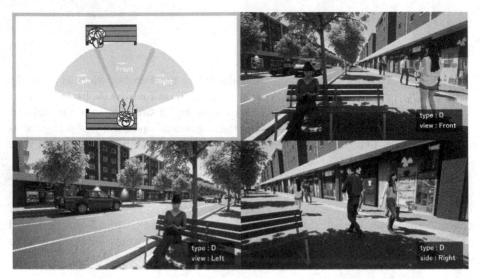

Fig. 3. Example of 3 images with different viewing directions

4.2 Evaluation

To evaluate the comfortableness, respondents were asked to rate the degree to which they could stay without worrying about the three factors of "other bench users," "passersby," and "behind themselves" on a 5-point scale. In addition, the 16 pairs of words shown in Table 1 were used as evaluation items of SD method, and respondents were asked to answer on a 7-point scale about their impression of sitting there.

5   Results/Considerations

5.1   Direct Effects

To examine the direct effects of bench placement angle, the evaluation items of comfortableness were analyzed. First, analysis of variance was conducted to check the significant difference in angles. As a result, significant differences in evaluation of "overall," "other users," and "passersby" were indicated. Second, the multiple comparisons were conducted for these three items, to investigate the combinations of angles with significant differences in evaluation. Table 1 shows the results of the analysis. The results indicate that combinations with larger changes in angle tended to show more differences in their ratings as well. Therefore, it is considered that the evaluation of "other users," which was found significant results even for combinations with small angle differences, was particularly affected by placement angles.

Table 1. Results of Multiple Comparisons

combination	overall	other users	passersby	behind
0 - 20	1.160	0.72 **	0.38	0.060
0 - 40	0.900	1.04 **	0.02	-0.160
0 - 90	1.620 **	1.56 **	-0.36	0.420
20 - 40	-0.260	0.32	-0.36	-0.220
20 - 90	0.460	0.84 **	-0.74 *	0.360
40 - 90	0.720	0.52 *	-0.38	0.580

*p < .05   **p < .01*

5.2 Factor Analysis

The conditions for the factor analysis are as follows. The number of factors was set to 3 because the eigenvalue was larger than 1 and scree plot criteria was met. In addition, the significance level of factor loadings was set at 0.4 or above. Table 2 shows the results of the analysis of the extracted factors based on these conditions, including the hypothesis before the experiment.

Table 2. Results of Factor Analysis

word:A	word:B	Factor1	Factor2	Factor3	commonality	hypothesis
unstable	stable	.981	-.133	-.216	.781	harmony
aneasy	easy	.739	-.011	.125	.590	affinity
ugly	beautiful	.698	.074	.181	.648	affinity
disorderly	orderly	.690	-.144	-.321	.393	harmony
inaccessible	accessible	.658	.190	.017	.632	affinity
scattered	serried	.259	-.722	.134	.359	territory
blind	clear	.093	.687	.020	.566	territory
close	open	.167	.634	.019	.568	territory
artificial	natural	.004	.520	-.046	.269	harmony
narrow	wide	.430	.490	.069	.716	territory
cheerless	cheerful	.151	.090	.780	.723	affinity
plain	colorful	-.038	-.178	.762	.577	activity
quiet	merry	-.196	-.056	.634	.396	activity
simple	complex	-.426	-.051	.606	.464	harmony
cool	warm	.521	-.156	.545	.587	activity
classical	modern	.001	.198	.431	.247	activity

First, Factor 1 shows the sense of "calmness" people feel when using benches. Starting with "unstable - stable" which has the highest loadings, "ugly - beautiful" and "disorderly - orderly " would be indicate balance and orderliness of the space elements. In other words, if there is little change in the environment when using benches, users would be more likely to feel a sense of safety and familiarity. Besides, Factor 2 was analyzed as indicating the "size" of spaces that users feel when sitting on benches. Moreover, Factor 3 indicates the "unusual" and, it is considered if users feel some movement in the space, user will have enjoyable impressions of there.

5.3   Indirect Effects

Analysis of variance was conducted to confirm for significant differences between the angles in each factor. Since there were significant differences among the angles for all three factors, multiple comparison was conducted to investigate the pairs of angles with large differences in evaluation. Table 3 shows the results of the multiple comparison. The results suggest that the installation angle influences the "calmness" and "spaciousness" factors, which showed significant differences even when the change in angle was small.

Additionally, correlations between the factor scores and the comfortableness items were investigated. Table 4 shows the results. The colored areas in the table indicate significant values. As a consideration, it is assumed that the score of "calmness" was related to feelings of "comfortableness" since the scenario presented was " a personal break with food and drink while shopping". On the other hand, it seems that the reason why the "size" factor correlated with the evaluation of comfortableness is that users' perception of space in front of them changes depending on bench placement angles.

Table 3. Results of Multiple Comparisons

combination	calmness	size	unusual
0 - 20	**0.421** *	**0.831** **	0.260
0 - 40	**-0.436** *	-0.243	0.419
0 - 90	**0.569** **	**0.503** **	-0.314
20 - 40	**-0.858** **	**-1.074** **	0.158
20 - 90	0.147	-0.328	**-0.574** **
40 - 90	**1.005** **	**0.747** **	**-0.733** **

$* \ p < .05$ $** p < .01$

Table 4. Results of Correlation Analysis

	Factor1	Factor2	Factor3
overall	0.58	0.48	0.25
0 degree	0.36	0.24	0.21
20 degree	0.57	0.40	0.35
40 degree	0.52	0.55	0.20
90 degree	0.74	0.55	0.40

$0.4 \le |r| \le 1.0$

6 Conclusion

In this study, we investigated the effect of bench placement angles on the "comfortableness" in a street space. In the experiment, comfortableness and impression evaluations were conducted for the 4 layouts with different bench placement angles, and each item was analyzed and investigated its mutual relationships. As a result of the survey for university students, it was revealed some details angle of placement affects the comfortableness evaluations. Specifically, it is considered to affect the evaluation of "other users" directly, and to have indirect effects on "comfortableness" by acting on the impressions of "calmness" and "spaciousness". From the above reasons, the results of the study imply that it is possible to improve comfortableness in street spaces adjusting bench placement angles.

In the future works, it is necessary to conduct the same experiment in actual environments. Also, there were not enough items to directly evaluate the "comfortableness". To solve this problem, the number of items will be increased. Based on these issues, we aim to improve the accuracy of evaluation in future studies.

References

1. Osaka City, Model Development for Street Space Realignment of Midousuji Avenue. https://www.city.osaka.lg.jp/kensetsu/page/0000378248.html. Accessed 17 Mar 2023
2. Ministry of Land, Infrastructure, Transport and Tourism, Street Design Guidelines Ver.2.0. https://www.mlit.go.jp/toshi/toshi_gairo_fr_000055.html. Accessed 17 Mar 2023
3. Ministry of Health, Labour and Welfare, Practical Examples of "New Lifestyle". https://www.mhlw.go.jp/content/000641913.pdf. Accessed 17 Mar 2023
4. Shinozaki, T.: A study on the influence of a human element to the stay action in urban outdoor public space. Jpn. Inst. Landsc. Archit. 65(5), 701–706 (2001)
5. Sueshige, Y., Saito, Y.: Influence of people's activities in public spaces on impression evaluation of urban landscape. AIJ J. Technol. 27(65), 464–468 (2021)
6. Kobayashi, S., Katsumata, R.: Effects of the directions of benches on the behavior of seated people in a street. Trans. AIJ J. Archit. Plan. Environ. Eng. 72(621), 69–75 (2007)
7. Takemoto, M., Nomaguchi, K., Izumiyama, R., Uozaki, K.: Study on change for the road function and demand change to the bench on the road. In: Proceedings of the 65th Faculty of Science and Technology Academic Lecture, Nihon University (2021)

Exploring the Learnability of Two Teleoperation Setups for Assembly Tasks

Theresa Prinz[1,2](✉) [iD] and Klaus Bengler[1,2] [iD]

[1] TUM School of Engineering and Design, Department of Mechanical Engineering, Chair of Ergonomics, Technical University of Munich, Munich, Germany
theresa.prinz@tum.de
[2] Munich Institute of Robotics and Machine Intelligence (MIRMI), Munich, Germany

Abstract. Teleoperation is being used in a variety of applications - from mobile systems in the aerospace, automotive, and maritime sector to static high-precision systems in medicine. Each application requires a carefully designed system for a set of defined tasks in a specific environment and highly trained users. In manufacturing, teleoperation can be used by process or product experts to interact with objects (e.g. machinery and new product parts) that are in another location. To facilitate access, the teleoperation system must be easy to use and should not require a long learning phase. In this study, we evaluate two different setups of teleoperation systems for assembly tasks with respect to learnability and usability. The two setups differ only in the way the remote location is presented to the human operator: direct or blocked view, in which case a video stream serves as visualization. Performance analysis shows a clear learning effect, as task completion time decreased for both setups over repetitions. The results indicate that novices in teleoperation systems can learn to use the system in a few interactions. However, more research is required to accurately describe the learning curve for both setups. The perceived usability was in the lower acceptance range, emphasizing the need for improvement.

Keywords: Teleoperation · Human-machine interface · Human-robot interaction · Learnability · Usability

1 Introduction

1.1 Motivation

Teleoperation has been a topic of research for several decades. It allows human operators to manipulate an object from a distance. It is used for multiple objectives in a variety of applications: to reach distant places such as in maritime [5]

The authors acknowledge the financial support by the Bavarian State Ministry for Economic Affairs, Regional Development and Energy (StMWi) for the Lighthouse Initiative KI.FABRIK (Phase 1: Infrastructure and the research and development program under grant no. DIK0249).

C. Stephanidis et al. (Eds.): HCII 2023, CCIS 1832, pp. 658–665, 2023.
https://doi.org/10.1007/978-3-031-35989-7_84

and space expeditions [12], to operate in dangerous environments such as mining [2], forestry [9], nuclear power plants [8], and the disposal of explosives [13], or to scale human movement as in surgery [11].

In many cases, the expertise, skills, and flexibility of the human operator are crucial to processes, making the human an essential element for successful task completion. In manufacturing and especially in assembly, processes are often either completely manual or fully automated. Human-robot collaboration has found its way into the industry only in recent years and aims to combine the benefits of both worlds [7]. Teleoperation in the manufacturing context can offer benefits by enhancing the temporal availability of experts across factory and national borders, allowing physical interaction with new parts that are produced in a distant plant, and teaching a robot new skills. Therefore, teleoperation in manufacturing has the potential to accelerate the time from the development of new variances and products to the implementation into the production workflow and to increase the productivity of process and product experts by empowering them to share their expertise faster. More broadly, teleoperation addresses the skilled labor shortage and increases sustainability by reducing the need for travel.

High usability and high reliability of the technical system are crucial in time-sensitive manufacturing processes. High usability results in intuitive handling and short task completion time (TCT). If a teleoperation system in manufacturing is to be used by process and product experts rather than by telerobotic specialists, it's ease-of-use is even more important. The usability of a system can be measured by the effective, efficient, and satisfactory interaction of the user with it, according to ISO 9241-11:2018 [3]. High learnability of a technical system can translate into quick onboarding, low costs and contribute to high user satisfaction [4]. This paper aims to investigate the learnability and usability of a teleoperation system for assembly tasks.

1.2   Contribution

The key contribution of this work is the evaluation and comparison of two different setups of teleoperation systems for assembly tasks. The two setups were developed for assembly tasks, and their suitability was tested in a pilot study. According to ISO 9241-11:2018 [3], the user performance (effectiveness and efficiency) can be quantified by measures of accuracy, completeness, and resource utilization; user satisfaction can be derived from satisfaction scales. According to previous research, the System Usability Scale is a highly robust tool for measuring perceived usability [1,6]. In this work, participants tested two versions of this system in an independent measures study design, differing in the visualization of the remote location. The effectiveness and efficiency dimensions were objectively addressed through task completion time (TCT) and satisfaction was subjectively measured with the System Usability Scale (SUS). The results of the evaluations aid in the development of intuitive and efficient human-machine interfaces (HMIs) for teleoperated assembly tasks.

2 Methods and Procedure

2.1 Ethics Statement

This research was carried out according to the principles embodied in the Declaration of Helsinki and according to the local statutory requirements of Bavaria, Germany. All participants gave their informed consent in writing to participate in the study. The study and all materials used were reviewed by the Ethics Committee of the Technical University of Munich for investigations involving human participants. No objections were raised and the research was approved by the review board under reference number 2022-663-S-NP.

2.2 Study Design

An experiment was conducted in a between-subjects study design to determine the usability of two different setups of teleoperation systems for assembly tasks. It was analyzed how the independent variable visualization method affects the dependent variables performance and perceived usability. The participants were randomly assigned to two groups, direct view (Baseline) and blocked view (Camera). Before the experiment, each participant volunteered, gave their consent, and was fully informed about the experiment. Participants received a tutorial on how to control the leader and a learning time (5 minutes) to experiment with the teleoperation setup and toy blocks. The main task consisted of an assembly and disassembly task, which needed to be repeated ten times (see Subsect. 2.3). After the treatment was completed, the participants completed the System Usability Scale (SUS) questionnaire to assess the usability of the system and operational comfort.

2.3 Task Description

Participants were asked to complete two consecutive tasks with ten repetitions: assembly and disassembly of two rotational symmetric parts of a gearbox. The completion time of the tasks was measured by the supervisor. For each task and trial, the robot moved to a defined starting position. For the assembly task, participants needed to locate the first part (ring), grasp it, and place it on the second part (box). When the participant was sure to have assembled the parts correctly through visual and/or acoustic feedback, he/she told the supervisor to stop timing. For the disassembly task, the assembled parts had to be located, the ring on top of the box had to be grasped and put on a defined position on the table. When the ring was placed in this position, the participant informed the supervisor to stop timing. To verify the measurements during the study, the measured times were verified using timestamps of a video recording.

2.4 Subject Sample

A total of 42 participants (N = 19 women, N = 23 men) were recruited for the experiment. The mean age of the subjects was 24.48 years (range 18 to 32 years, SD = 3.39). Two participants indicated to have previous experience with hand-guided robotic systems or teleoperated robotic systems. All participants reported normal or corrected-to-normal vision.

2.5   Teleoperation System

The teleoperation system consists of two Panda robot arms from Franka Emika^{TM} with a common two-finger parallel gripper (Franka Hand) as end effector, one acting as an input device in the local position (leader) and one as the output device in the remote location (follower). Both robots are connected via Ethernet cables and an 8-port gigabit desktop switch from TP-Link. Both robots are mounted on a desk. The connection allows for bilateral force feedback in real-time.

The participant stands in front of the leader, controlling the pose of the follower in realtime by moving the leader. To grasp/release an item, the participant manually pulls/pushs the fingers of the gripper apart/together. In contrast to the robot joints, the end effector does not provide force nor realtime feedback.

The two robots are positioned 1.70 m to the side and 1.80 m to the rear. Allowing a direct view at a distance of ca. 2.5 m for the participant from an egocentric perspective. In the camera setup (the direct view is blocked and substituted by a video stream), a partition wall blocks the direct view to the follower and the items to be handled. A camera, positioned at 1.53 m height simulating an egocentric perspective as if the participant stood in front of the follower, streams the image of the follower to a screen on the leader's table. Although blocking vision, the partition wall allows natural acoustic feedback.

The two teleoperation setups can be seen in Fig. 1 (Baseline setup) and in Fig. 2 (Camera setup).

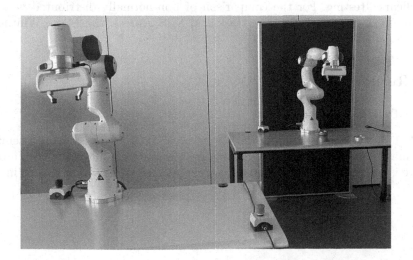

Fig. 1. Teleoperation setup with direct view.

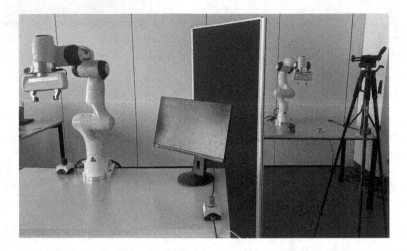

Fig. 2. Teleoperation setup with blocked view and video streaming.

2.6 Data Analysis

All data were plotted and analyzed using Microsoft Excel, the statistical programming language R, or the graphical user interface RStudio [10]. If a task could not be completed without the interference of the supervisor (e.g. because a part fell off the table and could not be recovered using the robot), the respective trial was excluded from the data set and from the analysis of TCTs. Shapiro-Wikl tests were conducted to test for normal distribution. For the normally distributed variables (mean TCT for the assembly task), a t-test was used for significance testing. For the comparison of non-normally distributed variables (mean TCT for the disassembly task and SUS scores), the Mann-Whitney U test was conducted.

3   Results

3.1   Task Completion Time

Table 1 shows the test statistics for the variables TCTs (assembly, disassembly). The mean TCTs of the assembly task are normally distributed for both groups. There is a significant difference between the mean TCTs of both groups in both tasks.

Table 1. Overview of descriptive data and test statistics of mean task completion times

Task	Mean (SD)	Shapiro-Wilk Test	Significance
Assembly	Baseline: 30.71 s (9.32) Camera: 44.84 s (9.43)	W = 0.93, p = 0.1211 W = 0.97, p = 0.7002	significant t = -4.8846, p = 8.549e-06
Disassembly	Baseline: 24.33 s (5.74) Camera: 35.68 s (10.43)	W=0.90, p=0.0387 W = 0.96, p = 0.6173	significant U = 74, z = -3.6853, p = 0.0002

For both groups and tasks, the mean TCTs have declined from the first to the last trial suggesting a learning effect. However, there is no consistent reduction of TCT from one trial to the next. In both tasks, the boxplots of the TCTs are consistently lower in every trial for the Baseline group as well as the range of TCTs. The Camera group shows a much broader range of individual TCTs, which persists throughout the trials. The TCTs for each trial and task are shown in Fig. 3.

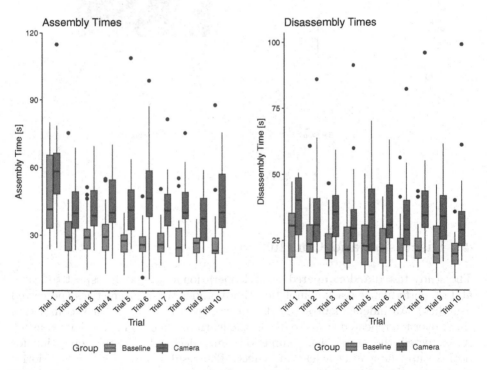

Fig. 3. Boxplots of task completion times of assembly task (left) and disassembly task (right)

3.2   Perceived Usability

The SUS score is in the lower acceptance level for both groups. According to the adjective ratings, the perceived usability of the respective teleoperation setups is OK (Baseline/Camera: mean 68.10/64.40, sd 9.81/7.78). The difference between the perceived usability of both teleoperation setups is not significant ($U = 291$, $z = -1.7832$, $p = 0.0745$). The range of the given scores is high in both groups: from 42.5/55.0 to 82.5/80.0 in the Baseline/Camera group. The SUS scores are shown in Fig. 4.

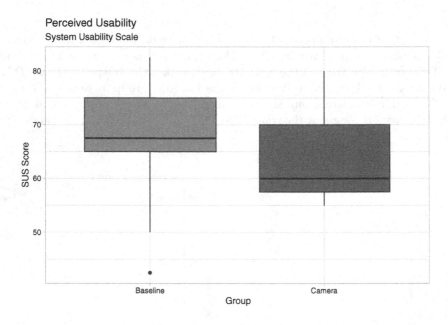

Fig. 4. Perceived Usability

4   Discussion and Conclusion

The study tested and compared two teleoperation setups with respect to learnability, performance (task completion time), and satisfaction metrics (perceived usability). An independent study design was used to measure task completion times over ten repeated trials to detect the learning effect of inexperienced users. As expected, the mean task completion times declined over the repetition for both setups, indicating a learning effect. The results show a clear superiority concerning learnability and performance for the Baseline setup, in which users had a direct view of the remote location rather than relying only on a two-dimensional video stream. However, although the study design facilitated the comparison of the learnability and performance metrics for first-time users, it diminished the informative value of the satisfaction metrics. To compare the perceived usability of the two setups, future studies should explore the difference in the evaluation of each user in a repeated measures (within-subject) design and after intense training (experienced users). The study gives a clear indication of the requirements of workplace and workflow design if teleoperation should be integrated into assembly lines. Any time pressure should be avoided. Moreover, the teleoperation human-machine interface has to be improved to increase the efficiency of teleoperation.

References

1. Bangor, A., Kortum, P.T., Miller, J.T.: An empirical evaluation of the system usability scale. Int. J. Hum.-Comput. Interact. **24**(6), 574–594 (2008). https://doi.org/10.1080/10447310802205776
2. Hainsworth, D.W.: Teleoperation user interfaces for mining robotics. Auton. Robot. **11**(1), 19–28 (2001). https://doi.org/10.1023/A:1011299910904
3. International Organization for Standardization: ISO 9241–11:2018(E): Ergonomics of human-system interaction part 11: Usability: Definitions and concepts (2018)
4. Joyce, A.: How to measure learnability of a user interface (2019). https://www.nngroup.com/articles/measure-learnability/
5. Khatib, O., et al.: Ocean one: a robotic avatar for oceanic discovery. IEEE Robot. Autom. Mag. **23**(4), 20–29 (2016). https://doi.org/10.1109/MRA.2016.2613281
6. Lewis, J.R.: The system usability scale: past, present, and future. Int. J. Hum.-Comput. Interact. **34**(7), 577–590 (2018). https://doi.org/10.1080/10447318.2018.1455307
7. Matheson, E., Minto, R., Zampieri, E.G.G., Faccio, M., Rosati, G.: Human-robot collaboration in manufacturing applications: a review. Robotics **8**(4), 100 (2019)
8. Mizuno, N., Tazaki, Y., Hashimoto, T., Yokokohji, Y.: A comparative study of manipulator teleoperation methods for debris retrieval phase in nuclear power plant decommissioning. Adv. Robot., 1–19 (2023). https://doi.org/10.1080/01691864.2023.2169588
9. Parker, R., Bayne, K., Clinton, P.W.: Robotics in forestry. NZ J. Forest. **60**(4), 8–14 (2016)
10. R Core Team, R.: A language and environment for statistical computing (2021). https://www.R-project.org
11. Richter, F., Orosco, R.K., Yip, M.C.: Motion scaling solutions for improved performance in high delay surgical teleoperation. In: 2019 International Conference on Robotics and Automation (ICRA), pp. 1590–1595 (2019). https://doi.org/10.1109/ICRA.2019.8794085
12. Ruoff, C.F.: Teleoperation and Robotics in Space, vol. 161. AIAA, Reston (1994). https://doi.org/10.2514/4.866333
13. Ryu, D., Hwang, C.S., Kang, S., Kim, M., Song, J.B.: Wearable haptic-based multi-modal teleoperation of field mobile manipulator for explosive ordnance disposal. In: IEEE International Safety, Security and Rescue Rototics, Workshop 2005, pp. 75–80 (2005). https://doi.org/10.1109/SSRR.2005.1501246

Usability Studies in Times of Pandemic: Different Solutions for the Remote Usability Tests of Research Digital Tools

Erasmo Purificato[1,2]([✉])[ID], Sabine Wehnert[1,2][ID],
and Ernesto William De Luca[1,2][ID]

[1] Otto von Guericke University Magdeburg, Magdeburg, Germany
{erasmo.purificato,sabine.wehnert,ernesto.deluca}@ovgu.de
[2] Leibniz Institute for Educational Media | Georg Eckert Institute,
Braunschweig, Germany
{erasmo.purificato,sabine.wehnert,deluca}@gei.de

Abstract. In this paper, we present the usability evaluation of three digital tools of the Leibniz Institute for Educational Media | Georg Eckert Institute, namely Curricula Workstation, GEI-Digital and International TextbookCat, compared with a Meta Search Engine (MSE) *search.gei.de* which shall replace the use of the individual tools. Due to the lockdown measures enforced by the German government at the end of 2021, we developed different solutions to adapt our usability test plans to remote settings. First, the MSE was compared with Curricula Workstation using recordings performed via Zoom. Second, we compared the MSE with GEI-Digital by leveraging mouse tracking data using a combination of Zoom with OBS Studio for recording the screen. Third, a comparison was made between International TextBookCat and the MSE with data collected via CamStudio. The experimental results showed that the individual tools are perceived as better than MSE mainly in terms of intuitive design and ease of learning, while MSE is more satisfying for users.

Keywords: Usability · Human-Centred Design · Remote Testing

1 Introduction

The Leibniz Institute for Educational Media | Georg Eckert Institute[1] (hereafter "GEI" or "the institute"), member of the Leibniz Association, conducts international, multidisciplinary and application-oriented research into educational media, focusing on approaches drawn from cultural and human-centred studies. Over the years, a large number of digital tools have been implemented at the GEI. These include several types of information services, e.g. for searching or browsing curricula or textbooks, which could only be accessed singularly with no uniform index for all the documents. In order to find all existing information

---

[1] https://www.gei.de/en/.

C. Stephanidis et al. (Eds.): HCII 2023, CCIS 1832, pp. 666–673, 2023.
https://doi.org/10.1007/978-3-031-35989-7_85

that could be relevant to one's own research questions, researchers would currently still have to access the relevant websites and familiarise themselves with the respective search logic. To deal with these challenges, a Meta Search Engine (MSE), named *search.gei.de* [7] has been developed as a new overarching tool.

In this work, we assess the usability of MSE, which shall replace the use of each individual search engine. We started a usability test planning process to evaluate the different possibilities of interacting singularly with the information services, namely Curricula Workstation [1,2], GEI-Digital [3,4] and International TextBookCat [5,6], compared to the overarching search.

Initially, in-lab studies were planned using an eye-tracking device, i.e. Tobii Pro Nano[2]. Due to the lockdown measures enforced by the German government at the end of 2021, we developed three different solutions to adapt our original usability test plans to remote settings. First, MSE is compared with Curricula Workstation, using recordings performed via Zoom to assess several usability goals, including intuitive design, ease of learning and subjective satisfaction. Second, we compare the Meta Search Engine with GEI-Digital evaluating intuitive design and subjective satisfaction, also leveraging mouse clicks using a combination of Zoom and OBS Studio for recording the video sessions. Third, a comparison is made between International TextBookCat and search.gei.de by leveraging mouse tracking collected with CamStudio. In the continuation of the paper, we will describe the digital tools analysed (Sect. 2) and then illustrate the conducted usability studies with related results (Sect. 3).

2   Analysed Tools

In this section, we briefly describe the digital tools of the GEI, which are objects of the presented usability studies.

2.1   Curricula Workstation

The **Curricula Workstation** [1,2] tool has been developed by the Research Library of the institute with the support of the German Research Foundation (DFG) funding line "Promotion of outstanding research libraries". Its aim is to provide a central access point to German and international curricula for humanities subjects. Curricula for the subjects of geography, history, social studies, politics and religion/ethics are permanently accessible. The majority of the documents are available for full-text online searches. The number of available texts is being continuously expanded, and historical curricula are gradually being added. The user interface (UI) provides a structured search function (Fig. 1) for curricula using the criteria of country, subject, level of education and year of publication. Free searches of the metadata and full texts of the digital curricula are also possible.

---

[2] https://www.tobii.com/products/eye-trackers/screen-based/tobii-pro-nano.

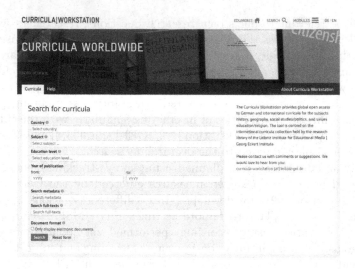

Fig. 1. Curricula Workstation UI

2.2 GEI-Digital

The creation and the development of the *digital textbook library*, known as **GEI-Digital** [3,4], has been developed at the institute and also funded by the DFG. This tool provides online access to the digitised full texts of the historical German textbook collection held by the GEI Research Library (the user interface is visible in Fig. 2). Textbooks from other libraries, which are often difficult to access, are also virtually captured, logged and brought together with other collections, making them available to a wider circle of users.

Fig. 2. GEI-Digital UI

2.3   International TextbookCat

The **International TextbookCat** (ITBC) [5,6] is a research tool that enables researchers to search textbook collections in new and more intuitive ways. It was created over two project phases to supplement the Research Library's OPAC[3], with the goal to expand the catalogue inventory accordingly. Two international institutions were therefore selected as partners: the University of Turin (Italy) and the National University of Distance Education (UNED - Madrid, Spain). The data records of the two international partners' textbook inventories were standardised in order for the ITBC to work as a common, cross-collection search tool. The ITBC uses the internal GEI classifications of the textbooks, which enable targeted searches by being categorised by country, education level and school subject (Fig. 3). Facets such as federal state and type of school are added for textbooks from Germany. The integrated international textbooks can also be filtered according to language. Lending and availability information is provided in the list of results for each search result that is not available directly online.

Fig. 3. International TextbookCat UI

2.4   The Meta Search Engine *search.gei.de*

The **Meta Search Engine**, referred to as MSE, has been implemented within the department "Digital Information and Research Infrastructures" with the aim of creating a central access point for retrieving all the data covered by the institute's digital services and tools. The related UI (Fig. 4) is developed with a minimalist design to enable a user-friendly experience.

---

[3] Acronym for "Online Public Access Catalogue".

Fig. 4. Meta Search Engine UI

3 Usability Studies

This section presents the three different remote solutions (including the related results) made in place to test the usability of the MSE against Curricula Workstation, GEI-Digital and ITBC, respectively.

3.1 Curricula Workstation compared to the Meta Search Engine

In this first test, the participants interact with the tools on their own laptops, and the sessions are recorded via Zoom[4]. In particular, they are asked to solve different tasks (T) and then answer questions (Q) related to specific usability goals (UG). The questionnaire is designed by leveraging 5-point Likert scale questions. Below, after illustrating the tasks and the corresponding questions to every usability goal, we show the resulting findings.

- *T1*: Search in all curricula for the subject "History";
- *T2*: Find all curricula from the years 1950 to 2000;
- *T3*: Find the oldest German curriculum containing the term "Demokratie".

- *UG1*: **Intuitive design** (*definition*: nearly effortless understanding of the architecture and navigation patterns of the site).
  - *Q1*: I felt confident in navigating through this tool;
  - *Q2*: I can easily solve the task using this tool.
- *UG2*: **Ease of learning** (*definition*: how fast a user who has never seen the UI before can accomplish basic tasks).
  - *Q3*: It was easy to learn the basic functions of this tool.
- *UG3*: **Subjective satisfaction** (*definition*: whether the user is satisfied with interacting with the tool).
  - *Q4*: This tool is pleasant to use;
  - *Q5*: I believe I would use this tool in future.

The results of the described test are shown in Table 1, where for each tool, the average of the answers to the questions is reported. We can see that Curricula Workstation is perceived as easier to use, but the Meta Search Engine provides greater user satisfaction.

---

[4] https://zoom.us/.

Table 1. Results of the questionnaire for the usability study where Curricula Workstation is compared with the Meta Search Engine. The best scores are in bold.

Usability goal	Question	Curricula Workstation	MSE
UG1	Q1	4.0	**4.125**
UG1	Q2	3.5	**3.75**
UG2	Q3	**4.375**	3.875
UG3	Q4	4.0	**4.125**
UG3	Q5	1.625	**2.375**

Table 2. Results of the questionnaire for the usability study where GEI-Digital is compared with the Meta Search Engine. The best scores are in bold.

Usability goal	Question	GEI-Digital	MSE
UG1	Q1	**3.0**	2.375
UG1	Q2	**3.125**	2.25

3.2 GEI-Digital Compared to the Meta Search Engine

In this experiment, the tools are compared *explicitly*, in terms of **ease of learning** (*UG1*) through a 4-point Likert scale questionnaire after solving a specific task (*T1*: Use the search function to find the first published German book which contains the word "Demokratie"), and *implicitly*, by analysing the **time spent** during the test and the **mouse clicks** needed for the operation. The participants interact with both tools remotely on their own machines, and the sessions are recorded via OBS Studio[5].

The questions provided to the participants to assess *T1* are the following:

- *Q1*: It was easy to learn the basic functions of this tool;
- *Q2*: It was easy to learn how to find the book I was searching for.

The results of the explicit and implicit analysis are displayed in Table 2 and Table 3, respectively. It is evident that the participants perceive GEI-Digital as easier to use, but the interaction with the Meta Search Engine needs fewer clicks to complete the task.

3.3 ITBC compared to the Meta Search Engine

For the third test, the participants are asked to compare ITBC and MSE by solving a specific task involving the use of filter necessarily (*T1*: Searching for the first digital resource in ITBC where the term "Demokratie". Then search for the same book on MSE. The procedure must involve the use of filters on both tools). The participants interact with both tools remotely on their own machines, and the sessions are recorded via CamStudio[6]. The usability goals assessed by

---

[5] https://obsproject.com/.
[6] https://camstudio.org/.

Table 3. Results of the implicit analysis (time spent and mouse clicks) where GEI-Digital is compared with the Meta Search Engine. The best scores are in bold.

Metric	GEI-Digital	Meta Search Engine
Time spent [seconds]	**1.63**	1.75
Mouse clicks [count]	11.5	**10**

Table 4. Results of the questionnaire for the usability study where ITBC is compared with the Meta Search Engine. The best scores are in bold.

Usability goal	Question	ITBC	Meta Search Engine
UG1	Q1	**3.718**	3.223
UG1	Q2	**3.432**	2.99
UG2	Q3	2.431	**3.334**
UG2	Q4	3.146	**3.334**

this test and the related post-session questions (provided in a 5-point Likert scale form) are listed below.

- *UG1*: **Intuitive design**
  - *Q1*: It was easy to find the filters on this tool;
  - *Q2*: Overall, the search process was intuitive.
- *UG2*: **Subjective satisfaction**
  - *Q3*: The tool was pleasant to use, and I found it as useful as my usual search engine to solve the same or a similar task;
  - *Q4*: I would use this tool again in future.

The results in Table 4 show how the participants found more intuitive to use the filters option while searching with ITBC, but overall, they are more satisfied while interacting with the Meta Search Engine.

4   Conclusion

In this paper, we presented the different solutions applied for three usability studies conducted in 2021. In particular, due to the pandemic period, the tests were conducted entirely remotely, leveraging different technologies. The main aim of the studies was to compare the usability of the Meta Search Engine *search.gei.de*, developed at the Leibniz Institute for Educational Media | Georg Eckert Institute, with each individual tool included in the unified Meta Search Engine, namely Curricula Workstation, GEI-Digital and International Textbook-Cat. The results of the conducted experiments showed, from different perspectives, that the users prefer the design and the ease of learning of the single tools, but at the same time, they are more satisfied by the interaction with a modern UI like the one proposed by the Meta Search Engine.

References

1. Drechsler, J., Strötgen, R., Chen, E.: Entwicklung eines informationssystems für lehrpläne-die curricula workstation. In: Informationsqualität und Wissensgenerierung. 3. DGI-Konferenz, 66. Jahrestagung, pp. 153–60 (2014)
2. Fuchs, A.: edumeres.net: Zehn jahre digitale vernetzung in der internationalen bildungsmedienforschung. In: Digital Humanities in der internationalen Schulbuchforschung: Forschungsinfrastrukturen und Projekte, pp. 191–206. V&R unipress GmbH (2018)
3. Hertling, A., Klaes, S.: "gei-digital" als grundlage für digital-humanities-projekte: Erschließung und datenaufbereitung. In: Digital Humanities in der internationalen Schulbuchforschung: Forschungsinfrastrukturen und Projekte, vol. 9, pp. 45–68. V&R unipress GmbH (2018)
4. Hertling, A., Klaes, S.: Historische schulbücher als digitales korpus für die forschung: Auswahl und aufbau einer digitalen schulbuchbibliothek. In: Digital Humanities in der internationalen Schulbuchforschung: Forschungsinfrastrukturen und Projekte, vol. 9, pp. 21–44. V&R unipress GmbH (2018)
5. Scheel, C.: Multilingualität in einem internationalen bibliothekskatalog. In: Digital Humanities in der internationalen Schulbuchforschung: Forschungsinfrastrukturen und Projekte, pp. 171–188. V&R unipress GmbH (2018)
6. Scheel, C., De Luca, E.W.: Fusing international textbook collections for textbook research. In: Kremers, H. (ed.) Digital Cultural Heritage, pp. 99–107. Springer, Cham (2020). https://doi.org/10.1007/978-3-030-15200-0_7
7. Scheel, C., Fallucchi, F., De Luca, E.W.: Visualization, interaction and analysis of heterogeneous textbook resources. Future Internet 12(10), 176 (2020). https://doi.org/10.3390/fi12100176

Use of Technology in the Context of Latin America

Carlos Ramos Galarza[1,2]([✉]), Omar Cóndor-Herrera[2], Mónica Bolaños-Pasquel[2], and Jorge Cruz-Cárdenas[3]

[1] Facultad de Psicología, Pontificia Universidad Católica del Ecuador, Av. 12 de Octubre y Roca, Quito, Ecuador
`carlosramos@uti.edu.ec`
[2] Centro de Investigación en Mecatrónica y Sistemas Interactivos MIST/Carrera de Psicología, Universidad Tecnológica Indoamérica, Av. Machala y Sabanilla, Quito, Ecuador
[3] Research Center in Business, Society, and Technology, ESTec, School of Administrative and Economic Science, Universidad Tecnológica Indoamérica, Quito, Ecuador
`jorgecruz@uti.edu.ec`

Abstract. The article reports national statistical data on the usage of information and communication technologies in Ecuador, illustrating a sample of what occurs across Latin American countries. The data was collected in the 28 cities from Ecuador. The respondents were 40, 814 people aged from 0 to 98 years old. Regarding gender, 20,110 (49.3%) participants identified as male and 20,704 (50.7%) as female. Regarding educational level, 1,570 (3.8%) participants did not report any level of education, 115 (0.3%) attended a literacy center, 8,492 (24.9%) primary school, 9,317 (25.8%) basic education, 7,041 (17.9%) secondary school, 5,239 (12.8%) high school, 717 (1.8%) non-university higher education, 4,860 (11.9%) university higher education, 320 (0.8%) postgraduate level. In the results, it was found that a large number of citizens do not have access to technological means in favor of activities such as education or to solve everyday life activities. The results are discussed in the context of Latin America and the need for greater investment in the technological accessibility and development of the region to improve the living conditions of its people.

Keywords: Latin America · technology · internet · education · Smartphone

1 Introduction

The use and access to technology is still a privilege in Latin America. The vast majority of countries in the region are characterized by not having technological devices in favor of education, medicine, basic and financial services, among others for the majority of the population.

Ecuador is a country in the region that is a clear example of this situation (Fig. 1), where access to technology is still a privilege. The aim of this article is to better understand how the Ecuadorian population access electronic devices and the Internet.

C. Stephanidis et al. (Eds.): HCII 2023, CCIS 1832, pp. 674–680, 2023.
https://doi.org/10.1007/978-3-031-35989-7_86

Fig. 1. Shaded in red in the South American region you can see Ecuador. (Color figure online)

In places such as Ecuador and other Latin American countries, it is necessary to highlight the existing gap in the use of technological resources to solve common problems. By looking into national surveys a better picture can be obtained so that solutions can be sought for this situation [1].

In the proposed context, the research objective is to describe the access that Ecuadorian citizens have to the internet, computer and smartphone in order to demonstrate the existing inequalities around use and access of technology in this region of the world [2].

2 Methodology

2.1 Sample

The respondents were 40, 814 people aged from 0 to 98 years old. Regarding gender, 20,110 (49.3%) participants identified as male and 20,704 (50.7%) as female. Regarding educational level, 1,570 (3.8%) participants did not report any level of education, 115 (0.3%) attended a literacy center, 3 (0.0%) nursery, 8,492 (21.9%) primary school, 9,317 (22.8%) basic education, 7,041 (17.3%) secondary school, 5,239 (12.8%) high school, 717 (1.8%) non-university higher education, 4,860 (11.9%) university higher education, 320 (0.8%) postgraduate level. From all the educational establishments that were reported only 7,664 have computers and only 7,046 have internet service (Fig. 2).

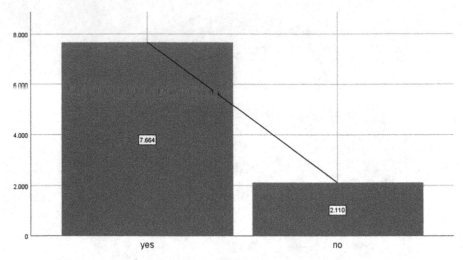

Fig. 2. Graphic representation of the question: Do you have a computer?

2.2 Measuring Instruments

The database from the Ecuadorian Institute of Statistics and Census, which is available for research purposes, was used. Specifically the surveys concerning access to technology and internet were selected. The information was collected [3].

2.3 Statistics Analysis

Descriptive statistical analysis techniques such as frequencies, mean, standard deviation, percentages, median and mode were applied. As inferential analysis, comparison of sample means was used. All analyzes were performed in the SPSS version 28.0 program.

3 Results

In terms of Smartphone use, 23,368 are active (Fig. 3), of which 16,375 participants have Internet access, 16,524 have access to social networks, 13,069 have an email on their Smartphone, 9,910 use GPS, and 12,049 use this device to download applications such as games. Regarding access in the last 12 months, 22,227 entered the Internet, of which 11,921 were to obtain information on the web, 6,774 were for general communication, 150 to buy and order products, 77 to use the bank, 2,021 for educational activities, 24 for transactions with government agencies, 515 for entertainment activities, 137 for music or movies, 60 for reading or downloading books, 492 for work activities, and 48 for scheduling medical appointments.

Regarding the frequency of Internet use, 18,940 use it at least once a day, 2,766 at least once a week, 431 at least once a month and 51 at least once a year (Fig. 4). As for installing and configuring new software on the computer 5787 has done this. In relation to transferring files between computers and other devices, it is found that 8073

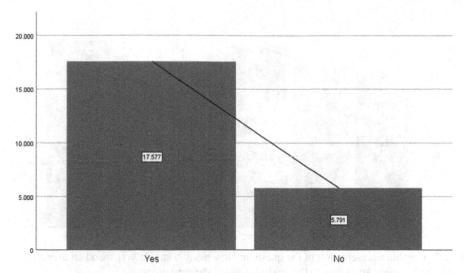

Fig. 3. Graphic representation of the question: Do you have a smartphone?

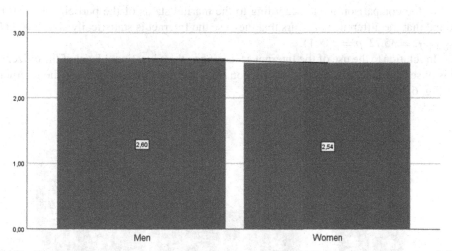

Fig. 4. Graphic representation of the question: How many hours do you spend on average daily using the Internet?

have done this action. Finally, when asking the participants if they have developed a computer program, 1759 they state that they have carried out this action.

When comparing the means between the hours that men and women use the Internet, it was found that this difference is statistically significant ($t_{(22225)} = 2.17, p = .01, d = 2.29$). The marital status of the population also has a direct influence on the number of hours that citizens use the Internet. The results found that single and divorced people have the most access to this network. The data can be seen in Fig. 5.

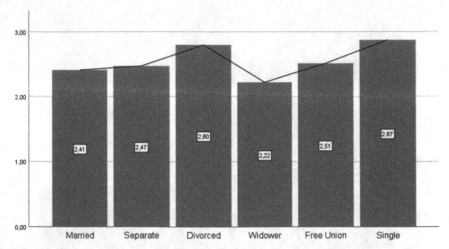

Fig. 5. Graphic representation of the question: How many hours do you spend on average daily using the Internet? According to the marital status of the participants.

In the comparison made according to the marital status of the participants, it was found that the difference in hours that they use the Internet is statistically significant ($F_{(5, 20431)} = 35.72, p = <.001$).

In relation to the use of the Internet according to the educational level of the citizens, it is observed that as the level of instruction rises, the more participants use the Internet. In Fig. 6 you can see this data.

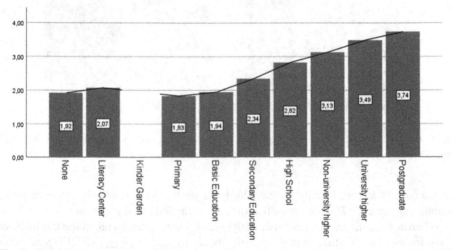

Fig. 6. Graphic representation of the question: How many hours do you spend on average daily using the Internet?.Data organized according to the educational level of citizens.

As in the previous analyses, the difference in the average number of hours used according to the academic level of the citizens was compared, finding that there are statistically significant differences in favor of a higher educational level and greater use of the Internet ($F_{(8, 22218)} = 211.88$, $p = <.001$).

Another aspect that influences the number of hours that a citizen uses the Internet is the ability to read and write. In this data it was found that people with reading and writing skills are the ones who use the internet the most. In Fig. 7 you can see this data.

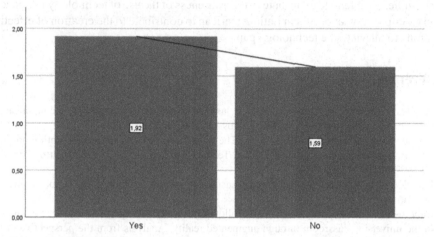

Fig. 7. The average number of hours of daily internet use is organized according to the reading and writing ability of the participants.

In relation to significant differences around the use of the Internet according to the reading and writing capacity of citizens, it was found that there is a statistically significant difference in this data ($t_{(7401)} = 2.63$, $p = .004$).

4   Conclusions

This research has analyzed the use of technology in Ecuador, a Latin American country. To achieve this objective, a representative sample of 28 cities from Ecuador was analyzed in order to have a better understanding of the usage and access to technology and the internet.

In Latin America there is still a deficit in access to technology and it is of vital importance that we can take actions that can help the population of this part of the world. For example, spaces such as education, medicine, finance and access to basic services need technological implementation to help the population advance, however, as seen in this research, in countries like Ecuador this access is still limited [4, 5].

In relation to the devices used, a restricted access of the population to the use of the Internet can be observed. There is a trend in relation to the use of technology as the academic level of the participants rises, with postgraduates being the ones who use the Internet the most [6].

Finally, as it can be seen, in Ecuador there is a high number of people who do not have access to computer technology or Smartphone to carry out educational or important activities in the lives of citizens. This example of what happened in Ecuador is a sample of what happens in the context of Latin America, where a limited number of human beings have access to technological development and thus be able to improve their social status.

Our future research will focus on several aspects: (a) analysis differences in accessing technology depending on gender, (b) use of technology in the various socioeconomic strata and (c) access to technology in the rural and urban context of the country. With these studies we intend to contribute to the awareness of the use of technology in Ecuador as an example of what occurs in Latin American to contribute to the creation of effective solutions to alleviate the technology gap.

References

1. Paredes, C., Morán, R.: Reflexiones sobre las tecnologías de la Información y comunicación (TIC) en el ámbito universitario. Encuentros **14**, 204–211 (2021)
2. Cóndor-Herrera, O., Ramos-Galarza, C.: The impact of a technological intervention program on learning mathematical skills. Educ. Inf. Technol. **26**(2), 1423–1433 (2020). https://doi.org/10.1007/s10639-020-10308-y
3. Ecuadorian Institute of Statistics and Census. https://www.ecuadorencifras.gob.ec/institucional/home
4. Cabero-Almenara, J., Vásquez-Cano, E., Villota-Oyarvide, W., López- Meneses, E.: Innovation in the university classroom through augmented reality. Analysis from the perspective of the Spanish and Latin American student. Revista Electronica Educare **25**(3), (2021)
5. Méndez-Porras, A., Alfaro-Velasco, J., Rojas-Guzmán, R.: Educational video games for girls and boys in preschool education using robotics and augmented reality. RISTI - Revista Iberica de Sistemas e Tecnologias de Informacao **2021**(42), 472–485 (2021)
6. Cóndor-Herrera, O., Acosta-Rodas, P., Ramos-Galarza, C.: Gamification teaching for an active learning. Intelligent human systems integration 2021. IHSI 2021. Adv. Intell. Syst. Comput. **1322** (2021)
7. Nadiia, R., Innola, N., Olesya, L., Oleksandr, N., Yulia, K., Yulia, H.: Socio-Economic processes functioning and innovation education development. In: Alareeni, B., Hamdan, A. (eds.) Innovation of Businesses, and Digitalization during Covid-19 Pandemic. ICBT 2021. LNNS, vol. 488, pp. 749–763. Springer, Cham (2021). https://doi.org/10.1007/978-3-031-08090-6_47

Assessing the Usability of Statistical Software Using Designed Experiments

Jacob Rhyne[(⊠)], Mark Bailey, Joseph Morgan, and Ryan Lekivetz

JMP Statistical Discovery, Cary, NC 27513, USA
{Jacob.Rhyne,Mark.Bailey,Joseph.Morgan,Ryan.Lekivetz}@jmp.com

Abstract. Modern statistical software is increasingly used by users with limited statistical training to address complex real-world problems. Yet, little work has been done on assessing the usability of such software [1]. This paper presents a usability case study for a design of experiments (DOE) tool in a commercially available statistical software product. The study focuses on an interface to specify factors for a designed experiment and discusses both qualitative and quantitative findings.

Keywords: Design of experiments · Usability · Statistical software

1 Introduction

Since the 1970s, several authors have addressed the validation of statistical software [6,7]. As it turns out, very little of this work has focused on assessing the usability of such software [1]. However, this is an increasingly important aspect of validating statistical software as ever more sophisticated capabilities are provided, sometimes by way of complex graphical user interfaces (GUI), to users who rely on these products to do their work. Furthermore, as these products become more pervasive and complex, both experienced users and those with limited statistical training may have even more difficulty using these products.

In this paper we present a usability case study for a tool within a commercial statistical software package (JMP) [3]. The focus of the study is a dialog from the design of experiments tool that is used to specify factors for an experiment. Factors are the independent variables that experimenters believe have an impact on the outcome of dependent variable(s) of interest to the experimenter. As can be seen from Fig. 1, factor specification is an activity in the initial step of the sequence of steps that are necessary for any experimental design.

This activity is critical because inadequate specifications can have a profound impact on the utility of an experiment. As a result, experimenters typically iteratively refine their factor specification to ensure that the factors are adequate for the experiment. To specify a factor, there are several attributes that the experimenter must consider, some of which have an impact on the category of design that can be constructed as well as the subsequent analysis.

Figure 2 is an example of a factor specification from the DOE tool in JMP. This is for an experiment to determine the factors and associated settings that

C. Stephanidis et al. (Eds.): HCII 2023, CCIS 1832, pp. 681–688, 2023.
https://doi.org/10.1007/978-3-031-35989-7_87

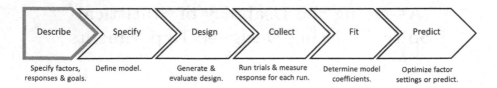

Fig. 1. DOE Workflow

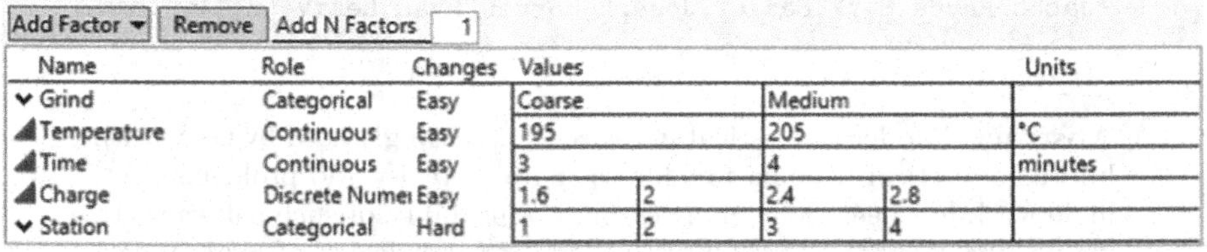

Name	Role	Changes	Values				Units
˅ Grind	Categorical	Easy	Coarse		Medium		
◢ Temperature	Continuous	Easy	195		205		°C
◢ Time	Continuous	Easy	3		4		minutes
◢ Charge	Discrete Numeri	Easy	1.6	2	2.4	2.8	
˅ Station	Categorical	Hard	1	2	3	4	

Add Factor ▾   Remove   Add N Factors   1

Fig. 2. Example of a factor list for an experiment to optimize the best tasting coffee.

determine the best tasting coffee. Note that simple attributes, such as factor name and units (i.e., °C, minutes, etc.), do not have an impact on the design. However, more complex attributes, such as factor type (referred to as **Role** in JMP), akin to a statistical type (i.e., continuous, categorical, discrete numeric, etc.), will have an impact on the resulting design. Note that for factor type the user must also decide on the values associated with the chosen type: a range for a continuous type, specific levels for categorical and discrete numeric types, and so on. Another attribute that has an impact on the design is changeability (referred to as **Changes** in JMP) which refers to whether a factor may be easily changed during the experiment.

2   Methodology

We began our study by compiling user feedback on the existing JMP DOE factor specification dialog (subsequently referred to as a factor list). It quickly became apparent that many user pain points had to do with discoverability, clarity and tedium when performing everyday tasks. However, some challenges were more fundamental, in that they indicated missing functionality. For example, users were unable to change the factor type after adding a factor. Similarly, users could not easily update the number of levels for a categorical or discrete numeric factor. Additionally, changing the order of factors was not possible and there was no undo or redo capability. Such limitations meant that simple tasks were difficult and often time-consuming.

With these observations in mind, the developers decided that a set of prototypes was needed to evaluate how various layout configurations would impact effectiveness [2] given a set of simple tasks gleaned from compiled user feedback. A configurable prototype offering 384 different configurations was built and it was decided that a designed experiment would be used to assess effectiveness, measured by task completion time.

For the designed experiment governing the study, the factors we considered represented the UI elements of the interface that could be varied, while the levels were the different settings for each factor (see Table 1). A run of the experiment would then represent a set of factor-level combinations that would define the configuration that a subject would be presented with.

For typical experimental design approaches in the human-computer interaction literature, counterbalancing (or, more generally, randomization) is accomplished through a Latin square approach [4]. The experimental design approach we used falls under a class of designs known as optimal experimental designs [5]. Our rationale for taking this approach is to allow consideration of a variety of factors that may each require a different number of levels. This is particularly useful when a full factorial design (i.e., using all possible combinations) is not feasible. Note that to generate an optimal design, an assumed model is required. For instance,

$$Y = \beta_0 + \beta_1 x_1 + \beta_2 x_2 + ... + \beta_m x_m + \epsilon \tag{1}$$

is such a model, where Y is the response, x_i represents the i'th effect and β_i its corresponding coefficient, with ϵ the random error, assumed to be normally distributed with mean 0 and variance σ^2. For nominal factors, we use a coding scheme (known as effects coding) where the sum of the levels is 0, so that β_0 represents the overall mean of the data.

By taking this approach, more factors can be accommodated than if a design catalog approach was adopted. Depending on the criterion used to generate an optimal design, the objective may be to minimize the average variance of prediction (known as I-optimality) versus more precise estimation of effect estimates (known as D-optimality) [5]. Here we opt for a D-optimal design, where we can estimate all effects, but also remove from the model and future experiments those effects and factors that are not significant. This concept of effect sparsity, or the Pareto principle, where not all factors are expected to influence the response, is an established concept in experimental design. We can also accommodate a learning effect by including a time-trend as a covariate. With our approach, a covariate is simply a factor that has its values/levels specified in advance, and while the values cannot be changed, they can be accounted for during design construction. Our approach allows us to evaluate task completion effectiveness as well as to determine the effects, whether they be main effects, interactions, or powers that have a significant impact on the layout configurations that we present to the subjects of our study.

3 Usability Case Study

3.1 Background

As developers mulled over the pain points from user feedback, several themes emerged. For example, the idea of a mini toolbar for addition, deletion, undo, redo, etc. emerged. Also, to address learnability and discoverability, the decision was made to use standard GUI elements/controls, such as buttons, input boxes, combo boxes, etc., wherever possible. The idea was to exploit known UI metaphors by using such controls. In addition, the developers decided to retain the grid layout of the existing interface (see Fig. 2) but with the requirement that rows should be draggable for rearranging, should be selectable to facilitate operations like deletion, and row highlighting should be supported. However, with the number of possible layout configurations that were possible, the developers decided to have an initial round of usability testing of a functional prototype built from available UI elements, before UX designers were able to provide a final design of icons and other UI elements. The study presented subsequently is for this initial usability study and so the screenshots presented do not reflect the final UX design.

3.2   UI Elements

The factor list prototype was designed with configurability in mind. One of the areas of focus of the study was to determine controls and icons that users would find intuitive as they attempted basic tasks. These tasks include the addition or removal of factors, changing the order of factors, as well as undoing or redoing changes. For example, there are two ways to delete a factor from the factor list. In one configuration, a user may select the row in the table for the factor they wish to delete, then click the Delete button (see control 2 outlined in orange in Fig. 3). In other configurations, the Delete button may be absent but a Trash Can icon would be present instead. In these configurations, the user could click the icon beside a row, then drag this icon upwards to the Trash Can icon, control 1 outlined in red in Fig. 3. There are also configurations in which both the Delete button and Trash Can icon may be included; thus, the user has the choice to use the control they prefer (or discover). Similarly, there are several ways to add factors. The Plus button (control 3 outlined in blue in Fig. 3) allows users to append a factor to the end of the factor list. Alternatively, the user may add factors using the Add N Factors control (control 5 outlined in purple in Fig. 3). This control allows a user to add multiple factors of the same predefined type. Again, there are configurations where the Plus button or the Add N Factors control may be used.

The prototype provides several additional UI elements for configuration. Given the number of possible configurations, a designed experiment was deemed necessary to allow the developers to assess the effectiveness of various UI elements.

3.3   Designed Experiment

For this iteration of the study, task completion time was the response, with minimization of task completion time the goal. Table 1 includes a summary of the eight factors that were identified, with the first seven factors indicating UI elements to be varied during the study.

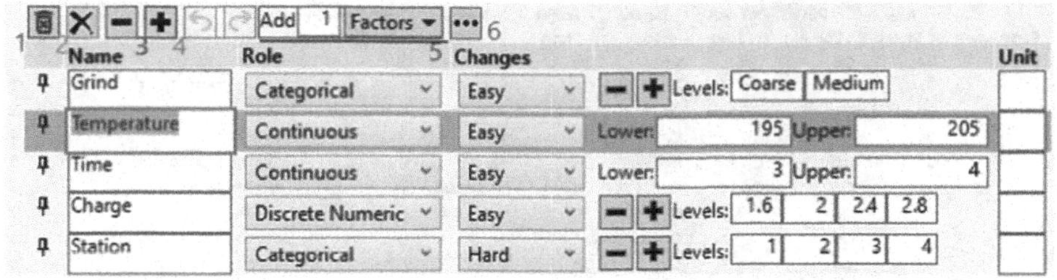

Fig. 3. Example of prototype including the (1) Trash Can icon, (2) Delete button, (3) Plus button, (4) Undo and Redo buttons, (5) Add N Factors control, and (6) Buffet Menu button.

Table 1. Factors for the factor specification dialog usability study

Name	Levels	Description
Pin Column	On, Off	Row icons (in)visible
Trash Icon	On, Off	Trash Can icon (in)visible
Delete Icon	On, Off	Delete icon (in)visible
Buffet Icon	On, Off	Buffet icon (in)visible
Toolbar Type	(+/−), Add N Factors, Both	Sets controls to add factors
Pin Col. Type	Pin, Oval, Copy, Oval+Copy	Sets row icons
Row States	On, Off	Sets row highlighting
Task	Delete, Change type, Change position	Sets tasks for subjects

Each row of the resulting design therefore determines a configuration of the prototype to be presented to subjects (see Fig. 4). Since the prototype is dynamically configurable, any configuration can be generated, on demand. As it turns out, some of the 384 possible configurations of the prototype cannot be used to complete every task. For example, to delete a factor, it would be impossible for a subject to complete the task if both the Trash icon and Delete button were set to Off. To account for such constraints, we make use of a "Disallowed Combinations" feature in the JMP DOE tool used for this exercise, to exclude factor combinations that make it impossible to complete the task.

Our statistical model allowed us to estimate all main effects and as many two-factor interactions as possible, given our run size restriction. Due to the time the pilot usability study took to complete, we decided that a 12-run design was a practical size for the usability study. Note that we used blocking to create four different versions of the study and recruited eight subjects, so that each version of the study would be completed twice. Finally, we decided that "Participant" and "Run Order" should be included as covariates in our design.

We aimed for a balanced representation of subjects by recruiting participants from three different personas: expert users of DOE and JMP, expert users of JMP who were new to DOE, and new users of both JMP and DOE. To deliver

Participant	Row States	Pin Column	Trash Icon	Delete Icon	Buffet Icon	Toolbar Type	Pin Column Type	Task	Run Order
1	On	Off	Off	On	On	Both	Pin	Delete	1
1	On	On	On	On	On	+/-	Copy	Change factor types	2
1	On	On	On	On	On	+/-	Oval+Copy	Delete	3
1	On	On	Off	On	Off	+/-	Oval+Copy	Delete	4
1	On	Off	Off	On	On	+/-	Oval+Copy	Change factor types	5
1	On	On	Off	On	On	Factor butt...	Pin	Change factor types	6
1	Off	On	On	On	Off	Factor butt...	Oval	Delete	7
1	Off	On	On	On	Off	+/-	Oval+Copy	Change factor types	8
1	Off	On	On	On	Off	Both	Oval	Change factor types	9
1	Off	On	On	Off	On	Both	Pin	Change factor types	10
1	On	On	Off	On	Off	+/-	Pin	Change position	11
1	Off	On	On	On	Off	Both	Oval+Copy	Change position	12

Fig. 4. Design for usability study completed by Participant 1.

the study to these participants, we developed a custom application that used the constructed designs to deploy an unmoderated study to each participant. In addition, an integrated questionnaire was included so that we could gather qualitative data.

4   Results

4.1   Qualitative Findings

Table 2 contains a summary of our qualitative data, with eight responses from subjects of the usability study plus two responses from subjects who completed the pilot study. Subjects overwhelmingly preferred the Plus button, as opposed to the Add N Factors control, though some subjects pointed out that they recognized the value of both options. Additionally, subjects were almost unanimous in their belief that the Trash Can icon was unnecessary.

Since we were interested in the utility of the undo and redo buttons, we asked subjects to indicate whether they used the undo button while completing the tasks. Six subjects used the undo button and two subjects pointed out that, while they did not need to use the button while completing the study, they liked that this option was included in the prototype.

Of the icons used for each row, the Pin icon was the most preferred, with five of ten subjects reporting it was their favorite. The Oval icon was preferred by only two subjects and three pointed out that they did not like any of the icons offered at the time the study was conducted.

Finally, only five subjects indicated that hover hints were easy to find, and four indicated that row icons did not make it clear that rows could be clicked. To our delight, eight of ten subjects indicated that the prototype was easy to learn and nine of ten preferred it to the existing interface.

4.2   Quantitative Findings

For our analysis (see Figs. 5 and 6), we used a stepwise regression procedure, available in the Generalized Regression platform of JMP, to determine the model

Table 2. Results from Questionnaire included in usability study

Outcome	Yes	No	N/A or Other
Preferred Plus button over Add N Factors control	9	1	0
Preferred the Delete button over the Trash icon	5	1	4
Believed the Trash icon was necessary	0	8	2
Used the undo button when completing the study	6	2	2
Preferred the Pin icon over the Oval icon	5	2	3
Hover hints were easy to find	5	5	0
Row icons signaled rows could be clicked	5	4	1
The user interface was easy to learn	8	0	2
Preferred prototype to existing interface	9	0	1

from our data. Since our response was task completion time (in seconds), and time cannot be negative, we used a LogNormal response distribution. In addition, we used the "Best Subset" method, which introduces an active effect into the model at each step and used the corrected Akaike Information Criterion (AICc) as our stopping rule.

Changing Factor Type: Subjects were asked to change a categorical factor to a blocking factor. Run Order turned out to be the only significant effect indicating that as subjects repeated the task, they were able to change factor type faster. Intuitively, this makes sense when you consider the task and how it was completed. To change factor type, one simply needs to select the appropriate type from a drop-down menu. As a result, different icon selections and methods of adding or removing factors should not influence task completion time.

Changing Factor Order: The second task considered in the study was to switch the order of two factors in the factor list. For this task, we found that Pin Column Type (the row icon used), the Trash icon, and Row States had a significant effect on task completion time. From Fig. 5 we see that the Oval icon was the optimal option. This seemingly contradicts the participants' stated preferences from the previous section. Recall that only two participants chose the Oval, yet subjects completed the tasks more efficiently using the Oval. Run Order did not have a significant effect for this task.

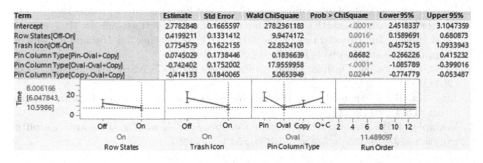

Term	Estimate	Std Error	Wald ChiSquare	Prob > ChiSquare	Lower 95%	Upper 95%
Intercept	2.7782848	0.1665597	278.2361183	<.0001*	2.4518337	3.1047359
Row States[Off-On]	0.4199211	0.1331412	9.9474172	0.0016*	0.1589691	0.680873
Trash Icon[Off-On]	0.7754579	0.1622155	22.8524103	<.0001*	0.4575215	1.0933943
Pin Column Type[Pin-Oval+Copy]	0.0745029	0.1738446	0.1836639	0.6682	-0.266226	0.415232
Pin Column Type[Oval-Oval+Copy]	-0.742402	0.1752002	17.9559958	<.0001*	-1.085789	-0.399016
Pin Column Type[Copy-Oval+Copy]	-0.414133	0.1840065	5.0653949	0.0244*	-0.774779	-0.053487

Fig. 5. Results for "changing factor order" task.

Deleting a Factor: The third task was to delete factors from the list. Our initial design was flawed, so we recruited additional participants for a follow-up study; the results of this can be seen in Fig. 6. The method used to remove factors and run order significantly affected task completion time. The time required to delete factors was minimized when the Delete button was used.

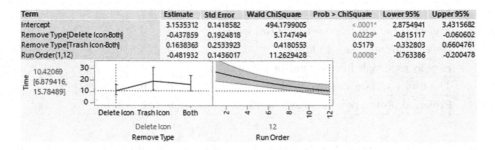

Term	Estimate	Std Error	Wald ChiSquare	Prob > ChiSquare	Lower 95%	Upper 95%
Intercept	3.1535312	0.1418582	494.1799005	<.0001*	2.8754941	3.4315682
Remove Type[Delete Icon-Both]	-0.437859	0.1924818	5.1747494	0.0229*	-0.815117	-0.060602
Remove Type[Trash Icon-Both]	0.1638363	0.2533923	0.4180553	0.5179	-0.332803	0.6604761
Run Order(1,12)	-0.481932	0.1436017	11.2629428	0.0008*	-0.763386	-0.200478

Fig. 6. Results for "deleting a factor" task.

Comparison of Prototype to Original Factor List: We wrapped up our study by having the subjects do the factor type change and factor order tasks with both the prototype and the original factor list. On average, the subjects took 68 s to complete the tasks when using the prototype but 316 s when using the original factor list, a dramatic and significant difference. Furthermore, for the original factor list, the average time was right-censored as two subjects reported giving up before completing the task.

References

1. Abbasnasab Sardareh, S., Brown, G.T., Denny, P.: Comparing four contemporary statistical software tools for introductory data science and statistics in the social sciences. Teach. Stat. **43**, S157–S172 (2021)
2. Bevan, N., Carter, J., Harker, S.: ISO 9241-11 revised: What have we learnt about usability since 1998? In: Kurosu, M. (ed.) HCI 2015. LNCS, vol. 9169, pp. 143–151. Springer, Cham (2015). https://doi.org/10.1007/978-3-319-20901-2_13
3. Carver, R.: Practical Data Analysis with JMP. SAS Institute (2019)
4. Eiselmayer, A., Wacharamanotham, C., Beaudouin-Lafon, M., Mackay, W.E.: Touchstone2: an interactive environment for exploring trade-offs in HCI experiment design. In: Proceedings of the 2019 CHI Conference on Human Factors in Computing Systems, pp. 1–11 (2019)
5. Goos, P., Jones, B.: Optimal Design of Experiments: a Case Study Approach. Wiley (2011)
6. Lekivetz, R., Morgan, J.: On the testing of statistical software. J. Stat. Theory Pract. **15**(4), 76 (2021)
7. Wampler, R.H.: A report on the accuracy of some widely used least squares computer programs. J. Am. Stat. Assoc. **65**(330), 549–565 (1970)

The Structure of Users' Satisfaction with Body-Worn Cameras: A Study of 181 Chinese Police Officers

Yan Shang[1,2,3], Xiaoyan Wei[4], Wenxuan Duan[1], and Jingyu Zhang[1,2(✉)]

[1] Institute of Psychology, Chinese Academy of Sciences, Beijing 100101, China
zhangjingyu@psych.ac.cn
[2] Department of Psychology, University of Chinese Academy of Sciences, Beijing 100049, China
[3] TD Tech Limited, Beijing 100102, China
[4] Chongqing Changan Automobile Co., Ltd., Chongqing 400000, China

Abstract. Recently, body-worn cameras (BWCs) have become a must-worn type of equipment for police officers to use in law enforcement. While the use of BWCs continues to increase, studies on the user experience of end users are still lacking. To understand how the multifaceted features are valued by the users (police officers) and identify the common dimensions behind these features, we conducted the present study by distributing a satisfaction questionnaire covering important features identified by a previous qualitative study. In total, 181 frontline police officers (Mage = 30.36, 86.7% are male) completed an online questionnaire in which they assessed their satisfaction with multiple features of BWCs, including waterproof, battery endurance, video quality, etc. Individual characteristics such as age, gender, working experience, and current position were also collected. Exploratory factor analysis revealed a three-factor structure: Adaptability, Portability, and Ease of use. We also found that all three factors significantly correlated with recommendation intention and overall satisfaction. These findings presented fresh and in-depth insights into how to design future BWCs. BWCs producers could increase technology satisfaction with police officer body-worn cameras by considering these factors and individual differences to enhance key features and provide personalized products and services.

Keywords: Factor analysis · Body-worn cameras · Adaptability · Portability · Ease of use

1 Introduction

Body-worn cameras (BWCs) are small wearable devices designed to capture an audio-visual record of police–citizen interactions. The recorded footage can then be used for investigatory and evidentiary purposes [1]. In many countries, BWCs were legally required for police officers to wear, and they played an active role in protecting the rights and interests of both the police and the citizens [2].

© The Author(s), under exclusive license to Springer Nature Switzerland AG 2023
C. Stephanidis et al. (Eds.): HCII 2023, CCIS 1832, pp. 689–694, 2023.
https://doi.org/10.1007/978-3-031-35989-7_88

In the past ten years, most studies related to BWCs focused on the societal consequences of using BWCs. For example, researchers have found that using BWCs can improve the transparency and legitimacy of the police, reduce legal disputes, and improve citizens' cooperation, which is the foundation for adopting BWCs at the societal level [3]. On a smaller scale, some studies have suggested that using BWCs may also result in privacy violation concerns or occasionally endanger the officers' safety [4].

Very recently, some researchers started to explore what can make a good BWC from the police officer's point of view. A study investigating police officers in Beijing found BWVC cannot fully meet the actual needs and expectations of the officers in battery life, stability, storage space, lens angle, and other issues. Also, it suggested that the most important concerns were battery life and BWVC reliability [5].

In addition, Suss and colleagues provided specific suggestions, from the perspective of ergonomists, to design better BWCs [6]. They suggested designers should pay attention to important features such as video quality, camera-mounting position, camera-mount stability, etc. However, studies are still lacking in showing why some features are important and how they are linked with users' satisfaction.

In the present study, we sought to establish a feature list for BWCs, and explore how the evaluation of these features is linked with overall satisfaction and actual usage by frontline police officers and how the evaluation of these features is linked with each other.

2 Methods

2.1 Participants

In total, 181 frontline police officers from China took part in an anonymous online survey. The included participants should be using or have used a BWC of any brand. The basic demographic information of the participants were shown in Table 1 below. Participants were paid ¥50 (US$7) for finishing the online questionnaire.

Table 1. The demographics of the 181 police officers

Categories	Counts
Age	
20–24 years	26
25–35 years	126
36–45 years	20
≥46 years	9
Gender	
Male	157
Female	24

(*continued*)

Table 1. (*continued*)

Categories	Counts
Education	
High school and lower	47
Undergraduate	118
Graduate and higher	16
Working experience	
1–5 years	116
6–10 years	35
>10 years	30

2.2 Measurement

Feature Evaluation. Based on a previous study on the design considerations of BWCs [6] and a previous qualitative study for Traffic Police [2], 24 features of user experience in the use of BWCs were identified (see Table 2). The respondents were asked to evaluate the performance of their most recently used BWCs on these features on a 5-point Likert scale, ranging from 1 (Very bad) to 5 (Very good).

Overall Satisfaction. The satisfaction of the overall BWCs product consists of three items adapted from a customer satisfaction questionnaire [7]. Respondents were asked to evaluate on a 7-point scale (from 1 to 7) about (1) to which degree they feel they were satisfied with the BWC, (2) to which degree the BWC fulfilled their needs, and (3) to which degree the BWC met their expectations. A higher score means higher satisfaction with the BWC.

Recommendation Intention. Recommendation intention has been a popular method to predict loyalty in recent years. Respondents were asked to evaluate "How likely is it that you would recommend this BWC to others?" on a 7-point scale, ranging from 1 (not recommend at all) to 7 (strongly recommend).

3 Results

An exploratory factor analysis (FA) was first performed to identify the common dimensions behind the 24 features. The value of KMO is 0.934, suggesting the data is appropriate for factor analysis. With the help of a scree plot, three factors were extracted using a principal component analysis (PCA) with Varimax rotation. By discarding features with low total loading (<0.5), 23 features were retained (see Table 2). The factors accounted for 58.6% of the variance in total. Factor 1 accounted for 27% of the variance and was named Adaptability because it tapped the diversified situations to use the key function that recoding evidence. Factor 2 accounted for 16.5% of the variance and was named Portability because it reflects portability and convenience. Factor 3 accounted for 15.1%

of the variance and was named Ease of use because it reflected the ease of wearing, learning, pressing, and so on.

Table 2. The Factor loadings of all 24 features on the three dimensions

Features	Adapt	Port	Ease
Video quality: the resolution of the shot video	.753		
Waterproof: the ability to protect the device from water	.744		
Visibility in dim light: the video shot in dim light can be identified	.735		
Anti-shake: can record clearly despite shaking	.727		
Authority-like appearance: the appearance can strengthen the authority	.708		
Wide angle: the view of the shot video is wide	.698		
Screen resolution: the display resolution of the device screen is high	.595		
Communication capability: clear voice and stable calling	.592		
Ease of battery changing: the battery is easy to be changed	.578		
Camera-mount stability: hard to fall off even during strong movement	.543		.542
Legibility under strong light: the display can be identified during strong light, such as the sunlight during the midday	.532		
Screen responsiveness: screen responds fast and accurately to touch	.516		
Firmness: the device is steady in accidents such as collisions and landing	.516		
Portability: the device is small enough to be portable		.762	
Lightweight: the device is light enough		.695	
System startup speed: the device startup is fast		.617	
Charge speed: the device can be charged in a short time		.566	
Battery life: the device can work for a long time after being fully charged		.543	
Ease of wearing: users easily mount the device on the body			.707
Accidental touch protection: can prevent unwanted touches			.704
Ease of learning: users can easily and quickly learn how to operate it			.660
Clarity of prompt: prompts such as low power are clear			.590
Ease of Pressing Buttons: the buttons can be easily and naturally pressed			.585
Ease of Filing: recorded files are easy to manage			

Note: Factor extraction method = PCA, rotation method = Varimax rotation

Spearman correlation (see Table 3) was conducted between the average item scores of the three factors with overall satisfaction and recommendation intention. All correlation coefficients are significant at the .001 level. All three factors significantly correlated with recommendation intention and overall satisfaction.

Table 3. Spearman correlation analysis

	Adaptability	Convenience	Ease of use
Overall satisfaction	.435**	.370**	.299**
Recommendation intention	.467**	.415**	.245**

Note: $^{**}p < .01$, significant correlation

4 Discussion

The present study explored the structure of users' evaluation of the 24 features of body-worn cameras among Chinese police officers. We found these features can be categorized into three dimensions, Adaptability, Portability, and Ease of Use, and they all contributed significantly to overall satisfaction and recommendation intention. Several aspects are worth further discussion.

Compared our findings with the Usefulness and Ease of Use dimensions in the Technology Acceptance Model (TAM) [8], it seems that both the Adaptability and the Portability factor are related to the usefulness concept. It seems that the two aspects are both important for a good BWC, i.e., it can be used in all contexts without a huge effort for carrying.

Second, we found that the three dimensions significantly correlated with overall satisfaction and recommendation intentions. While the relative importance of the three dimensions can be further delineated using larger consumer data and regressional approaches, it already suggests that the three dimensions can be considered the three pillars in defining a good BWC. Further analysis can help the brand to know its strengths and weaknesses and better define product strategies.

Based on these findings, producers can enhance user satisfaction with BWCs more effectively by considering this structure.

Acknowledgments. This study was supported by the National Natural Science Foundation of China (Grant No. T2192932) and TD Tech Limited.

References

1. Suss, J., Raushel, A., Armijo, A., White, B.: Design considerations in the proliferation of police body-worn cameras. Ergon. Design **26**(3), 17–22 (2018)
2. Duan, W., Shang, Y., Zhang, J., Wang, H., Zou, X.: Applying hierarchical task analysis to identify the needs of intelligent equipment for traffic police in China. In: Harris, D., Li, W.C. (eds.) Engineering Psychology and Cognitive Ergonomics. HCII 2022. LNCS, vol. 13307, pp. 6–7. Springer, Cham (2022). https://doi.org/10.1007/978-3-031-06086-1_13
3. White., M.D.: Police Officer Body-Worn Cameras: Assessing the Evidence, pp. 22–30. Office of Justice Programs, US Department of Justice, Washington, DC (2014)
4. Mateescu, A., Rosenblat, A., boyd, d:Police Body-Worn Cameras. Data & Society Research Institute, pp. 1–2, pp. 5–7 (2015)

5. Jiang, F., Xie, C., Ellis, T.: Police officers' perceptions of body-worn video Cameras in Beijing. Int. Crim. Just. Rev. **31**(5), pp.16–19 (2021). Special Issue: Bentham on Police & Policing (2020)
6. Suss, J., Raushel, A., Armijo, A., White, B.: Design considerations in the proliferation of police body-worn cameras. Ergon. Design **26**(3), 18–19 (2018)
7. Liu, L., Zhang, J., Zhang, L., Wang, J., Luo, X., Wang, Y.: Motive structure underlying the use of intelligent connected vehicles. In: CHI 2020: CHI Conference on Human Factors in Computing Systems, pp. 3–4 (2020)
8. Davis, F.D.: Perceived usefulness, perceived ease of use, and user acceptance of information technology. MIS Q. **13**, 11–12 (1989, September)

To Leave or Not to Leave? Understanding Task Stickiness in Smartphone Activity Recommendations

Lingyun Wan[1,2] , Jingyu Zhang[1,2(✉)], and Mengdi Liu[3]

[1] Institute of Psychology, Chinese Academy of Sciences, Beijing, China
zhangjingyu@psych.ac.cn
[2] Department of Psychology, University of Chinese Academy of Sciences, Beijing, China
[3] Huawei Device Co., Ltd., Shenzhen, China

Abstract. Recent intelligent smartphone assistants can provide proactive activity recommendations for what users might want to do in the upcoming moments. However, many of these recommendations may not be accepted because the ongoing tasks performed by users vary in their "stickiness" (reluctance to switch away). Past studies suggest that user states in their ongoing tasks might reflect task stickiness. Still, it has not been systematically tested among a comprehensive set of tasks for everyday smartphone users. In this study, we sought to examine the impacts of individual and task characteristics on users' task stickiness in the context of mobile recommendations based on a large set of tasks. In total, 220 participants completed an online evaluation assessing 55 everyday smartphone activities summarized from literature and interviews. They evaluated each task's perceived task load, involvement, and stickiness. Individual characteristics such as boredom proneness were also collected. Hierarchical linear modeling showed that: (1) Task load and involvement positively predicted task stickiness. Users may not accept new recommendations when their ongoing tasks are demanding and engaging. (2) Boredom proneness reduced the effect of task load. For people who are more likely to feel bored, their intention to stay in the current task was maintained even when the task load dropped. This study suggests that recommendation system designers should consider both task characteristics and individual differences to enhance contextual appropriateness and personalization.

Keywords: Activity Recommendation · Task Stickiness · Smartphone Usage

1 Introduction

Recent intelligent smartphone assistants, such as Siri and Celia, can provide proactive activity suggestions for what users might want to do in the upcoming moments. Such recommendations are now mainly based on users' habits of using the applications and external context information such as time of day and location. Although activity suggestions can potentially improve user interaction efficiency, low recommendation appropriateness is still an issue that impedes their effective utilization. Many of these

C. Stephanidis et al. (Eds.): HCII 2023, CCIS 1832, pp. 695–701, 2023.
https://doi.org/10.1007/978-3-031-35989-7_89

recommendations may not be accepted because the ongoing tasks performed by users vary in their "stickiness" (reluctance to switch away). The instantaneity of available activities and their possible interruptions to the ongoing task further emphasize the importance of considering users' task context for their acceptance of recommendations.

Past studies on notifications and interruption management suggest that user states in their ongoing tasks might reflect task stickiness. They found that users' interruptibility was lower when the current task was more complex, challenging, interesting, engaging, and enjoyable [1–3]. As for certain activity types, it might be inappropriate to disturb them during their work and study rather than during chores and idle time [2–4]. Critical task characteristics that may contribute to stickiness, such as load and involvement, can be derived from past research. However, these effects have not been systematically tested among a comprehensive set of tasks for everyday smartphone users that serve as scenarios for activity recommendations.

In addition, it may be effective but insufficient to consider the timing of recommendations based on a generic criterion of task characteristics. There is a wide diversity in people's intensity of use and interaction with smartphones [5]. Individuals could also exhibit different perceptual and behavioral patterns when presented with recommendations, which may constrain the possible ways to enhance the appropriateness of system behavior [6]. Beyond demographic characteristics, personal traits such as boredom have been found to correlate with smartphone addiction and flow experience [7] and were therefore included in the current study.

To improve our understanding of task stickiness in the context of smartphone recommendations, we examined the impacts of possible individual and task characteristics in this study based on a large set of tasks. We also discussed the implications of our results for application in this field.

2 Method

2.1 Participants

We recruited 267 smartphone users for this study, and they completed the questionnaires online. A total of 220 valid cases were retained after excluding participants with abnormal answering times and those who failed the attention checks embedded in the survey. The average age of the participants was 24.75 years (SD = 5.62), ranging from 18 to 55 years. 30.9% were male, and 98.2% had a college degree or higher. Their average daily mobile phone usage time ranged from 2 to 15 h (M = 6.75, SD = 2.38).

2.2 Materials

A list of 55 smartphone activities was developed through the following process:

1. Extracting and summarizing everyday activities proposed in the literature related to cell phone usage [7–16];
2. Making the necessary supplement and dismantling, and refining the task descriptions to unify the granularity of the tasks, which were performed by a research team with three members;

3. Inviting two experts to discuss further and adjust the entries where duplication and ambiguity existed.

In the evaluation survey for the above list of tasks, the participants rated each task using a seven-point Likert scale on three dimensions: perceived task load, involvement, and stickiness. In particular, the item of task stickiness was used to characterize to what degree the task was not easily disengaged and unsuitable for interruptions. The descriptions of each dimension given to the participants were as follows:

- Load: the extent to which performing the task takes up a person's mental and physical resources, concerning the difficulty you perceive in the task;
- Involvement: the extent to which the task meets your internal needs, interests, and values;
- Stickiness: the extent to which performing the task restricts you from using your phone for other activities.

In addition, several individual characteristics were collected:

- Demographic characteristics, including age, gender, education, etc.;
- Daily mobile phone usage time;
- Boredom proneness, measured by the Chinese version of the Short Boredom Proneness Scale (SBPS) [17, 18], 8 items, $\alpha = 0.91$.

2.3 Data Analysis

Task stickiness was predicted based on users' perceived load and involvement of tasks and selected individual characteristics with predictive effect. A hierarchical linear regression approach was adopted on account of the nested structure of data (multiple tasks assessed by different individuals), and the intra-class correlation was 15.87% in the null (intercept-only) model. Analyses were conducted with the *lmerTest* package in R. We obtained the marginal and conditional R^2 (i.e., the proportion of variance explained by fixed factors and both fixed and random factors) [19] of each model using the *bruceR* package. We also compared different models with deviance tests.

3 Results

We ran a series of mixed-effects models with task stickiness as the dependent variable. The following Table 1 presents a summary of fixed effects coefficients of them. An individual-level predictor, bored proneness, was first included in Model 1. The comparison between Model 1 and the intercept-only model showed a significant increase in goodness-of-fit ($\chi^2(1) = 7.52$, $p = .006$), which indicates that boredom proneness contributes to explaining an additional amount of variance in task stickiness. According to Table 1, higher boredom proneness was associated with increased task stickiness perceived by the participants ($\beta = .08$, $p < .01$).

Model 2 added the individual means of perceived load and involvement across the tasks, and the centered scores of their load and involvement were then entered into Model 3. We also considered the random effect of task load in Model 3, while that of task involvement was excluded because the relevant model failed to converge. The main effect of boredom proneness became insignificant after the inclusion of task evaluation predictors. Model 2 provided a better fit than Model 1 ($\chi^2(2) = 92.42, p < .001$). Both perceived task load ($\beta = .50, p < .001$) and involvement ($\beta = .11, p < .001$) positively predicted task stickiness. Model 3 also showed a significant improvement in fit compared to Model 2 ($\chi^2(4) = 5831.6, p < .001$), and the marginal and conditional R^2 were increased by 29.5% and 33.7%, separately.

Table 1. Hierarchical linear regression model predicting task stickiness.

	M1	M2	M3	M4
Level 2 variables				
Boredom proneness	.077 (.028)**	.033 (.023)	.033 (.023)	.033 (.023)
Mean load		.184 (.024)***	.184 (.024)***	.182 (.024)***
Mean involvement		.138 (.023)***	.138 (.023)***	.139 (.023)***
Level 1 variables				
Load			.500 (.007)***	.495 (.007)***
Involvement			.114 (.007)***	.119 (.007)***
Cross-level interaction				
Boredom proneness × Load				−.032 (.015)*
Marginal R^2	.006	.065	.360	.362
Conditional R^2	.164	.164	.501	.502

Note: N = 55 tasks (Level 1) evaluated by 220 participants (Level 2). Standard errors for the coefficients are given in parentheses. *p < .05; **p < .01; ***p < .001

Model 4, which included a cross-level interaction effect of boredom proneness and task load in consideration of the individual-specific effects of load on stickiness, showed an additional improvement in fit relative to Model 3 ($\chi^2(1) = 4.64, p = .031$). The results suggest that boredom proneness negatively moderated the effect of task load ($\beta = -.03, p = .015$). And the zero-order correlation between the boredom proneness index and the load coefficients estimated from the previous model was $-.14$ ($p = .032$). A simple slope test showed that the coefficients of load were significant for both high ($\beta = 0.47, p < .001$) and low ($\beta = 0.53, p < .001$) boredom proneness. However, for people with higher boredom proneness, task stickiness dropped more slowly when the task load dropped, as shown in Fig. 1.

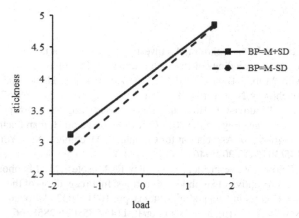

Fig. 1. Moderating effects of boredom proneness on load.

4 Discussion

In this study, we analyzed data from an evaluation of a large set of everyday smartphone activities to systematically test the impacts of individual and task characteristics on users' task stickiness. Results showed that task stickiness was positively related to perceived load and involvement in the task. Furthermore, we found that higher boredom proneness significantly reduced the effect of task load on stickiness and thus narrowed the gap between tasks with different load levels. In other words, people are more reluctant to switch away from the ongoing task when it is difficult and engaging. For those with a higher tendency to experience boredom, the decline in task stickiness is relatively slight, even when the task is simple and easy. A possible reason is that such people have a greater task-switching cost, as they more frequently suffer from overload and fatigue [20]. Boredom-prone individuals may also have difficulty choosing and launching into new activities [21].

The above results provide insights into the utilization of mobile activity recommendations. Pushing activity recommendations to users may not be appropriate when they are occupied by tasks with high load and involvement. People with different traits may also vary in the pattern of influence on task stickiness. Service providers could benefit from considering these factors to enhance the contextual appropriateness and personalization of activity recommendations.

There are some limitations in the current study. First, we relied simply on a subjective assessment method that may not directly reflect the actual outcomes of the recommendation acceptance decisions. Future research will need to generalize these effects to real recommendation settings. Second, the acceptance of a recommendation depends not only on the current task and individual characteristics but also on the content of the recommendation. In future work, researchers could further explore the joint influences of the ongoing and recommended tasks on acceptance.

Acknowledgments. This study was supported by the National Natural Science Foundation of China (Grant No. T2192932).

References

1. Pejovic, V., Musolesi, M., Mehrotra, A.: Investigating the role of task engagement in mobile interruptibility. In: Proceedings of the 17th International Conference on Human-Computer Interaction with Mobile Devices and Services Adjunct, pp. 1100–1105. Association for Computing Machinery, New York (2015). https://doi.org/10.1145/2786567.2794336
2. Yuan, F., Gao, X., Lindqvist, J.: How busy are you? Predicting the interruptibility intensity of mobile users. In: Proceedings of the 2017 CHI Conference on Human Factors in Computing Systems, pp. 5346–5360. Association for Computing Machinery, New York (2017). https://doi.org/10.1145/3025453.3025946
3. Mehrotra, A., Pejovic, V., Vermeulen, J., Hendley, R., Musolesi, M.: My phone and me: understanding people's receptivity to mobile notifications. In: Proceedings of the 2016 CHI Conference on Human Factors in Computing Systems, pp. 1021–1032. Association for Computing Machinery, New York (2016). https://doi.org/10.1145/2858036.2858566
4. Mehrotra, A., et al.: Understanding the role of places and activities on mobile phone interaction and usage patterns. In: Proceedings of the ACM on Interactive, Mobile, Wearable and Ubiquitous Technologies, vol. 1, no. 3, pp. 1–22 (2017). https://doi.org/10.1145/3131901
5. Falaki, H., Mahajan, R., Kandula, S., Lymberopoulos, D., Govindan, R., Estrin, D.: Diversity in smartphone usage. In: Proceedings of the 8th International Conference on Mobile Systems, Applications, and Services, pp. 179–194. Association for Computing Machinery, New York (2010). https://doi.org/10.1145/1814433.1814453
6. Gievska, S., Sibert, J.: Using task context variables for selecting the best timing for interrupting users. In: Proceedings of the 2005 Joint Conference on Smart Objects and Ambient Intelligence: Innovative Context-Aware Services: Usages and Technologies, pp. 171–176. Association for Computing Machinery, New York (2005). https://doi.org/10.1145/1107548.1107593
7. Leung, L.: Exploring the relationship between smartphone activities, flow experience, and boredom in free time. Comput. Hum. Behav. 103, 130–139 (2020). https://doi.org/10.1016/j.chb.2019.09.030
8. Atas, A.H., Çelik, B.: Smartphone use of university students: patterns, purposes, and situations. Malays. Online J. Educ. Technol. 7, 59–70 (2019). https://doi.org/10.17220/mojet.2019.02.004
9. Deng, T., et al.: Measuring smartphone usage and task switching with log tracking and self-reports. Mob. Media Commun. 7, 3–23 (2019). https://doi.org/10.1177/2050157918761491
10. Galletta, D., Dunn, B.: Assessing smartphone ease of use and learning from the perspective of novice and expert users: development and illustration of mobile benchmark tasks. AIS Trans. Hum.-Comput. Interact. 6, 74–91 (2014). https://doi.org/10.17705/1thci.00062
11. Jesdabodi, C., Maalej, W.: Understanding usage states on mobile devices. In: Proceedings of the 2015 ACM International Joint Conference on Pervasive and Ubiquitous Computing, pp. 1221–1225. Association for Computing Machinery, New York (2015). https://doi.org/10.1145/2750858.2805837
12. Nam, S.-Z.: Evaluation of university students' utilization of smartphone. Int. J. Smart Home 7, 175–182 (2013)
13. Smura, T., Kivi, A., Toyli, J.: Mobile data services in Finland: usage of networks, devices, applications and content. Int. J. Electron. Bus. 9, 138–157 (2011). https://doi.org/10.1504/IJEB.2011.040359
14. Tian, Y., Zhou, K., Lalmas, M., Pelleg, D.: Identifying tasks from mobile app usage patterns. In: Proceedings of the 43rd International ACM SIGIR Conference on Research and Development in Information Retrieval, pp. 2357–2366. Association for Computing Machinery, New York (2020). https://doi.org/10.1145/3397271.3401441

15. Verkasalo, H.: Analysis of smartphone user behavior. In: 2010 Ninth International Conference on Mobile Business and 2010 Ninth Global Mobility Roundtable (ICMB-GMR), Athens, Greece, pp. 258–263. IEEE (2010). https://doi.org/10.1109/ICMB-GMR.2010.74

16. Xu, Q., Erman, J., Gerber, A., Mao, Z., Pang, J., Venkataraman, S.: Identifying diverse usage behaviors of smartphone apps. In: Proceedings of the 2011 ACM SIGCOMM Conference on Internet Measurement Conference, pp. 329–344. Association for Computing Machinery, New York (2011). https://doi.org/10.1145/2068816.2068847

17. Struk, A.A., Carriere, J.S.A., Cheyne, J.A., Danckert, J.: A short boredom proneness scale: development and psychometric properties. Assessment **24**, 346–359 (2017). https://doi.org/10.1177/1073191115609996

18. Peng, J., et al.: Reliability and validity test of the Chinese vision of short boredom proneness scale. Chin. J. Clin. Psychol. **27**(2), 282–285 (2019). https://doi.org/10.16128/j.cnki.1005-3611.2019.02.014. (in Chinese)

19. Nakagawa, S., Schielzeth, H.: A general and simple method for obtaining R^2 from generalized linear mixed-effects models. Methods Ecol. Evol. **4**, 133–142 (2013). https://doi.org/10.1111/j.2041-210x.2012.00261.x

20. Whelan, E., Najmul Islam, A.K.M., Brooks, S.: Is boredom proneness related to social media overload and fatigue? A stress–strain–outcome approach. Internet Res. **30**, 869–887 (2020). https://doi.org/10.1108/INTR-03-2019-0112

21. Danckert, J.: Boredom: managing the delicate balance between exploration and exploitation. In: Ros Velasco, J. (ed.) Boredom Is in Your Mind, pp. 37–53. Springer, Cham (2019). https://doi.org/10.1007/978-3-030-26395-9_3

A Usability Study of a Research Institute Website with Eye-Tracking Devices

Sabine Wehnert[1,2] (ID), Erasmo Purificato[1,2](✉) (ID), and Ernesto William De Luca[1,2] (ID)

[1] Otto von Guericke University Magdeburg, Magdeburg, Germany
{sabine.wehnert,erasmo.purificato,ernesto.deluca}@ovgu.de
[2] Leibniz Institute for Educational Media, Georg Eckert Institute, Braunschweig, Germany
{sabine.wehnert,erasmo.purificato,deluca}@gei.de

Abstract. In this paper, we present the results of our study conducted at the Leibniz Institute for Educational Media | Georg Eckert Institute to assess the usability of the institute's website before the re-design of the same and the subsequent development of the new version. In particular, four specific pages are evaluated, i.e. *Home*, *Institute*, *Departments* and *Publications*. The aim of the presented usability studies is to uncover positive and negative usability findings in order to properly plan the potential corrective actions for the upcoming restyling. The experimental outcomes are displayed in form of aggregated heat maps and mainly focus on the ease of use of the different analysed sections.

Keywords: Usability · Human-Centred Design · Eye Tracking

1 Introduction

The Leibniz Institute for Educational Media | Georg Eckert Institute (from now on "GEI" or simply "the institute"), member of the Leibniz Association and sited in Brunswick, Germany, conducts international, application-oriented and multidisciplinary research into educational media, focusing on approaches drawn from cultural and human-centred studies.

To improve the overall user experience of its tools and websites, the institute initiated a series of actions to this end. One of the measures taken is the re-designing of the GEI website, taking into account user experience (UX) and usability aspects, which are often overlooked. For this, the version of the website in place in June 2022 has been assessed via multiple usability studies in order to derive positive and negative findings for guiding the future design process, which was completed in August 2022, when the new version of the GEI website[1] was released.

In this work, we describe the conducted usability studies for the main website's sections, namely the *Home* page, the *Institute* section, the *Departments* section

---

[1] https://www.gei.de/en/.

C. Stephanidis et al. (Eds.): HCII 2023, CCIS 1832, pp. 702–711, 2023.
https://doi.org/10.1007/978-3-031-35989-7_90

and the *Publications* page. In particular, four different in-lab usability tests were carried out. All the tests shared a standard structure: a briefing and pre-session interview questions, followed by the actual usability test tasks and ended with post-session interview questions. The participants in the tests made use of screen-based eye-tracking devices, i.e. Tobii Pro Nano[2]. The tasks were designed considering specific usability goals [2], including intuitive design, ease of use, ease of learning and subjective satisfaction. Both quantitative and qualitative evaluation approaches [4] have been used. For the former, success rate and time to task completion were employed. In contrast, gaze plots, heat maps, recorded pathways and answers to pre- and post-session interview questions were considered for the latter.

In this paper, we specifically present the usability findings derived from the qualitative analysis of heat maps and gaze plots. The methods shared in our paper and the insights gained from the analysed results can serve as a basis within the HCI community for future similar usability studies.

In the following, we will first describe the analysed sections of the institute's website (Sect. 2), and then we carefully explain the performed usability tests and the resulting findings (Sect. 3).

2   The Analysed GEI Website

In this section, we briefly introduce the main sections of the GEI website, which are subjects to the usability evaluation, in view of the re-design of the entire

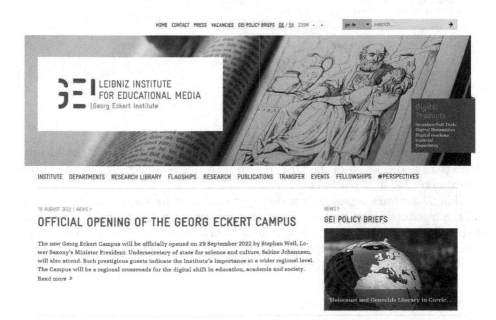

Fig. 1. GEI website - *Home* page (before the re-design)

---

[2] https://www.tobii.com/products/eyetrackers/screen-based/tobii-pro-nano.

website. In particular, the usability studies presented in this paper consider the four main pages (i.e. *Home*, *Institute*, *Departments* and *Publications*) from the latest version of the institute's website before the release, which was in place until August 2022.

The *Home* page (Fig. 1) displays in its central part the latest and/or most important news concerning the institute's activities. Links to all the other sections of the website are present.

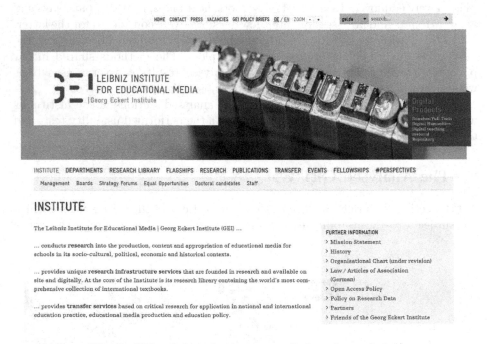

Fig. 2. GEI website - *Institute* page (before the re-design)

The *Institute* page (Fig. 2) displays all the information about the history, objectives and mission of the GEI. It also provides references to the institute's board and academic partners.

The *Departments* page acts mainly as a container for the individual pages of all the institute's departments. Every department page (such as the example in Fig. 3 displaying the department "Digital Information and Research Infrastructures") includes the description of the department and the list of its members in their own different roles.

Fig. 3. GEI website - *Departments* page (before the re-design)

PUBLICATIONS

THE LEIBNIZ INSTITUTE FÜR EDUCATIONAL MEDIA'S PRINT PUBLICATIONS

> Eckert. Die Schriftenreihe showcases outstanding work from the field of educational media rese-
arch. The series is published by V&R unipress, Göttingen.

> Early 2012 saw the creation of the new Eckert. Expertise series, which publishes practically rele-
vant, research-based expertise, recommendations and other studies.

> The Eckert. Beiträge series appears exclusively online and is a channel for findings from educatio-
nal media research. Each article is peer-reviewed by two independent experts.

CONTACT
publikationen [at] leibniz-gei.de

INSTITUTE PUBLICATION
> Textbooks between tradition and innova-
tion – A journey through the history of the
Georg Eckert Institute [PDF]

Fig. 4. GEI website - *Publications* page (before the re-design)

In the *Publications* page (Fig. 4), the articles published by the institute's members are listed and grouped by topic or associated project.

3 Usability Study

In this section, we describe the design of the usability tests which were carried out to evaluate the GEI website and discuss the related findings. For each page evaluated, we first describe the task that the participants are asked to solve, and then we report the results (in terms of either *heat maps* or *gaze plots*) from which the final conclusions are drawn.

Heat Maps: A *heat map* is a graphical representation of the user's mouse or eye movement (as in our usability studies) when using a product or service. Heat maps are helpful indicators of what grabs a user's attention, where the users are spending their time, and how much time is being spent on which areas [1,3]. Long dwelling times visualised as the "hotter" areas in a heat map therefore indicate attention, be it positive (e.g., appealing user interface elements) or negative (e.g., confusion). If in doubt, qualitative information - gathered from user surveys or

Fig. 5. Aggregate heat map of the usability tests of the *Home* page.

contextual interviews - offers evidence to interpret long dwelling times. Overall, heat maps can help determine which aspects of digital tools need to be improved.

Gaze Plots: Besides heat maps, gaze plots are another graphical representation of eye-tracking study results. When participants look at a specific location, the area they are looking at is marked by a circle. The longer the area is fixated, the bigger the circle is visualised. In the end, a series of numbered circles illustrate the movements of the eye. Thereby, different colours represent the eye movement of different participants. Between the circles, the eye's focus transitions to another location. This jump is called a *saccade*. During saccades, humans cannot see, but because these eye movements are very fast, humans are not aware of them.

3.1 *Home* Page

For the usability analysis of the *Home* page, the task assigned to the test participants is the following: "Find and read the most recent events of the institute". The heat map in Fig. 5 displays how the users are supposed to focus on the term *"events"* on the screen, but they overall look all around the page focusing all section headings, meaning that the layout is not straightforward and not very intuitive in presenting the latest and most important events at the GEI.

3.2 *Institute* Page

In testing the *Institute* page, the participants are required to locate the Mexican partner of the GEI. All users successfully completed the task, and the resulting heat map in Fig. 6 clearly shows the ease of use of the page, considering the unequivocal path followed by the testers to reach the correct item.

3.3 *Departments Page*

In this test, we ask the participants to visit the Research Library to borrow a book. In particular, they would have to check the address, opening hours and Covid-19 protocols for the visit[3] and note the book lending procedure. Only 25% of the testers were able to find out the Research Library regulations.

---

[3] The usability study was conducted in Spring 2022 when measures against Covid-19 were still in place.

Fig. 6. Aggregate heat map of the usability tests of the *Institute* page.

As shown in the heat map in Fig. 7, many participants missed the hyperlink to "Library Use". This is probably due to the unclear flow of information on the specific page and a poor intuitive design since the "Library Use" points to both "Library Regulations" and "Covid-19 Regulations".

3.4 *Publications* Page

On the *Publications* page, as the usability test task provided, the participants should reach the *Journal on Educational Media, Memory and Society* (JEMMS) section and search for the publication on "Holocaust" by Basabi Khan Banerjee and Georg Stöber. Due to previously known difficulties in locating the search

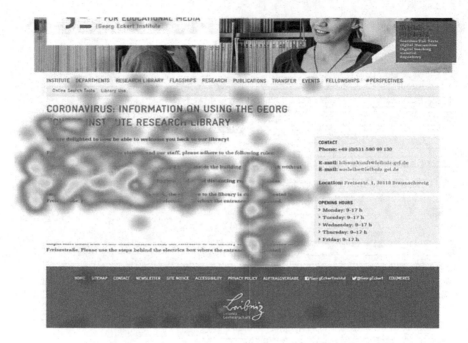

Fig. 7. Aggregate heat map of the usability tests of the *Departments* page.

bar of the web page, the users are also asked not to use the search functionality. The task was completed by 90% of the testers, but as shown in the heat map in Fig. 8, they went through the whole page before finding the correct links to get closer to the target. The main finding of this experiment is that it is paramount to make the search bar clearly visible on every page where a list of items or resources is displayed in order to improve ease of use and subjective satisfaction. In addition, filtering criteria to narrow down the topic can be considered.

Fig. 8. Aggregate heat map of the usability tests of the *Publications* page.

4 Conclusion

In this paper, we presented the main results of the studies carried out at the Leibniz Institute for Educational Media | Georg Eckert Institute to analyse the usability of the institute's website in view of the launch of a new version of the same. In particular, four specific sections were evaluated, namely *Home*, *Institute*, *Departments* and *Publications* pages, to discover positive and negative usability findings for planning the potential corrective actions for the novel restyling in progress. The experimental outcomes are displayed in form of aggregated heat maps and mainly show several issues concerning the ease of use of the different analysed sections.

References

1. Hirzle, T., Sauter, M., Wagner, T., Hummel, S., Rukzio, E., Huckauf, A.: Attention of many observers visualized by eye movements. In: Shic, F., et al. (eds.) ETRA 2022: Symposium on Eye Tracking Research and Applications, Seattle, WA, USA, 8–11 June 2022, pp. 65:1–65:7. ACM (2022). https://doi.org/10.1145/3517031.3529235
2. Jeng, J.: Usability assessment of academic digital libraries: effectiveness, efficiency, satisfaction, and learnability (2005)
3. Lamberti, F., Paravati, G., Gatteschi, V., Cannavò, A.: Supporting web analytics by aggregating user interaction data from heterogeneous devices using viewport-DOM-based heat maps. IEEE Trans. Ind. Inform. **13**(4), 1989–1999 (2017). https://doi.org/10.1109/TII.2017.2658663
4. Roy, S., Pattnaik, P.K., Mall, R.: A quantitative approach to evaluate usability of academic websites based on human perception. Egypt. Inform. J. **15**(3), 159–167 (2014)

Research on User Emotion Experience of Short Video Based on Cyclic Interaction Model

Meiyu Zhou[1], Changpeng Cai[1(✉)], Xiaomin Cui[2(✉)], and Rui Huang[3]

[1] School of Art Design and Media, East China University of Science and Technology, No. 130, Meilong Road, Xuhui District, Shanghai, People's Republic of China
y81220127@mail.ecust.edu.cn

[2] Architecture and Design College of Nanchang University, No. 999, Xuefu Road, Honggutan New District, Nanchang, Jiangxi, People's Republic of China
57842338@qq.com

[3] College of Fashion and Design, Donghua University, No. 1882, Yanan West Road, Changning District, Shanghai, People's Republic of China

Abstract. Purpose In the context of the gradual integration of self media into the life of the public, short videos have become a popular focus of entertainment. The purpose of this paper is to explore how to improve the emotional experience of we-media user interaction, so that we-media can be integrated into the public's Internet life in a better way. Methodology Based on the schematic energy theory and Hartson's cyclic interaction model, this paper explores the behavioral cycle of users' browsing short video works, constructs a user behavior framework of "planning-conversion-execution-result-evaluation", and looks for ways to enhance the emotional experience of short video by combining the influencing elements of users' emotional experience. Results The construction of a behavioral framework model of user interaction when browsing short videos can provide a more intuitive understanding of the connection between user behavior, media content and interaction and user emotional experience, and provide a reference for self media platforms to realize more comfortable and efficient human-computer interaction.

Keywords: Affordance · Cyclic interaction model · User emotional experience · User action framework · Human-computer interaction

1 User Emotional Experience

With the continuous popularity and development of the Internet, the number of mobile terminal users is increasing, and users are also pursuing a higher quality of Internet user experience. User experience is generated along with user behavior and is the subjective evaluation of users in human-computer interaction. As the research related to user experience continues to deepen, more and more scholars believe that emotion is one of the main factors of user experience.

Emotional design is centered on triggering cognitive pleasure and thus positive emotional value for the user. Theories of psychology that explain why people feel certain emotions and how they affect their ability to behave are key to theorizing the emotional experience of users.

The current research on user emotions covers many aspects. Some researchers have used relevant psychological models to corroborate the mechanism of generating a single user's emotion, and are expected to replicate it [1]. Meanwhile, more research has focused on users' emotional feedback for a certain type of product (or virtual product) in order to propose design solutions that make the user's emotional experience even better [2, 3]. Although there is no lack of series of studies on emotional experience in related research fields, such as the specific logic of generating emotion and emotional motivation during user operation, there is still a lack of a systematic theory to analyze the root cause of affecting emotional experience and how to improve it in a targeted way, in order to more accurately analyze and describe the subjective feelings of users during operation, especially in the field of human-computer interaction, and the relevant theory is essential to help In particular, in the field of human-computer interaction, relevant theories are important to help researchers and designers improve their designs to achieve better human-computer interaction.

2 Affordance Theory and Cyclic Interaction Model

The theory of demonstrative energy is the psychological basis of human-computer interaction, and the relevant theoretical model established on this basis can more comprehensively cover various details of users in the actual operation process, which provides a better entry point for analyzing users' emotional experience of using products.

2.1 Affordance Theory

In 1977, psychologist James Jerome Gibson, influenced by completion psychology, introduced the term Affordance to refer to the meaning and value that the environment provides to animals. Affordance is something that is actually present in the environment and can be directly perceived, not interpreted or guided by the perceiver. Donald Norman later introduced this concept into the field of product design, narrowing the definition of the oscillatory energy theory from animal and environment to human and product, making it more social and therefore more relevant to the problem of human-product interaction [4]. Norman proposed the concept of Perceived Affordance as a proxy for the surface features of a product, i.e., the user can understand how to operate it without any labels or prompts; and referred to Gibson's definition of Affordance as Real Affordances to show the difference [5]. Since then, many scholars have conducted extended research on this issue, and the theory of affordance has been improved, and a clear outline of usability cognitive system has been gradually outlined.

Rex Hartson considers that Norman's usability theory is still difficult to interpret affordance clearly and comprehensively in actual research and practice, and he redefines four complementary meanings of affordance without violating Gibson and Norman's guidelines: cognitive affordance, sensory affordance, physical affordance, and functional affordance (Fig. 1). The "cognitive affordance" is derived from Norman's "perceived affordance" and is related to the semantics of the user interface; the "physical affordance" is derived from the "real affordance" and is related to the "operability" feature of the user interface. "Sensory affordance" and "functional affordance" are his two new concepts. "Sensory affordance" is mainly a design feature that supports "cognitive affordance" and "physical affordance", and can be considered as an attribute of both. Functional affordance, on the other hand, links the utility and usability of a product [6].

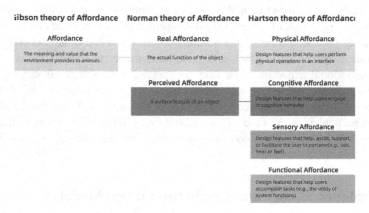

Fig. 1. Connotation Relationship Chart

2.2 Affordance Theory and Cyclic Interaction Model

Hartson also combined the demonstration of energy with Norman's linear stages-of-action model (Fig. 2) [6]. The linear stages-of-action model summarizes the typical interaction processes that occur when users interact with a product, and forms abstract functional hierarchies into concrete descriptions of system use that help classify and communicate usability issues. Users start by specifying behavioral goals, decompose the goals into specific intentions, intentions are mapped into action sequences, and users perform physical actions in sequences that cause changes in the state of the physical world, which are perceived by users through feedback, and users interpret and evaluate the feedback results by comparing them with the original goals as a way to determine whether the goals are achieved. Norman's model can often be used as a basis for usability checking, classification, or analysis in HCI design.

According to Hartson, in the seven stages of behavior, users need cognitive affordance most when mapping intentions to action sequences before performing the corresponding physical actions, and sensory affordance to know how to perform the action; users need cognitive affordance when evaluating the behavior by comparing system feedback with their goal intentions; physical affordance are needed during the execution stage of the action; in the stage of perceiving the results of the external world, the assistance of sensory affordance is needed. When the external world works and operates, it mainly demonstrates the role of functional affordance [6].

Further, based on the energy demonstration theory, Hartson abstracted, merged, and transformed Norman's behavioral stage model to form the cyclic interaction model. He combined Norman's stages of "goals" and intention determination into "planning"; the "sequence of actions" is called "translation"; the "execution of the action sequence" stage remains unchanged and refers to the execution of various physical behaviors; and the three stages of "perceiving the state of the world", "interpreting the perception", and "Evaluation of interpretations" are unified into "accessment" (Fig. 3). He also changed the term "the world" to "outcomes" in Norman's model. This process does not take place in the user interface, but is entirely internal to the system and does not include user actions. Even automated operating systems extract and input information from the external world by the system itself sensing it without user intervention. The four actions of "planning, translation, physical actions and accessment" are all subjective actions of users, while "outcomes" are the objective feedback of users' actions within the system. Thus, the "outcome" phase is the key node of the cyclic interaction model, where the outcome of each interaction between the user and the product influences the next plan, and the user reaches the initial goal through multiple iterations of the interaction.

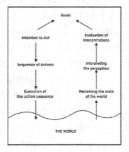

Fig. 2. Norman's (1990) Stages-of-action Model [4].

Hartson's model covers all the elements of Norman's behavioral stage model, but Norman's model tends to analyze the one-way human behavior in HCI, and the external world is independent and not subsumed into the seven stages of behavior; while Hartson analyzes it as a very important feedback (result) link in the cyclic interaction model, focusing more on the operational response relationship in HCI. The cyclic interaction model also introduces the four types of demonstrative energy mentioned above to analyze the demonstrative energy that each stage relies on. Therefore, Hartson's theory of oscillatory energy in HCI contexts is actually a "cognitive system consisting of a combination of external properties and internal perceptions".

2.3 The Relationship Between Affordance Theory, Cyclic Interaction Model and User Emotional Experience

Norman proposed the concept of emotional design and divided it into three levels: instinctive, behavioral and reflective levels [7]. The instinctive level of emotion is the first impression of the user's contact with the product through the visual perceptual performance of the product's appearance, color and touch with the user; the behavioral level: the sense of accomplishment and pleasure in efficient use; the reflective level of

Fig. 3. Hartson's (2003) cyclic interaction model [6].

design can give the user emotional enchantment in the long term. Thus, the factors that affect the user's emotional experience can be summarized into three factors: perceptual intuition, function and philosophy.

Specifically, perceptual intuition refers to the user's first impression in human-computer interaction, including the layout and color of the user interface, subjective feelings (visual, auditory and tactile) and the specific operating environment. Secondly, function refers to the various interactive functions of the product system, including usability, practicality, completeness and smoothness of the system. Finally, the philosophy is the additional meaning brought by the product system on the basis of its ability to respond to the user's human-computer operation smoothly, which specifically includes the persuasiveness of the whole product system of the user. It also includes the socio-cultural value brought to users by the product system, which is a deeper emotional resonance and cultural echo of the user's psyche, and can also cause users to reflect while satisfying their spiritual needs. The emotional experience generated by the reflection is the inherent emotional demand of users, and it can also connect the product with specific emotions.

Combining the above three main factors affecting user experience with the schematic energy theory and the cyclic interaction model, a mapping relationship between the three can be obtained (Fig. 4). In human embodied interaction in the real world, the oscillatory energy motivates the user's interaction behavior and further directs the behavior through the modulation of interaction feedforward. Schematic energy influences different aspects of the quality of the user's affective experience at different stages of the cyclic interaction model. This is important to reveal the user's emotional experience in actual human-computer interaction and the reasons for its generation.

Cognitive affordance help, support and facilitate users to think about or understand the function of something mainly in the planning, transformation and evaluation aspects of the cyclic interaction model, and give them intuitive operational cues to bring a good emotional experience. There are different ways of cognition during interaction. It relies heavily on cultural conventions to convey visual cues to users, and the basic mechanisms at play are symbols, constraints, and conventions. Usually, after repeated use, the information conveyed by the cognitive cues will be understood and remembered by novice users and thus transformed into their own subconscious mental activities. In the "planning" and "translation" stages, cognitive affordance mainly plays the role of prompting, supporting all users' learning and memory. In the final "accessment" stage, the user can evaluate the results of the feedback and determine whether the interaction was successful and whether the desired goal was achieved, thus enhancing the emotional experience of human-computer interaction.

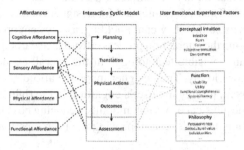

Fig. 4. The mapping relationship between affordance, cyclic interaction model and user emotional experience.

Sensory affordance can help designers enhance user perception during the planning, translation, physical action, and assessment phases. Until the system is thoroughly mastered, many of the user's interactions rely on the senses of sight, hearing, and sensation, including notability, legibility, legibility (in text), and audibility (in sound). Sensory performance often requires the cooperation of multiple senses to enhance the efficiency and accuracy of information conveyance [8], and the excellent interactive interface it brings can eliminate information transfer delays and execution gaps, and bring a good emotional experience in the experience at both intuitive and functional levels.

Physical affordance can help users perform physical behaviors efficiently mainly in physical actions [9], enhancing user experience in terms of usability, utility, and functional integrity. Cognitive and sensory affordance may be replaced by shallow conscious behaviors, but physical affordance is not. Even users who are already familiar with the system still have to interact through physical feedback such as sound, touch, and vision.

The functional affordance mainly reflects the system functional integrity in the result stage. The "outcomes" is the stage of feedback to the user's behavior and operation, which determines the user's overall interactive experience. It is also an effective means to enhance the feedback between the system and the user, so that the user can understand the internal logic of the product better and more comprehensively, and at the same time receive the feedback of the operation in a timely and effective manner [10]. Therefore, functional displays should be used with care to avoid the user's sense of loss of control caused by ambiguous, delayed or incorrect feedback. The difference between functional and sensory affordance and physical affordance is that the cues are used at the "outcomes" stage, and the purpose is to strengthen the transmission of feedback on the operation result.

3 Analysis of Users' Emotional Experience of Browsing Short Videos

Affordance theory is a tool that serves as a cue for designers to set behavioral guidelines in systems that focus on the connections between users, actions, and products or systems in design. The user's path from perception to cognition to action shows how each sign energy is involved in the learning and use of interaction with the product. Hartson has developed a User Action Framework (UAF) based on affordance theory and a cyclical interaction model that further decomposes user tasks and behaviors at each stage (including "outcomes"). The UAF is intended for designers and is about how interaction design can support users so that they can quickly grasp system processing and achieve operational goals. During the interaction process, affordance participates in the product's cognitive system as an "invisible technology" in the overall cyclic interaction model, linking all aspects more closely. The designer maps the affordance into the predefined user behavior framework, driving the user's cognition in the right direction, supporting the user to complete the physical behavior smoothly, reducing possible errors, increasing the variety of interaction methods, and improving the user experience.

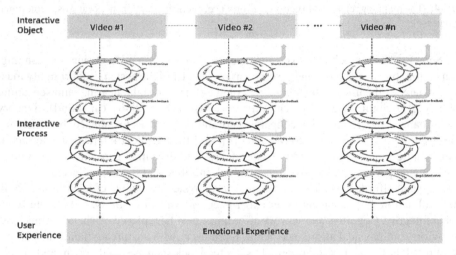

Fig. 5. The UAF of Users Watching Short Videos.

The user's behavior of watching short videos is subdivided into four stages: select video, enjoy video, giving feedback and continuing/ending. The user will decide whether to continue viewing the next video based on the viewing experience of the previous video and start the cycle of the next interaction process. Based on the cyclic interaction model and the four steps of video viewing, a UAF for users to browse short videos is established (Fig. 5). And the emotional experience is continuously accumulated in the process of each generated interaction (stage five of each cyclic interaction in the figure, the accessment stage), and the overall user experience of users browsing short videos this time can be derived through the accumulation of each interaction.

Through the user behavior framework constructed above combined with the schematic energy theory, it can be specific to the emotional experience of each step of user's operation in browsing short videos, and the causes can be further analyzed layer by layer and targeted improvement solutions can be proposed to enhance the emotional experience of the product and achieve better human-computer interaction.

4 Conclusion

In this paper, a circular interaction model based on the affordance is used to establish a mapping relationship between the three factors that affect the emotional experience. It further constructs a framework for users' behavior of browsing short videos. For researchers and designers in this field, the cyclic interaction model can help them better understand user behavior and make targeted construction and optimization of specific human-computer interaction in design solutions. In this process, the cyclic interaction model based on the affordance theory can accurately locate and analyze the interaction steps that affect the user's emotional experience. Although the comprehensive performance of emotion is not a single linear superposition, the subdivision steps of the model can still be used to accurately and quickly locate the interaction steps that affect the user's emotional experience when watching videos, and to solve the problem in a targeted manner.

References

1. Becattini, N., Borgianni, Y., Cascini, G., Rotini, F.: Investigating users' reactions to surprising products. Des. Study **69**, 100946 (2020)
2. Ma, C.X., Song, J.C., Zhu, Q., et al.: EmotionMap: visual analysis of video emotional content on a map. J. Comput. Sci. Technol. **35**(3), 576–591 (2020). https://doi.org/10.1007/s11390-020-0271-2
3. Gerdes, A.B.M., Wieser, M.J., Alpers, G.W.: Emotional pictures and sounds: a review of multimodal interactions of emotion cues in multiple domains. Front. Psychol. **5**, 1351 (2014)
4. Norman, D.: The Design of Everyday Things. Doubleday Business, New York (1990)
5. Norman, D.A.: Affordance, conventions, and design. Interaction **6**(3), 38–42 (1999)
6. Hartson, R.: Cognitive, physical, sensory, and functional affordances in interaction design. Behav. Inf. Technol. **22**, 315–338 (2003)
7. Norman, D.A.: Emotional Design: Why We Love (or Hate) Everyday Things. Basic Books, New York (2004)
8. De Paz, C., Travieso, D.: Sensory substitution: the affordance of passability, body-scaled perception, and exploratory movements. PLoS ONE **14**(3), e0213342 (2019)
9. Symes, E., Ellis, R.: Visual object affordances: object orientation. Acta Physiol. **124**, 238–255 (2007)
10. Pellicano, A., Iani, C.: Simon-like and functional affordance effects with tools: the effects of object perceptual discrimination and object action state. Q. J. Exp. Psychol. **63**, 2190–2201 (2010)

Author Index